THE ON-LINE STUDY OF

SENTENCE
COMPREHENSION

EDITED BY
MANUEL CARREIRAS AND
CHARLES CLIFTON, JR.

THE ON-LINE STUDY OF

SENTENCE COMPREHENSION

EYETRACKING, ERPs AND BEYOND

PSYCHOLOGY PRESS
NEW YORK • HOVE

Published in 2004 by
Psychology Press
270 Madison Avenue
New York, NY 10016
www.psychologypress.com

Published in Great Britain by
Psychology Press
27 Church Road
Hove, East Sussex
BN3 2FA
www.psychologypress.co.uk

10 9 8 7 6 5 4 3 2 1

Library of Congress Cataloging-in-Publication Data

The on-line study of sentence comprehension : eyetracking, ERPs, and beyond / edited by Manuel
Carreiras and Charles E. Clifton, Jr.
   p. cm.
  ISBN 1-84169-400-2 (hardcover : alk. paper)
  1. Psycholinguistics. 2. Comprehension. 3. Grammar, Comparative and general—Syntax.
4. Reading, Psychology of. 5. Eye—Movements. I. Carreiras, Manuel. II. Clifton, Charles,
1938-

P37.5.C6605 2004
401'.9—dc22

2003026652

Contributors
Information

Gerry T. M. Altmann
Department of Psychology
University of York, Heslington
York, YO10 5DD. England, U.K.

g.altmann@psych.york.ac.uk

Horacio Barber
Departamento de Psicologìa Cognitiva
Universidad de La Laguna
Campus de Guajara
s/n. 38205, La Laguna
Tenerife, Canary Islands, Spain
hbarber@ull.es

Moises Betancort
Departamento de Psicobiologìa y Metodologìa
Universidad de La Laguna
Campus de Guajara
s/n. 38205, La Laguna
Tenerife, Canary Islands
Spain
moibemo@ull.es

Julie E. Boland
University of Michigan
525 E. University Ave
Ann Arbor, 48109-1109, U.S.
jeboland@umich.edu

Ina D. Bornkessel
Max Planck Institute for Human Cognitive and Brain Sciences
P.O. Box 500355
D-04303 Leipzig, Germany

bornke@cbs.mpg.de

Sarah Brown-Schmidt
Department of Brain and Cognitive Sciences
The University of Rochester
River Campus
Meliora Hall
Rochester, NY 14627, U.S.
sschmidt@bcs.rochester.edu

Donna K. Byron
Department of Computer Science and Engineering
395 Dreese Laboratory
2015 Neil Avenue
Ohio State University
Columbus, Ohio 43210, U.S.
dbyron@cis.ohio-state.edu

C. Christine Camblin
Center for Cognitive Neuroscience &
Department of Psychological and Brain Sciences
Duke University
Durham, NC 27708-0999, U.S.
ccc9@duke.edu

Manuel Carreiras
Departamento de Psicologìa Cognitiva
Universidad de La Laguna
Campus de Guajara
s/n. 38205, La Laguna
Tenerife, Canary Islands, Spain
mcarreir@ull.es

Charles Clifton, Jr.
Department of Psychology
Tobin Hall
University of Massachusetts at Amherst
Amherst, MA 01003, U.S.
cec@psych.umass.edu

Matthew W. Crocker
Department of Computational Linguistics
Saarland University, Saarbrücken
Germany
crocker@coli.uni-sb.de

Peter F. Dominey
Institut des Sciences Cognitives
CNRS UMR 5015 CNRS-Universitè Lyon I
67, Bd PINEL. 69675 Bron Cedex. France
dominey@isc.cnrs.fr

Cathy Emmott
Department of English Language
University of Glasgow
12 Univeristy Gardens
Glasgow G12 8QQ
Scotland, U.K.
C.Emmott@englang.arts.gla.ac.uk

Christian J. Fiebach
(1) Max Planck Institute for Human Cognitive and Brain Sciences
Leipzig, Germany
(2) Department of Psychology and Helen Wills Neuroscience Institute
University of California, Berkeley
4143 Tolman Hall
Berkeley, CA 94720-5050, U.S.
christian@fiebach.org

Angela D. Friederici
Max Planck Institute for Human Cognitive and Brain Sciences
P.O. Box 500355
D-04303 Leipzig, Germany
angelafr@cbs.mpg.de

Steven Frisson
Department of Psychology
Tobin Hall
University of Massachusetts
Amherst, MA 01003, U.S.
steven.frisson@nyu.edu

Peter C. Gordon
Department of Psychology
University of North Carolina
Chapel Hill, NC 27599, U.S.
pcg@email.unc.edu

Ralf Greenwald
Department of Psychology
Box 351525
University of Washington
Seattle, WA 98195. U.S.
rgreen21@u.washington.edu

Michel Hoen
Institut des Sciences Cognitives
CNRS UMR 5015 CNRS-Universitè Lyon I
67, Bd PINEL. 69675 Bron Cedex. France
hoen@isc.cnrs.fr

Falk Huettig
Department of Psychology
University of York, Heslington
York, YO10 5DD. England
U.K.
f.huettig@psych.york.ac.uk

Kayo Inoue
Department of Psychology
Box 351525
University of Washington
Seattle, WA 98195. U.S.
ki@u.washington.edu

Albert Kim
Department of Psychology
Box 351525
University of Washington
Seattle, WA 98195. U.S.
alkim@u.washington.edu

Simon P. Liversedge
Department of Psychology
University of Durham
Durham DH1 3LE, U.K.
s.p.liversedge@durham.ac.uk

Scott A. McDonald
Department of Psychology
University of Edinburgh
7 George Square
Edinburgh EH8 9JZ, Scotland, U.K.
scott.mcdonald@ed.ac.uk

Brian McElree
Department of Psychology
New York University
6 Washington Place
NY, NY 10003, U.S.
brian.mcelree@nyu.edu

Judith McLaughlin
Department of Psychology
Box 351525
University of Washington
Seattle, WA 98195. U.S.
giuditta@u.washington.edu

Enrique Meseguer
Departamento de Psicologìa Cognitiva
Universidad de La Laguna
Campus de Guajara
s/n. 38205, La Laguna
Tenerife
Spain
emesegue@ull.es

Don C. Mitchell
School of Psychology
University of Exeter
Exeter, Devon, EX4 4QG. U.K.
d.c.mitchell@exeter.ac.uk

Lorna Morrow
Department of Psychology
University of Glasgow
Glasgow, G11 8QB
Scotland, U.K.
lorna@psy.gla.ac.uk

Linda Moxey
Department of Psychology
University of Glasgow
Glasgow, G11 8QB
Scotland, U.K.

linda@psy.gla.ac.uk

Lee Osterhout
Department of Psychology
Box 351525
University of Washington
Seattle, WA 98195. U.S.
losterho@u.washington.edu

Jamie Pearson
Department of Psychology
University of Edinburgh
7 George Square
Edinburgh EH8 9LW, Scotland, U.K.
jamie.pearson@ed.ac.uk

Martin J. Pickering,
Department of Psychology
University of Edinburgh
7 George Square
Edinburgh EH8 9LW, U.K.
Martin.Pickering@ed.ac.uk

Elena Salillas
Departamento de Psicologìa Cognitiva
Universidad de La Laguna
Campus de Guajara
s/n. 38205, La Laguna
Tenerife, Canary Islands, Spain
esalil@ull.es

Anthony Sanford
Department of Psychology
University of Glasgow
Glasgow, G11 8QB
Scotland, U.K.
tony@psy.gla.ac.uk

Christoph Scheepers
Department of Psychology
University of Dundee
Dundee DD1 4NH
Scotland, U.K.
C.scheepers@dundee.ac.uk

Matthias Schlesewsky
Junior Research Group Neurolinguistics
Department of Germanic Linguistics and Fine Arts
Philipps University Marburg
Wilhelm-Roepke-Str. 6A
D-35032 Marburg, Germany
schlesel@mailer.uni-marburg.de

Richard C. Shillcock
School of Philosphy, Psychology and Language Sciences
and School of Informatics
University of Edinburgh, Scotland, U.K.
2 Buccleuch Place
Edinburgh EH8 9LW
rcs@inf.ed.ac.uk

Patrick Sturt
Department of Psychology
University of Glasgow
Glasgow, G11 8QB
Scotland, U.K.
patrick@psy.gla.ac.uk

Tamara Y. Swaab
Department of Psychology and Center for Mind and Brain
University of California
One Shields Avenue
Davis, CA 95616-8686
tyswaab@ucdavis.edu

Michael K. Tanenhaus
Department of Brain and Cognitive Sciences
The University of Rochester
River Campus
Meliora Hall
Rochester, NY 14627, U.S.
mtan@bcs.rochester.edu

Matt Traxler
Department of Psychology
University of California at Davis
1 Shields Avenue
Davis, CA 95616, U.S.
mjtraxler@ucdavis.edu

Jos J. A. van Berkum (1,2,3)
berkum@psy.uva.nl
(1) University of Amsterdam
Department of Psychology (PN)
Roetersstraat 15, 1018 WB Amsterdam
The Netherlands
(2) F.C. Donders Centre for Cognitive Neuroimaging
(3) Max Planck Institute for Psycholinguistics

Roger P. G. van Gompel
Department of Psychology
University of Dundee
Dundee DD1 4NH
Scotland, U.K.
r.p.g.vangompel@dundee.ac.uk

Contributor Page

Gerry T. M. Altmann, *University of York, U.K.*

Horacio Barber, *Universidad de La Laguna, Spain*

Moisés Betancort, *University of Glasgow, U.K.*

Julie E. Boland, *University of Michigan, U.S.*

Ina D. Bornkessel, *Max Planck Institute of Cognitive Neuroscience, Germany*

Sarah Brown-Schmidt, *University of Rochester, U.S.*

Donna K. Byron, *Ohio State University, U.S.*

C. Christine Camblin, *Duke University, U.S.*

Manuel Carreiras, *Universidad de La Laguna, Spain*

Charles Clifton Jr. *University of Massachusetts at Amherst, U.S.*

Matthew W. Crocker, *Saarland University, Germany*

Peter F. Dominey, *CNRS-Université Lyon I, France*

Cathy Emmott, *University of Glasgow, U.K.*

Christian J. Fiebach, *Max Planck Institute of Cognitive Neuroscience, Germany*

Angela D. Friederici, *Max Planck Institute of Cognitive Neuroscience, Germany*

Steven Frisson, *University of Massachusetts at Amherst, U.S.*

Peter C. Gordon, *University of North Carolina at Chapel Hill, U.S.*

Ralf Greenwald, *University of Washington, U.S.*

Michael Hoen, *CNRS-Université Lyon I, France*

Falk Huettig, *University of York, U.K.*

Kayo Inoue, *University of Washington, U.S.*

Albert Kim, *University of Washington, U.S.*

Simon P. Liversedge, *University of Durham, U.K.*

Scott A. McDonald, *University of Edinburgh, U.K.*

Brian McElree, *New York University, U.S.*

Judith McLaughlin, *University of Washington, U.S.*

Enrique Meseguer, *Universidad de La Laguna, Spain*

Don C. Mitchell, *University of Exeter, U.K.*

Lorna Morrow, *University of Glasgow, U.K.*

Linda Moxey, *University of Glasgow, U.K.*

Lee Osterhout, *University of Washington, U.S.*

Jamie Pearson, *University of Edinburgh, U.K.*

Martin J. Pickering, *University of Edinburgh, U.K.*

Elena Salillas, *Universidad de La Laguna, Spain*

Anthony Sanford, *University of Glasgow, U.K.*
Christoph Scheepers, *University of Dundee, U.K.*
Matthias Schlesewsky, *Phillips-University Marburg, Germany*
Richard C Shillcock, *University of Edinburgh, U.K.*
Patrick Sturt, *University of Glasgow, U.K.*
Tamara Y. Swaab, *University of California–Davis, U.S.*
Michael K. Tanenhaus, *University of Rochester, U.S.A.*
Matthew J. Traxler, *University of California–Davis, U.S.*
Jos J. A. van Berkum, *University of Amsterdam, The Netherlands*
Roger P. G. van Gompel, *University of Dundee, U.K.*

Table of Contents

Preface

This book addresses core findings, assumptions, problems, hopes, and future guidelines concerning the use of advanced research techniques such as eyetracking and ERP, with some extensions to other techniques such as fMRI. Eyetracking and ERP have been widely used in the last two decades in the field of psycholinguistics. A vast amount of data has been collected and has advanced our knowledge of the cognitive mechanisms and processes involved in comprehending and producing language. The techniques used to probe these studies allow us to ask new questions designed to advance our theoretical knowledge. This book, written by leading researchers in the field of psycholinguistics who are also leading experts in the use of these methods, will help us to better understand the theoretical, methodological, and practical questions in this field.

The genesis of this project was the organization of the Eighth AMLaP (Architectures and Mechanisms for Language Processing) Conference held in Adeje, Tenerife, the Canary Islands, from September 19 to 21, 2002. The book is based on papers delivered by invited speakers for a special session and selected papers presented at the conference. The conference was organized by Manuel Carreiras, Carlos Alvarez, Enrique Meseguer, Moises Betancort, and Horacio Barber. They were helped by Margaret Gillon, Beneharo Jordan, and Ana Ravina, who made life easier for everybody. The organizers were also assisted by a program committee of reviewers that included Gerry Altmann, Kathryn Bock, Julie Boland, Marc Brysbaert, Chuck Clifton, David Corina, Martin Corley, Albert Costa, Matt Crocker, Marica di Vincenzi, Janet Fodor, Eva Fernández, Fernanda Ferreira, Victor Ferreira, Angela Friederici, Susan Garnsey, Ted Gibson, Jonathan Grainger, Barbara Hemforth, José Manuel Igoa, Yuki Kamide, Frank Keller, Gerard Kempen, Lars Konieczny, Vincenzo Lombardo, Mary Ellen MacDonald, Brian McElree, Don Mitchell, Thomas Munte, Wayne Murray, Lee Osterhout, Neil Pearlmutter, Manuel Perea, Martin Pickering, Dave Plaut, Joel Pynte, Keith Rayner, Christoph Scheepers, Shari Speer, Suzanne Stevenson, Patrick Sturt, Marcus Taft, Mike Tanenhaus, Matt Traxler, John Trueswell, Jos van Berkum, and Gabriella Vigliocco. The conference was financed by the University of La Laguna, Caja Canarias, the Ministry of Science and Technology, the Town Council of Adeje, and the Spanish Society for Experimental Psychology. The editors are very grateful to the conference organizers, the helpers, the reviewers of the program committee, and the financial supporters. They also like to deeply thank the contributing authors to the volume. They did a great job producing chapters, kindly answered our comments and suggestions, and were very efficient helping us to keep a tight schedule (on very few occasions some missed the first deadline but quickly caught up by the second!). Finally, we would like to express our gratitude to Yaiza Mena who assembled the camera-ready copy of the book to send to the publishers, and the people of Psychology Press who encouraged and helped us during the preparation of this volume, especially to Paul Dukes and Stacy Malyil.

Manuel Carreiras & Charles Clifton, Jr.
September 2003

Chapter 1
On the On-Line Study of Language Comprehension

MANUEL CARREIRAS AND
CHARLES CLIFTON, JR.

Language has been studied in many ways. It has been examined as an art, as a basis of philosophical investigations, and as a way of gaining insight into the human mind. During the past 50 years, practitioners of various scientific disciplines have developed objective ways of studying language. Linguists try to understand it through the construction of theories of abstract linguistic knowledge. Psycholinguists try to understand how language users engage this knowledge in comprehension and production. Neuroscientists have been digging into the biological substrate of language to study this exclusively human mental activity through identifying the time course of brain processes that are involved in language comprehension. This book provides a glimpse of how research done by linguists, psycholinguists, and neuroscientists can be brought to bear on a fundamentally psychological question—how language is comprehended in real time.

The topic of real-time comprehension of language has held center stage through most of the history of psycholinguistics. This is because psycholinguists have tried to develop theories of how language is comprehended that spell out the cognitive processes taking place when language is being understood. Such information-processing models are essentially claims about how mental representations are created, transformed, and stored, about what types of information are used in performing these operations, and about the architecture of the system that supports the proposed processes. A minimal (but difficult!) criterion for an adequate process model is whether or not it can create appropriate final outcomes; that is, can it create representations that adequately capture what readers and listeners understand sentences and texts to mean? Given that this has been met, even crudely, a second very challenging criterion can be addressed, which is posed by the following question: Is the model supported by "on-line" evidence about the temporal and logical flow of information, about the moment-by-moment processes that are claimed to take place between the presentation of auditory or written material and the achievement of understanding?

As a practical matter of psychological experimentation, these two criteria have traditionally been addressed by taking two types of measures: frequency of success on a task and performance speed. Reaction time has been one of the favorite dependent variables in cognitive psychology in general and psycholinguistics in particular. The use of reaction times to evaluate theories of cognitive processes can be traced to the 19th century when Donders (1868) invented the subtraction method to estimate the speed of internal cognitive processes. In more recent times, Sternberg's (1966, 1969) use of additive factors analysis and Posner's (1978) analysis of mental chronometry has stimulated a vast amount of theoretical and experimental work and has led to a notable increase in our understanding of the nature of cognition.

Psycholinguists commonly apply the experimental techniques of mental chronometry. For instance, when studying reading, they try to draw conclusions about what representations are formed, when, and on what basis, as a way of evaluating their claims about the architecture and operation of the reading system. Evidence for their conclusions has traditionally come from the speed and accuracy of responses in laboratory tasks such as lexical decision, word naming, self-paced reading, question answering, and sentence verification. While the evidence that these tasks provide has greatly increased our understanding of the process of language comprehension, they have not always proved adequate to discriminate between competing theoretical proposals. To take just one example, some theorists adopt modular positions following Fodor (1983) (e.g., Frazier & Rayner, 1982; Frazier, 1987); other theorists advocate more interactive positions (Marslen-Wilson & Tyler, 1987; MacDonald, Pearlmutter, & Seidenberg, 1994; Tanenhaus & Trueswell, 1995). Those who push modularity argue that certain types of information must be used and certain types of representations must be built in order for other types of information and representations to come into play. Those who argue for interactive processing envision a far less differentiated representational vocabulary and a far less constrained interplay among different types of information. This modular vs. interactive contrast would appear to have clear implications about the logical and temporal sequence of distinct processes in sentence comprehension. Although traditional measures of comprehension accuracy and speed have provided informative tests of these implications (see Mitchell, chapter 2, this volume), they have not provided evidence that settles the crucial questions to everybody's satisfaction.

Part of the problem with traditional methods is their relatively coarse granularity. Knowing how long it takes to read a sentence, or even a word, does not tell the researcher how long any particular component process took. More diagnostic evidence comes from patterns of eye movements observed while reading text for comprehension or memory, such as what words are fixated, how long each fixation lasts, and how often the eyes regress to previous part of the sentence. (See van Gompel et al., chapter 7, this volume, for an illustration of how the finer granularity of eyetracking measures can shed light on the underlying processes of comprehending anaphors.)

Another part of the problem with traditional measures (and with many uses of eyetracking) is their lack of specificity. An increase in comprehension time or a disruption in the eye-movement record is just an increase in time. It does not by itself carry any sort of signature about what processes gave rise to the disruption. Sometimes (e.g., Meseguer, Carreiras, & Clifton, 2002) the location or pattern of eye movements can carry hints about what processes are going on at some particular point in time—the eyes may well go to what the reader is thinking about at any moment. Similarly, the visual-world paradigm of measuring eye movements to visual scenes during listening (Tanenhaus, Spivey-Knowlton, Eberhard, & Sedivy, 1995) relies on the apparent fact that listeners tend to look at the referent of what they are hearing. Under this analysis, it can provide quite specific information about what a listener thinks a word or sentence refers to moment-by-moment (see Boland, chapter 4, this volume). Potentially, even more diagnostic information can come from measuring brain activity during reading or listening. Measures of evoked brain-related potentials (ERPs) can arguably provide information about what processes are taking place as well as when they occur (cf., van Berkum, chapter 13, this volume; Osterhout et al., chapter 14, this volume). Such measures, as well as measures of functional brain imaging, can provide information about what is happening in the sentence comprehension process, and (at least for ERP) when it is happening.

Measures of brain activity such as ERP and functional magnetic resonance imaging (fMRI), coming from the new interdisciplinary field of cognitive neuroscience, can in principle do even more. They can ground the cognitive processes of language comprehension, previously treated largely as abstract information processing operations, in the neural underpinnings of the brain (e.g., Posner & Raichle, 1994; Gazzaniga, 2000). Knowing what brain structures are involved in computing different kinds of linguistic information, and when, can place some constraints on what categories of cognitive processes are involved in different aspects of language comprehension. If two language comprehension phenomena involve different regions of the brain, they necessarily engage at least partly distinct cognitive processes; if two phenomena involve the same regions of the brain, they may involve overlapping processes. (See Fiebach et al., chapter 17, this volume, for an example of this reasoning.) Further, knowing what linguistic and nonlinguistic tasks involve which brain regions should place some constraints on the nature of the processes that engage these brain regions.

The methodological advances provided by various uses of eyetracking and measures of brain activity will not, by themselves, solve the problems of identifying the cognitive processes underlying language comprehension. They have to be combined with careful theoretical analyses of how the measures might be related to the presumed underlying processes (see Boland, chapter 4, this volume, and Tanenhaus, chapter 18, this volume, for discussions of *linking hypotheses*) and used in theoretically sophisticated experimentation. With the goal of highlighting current progress in using these new on-line methodologies and stimulating future progress in their use, the organizers of the Eighth Annual Meeting of Architectures and Mechanisms of Language Processing (AMLaP), which took place September 19 to 21, 2002, in Costa Adeje, Tenerife, Canary Islands, invited several distinguished researchers to present overviews of how eyetracking and cognitive neuroscience measures are advancing our knowledge of language comprehension. Each of these researchers was asked to consider the following questions in preparing their presentations:

- What is an on-line process?
- Why is on-line processing a very important theoretical issue?
- Are eyetracking and ERP good and useful on-line measures?
- Have these technologies helped theoretical knowledge advance?
- What theoretical debates have these technologies promoted?
- What theoretical questions have they helped us answer?
- What new theoretical questions can be asked with these technologies?

The resulting presentations appear as chapters in the present volume. They are complemented by written versions of several papers and posters that were presented at AMLaP. The editors of this book made a (sometimes difficult!) selection of papers and posters that illustrated informative uses of eyetracking and brain activity measures, and invited their authors to submit them to this book. The results, we trust, show that substantial progress is being made in understanding the on-line nature of language processing, and should stimulate even further progress.

We turn to a brief overview of the on-line measures emphasized in this book, and then return to an attempt to highlight the contributions made in the individual chapters. Readers familiar with the basics of eyetracking and measures of brain activity can skip the following sections without loss.

1.1 EYE MOVEMENTS

Eye-movement recoding has become a very popular technique, or better, a family of techniques. There are two sister techniques under the label of eye movements. One has been applied to measure eye movements during reading (see Rayner, 1998). The other has been used to measure eye movements to regions of a scene while participants listen to speech related to what the scene is about (Tanenhaus et al., 1995). Even though in both cases eye movements are recorded, assumptions about what each technique is tapping are different. (See Boland, chapter 4, this volume, for a description of both techniques.)

During reading, eyes do not sweep along a line of print, but advance through little jumps called saccades. A target word is brought to the fovea by a saccade; and the eyes then fixate on the word for something like a quarter of a second to identify it. About 90% of reading time is spent in fixations, including some regressions to an earlier misperceived word. The typical reader makes about three to four saccadic movements per second. Each movement lasts between 20 to 40 ms, and the eyes typically remain fixated for about 200 to 400 ms. Nearly 15% of the eye movements made by typical college students are regressive, meaning they go back to material previously fixated. The continuous recording of eye movements enables researchers to identify locations and durations of fixations during reading, allowing them to draw inferences about cognitive operations while reading.

A reader's fixation patterns vary greatly over a text, depending on the linguistic characteristics of the words. In developing their early model of text comprehension based on readers' eye movements, Just and Carpenter (1980) made two assumptions: the immediacy and the eye–mind assumptions. According to these assumptions, a word is the unit of processing, and processing occurs immediately and completely at the time the word is encountered. (See Pickering et al., chapter 3, this volume, for a discussion of these two assumptions.) Gaze duration, which is the summed duration of consecutive fixations on one word before the reader's eyes leave that word, is assumed to reflect processing time of that particular word.

A substantial amount of research on eye movements in reading was conducted early in the 20th century (see Huey, 1908; Tinker, 1946, 1958). By midcentury, research in this field had nearly stopped. However, prompted by the development of new methodologies and the appearance of information-processing theories of cognition, the study of eye movements in reading reappeared with vigor in the last third of the 20th century (see Rayner, 1998, for a review). Nowadays, eye-movement measures have been used successfully to understand the functioning of several components of language processing, such as phonological and orthographic processing (Lee, Binder, Kim, Pollatsek, & Rayner, 1999; Rayner, Pollatsek, Binder, 1998), the effects of neighborhood (Perea & Pollatsek, 1998), the processing of syllables (Ashby & Rayner, in press; Carreiras & Perea, 2004), lexical ambiguity (Duffy, Morris, & Rayner, 1988), morphological processing (Pollatsek, Hyona, & Bertram, 2000), syntactic processing (Carreiras & Clifton, 1999; Frazier & Rayner, 1982; Ferreira & Clifton, 1986; Trueswell, Tanenhaus, & Garnsey, 1994), plausibility (Pickering & Traxler, 1998), discourse context effects (Altmann, Garnham, & Dennis, 1992), and inference processing (O'Brien, Shank, Myers, & Rayner, 1988).

The recording of eye movements during reading to answer some theoretical questions about language processing and language architecture has helped us to better understand cognitive processes involved during on-line reading. On the one hand, results obtained with other laboratory techniques have generally been obtained with the eye-movement technique (see Mitchell, chapter 2, this volume). Converging evidence enhances our confidence in the phenomenon. On the other hand, due to its impressive temporal resolution and its ability to fractionate reading time into distinct components (long initial fixations, refixations on a word, regressions to earlier words, rereading a word after a regression, etc.), the eye- movement technique provides potentially useful detailed information about what cognitive processes might be occurring at any moment in time. (See Boland, chapter 4, this volume, and van Gompel et al., chapter 7, this volume, for illustrations.) The full value of eye-movement measures, however, will surely be realized only when we have a better understanding of how eye movements are controlled by various sorts of cognitive processes. Powerful and informative models of eye-movement control do exist (e.g., Reichle, Pollatsek, & Rayner, 1998; in press), but they emphasize how the location and timing of eye movements reflect lexical processing. They largely ignore processes of sentence parsing and interpretation. (See Boland, chapter 4, this volume, Perea & Carreiras, 2003, and Tanenhaus, chapter 18, this volume, for additional discussions of the need for models that link eye movements with higher cognitive processes.)

Eye-movement measures have recently been applied to questions about comprehension of spoken language. Making use of an old finding of Cooper (1974) that people strongly tend to look at the referents of words they are hearing, Tanenhaus and his colleagues and students (Tanenhaus et al., 1995) have created a new industry of visual-world studies. Participants' eye movements are measured while they are following instructions to manipulate objects in the real world or make decisions about (or simply observe) pictures on a video screen. (See Boland, chapter 4, this volume, for an overview.) It has been shown that the speed with which participants look at different objects or pictures can tell us a lot about how they use phonological information, how they create syntactic structures, how they use typical agents or objects, for example, of verbs, and how they integrate information about the visual world with the speech they are hearing, and so forth. The technique is yielding some very intriguing results (some of which are reported in chapters in the present volume), and at the very least allows researchers to examine in detail the effect that having a more or less specified world to talk about has on the process of language comprehension.

1.2 ERPS

Apart from neuropsychological studies of aphasia, psycholinguistic studies have usually proceeded in isolation from studies of the brain. The development of new methods for measuring the activity of the human brain has provided new tools to explore connections between cognitive processes and neural systems. Two of the most popular methods are event-related potentials (ERPs) and fMRI.

ERPs are tiny voltage changes measured at the surface of the scalp, reflecting brain activity that is triggered by sensory stimuli or by cognitive processes. This activity is normally buried in different spontaneous brain rhythms but can be revealed by averaging techniques. Through averaging, the activity that is time-locked to the stimulus is preserved, whereas the other activity cancels itself out for simple statistical reasons. This allows researchers to have a nonintrusive technique for recording signals of some brain processes. The resulting spatiotemporal map of the electrical activity has extremely high temporal resolution and, with some contentious assumptions, can be used to make inferences about what brain structures are active at any given moment. (See Van Berkum, chapter 13, this volume, and Osterhout et al., chapter 14, this volume, for descriptions of the method and its strengths and limitations.)

By varying information-processing requirements through the use of different tasks, it has been proved possible to identify some features of the flow of electrophysiological events that are related to different aspects of information processing. In the case of language comprehension, different ERP components appear to correlate with specific processes. For instance, it has been shown repeatedly that violations in expectancy that slow mental operations produce powerful electrical changes. Consider the sentence *Tom used to take his toast with butter.* The last word is highly primed and easily processed when it arrives because it fits so well with the context. However, if the expectancy is violated (e.g., with "socks"), one finds a negative-going wave form peaking around 400 ms after word onset (the N400) (e.g., Kutas & Hillyard, 1980, 1984; Kutas & Van Petten, 1994). Thus, difficulty with semantic integration is associated with the N400 component.

With respect to the processing of syntactic information, two different components have been identified: a left-anterior negativity (LAN) and a late centro-parietal positivity (P600/SPS [syntactic positive shift]). The LAN is a component with a left-anterior distribution starting at 250 ms that has been registered in response to syntactic (phase structure, subcategorization, etc.) and morphosyntactic violations (e.g., gender and number agreement) (Barber et al., chapter 15, this book; Friederici, Pfeifer, & Hahne, 1993; Rosler, Friederici, Pütz, & Hahne, 1993). The P600/SPS is a positive component (or family of distinct components) with a mainly posterior scalp distribution, characteristically starting about 500 ms after the onset of the target word (Friederici et al., 1993; Hagoort, Brown, & Groothusen, 1993; Osterhout & Holcomb, 1992; see also Ostherhout et al., chapter 14, this book; Barber et al., chapter 15, this book, Hoen & Dominey, chapter 16, this book). The P600 has been found, first, for words that are ungrammatical given the preceding sentence context (e.g., Coulson et al., 1998; Hagoort et al., 1993; Osterhout & Holcomb, 1992; Osterhout & Mobley, 1995); second, for words that are unexpected, given the preferred reading of the preceding context (garden-path sentences) (e.g., Hagoort & Brown, 2000; Carreiras et al., in press); and third, for sentences of more syntactic complexity (Friederici, Hahne, & Saddy, 2002; Kaan & Swaab, 2003).

Although ERPs have been useful in investigating the cognitive processes involved in language processing, many issues remain to be resolved in the use of this technique (see van Berkum, chapter 13, this volume; Osterhout et al., chapter 14, this volume). However, many of the results obtained with this technique do seem to reveal patterns that are similar to those obtained with behavioral methods. It is likely that the new advances that we are going to see in the near future regarding a better exploitation of the electrical signals of the brain (see van Berkum, chapter 13, this volume), together with cleverly designed experiments to answer insightful theoretical questions, will help us advance our knowledge of language processing.

1.3 FMRI

Neuroimaging methods such as functional magnetic resonance imaging have contributed to our understanding of the relationship between neural activity and language processing. The fMRI measures changes in blood oxygenation, which are used as indicators of where in the brain neuronal activity increases or decreases during the performance of one task compared to another. Using neuroimaging techniques such the fMRI, cognitive neuroscientists are beginning to map specific brain areas to several components of language (e.g., orthographic, phonological, syntactic, semantic processes, etc.). (See Binder & Price, 2001 for a recent review.) Clearly, neuroimaging studies are particularly important in the exploration of exclusively human mental activities such as language processing because no animal models of these functions can be obtained.

Nonetheless, it is important to bear in mind that neuroimaging techniques such as fMRI have their own limitations (see Osterhout et al., chapter 14, this volume). For instance, fMRI can reveal areas of the brain that are active during a particular mental function, indicating whether or not that activation is necessary for the execution of that function. But the hemodynamic response is slow, on the order of seconds, which means that fMRI has an unfortunately slow temporal resolution—too slow to capture the time course of very fast cognitive processes. Measuring the time course of processing is not, however, the only way to identify the cognitive processes involved in a task. Fiebach et al. (chapter 17, this volume) provide one interesting example of how fMRI can be used to gather evidence about whether two distinct tasks (attempting to understand complex sentences and ungrammatical nonsentences) involve the same or distinct processes.

1.4 USING THE TECHNIQUES

Each of the techniques we have discussed has its own strengths and weaknesses. Clever experimentation is needed to use these techniques properly, as is careful and explicit theorizing, including specification of the presumed links between cognitive processes and the data that can be observed in each technique. One promising way of allowing data to constrain theory is to combine the techniques in examining one particular problem. Sereno, Rayner, and Posner (1998) combined eyetracking and ERPs in analyzing the very early stages in the process of visual word recognition. Gordon et al. (chapter 8, this volume) combined the same measures in studying the comprehension of anaphors. Combining fMRI (a blood-flow technique of good spatial resolution but poor temporal resolution) with ERPs (a technique of poor spatial resolution but good temporal resolution) is another promising combination (see Osterhout et al., chapter 14, this book). Knowing both the timing of operations and their neural loci will help to isolate the conditions under which a particular process is operating. (See Friederici, 2002, for an example of a processing model of sentence processing based on the combined evidence of ERP and fMRI data.)

1.5 OVERVIEW OF THE BOOK

We had two goals editing this book: to illustrate different methodological approaches used by scientists to understand language processing, and to stimulate thought about how converging evidence from these approaches can lead to new insights and advances. Eyetracking, in its various guises, and ERPs are the current techniques of choice; fMRI holds great promise, and the future can be expected to bring new techniques that illuminate cognitive processes and their underlying brain processes in ways we cannot now imagine. The chapters that appear in this book provide evidence that researchers can use available techniques in a variety of creative ways to probe the language comprehension process and to explore its underlying brain processes.

In chapter 2, Don Mitchell sets the stage for examining how different techniques can illuminate questions of real-time processing by arguing that such questions have been with us nearly since the beginning of psycholinguistics. He argues that relatively cheap and simple techniques such as self-paced reading have, in fact, provided us with a great deal of information about on-line sentence comprehension. He provides a provocative discussion of the advantages and disadvantages of a wide variety of techniques for studying language processing and puts the new, sophisticated techniques that are the primary focus of this book in the context of other, arguably more efficient, techniques.

Pickering, Frisson, McElree, and Traxler describe some basic facts about measuring eye movements during reading in chapter 3. Their chapter lays out cautions about linking the various measures to possible cognitive processes (e.g., the problems of identifying early and late eyetracking measures with initial and noninitial cognitive processes). It continues by surveying a substantial number of experiments illustrating the use of eye movements to investigate semantic interpretation.

Julie Boland provides an overview in chapter 4 of how eye movements can be used to study both reading and listening. Her chapter addresses linking assumptions between eye-movement data and sentence comprehension processes, which clearly are different for the two eye-movement paradigms, and it discusses the strengths and limitations of each paradigm. The chapter also provides some provocative suggestions about how eye-movement measures might be used to distinguish between initial structure- building operations and ambiguity-resolution operations, among other processes.

Chapter 5 by McDonald and Shillcock measures eye movements during reading to demonstrate that knowledge of lexical co-occurrence frequencies are used on-line during reading. Eyetracking data showed an early influence of the transitional probabilities between words on various fixation duration measures, even in a range of transitional probabilities that is much lower than previous research has demonstrated to be effective. The authors advocate a Bayesian approach to integrating transitional probabilities with frequency of occurrence and argue that their findings fit well with other research using various techniques (including ERP and visual-world techniques) which show that language-processing systems are exquisitely sensitive to statistical information.

Chapter 6 by Betancort, Meseguer, and Carreiras, is the first of several chapters that study the on-line processing of anaphora. It describes two eyetracking experiments investigating the time course of different types of information in the assignment of an antecedent to PRO (the null pronoun in Spanish) during reading. It provides convincing evidence that PRO is bound very quickly, that plausibility plays an early role in parsing, and that there are biases toward taking the most recent NP as the antecedent of PRO when the opportunity exists (and that the parser obeys the grammar when the grammar dictates).

In chapter 7, van Gompel, Liversedge, and Pearson use eyetracking during reading to tease out the time course with which the antecedent of a nominal anaphor is identified. The basic question is, how does the typicality of the antecedent (e.g., "robin" vs. "goose") of an anaphor ("the bird") influence how the anaphor is interpreted. The research shows the power of eyetracking measures by showing how such measures can separate out distinct processes that are conflated using methods such as self-paced reading or whole-sentence reading time.

Chapter 8 by Gordon, Camblin, and Swaab continues the series of chapters on anaphor by showing the combined use of eyetracking and ERPs to address important issues in anaphora resolution, for example, the repeated name penalty and the process of extracting a singular antecedent from a conjoined or plural noun phrase. The authors argue that using both methods provides confirming as well as complementary evidence about the interpretation of anaphors.

In chapter 9, Sanford, Sturt, Moxey, Morrow, and Emmott take a different approach to studying plural anaphora, and more generally, the conceptual representation of multiple entities. They use both eyetracking and off-line production tasks to study the ways that semantic aspects of the situation being described and linguistic aspects of the description can influence how potential antecedents of an anaphor are represented and accessed. Their chapter presents a strong case for the position that on-line and off-line data can complement each other in helping us understand language processing.

Chapter 10 by Scheepers and Crocker uses the visual-world paradigm to examine how syntactic expectations formed during reading influence the interpretation of a following heard sentence. Listeners saw pictures depicting two events while they heard German sentences that were ambiguous in mentioning subject (agent) or object (patient) first. The structure of the sentence that had just been read was shown to influence the resolution of this ambiguity. In addition to showing that the visual-world technique can shed light on just how and when interpretive ambiguities are resolved, the paper provides some hints that measures of pupil diameter may provide information about momentary processing load.

Chapter 11 by Huettig and Altmann uses the visual-world paradigm to show that listeners were more likely to look at a visual foil that shares some salient physical characteristics with the referent of a target word than at foils that do not have such an identifiable physical similarity. A similar effect was observed for conceptual category membership (but not for physical properties that had to be supplied by conceptual knowledge rather than by the pictures). Further, listeners were more likely to look at the referent of the dominant meaning of a homophone (or to an object that shared a salient physical feature with this referent) than at unrelated objects, even when the context contained some information that biased the homophone toward its subordinate meaning. These sometimes-surprising results seem to shed light on the time course of extracting semantic information from what is heard and to coordinate that information with knowledge of what is seen.

In chapter 12 on anaphora by Brown-Schmidt, Byron, and Tanenhaus, the visual-world paradigm is used to study the discourse and reference conditions that govern the use of the demonstrative pronoun "that" (in contrast to "it"). The data show that the final interpretations of "that" and "it" differ, and that a *composite* object is a more attractive referent of either pronoun than a pair of objects side-by-side.

In chapter 13 van Berkum provides an illuminating overview of ERP research with a considerable amount of practical advice about doing such research and discusses the use of ERP research. In addition to serving as a very useful introduction to the value of ERP techniques in studying on-line language processing, the chapter illustrates how ERP research can be implemented very effectively to address crucial questions about the relation between discourse-level and sentence-level processing.

Chapter 14 by Osterhout, McLaughlin, Kim, Greenwald, and Inoue complements the previous chapter by providing another overview of ERP methods and research. It shows how EPRs can supplement other methods such as eye movements and fMRI in addressing core questions of language processing, such as the distinction between syntactic and semantic processing. Among other topics, it discusses the possible use of ERPs to localize sources, providing some promising evidence. Further, it summarizes some provocative research on second-language acquisition, suggesting that ERP measures can identify effects of learning earlier in the course of acquiring a language than can overt behavioral measures.

Chapter 15 by Barber, Salillas, and Carreiras reports one experiment with the use of ERPs to address the processing of semantic and grammatical gender-agreement violations in Spanish. It reports both a LAN and a P600 effect of similar size for grammatical gender violations as well as semantic gender violations, and also reports some intriguing differences between semantic and arbitrary gender sentences when there are no violations.

In chapter 16 Hoen and Dominey present some intriguing evidence about the similarity of three ERP components in natural language and in an artificial language. They provide evidence for a LAN-like effect in response to the occurrence of a symbol that indicates an upcoming reversal of the preceding sequence; an N400-like effect in response to an unexpected symbol; and a P600-like effect in response to a violation of the order in which the symbols should appear in the second half of the sequence. Generally comparable effects are shown for corresponding conventional types of violations in French sentences. Thus, they make the case that it appears to be possible to study ERPs in artificial languages whose properties can be well controlled.

In chapter 17 Fiebach, Schlesewsky, Bornkessel, and Friederici provide an interesting example of how fMRI, not generally thought of as an on-line task, can help us to understand better the on-line phenomena of processing difficult sentences and ungrammatical nonsentences. At least some behavioral tasks (for example, acceptability rating) do not exhibit a distinction between responses to ungrammatical strings and very difficult sentences. However, the fMRI data indicate a clear and informative difference between the brain regions that are strongly engaged in dealing with ungrammatical versus difficult items.

Finally, in chapter 18, Mike Tanenhaus presents an avowedly personal view of the past, present, and future of psycholinguistics. He discusses the roles that on-line measures of processing have played, emphasizing their varying relations to theoretical issues as these issues have shifted over the years. He provides an extended discussion of the need for explicit and justified *linking hypotheses* to relate on-line measures to theoretical events. In his comments, Tanenhaus highlights some of the contributions that other chapters in this volume make to contemporary issues in sentence processing, and he suggests how they may point the way to the future in their use of multiple converging measures of processing, their emphasis on measures of the neural events underlying sentence comprehension, and the movement seen in some chapters toward studying language in more natural, even interactive, environments.

References

Altmann, G. T. M., Garnham, A., & Dennis, Y. (1992). Avoiding the garden path: Eye movements in context. *Journal of Memory and Language, 31,* 685–712.

Ashby, J., & Rayner, K. (in press). Representing syllable information during silent reading: Evidence from eye movements. *Language and Cognitive Processes.*

Binder, J., & Price, C. (2001). Functional neuroimaging of language. In R. Cabeza & A. Kingstone (Eds.), *Handbook of functional neuroimaging of cognition.* Cambridge, MA: MIT Press.

Carreiras, M., & Clifton, C., Jr. (1999). Another word on parsing relative clauses: Eyetracking evidence from Spanish and English. *Memory and Cognition, 7,* 826–833.

Carreiras, M., & Perea, M. (2004). Effects of syllable neighborhood frequency in visual word recognition and reading: Cross-task comparisons. In L. Ferrand & J. Grainger (Eds.), *Psycholinguistique cognitive*. Brusselles, Belgium: De Boeck Université.

Carreiras, M., Salillas, E., & Barber, H. *Event-related potentials elicited during parsing of ambiguous relative clauses in Spanish. Cognitive Brain Research (in press).*

Cooper, R. M. (1974). The control of eye fixation by the meaning of spoken language: A new methodology for the real-time investigation of speech perception, memory, and language processing. *Cognitive Psychology, 6,* 61–83.

Coulson, S., King, J. W., & Kutas, M. (1998). Expect the unexpected: Event-related brain response to morphosyntactic violations. *Language and Cognitive Processes, 13,* 21–58.

Donders, F. C. (1868). Over de snelheid van psychische processen. Onderzoekingen gedaan in het Psyiologish Laboratorium der Utrechtsche Hoogeschool. *Twede Reeks, II,* 92–120. Translated by W. G. Koster (1969), *Acta Psychologica, 30,* 412–431.

Duffy, S. A., Morris, R. K., & Rayner, K. (1988). Lexical ambiguity and fixation times in reading. *Journal of Memory and Language, 27,* 429–446.

Ferreira, F., & Clifton, C. (1986). The independence of syntactic processing. *Journal of Memory and Language, 25,* 348–368.

Fodor, J. A. (1983). *The Modularity of mind.* Cambridge, MA: MIT Press.

Frazier, L. (1987). Sentence processing: A tutorial review. In M. Coltheart (Ed.), *Attention and performance* (pp. 559–586). Hillsdale, NJ: Erlbaum.

Frazier, L., & Rayner, K. (1982). Making and correcting errors during sentence comprehension: Eye movements in the analysis of structurally ambiguous sentences. *Cognitive Psychology, 14,* 178–210.

Friederici, A. D. (2002). Towards a neural basis of auditory sentence processing. *Trends in Cognitive Science, 6,* 78–84.

Friederici, A. D., Hahne, A., & Saddy, D. (2002). Distinct neurophysiological patterns reflecting aspects of syntactic complexity and syntactic repair. *Journal of Psycholinguistic Research, 31,* 45–63.

Friederici, A. D., Pfeifer, E., & Hahne, A. (1993). Event-related brain potentials during natural speech processing: Effects of semantic, morphological, and syntactic violations. *Cognitive Brain Research, 1,* 183–192.

Gazzaniga, M. S. (2000). *The new cognitive neurosciences.* Cambridge, MA: MIT Press.

Hagoort, P., & Brown, C. M. (2000). ERP effects of listening to speech compared to reading: The P600/SPS to syntactic violations in spoken sentences and rapid serial visual presentation. *Neuropsychologia, 38,* 1531–1549.

Hagoort, P., Brown, C., & Groothusen, J. (1993). The syntactic positive shift (SPS) as an ERP measure of syntactic processing. *Language and Cognitive Processes, 8,* 439–483.

Huey, E. B. (1968). *The psychology and pedagogy of reading.* Cambridge, MA: MIT Press. (Original work published 1908)

Just, M. A., & Carpenter, P. A. (1980). A theory of reading: From eye fixations to comprehension. *Psychological Review, 87,* 329–354.

Kaan, E., & Swaab, T. (2003). Repair, revision, and complexity in syntactic analysis: An electrophysiological differentiation. *Journal of Cognitive Neuroscience, 15,* 98–110.

Kutas, M., & Hillyard, S. A. (1980). Reading senseless sentences: brain potentials reflect semantic anomaly. *Science, 207,* 203–205.

Kutas, M., & Hillyard, S. A. (1984). Brain potentials during reading reflect word expectancy and semantic association. *Nature, 307,* 161–163.

Kutas, M., & Van Petten, C. K., (1994). Psycholinguistics electrified: Event-related brain potential investigations. In M. A. Gernsbacher (Ed.), *Handbook of psycholinguistics* (pp. 83–143). San Diego, CA: Academic Press.

Lee, Y., Binder, K. S., Kim, J., Pollatsek, A., & Rayner, K. (1999). Activation of phonological codes during eye fixations in reading. *Journal of Experimental Psychology: Human Perception and Performance, 25,* 948–964.

Marslen-Wilson, W. D., & Tyler, L. K. (1987). Against modularity. In J. Garfield (Ed.), *Modularity in knowledge representation and natural language understanding.* Cambridge, MA: MIT Press.

MacDonald, M. C., Pearlmutter, N. J., & Seidenberg, M. S. (1994). The lexical nature of syntactic ambiguity resolution. *Pyschological Review, 101,* 676–703.

Meseguer, E., Carreiras, M., & Clifton, C., Jr. (2002). Overt reanalysis strategies and eye movements during the reading of mild garden path sentences. *Memory and Cognition, 30,* 551–562.

O'Brien, E. J., Shank, D. M., Myers, J. L., & Rayner, K. (1988). Elaborative inferences during reading: Do they occur on-line? *Journal of Experimental Psychology: Learning, Memory, and Cognition, 14,* 410–420.

Osterhout, L., & Holcomb, P. J. (1992). Event-related brain potentials elicited by syntactic anomaly. *Journal of Memory and Language, 31,* 785–806.

Osterhout, L., & Mobley, L. A. (1995). Event-related brain potentials elicited by failure to agree. *Journal of Memory and Language, 34,* 739–73.

Perea, M., & Carreiras, M. (2003). Regressions and eye movements: When and where. *Behavioural and Brain Sciences, 26,* 497.

Perea, M., & Pollatsek, A. (1998). The effects of neighborhood frequency in reading and lexical decision. *Journal of Experimental Psychology: Human Perception and Performance, 24,* 767–779.

Pickering, M. J., & Traxler, M. (1998). Plausibility and the recovery from garden paths: An eyetracking study. *Journal of Experimental Psychology: Learning, Memory, and Cognition, 24,* 940–961.

Pollatsek, A., Hyona, J., & Bertram, R. (2000). The role of morphological constituents in reading Finnish compound words. *Journal of Experimental Psychology: Human Perception & Performance, 26,* 820–833.

Posner, M. I. (1978). *Chronometric explorations of mind: The third Paul M. Fitts lectures.* Hillsdale, NJ: Erlbaum.

Posner, M. I., & Raichle, M. E. (1994). *Images of mind.* New York: Scientific American Library.

Rayner, K. (1998). Eye movements in reading and information processing: 20 years of research. *Psychological Bulletin, 124,* 372–422.

Rayner, K., Pollatsek, A., & Binder, K. S. (1998). Phonological codes and eye movements in reading. *Journal of Experimental Psychology: Learning, Memory, and Cognition, 24,* 476–497.

Reichle, E. D., Pollatsek, A., & Rayner, K. (1998). Toward a model of eye movement control in reading. *Psychological Review, 105*(1), 125–156.

Reichle, E. D., Pollatsek, A., & Rayner, K. (2003). The E-Z reader model of eye movement control in reading: Comparisons to other models. *Behavioral and Brain Sciences, 26,* 445–526.

Rösler, F., Friederici, A. D., Pütz, P., & Hahne, A. (1993). Event-related brain potentials while encountering semantic and syntactic constraint violations. *Journal of Cognitive Neuroscience, 5,* 345–362.

Sereno, S., Rayner, K., & Posner, M. I. (1998). Establishing a time-line of word recognition: Evidence from eye movements and event-related potentials. *NeuroReport, 9,* 2195–2200.

Sternberg, S. (1966). High speed scanning in human memory. *Science, 153,* 652–654.

Sternberg, S. (1969). The discovery of processing stages: Extensions of Donders' method. *Acta Psychologica, 30,* 276–315.

Tanenhaus, M. K., Spivey-Knowlton, M. J., Eberhard, K. M., & Sedivy, J. C. (1995). Integration of visual and linguistic information in spoken language comprehension. *Science, 268,* 1632–1634.

Tanenhaus, M. K., & Trueswell, J. C. (1995). Sentence comprehension. In J. Miller & P. Eimas (Eds.), *Handbook of perception and cognition: Speech, language, and communication* (2nd ed., Vol. 11, pp. 217–262). San Diego CA: Academic Press.

Trueswell, J. C., Tanenhaus, M. K., & Garnsey, S. M. (1994). Semantic influences on parsing: Use of thematic role information in syntactic disambiguation. *Journal of Memory and Language, 33,* 285–318.

Tinker, M. A. (1946). The study of eye movements in reading. *Psychological Bulletin, 43,* 93–120.

Tinker, M. A. (1958). Recent studies of eye movements in reading. *Psychological Bulletin, 55,* 215–231.

Chapter 2
On-Line Methods in Language Processing: Introduction and Historical Review

DON C. MITCHELL

2.1 BACKGROUND

Within the community of researchers interested in understanding how humans process sentences, it has long been evident that there are important insights to be gained by taking "snapshots" of processing while a person is engaged in understanding or producing a sentence. Many theories propose that the burden of work fluctuates as the person progresses through different portions of the material. Some make assumptions about different hypotheses that might be entertained at different points in the sentence. Some posit very rapid or immediate use of any information that might contribute to the process of interpretation or production, whereas other more modular approaches argue for a more punctuated deployment of resources. To adjudicate between such theories, we need to make use of experimental methods that are capable of tracking variations in workload from moment to moment while a person is making sense of (or producing) a sentence. These have become known as *on-line methods*.

To address this need to track transitory events, researchers have developed an exotic array of methods ranging from the very simple and basic to those that are highly sophisticated and expensive to apply. Many chapters of this book aim to promote some of the more powerful and intricate methods. However, the approach adopted here will be more eclectic. A simple and apparently crude method is often all that is needed to answer a theoretical question. Historically, in this field, discoveries have almost always been made using simple techniques with the conclusions being corroborated later by more intricate high-tech methods. In selecting experimental methods, a researcher is well advised to consider fitness-for-purpose in the different techniques rather than opting directly for "nuclear weaponry."

The first section below will set out some of the on-line methods that have been used over the last 30 years or so. This will be followed by a brief consideration of the "naturalness" of a subset of the methods. I shall then present an analysis of the impact the various methods have had in the development of the field, ending with some observations about why some of the simpler methods have often been rather more influential than the more complex alternatives. The chapter ends with comment on how patterns of development are likely to change in the future.

2.2 WHY ARE ON-LINE METHODS IMPORTANT?

One observation that is consistently underlined by modern psycholinguistic work is that many of the operations involved in human language processing are completed in remarkably short periods of time (often measured in milliseconds) and are highly transitory in their effects. It follows that reliance on any method that "blinks" will miss much of what is interesting and important about the phenomena under scrutiny. I will illustrate the point by referring to just two theoretical debates: one classical and the other more current. Any number of other controversies in the field would serve equally well to make the point. The more traditional topic dates from the earliest years of psycholinguistic work within the cognitive tradition. It asks what happens when a person reads or hears an ambiguous word. Do the alternative meanings become available at the same time, or is just a single meaning retrieved from memory in the first place, perhaps followed by others after a short delay? Investigators like Bobrow (1970) demonstrated that only a single sense was *remembered* shortly after the sentence was finished, but this failed to establish that alternative meanings were entirely ignored during earlier phases of processing. Indeed, researchers like MacKay (1966) claimed they were, based on the evidence that partial sentences took longer to complete if they incorporated ambiguous words. This raised the possibility that some or all of the alternative meanings of an ambiguous word are considered shortly after the word's appearance, but that inappropriate senses are then rapidly suppressed, leaving no trace that they ever played any role in the comprehension process. At this point it became clear that there was no prospect of adjudicating between the different proposals without recourse to methods that make it possible to examine processing as it happens (i.e., while the sentence containing the ambiguous word is still being analyzed). Any method based on probing events after a delay would be subject to the criticism that it may have "missed the show." As a result of this, researchers set about devising methods of tapping into the processing of ambiguous words as soon as they made their appearance. As reported in all psycholinguistics textbooks, investigators (including, most influentially, Swinney, 1979, and Tanenhaus, Leiman, & Seidenberg, 1979) soon presented evidence that most or all meanings are initially activated and that the inappropriate ones are dumped within a few hundred milliseconds. From this, and a great deal of other work in the area, it follows that the process of lexical ambiguity resolution is one that cannot adequately be investigated without the use of tools that allow the experimenter to look in on processing as it happens and while the core activity (understanding the sentence) continues to proceed in an undisturbed way.

The second illustration of the importance of on-line psycholinguistic methods concerns a different aspect of sentence processing—namely, syntactic analysis. The particular question at issue is whether the earliest phases of syntactic processing can be influenced by prior discourse context. In a broad parallel to the Bobrow (1970) study mentioned above, Crain and Steedman (1985) showed that sentences were judged, on completion, to be more "grammatical" if and when the correct syntactic pathway was foreshadowed by discourse context. The question, as before, is whether this influence is brought to bear as the material is first being processed or whether the effect kicks in somewhat later (but still before the grammaticality judgment is exercised at the end of the sentence). Crain and his colleagues favored the former interpretation. But equally vehement were others—notably Rayner, Carlson, and Frazier (1983)—who maintained that early syntactic decisions were entirely independent of discourse context and that any effect this exerted on processing was during a later phase of "thematic processing" in which initial syntactic commitments were reappraised in the light of wider pragmatic information. What was needed to inform the dispute were methods capable of tracking processing *before* the end of the sentence (i.e., before Crain and Steedman's grammaticality assessment point). Given the challenge of refining such techniques, researchers set about the task with vigor and some assertiveness (Altmann & Steedman, 1988; Altmann, Garnham, & Henstra, 1994; Desmet, De Baecke, & Brysbaert, 2002; Mitchell, Corley, & Garnham, 1992; Rayner et al., 1983; van Berkum, Brown, & Hagoort, 1999; Zagar, Pynte, & Rativeau, 1997). Without getting drawn into discussing the *outcome* of the debate, it can be stated quite uncontroversially that the argument hangs on moment-to-moment changes as sentence analysis proceeds, and it is inconceivable that the controversy could be resolved without the imaginative use of on-line techniques.

As with the examples outlined here, there are extensive subareas of the study of language processing in which competing theoretical accounts of operations are expressed entirely in terms of events that begin and end as the process is unfolding. Without access to on-line methods, researchers would be blindfolded bystanders rather than full witnesses to such activities.

2.3 SURVEY OF MAJOR ON-LINE METHODS

Over the years, researchers have introduced and refined any number of different ways of attempting to tap into immediate language processes. Space does not permit me to attempt to compile a comprehensive catalog of these methods. Instead, I shall describe a variety of methods under three broad headings: (a) early methods that are no longer widely used, (b) long-standing methods still in active use, and (c) recent methods currently undergoing testing and evaluation.

2.4 METHODS THAT HAVE LARGELY FALLEN OUT OF FAVOR

One of the earlier methods designed to measure on-line processing loads was the click-migration task (Fodor & Bever, 1965; Garrett, Bever, & Fodor, 1966). In this task, subjects heard a sentence together with a very short burst of extraneous sound. Shortly afterwards, they were shown a printed version of the sentence and were instructed to mark with a pen the character or space in the sentence at which they thought the sound had occurred. As an on-line method, the potential of the task was based on the claim that the accuracy of click location varied as a function of the sentence processing load at the point when the click was sounded. In particular, the view held was that the local processing demands at different points in the sentence could be measured in terms of click discrepancy or migration scores. Another early and much more widely used method was the phoneme-monitoring task (Foss, 1969, 1970). In this case, subjects were instructed to press a key as soon as they heard a particular phoneme in a tape-recorded sentence. The response latency was taken as a direct measure of the linguistic processing at the point when the phoneme turned up. To test hypotheses about local processing demands, investigators merely designed materials in which the phoneme appeared at the sentence position of interest (along with foil materials with target phonemes appearing at other locations). In other tasks bearing some resemblance to phoneme monitoring, subjects were required to respond when they heard a word that *rhymed* with a target word (Tyler & Marslen-Wilson, 1977). An obvious limitation of a task in which a target is announced in advance is that this fact alone may alter the way in which the sentence is processed. Other methods avoided such preannouncement. For example, Jarvella (1971) interrupted tape-recorded material at unpredictable points in the sentence. Subjects were instructed in advance to listen to the sentence until this point and then to recall as many of the preceding words as possible. Variations in performance at different stopping points were used to address on-line questions. Other methods avoiding preannouncement had the subjects repeating back (shadowing) all the material played to them (Marslen-Wilson, 1973, 1975) or switching at a predefined point to a visual task designed to probe on-going sentence-processing activity (e.g., Tanen-haus et al., 1979).

While many of the results obtained using these methods are still broadly accepted, some of the findings have been questioned on the basis of distortions that might have been introduced by the task itself. Some almost certainly fell into disuse because of uncertainty in their interpretation. In other cases, investigators moved on not so much because the methods could not be used to tackle interesting questions but because other, often simpler, methods became available.

2.5 ON-LINE METHODS THAT HAVE STOOD THE TEST OF TIME

Next, we will consider methods that were first introduced 20 to 30 years ago and remain in regular use in current psycholinguistic work. The simplest of these is self-paced reading. In this task, the text is segmented into words, word strings, or phrases to be displayed one at a time, typically on a computer screen. The subject starts the process by pressing a key to see the first display. When the subject has read this, a second key-press initiates the second text segment, and so on until the end of the text. The main measure of interest for the researcher is the time between successive key-presses in specified regions of the text. This task was originally introduced independently by several different investigators (e.g., Aaronson & Scarborough, 1976; Mitchell & Green, 1978; Pynte, 1974), and has since been used in a variety of forms (e.g., Just, Carpenter, & Woolley, 1982; Kennedy & Murray, 1984). In some versions of the task, the display moves from left to right with successive key-presses so that each segment of the text occupies a position on the screen resembling that in the sentence displayed as a whole (the *moving-window* form of the task). In other (*stationary window*) versions, each successive segment overprints the previous one in the same location on the screen. In the moving-window version, the displays can be either be *cumulative* (with early segments remaining on-screen as others are added in turn) or *noncumulative* (in which old segments are removed as new ones are added). In either case, dashes or equivalent markers are often used to locate the position of text not currently on display). Of these alternatives, the use of the cumulative task is problematic because some subjects show an understandable tendency to press the key in rapid succession until the full sentence is on the screen, and then read the material at their leisure. The use of noncumulative task goes some way in avoiding this problem of decoupling key-pressing from linguistic processing. However, in all versions of the task there is some tendency for increments in processing time associated with material in one display to appear not immediately but in the reading latency for the following display (or even further downstream). Methods for minimizing *processing spillover* are discussed at further length in the following text.

Early users had to write their own software to run self-paced reading experiments, but this approach later became much easier to use when it was incorporated in standard experiment-generating packages (e.g., MEL, PsyScope, E-Prime, and DMASTR [later DMDX]). Currently, the simplest and cheapest way of doing this is to construct the experiment to run on DMDX (Ken and Jonathan Forster's experiment-generating software) that, at the time of this writing, can be downloaded at no cost from http://www.u.arizona.edu/~kforster/dmdx/dmdx.htm.

A second method that has been used for psycholinguistic on-line studies for almost 30 years is eyetracking (e.g., Rayner, 1975; Rayner & McConkie, 1976; Rayner, Sereno, Morris, Schmauder, & Clifton, 1989). The technical details of this task will be discussed at greater length by other contributors to this volume (e.g., Boland, chapter 4; Pickering, chapter 3). Suffice it to say that researchers have developed a variety of measures designed to quantify how difficult it is for people to read particular parts of the text (e.g., fixation duration, gaze duration, various regression measures, etc.). The method has been used to investigate numerous issues not only in comprehension (e.g., Rayner et al., 1989) but also in a much wider range of tasks (e.g., Rayner, 1998).

The third on-line method that has now established a secure track record is the use of event-related potentials (ERPs) in electroencephalography (EEG) studies (Kutas & Hillyard, 1980; Garnsey, 1993). This, too, will be discussed in much greater detail elsewhere in this volume (e.g., van Berkum, chapter 13), and so the outline here will be kept to a bare minimum. The basic method involves having the participant listen to or read text while EEG recordings are taken from a range of scalp positions. Waveforms collected over numerous trials are integrated after time-locking to a known stimulus event such as the arrival of a particular word in a test sentence. Kutas and Hillyard (1980) showed that the arrival of a semantically anomalous word produces a characteristic waveform with negative potential peaking at about 400 ms after the word (termed the N400 effect). Later researchers presented evidence that syntactic anomalies resulted in positive waveforms peaking at 600 ms or more after the triggering word (e.g., Osterhout & Holcomb, 1993; Hagoort, Brown, & Groothusen, 1993). Researchers have used evidence from these and other waveforms to examine a wide variety of issues in sentence processing. Compared with methods based exclusively on reading, a particular strength of this approach is that it offers a natural way of studying how material is processed when it is presented in the auditory modality.

2.6 METHODS INTRODUCED WITHIN THE LAST DECADE

Without question, the most influential on-line technique introduced over the last few years has been the adaptation of eyetracking to monitor eye movements not within a display of printed text but on visual arrays comprising collections of simple objects (or drawings of objects) (e.g., Tanenhaus, Spivey-Knowlton, Eberhard, & Sedivy, 1995; Eberhard, Spivey-Knowlton, Sedivy, & Tanenhaus, 1995). It turns out that as people listen to recorded sentences referring to the objects in the display, they tend to look from one object to another in a manner that is closely linked to the instructions played over the earphones (Cooper, 1974). By capitalizing on this and keeping an accurate spatial and temporal record of the pattern of fixations on the array, it is possible to learn a great deal about the linguistic processing of the auditory instructions. For example, Spivey, Tanenhaus, Eberhard, and Sedivy (2002) looked at the interpretation of the ambiguous phrase in the instruction *Put the apple on the towel* ... and were able to use eye-movement patterns to show that the precise content of the visual scene is capable of influencing the early interpretation of the phrase *on the towel* (either as modifying *apple* or as an argument of *put*). In a similar study using recorded statements rather than instructions, Altmann and Kamide (1999) showed that people are quicker to fixate on the picture of the sole edible object in an array (the cake) when they hear a sentence like *the boy will eat the cake* than if the verb *eat* is replaced by *move*. From this they argue that the selection restrictions of the verb exert an influence on processing at a point in time before the onset of the word that fills the object role.

One of the attractions of this task is that it offers a way of investigating auditory language processing without resorting to the use of a secondary task which is unnatural for the user (such as breaking off to complete an unrelated visual task). The secondary activity (scanning the visual scene) is an intrinsic part of the request to follow the instructions to move objects around within the visual array and, to this extent, can be regarded as providing an accurate reflection of realistic language behavior.

Another significant development in the last decade has been the increasing use of neuroimaging methods to study language processing. However, with a few exceptions, these methods are far too slow-acting to serve as on-line methods and will therefore only be mentioned in passing. In one such approach, positron emission tomography (PET) images are used in attempts to localize subcomponents of the language process (e.g., Stromswold, Caplan, Alpert, & Rauch, 1996). However, this approach is of no real value for on-line work because PET scans pinpoint neural activity by tracking local changes in blood flow—a process which can extend over several seconds and is likely to lead to marked smearing of image changes linked to successive linguistic operations. Similar problems occur with work based on functional magnetic resonance imaging (fMRI). With this method, it is acknowledged that the signal has "very limited temporal resolution" and may peak at up to 5 s after the triggering event (for a brief discussion of these features of the method see p. 121, Ni et al., 2000).

One neuroimaging method that may have the potential to measure up to the stringent timing requirements of on-line probes is work using magnetoencephalographic (MEG) methods (e.g., Harle, Dobel, Cohen, & Rockstroh, 2002). With this method, effects can be picked up within 200 ms or less. However, to date, there have only been very preliminary efforts to examine operations beyond the level of lexical processing, and it is much too early to comment on the potential value of this technique.

2.7 "NATURALNESS" OF DIFFERENT ON-LINE METHODS

Proponents of the more sophisticated on-line techniques typically maintain that their methods provide a more natural way of examining sentence processing than the alternatives. By this they usually mean that the normal operations involved in sentence processing are less likely to be distorted by the application of their preferred technique. For example, proponents of (print-driven) eyetracking point out that in contrast with the button-pressing measures used in self-paced reading, eye movements are a completely standard feature of normal silent reading and, moreover, the reading rates and levels of comprehension attained in this way are indistinguishable from those that occur in the absence of eyetracking (e.g., Rayner et al., 1989). In addition, the text on display need not be segmented in unnatural ways, and the reader is completely free to move both forward and backward while processing the material. Those who have more recently adapted eyetracking techniques to study processing in the auditory modality (e.g., Tanenhaus et al., 1995; Altmann & Kamide, 1999) emphasize the advantages of being able to examine the analysis of *spoken* rather than *printed* language, and of doing so in a situated context rather than in isolation from anything other than the text itself. Similarly, those advocating the use of ERP techniques often stress the benefits of being able to study spoken material.

There is no denying these strengths. However, in relation to traditional, fixed eyetracking systems (as opposed to more flexible head-mounted systems), it is worth pausing to consider how natural the reading is likely to be when head-clamps or bite-bars are used to prevent the reader from making head movements within the apparatus. Similarly, it is important to ask whether the way a person processes a spoken sentence might be influenced by the presence of an array of props or pictures in the visual environment. The mere presence of such an array may introduce demand characteristics that may completely alter the way individuals go about handling the linguistic material. This is not merely a fanciful and speculative possibility. In a famous "balloon-assisted serenade" demonstration now widely reproduced in intro-ductory texts, Bransford and Johnson (1973) showed that people processed identical printed passages in different ways depending on the details of an accompanying cartoon drawing. Text read in the presence of one picture was remembered much better than that linked with an alternative drawing—demonstrating that visual infor-mation can feed in and alter the course of linguistic processing. Interestingly, it was a core purpose of the paper by Spivey et al. (2002) to demonstrate precisely this point: that linguistic processing can be altered and guided by the contents of the visual display. A challenge for visual-world researchers will be to partial out the influence of such display-driven effects so that it is possible to say something about linguistic processing itself. It might be added that recent work suggests that this may be far from a trivial exercise. Huettig and Altmann (chapter 11, this volume) present evidence that in a visual-world task, the eyes may be drawn not only by sketches of the target object itself but also by other objects with a similar shape or color. The evidence is accumulating that the attention-directing process is itself extremely intricate, and cannot, by any means, be treated as a direct window on linguistic processing. This raises serious questions about the extent to which visual-world studies can throw light on core, context-invariant sentence processing, and the degree to which the results merely reflect the kinds of processing that occur in the presence of particular object-arrays. Granted, the proponents of this approach would almost certainly maintain that there is no such thing as "context-invariant sentence process-ing," but the problem remains that if context variation is acknowledged, there is little or nothing that such methods can tell us about sentence processing during reading or in the course of listening to prose in the absence of a relevant visual environment. These restrictions become particularly acute when it comes to investigating higher-level processes like anaphoric reference. Superficially, there might seem to be pros-pects of exploring co-indexing by tracking eye movements while people listen to sentences such as *George exchanged the CD for a cap because he no longer wanted it*. The whole process would almost certainly be distorted by the mere inclusion of the candidate pictures in the visual array as this would alter the salience of the potential antecedents.

   In relation to ERP studies, it is worth noting that the pace of presentation is often restricted to a metronomic 500–600 ms/word, which is both slower than natural speech and unnatural in its regularity. While this may assist investigators in the challenging problem of disentangling the longer latency waveforms triggered by successive words, it does beg the question about just how natural processing can be with material presented in such an unnatural way. For purposes of experimental convenience, researchers often try to minimize ambient light levels and discourage eye movements (which generate artifactual EEG patterns of their own). If real auditory sentence processing occurs in bright, animated social circumstances, it is at least worth pausing to ask whether these testing constraints represent a potential problem. Perhaps it is instructive that EEG researchers often have to pay participants more for their efforts than is typically the case for other on-line methods. This is not just to compensate for the inconvenience of having to wash the gel out of their hair after the experimental session: the onerous data requirements of EEG studies dictate that participants complete long and arduous sessions which may be six or more times longer than that commonly used in reading studies.

The point of these observations is that what appears "natural" to one group of investigators may seem profoundly unnatural to another. A case can even be made that conventional printed text was the preferred language-disseminating technology for just one period of time in history. In computer displays, advancing *is* typically achieved by pressing a key, and in cell-phone text messages the display is routinely restricted to just a few words. Arguably, in the 21st century, self-paced reading with truncated displays can be presented as the closest approximation we can currently offer to "normal" reading.

Since every task has both natural and unnatural features, the important thing is not to place excessive reliance on the results obtained using a single method. The most robust findings are those that reappear in experiments using a variety of different methods, and are therefore unlikely to be linked to the quirks or idiosyncrasies of any given technique.

2.8 SOME THEORETICAL QUESTIONS ADDRESSED IN EARLY ON-LINE WORK

It would be impossible to summarize all of the work that has been conducted using on-line methods. The coverage would extend to almost every issue that has been addressed in sentence processing. However, it is possible to pick up certain recurrent themes, and an interesting pattern emerges from this. With a few notable exceptions, the tendency is for an observation to be made by first using self-paced reading, then, after a delay of a couple of years, using an eyetracking method, and then, after a further delay, using ERP techniques. A few illustrations will suffice to make the point.

- When a reader encounters anomalous material, processing time increases in self-paced reading (Mitchell & Green, 1978), and there are also ERP N400 influences (Kutas & Hillyard, 1980), as well as increases in reading time in eyetracking studies (Frazier & Rayner, 1982; Rayner et al., 1983)
- Though the immediacy or otherwise of the influence remains contentious, the resolution of syntactic ambiguity can be shown to be influenced by changes in the discourse context. After a preliminary eyetracking failure to show the effect (Ferreira & Clifton, 1986), this was first demonstrated using self-paced reading (Altmann & Steedman, 1988) and later corroborated using eyetracking techniques (Altmann, Garnham, & Dennis, 1992) before eventually being tackled using ERP (P600) methods (van Berkum et al., 1999).
- End-of-sentence "wrap-up" effects—the demonstration that there is a processing increment associated with the final word or phrase of a sentence. This was first demonstrated using self-paced reading (Mitchell & Green, 1978) and confirmed a little later using eyetracking (Just & Carpenter,

1980). I am not aware of any ERP demonstrations of wrap-up effects to date.

- Cross-linguistic differences in (RC) attachment were demonstrated initially using self-paced reading (Cuetos & Mitchell, 1988) and later corroborated using eyetracking methods (Carreiras & Clifton, 1999). As we go to press, there has just been a very recent ERP investigation of RC-attachment in Spanish (Carreiras, Salillas, & Barber, in press). However, to date, there is no ERP study demonstrating cross-linguistic differences in RC-attachment.

- A slowing of processing with low-frequency words was demonstrated in off-line tasks many years ago, and was also quickly shown in on-line tasks, with an eyetracking demonstration (Rayner, 1977) perhaps coming in a few months earlier than the equivalent self-paced demonstration (Mitchell & Green, 1978).

- In some cases, the lag between demonstrations using different methods stretches to much longer intervals. An end-of-clause wrap-up effect was demonstrated using self-paced reading (Mitchell & Green, 1978) over 20 years before the equivalent eyetracking demonstration (Rayner, Kambe, & Duffy, 2000). ERP researchers have yet to tackle this issue.

Clearly, one could argue about the details, and no doubt there are exceptions to the rule-of-thumb that theoretically useful findings are demonstrated first with self-paced reading, later with eyetracking, and eventually (perhaps) with ERP methods. However, the pattern emerges often enough to suggest that there must be a good reason for precedence differences.

2.9 WHY IS SELF-PACED READING A TRAILBLAZING TECHNIQUE?

The answer to this question is almost certainly that there is nothing special about self-paced reading itself. It is just that the method is—and has always been—much cheaper and easier to implement than eyetracking of any kind, and certainly *very* much easier to set up and maintain than EEG-based methods. Experiments can readily be run on standard desktop (or laptop) computers using widely available experiment-generating packages (e.g., MEL, PsyScope, E-Prime, and DMASTR [later DMDX]), and so the method is available at very modest cost to almost every psycholinguistic investigator. In contrast, eyetracking apparatus is very much more expensive and, in the earlier years at least, experiments of this kind were considerably more difficult to program and run. ERP–EEG methods remain extremely expensive and technically challenging.

As a result of these technical differences, many more investigators have been able to run self-paced reading experiments, and it is probably true that there are still only a few dozen labs that are properly equipped to do modern ERP work. On this analysis, the common precedence of self-paced discoveries is probably a kind of statistical artifact. There is such a preponderance of researchers able to use straightforward methods of this kind and actually going ahead and conducting such experiments that there is a high statistical probability that any observation waiting to be made will first be made using this approach.

Low cost and ease of use are clearly strong selling points for self-paced reading. But what are the disadvantages to set against this? Is there any real justification for using expensive and technically demanding methods when alternative cheap and cheerful methods are available?

The main criticisms leveled against self-paced reading are (a) that it slows down the reading process with the implication that what is being studied may be qualitatively different from the "real" thing; (b) that it is subject to spill-over effects, with processing increments carrying over from one display to the next, and (c) that it is potentially subject to segmentation artifacts (with processing being influenced in some way by the fact that the material is segmented in an artificial way).

Each of these provides good reasons for treating self-paced reading findings with healthy skepticism but none proves to be particularly damaging in practice. It is unquestionably true that reading time is slowed down in the self-paced task, but no one has ever demonstrated that this changes the qualitative aspects of sentence processing in any important way. Indeed, as indicated in the brief summary of findings above, the standard pattern is for self-paced reading findings to be corroborated using other, faster techniques such as eyetracking. I know of no clear-cut demonstration that a self-paced finding has turned out to be misleading merely because it is associated with a lower pace of reading. As for spillover, this is an acknowledged problem discussed at length many years ago (e.g., Mitchell, 1984). Problems can be minimized by equating the lengths of displays immediately before critical test displays (so as to limit the variability of processing carryover) and, in particular, by avoiding the use of word-by-word versions of the task (see Mitchell, 1984, for a detailed discussion of this point). In any case, spillover is almost certainly a characteristic of sentence processing itself, and is frequently found both in eye-tracking studies (with anticipated differences emerging downstream of an expected test point) and in ERP methods (where entire waves of EEG activity spill over for varying amounts of time after the appearance of a critical word).

Perhaps the Achilles' heel of self-paced reading is the possibility that processing strategies might be influenced by the precise segmentation employed by the experimenter. Studies by Mitchell (1987), Gilboy and Sopena (1996), and others have demonstrated that processing can change from one segmentation to another, and this raises the possibility that any finding obtained using this method is somehow linked to a particular segmentation pattern. This in itself is not necessarily a fatal objection to the method. It merely means that the careful researcher should perhaps avoid going public before replicating an effect using a range of different segmentation patterns. If the finding in question reemerges with a variety of different segmentation patterns, then it seems safe to assume that it is not linked to any particular subdivision of the text.

In fact, there is remarkably little reason to suspect that self-paced segmentation artifacts are a serious problem, and I know of no clear-cut case in which a questionable finding has been traced to problems of this kind. In an illuminating case study, there were strong suspicions that this might have happened in my attempt to demonstrate that structural ambiguity resolution is not influenced by subcategorization information (Mitchell, 1987). In a subsequent attempt to replicate the findings of this study (but using *unsegmented* text and eyetracking methodology), Adams, Clifton, and Mitchell (1998) were unable to reproduce the finding and suggested that the original result may have been a segmentation artifact. However, since then, van Gompel and Pickering (2001) have identified possible problems with the materials used by Adams et al. (1998) and have succeeded in corroborating the original effect (using unsegmented materials and eyetracking). So the current best bet is that it is *not* safe to write off the original finding as a segmentation artifact. Since this has been the only documented case in which there were substantiated reasons for suspecting that there might have been a segmentation bias, and since these doubts have subsequently emerged as unfounded, there is no solid evidence that researchers have ever been misled by segmentation biases in the self-paced reading task.

So, to summarize, there does not seem to be good evidence that self-paced reading distorts processing in any important way. Given this, it would seem that the onus is on the proponents of the more expensive and complex on-line methods to justify setting aside what appear to be simple and reliable techniques for examining on-line sentence processing.

2.10 POSSIBLE JUSTIFICATIONS FOR USING "SOPHISTICATED" ON-LINE TECHNIQUES

One justification for employing such methods is that they provide a much richer body of data than the single key-pressing latency in self-paced reading. This may increase the sensitivity of the task (i.e., the chance of picking up a genuine psycholinguistic effect) and, perhaps more important, it can offer scope for differentiating between behavioral responses to subtly different classes of events. These potential contributions are evaluated in the following text. A second reason for using ERP and certain eyetracking tasks is that it is possible to use these methods to study the processing of *spoken* rather than printed sentences. Attempts have been made to use an auditory equivalent of self-paced reading (e.g., Ferreira, Anes, & Horine, 1996), but this suffers from the problem that, unlike printed text, the auditory representation of individual words is affected by the surrounding material, and so a context-independent segmentation of material is almost impossible. Visual-world eyetracking tasks and ERP are free to finesse this problem by making use of natural, unsegmented material. This capacity certainly trumps self-paced reading to the extent that auditory sentence processing is different from the analysis that occurs during reading; this is a good reason for exploring the use of alternative methods. Another benefit often claimed for ERP and reading eyetracking methods is the fact that informative data can be captured without the need to introduce any kind of competing concurrent task. This sets these methods apart from tasks in which one or more unusual decisions have to be made in the course of a task (e.g., a decision to press a button when ready to move on or to signal a match with probed information). It is certainly true that great care has to be taken in introducing extraneous tasks in this way. It is entirely possible that this may distort the linguistic processes that would otherwise be brought to bear in the core activity under investigation. However, there would be a much more compelling case for treating this as a selling point for single-task methods if there were clear-cut evidence that the theoretical conclusions drawn from them differ from those supported by dual tasks, and evidence, moreover, that it is the extraneous task that is the source of the difficulty. However, against this—as indicated previously—the pattern of results in the past shows that, far from challenging the results obtained using other methods, ERP and eyetracking findings typically *corroborate* earlier results. Where there are differences, it is typically too early to tell whether these should properly be attributed to weaknesses of the "extraneous task" method or methodological problems in the single-task study itself (as an example of such a debate, see the exchange between Brysbaert & Mitchell, 2000, and van Berkum, Hagoort, & Brown, 2000). In order to substantiate this claimed advantage, proponents of single-task techniques will have to provide more compelling evidence that additional tasks involved in other methods actually *modify* language-processing operations, and that their own tasks are entirely free from comparable criticism.

As indicated above, an important reason for using both eyetracking and ERP methods is that subtle qualitative differences in complex response pattern may potentially provide information about the *nature* of a problem at a fixed point in a sentence and not just the fact that there *was* a problem (identified by the fact that there was an increased reading latency). With the eyetracking methodology, the diagnostic potential lies in qualitative variation across the different measures routinely recorded (e.g., first-pass reading time, cumulative regression reading time, and percentage of regressions). For example, Boland (chapter 4, this volume; Boland & Blodgett, 2001) has presented evidence that when people read passages incorporating embedded anomalies, violations of semantic constraints only manifest themselves in some of the more *delayed* eyetracking measures (mostly involving regressions), whereas the appearance of an unexpected syntactic form (e.g., an NP [noun phrase] instead of a PP [prepositional phrase]) shows up not only in delayed measures but also in the form of amplified "early" first-pass reading measures. Distinct new patterns of combinations of effects are associated with other different kinds of syntactic anomaly (e.g., material with number violations). Another illustration of the diagnostic potential of eyetracking measures comes from a recent study by Meseguer, Carreiras, and Clifton (2002). The authors were interested in the way Spanish readers process temporarily ambiguous sentences in which an adverbial clause can initially be attached to one of two completing verb phrase (VP) sites. Attachment preferences were examined by comparing the reading patterns for sentences eventually resolved in favor of one or the other of the two competing attachment sites. The results showed that there was no obvious preference for either site—at least as revealed by the standard early reading measures typically used in eyetracking studies (e.g., first-fixation time, first-pass time). However, differences *were* evident when the investigators carried out a detailed analysis of the trajectories of regressive eye movements launched from the disambiguation point. That is, there was reliable evidence that the pattern of regression movements was altered depending upon which of the two readings turned out to be correct. If the Boland and Meseguer et al. findings above prove to be stable and generalizable, eyetracking measures may offer the promise of going beyond the mere *detection* of processing difficulties. In principle, the pattern and combination of effects may prove to be of diagnostic value in determining exactly what went wrong and, in that sense, the method offers at least the prospect of being considerably more informative than a simpler method that is capable of doing nothing more than detecting a processing problem.

Similar possibilities also arise from the use of ERP methods, as illustrated by two recent investigations of the EEG effects of syntactic violations. In the first study, Hopf, Bader, Meng, and Bayer (2003) compared the ERP patterns following critical words in fully and temporarily ungrammatical (i.e., garden-path) sentences. Whereas a simple measure of processing load could not draw a distinction between two scenarios, the use of an ERP method enabled the authors to claim that different kinds of processes were engaged in the two cases. Specifically, the duration and scalp distribution of ERP waveforms were demonstrably different in the two cases. In another similar, recent study, Kaan and Swaab (2003) compared ERP waveforms following a word signaling in one case fatal ungrammaticality and in another case unacceptability of an initially preferred analysis (i.e., the point at which an ambiguous sentence was disambiguated). The results showed that P600 waveforms evident in both cases were concentrated in different regions of the scalp: predominantly posterior in the first case and frontal in the second. Further examples of the use of detailed waveform analysis are provided by Osterhout and colleagues (chapter 14, this volume) and by van Berkum (in this case, see in particular the section, "Identity Inferences," chapter 13, this volume). In an inversion of the kind of argument just outlined, van Berkum (chapter 13, this volume) uses the *congruence* of waveforms generated by sentence-internal and discourse-induced anomalies as support for an inference that the two types of anomalies may be equivalent to one another. To the extent that differential ERP morphologies prove to be solid and replicable, they provide a clear demonstration that EEG methods are capable of picking up qualitatively different kinds of processing events at specific points in the sentence. Equally, congruence on all dimensions (polarity, peak-timing and variance, and scalp distribution) can be used to argue for processing equivalence. In these ways, they potentially provide a powerful way of tapping into the processes that are associated with sentence processing. Of course, to deliver on this promissory note, ERP researchers will have to demonstrate that the link between linguistic processing and EEG details can be relied upon to reappear in different tasks and situations and, in a further challenge, that the EEG signature in question is uniquely generated by a particular linguistic activity. If it emerges that there are many different ways of generating waveforms with the distributional characteristics in question, then it may turn out to be impossible to offer a unique interpretation of any given result.

A rather different kind of justification can be offered for tackling language processing using neuroimaging, as opposed to straightforward behavioral tasks. Methods of this kind may be able to tell us not just *what* is happening but also *where* the associated activity is located in the brain. Behavioral methods are simply not equipped to throw any light on these matters (and, in relation to ERP/EEG, the reliability of generator localization remains a contentious matter). Whether such mapping information is useful is largely a matter of the researcher's theoretical disposition. Traditional theories of language processing are agnostic about where individual processes might be seated in the brain, and as a result their adherents' response to locus-based claims of this kind is often one of disinterest. In contrast with this, new schools of thought are emerging in which the neural basis of language process is taken to be part of the very fabric of a viable theory of the operation (e.g., see Friederici, 2002; Gernsbacher & Kaschak, 2003). In view of these radical differences in the way in which different theories are currently being formulated, it is likely that the relative merits of the different approaches will ultimately be assessed almost entirely by the theoretical perspectives of the different protagonists.

2.11 SUMMARY, CONCLUSIONS, AND A GAUNTLET LAID DOWN

Looking back over the wide variety of on-line methods that have been introduced and tested, it is difficult not to be impressed by the inventiveness of researchers in this field—even more so in the case of individuals who have used virtually all of the methods mentioned here (and more). An encouraging fact is that there is an enormous amount of convergence of evidence concerning the theoretical conclusions drawn from most of the disparate methods discussed here, suggesting that as a community, we are on the right track. As modern methods become more refined and sophisticated, they raise the prospect of addressing increasingly subtle issues. However, having said this, it is a sobering fact that one of the most basic of the methods (i.e., self-paced reading) is rarely found wanting as an instrument for studying language processing, and rarely suggests conclusions that cannot be substantiated by other means. For those advocating the use of more sophisticated (and vastly more expensive) techniques, the challenge in the future will be to demonstrate unequivocally that their method of choice is capable of delivering insights that could not have been gained much more readily using a much simpler task. Why use a 3G video-enabled cell-phone when a Post-It note will do?

References

Aaronson, D., & Scarborough, H. S. (1976). Performance theories for sentence coding: Some quantitative evidence. *Journal of Experimental Psychology: Human Perception and Performance, 2,* 56–70.

Adams, B. C., Clifton, C., Jr., & Mitchell, D. C. (1998). Lexical guidance in sentence processing. *Psychonomic Bulletin and Review, 5,* 265–270.

Altmann, G. T. M., Garnham, A., & Dennis, Y. I. L. (1992). Avoiding the garden path: Eye movements in context. *Journal of Memory and Language, 31,* 685–712.

Altmann, G. T. M., Garnham, A., & Henstra, J. A. (1994). Effects of syntax in human sentence parsing: Evidence against a structure-based proposal mechanism. *Journal of Experimental Psychology: Language, Memory, and Cognition, 20,* 209–216.

Altmann, G. T. M., & Kamide, Y. (1999). Incremental interpretation at verbs: Restricting the domain of subsequent reference. *Cognition, 73,* 247–264.

Altmann, G. T. M., & Steedman, M. (1988). Interaction with context during human sentence processing. *Cognition, 30,* 191–238.

Bobrow, S. A. (1970). Memory for words in sentences. *Journal of Verbal Learning and Verbal Behavior, 9,* 363–372.

Boland, J. E., & Blodgett, A. (2001). Understanding the constraints on syntactic generation: Lexical bias and discourse congruency effects on eye movements *Journal of Memory and Language, 45,* 391–411.

Bransford, J. D., & Johnson, M. K. (1973). Consideration of some problems of comprehension. In W. G. Chase (Ed.), *Visual information processing* (pp. 383–438). New York: Academic Press.

Brysbaert, M., & Mitchell, D. C. (2000). The failure to use gender information in parsing: A comment on van Berkum, Brown, and Hagoort. *Journal of Psycholinguistic Research, 29,* 453–466.

Carreiras, M., & Clifton, C., Jr. (1999). Another word on parsing relative clauses: Eyetracking evidence from Spanish and English. *Memory and Cognition, 27,* 826–833.

Carreiras, S., Salillas, E., & Barber, H. (in press). Event related potentials elicited during parsing of ambiguous relative clauses in Spanish. *Cognitive Brain Research.*

Cooper, R. M. (1974). The control of eye fixation by the meaning of spoken language: A new methodology for the real-time investigation of speech perception, memory, and language processing. *Cognitive Psychology, 6,* 61–83.

Crain, S., & Steedman, M. (1985). On not being led up the garden path: The use of context in the psychological syntax processor. In D. R. Dowty, L. Kartunnen, & A. M. Zwicky (Eds.), *Natural language parsing* (pp. 320–358). Cambridge, UK: Cambridge University Press.

Cuetos, F., & Mitchell, D. C. (1988). Cross-linguistic differences in parsing: Restrictions on the use of the late closure strategy in Spanish. *Cognition, 30,* 73–105.

Desmet, T., De Baecke, C., & Brysbaert, M. (2002). The influence of referential discourse context on modifier attachment in Dutch. *Memory and Cognition, 30,* 150–157.

Eberhard, K. M., Spivey-Knowlton, M. J., Sedivy, J. C., & Tanenhaus, M. K. (1995). Eye-movements as a window into real-time spoken language comprehension in natural contexts. *Journal of Psycholinguistic Research, 24,* 409–436.

Ferreira, F., Anes, M. D., & Horine, M. D. (1996). Exploring the use of prosody during language comprehension using the auditory moving window technique. *Journal of Psycholinguistic Research, 25,* 273–290.

Ferreira, F., & Clifton, C. (1986). The independence of syntactic processing. *Journal of Memory and Language, 25,* 348–368.

Fodor, J. A., & Bever, T. G. (1965). The psychological reality of linguistic segments. *Journal of Verbal Learning and Verbal Behavior, 4,* 414–420.

Foss, D. J. (1969). Decision processes during sentence comprehension: Effects of lexical item difficulty and position upon decision times. *Journal of Verbal Learning and Verbal Behavior, 8,* 457–462.

Foss, D. J. (1970). Some effects of ambiguity upon sentence comprehension. *Journal of Verbal Learning and Verbal Behavior, 9,* 699–706.

Frazier, L., & Rayner, K. (1982). Making and correcting errors during sentence comprehension: Eye movements in the analysis of structurally ambiguous sentences. *Cognitive Psychology, 14,* 178–210.

Friederici, A. D. (2002). Towards a neural basis of auditory sentence processing. *Trends in Cognitive Sciences, 6,* 78–84.

Garnsey, S. M. (1993). Event-related brain potentials in the study of language—An introduction. *Language and Cognitive Processes, 8,* 337–356.

Garrett. M. F., Bever, T. G, & Fodor, J. A. (1966). The active use of grammar in speech perception. *Perception and Psychophysics, 1,* 30–32.

Gernsbacher, M. A., & Kaschak, M. P. (2003). Neuroimaging studies of language production and comprehension. *Annual Review of Psychology, 54,* 91–114.

Gilboy, E., & Sopena, J. M. (1996). Segmentation effects in the processing of complex NPs with relative clauses. In M. Carreiras, J. Garcia-Albea, & N. Sabastian-Galles (Eds.), *Language processing in Spanish* (pp. 145–187). Hillsdale, NJ: Erlbaum.

Hagoort P, Brown C, & Groothusen, J. (1993). The Syntactic Positive Shift (SPS) as an ERP measure of syntactic processing. *Language and Cognitive Processes, 8,* 439–483.

Harle, M., Dobel, C., Cohen, R., & Rockstroh, B. (2002). Brain activity during syntactic and semantic processing—A magnetoencephalographic study. *Brain Topography, 15,* 3–11.

Hopf, J. M., Bader, M., Meng, M., & Bayer, J. (2003). Is human sentence parsing serial or parallel? Evidence from event-related brain potentials. *Cognitive Brain Research, 15,* 165–177.

Jarvella, R. (1971). Syntactic processing of connected speech. *Journal of Verbal Learning and Verbal Behavior, 10,* 409–416.

Just, M. A., & Carpenter, P. A. (1980). A theory of reading: From eye fixations to comprehension. *Psychological Review, 87,* 329–354.

Just, M. A., Carpenter P. A., & Woolley, J. D (1982). Paradigms and processes in reading-comprehension. *Journal of Experimental Psychology—General, 111,* 228–238.

Kaan E., & Swaab, T. Y. (2003). Repair, revision, and complexity in syntactic analysis: An electrophysiological differentiation. *Journal of Cognitive Neuroscience, 15,* 98–110.

Kennedy, A., & Murray, W. S. (1984). Inspection times for words in syntactically ambiguous sentences under three presentation conditions. *Journal of Experimental Psychology—Human Perception and Performance, 10,* 833–849.

Kutas, M., & Hillyard, S. A. (1980). Reading senseless sentences: Brain potentials reflect semantic incongruity. *Science, 207,* 203–204.

MacKay, D. G. (1966). To end ambiguous sentences. *Perception and Psychophysics, 1,* 426–436.

Marslen-Wilson, W. D. (1973). Linguistic structure and speech shadowing at very short latencies. *Nature, 244,* 522–523.

Marslen-Wilson, W. D. (1975). Sentence perception as an interactive parallel process. *Science, 189,* 226–228.

Meseguer, E., Carreiras, M., & Clifton, C. (2002). Overt reanalysis strategies and eye movements during the reading of mild garden path sentences. *Memory and Cognition, 30,* 551–561.

Mitchell, D. C. (1984). An evaluation of subject-paced reading tasks and other methods for investigating immediate processes in reading. In D. Kieras, & M. A. Just (Eds.), *New methods in reading comprehension research* (pp. 69–89). Hillsdale, N. J.: Erlbaum.

Mitchell, D. C. (1987). Lexical guidance in human parsing: Locus and processing characteristics. In M. Coltheart (Ed.), *Attention and performance XII* (pp. 601–681). Hillsdale, NJ: Erlbaum.

Mitchell, D. C., Corley, M. M. B., & Garnham, A. (1992). Effects of context in human sentence parsing: Evidence against a discourse-based proposal mechanism. *Journal of Experimental Psychology: Learning, Memory, and Cognition, 18,* 69–88.

Mitchell, D. C., & Green, D. W., (1978). The effects of context and content on immediate processing in reading. *Quarterly Journal of Experimental Psychology, 30,* 609–636.

Ni, W., Constable, R. T., Mencl, W. E., Pugh, K. R., Fulbright, R. K., Shaywitz, S. E., et al. (2000). An event-related neuroimaging study distinguishing form and content in sentence processing. *Journal of Cognitive Neuroscience, 12,* 120–133.

Osterhout, L., & Holcomb, P. J. (1993). Event-related potentials and syntactic anomaly—evidence of anomaly detection during the perception of continuous speech. *Language and Cognitive Processes, 8,* 413–437.

Pynte, J. (1974). Une expérience automatisée en psycholinguistique. *Informatique et Sciences Humaines, 23,* 45–46.

Rayner, K. (1975). The perceptual span and peripheral cues in reading. *Cognitive Psychology, 7,* 65–81.

Rayner, K. (1977). Visual attention in reading: Eye movements reflect cognitive processes. *Memory and Cognition, 4,* 443–448.

Rayner, K. (1998). Eye movements in reading and information processing: 20 years of research. *Psychological Bulletin, 124,* 372–422.

Rayner, K., Kambe, G., & Duffy, S. A. (2000). The effect of clause wrap-up on eye movements during reading. *Quarterly Journal of Experimental Psychology Section A—Human Experimental Psychology, 53,* 1061–1080.

Rayner, K., Carlson, M., & Frazier. L. (1983). The interaction of syntax and semantics during sentence processing: Eye movements in the analysis of semantically biased sentences. *Journal of Verbal Learning and Verbal Behavior, 22,* 358–374.

Rayner, K., & McConkie, G. W. (1976). What guides a reader's eye movements? *Vision Research, 16,* 829–837.

Rayner, K., Sereno, S. C., Morris, R. K., Schmauder, A. R., & Clifton, C. (1989). Eye movements and on-line language comprehension processes. *Language and Cognitive Processes, 4,* 21–49.

Spivey, M. J., Tanenhaus, M. K., Eberhard, K. M., & Sedivy, J. C. (2002). Eye movements and spoken language comprehension: Effects of visual context on syntactic ambiguity resolution. *Cognitive Psychology, 45,* 447–481.

Stromswold, K., Caplan, D., Alpert, N., & Rauch, S. (1996). Localization of syntactic comprehension by positron emission tomography. *Brain and Language, 52,* 452–473.

Swinney, D. A. (1979). Lexical access during sentence comprehensiuon: (Re) consideration of context effects. *Journal of Verbal Learning and Verbal Behavior, 18,* 545–569.

Tanenhaus, M. K., Lieman, J. M., & Seidenberg, M. S. (1979). Evidence for multiple stages in the processing of ambiguous words in syntactic contexts. *Journal of Verbal Learning and Verbal Behavior, 18,* 427–440.

Tanenhaus, M. K., Spivey-Knowlton, M. J., Eberhard, K. M., & Sedivy, J. C. (1995). Integration of visual and linguistic information in spoken language comprehension. *Science, 268,* 1632–1634.

Tyler, L. K., & Marslen-Wilson, W. D. (1977). The on-line effects of semantic context on syntactic processing. *Journal of Verbal Learning and Verbal Behavior, 16,* 683–692.

van Berkum, J. J. A., Brown, C. M., & Hagoort, P. (1999). Early referential context effects in sentence processing: Evidence from event-related potentials. *Journal of Memory and Language, 41,* 147–182.

van Berkum, J. J. A., Hagoort, P., & Brown, C. M. (2000). The use of referential context and grammatical gender in parsing: A reply to Brysbaert and Mitchell (2000). *Journal of Psycholinguistic Research, 29,* 467–481.

van Gompel, R. P. G., & Pickering, M. J. (2001). Lexical guidance in sentence processing: A note on Adams, Clifton, and Mitchell (1998). *Psychonomic Bulletin and Review, 8,* 851–857.

Zagar, D., Pynte, J., & Rativeau, S. (1997). Evidence for early-closure attachment on first-pass reading times in French. *Quarterly Journal of Experimental Psychology: Section A—Human Experimental Psychology, 50,* 421–438.

Chapter 3
Eye Movements and Semantic Composition

MARTIN J. PICKERING, STEVEN FRISSON, BRIAN MCELREE, AND MATTHEW J. TRAXLER

Most research on language comprehension has focused on what we might consider the two ends of the process. One tradition is concerned with the "precursors" to interpretation—how people recognize words, how they decide which of the two unrelated meanings of a word is appropriate, and how they assign a syntactic analysis. The other tradition is predominantly concerned with the way in which interpretations of whole sentences are combined—how people determine the anaphoric links between sentences, what kinds of inferences they draw, and how they determine what texts are "about." Between these two extremes, there is another question (Frazier, 1999): How do people come up with the appropriate interpretation for complex expressions such as phrases and sentences? In this chapter, we seek to explore semantic composition by monitoring eye movements during reading.

We concentrate on two types of expression that we have considered in recent work. The first concerns the interpretation of *sense ambiguities*, where a word has two (or more) related interpretations. Although almost every word is ambiguous at the level of sense, the vast majority of psycholinguistic research on lexical ambiguity has concentrated on the rarer instances of *meaning ambiguity*, where a word (e.g., *bank, coach*) has unrelated interpretations (e.g., Swinney, 1979; Rayner & Duffy, 1986). Here, the main focus is on what has traditionally been termed metonymy: *Dickens* can refer literally to the man or metonymically to his writings, and *Vietnam* can refer literally to the country or metonymically to the Vietnam war. The second type of expression that we are concerned with is illustrated by *began the book*, which can be understood as "began reading the book," "began writing the book," or, indeed, as having other meanings (Jackendoff, 1997; Pustejovsky, 1995). Such ambiguities appear to arise when the semantic requirements of the verb are not met by the complement. In this case, the verb *began* requires a complement that denotes an event, but the actual complement is a noun phrase that denotes an entity. The processor resolves this problem by inserting relevant semantic content (reading, writing, etc.) via what has been termed *enriched composition*. An interesting theoretical question is the extent to which the resolution of sense ambiguity and the application of enriched composition can be related.

Many aspects of language comprehension take place without appreciable delay, and there is considerable evidence for what has often been termed *incrementality*—processing each new piece of information as soon as it is encountered (e.g., Marslen-Wilson, 1973; see Pickering, 1999, for a review). For example, it might have been the case that people did not interpret each word in a sentence incrementally, or interpreted words incrementally but only constructed a syntactic analysis at the end of the sentence, or only interpreted anaphora at the end of the sentence. However, we now know that people do not greatly delay such aspects of processing.

During language comprehension, any effect may in principle be immediate or delayed. Although there is certainly a continuum, some effects clearly occur without delay, and some clearly can be greatly delayed. For example, people are rapidly disrupted by a badly misspelled word, a nonword, or a word written using inappropriate capitalization, and they take longer reading a rare word than a frequent word (e.g., Rayner & Pollatsek, 1989). Hence, the aspects of processing that underlie these effects (e.g., lexical access) must be rapid, as well. In contrast, people often take a long time to realize that a difficult argument was illogical or based on false premises.

Just and Carpenter (1980) proposed the immediacy hypothesis, whereby readers try to interpret each content word as it is encountered. This means that they encode the word and select an interpretation (on the basis of frequency, context, etc.), assign it to its referent, and determine its status in the sentence and discourse. Though these claims are vague in many respects, what they appear to amount to is that the reader does not delay in performing lexical access, disambiguates the word with respect to context, constructs a syntactic representation that incorporates the word, and produces a semantic representation that is assessed with respect to background knowledge. All of this processing occurs before the reader starts processing the next word (assuming, of course, that the reader is successful).

In this chapter, we suggest that immediacy may be compromised for some aspects of semantic composition. This point is illustrated with reference to sense ambiguity resolution and semantic composition.

3.1 DETERMINING THE TIME COURSE OF PROCESSING USING EYE MOVEMENTS

When a reader encounters a rare word, for example, there may be immediate signs of processing difficulty. For this to happen, readers must be bound by two assumptions: *immediacy*, as already discussed, and what has been termed the *eye–mind assumption*, which is the assumption that people look at the thing they are thinking about. Jointly, the assumptions entail that if readers are looking at a particular word, for instance, then they are processing that word. If an effect linked to a word occurs while a reader fixates the word, then we can be certain that the relevant aspect of processing has occurred immediately (in accord with the immediacy hypothesis), and that the eye–mind assumption holds. So for instance, if people look at rare words longer than at frequent words (Just & Carpenter, 1980), we can infer that they perform lexical access while fixating that word and that rare words are more difficult to identify than frequent words.

However, if an effect is delayed or spills over onto the next word (Ehrlich & Rayner, 1981), then we cannot be certain whether immediacy does not hold (i.e., whether they delay processing) or whether that particular effect does not obey the eye–mind assumption. For example, some aspects of higher- level processing may require the reader to think about a discourse model, and fixating on a particular word for a longer time may not help with that process. Another possibility is that a reader may encounter difficulty at a particular point in a text but decide that it makes sense to continue moving forward normally, perhaps to see whether future information may resolve the problem. For example, in work discussed below, Frisson and Pickering (1999) found delayed difficulty with "A lot of Americans protested during Finland … ." Although readers may have immediately realized that they could not think of a relevant event associated with Finland, they may have kept moving forward to see if future information resolved their problem or because they realized that finding an event associated with Finland involved searching long-term memory and did not require any attention to a particular point in the text.

The implication is that it is not possible to use a delay in observed disruptions of the eye-movement record to unequivocally reject the immediacy hypothesis, as it is possible that, instead, the eye–mind assumption does not hold for that aspect of processing. Nevertheless, evidence that an effect does not show up immediately, when there is evidence that comparable effects do show up immediately, suggests that the cognitive processes underlying the effect are at least different from those involved in other processes that reveal immediate effects. More generally, differences in the time course and pattern of effects are likely to provide grounds for differentiating processes.

Recent experimental work in language comprehension using eye movements has employed many different measurements to determine the existence, locus, and time course of processing difficulty (see Liversedge, Paterson, & Pickering, 1998; Rayner, 1998; Rayner, Sereno, Morris, Schmauder, & Clifton, 1989). It is first necessary to define the region of interest, which almost always involves one or more words, because it is standard to assume that the word is the basic unit of analysis in sentence comprehension (rather than the character or morpheme, for instance). Analyses are almost entirely based on time spent in a region rather than length of saccade, as these measurements appear to be most sensitive to cognitive processing. An exception is analyses based on proportion of regressive eye movements. (Time spent during a saccade is usually excluded, but it probably does not matter greatly whether it is counted or not.) The earliest measure is *first fixation*, which is the time of the first fixation on a word. This appears to be sensitive to some cognitive processes (e.g., word frequency) and some gross syntactic anomalies. A slightly later measure that is probably more revealing for most issues in sentence comprehension is *first-pass time*, which is normally defined as the sum of all fixations beginning with the reader's first fixation in a region until the reader's gaze leaves the region (on one-word regions, first-pass time is equivalent to *gaze duration*, e.g., Rayner & Duffy, 1986). For both these measures, most researchers exclude trials in which readers "skip" the region during initial processing.

It is important to stress that first-pass effects cannot simply be equated with effects occurring during early phases of cognitive processing. This is because we do not typically know how to uniquely map cognitive events on to the different eye-movement measures, even when we have good grounds for believing that the eye–mind assumption generally holds. For example, even if both theoretical and empirical considerations strongly suggest that processing is split into two stages (initial analysis and reanalysis, lexical access and contextual integration, etc.), we cannot be certain that certain measures (e.g., first-pass time) exclusively measure the initial stage. Clearly, we would need a very specific hypothesis (backed up by relevant evidence) to link eye-movement patterns with underlying cognitive events.

An additional and more practical issue is that the linking is affected by the length of the region of interest. A first-pass effect for a long region (say, two or three words) will be clearly different from one that occurs on a single word. Another problem with drawing conclusions about long regions is that first-pass time finishes when the eye leaves the region in either direction, and so a regression from the first word of a long region back to an earlier region leads to a *short* first-pass time, although such a regression is presumably indicative of immediate processing difficulty. Hence, our preference has always been to define one-word critical regions wherever possible. Under such conditions, first-pass time, like first-fixation time, is spatially well-localized.

Other reading time measures capture somewhat later effects. Traditionally, these have included *total time*, defined as the sum of all fixations on a word, and *second-pass time*, which can be defined in slightly different ways. In our research, we have tended to define second-pass time as the time spent in a region after leaving the region (or after an initial skip of the region). However, just as it is dangerous to assume that first-pass time measures events that take place during initial cognitive processing, it is dangerous to assume that second-pass time measures reanalysis. A similar point holds for other definitions of second-pass (or rereading) time, such as time spent on a region following a regressive saccade.

Further measures have been developed and tested during recent years. The most important "new" measure, which often seems to capture interesting effects, is most commonly called *regression-path time*, though other older names exist (Brysbaert & Mitchell, 1996; Konieczny, Hemforth, Scheepers, & Strube, 1997; Liversedge, 1994; Traxler, Bybee, & Pickering, 1997). This includes all fixations from the first within a region until the first to the right of a region (again, with skips generally excluded). Hence, it includes fixations outside the target region when the reader has regressed to the left prior to fixating to the right of the region. It is striking how frequently this measure has been used in recent papers, suggesting that it is a particularly informative measure. One reason this is interesting is because we know that the reader has not looked at anything after the critical word. Regression-path time is sometimes interpreted as the time necessary for readers to process the text to a sufficient degree that they are prepared to input new information (and appears to correspond best to what readers can do during cumulative self-paced reading). However, note that some fixations included in the measure may be quite "late" because the reader may repeatedly fixate the beginning of the sentence after fixating the target word. Consequently, if first-pass time does not show any difference but regression-path time does, it must be that the effect is due to those trials on which a regression occurred from the region in question.

Finally, many papers report proportions (or numbers) of regressions. It is crucial to distinguish first-pass regressions from later measures of regressions. A first-pass *regression from a region* is a leftward movement from that region following a first-pass fixation in that region. Clearly an effect on first-pass regressions is an early effect because it demonstrates that readers have made a different decision for one condition over another during the time that they first spend in that region. In contrast, a measure of *regressions into a region* (i.e., back from a later region) is very akin to second-pass time and does not reflect early processing.

What do these different measures tell us about language comprehension? The answer is, of course, that they may tell us many different things. There is no single measure that should be preferred, and they are enormously affected by the characteristics of the regions chosen. If effects emerge on first-fixation or first-pass time for a single word of roughly normal length, we can be fairly confident that they emerged during the earliest stages of processing that eyetracking is likely to detect (discounting any preview effects, of course). First-pass regressions would also be informative of early effects if they occur on the target region. Very early spill-over effects (e.g., first fixation after the target word) must also be fairly early. Apart from this, it is not clear what can be said with certainty without a theory of how eye movements and cognitive processing interact. As noted above, it is very unlikely that there is a straightforward relationship between, on the one hand, first-pass and first-fixation measures and initial processing, and, on the other, between later measures and later processing. For the most part, we consider whether effects occur on early measures of processing or not, using the assumption that the combination of the immediacy and eye–mind hypotheses predicts that effects of linguistic processing should occur as soon as the relevant word is fixated.

3.2 SENSE RESOLUTION

As noted above, most work on lexical ambiguity resolution has been concerned with words with unrelated meanings (i.e., homonyms). For example, the two meanings of *bank* (roughly, repository for money, and side of a river) are largely unrelated. There has been a great deal of research on the on-line resolution of homonyms, using priming (Seidenberg, Tanenhaus, Leiman, & Beinkowski, 1982; Swinney, 1979; Tanenhaus, Leiman, & Seidenberg, 1979), eyetracking (Duffy, Morris, & Rayner, 1988; Rayner & Duffy, 1986; Rayner & Frazier, 1989), or a combination of the two (Sereno, 1995). This work has been greatly influenced by the "modularity" debate (Fodor, 1983) and has concentrated on the questions of whether all meanings are activated irrespective of context, and how and when the processor selects one meaning. Meaning resolution can be thought of as occurring before an interpretation is assigned to complex expressions. Context basically serves to select one meaning of a homonym, and this meaning is subsequently integrated with the context.

There has, in contrast, been very little work on the processing of words with related senses, but it is clear that sense resolution is very different from meaning resolution. Most words have only one or two meanings. In contrast, almost all words have very many senses, and it can be very hard to enumerate them. For example, *newspaper* can refer to the institution, the content of the newspaper over a number of editions, the day's edition, or a particular copy (e.g., Copestake & Briscoe, 1995), *window* can refer to the glass (*broke the window*) or to the aperture (*climbed through the window*), and even a proper name like *Julius Caesar* can refer to the man, a picture or statue of him, or even a speech by him, given appropriate context. It is also far from clear that either producers or comprehenders always determine exactly which sense is appropriate (e.g., Sanford & Sturt, 2002), and conversationalists often only resolve what they are talking about to a depth necessary for current purposes (Clark & Wilkes-Gibbs, 1986). However, sense resolution obviously can occur. For example, "I tore the newspaper" requires that *newspaper* refer to a particular copy. Although it is theoretically possible that sense resolution occurs like meaning resolution, a much more likely alternative is that it takes place as part of the process of assigning an interpretation to a complex expression.

There have been some attempts to study the representation of sense ambiguity, with Klein and Murphy (2001, 2002) arguing that different senses are represented in a largely independent manner, so that the distinction between sense and meaning representation is a matter of degree rather than kind. In contrast, Rodd, Gaskell, and Marslen-Wilson (2002) proposed clear differences between sense and meaning ambiguity with respect to their effects on comprehension time.

There have been few studies on the processing of sense ambiguities in sentence contexts. One important exception by Frazier and Rayner (1990) used eyetracking to investigate the processing of nouns with multiple senses (e.g., *novel*) and multiple meanings (e.g., *ball*), and compared them to unambiguous nouns like *door*. Their results showed that words with multiple meanings were processed differently from words with multiple senses, which behaved much more like unambiguous words. For example, when disambiguating information followed the ambiguous noun, nouns disambiguated to the subordinate meaning caused more difficulty than nouns disambiguated to the dominant meaning. Apparently people generally adopted the dominant meaning on, or soon after, encountering the word. However, words with multiple senses, which were disambiguated towards either the concrete or the abstract interpretation, did not show processing difficulties. Thus, they concluded that people did not perform immediate sense disambiguation in the absence of prior disambiguating context and that an abstract sense could be processed as fast as a concrete sense. Frazier and Rayner proposed a *minimal semantic commitment model* in which a single semantic value is only assigned immediately when two interpretations are incompatible.

To address the time course of sense ambiguity resolution, Frisson and Pickering (1999) turned to the consideration of metonymy. In metonymy, a salient aspect of an entity is used to refer to the entity as a whole or to some other part of the entity. In the following examples of metonymy, definitions of the relationship between the literal and metonymic interpretations are provided in parentheses:

(1) a. *I read Dickens whenever I can* (producer-for-product).
   b. *The wings took off from the runway* (part-for-whole or *synecdoche*).
   c. *Belgium will win the European cup* (whole-for-part).
   d. *The blasphemous woman had to answer to the convent* (place-for-institution).
   e. *They protested during Vietnam* (place-for-event).

Frisson and Pickering (1999) argued that metonymy was ideal for psycholinguistic investigation using eyetracking because it is generally localized to a single word. Hence, we can precisely determine the time course of metonymic processing. This contrasts with, for example, idioms and most metaphors, which are generally "dragged out" over a number of words. In such cases, it is often difficult to determine the precise point at which it becomes clear that the expression is not being used literally (consider, for example, *That's the way the cookie crumbles*).

Frisson and Pickering (1999) considered the processing of place-for-institution metonyms like *convent* in (1d) and place-for-institution metonyms like *Vietnam* in (1e). In Experiment 1, they contrasted literal versus metonymic uses of *convent* with the control word *stadium* that does not have a relevant metonymic use:

(2)   a. *These two businessmen tried to purchase the convent at the end of last April, which upset quite a lot of people.*
      b. *That blasphemous woman had to answer to the convent at the end of last March, but did not get a lot of support.*
      c. *These two businessmen tried to purchase the stadium at the end of last April, which upset quite a lot of people.*
      d. *That blasphemous woman had to answer to the stadium at the end of last March, but did not get a lot of support.*

Readers experienced no difficulty with *convent* in either the metonymic condition (2b) or the literal condition (2a). This suggests that the processor could rapidly access both senses. Although it is possible that the two senses were computed in parallel, with context then selecting between them, the lack of any correlation between sense frequency and processing difficulty makes this account unlikely, and so Frisson and Pickering proposed that readers initially accessed an underspecified representation that did not distinguish between the literal and metonymic senses (see also Frisson & Pickering, 2001). In contrast, readers experienced immediate difficulty with *stadium* in (2d) with the first-pass time on *stadium* being longer in (2d) than (2c). In accord with Just and Carpenter (1980), this effect is particularly early and suggests that effects of semantic incongruity can occur as soon as a word is fixated.

In Experiment 2, Frisson and Pickering (1999) contrasted literal versus metonymic uses of words like *Vietnam* with control words for places that were not associated with any event:

(3)   a. *During my trip, I hitchhiked around Vietnam, but in the end I decided to rent a car for a couple of days.*
      b. *A lot of Americans protested during Vietnam, but in the end this did not alter the president's decision.*
      c. *During my trip, I hitchhiked around Finland, but in the end I decided to rent a car for a couple of days.*
      d. *A lot of Americans protested during Finland, but in the end this did not alter the president's decision.*

Readers experienced no difficulty with (3a) or (3b), suggesting that they could access both senses without difficulty. They did experience difficulty with (3d), but the difficulty was delayed quite considerably (it appeared on regressions from an end-of-line region corresponding to *I decided to* or *this did not* for this example, and on late measures). A pretest indicated that (3d) was implausible (in comparison to 3c), though considerably less implausible than (2d). However, almost no one associated any event with Finland, so the manipulation could not have been stronger for this condition. Thus it appears that the delayed difficulty with (3d) is a genuine demonstration that a particular kind of incongruity effect is delayed.

These experiments suggest that established senses are interpreted straightforwardly and do not lead to any processing difficulty even if they are figurative. Pickering and Frisson (2003) considered whether it was also possible to make a novel sense familiar using appropriate context. They employed the producer-for-product rule (roughly, if X refers to a producer, then X also refers to that producer's characteristic product):

(4) a. *Not so long before she died, my great-grandmother met Dickens in the street. I heard that she often read Dickens when she had the time.*
   b. *My great-grandmother has all the novels written by Dickens in her library. I heard that she often read Dickens when she had the time.*
   c. *My great-grandmother confessed that she once kissed Dickens on the cheek. I heard that she often met Dickens when she had the time.*
   d. *Not so long before she died, my great-grandmother met Needham in the street. I heard that she often read Needham when she had the time.*
   e. *My great-grandmother has all the novels written by Needham in her library. I heard that she often read Needham when she had the time.*
   f. *My great-grandmother confessed that she once kissed Needham on the cheek. I heard that she often met Needham when she had the time.*

Texts (4a–c) employed a familiar producer, whereas (4d–f) employed an unfamiliar one (i.e., Needham was not identified as a writer). In the second sentence, (4c and f) used the name to refer to a person, whereas (4a, b, d, and e) used the name to refer to the product. We made two predictions. First, we predicted that on both first and second mentions of the names, *Dickens* would be easier to read than *Needham* because it is a more familiar name (names were matched for length). Name familiarity is presumably closely related to frequency (more familiar names being more frequent), and frequency effects occur during early processing (Just & Carpenter, 1980; Rayner & Duffy, 1986). Therefore we predicted effects of name familiarity should occur during early eyetracking measures (i.e., first-pass and first-fixation time), and they did.

Second, we predicted difficulty when a name was used to refer to a product, when readers were not aware that it referred to a producer. Clearly, no difficulty is predicted with the literal uses of either *Needham* or *Dickens* (i.e., with 4c or 4f) or with the metonymic use of *Dickens* (i.e., with 4a or 4b). In contrast, (4d) should be difficult because the context sentence does not introduce Needham as a writer, so the second reference to Needham (in *read Needham*) should be difficult in just the same way that the reference to *Finland* in (3d) was. Again, we found this pattern of results with effects occurring on late measures (specifically, second-pass time on and just before the name).

The most interesting condition is (4e), where the context sentence introduces Needham as a producer. We found that the target sentence was easier in (4e) than (4d). In fact, there was only weak evidence of any difficulty with (4e) at all (i.e., in comparison to 4f). This demonstrates that a single mention of a word in the appropriate sense can be enough for novel-sense learning. However, most strikingly, the first mention of Needham in (4e) is literal. The metonymic sense of Needham has never been encountered before. Hence, the new sense is learned not by repeated exposure but rather by application of the producer-for-product rule.

These three experiments provide evidence about the applicability of Just and Carpenter's hypotheses. We found immediate effects of the difference between *Needham* and *Dickens*, the difficulty of *answer to the stadium*, and delayed effects of *during Finland* and *read Needham*. The early name familiarity effect demonstrates the sensitivity of our experiments (i.e., it shows that we can detect early signs of difficulty). We propose that difficulty is delayed for *during Finland* and *read Needham* because they involve unsuccessful searches of their general knowledge. In other words, readers initially encounter these phrases and try to determine whether something relevant has ever happened in Finland and whether they have heard of a writer called Needham. In other words, they start to explore their general knowledge at this point. This search is sufficiently "detached" from the word *Finland* or *Needham* itself that the reader does not continue to fixate the word. Only after it becomes clear that the search is likely to be unsuccessful do readers refixate the critical word. Whether this account is right in detail or not, the results are incompatible with the immediacy hypothesis because the effects are localized but during second pass.

So why does immediate difficulty emerge with *answer to the stadium*? Intuitively, it appears to be that readers do not search general knowledge to determine if a stadium can be addressed. Instead, it appears to be part of the meaning of the word *stadium* that it is an inanimate object, and it is not plausible to address an inanimate object. Of course, it is possible to use stadium metonymically to refer to the people in the stadium, but this sense is not sufficiently familiar (without contextual support) for it to be accessed automatically. In other words, the difficulty with *answer to the stadium* appears to be due to the lexical representations of the words, whereas the difficulty with *during Finland* or *read Needham* appears to be one of reference. In any case, the results point to the complexity of determining which effects should occur on early processing measures and which should not. It is probably only because the regions are sufficiently small and well-defined that such distinctions can be drawn.

Finally, Pickering and Frisson (2001) considered the processing of verbs with multiple senses where the dominant sense was considerably more frequent than the subordinate sense. Pretests determined that the senses were closely related:

(5) a. *After the capture of the village, we disarmed almost every rebel and sent them to prison for a very long time* (supportive preceding context, dominant sense).

    b. *With his wit and humour, the speaker disarmed almost every critic who was opposed to spending more money on art* (supportive preceding context, subordinate sense).

    c. *Mr Graham is quite certain that they disarmed almost every rebel and sent them to prison for a very long time* (neutral preceding context, dominant sense).

    d. *Mr Graham is quite certain that they disarmed almost every critic who was opposed to spending more money on art* (neutral preceding context, subordinate sense).

The most important finding was that processing difficulty with the subordinate sense relative to the dominant sense did not emerge until much after the critical verb was first encountered. Similarly, prior disambiguating context reduced processing difficulty, but again this difference did not emerge until later processing. Again, these results are incompatible with immediacy. Interestingly, another experiment using verbs with two meanings (e.g., *ruled*) also showed delayed effects of meaning dominance, suggesting that verbs may be processed differently from nouns (where the subordinate bias effect occurs during initial processing; Duffy et al., 1988). However, verbs with multiple meanings and verbs with multiple senses were not processed in the same way; context had relatively rapid effects on meaning resolution but not on sense resolution.

3.3 SEMANTIC COMPOSITION

It is sometimes possible to derive the appropriate interpretation for a complex expression by simply combining key semantic properties of the individual words according to their syntactic position in the sentence (e.g., Jackendoff, 1997, 2002). In such circumstances, semantic properties retrieved from lexical representations and grammatical constraints associated with syntactic representations will uniquely determine the interpretation of the expression. Accordingly, the compositional mechanism—the critical interface between lexical and syntactic processing on one hand and discourse and text comprehension on the other—might merely consist of rules or principles for recursively combining semantic properties.

However, many common and seemingly simple expressions appear to require a richer form of composition (Jackendoff, 1997, 2002; Pustejovsky, 1991, 1995). An example of such an expression is *The boy began the book*. The verb *begin* (like start, enjoy, etc.) requires a complement with an event meaning (e.g., the fight, the assignment, the movie). However, the default interpretation of *the book* is an entity. In order to satisfy the semantic requirements of *begin*, it must be construed as an event. Typically, the complement is interpreted as an event by implicitly generating an activity that is commonly associated with the complement noun and compatible with the agent. Thus, *the boy began the book* is typically interpreted as the boy began reading the book, whereas *the author began the book* is typically interpreted as the author began writing the book (McElree, Traxler, Pickering, Seely, & Jackendoff, 2001; Traxler, Pickering, & McElree, 2002). To do this, the complement is type-shifted from an entity to an event interpretation, and unexpressed semantic content (e.g., reading, writing) must be introduced.

Piñango, Zurif, and Jackendoff (1999) presented some evidence for difficulty with enriched composition. Using a cross-modal lexical decision task, they found greater processing load after *the insect hopped effortlessly until …* versus *the insect glided effortlessly until …* . They argued that people interpreted *hopped* as referring to a point-action event with an intrinsic beginning and end, and were therefore forced to shift its aspectual form from point-action to repeated activity when they encountered *until*, whereas no such type-shift was necessary following *glided*. It is possible to interpret this difficulty as a kind of garden path where *hopped* is initially assigned the wrong aspectual form.

We now have good evidence for difficulty with enriched composition from a quite different source and also some suggestion that such difficulty is typically somewhat delayed. In a self-paced reading study, McElree et al. (2001) contrasted the following:

(6) a. *The author was starting the book in his house on the island.*
     b. *The author was writing the book in his house on the island.*
     c. *The author was reading the book in his house on the island.*

Sentence (6a) involves enriched composition, whereas (6b and c) do not. The verb in (6b) was employed in the most common interpretation of (6a) (i.e., started writing the book), and the verb in (6c) was employed in the next most common interpretation of (6a) (i.e., started reading the book), as assessed by a fill-in-the-blank pretest. McElree et al. found difficulty with (6a) at *book* and *in*, suggesting that enriched composition caused a noticeable processing cost.

Traxler et al. (2002) ran an eyetracking version of this experiment and also found difficulty with sentences similar to (6a) in comparison to controls like (6b and c). In this study, difficulty did not emerge on first-pass time on *the book*. Although there was some sign of a first-pass regressions difference on *the book*, there was no effect on regression-path time. The clearest effects occurred on regression-path time from the words immediately following *the book* and on other late measures. Because readers would have realized the need for enriched composition by *book*, these results again provide evidence against Just and Carpenter's assumptions and suggest that some semantic processing has delayed effects on the eye-movement record.

McElree et al. (2001) argued that an event-taking verb with an entity complement causes difficulty. However, it is possible that verbs like *starting* are difficult for some unrelated reason. To distinguish these possibilities, Traxler et al. contrasted event complements (e.g., *the fight*) with entity complements (e.g., *the puzzle*), and verbs that require an entity complement (e.g., *started*) with verbs that are compatible with either an entity or an event complement (e.g., *saw*):

(7) a. *The boy started the fight after school today.*
 b. *The boy saw the fight after school today.*
 c. *The boy started the puzzle after school today.*
 d. *The boy saw the puzzle after school today.*

In accord with our predictions, *started the puzzle* caused processing difficulty but *started the fight* did not. Overall, *started the fight* was processed similarly to *saw the fight*, but *started the puzzle* caused more difficulty than *started the fight* or *saw the puzzle*. This demonstrates that the cause of difficulty is the combination of entity-taking verb and event noun. In this experiment, difficulty was clearly delayed, with effects emerging on regressions from a post-target region (here, *after school*) and on second-pass and total-time measures on the noun phrase itself. A self-paced reading replication of this experiment showed this pattern of effects on *after* but not on *puzzle* or *fight*.

Although we can now conclude that the specific combination of event-taking verb with entity complement causes processing difficulty, there are different possible explanations for the difficulty. It could merely be due to anomaly detection, with the "clash" between the semantic type of the required and the actual complement causing difficulty. This would therefore be analogous to many garden-path effects in parsing, for instance, when an intransitive verb is followed by a noun phrase (e.g., Mitchell, 1987). Whereas anomaly detection may contribute to difficulty, it leaves unanswered the question of how the processor actually obtains the enriched interpretation for the expression.

Alternatively, difficulty may be due to ambiguity. Almost all cases of enriched composition are formally ambiguous, so that *start the puzzle* is probably most likely to mean "started solving the puzzle" but could mean "started making the puzzle" and can clearly have other meanings in appropriate contexts (e.g., "started painting the puzzle" in a context about an artist who was painting objects). In some cases, ambiguity is a source of processing difficulty. For example, it is more difficult to process nouns that have two meanings of roughly equal frequency (balanced nouns) than otherwise comparable unambiguous words in a context that does not provide disambiguation (Rayner & Duffy, 1986). Most likely, readers have difficulty deciding which interpretation to select for such ambiguous words. Could enriched composition be similar, with the difficulty being due to the process of selecting the appropriate interpretation?

There are a number of reasons why this explanation is unlikely to be correct. Ambiguity effects are quite limited, in that they appear to occur for balanced nouns with multiple meanings in neutral contexts alone. They may well not occur for syntactic ambiguity (Traxler, Pickering, & Clifton, 1998; van Gompel, Pickering, & Traxler, 2001) or for words with multiple senses (Frisson & Pickering, 1999) and require the two meanings to be of similar frequency (Rayner & Duffy, 1986). Duffy et al. (1988) found that a context that supported one interpretation removed the difficulty with the interpretation of balanced words. The ambiguity effects also appear to occur immediately, suggesting that the effect occurs during the process of selecting a meaning. In contrast, our effects are often somewhat delayed. More important, all our experiments involve highly biased items, with one interpretation (e.g., *the author started writing the book*) being much preferred to alternatives (as determined by fill-in-the-blank pretests).

Additionally, Traxler, McElree, Williams, and Pickering (2003) found that the difficulty is not attenuated by a context that provides strong support for the preferred interpretation. Participants read two-sentence texts in which the second sentence described an event using a coercing verb (8a, 8b) or a verb that corresponded to the coerced interpretation (8c, 8d) (i.e., coercing vs. control target). The first sentence either mentioned this event (8a, 8c) or did not (8b, 8d) (i.e., relevant vs. neutral context):

(8)   a. *The contractor had been building in the suburbs. That spring, he began a condominium next to the shopping center.*
      b. *The contractor had been looking for new jobs. That spring, he began a condominium next to the shopping center.*
      c. *The contractor had been building in the suburbs. That spring, he built a condominium next to the shopping center.*
      d. *The contractor had been looking for new jobs. That spring, he built a condominium next to the shopping center.*

In the neutral context conditions, we predicted difficulty for the coerced target sentence (8b) versus the control target sentence (8d). If a context mentioning the coerced event affected processing of the target sentence, we would not expect a similar difference in the relevant context conditions. In other words, (8a) should be no more difficult than (8c). In fact, we found the same difference between (8b) and (8d) as between (8a) and (8c). In other words, removing the ambiguity did not eliminate the coercion cost. More specifically, the experiment showed the coercion cost remained when there was a greatly preferred interpretation for the coerced expression and when context supported this interpretation by mentioning the event (building). Again, these effects primarily emerged on later measure such as total time (rather than, for example, first-pass time on *condominium*). We can therefore rule out an explanation of coercion cost in terms of ambiguity. The results also suggest that coercion does not appear to be a kind of bridging inference (Clark & Haviland, 1977) because the context should have provided the bridge. Instead, it appears to be due to language-internal semantic operations.

We might, however, predict that it would be possible to prime these semantic operations by repeating either the exact operation or its interpretation. Traxler et al. (2003) had participants read coercing targets (9a, 9b) or control targets (9c, 9d) following coercing contexts (9a, 9c) or control contexts (9b, 9d). The preferred interpretation of the coerced contexts and targets instantiated the same interpretation as the control contexts and targets, and hence the verb (*started* or *read*) was used transitively with the same entity serving as the object as in the target sentence. Most importantly, the context and target sentences involved the same interpretation of the complement:

(9)   a. *The student started a book in his dorm room. Before he started the book about the opium trade, he checked his e-mail.*
      b. *The student read a book in his dorm room. Before he started the book about the opium trade, he checked his e-mail.*

c. *The student started a book in his dorm room. Before he read the book about the opium trade, he checked his e-mail.*

d. *The student read a book in his dorm room. Before he read the book about the opium trade, he checked his e-mail.*

When participants read the coerced target, they had already interpreted the complement in the same way in the context sentence. In (9a), they had done this by performing the same coercion operation and therefore constructing the same complement to the coercing verb. In (9b), they had arrived at the same interpretation for the verb phrase in the context sentence via normal composition.

In fact, both forms of context removed the difficulty with the coerced target. More specifically, Traxler et al. (2003) found difficulty in reading the coerced context sentence versus the control context sentence (thereby confirming the basic pattern of difficulty with coercion), but no difficulty in reading the coerced target sentence versus the control target sentence in either condition (and, moreover, there was an interaction between context and target sentences). As before, the clearest effects emerged on total time, though this experiment did find evidence for an effect on the first noun region [i.e., *a book* in (9)] on regression-path time. In other words, the construction of the interpretation "read a book," whether via enriched or normal composition, removed the difficulty with assigning that interpretation to *started the book* in the following sentence. A further experiment found similar effects when the full noun phrase *the book* was replaced with an anaphor (*it*) in the target sentence.

These experiments suggest that the difficulty of performing coercion is attenuated by recent processing of the relevant event structure, either directly (e.g., *read a book*) or following coercion (e.g., *started a book*). In contrast, a relevant context that simply mentions the event [*building* in (8)] is not effective. Hence, simply facilitating the "bridging" inference is not enough to remove the difficulty. This suggests that coercion is a language-internal operation whose difficulty cannot be removed just by making the coercion more compatible with general context. However, it is possible to prime the actual mechanisms involved in the coercion.

3.4 DOES TYPE-SHIFTING CAUSE DIFFICULTY?

At this point, we have evidence for difficulty with the semantic operations involved in enriched composition and evidence for no difficulty with the semantic operations in understanding familiar metonymy. Indeed, the coercion studies find difficulty with the computation of a complement with an event interpretation, whereas Frisson and Pickering (1999) found no difficulty with interpreting *Vietnam* as an event. What is the difference between these cases, and what might it tell us about semantic composition?

Enriched composition appears to involve two operations: type-shifting itself and the insertion of new semantic structure. In *started the book*, the processor has to reinterpret the complement as an event and to insert the relevant meaning (e.g., *reading*). The experiments on metonymy (Frisson & Pickering, 1999; Pickering & Frisson, 2003) suggest that the act of type-shifting is not costly, so long as the type-shifted sense (e.g., *Vietnam* meaning the Vietnam war) is familiar. If so, it must have been the act of inserting the new semantic structure that was costly.

However, a direct comparison between the metonymy experiments and the coercion experiments is risky because the former involved proper names whereas the latter involved definite descriptions. To be more confident about the difference between metonymy and coercion and hence to be able to conclude that coercion involves an on-line process, we needed to make a direct comparison between the processes. Hence, we considered items with involving a literal expression (10a), a metonymic expression (10b), or a metonymic expression (10c) in a coerced context (McElree, Pickering, & Frisson, 2003):

(10) a. *The gentleman spotted Dickens while waiting for a friend to arrive.*
      b. *The gentleman read Dickens while waiting for a friend to arrive.*
      c. *The gentleman started Dickens while waiting for a friend to arrive.*

If type-shifting per se is the cause of processing difficulty, then (10b) and (10c) should be harder to process than (10a). If, instead, difficulty is caused by the insertion of new semantic structure, then (10c) should be difficult, but (10b) and (10a) should be similar in difficulty. In fact the results supported this latter prediction. Largely, on the total time measure, (10c) was harder than (10b) and (10a), which were somewhat similar in difficulty. These results therefore support the claim that familiar type-shifted senses can be stored, but that enriched composition has to take place on-line.

3.5 CONCLUSIONS

Our experiments suggest that type-shifting *per se* is not costly, but that the on-line generation of nonlexicalized senses is difficult. In *during Finland*, people have to generate an event sense for *Finland* or else come up with no interpretation for the expression. Similar conclusions hold for *reading Needham* in the absence of contextual support. Likewise, the generation of the appropriate sense for *started the book* causes difficulty. The fact that similar difficulty holds for *started Dickens* confirms our interpretation of the results.

Our experiments have generally found that these are "late" effects. In this respect, they contrast with frequency effects, some lexical effects (such as those that occur during the resolution of lexically ambiguous nouns), and some syntactic effects (such as the more extreme form of garden-path effects; e.g., Frazier & Rayner, 1982). The pattern of results also contrasts with *answering to the stadium*, where difficulty emerged immediately. It appears that some aspects of lexical, syntactic, and semantic processing do (largely) respect the immediacy and eye–mind assumptions (with some important caveats), but that many aspects of sentence interpretation are some-what delayed. Pickering and Frisson's (2001) findings confirm this, in that it takes time to settle on an interpretation of a sense-ambiguous verb. It may be that people have to perform extensive searches for semantic information (e.g., what event might have occurred in Finland?) and that this takes time. It may be that different experiments produce delayed effects for different reasons, and we must be mindful of the possibility that the absence of some early effects might simply reflect a failure to detect a real effect (perhaps because of insufficient power). Nevertheless, the pattern of results suggests that not all "deep" aspects of semantic processing have effects that emerge during initial processing of the relevant word.

Which hypothesis should we therefore relax? It appears that the main problems are with the immediacy hypothesis and that some aspects of processing simply take more time than the eye is prepared to wait. *Prima facie* it makes more sense to relax this hypothesis than the eye–mind hypothesis because the assumption that people look at the thing they are thinking about extends far beyond linguistic processing. However, more importantly, most of the late effects discussed above are relatively well localized during second-pass processing. In other words, readers do look at difficult words such as *Finland*, but they largely do this during later processing rather than during first pass.

The experiments discussed in this chapter provide some evidence that eye movements allow us to separate out different stages of processing. Because semantic processing may not occur all at once, and because eye movements are sensitive to different stages in comprehension, eyetracking experiments can help us determine what happens when and use this information to drive theoretical accounts of language comprehension.

3.6 ACKNOWLEDGMENTS

This research was supported by a University of Edinburgh Development Trust grant (awarded to MP), a National Institute of Mental Health grant MH57458 (awarded to BM), and a National Institute of Child Health and Human Development grant HD040865 (awarded to MT).

References

Brysbaert, M., & Mitchell, D. C. (1996). Modifier attachment in sentence parsing: Evidence from Dutch. *Quarterly Journal of Experimental Psychology, 49A,* 664–695.

Clark, H. H., & Haviland, S. (1977). Comprehension and the given-new contrast. In R. Freedle (Ed.), *Discourse production and comprehension* (pp. 1–40). Hillsdale, NJ: Erlbaum.

Clark, H. H., & Wilkes-Gibbs, D. (1986). Referring as a collaborative process. *Cognition, 22,* 1–39.

Copestake, A., & Briscoe, E. (1995). Semi-productive polysemy and sense extension. *Journal of Semantics, 12,* 15–67.

Duffy, S. A., Morris, R. K., & Rayner, K. (1988). The interaction of contextual constraints and parafoveal visual information in reading. *Journal of Memory and Language, 27,* 429–446.

Ehrlich, S. F., & Rayner, K. (1981). Contextual effects on word recognition and eye movements during reading. *Journal of Verbal Learning and Verbal Behavior, 20,* 641–655.

Fodor, J. A. (1983). *The modularity of mind.* Cambridge, MA: MIT Press.

Frazier, L. (1999). *On sentence interpretation.* Dordrecht, Netherlands: Kluwer.

Frazier, L., & Raynes, K. (1982).

Frazier, L., & Rayner, K. (1990). Taking on semantic commitments: Processing multiple meanings vs. multiple senses. *Journal of Memory and Language, 29,* 181–200.

Frisson, S., & Pickering, M. J. (1999). The processing of metonymy: Evidence from eye-movements. *Journal of Experimental Psychology: Learning, Memory, and Cognition, 25,* 1366–1383.

Frisson, S., & Pickering, M. J. (2001). Obtaining a figurative interpretation of a word: Support for underspecification. *Metaphor and Symbol, 16,* 149–171.

Jackendoff, R. (1997). *The architecture of the language faculty.* Cambridge, MA: MIT Press.

Jackendoff, R. (2002). *Foundations of language.* New York: Oxford University Press.

Just, M. A., & Carpenter, P. A. (1980). A theory of reading: From eye fixations to comprehension. *Psychological Review, 87,* 329–354.

Klein, D. E., & Murphy, G. L. (2001). The representation of polysemous words. *Journal of Memory and Language, 45,* 259–282.

Klein, D. E., & Murphy, G. L. (2002). Paper has been my ruin: Conceptual relations of polysemous senses. *Journal of Memory and Language, 47,* 548–570.

Konieczny, L., Hemforth, B., Scheepers, C., & Strube, G. (1997). The role of lexical heads in parsing: Evidence from German. *Language and Cognitive Processes, 12,* 307–348.

Liversedge, S. P. (1994). *Referential context, relative clauses, and syntactic parsing.* Unpublished Ph.D. thesis, University of Dundee, Dundee, UK.

Liversedge, S. P., Paterson, K. B., & Pickering, M. J. (1998). Eye movements and measures of reading time. In G. Underwood (Ed.), *Eye guidance in reading and scene perception* (pp. 55–75). Oxford, UK: Elsevier.

Marslen-Wilson, W. D. (1973). Linguistic structure and speech shadowing at very short latencies. *Nature, 244,* 522–523.

McElree, B., Pickering, M. J., & Frisson, S. (2003). *Enriched composition and sense extension.* Manuscript submitted for publication.

McElree, B., Traxler, M. J., Pickering, M. J., Seely, R. E., & Jackendoff, R. (2001). Reading time evidence for enriched semantic composition. *Cognition, 78,* B15–B25.

Mitchell, D. C. (1987). Lexical guidance in human parsing: Locus and processing character-istics. In M. Coltheart (Ed.), *Attention and performance XII* (pp. 601–618). Hillsdale, NJ: Erlbaum.

Pickering, M. J. (1999). Sentence comprehension. In S. Garrod & M. J. Pickering (Eds.), *Language processing* (pp. 123–153). Hove, UK: Psychology Press.

Pickering, M. J., & Frisson, S. (2001). Processing ambiguous verbs: Evidence from eye-movements. *Journal of Experimental Psychology: Learning, Memory, and Cognition, 27,* 556–573.

Pickering, M. J., & Frisson, S. (2003). *Learning novel senses by rule: Why reading Needham can be easy.* Manuscript submitted for publication.

Piñango, M. M., Zurif, E., & Jackendoff, R. (1999). Real-time processing implications of enriched composition at the syntax-semantics interface. *Journal of Psycholinguistic Research, 28,* 395–414.

Pustejovsky, J. (1991). The syntax of event structure. *Cognition, 41,* 47–81.

Pustejovsky, J. (1995). *The generative lexicon.* Cambridge, MA: MIT Press.

Rayner, K. (1998). Eye movements in reading and information processing: 20 years of research. *Psychological Bulletin, 124,* 372–422.

Rayner, K., & Duffy, S. A. (1986). Lexical complexity and fixation times in reading: Effects of word frequency, verb complexity, and lexical ambiguity. *Memory & Cognition, 14,* 191–201.

Rayner, K., & Frazier, L. (1989). Selection mechanisms in reading lexically ambiguous words. *Journal of Experimental Psychology: Learning, Memory, and Cognition, 15,* 779–790.

Rayner, K., & Pollatsek, A. (1989). *The psychology of reading.* Englewood Cliffs, NJ: Prentice Hall.

Rayner, K., Sereno, S. C., Morris, R. K., Schmauder, A. R., & Clifton, C. (1989). Eye movements and on-line comprehension processes. *Language and Cognitive Processes, 4,* 21–49.

Rodd, J. M., Gaskell, M. G., & Marslen-Wilson, W. D. (2002). Making sense out of ambiguity: Semantic competition in lexical access. *Journal of Memory and Language, 46,* 245–266.

Sanford, A. J., & Sturt, P. (2002). Depth of processing in language comprehension: not noticing the evidence, *Trends in Cognitive Sciences, 6,* 382–386.

Seidenberg, M. S., Tanenhaus, M. K., Leiman, J. M., & Bienkowski, M. (1982). Automatic access of the meanings of ambiguous words in context: Some limitations of knowledge-based processing. *Cognitive Psychology, 14,* 489–537.

Sereno S. C. (1995) Resolution of lexical ambiguity: Evidence from an eye movement priming paradigm. *Journal of Experimental Psychology: Learning, Memory, and Cognition, 21,* 582–595.

Swinney, D. A. (1979). Lexical access during sentence comprehension: (Re)consideration of context effects. *Journal of Verbal Learning and Verbal Behavior, 18,* 645–659.

Tanenhaus, M. K., Leiman, J. M., & Seidenberg, M. S. (1979). Evidence for multiple stages in the processing of ambiguous words in syntactic contexts. *Journal of Verbal Learning and Verbal Behavior, 18,* 427–440.

Traxler, M. J., Bybee, M. D., & Pickering, M. J. (1997). Influence of connectives on language comprehension: Eye-tracking evidence for incremental interpretation. *Quarterly Journal of Experimental Psychology, 50A,* 481–497.

Traxler, M. J., McElree, B., Williams, R., & Pickering, M. J. (2003). *Context effects in coercion: evidence from eye-movements.* Manuscript submitted for publication.

Traxler, M. J., Pickering, M. J., & Clifton Jr., C. (1998). Adjunct attachment is not a form of lexical ambiguity resolution. *Journal of Memory and Language, 39,* 558–592.

Traxler, M. J., Pickering, M. J., & McElree, B. (2002). Coercion in sentence processing: Evidence from eye-movements and self-paced reading. *Journal of Memory and Language, 47,* 530–547.

van Gompel, R. P. G., Pickering, M. J., & Traxler, M. J. (2001). Making and revising syntactic commitments: Evidence against current constraint-based and two-stage models. *Journal of Memory and Language, 45,* 283–307.

Chapter 4
Linking Eye Movements to Sentence Comprehension in Reading and Listening

JULIE E. BOLAND

Eyetracking paradigms in both written and spoken modalities are the state of the art for online behavioral investigations of language comprehension. But it is almost a misnomer to refer to the two types of paradigms by the same "eyetracking" label because they are quite different. Reading paradigms gauge local processing difficulty by measuring the participant's gaze on the very material that he or she is trying to comprehend. The critical sentence regions are determined spatially, and gaze is measured in terms of the time spent looking within a region of interest, the likelihood of a regressive eye movement out of the region, and so forth. In contrast, listening paradigms gauge how rapidly successful comprehension occurs by measuring how quickly people look, or how likely people are to look, at objects referenced by the linguistic material. In many cases, inferences can be drawn about the content of the listener's representation, based upon which of several objects are fixated.

This chapter summarizes some of the contributions of each paradigm, focusing on the development of linking assumptions between eye-movement data and sentence comprehension processes. I will also discuss some limitations that currently plague each paradigm and make a few suggestions for how we might get to the next level of investigation using these paradigms. The first half of the chapter focuses on reading, and the second half on listening. It will quickly become clear that the same linking assumptions will not serve us in both reading and listening paradigms. The cognitive processes under investigation include word recognition and syntactic/semantic analysis. The behaviors that we can measure in an eye-movement paradigm are the location, duration, and onset time of each fixation. Intuitively, the linkage between cognition and fixation is straightforward in reading paradigms: Reading comprehension involves visual attention, and visual attention requires fixation. However, it is less clear, on the face of it, why eye movements should be causally linked to language comprehension in a listening paradigm.

The linking assumptions between dependent measures and mental processes are worthy of discussion in and of themselves because these linking assumptions are essentially hypotheses about one's methodology rather than assumptions of the standard type. Unfortunately, these methodological hypotheses often go unstated and untested.

4.1 EYE MOVEMENTS AND READING

Eye-movement data from reading have been very influential for evaluating theories of human sentence processing. This is because the eye-movement record provides an on-line measure of processing difficulty with high temporal resolution, without relying on any secondary task to produce the dependent measures. Furthermore, we know much about the factors that influence the planning and execution of saccades and the duration of fixations, because eye movements have been carefully studied for several decades within the domains of vision, motor control, and language processing (see Rayner, 1998, for a recent review). For example, researchers have studied how our eyes move over meaningless strings and then examined how much of the variability in fixation duration and saccade landing site is linked to linguistic factors in actual text.

In fact, we have a pretty clear understanding of the amount of visual information processed during a fixation on text. During reading, factors such as a word's frequency, length, predictability, and ease of integration into the sentence influence how long it takes to access the lexical entry for that word and to incorporate the new lexical information into the structural and conceptual representations the reader is constructing for the sentence (e.g., Pollatsek & Rayner, 1990; Rayner, Sereno, & Raney, 1996). These same factors also influence whether the eyes fixate on a word and, if so, how long the fixation is maintained (Just & Carpenter, 1980; Rayner, Reichle, & Pollatsek, 1998; Rayner, Sereno, Morris, Schmauder, & Clifton, 1989; Reichle, Pollatsek, Fisher, & Rayner, 1998). In contrast, we do not understand how the different dependent measures that are commonly used (see Table 4.1) are linked to specific cognitive events. For example, long reading times on a word and regressive eye movements from the current word to earlier words are both presumably caused by processing difficulty associated with the current word. But when difficulty occurs, we do not know what determines how the difficulty will manifest itself in the eye-movement record. Reichle et al.'s E-Z Reader is probably the current state of the art in terms of precise models of eye movements during reading, but it models only "normal" undisrupted reading. They did not even attempt to model the probability of a regressive eye movement to an earlier region of the sentence.

Table 4.1. **Commonly Used Dependent Measures in Reading Studies**

First fixation:	The duration of the first fixation in a region
First-pass time:	The time spent in a region from first entering it until first leaving the region with a saccade in any direction
Regression path time:	The time from first entering a region until moving the eyes beyond (rightward) the region. If there were first-pass regressions, this will include time spent in earlier regions following the regression
Probability of a regression:	The percentage of regressive (leftward) eye movements out of a region; usually limited to first-pass regressions
Total time:	The sum of all fixations in a region, including secondary fixations

Note: A region is usually defined as a word or phrase.

4.1.1 Multiple Dependent Measures: Converging and Diverging Evidence

It is undoubtedly an advantage that we can carve the eye-movement record up in different ways. Most researchers analyze three or four different dependent measures in hopes of getting a complete view of the cognitive processes involved in sentence comprehension. Oftentimes, they find the same pattern in all the dependent measures, which makes for a coherent set of results. However, I will argue that we can learn more about the linking assumptions between eye-movement data and the cognitive events from sentence comprehension by studying experiments in which the dependent measures diverge.

An example of converging evidence is the classic paper by Frazier and Rayner (1982). Participants read garden-path sentences like those in (1). It is well known that readers and listeners develop structural (syntactic) and interpretive (semantic) representations of sentences incrementally as they read or hear each word. However, the structural position of *a mile* is temporarily ambiguous; it can either be the direct object of *jogs* as in (1a), or the subject of an embedded clause as in (1b).[1]

(1) a. *Since Jay always jogs a mile <u>this seems</u> like a short distance to him.*
     b. *Since Jay always jogs a mile <u>seems</u> like a short distance to him.*

The experimenters expected readers to adopt the direct object structure and to experience processing difficulty in (1b) at the point of disambiguation, which is underlined. As predicted, *seems* was fixated longer and regressive eye movements occurred more frequently in (1b) than in (1a). Some trials exhibited the effect in one dependent variable, some trials in the other, and some trials exhibited the effect in both dependent variables. The linking assumption here is fairly simple: A single type of cognitive event can result in various behavioral outcomes. The combination of long fixations and regressive eye movements at the point of disambiguation has become the hallmark of a garden path in eye-movement studies of reading, and such effects can be found even when the reader is unaware of any processing difficulty.

Much more recently, Traxler, Morris, and Seely (2002) found that the difficulty of reanalysis after a garden path in object relative sentences was mitigated by animacy. This pattern was seen as a trend in the first-pass data and was reliable in their other three dependent measures (quasi-first pass,[2] the likelihood of a regression, and total reading time). Findings like these, of which there are many, suggest that processing load increases are equally likely to be reflected in longer fixations, secondary fixations in the difficult region, and regressions to earlier segments.

Although the eye-movement record can be analyzed in different ways, it is important to keep in mind that we do not have four or five dependent measures that are derived independently. Within a region of interest, there are really just two behavioral measures: fixation duration and saccade extent/direction (i.e., does the eye leave the region on the saccade, and if so, does it move forward or backward?). Everything else is computed from that. For example, the probability of a first-pass regression impacts several different dependent measures, including the probability of a regression, regression path time, and total time.

Some research questions may be more easily answered when the various dependent measures do not all exhibit the same pattern.

- Do some types of constraints influence syntactic ambiguity resolution but not the initial generation of structural alternatives?
- Which constraints determine the structures that are initially accessed or constructed and how easy it is to do so?
- Are phrase structure, morphosyntactic, and semantic operations sequentially ordered or simultaneous?

It is fairly common in reading studies to contrast early (first-pass) effects with later (second-pass or total-time) effects. In doing so, one hopes to use the multiple dependent variables offered by the eye-movement record to distinguish early lexical and structure-building processes from later processes that make use of those representations. Importantly, different researchers have taken this contrast to reflect different cognitive events, depending upon their theoretical assumptions. Some researchers have argued that detailed lexical information is not part of the initial structure-building process (e.g., Mitchell, 1987), while others have argued that detailed lexical information forms the basis of the initial structure-building process (e.g., MacDonald, Pearlmutter, & Seidenberg, 1994). In my own research, I have argued that the architecture of the sentence comprehension system is restricted, such that lexical and syntactic constraints influence the initial construction of syntactic alternatives as each new word is integrated into the developing sentence structure. At the same time, I have maintained that constraints from higher levels of representation can influence syntactic ambiguity resolution when multiple structural alternatives are generated. The first of these two architectural claims was tested and supported by Boland and Blodgett (2001).

Boland and Blodgett (2001) embedded unambiguous target sentences like (2a) and (2b) in simple stories. The sentences contain a noun–verb homograph (*duck*), but its syntactic category is disambiguated by the preceding pronoun.

(2) Example target sentences from Boland and Blodgett (2001). Bars separate the regions used for analysis.
(a) Noun target. *She | saw his | duck and | chickens near | the barn.*
(b) Verb target. *She | saw him | duck and | stumble near | the barn.*

The examples in (2) are taken from a story about a girl visiting a boy on a farm. The sentence prior to the target sentence supported either a noun or verb meaning of the homograph: *Kate watched everything that Jimmy did.* Or *Kate looked at all of Jimmy's pets.* The type of context sentence and the type of target sentence were crossed to create two conditions that are discourse congruent and two that are not. In addition, the relative frequency of the noun and verb forms of the homograph were varied continuously to create a lexical frequency variable. Following the architectural assumptions outlined above, we predicted that the more frequent the appropriate form of the homograph, the easier it would be to integrate the homograph with the developing structural representation. In contrast, we expected that discourse congruency would not affect ease of structure building in this unambiguous syntactic context. Under the linking assumption in (3) then, only lexical frequency effects should be seen in the first-pass reading times of these unambiguous target sentences.

(3) **Linking assumption:** First-fixation duration reflects ease of structural integration but not pragmatic/discourse integration.

As predicted, there was a lexical frequency effect in the first fixation on the region *duck and*—the earliest possible location. In contrast, no discourse congruency effect was seen in the first-pass reading times. There was a discourse congruency effect in the likelihood of regressive eye movements, but this effect was downstream, in the region after the lexical frequency effect. There was also a very robust effect of discourse congruency in the second-pass reading times, distributed throughout most of the sentence. Note that in this contrast between early and late effects, there is a difference in both the dependent variables that exhibited the effects and the sentence region where the effect was found.

The early versus late contrast in Boland and Blodgett (2001) has theoretical implications because it suggests that lexical frequency influences the initial generation of structure but discourse congruency does not. The later effects of discourse congruency are assumed to reflect anomaly detection after the sentence structure has been determined. An important part of the argument is that discourse congruency *does* have rapid and local effects on structural ambiguity resolution. In temporarily ambiguous sentences like *She saw her duck ...* , Boland (1997) found effects of discourse congruency at the point of disambiguation (which was either the word following the ambiguous pronoun or downstream of the noun–verb homograph). This demonstrates that discourse congruency does resolve a syntactic ambiguity when a congruent and an incongruent structure are both syntactically possible, but that discourse congruency cannot determine what structures are possible, neither does it influence the initial structure-generating process.

4.1.2 Anomaly Detection

In Boland and Blodgett (2001), the discourse anomaly effects were observed relatively late in the eye-movement record. Under what circumstances should anomaly effects arise late? Would local structural anomalies reveal themselves earlier than discourse anomalies? To fully answer these questions, a detailed model of the mapping between the dependent measures and the underlying cognitive processes would be required. Athough no such model exists, some relevant evidence is reviewed in this section.

It should be noted that eye-movement research has not distinguished itself as much as some other methodologies in the area of anomaly detection. In particular, event-related potential (ERP) research has been quite promising in distinguishing anomaly detection processes in terms of the linguistic level of analysis at which the anomaly occurs (e.g., Ainsworth-Darnell, Shulman, & Boland, 1998; Friederici & Frisch, 2000; Gunter, Stowe, & Mulder, 1997; Hagoort, Brown, & Groothusen, 1993; Osterhout & Nicol, 1999). See van Berkum (chapter 13, this volume) and Osterhout et al. (chapter 14, this volume) for brief summaries of the N400, P600, and LAN components in semantic and syntactic anomaly detection studies. In fact, Friederici (1995) outlined a detailed processing architecture in which phrase structure construction (based on major syntactic category, as in Frazier's [1978, 1987] garden-path theory) precedes morphosyntactic and lexical-semantic processing. Her proposed architecture is motivated by differences in both the scalp location and the latency of ERP anomaly detection effects. Given the latency differences observed in the ERP record, should we not see similar distinctions in the eye-movement record, where we have more detailed temporal information?

There is surprisingly little evidence on "pure" anomaly detection in eye-movement studies. Most have focused on garden-path sentences rather than the globally anomalous sentences typically used in ERP research. A garden path occurs when a temporarily ambiguous region of a sentence is misanalyzed. In most cases, the initial analysis becomes anomalous when disambiguating words are encountered later in the sentence. For example, (1b) is a garden-path sentence in which *a mile* is structurally ambiguous and *seems* is the point of disambiguation. In some cases, the syntactically ambiguous phrase itself contains disambiguating semantic information. For example, in (4), the attachment of the prepositional phrase (PP) is ambiguous until the plausibility of using a revolver to see is evaluated against the plausibility of a cop having a revolver. Sentence (4) will cause a garden path if the reader initially attaches the PP to the verb phrase, as maintained by Rayner, Carlson, and Frazier (1983).

(4) *The spy saw the cop with a <u>revolver</u>, but the ... .*

As noted above, garden-path effects are characterized by increased looking time in the disambiguating region and higher probabilities of regressions out of the disambiguating region (e.g., Frazier & Rayner, 1982). Because garden paths are generally taken as evidence that the language-processing system pursues only one (incorrect) analysis of the ambiguous material, the linking assumption is that the cognitive phenomena of anomaly detection and syntactic reanalysis are collectively reflected in the eye-movement data as longer first-pass reading times, an increased probability of regressive eye movements, and the time spent re-reading earlier material following a regression. In fact, Frazier and Rayner suggested more specific linking assumptions between the cognitive processes, anomaly detection and reanalysis, and the dependent measures, fixation duration and regressions, respectively. They suggested that "there was an awareness at some level on the first fixation in the disambiguating region that something was wrong, as evidenced by a longer fixation duration" (p. 193). Because regressive eye movements often landed in the ambiguous region, Frazier and Rayner also suggested that such regressions "indicate that subjects have detected an error in their initial analysis of the sentence and have identified the source of the error" (p. 203).

These particular linking assumptions between eye movements and the underlying cognitive behavior have been widely accepted over the past two decades. However, there have been some cautionary notes and some conflicting conclusions as well. For example, Rayner et al. (1989) noted that regressions "could reflect not only the existence of an erroneous initial analysis, but also the relative plausibility of competing analyses, the syntactic differences between the initial and the revised analyses, and so on" (p. 38). In fact, Spivey-Knowlton and Tanenhaus (1998) attributed increased reading times to competition between parallel structures—not to anomaly detection and reanalysis. Their constraint-based lexicalist account allows such an attribution because, in contrast to Frazier and Rayner (1982), they assume that syntactic alternatives are postulated and evaluated in parallel. In short, despite some commonly held assumptions, there are many open research questions concerning the relationships between the dependent measures in eye-movement paradigms and the cognitive processes underlying sentence processing.

If noticing something anomalous is the initial component of processing difficulty in garden-path sentences, then one would expect to see anomaly effects in the first-pass measures on the anomalous words in both garden-path sentences and globally anomalous sentences. However, a review of the small eye-movement literature on unambiguous, globally anomalous sentences suggests that this is not always true. Table 4.2 provides a summary of anomaly detection effects from the eye-movement literature. Only local first-pass measures are considered here. This includes the first-pass reading time in the anomalous region and the probability of a regression out of the region during the first pass through the anomalous region. Sometimes the regression path duration is also taken to be a first-pass measure, but it is excluded here on the grounds that it includes processing time spent in multiple regions and is therefore not a strictly local measure. The shaded areas in Table 4.2 represent the types of anomalies that were investigated in each study. Unfortunately, there have not been many papers that investigate several types of anomalies within a single experiment. This makes it difficult to determine (in analogy to the ERP experiments) whether the gaze pattern in response to an anomaly differs depending upon linguistic level of anomaly.

Boland and Blodgett (2002) examined the broadest range of anomaly types. They used two sets of critical stimuli, an "argument structure set" and an "agreement set." The first set of stimuli contained verb argument structure violations on the indirect object. Examples are given in (5) and (6). Anomalous words are starred, and doubly anomalous words receive two stars. The critical word at which the potential anomaly is apparent is underlined. The anomalous indirect object was either of the wrong phrasal category—a noun phrase (NP) instead of a prepositional phrase (PP) as in (5b)—or had the wrong semantic properties (*signs*), or both. The anomalies in the agreement stimuli were either a syntactic subject/verb agreement violation as in (6b) or a semantic violation in which the sentential subject (*snake/s*) was not a suitable agent for the verb. Thus, in both stimulus sets, the semantically anomalous words were inconsistent with the thematic role that the verb assigned to one of its arguments. However, the syntactic violations were quite different. The syntactic anomalies in the agreement stimuli were morphosyntactic agreement violations similar to those used by Ni, Fodor, Crain, and Shankweiler (1998); Braze, Shankweiler, Ni, and Palumbo (2002); and Pearlmutter, Garnsey, and Bock (1999). In the argument structure stimuli, the violations reflected a conflict between the verb's argument structure and the phrasal category of the indirect object.

Table 4.2. **Anomaly Detection Results (Local First-Pass Measures)**

Experiment	Measure	Subcategory	Semantic	Morphosyntactic
Boland & Blodgett, 2002	Reading time	X		
	% Regression	X		X
Ni et al., 1998; Braze et al.,	Reading time			
2002	% Regression			X
Pearlmutter et al., 1999,	Reading time			
Exp 2	% Regression			X
Deutsch & Bentin, 2001	Reading time			X
Frisson & Pickering, 1999	Reading time		X	

(5) a. *Kim recommended Shakespeare to <u>everyone/*signs</u> after she saw Hamlet.*
   b. *Kim recommended Shakespeare *<u>everyone/**signs</u> after she saw Hamlet.*

(6) a. *The canary/*snake in the large cage <u>sings</u> beautifully.*
   b. *The *canaries/**snakes in the large cage <u>sings</u> beautifully.*

As noted above, there is some evidence from the ERP literature that phrasal category violations are recognized more rapidly (e.g., Friederici, Pfeifer, & Hahne, 1993), but there have been no previous attempts in the eye-movement literature to distinguish between morphosyntactic and phrasal category violations. Boland and Blodgett (2002) found that syntactic congruency affected first-pass reading time when the manipulation involved a phrasal category error, but not when it involved a morphological feature error. Both types of syntactic congruency influenced the likelihood of a first-pass regressive eye movement. Semantic congruency did not influence first-pass reading time, but it did affect the regression path duration.

Ni et al. (1998) investigated syntactic and semantic anomalies in unambiguous sentences like those in (7). Both the syntactic and semantic anomalies (illustrated in (7a) and (7b), respectively) led to more regressive eye movements than the control sentences (7c). The likelihood of an immediate regression, however, was higher for syntactic anomalies than for semantic anomalies. In contrast, only the semantic anomaly induced longer first-pass fixations, and only after (rather than during) the anomalous region. Ni et al. interpreted these results to suggest qualitative differences in the cognitive response to the two types of anomalies—differences that are directly reflected in the eye-movement patterns.

(7) a. **It seems that the cats won't usually <u>eating</u> the food ...*
   b. **It seems that the cats won't usually <u>bake</u> the food ...*
   c. *It seems that the cats won't usually <u>eat</u> the food ...*

More recently, Braze et al. (2002) focused on regressive eye movements in comparing morphosyntactic and semantic anomalies. They found that syntactic anomalies elicited an immediate peak in the percentage of regressive eye movements, while semantic anomalies led to a gradual rise in regressions that peaked at the end of the sentence.

Pearlmutter et al. (1999, Experiment 2) examined subject–verb agreement errors in sentences like (8). As in Ni et al. (1998) and Braze et al. (in press), the eye-movement pattern was dominated by regressions. However, Pearlmutter et al. *did* find longer first-pass fixations for some conditions on a subset of trials. The effect was not localized to the anomalous word alone (*were*), but became apparent when fixations on the anomalous word and the following word were summed. Furthermore, the effect was only observed after excluding the trials on which there was a regression out of that region (about 14% of trials) and excluding eight participants who either always or never made regressions out of that region.[3] I have not included the Pearlmutter et al. potential reading-time effect in Table 4.2 because it was not strictly localized to the anomalous word.

(8) a. *The key to the cabinet was/*were rusty ...*
     b. *The key to the cabinets was/*were rusty ...*

Deutsch and Bentin (2001) examined subject–verb gender agreement in Hebrew, a language that marks both gender and number in the verb morphology. In contrast to the English morphosyntactic results, they found an anomaly effect for mismatched gender in sentences like (9a) in the first-pass reading times on the verb. In (9a), the plural verb explicitly marks the gender of the subject. Only second-pass reading effects were observed for the unmarked (singular) form (9b). The authors did not analyze the probability of regressive eye movements. The authors also reported an ERP version of the experiment. They found a negative component 80–250 ms after incongruent verbs, regardless of markedness, and a P600 for marked incongruent verbs only.

(9) a. *I enjoyed seeing how the actors (*hasaxkaniot/hasaxkanim) were enchanting (maksimim) ...*
     b. *The woman saw that the boy/girl (*hayeled/hayalda) had fallen (nepal)* ...

Frisson and Pickering (1999) reported some early and some late semantic anomaly effects in their investigation of metonymic expressions. Familiar metonomy (*Americans protested during Vietnam.*) is handled easily; the authors report that readers were able to coerce the place (*Vietnam*) into an event (the Vietnam war) with no increase in processing difficulty over a literal control (*Americans hitchhiked around Vietnam.*). However, unfamiliar metonymic expressions seem to be treated as semantic anomalies, as in (10a), *Finland* condition. As in the Boland and Blodgett experiment, there was no evidence of an anomaly in the first-pass reading times for items like (10a). In contrast, Frisson and Pickering reported local first-pass reading time effects for semantic anomalies like those in (10b). The crucial difference between (10a) and (10b) is unclear. The authors suggest that *Finland* in (10a) initiates a search for relevant events, while there is a clear feature clash or selectional restriction in (10b). However, the details of such an account need to be carefully worked out. Why should unfamiliar "place-for-institution" metonomy violate a selectional restriction if unfamiliar "place-for-event" metonomy does not?

(10)   a. *A lot of Americans protested during *Finland/Vietnam* ...
       b. *The blasphemous woman had to answer to the *stadium/convent* ...

What generalizations can we make about these anomaly effects in unambiguous sentences? Can we generate any predictions about the types of anomalies that will generate local first-pass effects? There was only one study that examined phrasal category violations, and unfortunately, it is unpublished (Boland & Blodgett, 2002). Eye-movement evidence of the violations emerged in the first-pass reading times on the anomalous material. In fact, the results are predicted by most current sentence-processing theories, which maintain that verb subcategorization guides the initial structural analysis. However, not all syntactic violations led to local first-pass reading time effects. There was much more data on morphosyntactic errors, and within this group, most of the studies examined subject/verb agreement violations. The English studies consistently found morphosyntactic effects in the probability of a first-pass regression, while they did not find increased first-pass reading times on the anomalous word (Boland & Blodgett, 2002; Ni et al., 1998; Braze et al., 2002; Pearlmutter et al., 1999). In contrast, a Hebrew study did find first-pass reading time effects for some of the anomalous conditions—they did not analyze the probability of a regression (Deutsch & Bentin, 2001). The results regarding semantic/pragmatic violations are also mixed. Several studies found no local first-pass effects (Boland & Blodgett; Braze et al.; Ni et al.), but Frisson and Pickering (1999) did find first-pass reading time effects for certain semantic violations.

Based upon the anomaly detection results summarized in Table 4.2 as well as data from grammatical stimuli such as that in Boland and Blodgett (2001), I offer the linking assumption in (11) as a working hypothesis. "Structural integration" is intended here to mean adding the new constituent to the developing phrase-structure tree. When trouble arises, I assume that the reader will either maintain gaze or refixate the problematic word until either structural integration is complete or has been determined impossible. The English morphosyntactic violations represent an example in which structural integration proceeds normally but the agreement violation triggers reprocessing of earlier material.

(11)   **Linking Assumption:** The eyes do not leave a word until it has been structurally integrated. Therefore, constraints that control structure-building influence first-pass reading time.

The structure-building constraints that influence first-pass reading time would include syntactic category and subcategory, lexical frequency, morphological agreement in richly case-marked languages (like Hebrew, but not English), and semantics when it determines structure.[4] Note that the relevant constraints proposed here are different from the traditional first-pass assumptions by Frazier and colleagues in the garden-path literature (e.g., Frazier, 1978, 1987). In Frazier's garden-path model, neither detailed lexical information (such as verb subcategorization and the relative frequency of noun and verb forms of a homograph) nor semantics can influence the initial rule-generated parse.

The proposal that eye fixations are related to structural integration may seem to be quite a departure from the current models of eye movements such as E-Z Reader (Reichle et al., 1998). There are at least two issues here. The first issue is the assumed relationship between lexical access completion and syntactic analysis. E-Z Reader assumes the traditional distinction between lexical and syntactic processing embodied in Frazier's garden-path model. This sharp distinction allows E-Z Reader to predict eye movements based upon atomic lexical variables alone, such as the familiarity of the word in isolation, ignoring syntactic and high-level text factors. While this strategy simplifies the modeling task, it is at odds with the increasingly lexicalized nature of syntactic parsing theories (e.g., Ford, Bresnan, & Kaplan, 1982; Carlson & Tanenhaus, 1988; McElree, 1993). In many current approaches, word recognition within sentence context cannot be separated from structure assignment (e.g., Boland, 1997; Lewis, 2000; MacDonald et al., 1994; Novick, Kim, & Trueswell, 2003). That is, the identification of a single lexical form simultaneously completes word recognition and determines the local syntactic structure some or all of the time. Under such a view, the proposal that fixations are causally linked to structural integration is not a violation of E-Z Reader's core assumption that visual attention moves to the next word when lexical access of the current word is complete. Rather, such a view would require E-Z Reader to consider combinatory factors in addition to atomic lexical factors in predicting the time course of lexical access.

The second issue is the coupling of visual attention and fixation location. As in the linking assumption from (11), early theories of eye movements made a locality assumption, such that visual attention and eye fixation were tightly linked (Just & Carpenter, 1980; Morrison, 1984). In Morrison's theory, completion of lexical access on word n simultaneously prompted a shift in attention to word $n + 1$ and the planning of an eye movement to word $n + 1$. At some level of abstraction, a close relationship between visual attention and fixation location is absolutely necessary to explain reading behavior. However at a more precise level, the Morrison assumption is too constraining because it leaves us unable to model preview and spillover effects as well as refixations on the same word. To address these limitations, Reichle et al. (1998) decoupled visual attention shifts from saccade planning by assuming that there are two relevant events during lexical access. The first is completion of a familiarity check on the currently attended word, which signals an eye-movement program for a saccade to the next word. The second is completion of lexical access, which shifts attention to the next word. Thus, in apparent contrast to the linking assumption in (11), Reichle et al. do not assume that either structural integration or lexical access has been completed prior to eye-movement planning. Rather, it is the familiarity check that provides the important signal to the motor system.

To be clear, the proposed familiarity check is not an event that can be found in current theories of visual word recognition. Reichle et al. (1998) note that "The division of lexical access into two discrete serial stages, f (familiarity check) and lc (completion of lexical access), is largely a modeling convenience." (p. 133, parentheticals added here for clarity). To model the time course of the familiarity check,

Reichle et al. used log word frequency (Francis & Kucera, 1982) and predictability (essentially the cloze value of each word in a sentence), two variables that robustly predict lexical decision time, a common measure of lexical access. In other words, the function of the familiarity check is to estimate when lexical access will be complete, so that visual attention and fixation location will remain closely, but not exactly, synchronized. (In E-Z Reader, lexical access completion is more strongly affected than the familiarity check by the fixation location parameter and is assumed to require additional, but unspecified, processing beyond the familiarity check.)

To create a version of E-Z Reader that is consistent with the linking assumption in (11), factors that predict structural integration would have to be incorporated when modeling the time course of the "familiarity check." Unfortunately, the best way to do so is theory-dependent because the factors that affect structural integration are still hotly debated in the parsing literature. Nonetheless, some examples of the required changes are (a) to measure predictability in terms of the syntactic (and possibly semantic) categories of words, in addition to measuring the predictability of specific lexical items, and (b) to use the frequency of the required syntactic form instead of the base word frequency.

Of course, even if the proposed linking assumption in (11) is correct, it leaves much to be resolved. For example, what is the relationship between regressive eye movements out of a region and long or repeated fixations within that region? Why should first-pass reading time be linked to initial structure generation rather than complete understanding? The proposed linking assumption implies that only structure-determining factors will increase first-pass time, but there are obvious exceptions to that generalization, such as the discourse level effects reported by O'Brien, Shank, Myers, and Rayner (1988) and Garrod, Freudenthal, and Boyle (1994). If the proposed linking assumption is to be maintained, one must identify the conditions that govern how quickly such discourse level effects arise.

4.1.3 The Promise and Limitations of Reading Paradigms

Most of eye-movement research in reading has focused on garden-path sentences, leading to many insights about syntactic ambiguity resolution. However, because garden paths involve both anomaly detection and reanalysis, it is difficult to establish the mapping between cognitive events and eye-movement behaviors. In this chapter, I have focused on eye-movement patterns over *unambiguous* sentences as a means to contrast constraints on initial syntactic generation with constraints on other processes, such as syntactic ambiguity resolution, morphological agreement (in languages like English), and semantic/pragmatic felicity. I have argued that first-fixation and first-pass reading times in unambiguous sentences may provide a relatively pure index of syntactic generation. Thus, first-pass duration is influenced by lexical frequency but not discourse congruency (Boland & Blodgett, 2001), consistent with an architecture in which structure generation is largely lexical, with discourse constraints operating upon the lexically generated structures. Likewise, within anomaly detection paradigms, first-pass duration is influenced by (sub)category and other structure-determining constraints.

Despite some measure of promise, it should be clear that there has been no definitive mapping between specific cognitive processes and eye behavior. Many questions remain unanswered. Do (specific) cognitive events trigger a saccade? Is there some cognitive event that causes the eyes to regress rather than move forward? How much cognitive processing occurs in the parafovea? The answer to this last question is linked to another set of questions: Is attention limited to the currently fixated word? Do attention and gaze always shift in unison? To what degree are words recognized and structured in parallel? If there is some degree of parallelism, should we still think of the first fixation on a word as the earliest possible measure of processing for that word? Are nonfixations on a word cognitively meaningful?

In contrast to the ERP literature, there is no evidence that syntactic anomalies disrupt the eye-movement record in one way and semantic anomalies disrupt it in another. We may always have to rely upon converging evidence from ERP or MEG to understand which levels of representation have registered an anomaly. Although eyetracking paradigms lack precision in addressing that kind of "how" question, they excel at answering the "when" questions, providing a detailed temporal record of local processing difficulty.

An inherent limitation is actually the reading itself. When relying upon reading as an intermediary skill in order to measure language comprehension, one immediately limits one's population to that of skilled readers (omitting children, language-disordered populations, etc.). Furthermore, many interesting questions about language comprehension can only be answered within listening paradigms and by "situating" language within a real-world context. Ideally, one would like to study language comprehension in conversation, its original and most natural context. To address these kinds of concerns, spoken language paradigms have a great deal of appeal.

4.2. EYE MOVEMENTS AND LISTENING

Over the last 5 to 10 years, psycholinguists have been exploiting Cooper's (1974) finding that we tend to look at things as they are mentioned. Cooper used a passive listening task; he presented a set of pictures in a grid and found that listeners' looks to objects were time-locked to mention of those objects in a story. In more recent studies, some researchers have made the link between mentioning an object and looking at it more explicit by asking listeners to move or point to objects within a directed action paradigm. Regardless of the task (directed action versus passive listening), eye movements in listening paradigms do not provide the multilayered dependent measures found in reading paradigms (as in Table 4.1) because the looks of interest are not integrated within some regular sequence of eye movements as they are in reading. In listening paradigms, the dependent measures are usually limited to the probability and duration of a look to a relevant object within some temporal interval.

In reading research, a natural starting point was to study how the eyes move over meaningless strings and then examine how the variability in fixations and saccades is associated with linguistic factors in actual text. No comparable approach has been taken in the listening literature, though one could—and perhaps ought to—in the struggle to outline the linking assumptions between visual attention and listening comprehension. For now, the most we can do is look to the substantial literature on scene perception in order to ground our predictions about when and how eye movements should occur.

Research on scene perception has established that scenes are identified within the first fixation (Biederman, Mezzanotte, & Rabinowitz, 1982; Boyce & Pollatsek, 1992; Hollingworth & Henderson, 1998). That is, basic global information about the scene is absorbed within a single fixation. The mean fixation duration in scene perception is about 330 ms, with a mode of 230 ms (Henderson & Hollingworth, 1999). The initial fixation patterns are quite similar across participants, but variance increases rapidly over time (Mannan, Ruddock, & Wooding, 1995). The locations of the initial fixation on a scene are based on visual, not semantic, features (Henderson & Hollingworth). However, the likelihood of refixation is based upon task-dependent informativeness (Henderson & Hollingworth). Finally, our working memory representation of scene is abstract/conceptual rather than strictly visual (Henderson & Hollingworth).

The scene perception literature suggests that gaze during the first second or so of looking at a scene is driven by visual parameters, with little variance in performance.[5] In language comprehension experiments, the time interval of interest generally follows scene presentation by several seconds, so we should expect listeners to have already scanned the scene and have an abstract representation of it. This mental representation allows listeners to look at maximally informative regions of the scene in response to linguistic input. In fact, the Cooper (1974) results suggest a simple linking assumption: *The probability of looking at an object increases when the object is mentioned.* This linking assumption has ecological validity in conversation because we need to know properties of referents beyond their linguistic label. Directed action tasks further increase the probability of a look by using eye–hand coordination to mediate comprehension and eye movements. That is, it is difficult to manipulate or point to an object without first looking at it.

In short, listeners have reason to look at referents as they are mentioned in both passive listening and directed action tasks. This phenomenon has proven useful and informative in a variety of domains, as illustrated in Table 4.3. Research on spoken language comprehension has shown that eye fixations are time-locked to lexical access of isolated words (e.g., Allopenna, Magnuson, & Tanenhaus, 1998), identification of referents for syntactically ambiguous phrases (e.g., Tanenhaus, Spivey-Knowlton, Eberhard, & Sedivy, 1995), and pronoun resolution in discourse context (e.g., Arnold, Eisenband, Brown-Schmidt, & Trueswell, 2000). Eyetracking experiments investigating language comprehension have been conducted on children (Trueswell, Sekerina, Hill, & Logrip, 1999b) and in the context of conversation among adults (Brown-Schmidt, Campana, & Tanenhaus, 2002).

Clearly, measuring eye movements in a listening paradigm can provide a sensitive index of referential success or ambiguity resolution once linguistic input has been comprehended. However, it is not obvious that eye fixations are time-locked to developing syntactic and semantic representations in a manner that can be distinguished from the listener's ultimate conceptual representation of the linguistic

Table 4.3. **Important Contributions From Listening Paradigms**

Cohort competition and frequency effects in lexical access	Allopenna, Magnuson, and Tanenhaus, 1998; Dahan, Magnuson, and Tanenhaus, 2001
Incremental reference assignment	Cooper, 1974; Eberhard, Spivey-Knowlton, Sedivy, J. C., and Tanenhaus, 1995
Visual referential context influences ambiguity resolution	Tanenhaus, Spivey-Knowlton, Eberhard, and Sedivy, 1995
Young children do not use visual context as efficiently in ambiguity resolution	Trueswell, Sekerina, Hill, and Logrip, 1999
Initial forays into conversational interaction	Brown-Schmidt, Campana, and Tanenhaus, 2002

input. Can this research paradigm be used to investigate how people develop linguistic representations of spoken language input? Can we use it to unpack the cognitive operations in syntactic processing? Is it on-line enough to investigate parsing?

4.2.1. Anticipatory Looks

Intriguingly, reference resolution is sometimes completed prior to actual mention of the referent. For example, Sedivy, Tanenhaus, Chambers, and Carlson (1999) found that when listeners were asked to *Pick up the tall glass ...* , they often planned an eye movement to the glass during the adjective, prior to hearing *glass*. Instead of waiting for bottom-up evidence that the target object is being mentioned, listeners used the current visual context (i.e., presence of a tall/short contrast set) to select the pragmatically appropriate referent. In a more recent study, Sussman, Campana, Tanenhaus, and Carlson (2002) found that listeners made an eye movement to an appropriate instrument (a pencil) when hearing *Poke the dolphin* but not *Touch the dolphin*. Thus, even though no instrument was mentioned, listeners used their knowledge about the two verbs to decide whether to manipulate the dolphin with their finger or a pencil in the real-world environment. Listeners in the Sussman et al. study were also sensitive to contextual factors that altered verb meaning. For example, they looked at a potato peeler when asked to *Peel the potato*, but not when asked to *Peel the banana*.

4.2.2 Does Argument Structure Implicitly Introduce New Entities Into Discourse?

Anticipatory looks such as those in the foregoing discussion may provide clues to intermediate representations. For example, Sussman et al. (2002) concluded that hearing a verb provides access to its thematic grids and listeners then use context to select the appropriate grid. If the relevant thematic grid contained an instrument, eye movements were observed to an appropriate instrument in the environment. A related phenomenon has been reported in reading studies (Mauner, Tanenhaus, & Carlson, 1995, implicit agents; Carlson & Tanenhaus, 1988, open thematic roles). Just as in Sussman et al., it was argued that thematic role information from verb argument structure was accessed during word recognition. In Mauner et al.'s reading studies, the thematic roles guided comprehension even if an argument was not explicitly mentioned. Together, these studies suggest that the thematic roles accessed during verb recognition can be used both to interpret current discourse entities and to introduce new entities into the discourse.

Of course, directed action tasks such as that used by Sedivy et al. (1999) and Sussman et al. (2002) give rise to the concern that listeners are strategically guessing the speaker's intent rather than allowing language processing to proceed automatically. Arguably, normal conversation involves a great deal of strategic guessing about the speaker's intent, so this is not a problem if the goal is to study the complete comprehension process. However, if there are some partially or fully automatized aspects of syntactic and semantic processing, the directed action paradigm is not ideal for studying the representations that result from those automatized processes alone. For example, one might question whether the recognition of "poke" *obligatorily* introduces an instrument into the discourse model. And importantly, are the discourse elements that can be introduced by the verb limited to members of its thematic grids? (See Koenig, Mauner, & Bienvenue, 2003, for one current approach to understanding how semantic participants are lexically encoded.) In other words, do the verb's arguments hold a privileged status or are all related words and concepts accessed in the same way?

Encouragingly, work from Gerry Altmann's lab, as well as some of my own recent work, provide converging evidence for the automatic activation of thematic role information from passive listening tasks. In an extremely interesting study, Altmann and Kamide (1999) had people listen to a sentence like *The boy will move/eat the cake* while looking at a semirealistic scene with a boy, a cake, and other movable but not edible objects. Altmann and Kamide found faster looks to the cake following *eat* compared to *move*. In fact, participants often looked at *cake* in the *eat* condition prior to the onset of the noun. Altmann and Kamide concluded that the verb's thematic roles were used to proactively restrict the domain of subsequent reference.

Even in a passive listening task, it is difficult to identify the cause of the anticipatory fixations on the cake because both linguistic and general-world knowledge could have contributed to the effect. If it is solely the verb's argument structure that is driving eye movements, then listeners should not look at a bed upon hearing *The girl slept* because *bed* cannot be an argument of *slept*. However, beds are part of a prototypical sleeping event and are thus conceptually related to *sleep*. Furthermore, discussions about sleep often include mention of a bed, so linguistic co-occurrence frequency is high and the co-occurrence of sleeping and beds in participants' actual experience is likely to be extremely high. One might consider an account of Altmann and Kamide's (1999) effect that is akin to semantic priming—a conceptual, essentially intralexical, process. However, in more recent work, Kamide, Altmann, and Haywood (2003) found that combinatory semantics rather than simple lexical relationships influenced eye movements. For example, when viewing a carnival scene, listeners looked at a motorcycle upon hearing *The man rode ...* and looked at a merry-go-round upon hearing *The girl rode. ...* Thus, something higher-level than simple lexical associations influenced the pattern of eye movements.

Using a similar paradigm, Boland (2003) investigated the hypothesis that the use of a verb would implicitly introduce relevant entities (linguistic arguments) that had not yet been mentioned, and thus a picture corresponding to such an entity would draw anticipatory looks. For example, upon hearing ... *mother suggested ...*, participants would look at a potential recipient of the suggestion. The first experiment manipulated both the argument structure of the verb and the typicality–co-occurrence frequency of the target argument or adjunct, in order to distinguish between anticipatory looks to arguments specifically and anticipatory looks to pictures that were strongly associated with the verb but did not have the linguistic status of argument. Example stimuli are in (13). The intransitive-location stimuli provide a clear case of an adjunct target (*bed/bus*), the dative-recipient stimuli provide a clear case of an argument target (*teenager/toddler*), and the action-instrument stimuli provide an intermediate case in which the targets are arguably adjuncts (*stick/hat*). Acceptability ratings insured that sentences with typical targets were judged more acceptable than sentences with atypical targets. Furthermore, typical targets were more likely to co-occur with their verbs.[6] Importantly, there was no evidence that typical recipients had a higher co-occurrence frequency than typical locations—if anything, the opposite was true.

(13) Example stimuli from Boland (2003), Experiment 1. The typical/atypical target is underlined.

  a. Intransitive-Location: *The girl slept for a while on the <u>bed/bus</u> this afternoon.* (pictures: girl, bed/bus, pillow, toy car)

  b. Action-Instrument: *The donkey would not move, so the farmer beat it vigorously with a <u>stick/hat</u> every day.* (pictures: donkey, farmer, stick/hat, grass)

  c. Dative-Recipient: *The newspaper was difficult to read, but the mother suggested it anyway to her <u>teenager/toddler</u> last week.* (pictures: newspaper, mother, teen/toddler, dictionary)

The primary finding was that dative verbs prompted more anticipatory looks to potential recipients than transitive action verbs prompted to potential instruments or intransitive verbs prompted to potential locations. This argument status effect began about 500 ms after verb onset, suggesting that it occurred soon after lexical access of the verb. If verbs specify the syntactic and semantic constraints on their arguments, recognizing a verb would make available knowledge about that verb's arguments, and likely candidates (entities that satisfy the syntactic and semantic constraints) could be identified in the current discourse model or the situational context. No overall typicality effects were found, in contrast with Kamide et al. (2003). This apparent discrepancy may be due to a difference in the way the visual stimuli were presented. In Kamide et al., argument structure knowledge introduced an abstract ridable object into the discourse. In the visual scene, there were two ridable objects (a motorcycle and a merry-go-round), so real-world knowledge guided the viewer to the most plausible one. In Boland's experiment, the argument structure of the dative verbs introduced an abstract recipient, but there was only one potential referent pictured. In both the typical and atypical conditions, the potential referent met the lexical constraints on recipients for that particular verb. Thus, plausibility had no opportunity to play a role if we assume that verb argument structure is first used to identify possible referents. (If verb argument structure and plausibility simultaneously and jointly constrain referent identification, then typicality effects would be expected even if only one possible referent were pictured.) This explanation is consistent with prior findings that pragmatic constraints influence ambiguity resolution but not the generation of linguistic structure (Boland, 1997).

Boland (2003) reports a follow-up experiment that supports this explanation of the discrepancy with Kamide et al. (2003). For some participants, the sentences from the first experiment were used again, but both typical and atypical targets were pictured on each trial. Another group of participants viewed the slides while listening to music, instead of the sentences, to establish baseline looking rates for each of the pictures. The argument status effect from the first experiment was replicated, even after a general bias to look at the recipient pictures was taken into account. A typicality effect comparable in size to those of Kamide et al. also emerged for recipients, but not for instruments or locations.

The argument status effect was replicated again in Boland's (2003) third experiment, in which a single animate NP (and the corresponding picture) served as an argument in the dative condition (14a) and as an adjunct in the action verb condition (14b). No instrument was mentioned in the critical trials, though a prototypical instrument for the action verb was always pictured and, in filler trials, pictured instruments were mentioned. There were no reliable differences in co-occurrence frequency among the dative-recipient, action–benefactor, and action–instrument pairs.

(14) *One window was broken, so the handyman* ... (pictures: window, handy-man, couple, tools)
    a. *mentioned **it right away to the <u>owners</u>**.* (Recipient-Argument)
    b. *fixed **it hurriedly for the <u>owners</u>**.* (Benefactor-Adjunct)

As in the first two experiments, there were more looks to the target picture when it was an argument (recipient) than when it was an adjunct (benefactor, instrument) during the interval 500–1000 ms after the onset of the verb. There was no difference in the probability of a look to a prototypical adjunct (*fix*-tools) and an improbable adjunct (*mention*-tools). Thus, the results from all three experiments indicate that linguistic constraints play a privileged role in guiding visual attention in this passive listening paradigm. Co-occurrence frequency does not provide an alternative explanation. These argument status effects suggest an important distinction between adjuncts and arguments in terms of how verbs introduce associated entities into the discourse.

4.2.3 Limitations and Open Questions in Listening Paradigms

Listening paradigms provide an exciting opportunity to investigate spoken language comprehension in an on-line manner. While the paradigm is largely limited to referential processing, it has been used to address a wide range of questions in word recognition, sentence analysis, and discourse processing. Because listening paradigms do not require reading, they offer the opportunity to study language processing in children and other populations that include less skilled readers. Perhaps most importantly, listening paradigms allow, at least in principle, for investigations of language processing within conversational contexts.

Despite some clear advantages over reading paradigms, listening paradigms share the lack of an explicit model linking sentence comprehension to eye movements. In fact, this problem seems worse within listening paradigms, which have not benefited from the same degree of scientific scrutiny over the past several decades. On the bright side, we are likely to make some progress if we examine and test our linking assumptions in a rigorous fashion. Some of the open questions include the following:

- How do directed action and passive listening tasks differ? Does the task influence the eye movements above and beyond the linguistic material?
- What cognitive events prompt a saccade to an object? How does this interact with task, local syntactic ambiguity, and other factors?
- Can we integrate models of scene perception to explain more variance in passive listening paradigms?
- How can we measure the likelihood that an object will be mentioned? How do we decide the appropriate label for an object when measuring likelihood?
- Are all of the effects essentially referential—that is, at the level of the discourse model? Could we find a syntactic complexity effect? Could we find a lexical bias effect (e.g., ease of integrating noun–verb homophones)?

4.3 CONSIDERING READING AND LISTENING TOGETHER

Thus far, I have considered reading and listening eye-movement paradigms separately for reasons outlined in the introduction: the two approaches are very different. To the extent that they measure comparable aspects of language comprehension, the two classes of paradigms might provide converging evidence for particular processing models or phenomena. In fact, there is growing evidence of this type of convergence in the literature.

One example of complementary reading and listening data is the argument–adjunct line of research from my own laboratory. Using the stop-making-sense task (Boland & Boehm-Jernigan, 1998), word-by- word reading (Blodgett & Boland, 2004), and eyetracking (Boland & Lewis, 2001), reading studies have found consistent support for the view that argument structures largely determine the strength with which competing analyses are initially made available. For example, Boland and Boehm-Jernigan investigated temporarily ambiguous dative sentences like those in (15). Following a theme-NP, like *the letter, give* licenses a recipient argument beginning with the preposition *to*. This argument structure constraint predicts a garden path in (15b), but not in (15c) or (15d). However, there is another possibly relevant constraint that is not related to argument structure: the prepositions *to, for,* and *about* differ in the likelihood of verb phrase (VP) attachment. Making a VP attachment in either case would render the recipient in PP2 ungrammatical (or at least very awkward) because an adjunct cannot precede an argument. In fact, the argument structure constraint produced the expected garden-path effect at *his*, with only (15b) differing from the control condition, indicating the primacy of the argument structure constraint. In addition, there was evidence of a garden path in (15c) one word later, indicating that the preposition's attachment bias is stored in the lexicon and plays some role during syntactic ambiguity resolution. These data complement the listening data from Boland (2003) in demonstrating how argument structure is used during comprehension.

(15) *Which friend did John give a letter* ...

    a. ... *to ___ for his son a month ago?* (early gap control condition)

    b. ... *to his son to___ a month ago?* (garden-path condition)

    c. *for his son to ___ a month ago?* ("for" is equibiased for NP and VP attachment)

    d. *about his son to ___ a month ago?* ("about" has strong NP attachment bias)

In other respects, convergence has not yet been achieved, but efforts toward that goal are likely to lead to some important insights. For example, I have suggested that the text-based statistics commonly used to predict reading time in recent constraint-based lexicalist studies are inappropriate for evaluating anticipatory looks in listening studies. Compare the reading study of McDonald and Shillcock (chapter 5, this volume) to the Boland (2003) listening study described in the preceding text. McDonald and Shillcock found that the higher the transitional probability of a noun, given a verb, the shorter the first fixation duration on that noun when it followed that verb in a sentence. Because they were measuring fixations on a linguistic object (a printed noun), they measured the transitional probabilities of that object, given another linguistic object (a printed verb) in text corpora. The assumption is that both the transitional probability and the fixation duration are directly related to the time it takes to access and integrate that noun. In contrast, Boland measured looks to an unlabeled picture following a verb in a spoken sentence. In such a case, probability may play some role in guiding eye movements, but it is not clear that the relevant probabilities can be obtained from a text corpus. The dependent measure assumes that the verb has been recognized, but it does not require accessing and integrating a specific word or lexical category associated with the picture because the relevant words have not yet been uttered. Rather, the dependent measure probably reflects attention to some conceptual domain that has been made salient by the pictured material and made relevant by the linguistic input thus far. Whatever the appropriate measure of probability is, it should take into account the visual display as well as the linguistic material.

My point in comparing McDonald and Shillcock (chapter 5, this volume) with Boland (2003) is this: In reading studies, we can account for a substantial portion of the variance in reading time by assuming that the linguistic context is the entire context, for all practical purposes. Furthermore, we generally assume that syntactic and semantic processing of some portion of text begins sometime after that text is initially fixated. However, the listening paradigm forces us to wrestle with aspects of syntactic and semantic processing that begin prior to bottom-up word recognition, and with the fact that most real-life contexts are considerably richer than the linguistic context alone. While these additional layers of complexity complicate the experimental logic, they also bring some degree of real-world validity to the experiment. And it is likely that many of the insights to be gained from the listening studies will be relevant for reading studies as well.

4.4 SUMMARY

Eye-movement data in both visual and auditory modalities have excelled in addressing "when" questions, such as how early during comprehension we have access to lexical information or how early a particular constraint is used. In this chapter, I highlighted some promising findings in each modality that push the linking assumptions between eye and mind a little further than the current state of affairs. First I suggested that, when reading unambiguous sentences, the first-fixation or first-pass reading time may be closely tied to syntactic generation (the access to, or construction of, possible syntactic structures). Second, I offered evidence that argument-structure knowledge allows us to focus on relevant entities as soon as spoken verbs are recognized, based on anticipatory looks to objects that might be event participants. Nonetheless, neither reading nor listening paradigms may be capable of distinguishing among linguistic (e.g., syntactic vs. semantic) levels of representation, unlike ERPs which have proven sensitive to syntactic–semantic distinctions.

4.5 ACKNOWLEDGMENTS

This chapter is based upon a presentation to the 8th Annual AMLaP conference, held in Tenerife, Canary Islands, in September, 2002. I would like to thank the members of the audience and the other presenters for their comments. As I was preparing for the talk and writing this chapter, I benefited from the contributions of my collaborators, students, and colleagues, especially Allison Blodgett, David Thomas, Meghan Ahern, Alicia Seifers, and the University of Michigan Psycholinguistics Research Group.

References

Ainsworth-Darnell, K., Shulman, H. G., & Boland, J. E. (1998). Dissociating brain responses to syntactic and semantic anomalies: Evidence from event-related potentials. *Journal of Memory and Language, 38*(1), 112–130.

Allopenna, P. D., Magnuson, J. S., & Tanenhaus, M. K. (1998). Tracking the time course of spoken word recognition: Evidence for continuous mapping models. *Journal of Memory and Language, 38,* 419–439.

Altmann, G. T. M. (1994). Regression-contingent analyses of eye movements during sentence processing: Reply to Rayner and Sereno. *Memory and Cognition, 22,* 286–290.

Altmann, G. T. M., Garnham, A., & Dennis, Y. (1992). Avoiding the garden path: Eye movements in context. *Journal of Memory and Language, 31,* 685–712.

Altmann, G. T. M., & Kamide, Y. (1999). Incremental interpretation at verbs: Restricting the domain of subsequent reference. *Cognition, 73*(3), 247–264.

Arnold, J. E., Eisenband, J. G., Brown-Schmidt, S., & Trueswell, J. C. (2000). The rapid use of gender information: Evidence of the time course of pronoun resolution from eyetracking. *Cognition.*

Biederman, I., Mezzanotte, R. J., & Rabinowitz, J. C. (1982). Scene perception: Detecting and judging objects undergrouping relational violations. *Cognitive Psychology, 14,* 143–177.

Blodgett, A., & Boland, J. E. (2004). Differences in the timing of implausibility detection for recipient and instrument prepositional phrases. *Journal of Psycholinguistic Research, 33,* 1–24.

Boland, J. E. (1997). The relationship between syntactic and semantic processes in sentence comprehension. *Language and Cognitive Processes, 12,* 423–484.

Boland, J. E. (2003). *Visual arguments.* Manuscript submitted for publication.

Boland, J. E., & Boehm-Jernigan, H. (1998). Lexical constraints and prepositional phrase attachment. *Journal of Memory and Language, 39,* 684–719.

Boland, J. E., & Blodgett, A. (2001). Understanding the constraints on syntactic generation: Lexical bias and discourse congruency effects on eye movements. *Journal of Memory and Language, 45*(3), 391–411.

Boland, J. E., & Blodgett, A. (2002). *Eye movements as a measure of syntactic and semantic incongruity in unambiguous sentences.* Unpublished manuscript, University of Michigan at Ann Arbor.

Boland, J., & Lewis, R. (2001). *Distinguishing generation and selection of modifier attachments: Implications for lexicalized parsing and competition models.* Paper presented at the 14th Annual CUNY Conference on Human Sentence Processing, Philadelphia, PA.

Boyce, S. J., & Pollatsek, A. (1992). Identification of objects in scenes: The role of scene background in object naming. *Journal of Experimental Psychology: Learning, Memory, and Cognition, 18,* 531–543.

Braze, D., Shankweiler, D., Ni, W., & Palumbo, L. C. (2002). Readers' eye movements distinguish anomalies of form and content. *Journal of Psycholinguistic Research,* 31–25–44.

Brown-Schmidt, S., Campana, E., & Tanenhaus, M. K. (2002). *Reference resolution in the wild: How addresses circumscribe referential domains in real time comprehension during interactive problem solving.* Paper presented at the 15th Annual CUNY Conference on Human Sentence Processing, New York.

Carlson, G. N., & Tanenhaus, M. K. (1988). Thematic roles and language comprehension. In W. Wilkins (Ed.), *Syntax and Semantics: Vol. 21. Thematic Relations.* San Diego, CA: Academic Press.

Cooper, R. M. (1974). Control of eye fixation by meaning of spoken language—new methodology for real-time investigation of speech perception, memory, and language processing. *Cognitive Psychology, 6*(1), 84–107.

Dahan, D., Magnuson, J. S., & Tanenhaus, M. K. (2001). Time course of frequency effects in spoken-word recognition: Evidence from eye movements. *Cognitive Psychology, 42*(4), 317–367.

Deutsch, A., & Bentin, S. (2001). Syntactic and semantic factors in processing gender agreement in Hebrew: Evidence from ERPs and eye movements. *Journal of Memory and Language, 45*(2), 200–224.

Eberhard, K. M., Spivey-Knowlton, M. J., Sedivy, J. C., & Tanenhaus, M. K. (1995). Eye movements as a window into real-time spoken language comprehension in natural contexts. *Journal of Psycholinguistic Research, 24,* 409–436.

Ford, M., Bresnan, J., & Kaplan, R. M. (1982). A competence-based theory of syntactic closure. In J. Bresnan (Ed.), *The mental representation of grammatical relations.* Cambridge, MA: MIT Press.

Francis, W. N., & Kucera, H. (1982) *Frequency Analysis of English Usage: Lexicon and Grammar.* Houghton Mifflin Co., Boston.

Frazier, L. (1978). *On comprehending sentences: Syntactic parsing strategies.* Unpublished doctoral dissertation, University of Connecticut, Storrs.

Frazier, L. (1987). Theories of sentence processing. In J. L. Garfield (Ed.), *Modularity in knowledge representation and natural language understanding.* (pp. 291–307). Cambridge, MA: MIT Press.

Frazier, L., & Rayner, K. (1982). Making and correcting errors during sentence comprehension: Eye movements in the analysis of structurally ambiguous sentences. *Cognitive Psychology, 14*(2), 178–210.

Friederici, A. D. (1995). The time course of syntactic activation during language processing: A model based on neuropsychological and neurophysiological data. *Brain and Language, 50,* 259–281.

Friederici, A. D., & Frisch, S. (2000). Verb argument structure processing: The role of verb-specific and argument-specific information. *Journal of Memory and Language, 43,* 476–507.

Friederici, A. D., Pfeifer, E., & Hahne, A. (1993). Event-related brain potentials during natural speech processing: Effects of semantic, morphological, and syntactic violations. *Cognitive Brain Research, 1*(3), 183–192.

Frisson, S. P., & Pickering, M. J. (1999). The processing of metonymy: Evidence from eye movements. *Journal of Experimental Psychology: Learning, Memory, and Cognition, 25,* 1366–1383.

Garrod, S., Freudenthal, D., & Boyle, E. (1994). The role of different types of anaphor in the online resolution of sentencs in a discourse. *Journal of Memory and Language, 33,* 39–68.

Griffen, Z. M., & Bock, K. (2000). What the eyes say about speaking. *Psychological Science, 11,* 274–279.

Gunter, T., Stowe, L. A., & Mulder, G. (1997). When syntax meets semantics. *Psychophysiology, 34,* 660–676.

Hagoort, P., Brown, C., & Groothusen, J. (1993). The syntactic positive shift (SPS) as an ERP measure of syntactic processing. *Language and Cognitive Processes, 8*(4), 439–483.

Henderson, J. M., & Hollingworth, A. (1999). High-level scene perception. *Annual Review of Psychology, 50,* 243–270.

Hollingworth, A., & Henderson, J. (1998). Does consistent scene context facilitate object perception? *Journal of Experiment Psychology: General, 127,* 398–415.

Just, M. A., & Carpenter, P. A. (1980). A theory of reading: From eye fixations to comprehension. *Psychological Review, 87,* 329–354.

Kamide, Y., Altmann, G. T. M., & Haywood, S. (2003). Prediction and thematic information in incremental sentence processing: Evidence from anticipatory eye-movements. *Journal of Memory and Language, 49,* 133–156.

Koenig, J.-P., Mauner, G., & Bienvenue, B. (2003). Arguments for adjuncts. *Cognition, 89,* 67–100.

Lewis, R. L. (2000). Specifying architectures for language processing: Process, control, and memory in parsing and interpretation. In M. W. Crocker, M. Pickering, & C. Clifton, Jr. (Eds.), *Architectures and mechanisms for language processing.* New York: Cambridge University Press.

MacDonald, M. C., Pearlmutter, N. J., & Seidenberg, M. S. (1994). The lexical nature of syntactic ambiguity resolution. *Psychological Review, 101,* 676–703.

Mannan, S. K., Ruddock, K. H., & Wooding, D. S. (1995). Automatic control of saccadic eye movements made in visual inspection of briefly presented 2-D visual images. *Spatial Vision, 9,* 363–386.

Mauner, G., Tanenhaus, M. K., & Carlson, G. N. (1995). Implicit arguments in sentence processing. *Journal of Memory and Language, 34,* 357–382.

McElree, B. (1993). The locus of lexical preference effects in sentence comprehension: A time-course analysis. *Journal of Memory and Language, 32,* 536–571.

Mitchell, D. C. (1987). Lexical guidance in human parsing—locus and processing characteristics. *Attention and Performance, 12,* 601–618.

Morrison, R. E. (1984). Manipulation of stimulus onset delay in reading: Evidence for parallel programming of saccades. *Journal of Experimental Psychology: Human Perception and Performance, 10,* 667–682.

Ni, W., Fodor, J. D., Crain, S., & Shankweiler, D. (1998). Anomaly detection: Eye movement patterns. *Journal of Psycholinguistic Research, 27*(5), 515–539.

Novick, J. M., Kim, A., & Trueswell, J. C. (2003). Studying the grammatical aspects of word recognition: Lexical priming, parsing, and syntactic ambiguity resolution. *Journal of Psycholinguistic Research, 32*(1), 57–75.

O'Brien, E. J., Shank, D. M., Myers, J. L., & Rayner, K. (1988). Elaborative inferences: Do they occur on-line? *Journal of Experimental Psychology: Learning, Memory, and Cognition, 3,* 410–420.

Osterhout, L., & Nicol, J. (1999). On the distinctiveness, independence, and time course of the brain responses to syntactic and semantic anomalies. *Language and Cognitive Processes, 14*(3), 283–317.

Pearlmutter, N. J., Garnsey, S. M., & Bock, K. (1999). Agreement processes in sentence comprehension. *Journal of Memory and Language, 41,* 427–456.

Pollatsek, A., & Rayner, K. (1990). Eye movements and lexical access in reading. In D. A. Balota, G. B. Flores D'Arcais, & K. Rayner (Eds.), *Comprehension processes in reading* (pp. 143–163). Hillsdale, NJ: Erlbaum.

Rayner, K. (1998). Eye movements in reading and information processing: 20 years of research. *Psychological Bulletin, 124,* 372–422.

Rayner, K., Carlson, M., & Frazier, L. (1983). The interaction of syntax and semantics during sentence processing: Eye movements in the analysis of semantically biased sentences. *Journal of Verbal Learning and Verbal Behavior, 22,* 358–374.

Rayner, K., Reichle, E. D., & Pollatsek, A. (1998). Eye movement control in reading: An overview and model. In G. Underwood (Ed.), *Eye guidance in reading and scene perception* (pp. 243–268). New York: Elsevier.

Rayner, K., & Sereno, S. C. (1994a). Regressive eye movements and sentence parsing: On the use of regression-contingent analyses. *Memory and Cognition, 22,* 281–285.

Rayner, K., & Sereno, S. C. (1994b). Regression-contingent analyses: A reply to Altmann. *Memory and Cognition, 22,* 291–292.

Rayner, K., Sereno, S. C., Morris, R. K., Schmauder, R. A., & Clifton, C., Jr. (1989). Eye movements and on-line language comprehension processes. *Language and Cognitive Processes, 4,* 21–50.

Rayner, K., Sereno, S. C., & Raney, G. E. (1996). Eye movement control in reading: A comparison of two types of models. *Journal of Experimental Psychology: Human Perception and Performance, 22,* 1188–1200.

Reichle, E. D., Pollatsek, A., Fisher, D. L., & Rayner, K. (1998). Toward a model of eye movement control in reading. *Psychological Review, 105,* 125–157.

Sedivy, J. C., Tanenhaus, M. K., Chambers, C. G., & Carlson, G. N. (1999). Achieving incremental semantic interpretation through contextual representation. *Cognition, 71*(2), 109–147.

Spivey-Knowlton, M., & Tanenhaus, M. K. (1998). Syntactic ambiguity resolution in discourse: Modeling effects of referential context and lexical frequency within an integration-competition network. *Journal of Experimental Psychology: Learning, Memory, and Cognition, 24,* 1521–1543.

Sussman, R. S., Campana, E., Tanenhaus, M. K., & Carlson, G. M. (2002). *Verb-based access to instrument roles: Evidence from eye movements.* Poster session presented at the 8th Annual Architectures and Mechanisms of Language Processing Conference, Tenerife, Canary Islands, Spain.

Tanenhaus, M. K., Spivey-Knowlton, M. J., Eberhard, K. M., & Sedivy, J. C. (1995). Integration of visual and linguistic information in spoken language comprehension. *Science, 268,* 1632–1634.

Traxler, M. J., Morris, R. K., & Seely, R. E. (2002). Processing subject and object relative clauses: Evidence from eye movements. *Journal of Memory and Language, 47,* 69–90.

Trueswell, J. C., Sekerina, I., Hill, N. M., & Logrip, M. L. (1999). The kindergarten-path effect: Studying on-line sentence processing in young children. *Cognition, 73,* 89–134.

Notes

1. Some readers will be bothered by the absence of a comma in these sentences. However, similar garden-path effects are found in other structures without "the comma problem."
2. Quasi-first pass time is similar to the regression path duration, except that it does not include time spent in prior regions. It is the sum of all fixations with a region from the time the region is first entered until the reader fixates on a region to its right.
3. Much ink has been spilled on the validity of regression-contingent analyses of reading time (Altmann, Garnham, & Dennis, 1992; Altmann, 1994; Rayner & Sereno, 1994a & b). I remain an agnostic on that issue.
4. None of the semantic anomalies illustrated above are structure-determining. For example, in (6a), syntax dictates that *canary* or *snake* must be the subject of *sings*. Whether or not the animal can plausibly sing is irrelevant to the sentence's structure. In contrast, the sentences in (12), adopted from Boland (1997), illustrate how semantic properties can govern sentence structure in English. A reading event can involve a reader, the thing being read, and a listener. This can be stated in one of two syntactic forms: "The reader read the material to the listener" or "The reader read the listener the material." In (12), the semantic properties of the *wh*-phrase determine whether it will be interpreted as the listener or the material at the verb (recognition of "read" presumably makes its thematic roles available), but the syntactic form of the sentence is not determined until the last word in the sentence. The syntactic position of the

wh-phrase is represented by the blank line in the examples. Examples (12b) and (12c) both become ungrammatical because *Suzie/Hamlet* satisfies the same set of semantic constraints as the *wh*-phrase, thereby competing for the same syntactic position. Because semantics determines structure, I would expect to find long reading times for the underlined phrases in (12b) and (12c) compared to the same phrases in (12a) and (12d).

(12) a. *Which poem did the babysitter read Suzie* ___?
     b. **Which child did the babysitter read <u>Suzie</u>* ___?
     c. **Which poem did the babysitter read* ___ *"Hamlet"*?
     d. *Which child did the babysitter read* ___ *"Hamlet"*?

In well-known examples like *The spy saw the cop with the revolver* from Rayner et al. (1983), the semantics of *revolver* is not structure-determining in the intended sense. The syntactic analysis of *revolver* itself is unambiguous—it must be the daughter of the PP. Of course, if a PP is constructed and VP-attached at *with*, then *revolver* would be semantically anomalous and the PP might be reanalyzed as modifying *the cop*. However, I am trying to identify the factors determining the initial structure rather than the factors that prompt reanalysis of earlier material.

5. In fact, Griffen and Bock (2000) compared a picture inspection task with a picture description task, using simple line drawings with two participants (e.g., a mouse squirting a turtle). They found an equal number of looks to the two participants during the first 1300 ms of the picture inspection. In contrast, people who were describing the pictures tended to look at the first-mentioned participant during this same time interval. Thus, the nature of the experimental task can clearly influence looking patterns during the initial seconds of picture viewing.

6. Counting co-occurrence frequency in an "anticipatory looking" paradigm presents an interesting problem. The dependent measure is an anticipatory look to a photograph, prior to hearing the target phrase. Thus, the frequency measures that are often used in parsing/reading research are inappropriate. In reading studies, the co-occurrence frequency between a verb and a phrase of a particular class (e.g., a PP beginning with *to* or a phrase that is assigned a particular thematic role) is often used to predict processing difficulty for a phrase of the same class (e.g., McDonald & Shillcock, chapter 5, this volume). In contrast, what we need to know here is, given a particular verb, how likely is the occurrence of an object or person like the one in the target picture. Boland (2003) used two different methods to compute co-occurrence frequency, but it is likely that this research problem will require continued attention.

Chapter 5
Lexical Predictability Effects on Eye Fixations During Reading

SCOTT A. MCDONALD AND RICHARD C. SHILLCOCK

5.1 INTRODUCTION

The speed and accuracy with which readers can extract the meaning from written language is remarkable given the relative infancy of reading on the evolutionary time-scale. Because of reading's late cultural emergence, the efficiency of reading cannot be explained by specialized neural mechanisms. Instead, it must be attributed to processing mechanisms that already exist for other purposes. Reading for comprehension is a highly complex task that involves a number of levels of processing, from basic visual perception through syntactic analysis and semantic interpretation, and it would be surprising if cognitive mechanisms deployed for solving other problems had not also been co-opted for reading.

One type of cognitive mechanism that could assist reading is a mechanism that takes advantage of statistical (frequency-based) knowledge present in the linguistic environment in order to make informed predictions about upcoming words. The brain is sensitive to frequency information at many levels, from Hebbian learning at the neural level to different meanings of homophones in speech at a higher, cognitive level, and it is conceivable that the processes involved in skilled reading are also dependent on frequency-based information. In this chapter, we review the role of statistical information in language comprehension, and then present empirical evidence for the exploitation of lexical contingency statistics by the processor during reading.

Statistical/probabilistic models of a range of language processing phenomena (e.g., Corley, 1998; Crocker & Corley, 2002; Jurafsky, 1996; McDonald & Brew, 2001) are currently enjoying a renaissance due in part to the availability of large amounts of text in electronic form, and to complementary research in the psychology of memory and reasoning (e.g., Anderson, 1990; Tenenbaum & Griffiths, 2001). Although these models emphasize the roles of different types of linguistic knowledge (lexical, syntactic, categorical, etc.), most are ultimately derived from occurrence and co-occurrence frequencies extracted from large corpora (for a review see Jurafsky, 2003).

We propose that the relative likelihoods of words appearing after other words is a potential source of statistical knowledge that could be exploited during reading. *Transitional probabilities* (also known as word-to-word contingency statistics) are easily computable from a large sample of readers' input. The transitional probability between any pair of words can be estimated by simply counting the number of times *word*$_1$ and *word*$_2$ co-occur in a text corpus, and dividing this figure by the frequency of *word*$_1$ in the same corpus. The result is an estimate of how likely it is for *word*$_2$ to appear, given that *word*$_1$ has just been encountered.

There is substantial variability within a language with respect to the transitional probabilities between words; on one extreme, there are combinations that have high transitional probabilities, such as *preside over* and *recent years*, entailing that the occurrence of the second element can be confidently predicted from the occurrence of the first. On the other extreme, there are word sequences that are produced with extremely low probabilities, such as *infant vote* and *think around*—such cases may be due to a number of factors, such as the syntactic incompatibility of certain lexical categories or the semantic implausibility of the combination of meanings conveyed by the words. The purpose of this chapter is to evaluate the potential contribution of lexical statistics to the processing of individual words in reading. The principal hypothesis to be tested is that words with high transitional probabilities are easier to process than words with low transitional probabilities, all else being equal. After demonstrating an independent influence of transitional probability on various eye-fixation measures, we then show that a more parsimonious treatment of the data is provided by combining transitional probability with word frequency, which captures the more general notion of *lexical predictability*.

5.1.1 Prediction Is a Component of Sentence Comprehension

Prediction would appear to be a pervasive cognitive strategy for the processing of both written and spoken language.[1] A number of recent eyetracking studies using the *visual-world* paradigm (Eberhard, Spivey-Knowlton, Sedivy, & Tanenhaus, 1995; Tanenhaus, Spivey-Knowlton, Eberhard, & Sedivy, 1995) have shown time course effects consistent with the on-line prediction of semantic and syntactic information associated with the next word in the unfolding speech stream (e.g., Altmann & Kamide, 1999; Huettig & Altmann, this volume; Kamide, Scheepers, Altmann, & Crocker, 2002). For instance, given a restricted set of objects in the visual scene and an auditory stimulus such as "The boy will eat the … ," participants are more likely to start directing their gaze towards the objects in the scene that satisfy the selectional restrictions of the verb *eat* than towards alternative items, before the noun (e.g., *cake*) is realized in the input (Altmann & Kamide, 1999). A similar study tested the on-line prediction of a particular meaning of an ambiguous word such as *boxer*; when the context biased the subordinate meaning ("type of dog"), participants spent more time looking at the picture illustrating this meaning than the picture of the dominant meaning, even before *boxer* was heard (Huettig & Altmann, this volume).

A third experiment, which examined the processing of German verbs that conveyed a distinct meaning if combined with a subsequently occurring particle, demonstrated that prior context, world knowledge, and frequency information were rapidly integrated to arrive at the "best guess" interpretation of the verb meaning, well before the disambiguating particle was encountered (Muckel, Scheepers, Crocker, & Müller, 2002). In all three cases, findings are consistent with the on-line, incremental processing of semantic information, with predictions about upcoming lexical items being formed as early as possible.

Syntactic information (e.g., case-marking) can also influence eye movements directed towards an object in the scene before its name is realized acoustically. Using German sentence stimuli that were identical except for the case-marking of the subject and object noun phrases, Kamide et al. (2002) found that gaze was more often directed towards items that were plausible fillers of the verb's remaining case role than to items that were implausible.

Converging evidence for prediction as an integral part of language comprehension is supplied by recent research employing the event-related potential (ERP) methodology. Kutas and Federmeier (2000) propose that the human language processor builds expectations about the meaning of upcoming words; predictions are formed by combining information invoked from the prior context with context-independent semantic knowledge. Using ERP techniques in conjunction with a sentence-reading task, Federmeier and Kutas (1999) found that sentence-final words that were highly predictable from the context caused the least processing disruption, followed by sentence endings that were members of the same semantic category as the predicted ending and, lastly, unpredictable final words from a different category. The authors propose that their results are compatible with a prediction mechanism where the semantic properties of an upcoming word are compared on-line with expectations about its meaning.

Syntactic information associated with the upcoming word can also influence current processing. van Berkum, Kooijman, Brown, Zwitserlood, and Hagoort (2002) report results of a Dutch ERP study using auditory presentation that is consistent with the grammatical gender of an upcoming noun being available before the noun was heard, if it was highly predictable from context. Discourse-level information led the listener to anticipate a specific noun; the critical manipulation was the gender of the adjective preceding the noun. There was a small but reliable ERP effect during the processing of the adjective if its gender mismatched the gender of the yet-unrealized noun. This study provides compelling electrophysiological evidence for a lexical prediction mechanism as an integral component of spoken language comprehension.

5.1.2   The "Grain" of Contingency Statistics

Sensitivity to contingency statistics at a sublexical level of linguistic description has been put forward as an account of how segmentation of the speech stream is achieved by infants (Saffran, Aslin, & Newport, 1996), and adults learning an artificial language are also influenced by the manipulation of transitional probability (Saffran, Newport, & Aslin, 1996). In these studies, between-syllable contingency statistics provided strong cues as to whether a sequence of syllables straddles a word boundary or not; both infants and adults proved to be sensitive to these contingencies after only a small amount of exposure.

There is also evidence that the language processor is sensitive to statistical information of a coarser "grain" than the word level. Crocker and Corley (2002) report that the probability of encountering combinations of lexical categories (e.g., noun followed by verb) as estimated, using a part-of-speech tagged text corpus, was predictive of parsing difficulty and syntactic reanalysis. They discuss the results of two self-paced reading experiments that suggested that statistical knowledge of the likelihoods of an ambiguous word being a given lexical category can affect reading times even in the presence of (incompatible) syntactic constraints. The first experiment showed that lexical-category frequency (noun vs. verb) influenced the reading of ambiguous words, with longer reading times in the disambiguating region when the category of the ambiguous item was constrained to its less frequent category. The second experiment showed that a constraining syntactic context did not override the frequency bias, at least initially.

Finally, MacDonald (1993) investigated the influence of a dichotomized co-occurrence probability measure by comparing the processing of word pairs that occurred in a corpus (e.g., *miracle cures*) with combinations that did not (e.g., *shrine cures*). The second element of the pair was ambiguous between a noun and a verb; a self-paced reading task using sentences that enforced the verb reading indicated longer reading times when the words co-occurred in the corpus, suggesting that the processor initially adopted the nominal interpretation of the second word. Because *cures* (as a noun) is more probable following *miracle* than following *shrine*, MacDonald's results suggest that it is more difficult for the processor to adopt the verbal reading when the preceding lexical context provides a conflicting statistical cue.

To summarize, accumulating evidence from a variety of language processing studies employing diverse methodologies indicates that the human language processor is sensitive to probabilistic/statistical information at several levels of description: syntactic, semantic, and lexical (where some of the types of information may even be specific to certain languages), and that contingency statistics in particular could form the input to a prediction mechanism that operates in an incremental, rapid, and on-line fashion. We propose that the prediction of upcoming structure, content, and form constitutes an integral part of language comprehension. Next, we focus on testing the hypothesis that statistical knowledge about the likelihoods of upcoming words can influence eye-movement behavior during reading.

5.2 EMPIRICAL STUDIES

The results reported in this chapter are based on eye-movement data collected in two eyetracking studies. In the first, the transitional probabilities of verb + noun sequences were manipulated in a controlled sentence-reading experiment (McDonald & Shillcock, 2003a). A subexperiment tested the effect of manipulating the transitional probabilities between verbs and function words. The second study required participants to read excerpts from contemporary newspaper articles totalling

2,300 words. These data were used to investigate the influence of transitional probability on eye movements for all combinations of lexical categories (i.e., not just involving verbs), and to evaluate a Bayesian method for integrating transitional probability with word frequency (McDonald & Shillcock, 2003a).

5.2.1 Methods

Of the 24 young adults participating in the sentence-reading study, 20 took part in the passage-reading study. Each was paid £5; all were native English speakers and had normal or corrected-to-normal vision. Participants were seated at a viewing distance of 75 cm from a 15-in. RM VGA monitor. Stimuli were displayed in a monospaced font as light cyan on a black background. One degree of visual angle corresponded to 3.8 characters. In the sentence-reading study, each sentence occupied a single line of the display; in the passage-reading study, an article excerpt occupied between one and four display pages, each page containing up to 10 double-spaced lines of text. Filler sentences ($n = 20$) in the sentence-reading study and each article in the passage-reading study were followed by an untimed yes–no comprehension question. Eye movements were recorded from the right eye using a Fourward Technologies Generation 6.3 Dual Purkinje Image eyetracker interfaced to a 486 PC. Gaze position was sampled every millisecond. In order to reduce head motion as much as possible, a forehead rest and bite-bar were employed. Calibration of the eyetracker was verified and adjusted periodically throughout the course of the studies. Experimental sessions lasted 30–45 min.

5.2.2 Computation of Lexical Statistics

Word frequencies were extracted from the 100-million-word British National Corpus (BNC) (Burnage & Dunlop, 1992). Besides word form frequency, we also computed base frequencies (which sum together the frequencies of all inflectional variants of a word) using a lemmatized version of the same corpus. Transitional probabilities for the sentence-reading study were estimated from the BNC as follows:

$$P(word_2 | word_1) = \frac{freq(word_1, word_2)}{freq(word_1)}$$

We used the CMU-Cambridge language modelling toolkit (Clarkson & Rosenfeld, 1997) to estimate the transitional probabilities for all words in the passage-reading materials from the BNC. We employed the software's Good-Turing smoothing option to estimate the probabilities for ($word_1$, $word_2$) pairs that did not occur in the BNC. Note that in the regression analyses described below, all transitional probability values were first transformed by converting to natural logarithms.

5.2.3 Verb + Noun Pairs

In this study, participants were required to read sentences containing verb + noun sequences with either high or low transitional probabilities. There were 48 sentence pairs; each sentence in a pair was composed around the same verb followed by either a more probable or a less probable (but still plausible) noun object. For each item, the length and corpus frequency of the target noun were closely matched, and the context prior to the verb (and for several items, the context following the noun) was the same in both sentences. The two sets of nouns also did not reliably differ in base frequency: paired $t(47) = 1.11$, $p > .2$; in fact, the mean base frequency of the High set was slightly lower than the mean frequency of the Low items. Transitional probability was computed using the BNC (High: mean = 0.0101, Low: mean = 0.0004), and was the sole variable manipulated. An example item is shown in Table 5.1.

An independent group of 26 participants judged the candidate sentences for plausibility using a 7-point scale, where a 7 meant "highly plausible" and 1 meant "highly implausible." Mean plausibility did not differ between the two conditions (High: mean = 5.3, Low: mean = 5.2; paired $t(47) = .62$, $p > .5$), confirming that the High and Low transitional probability items were closely matched on this variable. In order to estimate how strongly the preceding context constrained the selected nouns, we assessed the conventional notion of predictability by having a second group of 16 participants perform a cloze procedure (Taylor, 1953). Participants were given the sentences up to and including the verb, and asked to supply the first word that came to mind that plausibly continued the sentence. The proportion of participants supplying either of the selected nouns was very small; the High noun was produced by 7.96% of the participants on average, compared with .79% for the Low noun. Note that those studies reporting a predictability effect on eye-movement measures employed cloze differences of an order of magnitude larger (e.g., Binder, Pollatsek, & Rayner, 1999; Rayner & Well, 1996). Hyönä (1993) did not observe any influence on first-pass measures using a moderate 65/32% High/Low contrast.

Several first-pass reading measures calculated from the eye-movement data are presented in Table 5.2. The most interesting result was the reliable 11-ms effect of transitional probability on the duration of the first fixation made on the target noun (FirstF): $F1(1, 23) = 4.88$, $p < .05$; $F_2(1, 47) = 4.30$, $p < .05$ (see Figure 5.1). We report two other duration measures: the fixation duration on words receiving a single fixation only (SingleF), and the summed duration of all fixations made on the word

Table 5.1. **Examples of the Paired Sentence Materials With Matched High and Low Transitional Probability Target Words**

Condition	Example Sentence
Verb + noun	
High	One way to avoid **confusion** is to make the changes during vacation.
Low	One way to avoid **discovery** is to make the changes during vacation.
Verb + function word	
High	Today she is to preside **over** morning coffee while her boss attends the meeting.
Low	Today she is to preside **from** morning coffee to noon over two public meetings.

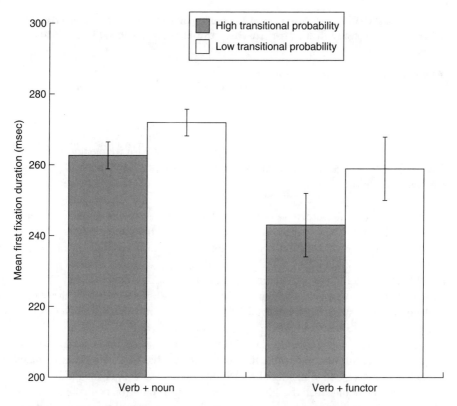

Figure 5.1. Mean first fixation duration as a function of transitional probability for the verb + noun and verb + functor experiments. Bars indicate standard errors.

(Gaze). The influence of transitional probability on the SingleF measure was also reliable: $F_1(1, 23) = 7.08$, $p < .05$, $F_2(1, 47) = 3.75$, $p < .06$; the effect on Gaze was only marginally significant: $F_1(1, 23) = 3.01$, $p < .10$, $F_2(1, 47) = 2.81$, $p = .10$. For all three measures, fixation durations on the High noun were shorter than on the Low noun. Nouns that were more probable given the immediately preceding verb were easier to process than less probable nouns.

Interestingly, there was no effect on the probability of skipping the target noun: $F_1(1, 23) = 1.33$, $p > .2$; $F_2(1, 47) < 1$. Because the *a priori* probability of word skipping is higher the shorter the word (e.g., Brysbaert & Vitu, 1998; Just & Carpenter, 1980), it is possible that the lack of skipping effect was due to the relatively long target nouns employed (mean length: 7.2 letters). We tested the hypothesis that transitional probability influenced the probability of skipping the short target nouns. We conducted a separate analysis on the shorter items only (word lengths from 4–6 letters; $n = 21$). There was no evidence of a skipping effect for this subset of the materials (High: mean = .195, Low: mean = .166; $F_1(1, 23) < 1$, $F_2(1, 20) = 1.03$, $p > .3$). Due to visual acuity constraints, skipping is also more likely the nearer the previous fixation (Rayner, Sereno, & Raney, 1996); we divided the data into two groups according to a median split of launch distance (the distance

Table 5.2. **First-Pass Eye-Movement Measures on the Verb + Noun and the Verb + Functor Sentence Stimuli, for the High and Low Transitional Probability Conditions**

Verb + Noun		Verb + Functor		
High		**Low**	**High**	**Low**
First fixation duration	261	272	239	258
Single-fixation duration	261	274	239	259
Gaze duration	291	303	239	263
Probability of skipping	0.114	0.095	0.606	0.594

Note: Fixation durations are in milliseconds. All figures represent the mean value for each participant averaged across participants.

in characters from the previous fixation to the space before the target word), and analyzed the "near" launch distance group separately. There was again no evidence for a transitional probability effect on skipping probability: (High: mean = .185, Low: mean = .148; $F_1(1, 23) < 1$, $F_2(1, 47) < 1$).

Are there alternative explanations for the fixation duration results? There are two possibilities that could account for the obtained effect that have nothing to do with contingency statistics or predictability. The first is a relationship between spatial and temporal factors termed the *Saccade Distance Effect* (Vitu, McContie, Kerr, & O'Regan, 2001; Radach & Heller, 2000): the further away the previous fixation, the longer the duration of the current fixation. If it was the case that the size of the saccade landing in Low transitional probability nouns was longer than the saccades landing in High nouns, then the advantage for the High condition could be explained. However, the mean distance from the previous fixation to the target noun was actually slightly *longer* in the High condition, which would predict the duration of the first fixation on High nouns to be longer than on Low nouns. Mean launch distance was 5.08 and 4.82 characters for the High and Low conditions, respectively. This difference was not reliable: $F_1(1, 23) = 2.42$, $p > .10$; $F_2(1, 47) = 1.43$, $p > .20$.

A second possibility that could explain the transitional probability effect is the influence of fixation location on fixation duration: the *Inverted Optimal Viewing Position* (IOVP) effect (Vitu et al., 2001). The IOVP describes an inverse U-shaped function of location on duration; fixations made at word-centre tend to be longer than fixations made at either word-beginning or word-end. If initial landing position was affected by the transitional probability manipulation so that the first fixation made on the Low nouns tended to be closer to word-centre than the first fixation made on the High nouns, then a fixation duration difference would not be surprising. There was no evidence for such a difference, however. Figure 5.2 displays the distributions of normalized landing positions on the target noun (letter positions are converted to "fixation zones" in order to display data for different word lengths in the same plot (see Vitu et al.). For example, fixation zone 1 corresponds to the space before a 5-letter target word; zone 6 corresponds to the final letter). There is very little difference in the shapes of the two distributions.

The first-pass results have demonstrated an early influence of transitional probability. Is there evidence that second-pass (or later) reading was also affected?

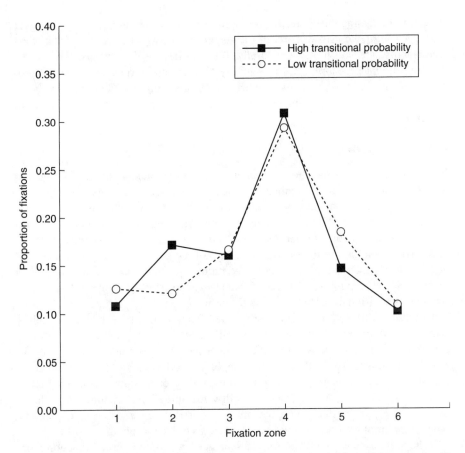

Figure 5.2. The distribution of landing positions in the target noun (of the verb + noun stimuli) as a function of transitional probability. Landing positions are converted to fixation zones in order to collapse together the data for words of different lengths (see text for details).

For instance, encountering a less predictable noun compared with an expected noun after the verb may trigger more regressive saccades to earlier parts of the sentence. Re-inspection of either the verb or the target noun would suggest that comprehension had been disrupted sufficiently for the processor to demand a "second look."

Table 5.3 displays a number of "late" eye-movement measures. There were reliable effects of transitional probability on second-pass reading time (the total amount of time spent re-reading the target word, i.e., including both regressive and progressive saccades into the target word) and the probability of making a regressive saccade to the noun: $F_1(1, 23) = 5.34$, $p < .05$, $F_2(1, 47) = 8.37$, $p < .01$; and $F_1(1, 23) = 15.63$, $p < .001$, $F_2(1, 47) = 9.97$, $p < .01$, respectively. There was no significant influence on re-reading time on the verb, $F_1(1, 23) = 2.67$, $p > .1$; $F_2(1, 47) = 2.37$, $p > .1$; however, there was a marginally significant effect on the probability of making a regression to the verb: $F_1(1, 23) = 4.00$, $p < .06$; $F_2(1, 47) = 3.76$, $p < .06$.

Considering the first- and second-pass results together, we can conclude that the transitional probability manipulation was sufficient to influence the very first stages of lexical processing during reading, as well as to cause enough difficulty to trigger re-inspection of the critical parts of the sentence. Clearly, the effects of statistical predictability are not limited temporally to the earliest reading stages. We suggest that transitional probability has a primarily "bottom-up" influence on lexical processing, facilitating comprehension when the current word is highly probable given the previous word, and making comprehension problematic when the current word is surprising.

5.2.4 Verb + Function Word Pairs

The prototypical high-transitional probability words are found in the class of function (or *closed-class*) words. These include lexical categories such as particles (e.g., pick *up*, rely *on*) and prepositions (e.g., arrive *at*; dozen *of*). In some cases the functor can be seen as part of the lexical item, forming an integral part of its meaning (in languages such as English and German, verbs can convey substantially different meanings depending on the presence/absence of a particle, e.g., pick vs. pick *up*), or may simply have a high co-occurrence probability (e.g., browse *through*, revert *to*, salt *and*). The purpose of this experiment was to investigate the influence of a stronger transitional probability manipulation than used in the verb + noun experiment, with two aims: (1) to confirm the fixation time transitional probability effect using target words drawn from lexical categories other than nouns, and (2) to determine whether skipping rate can be influenced. Because the function words we tested were shorter (mean length: 3.6, range: 2–7 letters) than the target nouns in the previous experiment, their a priori probability of skipping is much higher. Moreover, if a strong transitional probability manipulation is required in order to observe a skipping effect, then the much larger difference in mean transitional probability employed here should be adequate to induce skipping.

The stimuli consisted of 24 sets of sentences containing verb + function word pairs, where the length and corpus frequency of the High and Low transitional probability function word was closely matched on a pairwise basis. Mean transitional probabilities were 0.461 and 0.007 for the High and Low items, respectively. A sample item is provided in Table 5.1. Because of the strong transitional probability manipulation, creating items that were equivalent in rated plausibility was much

Table 5.3. **Second-Pass Eye-Movement Measures for the Verb + Noun and the Verb + Functor Sentence Stimuli, for the High and Low Transitional Probability Conditions**

Verb + Noun			Verb + Functor	
	High	**Low**	**High**	**Low**
Re-reading time on verb	45	58	39	70
Re-reading time on noun/functor	42	67	46	63
Probability of regression to verb	0.212	0.288	0.066	0.156
Probability of regression to noun/functor	0.146	0.274	0.139	0.142

Note: Re-reading times are in milliseconds and are not conditional on a regression being made. All figures represent the mean value for each participant averaged across participants.

more difficult than for the verb + noun materials. Mean plausibility as rated by an independent group of 13 participants was 5.5 and 5.1 for the High and Low items, respectively: this difference was marginally significant, paired $t(23) = 1.84, p = .078$. Also, the cloze difference between the two conditions was larger than for the verb + noun stimuli (42.99% vs. .78% for the High and Low items), approaching the size of the cloze manipulations employed by previous studies.[2]

Table 5.2 summarizes the results of the first-pass analysis, with FirstF, SingleF, and Gaze duration as dependent measures. Transitional probability was significant in the Gaze analysis, but only by subjects: $F_1(1, 23) = 4.85, p < .05; F_2(1, 22) = 1.22; p > .2$. Both FirstF and SingleF were marginally significant in the by-subjects analyses: $F_1(1, 23) = 3.47, p < .1; F_2(1, 22) < 1; F_1(1, 23) = 3.71, p < .1; F_2(1, 22) < 1$, respectively. The overall high skipping rate (~60%) meant that there were fewer fixation-duration data points than in the verb + noun experiment, and consequently lower statistical power. However, the effects were in the expected direction and were numerically larger than the effect sizes obtained using the verb + noun stimuli.

There was no evidence for an overall skipping probability effect: $F_1(1, 23) < 1, F_2(1, 23) < 1$. Because the overall skipping probability was high (the average functor length being less than four letters), it is possible that this global analysis might have obscured a skipping effect restricted to the closer launch distances. However, a comparable analysis of the "near" data only (operationalized using a median split on launch distance) also indicated a null result.

Table 5.3 displays several second-pass reading measures as a function of transitional probability. There was a significantly higher likelihood of making a regression to the verb from a later point in the sentence in the Low condition than in the High condition: $F_1(1, 23) = 21.72, p < .001$ $F_2(1, 23) = 19.15, p < .001$. Accordingly, second-pass reading times were also 31 ms longer on average for the Low condition: $F_1(1, 23) = 13.70, p < .001$ $F_2(1, 23) = 14.74, p < .001$. There was no effect of transitional probability on the probability of regressing to the functor: $F_1(1, 23) < 1, F_2 = 1.78, p > .1$; or on second-pass reading time on the functor: $F_1(1, 23) = 2.28, p > .1$ $F_2(1, 23) = 2.36, p > .1$.

To summarize: results were suggestive of an effect of transitional probability on fixation durations during first-pass reading, using sentence stimuli constructed around matched verb + functor sequences, but statistical significance was not achieved. The effect sizes obtained (see Table 5.2) of ~20 ms were also smaller than anticipated, given the strong transitional probability manipulation. There were, however, reliable re-reading effects on the critical verb. Because of the strong syntactic dependence between many of the verb + functor pairs employed, and the corresponding cloze difference, it is not possible to uniquely attribute the processing disruption triggering a regressive saccade to the transitional probability manipulation.

The lack of an influence of transitional probability on skipping rate in both sentence-reading experiments suggests that the effects of contingency statistics are qualitatively different from the effects of cloze-type predictability. The latter type of predictability effect is typically attributed to "top-down" processing, and is assumed to involve high-level semantic and syntactic integration of the target word with preceding context (e.g., Calvo & Meseguer, 2002; Morris, 1994). We might describe the effects of transitional probability as "bottom-up" processing, where a high transitional probability facilitates lexical processing but does not affect the selection of the next saccade target. It is possible that the two types of predictability effect differ in their locus, with lexical statistical information coming into play very early during sentence comprehension, and cloze-type predictability primarily influencing later processing. More work is needed in order to clarify the distinction between the two sources of predictability.

5.2.5 Passage-Reading Study

In this study, participants' eye movements were monitored in a more natural passage-reading situation. The data gathered from this experiment allowed us to address the question of whether the effect of transitional probability observed on fixation duration in the sentence-reading experiments is found across all combinations of lexical categories. We anticipated that the influence of contingency statistics on reading behavior is not restricted to a small set of category combinations, but rather is a general phenomenon that applies pervasively throughout the language.

The passage-reading eye movement corpus was first filtered to exclude data recorded for the first and last words on a line, words preceded or followed by punctuation marks, the first fixation made on a line, and very long fixations (> 700 ms). In presenting the analyses of this data, we focus on first-pass fixation duration measures only.[3] We used multiple linear regression methods (Lorch & Myers, 1990, Method 3) to first remove between-subject variance and to control for other factors known to influence fixation durations: word length (e.g., Just & Carpenter, 1980) and launch distance (Vitu et al., 2001). Word frequency—probably the most widely reported influence on fixation-duration measures (e.g., Just & Carpenter, 1980; Rayner, 1998; Rayner, Sereno, & Raney, 1996)—was also included as a predictor variable.

After controlling for variability due to participants, word length, and launch distance (log-transformed) transitional probability was a reliable predictor of first fixation, single fixation, and gaze duration: $F(1, 19) = 79.68, p < .0001; F(1, 19) = 93.86, p < .0001; F(1, 19) = 69.31, p < .0001$, respectively. The higher the transitional probability, the shorter the duration; regression coefficients were -2.82, -3.15 and -3.63 for the three measures. The picture did not change if frequency was additionally partialled out: $F(1, 19) = 45.43, p < .0001; F(1, 19) = 56.52, p < .0001; F(1, 19) = 16.22, p < .001$, for FirstF, SingleF, and Gaze, respectively.

The results of the passage-reading study confirmed that statistical information about word-to-word contingencies influenced the early stages of sentence comprehension during reading: fixation durations were reliably shorter the higher the transitional probability between the target and immediately preceding word. This effect proved to be distinct from the effect of word frequency even though the two measures are naturally highly intercorrelated. Based on the conceptual similarity of transitional probability and frequency—frequency can be easily interpreted as the prior probability of a word occurring, irrespective of context—and evidence suggesting that their influences on fixation duration have a common time course (cf. McDonald & Shillcock, 2003a), we next sought to investigate ways of integrating the two measures.

5.2.6 Combining Transitional Probability With Frequency

As we have seen, transitional probability provides a computationally straightforward estimate of the probability of an upcoming word in text given its immediate context. The amount of evidence determining the value does not, however, enter into the equation; identical transitional probabilities can result from vastly different amounts of evidence. For example, if *word₁* has a frequency of 10, and *word₂* co-occurs three times with *word₁* in the corpus, then $P(word_2|word_1) = .3$. This value is also obtained if *word₁* has a frequency of 1000 and *word₂* co-occurs 300 times with *word₁*. It is clear that the second case provides a more reliable estimate for the value of *word₁* as contextual evidence for *word₂* than the first.

McDonald and Shillcock (2003a) demonstrated how Bayes' Law provides a principled approach for weighting and combining the evidence for the appearance of a particular upcoming word with prior information, in order to compute the *posterior probability* of the word occurring given the evidence. This posterior probability measure also weighted the contextual evidence for a word with its prior probability of occurrence. A high transitional probability may be offset by a low prior probability; for example, $P(havoc|wreak)$ is very high, because *wreak* is nearly always followed by *havoc*, but the frequency of *havoc* is very low. We tested the hypothesis that eye-fixation behavior reflects an integration of both types of probabilistic information.

In order to compute a word's posterior probability using Bayes' Law, we modeled its occurrence in context as a Binomially distributed random variable, where transitional probability is interpreted as the number of successful outcomes (e.g., if *wreak* occurs 200 times in a corpus, and the relative frequency of *havoc* following *wreak* is 70/200, then s[successes] = 70 and f[failures] = 130.). By assuming a Beta prior distribution (the conjugate prior for the Binomial), the expected value of the posterior density is computed as follows (cf. Schmitt, 1969):

$$E\left[P(word_2|word_1)\right] = \frac{\alpha \cdot s_{prior} + s_{evidence} + 1}{\alpha \cdot f_{prior} + f_{evidence} + 2}$$

In this equation, s_{prior} is set to $freq(word_2)$ and f_{prior} is set to $[N\ freq(word_2)]$, where N is the number of words in the corpus. The weighting parameter α encodes the relative importance of prior knowledge and contextual evidence. This parameter was set by finding the optimal linear fit to the first fixation-duration data collected from the filler items in the sentence-reading study ($\alpha = .0001$). This approach has the advantage of being simple, but is not the final story, as α itself could be allowed to vary according to a density function that models its dependence on other variables.

We evaluated the Bayesian measure using the passage-reading eye-movement data and multiple regression analysis. As above, participants, word length, and launch distance were entered first into the regression, followed by either posterior probability, frequency, or transitional probability. Posterior probability proved to be the best single predictor of first fixation, single fixation, and gaze duration: $\beta = .126$, $F(1, 19) = 81.02$, $p < .0001$; $\beta = .136$, $F(1, 19) = 82.67$, $p < .0001$; $\beta = .144$, $F(1, 19) = 99.60$, $p < .0001$, respectively.[4] Posterior probability also provided a more parsimonious account of the fixation-duration data than frequency and transitional probability: a single variable accounted for as much variability as two. The total amounts of FirstF, SingleF, and Gaze variance explained by the regression equations containing posterior probability were 14.5%, 16.3%, and 15.4%, respectively; the corresponding amounts of variance explained by the regression models incorporating both frequency and transitional probability was 14.5%, 16.3%, and 15.5%, respectively.[5]

5.3 DISCUSSION

In this chapter we discussed the results of three eyetracking experiments that tested the hypothesis that statistical information in the form of transitional probabilities has an influence on eye fixations during reading. Manipulating the transitional probability of verb + noun sequences gave reliable early fixation-duration effects on the noun. Second-pass eye-movement measures were also sensitive to the manipulation; there was a higher likelihood of re-reading the target noun in the Low transitional probability condition. These results were largely confirmed by two further experiments that considered matched verb + functor sequences and unrestricted combinations of lexical categories. The transitional probability effect appears to be pervasive across all lexical categories.

We then considered whether contingency statistics—which estimate the probability distribution over potential upcoming words given the presence of the current word—could be integrated with the prior probability of the upcoming word (estimated using its relative frequency of occurrence). We tested a Bayesian approach to integrating these two sources of probabilistic information, which gave a more parsimonious explanation of the fixation-duration data than considering frequency and transitional probability as independent factors.

We have suggested that lexical statistical information is exploited by the processor during reading in order to facilitate the processing of upcoming words in the unfolding text. This proposal is consistent with recent eyetracking and ERP evidence for the on-line, incremental anticipation of the semantic, syntactic, and categorical properties of words in listeners' auditory input (e.g., Altmann & Kamide, 1999; Crocker & Corley, 2002; Federmeier & Kutas, 1999; Huettig & Altmann, chapter 11, this volume; Kamide et al., 2002; Muckel et al., 2002; van Berkum et al., 2002).

Besides prediction, are there other reasons why the processor might take advantage of contingency information? For one, this type of statistical knowledge can often be seen as approximating "high-level" semantic knowledge. High transitional probability word sequences, such as verb + noun, are a good cue that the noun is a semantically plausible object of the verb. A processing mechanism operating on statistical information alone provides a computationally inexpensive alternative to complex (and, conceivably, more costly) cognitive processing (Fodor, 1983).

5.3.1 Principles for Comprehension

Based on the converging empirical evidence for the use of statistical mechanisms and contingency information by the processor during natural language comprehension, we outline three guiding principles:

The Contingent Learning Principle: Elements of language (e.g., phonemes, bound morphemes, words) are rarely encountered in isolation; rather, they occur in context, and so learning these items also involves encoding their context to some extent. Contingency information is therefore learned with (and is perhaps even a by-product of) language exposure. Note that this type of learning is not restricted to language; the brain appears to employ contingency information for a variety of motor and cognitive tasks, and at many levels of processing.

The Integration of Statistical Predictors Principle: The best solution to a problem often involves making use of all the information available. If independent statistical sources of information (visual, linguistic, and otherwise) exist for predicting the outcome of an event, the greatest predictive accuracy may be achieved by combining predictors in a principled way.

The Principle of Incremental Processing: Both written and spoken language processing proceed incrementally; new words are encountered and integrated into continually evolving representations of the semantic, syntactic, and discoursal structure of the input. The exigencies of phonological processing in spoken-word recognition (e.g., the limitations on storing a "raw" representation of speech, and the need to combine speech perception with gestural perception) make incremental interpretation an important goal for the speech processor, which it achieves by the processor's exquisite sensitivity to a wide range of cues (such as contingency statistics); reading shares this incremental processing.

We propose that recognition of these three principles places realistic constraints on models of reading. For instance, the Principle of Incremental Processing eliminates certain classes of models from consideration, such as any model that assumes semantic processing is delayed until the end of the clause is reached. The Contingent Learning Principle suggests the modification of those lexical processing models that assume statistical independence between a given word and its context. More generally, any model of the temporal characteristics of eye movements during reading needs to account for the effects of statistical predictability on fixation durations.

5.4 CONCLUSIONS

Reading is a complex activity for which specialized neural mechanisms could not have evolved. The use of statistical information present in the input, such as transitional probabilities, is computationally inexpensive and it would be surprising if it was not exploited for highly practiced skills such as reading. We suggest that the on-line formation of lexical predictions is a functional (and perhaps inevitable) component of normal reading, and more generally, language comprehension. The accumulating evidence from eyetracking, ERP, and other experimental paradigms points towards the conclusion that readers and listeners are able to exploit context-dependent and context-independent statistical knowledge in order to anticipate the upcoming words. Furthermore, they appear to integrate these sources of information in a principled way that can be naturally modeled as a Bayesian combination of probabilistic variables.

5.5 AUTHOR NOTE/ACKNOWLEDGMENTS

Correspondence should be sent to Scott McDonald, Department of Psychology, University of Edinburgh, 7 George Square, Edinburgh, Scotland EH8 9JZ. Fax: + 44 131 650 3461. E-mail: Scott.McDonald@ed.ac.uk. This research reported in this chapter was supported by the Wellcome Trust (project grant GR064240AIA).

References

Altmann, G. T. M., & Kamide, Y. (1999). Incremental interpretation at verbs: Restricting the domain of subsequent reference. *Cognition, 73,* 247–264.

Anderson, J. R. (1990). *The adaptive character of thought.* Hillsdale, NJ: Erlbaum.

Binder, K. S., Pollatsek, A., & Rayner, K. (1999). Extraction of information to the left of the fixated word in reading. *Journal of Experimental Psychology: Human Perception and Performance, 25,* 1162–1172.

Burnage, G., & Dunlop, D. (1992). Encoding the British National Corpus. In J. M. Aarts, P. de Haan, & N. Oostdijk (Eds.), *English language corpora: Design, analysis, and exploitation* (pp. 79–95). Amsterdam: Rodopi.

Calvo, M. G., & Meseguer, E. (2002). Eye movements and processing stages in reading: Relative contributions of visual, lexical, and contextual factors. *The Spanish Journal of Psychology, 5,* 1138–7416.

Clarkson, P. & Rosenfeld, R. (1997) Statistical language modeling using the CMU-Cambridge Toolkit. *Proceedings of Eurospeech '97.* Rhodes, Greece.

Corley, S. (1998). *A statistical model of human lexical category disambiguation.* Unpublished Ph.D. dissertation, University of Edinburgh, Scotland.

Crocker, M. W., & Corley, S. (2002). Modular architectures and statistical mechanisms: The case from lexical category disambiguation. In P. Merlo & S. Stevenson (Eds.), *The lexical basis of sentence processing.* Amsterdam: John Benjamins.

Eberhard, K., Spivey-Knowlton, S., Sedivy, J., & Tanenhaus, M. (1995). Eye movements as a window into real-time spoken language processing in natural contexts. *Journal of Psycholinguistic Research, 24,* 409–436.

Ehrlich, S. F., & Rayner, K. (1981). Contextual effects on word perception and eye movements during reading. *Journal of Verbal Learning and Verbal Behavior, 20,* 641–65.

Federmeier, K. D., & Kutas, M. (1999). A rose by any other name: Long-term memory structure and sentence processing. *Journal of Memory and Language, 41,* 469–495.

Fodor, J. A. (1983). *The Modularity of Mind.* Cambridge, MA: MIT Press.

Hyönä, J. (1993). Effects of thematic and lexical priming on readers' eye movements. *Scandinavian Journal of Psychology, 34,* 293–304.

Jurafsky, D. (2003). Probabilistic modeling in psycholinguistics: Linguistic comprehension and production. In R. Bod, J. Hay, & S. Jannedy (Eds.), *Probabilistic linguistics.* MIT Press.

Jurafsky, D. A. (1996). A probabilistic model of lexical and syntactic access and disambiguation. *Cognitive Science, 20,* 137–194.

Just, M. A., & Carpenter, P. A. (1980). A theory of reading: From eye fixations to comprehension. *Psychological Review, 87,* 329–354.

Kamide, Y., Scheepers, C., Altmann, G., & Crocker, M. (2002). *Integration of syntactic and semantic information in predictive processing: Anticipatory eye movements in German.* Paper presented at the 15th CUNY Conference on Human Sentence Processing, New York.

Kutas, M., & Federmeier, K. D. (2000). Electrophysiology reveals semantic memory use in language comprehension. *Trends in Cognitive Sciences, 4,* 463–470.

Lorch, R. F., & Myers, J. L. (1990). Regression analyses of repeated measures data in cognitive research. *Journal of Experimental Psychology: Learning, Memory, and Cognition, 16,* 149–157.

MacDonald, M. (1993). The interaction of lexical and syntactic ambiguity. *Journal of Memory and Language, 32,* 692–715.

McDonald, S., & Brew, C. (2001). *A rational analysis of semantic processing by the left cerebral hemisphere.* First Workshop on Cognitively Plausible Models of Semantic Processing (SEMPRO-2001), Edinburgh, Scotland, July 31, 2001.

McDonald, S. A., & Shillcock, R. C. (2003a). Eye movements reveal the on-line computation of lexical probabilities. *Psychological Science, 14,* 648–652.

McDonald, S. A., & Shillcock, R. C. (2003b). Low-level predictive inference in reading: the influence of transitional probabilities on eye movements. *Vision Research, 43,* 1735–1751.

Morris, R. K. (1994). Lexical and message-level sentence context effects on fixation times in reading. *Journal of Experimental Psychology: Learning, Memory, and Cognition, 20,* 92–103.

Muckel, S., Scheepers, C., Crocker, M., & Müller, K. (2002). *Anticipating German particle verb meanings: Effects of lexical frequency and plausibility.* Paper presented at the 8th Conference on Architectures and Mechanisms for Language Processing (AMLaP-2002), Tenerife, Canary Islands, Spain.

Radach, R., & Heller, D. (2000). Spatial and temporal aspects of eye movement control. In R. Radach, D. Heller, & J. Pynte (Eds.), *Reading as a perceptual process* (pp. 165–191). Oxford: Elsevier.

Rayner, K. (1998). Eye movements in reading and information processing: 20 years of research. *Psychological Bulletin, 124,* 372–422.

Rayner, K. Sereno, S. C., & Raney, G. E. (1996). Eye movement control in reading: A comparison of two types of models. *Journal of Experimental Psychology: Human Perception and Performance, 22,* 1188–1200.

Rayner, K., & Well, A. D. (1996). Effects of contextual constraint on eye movements in reading: A further examination. *Psychonomic Bulletin and Review, 3,* 504–509.

Saffran, J. R., Aslin, R. N., & Newport, E. L. (1996). Statistical learning by 8-month old infants. *Science, 274,* 1926–1928.

Saffran, J. R., Newport, E. L., & Aslin, R. N. (1996). Word segmentation: the role of distributional cues. *Journal of Memory and Language, 35,* 606–621.

Schmitt, S. A. (1969). *Measuring uncertainty: An elementary introduction to Bayesian statistics.* Reading, MA: Addison-Wesley.

Tanenhaus, M., Spivey-Knowlton, S., Eberhard, K., & Sedivy, J. (1995). Integration of visual and linguistic information in spoken language comprehension. *Science, 268,* 1632–1634.

Taylor, W. L. (1953). "Cloze Procedure": A new tool for measuring readability. *Journalism Quarterly, 30,* 415–433.

Tenenbaum, J. B., & Griffiths, T. L. (2001). Generalization, similarity, and Bayesian inference. *Behavioral and Brain Sciences, 24,* 629–640.

van Berkum, J. J. A., Kooijman, V., Brown, C. M., Zwitserlood, P., & Hagoort, P. (2002). *Do listeners use discourse-level information to predict upcoming words in an unfolding sentence? An ERP study.* Poster presented at CNS 2002 (The Annual Computational Neuroscience Meeting), Chicago.

Vitu, F., McConkie, G., Kerr, P., & O'Regan, J. K. (2001). Fixation location effects on fixation durations during reading: an inverted optimal viewing position effect. *Vision Research, 41,* 3513–3533.

Notes

1. We do not mean prediction is the sense of being explicit, conscious, or strategic.
2. Because of the imperfect plausibility match and the larger discrepancy in cloze probability between the two conditions, we cannot be as confident as we were for the previous experiment that any observed transitional probability effect was independent of higher-level (semantic/syntactic) factors.
3. For a more comprehensive analysis of an expanded version of this corpus, including fixation duration, skipping probability, and initial landing position measures, see McDonald and Shillcock (2003b).
4. This conclusion is based on model fit; R^2 for the regression model containing posterior probability was larger than the R^2 values for the models containing either frequency or transitional probability.
5. Posterior probability does not completely subsume the other two variables; although adding frequency to the regression model containing posterior probability did not increase the amount of FirstF or SingleF variance explained: $F(1, 19) = 1.18, p > .10$; $F(1, 19) = 2.70, p > .10$, respectively, adding transitional probability resulted in a slight improvement in model fit: $F(1, 19) = 4.61, p < .05$; $F(1, 19) = 6.83, p < .05$, respectively.

Chapter 6
The Empty Category PRO: Processing What Cannot Be Seen

MOISÉS BETANCORT, ENRIQUE MESEGUER, AND MANUEL CARREIRAS

6.1 INTRODUCTION: THE EMPTY CATEGORY PRO

An *Empty Category* PRO (henceforth EC-PRO) is an element standing at the subject position of infinitive constructions that lacks phonological realization.[1] This element must establish a relationship with an *antecedent* in order to acquire its meaning.[2] As shown in example (1), the EC-PRO must be related to the noun phrase (NP) *Max* in order to be the grammatical subject of the predicate *to eat*.

(1) *Max$_i$ tried* [PRO$_i$ *to eat apples*].

The study of EC-PRO is interesting for various reasons. First, as noted, it lacks phonological realization. Second, it does not involve a moved element (as in NP-trace or wh-trace), so readers have no warning about the empty element downstream in the sentence. Finally, PRO as an anaphoric element needs to be linked to an antecedent. These special features of EC-PRO provide an attractive structure to test predictions from different models of syntactic processing (Fodor, 1989). Nonetheless, the empirical evidence on how readers resolve EC-PRO on-line is far from conclusive (e.g., Featherston, 2001).

One of the first experimental references to a type of strategy dealing with EC-PRO appears in C. Chomsky (1969). She observed that children prefer to take the last NP as controller (grammatical subject) of PRO independently of the lexical properties of the main verb (subject control verbs such as *promise*). She attributes this to the Minimal Distance Principle (MDP) which was proposed previously by Rosenbaum (1967). This principle states that the controller of a subordinate verb's missing subject position is the noun phrase that is most contiguous to it in the linear word order of the sentence.

Later on, this idea was invoked in the experiments carried out by Frazier, Clifton, and Randall (1983). It was the first attempt to propose a syntactic strategy in the processing of empty categories. Frazier et al. studied how rapidly readers use the verb control information by giving a speeded comprehension task.[3] They presented sentences such as (2) to (5) in which they manipulated the type of main verb (subject vs. object control) and the ambiguity of the sentences with respect to the control verb information (ambiguous control vs. unambiguous control).

(2) Subject Control_unambiguous
     Everyone liked the woman who the little child started $_{[PRO]}$ *to sing those stupid French songs for_last Christmas.*

(3) Object Control—unambiguous
     Everyone liked the woman who the little child forced$_{-[PRO]}$ *to sing those stupid French songs last Christmas.*

(4) Subject Control—ambiguous
     Everyone liked the woman who the little child begged $_{[PRO]}$ *to sing those stupid French songs for_last Christmas.*

(5) Object Control—ambiguous
     Everyone liked the woman who the little child begged$_{-[PRO]}$ *to sing those stupid French songs last Christmas.*

It was found that reading times were faster for (2) and (4) than for (3) and (5). Frazier et al. argued for the application of the Most Recent Filler Strategy (MRFS), according to which, when readers encounter the empty infinitive verb subject position, they will prefer the recent potential filler noun phrase (NP) instead of the more distant NP to fill the empty position. Since the same result was found in both the ambiguous and the unambiguous conditions, they concluded that control information is accessed later in the parsing process. Subsequently, the MRFS was replaced by the Active Filler Strategy (AFS) (Frazier & Flores D'Arçais, 1989). Finally, De Vincenzi (1991, 1996) reformulated the AFS into a more general strategy called the Minimal Chain Principle (MCP). The MCP holds that the parser will prefer the shortest chains and that the preference for a short chain will produce Active Filler Strategy effects.

The conclusions reached by Frazier et al. (1983) provoked a great deal of interest in EC phenomena as well as in testing the validity of the MRFS. J. Nicol and Lee Osterhout (1988) and Lee Osterhout and J. Nicol (1998) (reported in Nicol and Swinney, 1989) presented evidence about the identification of the controller of PRO using cross-modal lexical priming (CMLP).[4] The main point they raised was that semantic and pragmatic information would be necessary to recover the antecedent of PRO since it *behaves* as a pronoun.[5] They presented sentences with two potential antecedents in transitive–intransitive and active–passive constructions. An example of such a sentence is presented in (6).[6] The symbol (*) indicates the test points.

(6)   *The actress invited the dentist$_i$ from the new medical center* PRO$_i$ *to * go to the par * ty at the * mayor's * house*.*

The data showed that there was not only activation of the recent filler *dentist* in (6), but contrary to the MRFS predictions, all potential antecedents were reactivated.

Although empty category constructions are common in Spanish (a null-subject language), psycholinguists have paid little attention to them (Alonso-Ovalle, Fernández-Solera, Frazier, & Clifton, 2002; Betancort, Carreiras, & Acuña, 2004; Demestre, Meltzer, García-Albea, & Vigil, 1999). However, only the studies by Betancort et al. (2004) and Demestre et al. (1999) have investigated the EC-PRO in subordinate infinitival sentences. In an ERP (event-related potentials) study, Demestre et al. (1999) tested how fast readers activated the legal antecedent of an EC-PRO in sentences like (7) and (8). They manipulated the sentences along two dimensions: (a) the number of potential antecedents [i.e., either one (7) or two (8)], and (b) the agreement in gender with an adjective at the end of the sentence (i.e., either matching or mismatching). Mismatched sentences are indicated by (*).

(7)   *Pedro/*María quiere* [PRO] *ser rico.*
      Peter/*Mary wants [PRO] *to be rich* (mas).

(8)   *Pedro/María ha aconsejado a María/*Pedro* [PRO] *ser educada* (fem) *con los trabajadores.*
      Peter/Mary has advised Mary/*Peter [PRO] *to be polite* (fem) *with the workers.*

In the mismatched conditions, the authors found an early negativity distributed over frontal and central scalp regions following the mismatched target (*rich/polite*). They concluded that this pattern of electrophysiological response reflected the rapid detection of gender agreement violations in infinitival clauses, which implies that the parser had established the coreference relation between the null subject (PRO) and its antecedent. (See also Barber, Salillas, & Carreiras, chapter 15, this volume, for a left-anterior negativity effect during noun–adjective gender agreement violations).

In an eyetracker experiment, Betancort et al. (2004) manipulated subject control verb (9a, b) and object control verb (10a, b) sentences. The gender of an adjective which appeared later in the sentence could either match or mismatch the gender of the PRO antecedent dictated by the verb of the main clause, so that mismatching sentences were ungrammatical. The aim of the experiment was to test (a) how fast readers use the verb control information, and (b) when readers make their decisions during sentence processing.

(9) a. *Maríai prometió a Pedroj* [PRO$_i$] *ser bastante cauta con los comentarios.*

Maryi promised Peter [PRO$_i$] *to be quite careful* (fem) *with her comments.*

(9) b. * *María$_i$ prometió a Pedro$_j$* [PRO$_i$] *ser bastante cauto con los comentarios.*

* *Mary$_i$ promised Peter* [PRO$_i$] *to be quite careful* (mas) *with her
comments.*

(10) a. *María$_i$ exigió a Pedro$_j$* [PRO$_j$] *ser bastante cauto con los comentarios.*
Mary$_i$ demanded that Peter [PRO$_j$] *be quite carefu l* (mas) *with his
comments.*

(10) b. * *María$_i$ exigió a Pedro$_j$* [PRO$_j$] *ser bastante cauta con los comentarios.*
* *Mary$_i$ demanded that Peter$_j$* [PRO$_j$] *be quite careful* (fem) *with his
comments.*

Betancort et al. (2004) found that readers made use of the control information
provided by the matrix verb and engaged in differential processing of subject-control
versus object-control structures. They also found that it was harder to process the
adjective in mismatched sentences than in matched sentences. This allowed the
authors to conclude that readers had made a commitment to one NP as controller
of PRO before reaching the adjective region. Thus, it seems that when readers got
to the adjective region, they already had enough information to select the subject or
the object of the main clause as subject of PRO. This commitment had to be grounded
in the matrix verb and its control properties to select the right antecedent for PRO.

The study of the EC-PRO in Spanish has largely been restricted to control
structures (Demestre et al., 1999; Betancort et al., 2004). Control is a lexical quality
of verbs such as *promise* or *force* (Chomsky, 1981; Jackendoff, 1972, 1974; Bresnan,
1982; Cattell, 1984; Chierchia, 1988; Sag & Pollard, 1991). In this chapter, we report
two experiments that investigated the EC-PRO in gerund (Experiment 1) and infinitive (Experiment 2) clauses using *perception* main verbs such as *see*.

The gerund structure creates an interesting syntactic ambiguity in Spanish, as
shown in example (11). The ambiguity arises with perception verbs in the main
clause, allowing either *Juan* or *María* to be the antecedent of the EC-PRO.

(11) *Juan$_i$ vio a María$_j$ [?$_{ij}$ comprando en la tienda]*
John saw Mary [? shopping in the market]

The most accepted analysis in Spanish is that the gerund clause creates an EC-PRO
related to either *"Juan"* or *"Maria"* in the main clause, as in (12).

(12) *Juan$_i$ vio a María$_j$ [PRO $_{ij}$ comprando en la tienda].*
John$_i$ saw Mary$_j$ [PRO $_{ij}$ shopping in the market].

The gerund clause holds an EC-PRO as subject of the subordinate clause, which could be controlled either by the subject or by the object of the main verb. The ambiguity created in the gerund clause will give us the opportunity to test whether the MRFS applies to the resolution of EC-PRO or whether other variables such as plausibility have an initial impact. This type of syntactic ambiguity arises due to the possibility of referring to the NP1 or to the NP2.[7]

Although the syntactic analysis of perception predicates is controversial (see Hernanz, 1999, pp. 2238–2247; see Fillmore, 1963; Rosenbaum, 1967; Fiengo, 1974; Akmajian, 1977; Declerck, 1983a; San Martin, 2002; Landau, 1999; Abney, 1987; Johnson, 1988; Milsarck, 1988; Reuland, 1983 and the references cited there), we take these verbs to license complement clauses with PRO subjects. This means that the recovery of the EC-PRO is regulated by a coreferential relationship of control from a constituent in the matrix clause (NP1 or NP2). This means two things:

1. These structures are different from ECM (extracellular matrix) structures containing verbs like *believe* or *want,* in that in these the intervening NP (NP2) is not really an argument of the matrix verb from which it nevertheless receives "extraordinary case marking" in the accusative. The intervening NP (or PP) occurring with perception predicates is taken to be an argument of the matrix verb. In fact, these verbs are often called *direct perception predicates* when they take nonfinite complements just to make it clear that the perception of the event denoted in the nonfinite clause is indeed direct and simultaneous with that event. (By contrast, when these verbs license full that-clauses as complements, they often involve "intellectual" perception: *I saw that the house had been repainted* means rather that the perceiver "realized" that, and that the realization took place after the painting.) For further differences between perception predicates and ECM predicates, see Felser (1998, 358 ff.).

2. Since control is used to refer to a relation of referential dependency between an unexpressed subject (the controlled element) and an expressed or unexpressed constituent (the controller) (Bresnan, 1982, p. 372) and such a dependency is lexically specified (Chomsky, 1981; Jackendoff, 1972, 1974; Bresnan, 1982; Cattell, 1984; Chierchia, 1988; Sag & Pollard, 1991), the subject or object orientation of that referential dependency does not affect the syntactic tree. This means that even if the *-ing* structures of our first experiment are seen as different from the infinitival structures to be used in the second, the nature of the referential tie would be unaffected (see Felser, 1998, p 355). It is worth keeping in mind that even if *-ings* are seen as participial adjuncts (not complements) of the matrix or as some kind of verbal small clause, the kind of control established between the matrix constituent and the unexpressed subject of the nonfinite clause is obligatory control like in (1) above (see Haegeman, 1994, p. 262).

6.2 THE ROLE OF PLAUSIBILITY IN PROCESSING GAPS

As we mentioned before, the MRFS stated that when readers are faced with an EC, they apply a syntactic strategy according to which they prefer to take the most recent NP instead of a more distant NP to fill the EC. This syntactic principle quickly generated a great deal of research to test whether or not this type of strategy is initially applied in the resolution of filler-gap dependencies. In particular, several experiments were conducted to investigate the role played by constraints (e.g., verb argument structure, transitivity of the main verb, main verb control information, and plausibility) in the gap-filling process (Tanenhaus, Stowe, & Carlson, 1985; Stowe, Tanenhaus, & Carlson, 1991; Stowe, 1986; Boland, Tanenhaus, & Garnsey, 1990; Boland, Tanenhaus, Garnsey, & Carlson, 1995).

An initial effect of plausibility in the verb prior to the gap has been obtained in several experiments. Boland et al. (1995) found plausibility effects in sentences such as *which prize/client did the salesman visit ... ?* Using a word-by-word makes-sense judgment reading task, they found a plausibility effect in the matrix verb. The percentage of *non-sense* responses was higher in the matrix verb of the implausible filler *which prize* than in the plausible filler *which client*. In contrast, this effect disappeared with verbs like *notify* in which a complement sentence could contain the gap. Similar effects of plausibility have also been shown in other experiments (Tanenhaus, Carlson, & Trueswell, 1989; Boland et al., 1990; Stowe et al., 1991; Garnsey, Tanenhaus, & Chapman, 1989 for an ERP study). Nevertheless, the task used in some of these experiments could have modulated the findings notably because readers had to decide whether the presented sentences were meaningful or not. This task differs greatly from normal reading.

Traxler and Pickering (1996), using a more natural reading experimental technique, ran two eyetracker experiments in which they manipulated the plausibility of the *wh*-filler and showed an early plausibility effect (first-fixation and first-pass time, Experiment 1). This effect led the authors to conclude that an unbounded dependency is immediately formed when readers encounter the verb regardless of plausibility. (See Mitchell, chapter 2, this volume, for the consequences of using different tasks in theoretical development.) Nonetheless, none of these experiments investigated plausibility in the resolution of PRO sentences. Importantly, gerund and infinitive EC-PRO clauses are different from *wh*-type EC constructions because there is no cue that a gap will appear later.[8] Previous results showed that recovery of the antecedent seemed to be initially guided by the lexical properties of the main verb in controlled PRO (Betancort et al., 2004). In the present experiments, we aim to test the effect of plausibility in the recovery of the antecedent (controller) of EC-PRO in ambiguous subordinate gerund (Experiment 1) and unambiguous infinitive clauses (Experiment 2). The use of an infinitive complement clause in Experiment 2 makes sentences unambiguous. With regard to grammar, only the grammatical object NP of the main sentence can be the controller of the PRO subject of the infinitive subordinate verb.

In Experiment 1, we investigated the effect of noun phrase plausibility when readers faced the ambiguity created by the subordinate gerund clause. Gerund clauses were constructed with two potential antecedent noun phrases for the EC-PRO and, importantly, the ambiguity created by perception verbs allows a good test for checking if, and how, plausibility modulates any initial preference for the PRO's antecedent. Furthermore, in Experiment 2 we tested if plausibility could be useful or initially computed even in a syntactically unambiguous EC-PRO structure (using infinitive verbs instead of gerund verbs). Constraint-satis-faction models would assume the initial use of semantic plausibility (among other extra-syntactic information) in the earliest stage of processing, while the garden-path model (MRFS; AFS) would propose that readers initially prefer the recent filler instead of the distant filler in resolving empty-category construc-tions.

6.2.1 Experiment 1

The goal of this experiment was to test the time course of processing the EC-PRO in Spanish subordinate gerund sentences. The main questions we wanted to address were: (a) To what extent does the plausibility of an NP guide the initial syntactic analysis, and (b) What is the role played by recency as a syntactic strategy in the processing of these types of sentences?

The questions presented above are directly related to the MRFS proposed in Frazier et al. (1983) to account for the processing of sentences with an empty element. The MRFS puts forward that when readers find a gap in the syntactic tree, they prefer to fill it with the most recent NP as the antecedent of the empty category, instead of with a more distant NP. This means that in our sentences, there should be a preference for the recent filler (NP in object position) as the antecedent of PRO rather than the distant filler which is in the subject position.

Each item contains a main sentence in which two NPs (the subject or the object) could act as grammatically correct antecedents of EC-PRO. Nevertheless, in order to test the role that plausibility plays as an initial constraint in parsing operations, one NP was more plausible as an antecedent of PRO. The plausibility of the NPs was obtained by means of the decisions made by three judges. The judges read a pool of gerund subordinate sentences with two potential antecedents. They decided which of the two potential antecedents could unequivocally act as the plausible agent of the gerund verb and then as the antecedent of PRO. We rejected sentences in which there was a doubt in any of the judgments.

In order to test at what point in the sentence the readers have chosen the NP that controls PRO, we introduced an adjective phrase in the region immediately following PRO that either matched or failed to match the controlling NP in gender (see an example of the material in Table 6.1).

The predictions of garden-path and constraint satisfaction models do not differ greatly for the present experiment. In fact, both models seem to make quite similar predictions though for very different theoretical reasons. The gar-den-path model assumes that a single analysis is initially chosen based on structural information only. If the initial analysis is based only on structural

Table 6.1. **Example of Material Used in Experiment 1**

CONDITION 1

Object-Plausibility-Matched (Objplau-Match)

La abogada/oyó/al juez/[*PRO*] sentenciando/muy seguro/al acusado de homicidio.

The lawyer (fem.) heard the jugde (mas.) *[PRO] sentencing very confident* (mas.) *to the accused of homicide.*

CONDITION 2

Subject-Plausibility-Matched (Subjplau-Match)

El juez/oyó/a la abogada/[PRO] sentenciando/muy seguro/al acusado de homicidio.

The judge (mas.) *heard the lawyer* (fem.) *[PRO] sentencing very confident* (mas.) *to the accused of homicide.*

CONDITION 3

Object-Plausibility-Mismatched (Objplau-Mismatch)

La abogada/oyó/al juez/[PRO] sentenciando/muy segura/al acusado de homicidio.

The lawyer (fem.) heard the judge (mas.) *[PRO] sentencing* (gerund) *very confident* (fem.) *to the accused of homicide.*

CONDITION 4

Subject-Plausibility-Mismatched (Subjplau-Mismatch)

El juez/oyó/a la abogada/[PRO] sentenciando/muy segura/al acusado de homicidio.

The judge (mas.) heard the lawyer (fem.) *[PRO] sentencing* (gerund) *very confident* (fem.) *to the accused of homicide.*

---

information (MRFS), readers should take the most recent NP (second NP) as the antecedent of PRO in all cases, independent of its plausibility in acting as the subject of the gerund. Therefore, this provides no grounds for predicting differences in early measures in the verb region. However, more difficulty in late measures would be expected in the condition in which the most recent NP does not fit with the plausibility information that would cause a reanalysis. However, Traxler and Pickering's (1996) findings showing that plausibility could be evaluated very early by the system suggest that the implausible filler could be computed and immediately assigned as a good agent for the gerund verb, but the rapid evaluation of plausibility would cause slowing even in the early eyetracking measures. In summary, sentences in which the plausible antecedent is in object position (recent filler) will be easier to process than sentences in which the plausible antecedent is located in subject position (distant filler). Reanalysis should therefore be the key that shows us if recency is initially followed. In addition, a mismatch effect is expected when the gender of the adjective does not agree with the right antecedent if this has already been assigned. (See Boland, chapter 4, this volume, for a discussion about eye-movement measures and their mapping on cognitive events.)

On the other hand, constraint satisfaction models would claim that plausibility is initially computed when readers reach the gerund verb, as a constraint to guide the selection of the right antecedent of PRO. If this happens, we should anticipate a competition between recency and plausibility in the region of the verb in the conditions of subject plausibility, provided that recency is computed as another constraint. This competition should produce a higher load at early stages for distant filler sentences (subject plausibility) as compared to recent filler sentences (object plausibility) which should be present at early stages. In the adjective region, constraint models should predict a mismatch effect and mismatched sentences should produce an increased reading time as compared to matched sentences.

6.2.2 Method

6.2.2.1 Participants

A total of 24 undergraduate students of the University of La Laguna (Canary Islands, Spain) participated in the experiment for course credit.

6.2.2.2 Materials and Design

A total of 40 sentences with the structure NP1-VP1-NP2-[PRO-gerund]-AdjP-PP, like those displayed in Table 6.1, were constructed. For each sentence, four versions were created—two sentences with subject plausibility and two sentences with object plausibility. While the gender of the adjective matched the gender of the more plausible antecedent in one of the sentences, it simultaneously mismatched the gender of the correct antecedent in the other sentences. The manipulation of the gender in the AdjP region will allow us to test how fast participants relate the EC-PRO with the correct antecedent. In addition, another 92 sentences with different types of structures were written to serve as fillers, as well as 10 sentences for practice trials.

6.2.2.3 Apparatus and Procedure

The sentences were presented in lowercase letters on a video screen interfaced with a PC-compatible computer. The monitor displayed up to 80 characters per line. All the sentences had less than 80 characters, so they were displayed on one line. Participants were seated 73 cm away from the monitor, and three characters equated one degree of visual angle. Participants' eye movements were monitored by a Fourward Technologies Dual Purkinje Eyetracker which was interfaced to a computer. The eyetracker has a resolution of 10 min of arc (half a character). Viewing was binocular, with the eye position recorded from the right eye only. The signal from the eyetracker was sampled every millisecond by the computer.

When participants arrived for the experiment, they were seated in front of the monitor with their heads in a chin rest to stabilize head movements. The initial calibration of the eyetracking system generally required about 5 min. The participants were asked to read sentences displayed on the monitor and were told that they would be questioned about the sentences and that they should read for comprehension. Questions were asked on approximately a third of the trials. Prior to reading each sentence, the participants were instructed to look at a fixation box that outlined the first character position of the sentence. A red dot within the square indicated to them that they were correctly looking at the first square and were ready to read, so they could press a button to display the sentence. When they pressed the button, a sentence immediately appeared on the screen. After reading the sentence, the participants again pressed a button that could cause the presentation of a question or of a row of squares. When a question appeared on the screen, participants had to press one of the two buttons to answer yes or no. Each of them initially read 10 practice sentences to become familiar with the procedure. Then they read the 40 experimental sentences intermixed randomly with the 92 filler sentences.

6.2.2.4 Data Analysis

We will report results for three different eye-movement measures. *First-pass reading times* is used as an index of early processing and represents the sum of all fixations from the time when the reader first enters a region to the left until the region is first exited either to the right or left. *Regression-path times* is the sum of all fixations from the first time a region is accessed until the first time the reader leaves the region to the right, including fixations due to regressions. This measure is sometimes, although not always, considered as an early measure (Brysbaert & Mitchell, 1996; Duffy, Morris, & Rayner, 1988; Konieczny, Hemforth, Scheepers, & Strube, 1997; Traxler, Pickering, & Clifton, 1998). *Total-reading times* is used as an index of late processing and is the sum of all fixations that occurred in a particular region.

6.2.3 Results

For the purpose of the analyses, the texts were segmented as shown with slashes in Table 6.1; the first region contained the first NP (*La abogada/el juez*), the second comprised the VP1 (*oyó*), the third consisted of the next NP (*al juez/a la abogada*), the fourth included the PRO-gerund ([PRO] *sentenciando*), the fifth contained the adjective (*muy segura/o*), and the sixth comprised the PP (*al acusado de homicidio.*) at the end of the sentence. Reading times that were calculated according to the measures described above were entered into different ANOVA (analysis of variance) tables for each region. The ANOVAs included type of plausibility (subject vs. object) and gender agreement (match vs. mismatch) as repeated measure factors.

First-pass reading times. The ANOVAs by subjects and by items were carried out separately in the region of the PRO-verb (*sentenciando*) and showed a significant plausibility effect [$F1(1, 23) = 9.17$, $p < .05$; $F2(1, 39) = 5.77$, $p < .05$]. Sentences in which the plausible antecedent was situated in the distant position (grammatical subject of the main clause) were slower than sentences in which the plausible NP was located in the object position (recent filler NP). Further regions did not show any reliable effect in the first pass-reading time (see Figure 6.1).

Regression-path time. The ANOVAs by subjects and by items carried out in the region of the PRO-verb (*sentenciando*) did not show any significant effect [$Fs < 1$]. The analysis of the adjective region did not show any significant effect [$Fs < 1$].

The PP region showed that the two main effects and the interaction were significant. The effect of plausibility was significant as a main factor but only in the between-participants analysis [$F1(1, 23) = 5.55$, $p < .05$; $F2(1, 39) = 1.66$, $p > .1$]; object plausibility sentences were read faster than subject plausibility

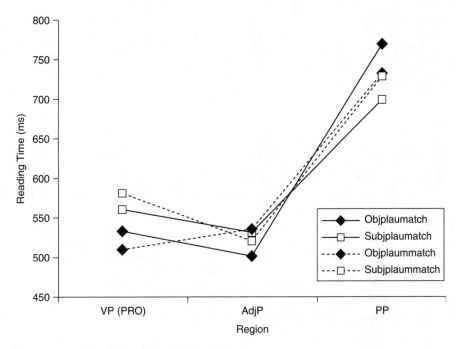

Figure 6.1. First-pass reading time from Experiment 1.

sentences. The effect of mismatch was significant both by participants and by items [$F1(1, 23) = 12.64$, $p < .01$; $F2(1, 39) = 34.41$, $p < .01$]. Mismatched sentences were harder to read than matched sentences. The interaction between plausibility and matching was significant [$F1(1, 23) = 4.64$, $p < .05$; $F2(1, 39) = 9.89$, $p < .05$]. Further analysis showed that object-plausibility-matched sentences were read faster than subject-plausibility-matched sentences [$F1(1, 23) = 10.76$, $p < .05$; $F2(1, 39) = 7.31$, $p < .05$]. At the same time, object-plausibility-matched sentences were read faster than object-plausibility-mismatched sentences [$F1(1, 23) = 14.04$, $p < .05$; $F2(1, 39) = 46.52$, $p < .05$]. On the other hand, the difference between subject-plausibility-matched and subject-plausibility-mismatched sentences showed a significant effect, but only in the analysis by items [$F1(1, 23) = 2.05$, $p > .1$; $F2(1, 39) = 4.19$, $p < .05$]. See Figure 6.2 below.

Total-reading times. The ANOVAs by subjects and by items carried out separately in the region of the PRO-verb (*sentenciando*) showed a significant mismatch effect [$F1(1, 23) = 5.01$, $p < .05$; $F2(1, 39) = 13.43$, $p < .05$]. Readers spent more time reading mismatched sentences than matched sentences. The analysis of the AdjP region (*muy segura/o*) showed a significant mismatch effect [$F1(1, 23) = 9.77$, $p < .05$; $F2(1, 39) = 20.02$, $p < .05$]. Mismatched sentences were harder to process than matched sentences. However, this effect was qualified by the interaction between the two factors [$F1(1, 23) = 5.73$, $p < .05$; $F2(1, 39) = 18.22$, $p < .05$]. Further analysis showed that object-plausibility-mismatched sentences took more time than object-plausibility-matched sentences [$F1(1, 23) = 15.02$, $p < .01$;

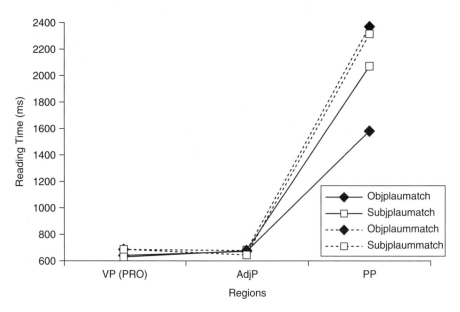

Figure 6.2. Regression-path time from Experiment 1.

$F2(1, 39) = 35.59$, $p < .01$]. However, subject-plausibility-matched and subject-plausibility-mismatched sentences did not differ [$Fs < 1$]. In addition, subject-plausibility-matched-sentences took more time to read than object-plausibility-matched sentences [$F1(1, 23) = 5.60$, $p < .05$; $F2(1, 39) = 13.68$, $p < .05$]. Finally, at the PP region there was a mismatch effect—only reliable in the analysis by items [$F1(1, 23) = 2.29$; $p = .08$; $F2(1, 39) = 5.9$, $p < .05$]. The interaction was also reliable in the analysis by items [$F1(1, 23) = 3.12$, $p = .09$; $F2(1, 39) = 5.6$; $p < .05$]. Object plausibility sentences were read more rapidly in the matched condition as compared to the mismatched condition [$F1(1, 23) = 4.34$, $p < .05$; $F2(1, 39) = 13.8$, $p < .01$], but no differences were obtained for the mismatched sentences [both $Fs < 1$]. See Figure 6.3.

6.2.4 Discussion

The effects obtained in regression-path time and total-reading time showed that readers made a commitment for the antecedent of PRO. A clear gender-mismatch effect was obtained in total time in the verb region. Furthermore, the interactions found in the adjective region in total time and in the PP region in the regression-path time could still show a competition between plausibility and recency. For the match condition, object plausible sentences were read faster than subject plausible sentences. It seems that when the two factors that can guide the selection of the antecedent of PRO (plausibility and recency) run in the same direction (condition 1), they have a dramatic effect on the time readers spend re-reading the final part of the sentence as compared to when plausibility is against recency. Thus, plausibility and recency seem to be at work during sentence processing.

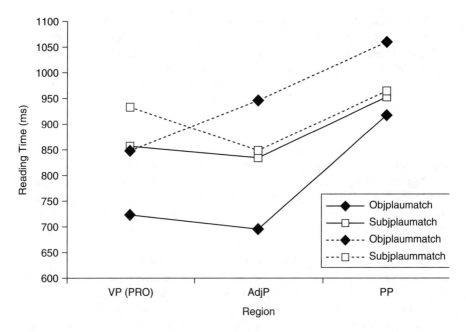

Figure 6.3. Total-reading times from Experiment 1.

In addition, the present data show a plausibility effect in first-pass reading times in the gerund verb region (*sentenciando*). When the most plausible antecedent was in the most recent position, it was easier to recover it than when it was in a distant position. (See Traxler & Pickering, 1996; Traxler, Morris, and Seely, 2002 and Boland, chapter 4, this volume, for early influences of semantic variables such as plausibility or animacy.) Several explanations can be postulated to account for this result.

First, as predicted by the constraint satisfaction models, plausibility may have an early effect because the processor was considering it from earlier stages of processing, together with recency.

Second, two stage garden-path models could account for the early effect of plausibility if implausibility at the gerund (verb) quickly triggered reanalysis. The low plausibility of the nearby NP (e.g., *the lawyer*) as the subject of the subordinate verb (e.g., *sentencing*) as compared with the high plausibility of the distant NP (e.g., *the judge*) could have triggered the reanalysis. As mentioned above, these constructions with gerund verbs are ambiguous and they allow the possibility of taking either the subject or the object of the main sentence as the subject. According to this interpretation of the effect, readers take the most recent NP to fill the PRO, but plausibility is quickly consulted to confirm or disconfirm this syntax-guided decision. The plausibility effect obtained for gender-match sentences in regression-path times in the last region and in the total times in the adjective region can to some extent support this explanation of the first-pass effect. Of course, it could also be the case that plausibility is an effect that had started very early and is long lasting instead of a reanalysis process.

Third, it could have been simply caused by lexical facilitation. Some experiments have shown that when two semantically related words are presented in the same sentence-frame, the processing of the second word is faster (Fischler & Bloom, 1979, 1980; Schuberth & Eimas, 1977; Stanovich & West, 1979, 1981, 1983b; West & Stanovich, 1982; O'Seaghdha, 1989). For example, when a participant reads sentences such as *The author of the book/floor*, lexical decision responses to the word *book* are faster than to a nonrelated word such as *floor* (O'Seaghdha, 1989). Duffy, Henderson, and Morris (1989) obtained similar data as readers were faster at processing *mustache* when preceded by a context such as *The barber trimmed the ...*, than when preceded by a context such as *The woman trimmed the ....*

The plausibility effect found in our first experiment could be a lexical facilitation (priming effect) due to the semantic relations between the two adjacent words. In an item like *The lawyer saw the judge* [PRO] *sentencing ...*, it is possible that the faster reading time found in the verb region when it was preceded by the NP *the judge* instead of when it was preceded by *the lawyer* is due to lexical semantic activation between *judge* and *to sentence*. Early plausibility data obtained in first-pass reading time in Experiment 1 showed that the verb *sentenciando (sentencing)* is read more quickly when preceded by the noun phrase *el juez (the judge)*.

In order to disentangle this plausibility versus lexical facilitation confound, we conducted a second experiment in which we separated the recent filler from its close position to the embedded verb and made the choice of antecedent of PRO syntactically unambiguous. We reversed the canonical order in the main sentences as to an object–verb–subject (O–V–S) structure and used an infinitive complement structure that demanded the object as the antecedent of PRO. Thus, the object is located as distant filler and the subject as recent filler. This allows us to test whether the verb *to sentence* is processed still faster when *the judge* (see condition 1 and 3 in Table 6.2) is located in a more distant position, but grammatical rules dictate that it is the object of the main sentence, and therefore, the filler of PRO. We used an infinitive verb instead of a gerund verb because this commits readers to take the object NP of the main sentence (the distant one in our material) as the grammatical subject of the infinitive verb. It is important to note that these sentences are unambiguous because the object of the main sentence is the antecedent of PRO.

6.2.5 Experiment 2

In this experiment, our focus was to separate the initial plausibility effect from the lexical facilitation effect. We used the same materials as in Experiment 1 except for two changes: (1) The form of the verb was now infinitive, and (2) The main sentences now had an object–verb–subject structure. It is important to note that mismatched sentences (3) and (4) are ungrammatical. The use of an infinitive makes the sentences unambiguous with respect to the antecedent of PRO. In this case, the grammar dictates that when we have an infinitive verb in the subordinate clause, only the direct object of the main sentence can be the subject of PRO. This makes our material unambiguous. An example of the material is shown in Table 6.2.

Similar to Experiment 1, garden-path and constraint satisfaction models will make very close predictions regarding the reading times in our materials. The garden-path model assumes that only syntactic information is used initially. Readers should follow the grammar, according to which the object of the main sentence is the subject (controller) of the infinitive verb *al juez* in conditions 1 and 3, and *la abogada* in conditions 2 and 4 (see Table 6.2). However, if plausibility very quickly affects the initial evaluation of the gap (Traxler & Pickering, 1996), it should produce an increased reading time in the infinitive verb region for sentences with implausible NPs (such as *la abogada*) acting as agent of the infinitive (conditions 2 and 4). We should expect differences in the infinitive verb region due to a rapid evaluation of the plausibility of the NP as agent of the verb. In addition, a mismatch effect is expected in the adjective region.

Constraint satisfaction models would predict that the grammar and plausibility are computed as constraints that initially guide the parsing. Thus, at the infinitive verb when readers encounter the empty category, sentences in which plausibility and grammar converge in the same direction (conditions 1 and 3, see material in Table 6.2) should be easier than sentences in which grammar and plausibility compete as constraints (condition 2 and 4 see material in Table 6.2). On the other hand, an effect of mismatch is expected in the adjective region or later.

6.2.6 Method

6.2.6.1 Participants

A total of 24 undergraduate students of the University of La Laguna (Canary Islands, Spain) participated in the experiment for course credit.

Table 6.2. **Example of Material Used in Experiment 2**

CONDITION 1
Plausible-Match (Plau-Match)
Al juez/lo oyó/la abogada/[PRO] sentenciar/muy seguro/al acusado de homicidio.
To the judge (acc. mas.) *heard the lawyer* (nom. mas.) [PRO] *to sentence* (infinitive) *very confident* (mas.) *to the defendant.*

CONDITION 2
Implausible-Match. (Implau-Match)
A la abogada/la oyó/el juez/[PRO] sentenciar/muy segura/al acusado de homicidio.
To the lawyer (acc. fem.) *heard the judge* (nom. mas.) [PRO] *to sentence* (infinitive) *very confident* (fem.) *to the defendant.*

CONDITION 3
Plausible-Mismatch. (Plau-Mmatch)
Al juez/lo oyó/la abogada/[PRO] sentenciar/muy segura/al acusado de homicidio.
To the judge (acc. mas.) *heard the lawyer* (nom. fem.) [PRO] *to sentence* (infinitive) *very confident* (fem.) *to the defendant.*

CONDITION 4
Implausible-Mismatch. (Implau-Mmatch)
A la abogada/la oyó/el juez/[PRO] sentenciar/muy seguro/al acusado de homicidio.
To the lawyer (acc. fem.) *heard the judge* (nom. mas.) [PRO] *to sentence* (infinitive) *very confident* (mas.) *to the defendant.*

6.2.6.2 Materials and Design

A total of 40 groups of sentences with the structure NP1 (*accusative*)-VP1-NP2 (*nominative*)-[PRO-infinitive]-AdjP-PP, like those displayed in Table 6.2, were constructed. In addition, another 68 sentences with different types of structures were written to serve as fillers, as well as 10 sentences for practice trials.

6.2.6.3 Apparatus and Procedure

These were the same as used in Experiment 1.

6.2.6.4 Data Analysis

We will report the same measures reported in Experiment 1.

6.2.7 Results

For the purpose of the analyses, the texts were segmented with slashes as shown in Table 6.2: the first region contained the first NP (*Al juez/a la abogada*), the second comprised the VP1 (*lo/la oyó*), the third consisted the next NP (*la abogada/al juez*), the fourth included the PRO-infinitive ([PRO] *sentenciar*), the fifth was the adjective (*muy seguro/a*), and the sixth contained the head of the PP (*al acusado de homicidio*). Reading times calculated according to the measures described above were entered into ANOVAs. The ANOVAs included type of plausibility (plausible vs. implausible) and gender agreement (match vs. mismatch) as repeated measure factors. In comparison to Experiment 1, sentences were unambiguous. Thus sentences in which the obligatory object antecedent was not plausible as PRO will be referred to simply as implausible sentences.

First-pass reading times. The ANOVAs by subjects and by items that were carried out separately did not show any effect of plausibility [$Fs < 1$] in the PRO-verb region (*sentenciar*). In order to capture any trend of plausibility effect, we analyzed the probability of receiving a first-pass fixation in this region as an early measure that can be potentially sensitive to predictability due to plausibility (Starr & Rayner, 2001). The effect on this measure was significant [$F1(1, 23) = 8.07, p < .05; F2(1, 39) = 8.55, p < .05$]. Plausible sentences showed a lower probability of receiving a first-pass fixation than implausible sentences (89.5 vs. 94.0). Thus, it appears that plausible sentences were skipped more often than implausible sentences. The analysis in the next region (AdjRegion) *muy seguro/a* showed a main effect of agreement in first-pass time, although the effect was significant only in the analysis by subjects [$F1(1, 23) = 4.09, p < .05; F2(1, 39) = 2.56, p = .11$]. Mismatched sentences were harder to process than matched sentences (see Figure 6.4).

Regression-path time. The ANOVAs by subjects and by items carried out separately in the region of the PRO-verb (*sentenciar*) did not show any significant effect [$Fs < 1$]. The analysis of the AdjP region (*muy segura/o*) showed a main effect of agreement [$F1(1, 23) = 5.71, p < .05; F2(1, 39) = 5.36, p < .05$]. Mismatched sentences were harder to process than matched sentences. Finally, the PP region showed a main effect of agreement [$F1(1, 23) = 10.49, p < .01; F2(1, 39) = 15.01$,

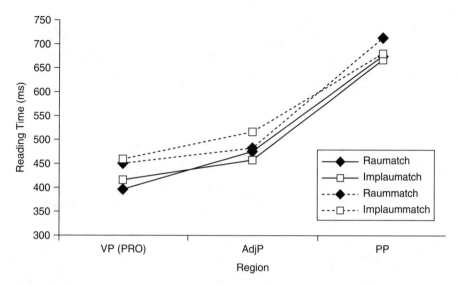

Figure 6.4. First-pass reading times from Experiment 2.

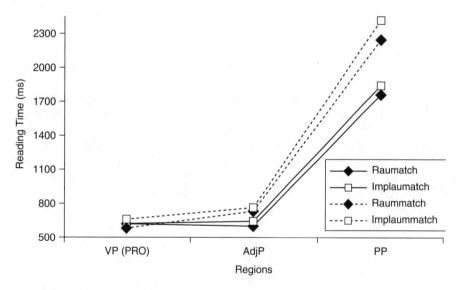

Figure 6.5. Regression-path times from Experiment 2.

$p < .01$]. Mismatched sentences were harder to process than matched sentences (see Figure 6.5).

Total-reading times. The ANOVAs by subjects and by items carried out separately in the region of the PRO-verb (*sentenciar*) showed an effect of plausibility that was significant by participants but only marginally significant by items [$F1(1, 23 = 7.45, p < .05; F2(1, 39) = 3.70, p = .06$]. Sentences in which the plausible antecedent was the grammatical object of the main clause were read faster. The

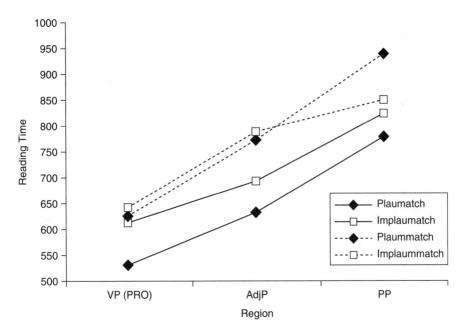

Figure 6.6 Total-reading times from Experiment 2.

agreement factor reached significance in this region too [$F1(1, 23 = 4.86, p < .05$; $F2(1, 39) = 7.74, p < .05$]. Mismatched sentences had longer reading times in the infinitive verb than matched sentences. The interaction between the two factors was not significant. The analysis of the AdjP region (*muy segura/o*) showed a main effect of agreement [$F1(1, 23) = 11.34, p < .05$; $F2(1, 39) = 11.66, p < .05$]. Mismatched sentences were harder to process than matched sentences. The interactions of both factors did not reach significance. Finally, the PP region showed a significant effect of agreement [$F1(1, 23) = 4.41, p < .05$; $F2(1, 39) = 10.81, p < .05$]. Mismatched sentences were slower than matched sentences. However, this effect was qualified by an interaction between both factors [$F1(1, 23) = 3.93, p = .06$; $F2(1, 39) = 5.97, p < .05$]. Further analysis showed that plausible matched sentences were easier to process than plausible mismatched sentences [$F1(1, 23) = 6.66, p < .05$; $F2(1, 39) = 14.05, p < .01$]. There were no differences between matched and mismatched implausible sentences [$Fs < 1$] (see Figure 6.6).

6.2.7 Discussion

The mismatch effect consistently appears in first-pass reading time (although in this measure, only in the by- participants analysis), regression-path time, and total-reading time, which shows that readers do not delay the recovery of the PRO antecedent. Second, our data show that the first-pass reading time did not show plausibility differences in the verb region (*sentenciar/to sentence*) when the sentences have an object–verb–subject structure. We did not find any facilitation effect for the verb *sentenciar/to sentence* when it was immediately preceded by the noun phrase *el juez/the judge* as compared to when the same verb was immediately preceded by the noun phrase *la abogada/the lawyer*. The lack of an effect in first-pass reading time seems to suggest that plausibility does not have an initial effect in parsing an empty category such as PRO when the syntactic structure does not favor the role of plausibility. However, this absence of a first-pass effect of plausibility in the verb does not allow us to rule out the possibility of a lexical facilitation in Experiment 1.

The lack of plausibility effects in the second experiment could be due to the simultaneous action of two counteracting factors: lexical facilitation in conditions 2 and 4, and plausibility facilitation (lack of implausibility disruption) in conditions 1 and 3. Thus, there still remains the possibility that the effect found in Experiment 1 in the PRO-verb region could have been a lexical facilitation effect (O'Seghadha, 1989). Nonetheless, a pure lexical facilitation effect should produce opposite effects in Experiments 1 and 2. On the other hand, a more detailed analysis has shown that plausible sentences are skipped more often than implausible sentences, which can be seen as a predictability effect. When readers parafoveally detect a verb that fits with the semantic characteristics of the direct object of the main sentence, they tend to skip it. But when the semantic features of the infinitive verb and the direct object do not fit, readers tend to fixate on the infinitive verb to confirm the decision taken in terms of grammar.

In comparison, plausibility produced late effects. Total reading times showed a late plausibility effect. Implausible sentences (see Table 6.2, Conditions 2 and 4) were harder to process than plausible sentences (see Table 6.2, Conditions 1 and 3). Thus, there is an ongoing competition between plausibility and grammar. Grammar selects a noun phrase as antecedent of an infinitive clause (the object of the main sentence), and when this decision does not completely agree with semantic information (plausibility), readers spend more time re-reading these sentences. Since infinitive sentences are unambiguous, readers seem to check the activated syntactic structure with plausibility information which may not be a proper reanalysis due to the lack of ambiguity.

In summary, Experiment 2 suggests that readers activate the object–verb–subject structure and take the grammatical object NP as subject of the infinitive verb—a strategy that is mildly modulated by plausibility at this early stage. Grammar seems to strongly guide the reactivation of antecedent of PRO embedded in an infinitive subordinate clause. In that sense, it is important to bear in mind that there is no ambiguity in infinitive clause sentences as there is in gerunds about what is the antecedent of PRO, and no clear control information as in *promise*-verb type is obtained from the main verb (we have used perception verbs in this experiment).

6.2.8 General Discussion

The aim of the study was to examine how readers recover the antecedent of an EC-PRO in Spanish. Eye-movement technology has proved effective in uncovering the on-line processing of EC-PRO. Readers do not seem to delay the selection of an antecedent of PRO. Data consistently obtained throughout the two experiments showed an agreement effect in the adjective postverbal region, which allows us to conclude that when readers arrive at the EC-PRO, they begin a search for the antecedent of PRO. This search seems to be carried out quickly as agreement effects show (see also Demestre et al., 1999; Betancort et al., 2004).

The second main goal was to investigate the role of plausibility. Data obtained from Experiment 1 showed that readers analyze an ambiguous subordinate gerund clause as referring to the recent NP (object of the main clause) rather than to the distant NP (subject of the main clause), but they also consider how plausible the antecedent will be. This result extends previous findings about the preference for recent as opposed to distant NPs when the parser encounters an embedded inflected verb's empty subject position (Frazier et al., 1983; Clifton & Frazier, 1986). When the main clause includes two potential antecedents for EC-PRO, readers prefer the antecedent that occupies the position of the direct object of the main sentence and that fits better (the more plausible) as the agent of the embedded subordinate verb (gerund or infinitive). This preference was first detected in Experiment 1 in early (first-pass time) and late (regression-path time and total-reading time) measures. This outcome could be interpreted as an initial preference, a reanalysis effect, or a lexical facilitation effect (e.g., *judge-to sentence* vs. *lawyer-to sentence*).

In Experiment 2, we changed the canonical order of the constituents in order to tease out any effect of lexical facilitation. The effect of plausibility was not observed in first-pass time in the second experiment, although it was apparent in other early measures (such as the probability of a first fixation) as well as in a late measure (e.g., total time). In any case, the plausibility effect was much more reduced in Experiment 2. The present data do not allow us to deny that some lexical facilitation effects could be contributing to the plausibility obtained in Experiment 1 since both factors were in the same direction, but what seems to be clear from Experiment 2 is that there is only an early influence of plausibility.

How do the models discussed so far account for these plausibility effects? The garden-path model assumes that readers check the initial syntactic analysis against semantic information. However, in Experiment 2, they cannot be really reanalyzing the syntactic structure initially computed because it is the only possible syntactic structure (recall that infinitive constructions are not ambiguous). The garden-path model could argue that when the parser tackles a syntactic decision with the semantic information, this decision will not always trigger a reanalysis. Thus, the garden-path model could assume that the early (Traxler & Pickering, 1996) and late plausibility effects were reanalysis effects in Experiment 1 and rechecking effects in Experiment 2.

What about constraint satisfaction models? They can easily account for the data of Experiment 1, according to which plausibility effects occur early as reflected in first-pass reading times. In Experiment 2, the effect of plausibility did not appear in first-pass time but did in the probability of a first-pass fixation, so the early influence is manifested in such a measure (infinitive verbs with a plausible subject were skipped more often). Thus, plausibility, as a constraint seems to be acting from the very beginning of parsing.

The change in the syntactic structure in Experiment 2 modulates the effect of plausibility which emerges in Experiment 1 in the PRO region. While the gerund sentences are ambiguous regarding the subject of the infinitive, the subordinate infinitive sentences are unambiguous; so, in this case, only the grammar seems to initially guide the selection of the antecedent of PRO. Both experiments showed an early plausibility effect (first-pass time in Experiment 1 and probability of a first-pass fixation in Experiment 2) that should not be ignored. It seems that plausibility is an important feature that qualifies parsing decisions at very early stages with different strengths depending on, among other things, the strength of the grammatical constraints.

In summary, the present data provides convincing evidence that PRO is bound very quickly, that plausibility plays an early role in parsing, that there are biases toward taking the most recent NP as the antecedent of PRO when the opportunity exists, and that the parser obeys the grammar when the grammar dictates this.

6.3 ACKNOWLEDGMENTS

Preparation of this chapter was supported by grant BSO2001-3492-C04-03 (Spanish Ministry of Science and Technology). We would like to thank Carlos Acuña and Chuck Clifton for comments on an earlier draft of this chapter.

References

Abney, S. (1987). *The English noun phrase in its sentential aspects.* Unpublished Ph.D. dissertation, MIT, Cambridge, MA.

Akmajian, A. (1977). The complement structure of perception verbs in an autonomous syntax framework. In P. Cullicover, T. Wasow, and A. Akmajian (Eds.), *Formal Syntax.* (pp. 427–460) New York: Academic Press.

Alonso-Ovalle, L., Fernández-Solera, S., Frazier, L., & Clifton, C., Jr. (2002). Null vs. overt pronouns and the topic-focus articulation in Spanish. *Journal of Italian Linguistics,* 14:2, 151–169.

Betancort, M., Carreiras, M., & Acuña, C. (2004). Processing controlled PROs in Spanish.

Boland, J. E., Tanenhaus, M. K., & Garnsey, S. M.(1990). Evidence for the immediate use of verb control information in sentence processing. *Journal of Memory and Language,* 29, 413–432.

Boland, J., Tanenhaus, M. K., & Garnsey S. M. (1990). Lexical structure and parsing: Evidence for the immediate use of verb control information in sentence processing. *Journal of Memory and Language, 29,* 413–432.

Boland, J., Tanenhaus, M. K., Garnsey S. M., & Carlson, G. (1995). Verb argument structure in parsing and interpretation: Evidence from Wh-questions. *Journal of Memory and Language, 34,* 774–806.

Bresnan, J. (1982). *The theory of complementation in English syntax.* Unpublished Ph.D. dissertation, MIT, Cambridge, MA.

Brysbaert, M., & Mitchell, D. C. (1996). Modifier attachment in sentence processing: Evidence from Dutch. *Quarterly Journal of Experimental Psychology, 49A,* 664–695.

Cattell, R. (1984). *Composite predicates in English.* New York: Academic Press.

Chierchia, G. (1988). Structured meanings, thematic roles, and control. In G. Chierchia, B. Partee, & R. Turner (Eds.), *Properties, types, and meaning.* (Vol 2, pp. 131–136). Dordrecht, Netherlands: Kluwer.

Chomsky, C. (1969). *The acquisition of syntax in children from 5 to 10.* Cambridge, MA: MIT Press.

Chomsky, N. (1981). *Lectures on Government and Binding.* Dordrecht, Netherlands: Foris.

Chomsky, N. (1986). *Knowledge of language: its nature, origin, and use.* New York: Praeger.

Chomsky, N. (1995). *The minimalist program.* Cambridge, MA: MIT Press.

Clifton, C., Jr., & Frazier, L. (1986). The use of syntactic information in filling gaps. *Journal of Psycholinguistic research, 15,* 209–224.

Declerck, R. (1984). The structure of infinitival perception verb complements in a transformational grammar. In L. Tasmowski & D. Willems (Eds.), *Problems in syntax.* Ghent, Belgium: Plenum. Also in *Communication and Cognition, 15:* 383–406.

De Vincenci, M. (1991). Filler-gap dependencies in a null subject language: Referential and nonreferential Whs. *Journal of Psycholinguistics Research, 20,* 197–213.

De Vincenci, M. (1996). Syntactic analysis in sentence comprehension: Effects of dependency types and grammatical constraints. *Journal of Psycholinguistic Research 25,* 117–133.

Demestre, J., Meltzer, S., García Albea, J. E., & Vigil, A. (1999). Identifying the null subject: Evidence from event-related brain potential. *Journal of Psycholinguistic Research, 28,* 293–312.

Duffy, S. A., Morris, R. K., & Rayner, K. (1988). Lexical ambiguity and fixation times in reading. *Journal of Memory and Language, 27,* 429–446.

Duffy, S., Henderson, J. M., & Morris, R. K. (1989). Semantic Facilitation of Lexical Access During Sentence Processing. *Journal of Experimental Psychology: Learning, Memory & Cognition. 15,* 791.

Featherston, S. (2001). *Empty categories in sentence processing.* Amsterdam: John Benjamin.

Felser, C. (1998). Perception and control: A minimalist analysis of English direct perception complements. *Journal of Linguistics, 34,* 351–385.

Fiengo, R. (1974). Semantic conditions on surface structure. Ph.D. dissertation, MIT, Cambridge, MA.

Fillmore, C. (1963). The position of embedding transformations in a grammar. *Word, 19,* 208–231.

Fischler, I., & Bloom, P. A. (1979). Automatic and attentional processes in the effects of sentence contexts on word recognition. *Journal of Verbal Learning and Verbal Behavior, 10,* 1–20.

Fischler, I., & Bloom, P. A. (1980). Rapid processing of the meaning of sentences. *Memory and Cognition, 8,* 216–225.

Fodor, J. D. (1989). Empty categories in sentence processing. In G. Altman (Ed.), *Special Issue on Language and Cognitive Processes. Parsing and Interpretation, 4*(3,4), SI 155–209.

Frazier, L., Clifton, C. Jr., & Randall, J. (1983). Filling gaps: Decision principles and structure in sentence comprehension. *Cognition, 13,* 187–222.

Frazier, L., & Flores D'Arçais, G. (1989). Filler-driven parsing: A study of gap filling in Dutch. *Journal of Memory and Language, 28,* 331–344.

Garnsey, S. M., Tanenhaus, M. K., & Chapman, R. M. (1989). Evoked potential and the study of comprehension. *Journal of Psycholinguistic Research, 18,* 51–60.

Haegeman, L. (1994). *Introduction to government and binding theory* (2nd ed.). Oxford: Blackwell.

Hernanz, M. Lluïsa. (1999). El infinitivo. In I. Bosque & V. Demonte (Eds.). *Gramática Descriptiva de la Lengua Española* (Vol. 2). Madrid: Espasa.

Jackendoff, R. (1972). Semantic interpretation in generative grammar. Cambridge, MA: MIT Press.

Jackendoff, R. (1974). A deep structure projection rule. *Linguistic Inquiry, 5,* 481–506.

Johnson, K. (1988). Clausal gerunds, the ECP, and government. *Linguistic Inquiry, 19,* 583–610.

Konieczny, L., Hemforth, B., Scheepers, C., & Strube, G. (1997). The role of lexical heads in parsing: evidence from German. *Language and Cognitive Processes, 12,* 307–348.

Landau, I. (1999). *Element of Control.* Unpublished doctoral dissertation, MIT, Cambridge, MA.

Milsark, G. (1988). Singl-ing. *Linguistic Inquiry, 19,* 611–634.

Nicol, J., & Osterhout, L. (1998). Reactivating antecedent of empty categories during parsing. Unpublished Manuscript.

Nicol, J., & Swinney, D. (1989). The role of structure in coreference assignment during sentence comprehension. *Journal of Psycholinguistic Research, 18,* 5–19.

O'Seaghdha, P. G. (1989). The Dependence of lexical relatedness effects on syntactic connectedness. *Journal of Experimental Psychology: Learning, Memory, and Cognition, 15,* 73–87.

Osterhaut, L., & Nicol, J. (1998). The time course of antecedent activation following empty subject. Unpublished manuscript.

Polland, C., & Sag, I. A. (1994). *Head-driven phrase structure grammar.* Chicago: University of Chicago Press.

Reuland, E. (1983). Governing-ing. *Linguistic Inquiry, 14,* 101–136.

Rosenbaum, P. (1967). *The grammar of English predicate complement constructions.* Cambridge, MA: MIT Press.

San Martin, I. (2002). *On subordination and the distribution of PRO.* Unpublished doctoral dissertation, University of Maryland, College Park.

Sag, I., & Pollard, C.(1991). An integrated theory of complement control. *Language, 67,* 63–113.

Schuberth, R. E., & Eimas, P. D. (1977). Effects of context on the classification of words and nonwords. *Journal of Experimental Psychology: Human Perception and Performance, 3,* 27–36.

Stanovich, K. E., & West, R. F. (1979). Mechanisms of sentence context effects in reading: Automatic activation and conscious attention. *Memory and Cognition, 7,* 77–85.

Stanovich, K. E., & West, R. F. (1981). The effect of sentence context on ongoing word recognition: Test of a two-process theory. *Journal of Experimental Psychology: Human Perception and Performance, 7,* 658–672.

Stanovich, K. E., & West, R. F. (1983b). On priming by a sentence context. *Journal of Experimental Psychology: General, 112,* 1–36.

Starr, M. S., & Rayner, K. (2001) Eye movements during reading: Some current controversies. *Trends in Cognitive Science, 5,* 156–163.

Stowe, L. (1986). Parsing Wh-constructions: Evidence for on-line gap location. *Language and Cognitive Processes, 1,* 227–245.

Stowe, L., Tanenhaus, M., & Carlson, G. (1991). Filling gap on-line: Use of lexical and semantic informtion in sentence processing. *Language and Speech, 34,* 319–340.

Tanenhaus, M. K., Stowe, L., & Carlson, G. (1985). The interaction of lexical expectation and pragmatic in parsing filler-gap constructions. *Proceeding of the Seventh Annual Cognitive Science Society* Meeting, Irvine, California. pp. 361–365.

Tanenhaus, M.K., Carlson, G., & Trueswell, J. C. (1989). The role of thematic structure in interpretation and parsing. *Language and Cognitive Processes, 4,* 211–234.

Traxler, M. J., & Pickering, M. J. (1996). Plausibility and the processing of unbounded dependencies: An eye-tracking study. *Journal of Memory and Language, 35,* 454–475.

Traxler, M. J., Pickering, M. J., & Clifton, C., Jr. (1998). Adjunct attachment is not a form of lexical ambiguity resolution. *Journal of Memory and Language, 39,* 558–592.

Traxler, M. J., Morris, R. K., & Seely, R. E. (2002). Processing subject and object relative clauses: Evidence from eye movements. *Journal of Memory and Language, 47,* 69–90.

West, R. F., & Stanovich, K. E. (1982). Source of inhibition in experiments on the effect of sentence context on word recognition. *Journal of Experimental Psychology: Learning, Memory and Cognition, 8,* 385–399.

<3F55B7F7.2050808@ull.es>
<001701c37200$57a01020$3159d182@psy.gla.ac.uk> <3F55C424.8080005@ull.es>
<002401c3720a$b5264750$3159d182@psy.gla.ac.uk> <3F55CC59.2090705@ull.es>
<002f01c3720c$5168c2e0$3159d182@psy.gla.ac.uk> <3F55D33C.4080106@ull.es>
<005701c37210$a43adc70$3159d182@psy.gla.ac.uk> <3F55D4A5.2010005@ull.es>
<00a701c37216$848547c0$3159d182@psy.gla.ac.uk> <3F564581.7020409@ull.es>

Notes

1. In this chapter, we adopt the Principle and Parameters Theory (PPT) of grammar proposed by Chomsky (1981, 1986, 1995). However, there are other grammars such as Head-Driven Phrase Structure Grammar (HPSG) (Pollard & Sag, 1987, 1994) that do not assume the existence of PRO and, instead, present another type of account to deal with the subject of uninflected verbs.
2. The PPT proposes two types of PROs: arbitrary PRO and controlled PRO. The former does not require an antecedent in the main sentence in order to be interpretated, but the latter must have an antecedent (the subject or the object) in the main sentence to obtain its interpretation. We are focusing only on the latter type of PRO.
3. In the speeded comprehension task, readers are faced with a word-by-word sentence presentation, and then they need to make a sentence-final "got it" or "missed it" decision. In the experiment of Frazier et al. (1983), subjects read sentences in a 300 ms word-by-word presentation.
4. In the CMLP task, participants listen to sentences, and at different points of the text they make a lexical decision on visually presented targets. Targets are usually semantic associates of the antecedent and a matched unrelated control.
5. Although obligatory controlled PROs behave more like an anaphora such as *himself* and not like a pronoun such as *him*, Nicol and Osterhout (1988) seem to conclude that the recovery of the antecedent of PRO is delayed and there is not a quick commitment to one antecedent in the higher clause.
6. For convenience we present only one sentence type. For a comprehensive presentation of the whole design, see Nicol and Swinney (1989).
7. Accepting that the perception verbs behave as control verbs and are subcategorized for PRO in subordinate gerund sentences, the syntactic tree proposed for this structure is as following: $_S[_{NP}[Juan]_{VP}[[_v vio]_{PP}[a María]_{COMP}[comprando en el mercado.]]$ (John saw Mary shopping in the mall).
8. It is important to notice that the generalization of the MRFS (Frazier et al., 1983) to the AFS (Frazier & Flores D'Arçais, 1989) and lastly to the Minimal Chain Principle (De Vinzenci, 1991, 1996) was motivation for research on structures in which there was an element that pointed out the presence of a gap later on the syntactic string. In our case, as pointed out in the text, the EC-PRO does not have a previous element which signals the presence of a gap. This is because we refer to MRFS as the original strategy proposed to resolve this type of construction (see Frazier et al., 1983).

Chapter 7
Antecedent Typicality Effects in the Processing of Noun Phrase Anaphors

ROGER P. G. VAN GOMPEL, SIMON P. LIVERSEDGE, AND JAMIE PEARSON

7.1 INTRODUCTION

When we read, we usually process sentences in the context of other sentences. For example, when we read a book, we do not simply process each sentence in isolation. Instead, we integrate each new sentence into the discourse representation that we have constructed on the basis of the text that we have read so far. A crucial part of forming a coherent representation of a text is the comprehension of coreference relations that exist between elements of that text. These coreference relations must be fully processed for the reader to attain complete discourse coherence. For example, to understand what the mini text in (1a) is about, the reader has to work out that the anaphor *the bird* refers to the same thing as the antecedent *a robin*. Without establishing a coreference relation between these two noun phrases, the reader cannot construct a coherent representation of (1a).

(1) a. *A robin would sometimes wander into the house. The bird was attracted by the larder.*

Psycholinguistic research has shown that many linguistic factors influence the ease with which readers establish a coreference relation between an anaphor and its antecedent (see Garnham, 2001, for an overview). One factor that influences anaphoric processing is the typicality of the antecedent as an instance of the anaphor. For example, in (1a), the antecedent *a robin* is a very typical type of bird, but in (1b), *a goose* is a much less typical type of bird (at least according to typicality norms, e.g., Battig & Montague, 1969; Rosch, 1975).

(1) b. *A goose would sometimes wander into the house. The bird was attracted by the larder.*

In this chapter, we will discuss theories of how readers process noun phrase anaphors such as *the bird* in (1a) and report an eye-movement experiment that tested these theories.

7.2 ANTECEDENT TYPICALITY EFFECTS IN ANAPHORIC PROCESSING

Reading studies have shown that the typicality of an antecedent as an instance of an anaphor affects the ease with which a coreference relation is established. In an early study, Garrod and Sanford (1977) investigated how sentences such as (1) are processed, and observed that self-paced reading times for the sentence containing the anaphor were longer when its antecedent was atypical (*goose*) than when it was typical (*robin*). Garrod and Sanford proposed what we will term the *semantic overlap theory*. They argued that the typicality effect occurs because it is easier to identify an antecedent when it has a high semantic overlap with the anaphor than when the semantic feature overlap between anaphor and antecedent is small.

Garrod and Sanford also tested an alternative explanation of the typicality effect. In theory, it is possible that processing *the bird* in (1a) is easier than in (1b) because lexical-semantic priming between *robin* and *bird* is larger than between *goose* and *bird*. Single-word lexical-priming studies have shown that the larger the semantic feature overlap between a prime and a target word, the easier it is to process the target word (e.g., Meyer & Schvaneveldt, 1971). In order to test this alternative explanation, Garrod and Sanford investigated processing of sentences such as in (2).

(2) *A bus/tank came roaring around the corner. It nearly hit a horse-drawn vehicle.*

Here, *vehicle* cannot be coreferent with either *bus* or *tank*. Therefore, no effect of antecedent typicality should occur for the sentence containing *vehicle*. In contrast, the lexical priming account predicts that *vehicle* should be primed by the typical vehicle *bus*, but not (or much less) by the atypical vehicle *tank*. However, Garrod and Sanford (1977) did not observe any effect of typicality for (2), even though they did observe the typicality effect for very similar sentences such as (3).

(3) *A bus/tank came roaring around the corner. A pedestrian was nearly killed by the vehicle.*

Hence, they concluded that the typicality effect is not due to lexical priming, but reflects processes that occur during anaphor resolution.

The semantic overlap account that was proposed by Garrod and Sanford (1977) has received further support from later eye-movement studies (Duffy & Rayner, 1990; Rayner, Kambe, & Duffy, 2000). The advantage of using eye-movement methodology compared with self-paced reading is that it provides a detailed record of the time course of processing. An eye-movement record consists of individual fixations on words, resulting in a high level of granularity. This permits the researcher to conduct a detailed examination of different groupings of fixations over time and space that reflect different psychological processes. Furthermore, eye-movement methodology is more naturalistic than self-paced reading because participants do not need to press a button to proceed through the text or sentence, and previously read text does not disappear.

Duffy and Rayner (1990) manipulated antecedent typicality in short texts such as (4). (The antecedent and anaphor were not underlined in the actual experiment.)

(4) *It was a sunny afternoon. Judy was walking home from school, daydream-ing about herself. She crossed the busy street at the light. She stopped to watch the traffic while she gathered her thoughts. She had just decided she was going to be a <u>doctor/writer</u> when she grew up. <u>The profession</u> seemed to be an exciting one. She knew she would have to work hard at school.*

They also manipulated the distance between the anaphor and antecedent. In (4), the antecedent is close to the anaphor, whereas in two further conditions, the ante-cedent was much earlier, in the second sentence of the text.

Duffy and Rayner (1990) observed an interaction between antecedent typicality and distance in first-pass reading times for the anaphor (*the profession*). Anaphors with typical antecedents were read faster than anaphors with atypical antecedents when the antecedent was distant, although no effect of typicality occurred when the antecedent was close. In the region following the anaphor (*seemed to be an*), Duffy and Rayner observed a main effect of typicality in first-pass times, but no distance effect and no interaction. This preference for anaphors with typical antecedents in Duffy and Rayner's eye-movement study is consistent with the predictions of semantic overlap theories (e.g., Garrod & Sanford, 1977).

In another eye-movement study, Rayner et al. (2000) also observed that anaphors with typical antecedents were easier to read than anaphors with atypical antecedents. Participants in their study read sentences such as (5).

(5) *Joey wanted to learn to play the clarinet/harmonica. Since his friend owned the instrument already, he was able to find out where to get one.*

First-pass reading times for the anaphor (*the instrument*) were longer when the antecedent was atypical (*the harmonica*) than when it was typical (*the clarinet*). However, in contrast to Duffy and Rayner's (1990) experiment, no effect of typicality was observed in the region following the anaphor (*already*). Possibly, this analysis region was too short to detect an effect, and perhaps the effect was masked because the region was at a sentence boundary (See Rayner et al., 2000, for details).

In summary, the studies discussed so far provide clear evidence for the semantic overlap account, which predicts that identifying an antecedent should be easier the more semantic features the anaphor and antecedent have in common. The results also support more recent proposals by O'Brien and colleagues, who claim that anaphoric processing is a kind of resonance process (e.g., Myers & O'Brien, 1998; O'Brien, Albrecht, Hakala, & Rizzella, 1995; O'Brien & Albrecht, 1992; O'Brien, Raney, Albrecht, & Rayner, 1997). When an anaphor is encountered, it resonates with possible antecedents. The larger the featural overlap between anaphor and antecedent, the more the anaphor resonates and the easier it is to establish a coreference relation.

7.3 THE REPEATED NOUN PHRASE PENALTY

Semantic overlap between an anaphor and its antecedent is not the only factor that affects the processing of anaphors. Many studies have found that a repeated reference with a noun phrase anaphor can be harder to process than a reference with a pronoun, even though the semantic overlap between the anaphor and antecedent is larger in the former case than in the latter (Almor, 1999; Garrod, Freudenthal, & Boyle, 1994; Gordon, Grosz, & Gilliom, 1993; Gordon & Chan, 1995; Gordon & Scearce, 1995; Kennison & Gordon, 1997). For example, Gordon and Chan (1995) showed that self-paced reading times for the second sentence in (6) were longer when the anaphor was a repeated name than when it was a pronoun, even though the semantic overlap between *Susan* and *Susan* is clearly larger than between *Susan* and *she*.

(6)   *Susan decided to give Fred a hamster. She/Susan was questioned at length by Fred about what to feed it.*

Gordon and his colleagues have dubbed this effect the *repeated name penalty* (Gordon et al., 1993; Gordon & Scearce, 1995; Gordon, Swaab, & Camblin, this volume). However, it may be more appropriate to refer to it as the *repeated noun phrase penalty* because there is evidence that the penalty also occurs when the anaphor is a definite noun phrase rather than a name (Almor, 1999; cf. Garrod et al., 1994).

Gordon et al. (1993) showed that the repeated noun phrase penalty is modulated by the syntactic position of the antecedent. In sentences such as (7), where *he/George* is coreferent with the syntactic subject of the preceding sentence, reading times were much longer when the anaphor was a name (*George*) than when it was a pronoun (*he*).

(7)   *George jumped out from behind a tree and frightened Debbie. He was surprised at her hysterical reaction. He/George never thinks about how others might feel.*

In contrast, when the antecedent not a subject, as in (8), the difference between name and pronoun was much reduced and nonsignificant.

(8) *George jumped out from behind a tree and frightened Debbie. He was*
     surprised at her hysterical reaction. She/Debbie screamed loudly and ran
     away.

Gordon et al. (1993) argued that the subject is the syntactic role that receives
most focus in the sentence (the highest ranked *forward-looking centers* in their
terms), whereas other grammatical roles receive much less focus (lower-ranked
forward-looking centers). The repeated noun phrase penalty occurs when a repeated
noun phrase anaphor refers to an antecedent that is in focus, but no such penalty
occurs when the antecedent is out of focus.

Gordon and colleagues have argued that the repeated noun phrase penalty
provides evidence for *centering theory* (Grosz, Joshi, & Weinstein, 1983, 1995;
Gordon et al., 1993; Gordon & Chan, 1995; Gordon & Scearce, 1995; Walker,
Joshi, & Prince, 1998). More generally, their findings fit well with theories which
claim that anaphoric expressions differ with respect to the accessibility of the
antecedents that they normally refer to (e.g., Ariel, 1990; Givón, 1983; 1987;
Gundel, Hedberg, & Zacharski, 1993; van Hoek, 1997). According to these theories, anaphors can be ranked on a continuum reflecting the relative accessibility
of their antecedents. For example, pronouns are high on the accessibility scale
because they usually refer to antecedents that are highly accessible. In contrast,
noun phrase anaphors are low on the scale because they tend to refer to antecedents
that are relatively inaccessible. Generally, anaphors that are high on the accessibility scale (e.g., pronouns) provide less information about the discourse entity
than anaphors that are low on the scale (e.g., noun phrase anaphors). The repeated
noun phrase penalty can be explained by assuming that repeated noun phrase
anaphors are infelicitous when they refer to an antecedent that is highly accessible.
In such cases, the anaphor is *overspecified*: The repeated noun phrase anaphor
provides more information about the discourse entity than is required to identify
the antecedent. This results in a violation of Grice's maxim of quantity (Grice,
1975), which states that speakers and writers should not provide more information
than is required.

7.4 THE INFORMATIONAL LOAD HYPOTHESIS (ILH)

In order to account for overspecification and antecedent typicality effects in a
single theory of anaphoric processing, Almor (1999) proposed the *informational
load hypothesis (ILH)*. According to the ILH, every anaphor has a processing cost
which is determined by the informativeness of the anaphor relative to its antecedent. This processing cost is called the anaphor's *informational load*. In order to
determine an anaphor's informational load, it has to be mapped into a conceptual-
semantic space relative to its antecedent. For instance, in Figure 7.1, the anaphor
the bird is presented in a conceptual-semantic space relative to possible antecedents (*the crippled goose, the goose, the robin, the bird, the animal, the creature*).
For clarity, the anaphor is presented as a square and the possible antecedents as
circles. Antecedents that are more informative or specific than the anaphor occupy

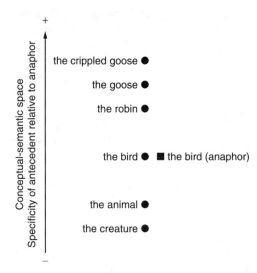

Figure 7.1. The mapping of the anaphor *the bird* in conceptual-semantic space relative to potential antecedents.

a position in conceptual space that is higher than the anaphor's position, whereas antecedents that are less informative occupy a lower position. For example, *the goose* is more specific or informative than *the bird*, and therefore *the goose* occupies a position higher in conceptual-semantic space than *the bird*. In contrast, *the animal* is less informative than *the bird* and therefore occupies a position lower in conceptual space. Furthermore, the more informative the antecedent is with respect to the anaphor, the higher the antecedent's position in conceptual space. For example, because *the crippled goose* is more informative than *the goose*, *the crippled goose* occupies a position in conceptual space that is higher than the position of *the goose*. Similarly, *the animal* is more informative than *the creature*, and therefore *the animal* is higher in conceptual space than *the creature*. Finally, the larger the semantic distance between the anaphor and its antecedent, the further apart they are in conceptual space. For example, the distance between *the goose* and *the bird* is larger than that between *the robin* and *the bird* because *goose* and *bird* are semantically less similar than *robin* and *bird* (Rips, Smith, & Shoben, 1973; Rosch, 1975).

In order to define the informational load of an anaphor, Almor (1999) first defines an intermediate concept, the *c-difference* between the anaphor and its antecedent:

Definition I: C-difference = anaphor's position in conceptual space-antecedent's position in conceptual space.

Because the axis in Figure 7.1 is positive upward, Definition I results in negative numbers when the antecedent is higher in conceptual-semantic space than the anaphor, and in positive numbers when the antecedent is lower in conceptual-semantic space. Almor (1999) then defines informational load as:

Definition II: Informational load of anaphor = A monotonic increasing function of the c-difference between the anaphor and its antecedent.

In other words, the larger the c-difference between an anaphor and its antecedent, the larger the anaphor's informational load.

Let us first consider cases where the anaphor is *higher* in conceptual space than its antecedent. In such cases, the larger the distance between the anaphor and its antecedent, the larger the c-difference, and therefore the larger the informational load of the anaphor. For example, the c-difference between *the bird* and *the creature* is larger than between *the bird* and *the animal*. As a result, the informational load of *the bird* is higher when it refers to *the creature* than when it refers to *the animal*. This contrasts with cases where the anaphor is *lower* in conceptual space than its antecedent. In such cases, the larger the distance between the anaphor and its antecedent, the smaller the c-difference, and the smaller the informational load of the anaphor. For example, the c-difference between *the bird* and *the crippled goose* is smaller, that is, more negative, than the c-difference between *the bird* and *the goose*. As a result, the informational load of *the bird* is smaller when the antecedent is *the crippled goose* than when it is *the goose*. Similarly, the c-difference between *the bird* and *the goose* is smaller (i.e., more negative) than the c-difference between *the bird* and *the robin*, and therefore, the informational load of *the bird* is smaller when the antecedent is *the goose* than when it is *the robin*.

The ILH claims that the higher an anaphor's informational load, the higher the processing cost. However, two factors interact with informational load, because they can give a functional justification to anaphors that have a high informational load. The first factor is the accessibility of the antecedent. Almor (1999) argues that one of the functions of an anaphor with a high informational load may be to aid the identification of its antecedent. If an antecedent is hard to identify because it is relatively inaccessible, an anaphor with a high informational load may help the processor to identify the antecedent. In such cases, an anaphor with a high informational load may actually be easier to process than an anaphor with a low informational load. The second factor that interacts with informational load is the amount of new information that is added by the anaphor. Almor claims that anaphors can also function as devices that predicate further information about an entity in the discourse. This can provide another functional justification for a high informational load: When an anaphor has a high informational load but contributes new information, it may be no harder to process than an anaphor with a low informational load. For example, *the bird* has a higher informational load when it refers to *the creature* than when it refers to *the animal*, but also adds more new information because the difference in specificity between *the bird* and *the creature* is larger than between *the bird* and *the animal*. Because a high informational load makes an anaphor harder to process but adding new information makes it easier, the ILH does not make any prediction concerning the differences in processing cost in such cases.

The ILH explains why a repeated noun phrase penalty (Gordon et al., 1993; Gordon & Chan, 1995) occurs when the anaphor's antecedent is in focus and highly accessible, but does not occur when it is out of focus and inaccessible. Figure 7.2

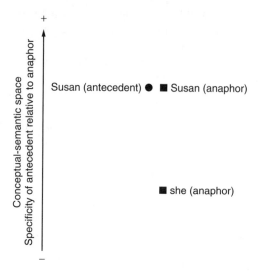

Figure 7.2. The mapping of the antecedent *Susan* in conceptual-semantic space relative to the anaphors *Susan* and *she*.

represents a pronoun (*she*) and a repeated noun phrase anaphor (*Susan*) in conceptual space relative to their antecedent *Susan*.

According to Definitions I and II, the informational load of *Susan* relative to *Susan* is larger than the informational load of *she* relative to *Susan*. When the antecedent is in focus, this should result in a greater processing cost for the repeated noun phrase *Susan* than for the pronoun *she*. In such cases, there is no functional justification for the use of the repeated noun phrase. First, the repeated noun phrase does not aid identification because the antecedent is in focus and easy to identify. Second, it does not add any new information. Thus, the ILH predicts that processing a repeated noun phrase should be harder than processing a pronoun when the antecedent is in focus. This contrasts with cases where the antecedent is out of focus. Because the antecedent is harder to identify in such cases, the repeated noun phrase has a functional justification: The use of a repeated noun phrase makes the antecedent easier to identify relative to the use of a pronoun. Therefore, when the antecedent is out of focus, a repeated noun phrase anaphor is no harder to process than a pronoun, and may even be easier.

The ILH also deals with antecedent typicality effects and makes a new and quite surprising prediction. Figure 7.3 shows two possible antecedents for the anaphor *the bird*.

The figure shows that both *the goose* and *the robin* are represented higher in conceptual-semantic space than their antecedent *the bird*, because both are more specific than their antecedent. However, the position of *the goose* in conceptual-semantic space is higher than the position of *the robin*, because the semantic distance between *goose* and *bird* is larger than between *robin* and *bird*. Given that the c-difference between an anaphor and its antecedent is defined as the anaphor's position in conceptual space minus the antecedent's position (Definition I) and given

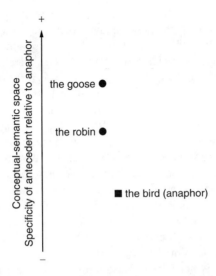

Figure 7.3. The mapping of the anaphor *the bird* in conceptual-semantic space relative to the potential antecedents *the robin* and *the goose*.

that an anaphor's informational load is a monotonic increasing function of the c-difference (Definition II), the informational load for *the bird* after *the robin* is higher than after *the goose*. When the antecedent is focused and easy to identify as in (9), there is no functional justification for the high informational load that occurs when the antecedent is typical (*the robin*), because the antecedent is easy to identify and the anaphor does not add new information. As a result, *the bird* should be *harder* to process in (9a) than in (9b).

(9) a. *What the novelist spotted was the robin. The bird was not far away.*
     b. *What the novelist spotted was the goose. The bird was not far away.*

We will henceforth call this effect the *inverse typicality effect* (Garnham, 2001).

In contrast, when the antecedent is out of focus, as in (10), the ILH predicts that noun phrase anaphors with typical antecedents are easier to process than those with atypical antecedents.

(10) a. *It was the novelist who spotted the robin. The bird was not far away.*
      b. *It was the novelist who spotted the goose. The bird was not far away.*

The reason for this is that the high informational load in (10a) relative to (10b) has a functional justification. Because the antecedent is out of focus and relatively inaccessible, the high semantic overlap between *the bird* and *the robin* helps the identification of the antecedent. As a result, the ILH predicts that *the bird* in (10a) should be easier than in (10b).

Clearly, the predictions of the ILH are very different from the predictions of semantic overlap theories (e.g., Garrod & Sanford, 1977; Myers & O'Brien, 1998;

O'Brien et al., 1995), which predict that anaphors with atypical antecedents should always be harder to process than typical antecedents, regardless of the accessibility of the antecedent. However, Almor (1999) provided support for the ILH in a self-paced reading experiment. Reading times for *the bird* were significantly longer in (9a) than in (9b). In contrast, the pattern for (10) was different: Reading times for *the bird* were longer in (10b) than in (10a), although this effect was marginal.

The results from Almor's (1999) experiment are very surprising in the light of other findings on antecedent typicality effects (Duffy & Rayner, 1990; Garrod & Sanford, 1977; Rayner et al., 2000), which showed that noun phrase anaphors with typical antecedents were easier to process than those with atypical antecedents. Almor argued that the apparent conflict between these results and the predictions of the ILH occurs because previous studies did not systematically manipulate the focus of the antecedent. Indeed, it is possible that the antecedent in some of the other studies was out of focus, in which case the ILH predicts that noun phrase anaphors with typical antecedents are easier than those with atypical antecedents. In the example that Duffy and Rayner give [see (4)], the antecedent in the near antecedent condition is not in the clause immediately preceding the anaphor, and the antecedent is not a syntactic subject. Hence, it is likely that the antecedent is relatively inaccessible even though it is close to the anaphor. Furthermore, in the distant condition, the antecedent is clearly out of focus because there are several sentences intervening between the anaphor and antecedent. Similarly, the list of materials from Rayner et al. (2000) shows that the antecedent is not a syntactic subject, and it is therefore likely to be out of focus and relatively inaccessible [cf. (5)].

However, Almor's ILH has difficulty dealing with the results from Garrod and Sanford's (1977) study because their example [see (1)] shows that the antecedent is the subject of the clause preceding the anaphor, and it should therefore receive sentence focus. If Garrod and Sanford's example is representative for their materials, the ILH cannot account for their results.

In summary, the results from studies investigating antecedent typicality effects show seemingly conflicting results. Almor's (1999) study showed that anaphors with typical focused antecedents are harder to process than anaphors with atypical focused antecedents, but Garrod and Sanford's (1977) study showed exactly the opposite pattern. Furthermore, the predictions of the ILH and semantic overlap theories are very different. Semantic overlap theories predict that anaphors with typical anteced-ents should be easier to process than anaphors with atypical antecedents, whereas the ILH predicts an inverse typicality effect when the antecedent is in focus. The ILH can account for the results from Almor (1999) and possibly for the results from Duffy and Rayner (1990) and Rayner et al. (2000), but it is unclear how it explains the results from Garrod and Sanford. In contrast, semantic overlap theories account for the results from Garrod and Sanford, Duffy and Rayner (1990), and Rayner et al. (2000), but cannot account for the findings from Almor's (1999) study.

7.5 AN EYE-MOVEMENT EXPERIMENT INVESTIGATING ANTECEDENT TYPICALITY EFFECTS

In order to test the contrasting predictions of the ILH and semantic overlap theories, we conducted an eye-movement experiment to investigate antecedent typicality effects during reading. Because eye-movement methodology can provide a much more detailed insight into the time course of language processing than self-paced reading, we anticipated that our experiment might be able to resolve the conflict between Almor's (1999) and Garrod and Sanford's (1977) self-paced reading results. Although Duffy and Rayner (1990) and Rayner et al. (2000) also conducted eye-movement studies investigating the typicality effect, their data do not distinguish between the ILH and semantic overlap theories because, in their experiments, the antecedent was always out of focus. As argued by Almor (1999), in such cases the ILH makes the same predictions as semantic overlap theories.

We therefore employed materials such as (11), in which the typical or atypical antecedent (*the coal/the peat* respectively) was the focus of the sentence preceding the anaphor (*the fuel*).

(11)   a. *It was the coal that was ordered in great quantities before the winter. Obviously, the fuel was in great demand.*
       b. *It was the peat that was ordered in great quantities before the winter. Obviously, the fuel was in great demand.*
       c. *The coal was ordered in great quantities before the winter. Obviously, the fuel was in great demand.*
       d. *The peat was ordered in great quantities before the winter. Obviously, the fuel was in great demand.*

The first sentences in (11a–b) are clefted structures in which the antecedent *the coal/peat* is the clefted constituent (Davidse, 2000; Delin, 1995; Delin & Oberlander, 1995; Prince, 1978). Psycholinguistic research has shown that clefted constituents are more salient than constituents that are not clefted (Brédart & Modolo, 1988; Langford & Holmes, 1979; Morris & Folk, 1998). Following Almor (1999), we used this construction as a means of making the antecedent highly accessible for anaphor resolution. However, clefted structures are relatively infrequent, especially when they occur without a preceding context, and they serve very specific discourse functions. Therefore, in order to determine whether Almor's results were specific to clefts, we also used non-clefted sentences such as in (11c–d). In these sentences, the antecedent was the syntactic subject. Several studies have shown that a sentence-initial subject is the most accessible noun phrase for subsequent anaphor resolution (e.g., Gernsbacher & Hargreaves, 1988; Gordon et al., 1993; Stevenson, Nelson, & Stenning, 1995), so Almor's ILH predicts that the typicality effect for the nonclefted structures should be similar to that for clefted structures. For both types of structures, anaphors with typical antecedents should be harder to process than anaphors with atypical antecedents (though the size of the effect may differ if the antecedent receives more focus in clefts than in nonclefts).

Semantic overlap theories (e.g., Garrod & Sanford, 1977) make the opposite prediction. They predict that the larger the semantic overlap between anaphor and antecedent, the easier it should be to identify the antecedent and establish the coreference relation. Consequently, anaphors with typical antecedents should be easier to process than those with atypical antecedents, regardless of whether the antecedent is in focus.

We conducted an eye-movement study with 36 participants and 32 materials similar to (11) to contrast the two theories. The anaphor-antecedent pairs were pretested for typicality: For all materials, a different group of participants had indicated that the typical antecedent was a more typical instance of the anaphor than the atypical antecedent.

In order to investigate the time course of the typicality effect, we divided the sentence containing the anaphor into four regions of interest: The region preceding the anaphor (*Obviously*), the anaphor (*the fuel*), the postanaphor region (*was in great*), and the final region (*demand*). Furthermore, we analyzed five different eye-movement measures. *First-fixation time* was defined as the first fixation in a region provided the participant had not previously fixated subsequent text. *First-pass reading time* was the sum of fixations from the first fixation in the region until the first fixation outside the region, provided that the participant had not fixated subsequent text. *First-pass regressions* were defined as the percentage of times participants made a regression to a preceding region immediately following a first-pass fixation. *Regression-path time* was the sum of fixations from the first fixation in the region until fixating a subsequent region, provided that the participant had not fixated subsequent text. Thus, this measure potentially includes fixations after a regression was made from the region of interest. Finally, *total reading time* was defined as the sum of all fixations in a region.

None of the eyetracking measures and regions showed a significant effect of structure (cleft vs. noncleft), nor an interaction between typicality and structure, indicating that anaphoric processing was very similar regardless of whether the antecedent was or was not a clefted constituent. In the anaphor region, none of the eyetracking measures showed an effect of typicality. However, first-pass times in the post-anaphor region (*was in great*) and regression-path times in the final region (*demand*) did show typicality effects that were significant ($p < 0.05$) by subjects and items.[1] First-pass times are presented in Figure 7.4 and regression-path times in Figure 7.5.

First-pass times for the post-anaphor region (*was in great*) showed that anaphors with typical antecedents were easier to read than anaphors with atypical antecedents. A similar pattern was observed in first fixation times for this region, but the effect was only significant by subjects. These results support semantic overlap theories but are inconsistent with the predictions of the ILH. However, regression-path times for the final region showed a very different pattern: They were longer when the anaphor had a typical antecedent than when it had an atypical antecedent. Thus, the results from this measure are consistent with the ILH, but inconsistent with semantic overlap theories.

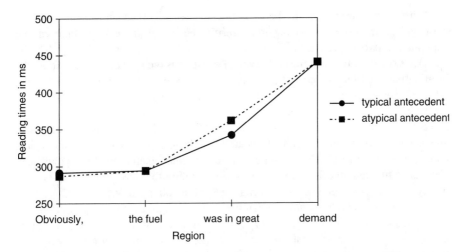

Figure 7.4. First-pass reading times for sentences with a noun phrase anaphor referring to a typical or a typical antecedent, collapsed across clefted and nonclefted structures.

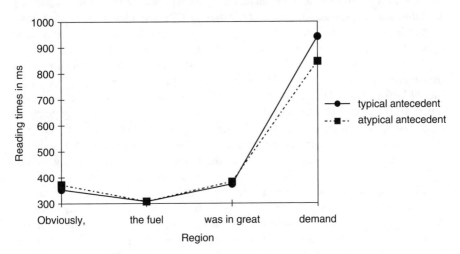

Figure 7.5. Regression-path reading times for sentences with a noun phrase anaphor referring to a typical or atypical antecedents, collapsed across clefted and nonclefted structures.

7.6 PROCESSING STAGES IN THE RESOLUTION OF NOUN PHRASE ANAPHORS: ANTECEDENT IDENTIFICATION AND SEMANTIC OVERSPECIFICATION

The results from our eyetracking experiment indicate that (at least) two different types of processes occur during the resolution of noun phrase anaphors. During an initial stage of processing, anaphors with typical antecedents are easier to process than anaphors with atypical antecedents, but during a subsequent processing stage, the pattern reverses.

What type of processes do the two effects reflect? The advantage for anaphors with typical antecedents that occurred during the initial processing stage can be explained in two ways.

One explanation is that the early typicality effect is the result of lexical-semantic priming between the antecedent and anaphor (e.g., Collins & Loftus, 1975; Neely, 1991; Meyer & Schvaneveldt, 1971). When the antecedent is a typical instance of the anaphor, the semantic overlap between the two nouns is larger than when the antecedent is an atypical instance (Rips et al., 1973; Rosch, 1975). Therefore, typical antecedents may result in stronger semantic priming to the anaphor than atypical antecedents, and this would facilitate lexical access for anaphors with typical antecedents. If this hypothesis is correct, this would imply that the typicality effect is a purely lexical effect, independent of higher level anaphoric processing.

However, researchers have previously argued against this explanation. As mentioned earlier, Garrod and Sanford (1977) showed that the typicality of a noun phrase as an instance of a following noun phrase did not have an effect when the two noun phrases were not coreferent. Although we believe that care should be taken when interpreting self-paced reading results, this suggests that coreference is a prerequisite for the typicality effect and that the typicality effect is not caused by lexical-semantic priming. Duffy and Rayner (1990) provided further arguments against lexical-semantic priming as an explanation for the antecedent typicality effect. They argued that most word-recognition studies show that lexical-priming effects are very short-lasting. In single-word lexical-decision experiments, priming effects disappear when one word intervenes between prime and target (e.g., Feldman, 2000; Masson, 1995; Zeelenberg & Pecher, 2002). Furthermore, in an eye-movement experiment, Carroll and Slowiaczek (1986) showed that semantic priming occurred when prime and target occurred in the same clause, but not when they were in different clauses. As the antecedent and anaphor were in different sentences in our experiment and several words intervened, the findings from these priming studies suggest that our results were probably not due to lexical-semantic priming.

Finally, probably the most convincing argument against a lexical-priming explanation is the time course of the typicality effect in our experiment. We observed the typicality effect in first-pass times for the region following the anaphor. To our knowledge, all eye-movement studies on lexical-semantic priming show that this effect occurs earlier, in first-pass or even first-fixation times for the primed word (Carroll & Slowiaczek, 1986; Morris, 1994; Morris & Folk, 1998). Generally, word-level effects such as lexical frequency and lexical ambiguity are observed in first-pass or first-fixation times on the word itself and are not delayed until the next words (e.g., Duffy, Morris, & Rayner, 1988; Rayner & Duffy, 1986; Schilling, Rayner, & Chumbley, 1998). Therefore, although we cannot rule out a lexical-priming explanation on the basis of our experiment alone, we believe that the results from other studies strongly suggest that this is not the most plausible explanation for the antecedent typicality effect.

A second, and we believe more plausible, explanation is that the early typicality effect reflects identification of the antecedent. When the semantic overlap between anaphor and antecedent is large because the antecedent is a typical instance of the anaphor, it is easier to identify the antecedent and to establish a coreference relation than when the antecedent is atypical. This results in faster reading times following anaphors with typical antecedents than atypical ones. This explanation is the same as the explanation that semantic overlap theories (e.g., Garrod & Sanford, 1977) provide. However, these theories do not explain why we observed the inverse typicality effect in the final region of the sentence.

We propose that the late, inverse typicality effect that we observed in regression-path times for the final region is a semantic overspecification effect. After the processor has established a coreference relation, it checks whether the anaphor is semantically appropriate. If the anaphor is semantically very similar to its antecedent, it is infelicitous because the two referring expressions provide very similar information about the discourse entity that they refer to. The semantic information that the anaphor provides is redundant because it has already been introduced by the antecedent. As a result, the anaphor violates Grice's maxim of quantity (Grice, 1975), which states that speakers and writers should not provide more information than is required. For example, when the antecedent is *the coal*, the processor accesses semantic information related to fuel, and when the anaphor *the fuel* is subsequently encountered, it merely provides redundant information. In contrast, when the semantic information that is accessed at the antecedent is different from the information that is accessed at the anaphor, no semantic overspecification occurs. For example, when the antecedent is *the peat*, semantic information related to boggy places and plants is strongly activated, but semantic information related to fuel is only relatively weakly activated. In this case, the anaphor provides only minimal redundant information, and is therefore semantically more felicitous.

Clearly, the explanation that we have suggested for the inverse typicality effect in regression-path times for the final region is very similar to Almor's (1999) explanation. Almor claims that the informational load of *the fuel* is higher when the antecedent is *the coal* than when it is *the peat*. When the antecedent is in focus, the high informational load after typical antecedents has no functional justification, and therefore the anaphor should be harder to process when the antecedent is typical than when it is atypical. Like our account of the inverse typicality effect, the ILH claims that anaphors with typical antecedents are hard to process because the high semantic overlap between anaphor and antecedent is unnecessary.

However, there is an important difference between our account of antecedent typicality effects and Almor's (1999) ILH. According to our account, the anaphoric processor operates in (at least) two stages: An antecedent identification stage and a subsequent stage during which the semantic felicity of the anaphor is checked. This distinction between two separate stages in the processing of anaphors bears resemblance to Sanford and Garrod's (1989; cf. Garrod & Terras, 2000) distinction between *bonding* processes, which involve finding a match between an anaphor's properties and possible antecedents, and subsequent *binding* processes, which involve the instantiation of a semantic relationship between the anaphor and its antecedent. In contrast, the ILH assumes that anaphor resolution occurs in a single stage of processing, during which the informational load of the anaphor and antecedent accessibility interact. The ILH does not explain why the pattern of results in first-pass reading times for the postanaphor region was different from the pattern of results for the final region. To uphold the ILH, one could assume that the results from the postanaphor region do not reflect anaphoric processes but reflect lexical-semantic priming between antecedent and anaphor. However, as discussed before, there are various reasons why this does not seem the most plausible explanation of this effect.

The results from our study clearly show the importance of using eye-movement methodology to investigate anaphoric processing because it enabled us to discriminate between processes that occurred at the postanaphor region and processes that occurred at the end of the sentence. Previous studies that investigated typicality effects for in-focus antecedents (Almor, 1999; Garrod & Sanford, 1977) possibly failed to observe the two stages of anaphoric processing because they employed self-paced reading methodology, a method that makes it very hard or impossible to investigate the time course of processing in detail.

In Garrod and Sanford's (1977) self-paced reading study, reading times were measured for the complete sentence containing the anaphor. Hence, their method did not allow them to distinguish between anaphoric processes that occur at different points in time, and it is likely that the two processing stages that we observed in our study were conflated in Garrod and Sanford's study. If the early antecedent identification effect in Garrod and Sanford's study was larger than the later semantic overspecification effect, this would explain why they observed a preference for anaphors with typical antecedents.

Almor's (1999) self-paced reading method was, at least in principle, slightly more sensitive to the time course of anaphoric processing because reading times for the anaphor and the rest of the sentence were measured separately (though reading times for the rest of the sentence were not reported). However, it is likely that reading times for the anaphor still conflated the identification and semantic overspecification effect. Due to motor processes that are required for pressing the button in a self-paced reading task, reading times are generally slower than during normal reading. As a result, self-paced reading times often include both early and late processes (e.g., Clifton & Ferreira, 1989). Furthermore, Almor's method of presenting the anaphor separately from the rest of the sentence may have induced specific unnatural reading strategies. For example, it may have caused participants to complete both antecedent identification and the later semantic appropriateness check before they pressed the button to see the rest of the sentence. This would have made it impossible to distinguish between these two processing stages. If readers completed the semantic appropriateness check before pressing the button, this would also explain why Almor observed the inverse typicality effect at the anaphor, whereas in our eye-movement experiment, this effect occurred much later in the final region of the sentence. Finally, the preference for atypical antecedents in Almor's study can be explained by assuming that the semantic overspecification effect was stronger than the earlier antecedent identification effect.

The results from our eye-movement experiment suggest an explanation for the conflicting findings of Garrod and Sanford's (1977) and Almor's (1999) study. Because these studies used different materials and a different presentation method, the antecedent identification effect may have been stronger than the semantic over-specification effect in Garrod and Sanford's experiment, whereas the opposite may have been the case in Almor's experiment. Because we used eye-movement methodology, which is much more sensitive to the time course of different effects, we observed both effects in our experiment.

AUTHOR NOTE

This research was supported by British Academy Grant SG-35247. We would like to thank Maria Nella Carminati and Leila Kalliokoski for comments on an earlier draft of this chapter.

References

Almor, A. (1999). Noun-phrase anaphora and focus: The informational load hypothesis. *Psychological Review, 106,* 748–765.

Ariel, M. (1990). *Accessing noun-phrase antecedents*. London: Routledge.

Battig, W. G., & Montague, W. E. (1969). Category norms for verbal items in 56 categories: A replication and extension of the Connecticut Category Norms. *Journal of Experimental Psychology, 80.*

Brédart, S., & Modolo, K. (1988). Moses strikes again: focalization effect on a semantic illusion. *Acta Psychologica, 67,* 135–144.

Carroll, P., & Slowiaczek, M. L. (1986). Constraints on semantic priming in reading: A fixation time analysis. *Memory and Cognition, 14,* 509–522.

Clifton, C. J., & Ferreira, F. (1989). Ambiguity in context. *Language and Cognitive Processes, 4,* SI 77–103.

Collins, A. M., & Loftus, E. F. (1975). A spreading-activation theory of semantic processing. *Psychological Review, 82,* 407–428.

Davidse, K. (2000). A constructional approach to clefts. *Linguistics, 38,* 1101–1131.

Delin, J., & Oberlander, J. (1995). Syntactic constraints on discourse structure: The case of it-clefts. *Linguistics, 33,* 465–500.

Delin, J. (1995). Presupposition and shared knowledge in it-clefts. *Language and Cognitive Processes, 10,* 97–120.

Duffy, S. A., Morris, R. K., & Rayner, K. (1988). Lexical ambiguity and fixation times in reading. *Journal of Memory and Language, 27,* 429–446.

Duffy, S. A., & Rayner, K. (1990). Eye movements and anaphor resolution: Effects of antecedent typicality and distance. *Language and Speech, 33,* 103–119.

Feldman, L. B. (2000). Are morphological effects distinguishable from the effects of shared meaning and shared form? *Journal of Experimental Psychology: Learning, Memory, and Cognition, 26,* 1431–1444.

Garnham, A. (2001). *Mental models and the interpretation of anaphora*. Hove, UK: Psychology Press.

Garrod, S., Freudenthal, D., & Boyle, E. (1994). The role of different types of anaphor in the online resolution of sentences in a discourse. *Journal of Memory and Language, 33,* 39–68.

Garrod, S., & Sanford, A. (1977). Interpreting anaphoric relations: The integration of semantic information while reading. *Journal of Verbal Learning and Verbal Behavior, 16,* 77–90.

Garrod, S., & Terras, M. (2000). The contribution of lexical and situational knowledge to resolving discourse roles: Bonding and resolution. *Journal of Memory and Language, 42,* 526–544.

Gernsbacher, M. A., & Hargreaves, D. J. (1988). Accessing sentence participants: The advantage of first mention. *Journal of Memory and Language, 27,* 699–717.

Givón, T. (1983). Topic continuity in discourse: An introduction. In T. Givón (Ed.), *Topic continuity in discourse: A quantitative cross-language study.* Amsterdam: John Benjamins.

Givón, T. (1987). *On understanding grammar.* New York: Academic Press.

Gordon, P. C., Grosz, B. J., & Gilliom, L. A. (1993). Pronouns, names, and the centering of attention. *Cognitive Science, 17,* 311–347.

Gordon, P. C., & Scearce, K. A. (1995). Pronominalization and discourse coherence, discourse structure, and pronoun interpretation. *Memory and Cognition, 23,* 313–323.

Gordon, P. C., & Chan, D. (1995). Pronouns, passives, and discourse coherence. *Journal of Memory and Language, 34,* 216–231.

Grice, H. P. (1975). Logic and conversation. In P. Cole & J. Morgan (Eds.), *Syntax and Semantics: Vol. III. Speech acts* (pp. 41–58). New York: Academic Press.

Grosz, B. J., Joshi, A. K., & Weinstein, S. (1983). Providing a unified account of definite noun phrases in discourse. *Proceedings of the 21st Annual Meeting of the Association for Computational Linguistics,* Cambridge, MA.

Grosz, B. J., Joshi, A. K., & Weinstein, S. (1995). Centering: A framework for modeling the local coherence of discourse. *Computational Linguistics, 21,* 203–226.

Gundel, J. K., Hedberg, N., & Zacharski, R. (1993). Cognitive status and the form of referring expressions in discourse. *Language, 69,* 274–307.

Kennison, S. M., & Gordon, P. C. (1997). Comprehending referential expressions during reading: Evidence from eyetracking. *Discourse Processes, 24,* 229–252.

Langford, J., & Holmes, V. M. (1979). Syntactic presupposition in sentence comprehension. *Cognition, 7,* 363–383.

Masson, M. E. J. (1995). A distributed memory model of semantic priming. *Journal of Experimental Psychology: Learning, Memory, and Cognition,* 3–23.

Meyer, D. E., & Schvaneveldt, R. W. (1971). Facilitation in recognizing words: Evidence of a dependence between retrieval operations. *Journal of Experimental Psychology, 90,* 227–235.

Morris, R. K. (1994). Lexical and message-level sentence context effects on fixation times in reading. *Journal of Experimental Psychology: Learning, Memory, and Cognition, 20,* 92–103.

Morris, R. K., & Folk, J. R. (1998). Focus as a contextual priming mechanism in reading. *Memory and Cognition, 26,* 1313–1322.

Myers, J. L., & O'Brien, E. J. (1998). Accessing the discourse representation during reading. *Discourse Processes, 26,* 131–157.

Neely, J. H. (1991). Semantic priming effects in visual word recognition: A selective review of current findings and theories. In D. E. Besner & G. W. Humphreys (Eds.), *Basic processes in reading: Visual word recognition* (pp. 264–336). Hillsdale, NJ: Erlbaum.

O'Brien, E. J., & Albrecht, J. E. (1992). Comprehension strategies in the development of a mental model. *Journal of Experimental Psychology: Learning Memory and Cognition, 18,* 777–784.

O'Brien, E. J., Albrecht, J. E., Hakala, C. M., & Rizzella, M L. (1995). Activation and suppression of antecedents during reinstatement. *Journal of Experimental Psychology: Learning Memory and Cognition, 21,* 626–634.

O'Brien, E. J., Raney, G. E., Albrecht, J. E., & Rayner, K. (1997). Processes involved in the resolution of explicit anaphors. *Discourse Processes, 23,* 1–24.

Prince, E. (1978). A comparison of wh-clefts and it-clefts in discourse. *Language, 54,* 883–906.

Rayner, K., & Duffy, S. A. (1986). Lexical complexity and fixation times in reading: Effects of word frequency, verb complexity, and lexical ambiguity. *Memory and Cognition, 14,* 191–201.

Rayner, K., Kambe, G., & Duffy, S. A. (2000). The effect of clause wrap-up on eye movements during reading. *Quarterly Journal of Experimental Psychology, 53A,* 1061–1080.

Rips, L. J., Shoben, E. J., & Smith, E. E. (1973). Semantic distance and the verification of semantic relations. *Journal of Verbal Learning and Verbal Behavior, 12,* 1–20.

Rosch, E. (1975). Cognitive representations of semantic categories. *Journal of Experimental Psychology: General, 104,* 192–233.

Sanford, A. J., & Garrod, S. C. (1989). What, when, and how? Questions of immediacy in anaphoric reference resolution. *Language and Cognitive Processes, 4,* 235–262.

Schilling, H. E. H., Rayner, K., & Chumbley, J. I. (1998). Comparing naming, lexical decision, and eye fixation times: Word frequency effects and individual differences. *Memory and Cognition, 26,* 1270–1281.

Stevenson, R. J., Nelson, A. W. R., & Stenning, K. (1995). The role of parallelism in strategies of pronoun comprehension. *Language and Speech, 38,* 393–418.

van Hoek, K. (1997). *Anaphora and conceptual structure.* Chicago: University of Chicago Press.

Walker, M. A., Joshi, A. K., & Prince, E. F. (1998). *Centering theory in discourse.* Oxford: Clarendon.

Zeelenberg, R., & Pecher, D. (2002). False memories and lexical decision: Even twelve primes do not cause long-term semantic priming. *Acta Psychologica, 109,* 269–284.

Note
1. First-pass regressions and total reading times did not show any significant results in these regions.

Chapter 8
On-Line Measures of Coreferential Processing

PETER C. GORDON, C. CHRISTINE CAMBLIN, AND TAMARA Y. SWAAB

8.1 INTRODUCTION

One reason that the comprehension of reference and coreference is an important topic in language research is that it allows examination of critical aspects of the interaction between language and memory. In order to process coreferential relations, a listener or reader must establish a representation of linguistic input in memory during initial referential processing and then must access that representation during the processing of a subsequent coreferential expression. Clearly, performing this task involves the three major facets of memory: encoding, storage, and retrieval. The task also brings central questions of language structure into play because syntactic factors have been shown to have a very strong impact on how coreferential expressions are interpreted and even on whether two expressions can be interpreted as refering to the same thing. In this chapter we examine the online processing of reference and coreference in order to gain understanding of the memory load induced by maintaining a representation of an antecedent in memory and in order to understand how such a representation is accessed during the processing of a subsequent coreferential expression.

Our attempts to gain this understanding have involved coordinated studies of reading comprehension using eyetracking and ERPs as online measures of referential processing. As noted elsewhere in this volume, eyetracking during reading provides a sensitive measure of the timing of the input to language comprehension as it occurs when participants have strategic control over reading (Boland, this volume; Mitchell, this volume; Sanford, Sturt, Moxey, & Morrow, this volume; van Gompel, Liversedge, & Pearson, this volume). ERPs provide a continuous neural measure that can tap into these language processes as they unfold in real time (Osterhout, McLaughlin, Kim, Greenwald, & Inoue, this volume; van Berkum, this volume). In this chapter we focus on the presentation of results from an eyetracking experiment, but we also discuss the merits of the two methods and results from ERP experiments that complement our current eyetracking experiment.

Eyetracking. Eyetracking has been extensively used as a measure of reading in general (Just & Carpenter, 1980; Rayner, 1978; 1998) and has also been applied successfully to issues concerning the comprehension of referential expressions

(Ehrlich, 1983; Ehrlich & Rayner, 1983; Duffy & Rayner, 1990; Garrod, Freudenthal, & Boyle, 1994; Kennison & Gordon, 1997; Rayner, Kambe, & Duffy, 2000; Sanford et al., this volume; van Gompel et al., this volume). It provides an online behavioral measure with fine-grained temporal resolution of reading under relatively natural circumstances. Eyetracking research has yielded strong models of the interaction of lexical processes and eye-movement control (Reichle, Pollatsek, Fisher, & Rayner, 1998), but as yet detailed models have not been developed to account for the contribution of higher-level language processes to the control of eye movements during reading.

ERPs. ERPs provide information with very fine temporal resolution about the neural processing induced by stimuli. Because separable ERP components are sensitive to separable aspects of language processing (e.g., semantics vs. syntax), they can give a direct indication of the component mechanisms of language comprehension processes. Of particular relevance to our research are the N400 and the P600. With respect to the processing nature of the N400, there is evidence that in the context of a sentence or a word, the modulation of the N400 amplitude is dependent upon the ease or difficulty with which a word can be integrated into the preceding context (Rugg, Furda, & Lorist, 1988; van Petten & Kutas, 1990; Brown & Hagoort, 1993; Holcomb, 1993; Chwilla, Brown, & Hagoort, 1995). Its amplitude is reduced to words that are easily integrated into a higher-order representation of the preceding context. The P600 is an index of syntactic processing difficulty, including repair and revision (Kaan & Swaab, 2003); it is prompted by garden-path sentences (Osterhout & Holcomb, 1992), difficult syntactic ambiguities (Osterhout, Holcomb, & Swinney, 1994), complex, but syntactically correct and preferred continuations (Kaan, Harris, Gibson, & Holcomb, 2000), ungrammatical coreference (Osterhout & Mobley, 1995), and by ungrammatical continuations of a sentence fragment (Osterhout, Holcomb, & Swinney). Research using ERPs to investigate the processing of referential expressions (Harris, Wexler, & Holcomb, 2000; Osterhout & Mobley; Streb, Rosler, & Hennighausen, 1999; van Berkum, Brown, & Hagoort, 1999a,b) has successively shown that it can affect the N400 and P600.

8.1.1 Eyetracking and Coreferential Processing

Our research here focuses on a fairly straightforward pair of manipulations of reference as illustrated in (1) below, where each of the two types of initial clauses can be paired with each of the two types of final clause.

(1) Pam washed the dishes while ... ... she talked about politics.

  Pam and Joe washed the dishes while ... ... Pam talked about politics.

The first manipulation is whether the initial clause of the sentence has a subject noun phrase that is a single name or a pair of conjoined names. This provides a way of manipulating memory load during sentence comprehension since either one or two names must be remembered as the sentence is being understood. It also provides a way of manipulating the linguistic prominence of the first name in the sentence since a referent that is realized by the subject of a sentence is more prominent than one that is embedded within a complex NP (see Albrecht & Clifton, 1998; Gordon & Hendrick, 1997, 1998; Gordon, Hendrick, Ledoux, & Yang, 1999 for discussions). Considerable research has previously been done examining the processing of sentences with plural antecedents and has examined a number of issues: how different forms of conjunction and types of NPs are mapped into common role-slots in the mental scenarios created in discourse comprehension (Sanford & Lockhart, 1990; Sanford et al., this volume), the nature of the representations of the entities that make up the plural antecedent (Carreiras, 1997; Kaup, Kelter, & Habel, 2002; Koh & Clifton, 2002; Sanford et al., this volume), and the difficulty of splitting a conjoined antecedent with singular reference (Albrecht & Clifton; Gordon et al.).

The second manipulation is whether the anaphoric expression in the second clause is a pronoun or a repeated name; the anaphoric expression must in some way be matched with the earlier mention of the referent. Standard notions in the memory literature would lead to the expectation that a repeated name would be a better stimulus for memory retrieval than a pronoun would be because it provides more cues that match the original stimulus (Gernsbacher, 1989). However, a considerable amount of research in linguistics indicates that pronouns are often the preferred form for coreference, especially when the referent is prominent. Psycholinguistic research (e.g., Cloitre & Bever, 1988; Gordon, Grosz, & Gilliom, 1993) has provided support for this idea, and some of our previous research has used self-paced reading to look at just the sort of manipulations described above (Gordon et al., 1999).

One of our goals in conducting the current research was to provide evidence regarding people's expectations about the characteristics of sentences that begin either with a name or a pair of conjoined names. We were particularly interested in the extent to which people expected the second clause to include coreference to the named characters and, if so, what kind of coreference they expected. In order to address this question we conducted a completion study in which participants were presented with the initial clause and clausal connective of sentences like those in (1) and asked them to write a natural-sounding completion for the sentence. The use of a completion task to study coreference in the presence of a plural antecedent has previously been undertaken by Sanford and Lockhart (1990) who were concerned with how different methods of conjoining ("and" *vs.* "with") and different types of noun phrases (names *vs.* descriptions) would influence the subsequent use of plural coreference. The results of our study, shown in Table 8.1, indicate that around half of the completions involved coreference to the initial noun phrase of the first clause. This shows that coreference is fairly natural in this type of sentence. The results are also very clear in showing that pronouns relative to names are overwhelmingly the preferred form of coreferential expression though the type of pronoun used depends on the characteristics of the subject noun phrase: singular pronouns are used following a singular subject while plural pronouns are used following a subject consisting of a pair of names conjoined with "and." Our plural condition replicates Sanford and Lockhart's *name-and-name condition*. They found slightly over 50% of continuations included plural coreference while we found almost 44% of continuations included plural coreference, results that seem quite

Table 8.1. **Results from a Completion Study Following Clauses with One-Name (Singular) NPs and Two-Name (Plural) NPs as the Subject of the Initial Clause**

	Singular Pronoun (He/She)	Plural Pronoun (They)	Repeated Name	Other
Singular antecedent	49%	1.6%	0.2%	47.4%
Plural antecedent	0.8%	43.8%	0.6%	54.8%

similar, given that the specific continuation materials were different. Of particular importance to our present concerns, repeated names are hardly used at all. This leads to the view that for the stimuli included in our experimental design, the only type of coreferential condition that matches prior expectations is a singular pronoun following a singular subject NP. For the other three conditions (singular pronoun following conjoined names, and repeated name following either conjoined or singular name), the completion rates for singular pronouns and repeated names are all under 1%. To the extent that expectations play a role in our experiment, we would expect the singular-pronoun condition to stand out from the other three. In the following text we describe the methods and results for an experiment that used eyetracking to examine the reading of sentences like those we examined for completion responses.

Participants, Stimuli, and Procedure. The experimental sentences had two clauses as shown in example 1. The first clause introduced one or two named characters, and the subject of the second clause was reasonably interpreted as coreferential with the initial name in the first clause. At the University of North Carolina-Chapel Hill, 16 undergraduates were tested as part of a course requirement. A total of 48 sentences were presented in four conditions as shown in example 1, with assignment of sentences to conditions counterbalanced across participants. Participants were asked to read the sentences at a natural pace (while their eye movements were being recorded by an SMI EyeLink eyetracker) and answer a comprehension question after each sentence. There was an initial warm-up block of unrelated filler sentences, and the experimental sentences were interspersed with an equal number of unrelated filler sentences.

Results and Discussion. The questions of principal interest relate to reading of the coreferential expression and of the words between the antecedent and coreferential expressions. To address those questions we look at a number of measures. First, we examine gaze duration, which is the sum of fixation durations from the first time a word has been fixated until a different word is fixated, given that no subsequent word has already been fixated. Gaze duration provides a measure of first-pass reading of a word. Second, we look at the duration of re-reading words. Finally, we examine the probability of a regressive eye movement to a region and from a region.

The first question of interest concerns the effects of the type of subject noun phrase (one name vs. a pair of conjoined names). In the one-name (singular) case there is less information to remember while the sentence is being understood than there is in the two-name (plural) case. In general, processing difficulty goes up with memory load, so we might expect that eyetracking measures would show evidence of greater difficulty in the two-name than in the one-name condition. This was assessed by looking at the gaze duration for the region of text after the initial subject NP up until the connective to the second clause. These portions of text are exactly matched in the two conditions. (For example 1, this region corresponds to the phrase "washed the dishes"). There was a tendency for gaze duration to be longer in the two-name (plural) condition than in the one-name condition (602 *vs.* 572 ms; $F_1(1, 15) = 4.05$, $p = .06$; $F_2(1, 47) = 3.71$, $p = .06$). While this difference does not quite reach conventional levels of significance, it is in the expected direction of more difficulty processing in the higher-memory load (two-name) condition than in the lower memory load (one-name) condition. The pattern is in the opposite direction from what would be expected under general characterizations of the effect of position in a sentence on reading time. Ferreira and Henderson (1995) showed that, in general, the time spent reading a region of text decreases as that text occurs later in a sentence. Our load results buck that particular trend since the matched regions occur later in the two-name condition than in the one-name condition.

The second question of interest concerns the reading of the critical coreferential expression as shown in Table 8.2. For gaze duration, there was a significant main effect such that pronouns were read more slowly than repeated names ($F_1(1, 15) = 8.43$, $p < .02$, $F_2(1, 47) = 12.97$, $p < .01$); there was no effect of singular-plural nor did the experimental factors interact. The surprising finding that pronouns have longer gaze durations than repeated names needs to be understood in relation to the probability of fixating these expressions. Because the coreferential expressions were short (pronouns or three-letter names), they were frequently skipped as is shown in Table 8.2. (This skipping was more apparent for pronouns than for names, an effect that was close to significant by subjects ($F_1(1, 15) = 4.24$, $p < .06$) and significant by items $F_2(1, 47) = 5.54$, $p < .05$).

Table 8.2. **Eyetracking Results for the Reading of Coreferential Expressions (Repeated Name or Pronoun)**

	Singular		Plural	
	Name	Pronoun	Name	Pronoun
Gaze duration on coreferential word (ms)	178	198	176	195
Proportion first-pass fixation on coreferential word	.510	.437	.505	.406
Gaze duration on coreferential plus preceding word (ms)	309	280	306	262
Rereading duration on coreferential word (ms)	91	44	68	70
Probability of regression into region	0.230	0.129	0.129	0.176
Probability of regression out of region	0.102	0.035	0.059	0.074

It is commonly argued that words are skipped because they are processed while viewing the preceding word. Thus, a region of reading was defined that consisted of the critical referring expression and the word that preceded it. As shown in Table 8.2, gaze durations were longer in the repeated name condition than in the pronoun condition ($F_1(1, 15) = 27.8, p < .01$; $F_2(1, 47) = 11.96, p < .01$); neither singular–plural nor the interaction of singular–plural and type of referring expression showed significant differences. As such, it appears that on first-pass reading, clauses with pronouns are read more quickly than those with names, though there is no evidence of an interaction of this effect with the prominence of the antecedent. Interpretation of this effect by itself is difficult because it could be due to processing of coreference or it could be due to inherent differences in processing names and pronouns.

With respect to measures of later processing, the effect of the prominence of the antecedent is quite clear. The time spent re-reading the critical coreferential word showed a strong interaction between the singular–plural and name–pronoun manipulations ($F_1(1, 15) = 12.08, p < .003$; $F_2(1, 47) = 5.44, p < .05$). Re-reading times were longer in the singular-name condition than in plural-name condition, and were longer in the plural-pronoun condition than in the singular-pronoun condition. Consistent with the findings on re-reading, the probability of regressions onto the critical coreferential word also showed this interaction ($F_1(1, 15) = 17.87, p < .005$; $F_2(1, 47) = 6.74, p < .02$). Finally, the probability of regressions from the critical coreferential word to an earlier point in the sentence showed the same pattern of difficulty ($F_1(1, 15) = 11.67, p < .005$; $F_2(1, 47) = 5.28, p < .05$).

With respect to processing the coreferential expression, the results show facilitated processing for pronouns that corefer with nonembedded expressions while repeated names exhibit the opposite pattern. This interaction is consistent with the predictions of the discourse-processing model of Gordon and Hendrick (1998) which ties together findings and ideas from linguistic research on binding with psycholinguistic research on coreferential processing. This interaction is not consistent with the notion that ease of coreferential processing in sentences like those in example 1 reflect expectations about how a sentence is going to be completed. Our completion data (Table 8.1) shows that the singular-pronoun condition is highly expected but that the other three conditions (singular-name, plural-pronoun, and plural-name) are not expected based on the first clause of the sentence. Thus, predictions based on expectations alone are not consistent with the specific form of the interactions that we find.

The relevant interaction is found clearly in late measures of comprehension (re-reading of the coreferential word and regressions to and from the coreferential word). This pattern is similar to what we have observed previously for similar materials in studies using self-paced reading (Gordon et al., 1999). The finding that pronouns are more readily understood when they corefer with a singular name rather than when they corefer with a name that is embedded in a conjoined phrase has also been shown by Albrecht and Clifton (1998).

8.1.2 ERPs and Coreferential Processing

As part of our effort to do coordinated studies of reading using eyetracking and ERPs, we have conducted an ERP study, reported in Swaab, Camblin, and Gordon (in press), that parallels the eyetracking study reported above. The coordinated use of eyetracking and ERPs is, in our view, a strong approach to study the time course and nature of the processes that underlie normal language comprehension because these methods are very complementary (e.g., Sereno, Rayner, & Posner, 1998).

Whereas eyetracking provides us with a measure of strategic eye movements during natural reading, ERP studies need RSVP (Rapid Serial Visual Presentation) to help prevent eye-movement artifacts in the electroencephalography (EEG) RSVP allows the time-locked analysis of each word, without the risk that critical words of interest may not contain a fixation. However, the unnatural aspect of slow-rate RSVP presentation has to be considered when interpreting ERP data. The ERP experiment described in Swaab et al. (in press) used a presentation rate of 500 ms (300 ms stimulus duration plus 200 ms ISI (inter-stimulus interval)). This presentation rate is reasonably common in the ERP literature because the separation between the words allows some ERP components of interest to be observed without overlap of ERPs to preceding and subsequent words. (Nonetheless, faster presentation rates have been successfully used with both visual and auditory presentation of sentence material, e.g., Swaab, Brown, & Hagoort, 1997). The use of this presentation rate is slower than typical reading rates, and may therefore affect normal reading processes, especially since readers have no preview of the upcoming words when RSVP is used.

ERPs, on the other hand, can provide us with a way of understanding the qualitative nature of experimental manipulations because separate ERP components have been linked to specific aspects of language processing and can therefore go beyond the level-of-difficulty information provided by eyetracking. This will be illustraded by the ERP study of coreferential processing discussed below.

The ERP components of primary interest in our study of coreferential processing were the N400 and the P600. As described earlier, the N400 amplitude depends on the ease with which a word can be integrated with the preceding context. In contrast, the P600 seems to be elicited primarily by difficulties in syntactic processing. Our results (Swaab et al., in press) were very clear with respect to how patterns of coreference affected ERPs (see Figure 8.1). For repeated names the N400 was consistently reduced in the plural relative to the singular condition; this effect had the posterior distribution that is characteristic of the N400. The overall pattern is consistent with the idea that there is greater difficulty in integrating the meaning of a repeated name following a singular antecedent than following a plural antecedent, a pattern that matches what we found in the eyetracking data reported above. But, in addition, we did not find evidence for a syntactic P600 effect. The finding of an N400 effect but no syntactic P600 effect is consistent with the idea that a semantic level of coreferential processing, not a syntactic one, is influenced by the structure of the antecedent. With respect to the pronoun condition, the findings are quite different, showing no significant effects of the type of antecedent (singular vs. plural) on the ERPs to the singular pronouns. This finding contrasts with the eyetracking results where it is seen that pronouns are more readily understood after singular antecedents than after plural antecedents (a finding also shown in self-paced reading studies; Albrecht & Clifton, 1998; Gordon et al., 1999).

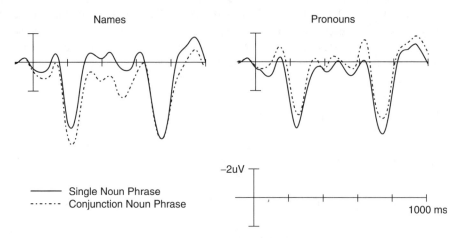

Figure 8.1. Grand average ERPs ($N = 20$) for electrode Cz to critical names (left) and critical pronouns (right) preceded by a singular noun phrase (solid line) or by a conjoined noun phrase (dotted line). The amplitude of the ERPs is on the vertical axis in microvolts, and the time in milliseconds is on the horizontal axis. ERP waveforms are displayed with a 100-ms pre-stimulus baseline. Negative polarity is depicted upwards. Whereas a clear difference can be seen between conditions for the names in the single versus conjunction conditions in the 300–500 ms N400 time window, this effect is absent for the pronouns.

8.1.3 Eyetracking, ERPs, and Coreferential Processing

Our studies using eyetracking and ERPs to study coreferential processing have, at least in our view, validated the wisdom of using these techniques to obtain converging evidence about language comprehension. A major finding in both eyetracking and ERP studies is that coreference with a repeated name is more difficult when the antecedent is a singular NP than when it is embedded within a pair of conjoined NPs. The results of the eyetracking experiment reported here show clearly that this difficulty occurs in later stages of processing. Those results are less clear with respect to whether the difficulty occurs in earlier stages of processing. Standard measures of first-pass reading did not show significant effects but the names used in the experiment were very short and were frequently skipped; a more expansive measure of first-pass reading did show a significant effect. The absence of a significant difficulty in traditional measures of first-pass reading is a null result and care must be taken before it is accepted. Further studies using longer names and additional controls should be able to provide a stronger basis for determining whether the repeated-name difficulty occurs in early measures of comprehension as measured using eyetracking. Whereas on the one hand, the eyetracking study provided evidence that the effects of coreference occurred in later stages of processing during natural reading, the ERP study, on the other hand, provided important evidence about the nature of the effects of focus on coreferential processing: That the repeated name manipulation affected the N400 rather than the P600 indicates that the effect has to do with integration of a semantic sort and not with the recovery from a problem in parsing (Swaab et al., in press).

Our studies also provide two instances where the results of the eyetracking and ERP research do not align. Eyetracking provided some evidence of a memory-load effect where reading times were slower in the words following the plural (two names) condition than following the singular (one name) condition. The existence of such an effect was difficult to assess in our ERP experiment because of the confound between the singular/plural manipulation and the sentential position of the subsequent words. Sentence position has a strong effect on ERPs. In addition, the eyetracking study showed that pronouns were more readily understood following a singular name than following a pair of conjoined names. This manipulation did not affect the ERPs to pronouns. The absence of an ERP effect on pronouns could be due to a number of factors: It has been shown that the N400 is less sensitive to closed- class words than to open-class words (e.g., Kutas and Hillyard, 1983; Neville, Mills, & Lawson, 1992; Nobre and McCarthy, 1994; Osterhout, Bersick, & McKinnon, 1997), and, additionally, the effects of pronouns may have been masked by the slower presentation rate in the ERP study. Experimental analysis of those possibilities may provide greater insight into the processing of pronominal reference.

Understanding coreferential processing is essential to understanding how people determine meaning during language comprehension. Coreferential processing also provides an excellent opportunity for studying the interaction of language and memory as processing occurs. In this chapter we illustrated a new methodological approach to study this, namely the coordinated use of eyetracking and ERPs. Our results on coreferential processing illustrated that these methods can provide unique as well as complementary data, which can enhance our understanding of the interaction between language and memory processes.

8.2 ACKNOWLEDGMENTS

This research was supported by NSF grants BCS-0112231 to PCG and SES-0074634 to TYS, as well as by NIH 1-R01-MH066271-01A1 to PCG and TYS. Direct correspondence to Peter C. Gordon, Department of Psychology, University of North Carolina, Chapel Hill, NC 27599-3270, pcg@email.unc.edu. We thank Adriane Boyd and Marcus Johnson for help with this work.

References

Albrecht, J. E., & Clifton, C. K. (1998). Accessing singular antecedents in conjoined phrases. *Memory and Cognition, 26,* 599–610.

Brown, C. M., & Hagoort, P. (1993). The processing nature of the N400: evidence from masked priming. *Journal of Cognitive Neuroscience, 5,* 34–44.

Carreiras, M. (1997). Plural pronouns and the representation of their antecedents. *European Journal of Cognitive Psychology, 9,* 53–87.

Chwilla, D. J., Brown, C. M., & Hagoort, P. (1995). The N400 as a function of the level of processing. *Psychophysiology, 32,* 274–285.

Cloitre, M., & Bever, T. G. (1988). Linguistic anaphors, levels of representation, and discourse. *Language and Cognitive Processes, 3,* 293–322.

Duffy, S. A., & Rayner, K. (1990). Eye movements and anaphor resolution: Effects of antecedent typicality and distance. *Language and Speech, 33,* 103–119.

Ehrlich, K. (1983). Eye movements in pronoun assignment: A study of sentence integration. In K. Rayner (Ed.), *Eye movements in reading: Perceptual and language processes.* New York: Academic Press.

Ehrlich, K., & Rayner, K. (1983). Pronoun assignment and semantic integration during reading: Eye movements and immediacy of processing. *Journal of Verbal Learning and Verbal Behavior, 22,* 75–87.

Ferreira, F., & Henderson, J. M. (1995). Reading processes during syntactic analysis and reanalysis. In J. M. Henderson & M. Singer (Eds.), *Reading and language processing* (pp. 119–147). Hillsdale, NJ: Erlbaum.

Garrod, S., Freudenthal, D., & Boyle, E. A. (1994). The role of different types of anaphor in the on-line resolution of sentences in a discourse. *Journal of Memory and Language, 33*(1), 39–68.

Gernsbacher, M. A. (1989). Mechanisms that improve referential access. *Cognition, 32*(2), 99–156.

Gordon, P. C., Grosz, B. J., & Gilliom, L. A. (1993). Pronouns, names, and the centering of attention in discourse. *Cognitive Science, 17,* 311–347.

Gordon, P. C., & Hendrick, R. (1997). Intuitive knowledge of linguistic coreference. *Cognition, 62,* 325–370.

Gordon, P. C., & Hendrick, R. (1998). The representation and processing of coreference in discourse. *Cognitive Science, 22,* 389–424.

Gordon, P. C., Hendrick, R., Ledoux, K., & Yang, C. L. (1999). Processing of reference and the structure of language: An analysis of complex noun phrases. *Language and Cognitive Processes, 14,* 353–379.

Harris, T., Wexler, K., & Holcomb, P. (2000). An ERP investigation of binding and coreference. *Brain and Language, 75,* 313–346.

Holcomb, P. J. (1993). Semantic priming and stimulus degradation: Implications for the role of the N400 in language processing. *Psychophysiology, 30,* 47–61.

Just, M. A., & Carpenter, P. A. (1980). A theory of reading: from eye fixations to comprehension. *Psychological Review, 87,* 329–354.

Kaan, E., Harris, A., Gibson, E., & Holcomb, P. (2000). The P600 as an index of syntactic integration difficulty. *Language and Cognitive Processes, 15*(2), 159–201.

Kaan, E., & Swaab, T. Y. (2003). Repair, revision, and complexity in syntactic analysis: An electrophysiological differentiation. *Journal of Cognitive Neuroscience, 15,* 98–110.

Kaup, B., Kelter, S., & Habel, C. (2002). Representing referents of plural expressions and resolving plural anaphors. *Language and Cognitive Processes, 17*(4), 405–450.

Kennison, S. M., & Gordon, P. C. (1997). Comprehending referential expressions during reading: Evidence from eyetracking. *Discourse Processes, 24,* 229–252.

Koh, S., & Clifton, C. A. (2002). Resolution of the antecedent of a plural pronoun: Ontological categories and predicate symmetry. *Journal of Memory and Language, 46,* 830–844.

Kutas, M., & Hillyard, S. A. (1983). Event-related brain potentials to grammatical errors and semantic anomalies. *Memory and Cognition, 11,* 539–550.

Neville, H. J., Mills, D. L., & Lawson, D. S. (1992). Fractionating language: different neural subsystems with different sensitive periods. *Cerebral Cortex, 2,* 244–258.

Nobre, A. C., & McCarthy, G. (1994). Language-related ERPs: scalp distributions and modulation by word type and semantic priming. *Journal of Cognitive Neuroscience, 6,* 233–55.

Osterhout, L., Bersick, M., & McKinnon, R. (1997). Brain potentials elicited by words: word length and frequency predict the latency of an early negativity. *Biological Psychology, 46,* 143–68.

Osterhout, L., & Holcomb, P. J. (1992). Event-related brain potentials elicited by syntactic anomaly. *Journal of Memory and Language, 31,* 785–806.

Osterhout, L., Holcomb, P. J., & Swinney, D. A. (1994). Brain potentials elicited by garden-path sentences: Evidence of the application of verb information during parsing. *Journal of Experimental Psychology: Learning, Memory, and Cognition, 20,* 786–803.

Osterhout, L., & Mobley, L. A. (1995). Event-related brain potentials elicited by failure to agree. *Journal of Memory and Language, 34,* 739–773.

Rayner, K., Kambe, G., & Duffy, S. A. (2000). The effect of clause wrap-up on eye movements during reading. *The Quarterly Journal of Experimental Psychology, 53A*(4), 1061–1080.

Rayner, R. (1978). Eye movements in reading and information processing. *Psychological Bulletin, 85,* 618–660.

Rayner, R. (1998). Eye movements in reading and information processing: 20 years of research. *Psychological Bulletin, 124,* 372–422.

Reichle, E. D., Pollatsek, A., Fisher, D. L., & Rayner, K. (1998). Toward a model of eye movement control in reading. *Psychological Review, 105*(1), 125–157.

Rugg, M. D., Furda, J., & Lorist, M. (1988). The effects of task on the modulation of event-related potentials by word repetition. *Psychophysiology, 25,* 55–63.

Sanford, A. J., & Lockhart, F. (1990). Description types and method of conjoining as factors influencing plural anaphora: A continuation study of focus. *Journal of Semantics, 7,* 365–378.

Sereno, S. C., Rayner, K., & Posner, M. I. (1998). Establishing a time-line of word recognition: Evidence from eye movements and event-related potentials. *Neuroreport, 9*(10), 2195–2200.

Streb, J., Roesler, F., & Hennighausen, E. (1999). Event-related responses to pronoun and proper name anaphors in parallel and nonparallel discourse structures. *Brain and Language, 70*(2), 273–286.

Swaab, T. Y., Brown, C., & Hagoort, P. (1997). Spoken sentence comprehension in aphasia: Event-related potential evidence for a lexical integration deficit. *Journal of Cognitive Neuroscience, 9,* 39–66.

Swaab, T. Y., Camblin, C. C., & Gordon, P. C. (in press). Electrophysiological evidence of reversed lexical repetition effects in language processing. *Journal of Cognitive Neuroscience.*

van Berkum, J. J. A., Brown, C. M., & Hagoort, P. (1999a). Semantic integration in sentences and discourse: evidence from the N400. *Journal of Cognitive Neuroscience, 11,* 657–671.

van Berkum, J. J. A., Brown, C. M., & Hagoort, P. (1999b). Early referential context effects in sentence processing: Evidence from event-related brain potentials. *Journal of Memory and Language, 41*(2), 147–182.

van Petten, C., & Kutas, M. (1990). Interactions between sentence context and word frequency in event-related brain potentials. *Memory and Cognition, 18,* 380–393.

Note

1. One way of combining gaze duration and skipping into a single measure of first-pass reading is to compute averages based on all the opportunities that a reader has to read a word (as was done by Just & Carpenter, 1980). Thus, if the reader skips the word, a duration of zero is averaged in for that trial. Using this method of calculation, the first-pass reading times for the critical referring expressions showed no significant effects as a function of experimental conditions (all $F_s < 1$). It should also be noted that the first-pass reading times that we report are relatively brief. So as not to further inflate the skipping rates for the short words of interest, we did not exclude very brief fixations as is sometimes done.

Chapter 9
Production and Comprehension Measures in Assessing Plural Object Formation

ANTHONY J. SANFORD, PATRICK STURT,
LINDA MOXEY, LORNA MORROW, AND
CATHY EMMOTT

Whenever two or more individuals are mentioned in a text, it is subsequently possible to refer to some or all of these individuals using plural anaphoric expressions like *they*. Although there is a long tradition of research on singular anaphoric reference in language comprehension, surprisingly little work has been done on the mechanisms and representations that underlie plural reference. In this chapter, we outline the main research problems in plural reference and evaluate the utility of two experimental techniques that can be used to tackle these problems: eye-movement monitoring during reading and off-line sentence completion.

9.1 RESEARCH PROBLEMS IN PLURAL REFERENCE

The representation of plural objects is an underresearched topic in both theoretical semantics and psycholinguistics. In this section, we will outline some of the main issues surrounding this topic, with an emphasis on those that are of interest from the processing point of view. What kind of representation does the comprehender construct for a conjoined noun phrase like *John and Mary*, or for plural noun phrase like *the boys*? One question is whether there is a separate representation for each of the individuals that are denoted by the plural or conjoined phrase. For example, in the representation of *the boys*, is each boy ever represented separately, or is there always a single representation that denotes the whole set without individuating each boy? The issue at stake, which has recently been discussed in detail by Kaup, Kelter, and Habel (2002), can be seen more clearly when a noun phrase like *the boys* is combined with a predicate to form a sentence like *The boys enjoyed the film*. If there is a single nonindividuating representation for *the boys,* then the whole assemblage of boys is predicted of *enjoyed the film* (Kaup et al. call this the *assemblage token* view). On the other hand, if each boy is represented separately, then the sentence effectively describes a conjunction of many events, each of which involves a single boy enjoying the film (Kaup et al. call this the *atomic tokens* view). Collective predicates like *assemble* lend support to the idea that *the boys* is represented as a single, nonindividuating whole. This is because a sentence like *The boys assembled at the cinema* cannot mean that each boy individually assembled because *assemble* requires a plural subject. Kaup et al. point out, however, that whether or not a plural noun phrase is represented in an individuated way depends partly on the form of the noun phrase itself. So, if the determiner of the noun phrase is *each*, the individuated interpretation is encouraged, leading to an individuated interpretation of sentences like *each boy enjoyed the film*. This suggests that, given a number of individuals in the domain of discourse, the language processing system is capable of representing this collection of individuals in at least two different ways: as an unindividuated group or as a collection of individuated entities.

This distinction can be seen particularly clearly in the case of *split antecedents*, where the referents of a plural anaphor can be introduced separately, as in (1) and (2):

(1)   *Richard and Jill bought food from local shops.*
(2)   *He/She/They were preparing a dinner party.*

In (1), *Richard* and *Jill* are mentioned, and in (2), it is possible to refer to either of the two individuals separately, using singular pronouns (*he* or *she*), or to refer to them collectively, using a plural pronoun (*they*). What kind of semantic representation of *Richard* and *Jill* is necessary for these anaphoric references to be made? One widely accepted view is that, in order for a plural anaphor like *they* to refer successfully, there must be a complex plural reference object in the mental representation of the discourse (Eschenbach, Habel, Herwe, & Rehkamper 1989; Koh & Clifton, 2002; Kaup et al., 2002). This would mean that to use *They* in (2), for example, there must be some representation in which *Richard* and *Jill* are treated as a single grouped object akin to the *assemblage token* interpretation discussed above.

A number of interesting questions can be asked about complex reference objects and their role in processing. For example, exactly what information is represented in a complex reference object? There have been various proposals for the representation of plural reference objects in the literature. One possibility is to treat plural reference objects as atomic named individuals (for a proposal within the framework of discourse representation theory, see Gordon, Camblin, & Strau, chapter 8, this volume; also Gordon & Hendrick, 1998), and there are various other possibilities, some of which are discussed in Koh and Clifton (2002). However, from the processing point of view, all of these theoretical treatments share the prediction that, when a plural reference object exists in a mental representation, the totality of individuals will be more accessible to reference than any of the separate individuals involved. This means that in (1), for example, if people form a plural reference object after reading *Richard and Jill*, then subsequent processing in (2) should be relatively easy when the pronoun *they* is used because this pronoun can refer to the plural reference object, which is salient in the representation. If, on the other hand, a singular pronoun is used (*he* or *she*), then more processing effort would be expected since this refers to one of the separate individuals rather than the assemblage of individuals denoted by the plural reference object. This predicted difference in accessibility is crucial in the experimental evaluation of theories of plural reference.

A second important research issue concerns the conditions under which plural reference objects are formed or not formed. According to one possible account, set out in Albrecht and Clifton (1998), plural reference objects are formed in response to syntactic cues. One strong cue is noun phrase coordination: Conjoined noun phrases like *Richard and Jill* in (1) provide a strong cue towards forming a plural reference object. According to such theories, readers will be more likely to form a plural reference object when reading (1, repeated below) than when reading (3), simply because in (1) *Richard* and *Jill* are conjoined into a single constituent, while in (3) they are not:

(1)   *Richard and Jill bought food from local shops.*
(3)   *Richard bought food from local shops with Jill*

Thematic and discourse roles provide another clue towards the formation of plural reference objects. Sanford and Moxey (1995) presented an account of plurality and individuation with the Sanford and Garrod (1981, 1998) scenario-mapping theory as its basis. Within scenario-mapping theory, sentences find a fundamental interpretation by their elements being mapped into a data-structure (scenario) in long-term memory. So, if *Richard and Jill bought food from the local shops*, then both *Richard* and *Jill* will be mapped into a scenario of food shopping at local shops. Are *Richard* and *Jill* represented separately or together? According to the Sanford–Moxey account, both. To some extent they form an indistinguishable complex because they map into the same role in the shopping scenario. On the other hand, because they map into separate data-structures (e.g., Richard > + male; Jill > + female), they are also differentiated to some extent.

Sanford and Moxey assume that the equivalent of a complex object occurs when two or more elements share a common mapping, and that when the mapping is prominent in the discourse, it is readily accessed by a plural pronoun. Common roles may occur at several levels. For instance, at the sentence level, two elements may share a thematic role. So, if *John and Mary painted the room*, then the protagonists share the co-agent role. Of course, determination of thematic role may depend upon interpretation. Consider a case like *John painted the room with Mary*. One set of mappings would make them co-agents, while another might put *Mary* into the role of instrument, as in the case of action-painting using a human being as a means of applying paint. For this to happen, general knowledge or frequency information has to be applied in the form of possible or likely situations that might offer the alternative mappings, and of course, one will typically be more available or more easily construed than another. The tendency to produce a common mapping and focus on this mapping should be enhanced by the use of noun phrase coordination because two noun phrases conjoined by *and* will typically be assigned the same thematic role as is the case in (1). Note, however, that this is not an absolute restriction; cases like (4), in which each conjunct is assigned a different thematic role, are grammatically possible:

(4)   *Richard and Jill bought food and washed the car, respectively.*

However, the stylistic awkwardness of (4) suggests that, although grammatically possible, there is a very strong bias against individual conjuncts being assigned different thematic roles.

9.2 EXPERIMENTAL TECHNIQUES IN THE STUDY OF PLURALITY: COMPLETION PRODUCTION

As we have seen above, two of the current research problems in plural reference concern, on the one hand, how plural reference objects are represented, and on the other hand, in what circumstances representations of singular individuals might be combined into plural reference objects. In this section, we consider one of the simplest possible experimental techniques that can be used to look at these questions: completion production. In this technique, the experimental participant is required to produce a continuation (either spoken or written) for the initial part of a stimulus. The content of the continuation that the participant writes, or says, is then analyzed according to preset criteria in order to evaluate the experimental hypothesis.

Several aspects of the completion-production task make it ideal for studying plural reference. The first of these reasons is that the relative proportions of pronouns and nonpronominal noun phrases used in the continuation can be informative about discourse focus. Second, the actual content of the continuation can be informative about the thematic or discourse roles that have been assigned to the individuals mentioned in the given text. For example, consider example (1). If (1) is used as the given text in a completion- production task, then (a, b, and c) represent different possible continuations:

a. *They were preparing a dinner party.*
b. *He always preferred not to go to the big out-of-town supermarkets.*
c. *Richard was quite happy about that.*

Continuations (a) and (b) both begin with referential pronouns. According to standard assumptions (Grosz, Joshi, & Weinstein 1995), this implies that the referents of the pronouns are in discourse focus. The use of the plural pronoun in (a) suggests that the reference object combining *Richard* and *Jill* is in focus, while the use of the singular pronoun *he* in (b) suggests that *Richard* is in discourse focus. On the other hand, the use of the repeated name in (c) would suggest that *Richard* was not in focus when the participant made this continuation because repeated names represent a less preferred means of referring to focused individuals (Grosz et al., 1995). Therefore, if we collect a large number of continuations, then the relative frequencies of continuations like (a), (b), or (c) will be informative about whether the plural reference object or one or other of the individuals are in discourse focus. This means that the technique can be used to test theories about the conditions that lead to the formation of plural reference objects; sentence types that lead to the formation of plural reference objects should induce more *they* continuations and fewer *he* or *she* continuations in comparison to sentence types that do not lead to the formation of plural reference objects. This is because the formation of a plural reference object results in a lower accessibility for each separate individual denoted by the object. Also, any singular references following sentence types that lead to plural reference objects, again, should tend to use proper names rather than pronouns because the singular individual should not be in focus. So, completion production can give us clues about which individuals or groups of individuals are and are not in discourse focus following the processing of a section of text.

9.3 EYETRACKING AND OTHER ON-LINE TASKS

While off-line tasks like continuation production are certainly informative about interpretation, they tell us nothing about the time course of processing; this information is only available if we use an on-line task. In this chapter, we will consider eyetracking during reading as an example of an on-line technique that gives detailed time-course information. Eyetracking allows a continuous measurement of reading time through a sentence or text. As the subject does not have to press a button to move through the text, the technique allows a greater approximation to normal reading than is available in self-paced reading, and reading speeds do not differ from a normal reading situation. Another on-line technique that has proved fruitful in the study of plural anaphora is *speeded completions* (Carreiras, 1997). In Carreiras' study, participants were presented with short texts, followed by a sentence-initial pronoun. The task was to use the pronoun to start a spoken completion of the text. The time between the presentation of the pronoun and the onset of the response was recorded. In one study, Carreiras manipulated whether two individuals in the discourse were described as being in close in physical space (e.g., both in Madrid) relative to a third character, or as being in distant in physical space (e.g., *Thomas* in Madrid and *Sophie* in Barcelona). When completions began with a plural pronoun, completion onsets were slower in the different location condition than in the same location condition. However, this difference was not obtained for the singular pronouns. These results support the idea that plural reference is facilitated when two individuals play a role in the same scenario. The speeded completion technique is useful for taking "snapshots" of the state of processing at particular points in reading. However, what it lacks is a way of looking at the *dynamics* of processing or how preferences change over time. Similar remarks could be made for the whole-sentence self-paced reading technique, which has also been usefully applied to the study of plural reference (Gordon, Hendrick, Ledoux, & Yang, 1999). In this technique, reading times are recorded for whole sentences. Although the technique is useful for looking at *global* differences in processing difficulty, it does not yield information about how these differences emerge or change over time.

Eyetracking during reading is particularly well suited to testing how differences in processing difficulty unfold over time. This means that we can use the technique to study plural reference by making references to individuals or groups of individuals in contexts where the referents are predicted to be more or less accessible. The assumption is that in cases where a pronoun refers to an antecedent that is relatively inaccessible, there should be processing difficulty in relation to cases where the antecedent is more accessible. So, for example, other things being equal, it should be relatively difficult to process a singular pronoun following a sentence in which it is hypothesized that a plural reference object has been created, like *Richard and Jill went bought food at the local shops. He ... .* This experimental logic was used by Albrecht and Clifton (1998) using eyetracking, and by Gordon et al. (1999) using whole-sentence self-paced reading. In the case of eyetracking, the eye-movement-record will give us very fine-grained information about the time course with which this effect manifests itself, information that is not available in the continuation production method.

In the following text, we look at three research problems that we have addressed using eyetracking and continuation methodologies in our laboratory.

9.4 PROBLEM 1: SYNTACTIC GROUPING AND THEMATIC ROLES

Moxey, Sanford, Sturt, and Morrow (2004) investigated the influence of common role as a determinant of performance with plural references. They also investigated the effect of syntactic grouping using materials such as the following:

(5) a. Conjoined, common role: *Mary and John cleared up the garden.*
    b. Common role: *Mary cleared up the garden with John.*
    c. Benefactive: *Mary cleared up the garden for John.*

The common-role condition (5b) represented a situation where the preferred default interpretation is one in which both *Mary* and *John* are assigned the agent thematic role (or co-agent interpretation). The conjoined (5a) condition added to this the extra constraint of syntactic grouping. In the case of the benefactive condition (5c), *Mary* and *John* are clearly assigned different thematic roles. Consider first the production of continuations. Our prediction was that the benefactive (5c), by inducing different roles, should not encourage the construction of a plural reference object. This would mean that plural pronominal reference would be very rare in continuations in this condition. In contrast, plural reference objects should often be created during the processing of the common role materials (5b), leading to a greater number of continuations with plural pronouns. Finally, if the common-role interpretation is enhanced by the use of *and*, then the conjoined condition (5a) should make plural pronoun continuations even more likely. If our assumptions about common roles are wrong, then the common-role and the benefactive conditions should lead to similar patterns of pronoun usage.

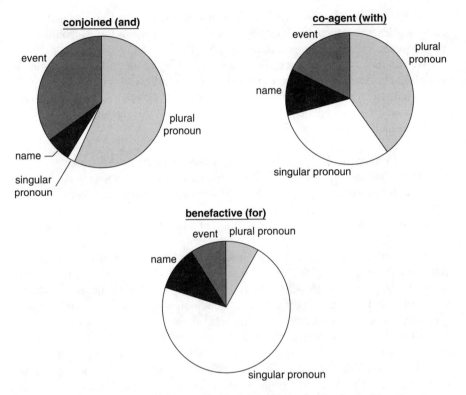

Figure 9.1. Pie-chart showing the principal continuation categories for problem 1.

There were significant differences between each of the conditions, as shown in Figure 9.1. For example, there were more plural pronominal references in the conjunction condition (5a) than in the common-role condition (5b), and there were very few at all in the benefactive (5c) condition. In contrast, there were virtually no singular pronominal references in the conjunction condition (5a) and intermediate number in the common-role condition (5b), and these responses predominated in the benefactive condition (5c). These findings are consistent with the idea that a common role leads to plural pronominal reference, and that the syntactic grouping enhances this effect. There appears to be an asymmetry between the level of singular pronoun responses in the benefactive case (72%) and the level of plural pronouns in the conjoined case (57%), suggesting that while the benefactive case leads to strong singular reference objects, the conjoined case leads to somewhat weaker or less available plural reference objects. This result (echoing an earlier finding by Sanford & Lockhart, 1990) might be taken to suggest that singular and plural reference objects are both available in the conjoined condition. However, there are almost no singular pronominal references used in the conjoined case, so this seems to be unlikely. Rather, the lack of plural pronominal continuations seemed to be due to people electing to continue by producing some detail of the action depicted in the stimulus sentence, rather than anything else. Continuations of this sort tacitly assume that both individuals are acting together and are thus consistent with a strong plural reference object. This is not consistent with the idea that both singular and plural entities are in focus and thus supports the idea that the use of the conjunction almost forces the use of a plural reference object.

We can look at similar questions using eyetracking as an on-line technique. In this case, the same initial sentences (5a–c) would be followed by a second sentence that included a pronominal reference, and the number of the pronoun (singular versus plural) would be manipulated. Moxey et al. (2004) did this, resulting in materials similar to the following:

(5) a. Conjoined: *Mary and John cleared up the garden.*
    b. Common role: *Mary cleared up the garden with John.*
    c. Benefactive: *Mary cleared up the garden for John.*

(6) SENTENCE 2:   *She/They enthusiastically made a bonfire.*

It was predicted that processing difficulty should be found at or immediately following the pronoun in the second sentence (6), in cases where the pronoun is forced to refer to an unfocussed antecedent. Thus, the plural pronoun should be relatively easy to process in the conjoined condition where it is hypothesized that a plural reference object has been created, and it should be relatively hard to process in the benefactive case where it is hypothesized that a plural reference object has not been created. The reverse pattern should be found when a singular pronoun is used; processing difficulty should be greatest in the conjoined condition because the discourse focus should consist of the plural reference object rather than any of the singular individuals that make it up. Processing difficulty should be easiest in the benefactive condition where a plural reference object is hypothesized to be least likely to have been formed and where it is very likely that the first-mentioned individual is in discourse focus. Earlier attempts to uncover reading-time differences in the case of plural pronoun resolution as a function of conditions related to same or different theta role failed. Clifton and Ferreira (1987) used self-paced reading of text segments and found no effects, while in an unpublished study, Huitema (1989) used eyetracking but also failed to find significant effects, possibly because the critical region in many of the experimental items was close to the left margin of the line of text, a problem that Moxey et al. (2004) avoided.

In Moxey et al's study, the predicted pattern was obtained. At the adverb immediately following the pronoun in the second sentence, first-pass eye-movement measures (first-pass reading times and regression-path times) showed an interaction between the two factors of antecedent sentence type (conjoined, co-agent, and benefactive) and pronoun number (singular versus plural). The interaction showed particularly long processing time for the singular conjoined condition. Figure 9.2 shows this interaction in the regression-path times on this adverb (regression-path times consist of the sum of fixations from the time the region is first entered from the left to the time the region is first exited to the right). The plot of the interaction in Figure 9.2 shows that the two conjoined conditions ("and") differ in processing difficulty, with longer reading times on the singular than the plural. However, singular and plural conditions did not differ for the co-agent ("with") or benefactive ("for")

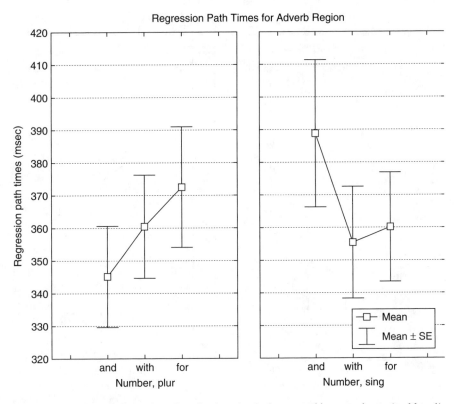

Figure 9.2. Regression-path times for adverb region in the eyetracking experiment (problem 1).

conditions. In the last region of the sentence, there was evidence for processing difficulty in the plural benefactive condition relative to the other plural conditions, as can be seen in Figure 9.3. This figure shows differences among the plural conditions; regression path times were significantly longer for the plural benefactive condition ("for") compared with both the plural conjoined condition ("and") and plural co-agent condition ("with"). The figure also illustrates a general trend for sentences with singular pronouns to be read more slowly than sentences with plural pronouns.

The eyetracking study can tell us many things over and above the continuation study. First, we know that in the conjoined conditions, the plural reference object is available very soon after participants begin to read the second sentence. We know this because the first-pass eye-movement measures show a statistical interaction on the word immediately following the pronoun (Figure 9.2). There are two possible explanations for this interaction. First, it could be the case that plural reference objects are only constructed retrospectively when a pronoun is processed, and the relative ease or difficulty of this retrospective process depends on properties such as role assignment or syntactic structure. The alternative explanation is that these role-based or syntactic cues influence the decision of whether to build a plural reference object *before* the pronoun is processed. The obtained pattern of results

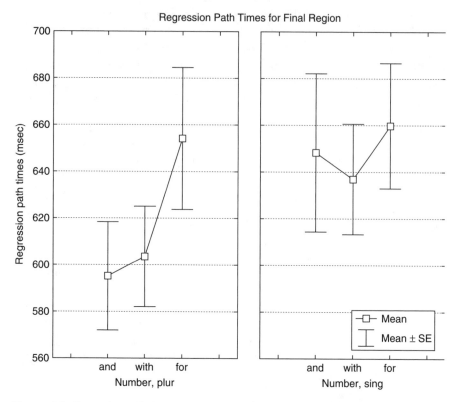

Figure 9.3. Regression-path times for final region in the eyetracking experiment (problem 1).

suggests that, at least in the conjoined conditions, the plural reference object is constructed during the processing of the first sentence. If plural reference objects were constructed retrospectively, it would be difficult to explain the processing cost associated with the singular pronoun in the conjoined condition in the early eye-movement measures; why would the processor attempt to construct a plural reference object on encountering a singular pronoun? In the completion-production experiment, by contrast, although we can infer that the formation of plural reference objects did differ according to condition, we cannot know when these objects were formed. For example, participants might have interpreted the first sentence without ever forming plural reference objects even in the conjoined condition and only later formed plural reference objects once they had thought about a suitable continuation. A second piece of information from eyetracking, but not from continuation, concerns differences between the plural and singular conditions. In some of the measures in the regions of the second sentence, effects were found suggesting that sentences with singular pronouns were read more slowly than sentences with plural pronouns. This effect was particularly apparent at the final region of the sentence (see Figure 9.3). One possible interpretation of this difference is that it reflects differences in the depth of processing between singular and plural anaphors. For example, resolution of singular anaphors might be obligatory and detailed, requiring greater processing resources.

However, it is only by combining the on-line and off-line data that we can gain a full picture that includes information about the focus properties of plural reference, the effect on interpretations, and the time course of the processes involved. The continuation study appeared to rule out the possibility that atomic individuals were in focus along with complex reference objects under the conjoined condition. Also, the continuations provided a rich source of information about possible interpretations for the common-role condition. Where singular pronouns were used in continuations, interpretations showing different role mappings for the two atomic individuals were apparent. For example, after reading the sentence *Mary cut the grass with John*, subsequent completions occasionally yielded examples like *She should have used a lawnmower instead*, in which case one may conclude that the instrumental role has been assigned. The incidence of such cases in the common-role condition is consistent with the idea that plural reference objects require common-role mapping of atomic individuals for their formation, and that the alternative mappings may be the reason for the failure of the common-role case to have the same effect as the conjoined case in encouraging the formation of plural reference objects.

9.5 PROBLEM 2: MIXING DESCRIPTION TYPES WITHIN GROUPS

It is possible that the provision of grounds for making a contrast between two atomic individuals might reduce the likelihood of those individuals being given interpretations that put them into a common role. Indeed, there are some cases where it is quite difficult to put individuals into a common role, cases of mixed ontology like *Martha and the brandy* (see Sanford & Moxey, 1995, for a discussion; also Koh & Clifton, 2002, for related issues). We shall not deal with such extreme cases here but rather focus on the effect of describing two humans by different means: proper name and role description. In earlier work using continuations, Sanford and Lockhart (1990) found that plural continuations were produced much less often in Name + Role cases like *Martha and the car dealer* than in Name + Name cases like *Martha and David*. Moxey et al. (2003) examined this finding further, using both continuation-production and eyetracking measures.

Continuations were obtained to sentences headed by Name + Name and Name + Role conjoined noun phrases. The results replicated Sanford and Lockhart (1990) in that the proportion of plural pronominal continuations was 50% for the Name + Name continuation, falling to only 27% in the Name + Role condition. As with the continuation study mentioned above, there were very few singular pronominal continuations and many simple event continuations for the Name + Name condition, so we conclude again that in this condition, a complex plural reference object is in focus. However, in the Name + Role condition, there was an increase in both the number of pronominal references and in the number of (singular) repeat name or repeat role-descriptions. This suggested an increase in the tendency to want to refer to the individuals separately, and at least a weak licensing of the use of a pronoun to do this. There was also a strong tendency to refer to the named character rather than the role-described character. Elsewhere (Sanford, Moar, & Garrod, 1998), evidence was found for just such a preference in other types of text. This shows that a difference in the form of referring to characters triggers a tendency to want to refer to them separately in continuation production.

What does this predict for eyetracking? First, plural pronominal anaphors should be easier to process than singular pronominal anaphors for the Name + Name condition. Second, if the Name + Role condition is harder to process when the description itself is encountered, then this should be reflected in the eye-movement pattern prior to a pronoun being encountered. We might also expect some differences between Name + Role and Name + Name conditions in terms of the relative ease of processing singular and plural pronominal anaphors, particularly if there is a reduced tendency to produce a focused complex plural reference object in the case of Name + Role; resolving plural pronouns should perhaps be more difficult in Name + Role case, while the ease of resolving singular references should be easier. However, we note that although there is a reliable tendency for more singular pronouns to be used in the Name + Role continuations, numerically the incidence of singular pronouns in that condition is not that high—at about 15%—so what was revealed in continuations may not be reflected in eyetracking measures.

In the eyetracking study, Moxey et al. (2004) used materials like (7a) and (7b). The slashes indicate regions of analysis, and alternatives that differed according to the experimental manipulation are enclosed in square brackets.

(7) a. Conjoined format
        Mary and [John\the landlord]/painted the room./
        The ladder annoyed/[her\them] because/it was hard to move./
        The paint fumes lingered for days./

     b. Co-agent format
        Mary painted the room with [John\the landlord]./
        The ladder annoyed/[her\them] because/it was hard to move./
        The paint fumes lingered for days./

There were several interesting findings. First, in the second region of the conjoined condition [*painted the room* in (7a)], a variety of measures (e.g., regression-path time, proportion of first-pass regressions, total times) showed longer reading times as well as more and longer regressions in the Name + Role than in the Name + Name condition. So the idea that the former combination (e.g., *Mary and the landlord*) is harder to process is vindicated. Second, region 3 (*her/them because*) was analyzed as a function of description type, format (conjoined versus co-agent), and pronoun number (singular or plural). In total times and first-pass reading times, there was an interaction of format (conjoined vs. co-agent) with pronoun (singular vs. plural), such that plural pronouns were more difficult to resolve under co-agent than under conjoined format, while singular pronouns were more difficult to resolve under conjoined than under co-agent format. However, there were no interactions involving description type. This suggested that plural reference objects are formed under both description types, but the Name + Role description type initially causes some processing difficulty. However, at the time of reading, the Name + Role description type does not put atomic individuals into focus.

Putting together the two studies, we can say that the tendency for Name + Role to increase the separation of atomic individuals is reflected in the longer-term tendency to want to refer to the named character; however, this does not happen during integration of the pronoun during reading.

9.6 PROBLEM 3: CANONICAL ORDERING OF ELEMENTS

Judgments of descriptions using examples like (8a) or (8b) suggest that (8b) is the more unusual method of description:

(8) a. *Mary and the doctor discussed the problem.*
     b. *The doctor and Mary discussed the problem.*

Examination of naturally occurring examples of mixed descriptions in literary writing (Morrow, Sanford, & Emmott, 2004) reveals that cases of the order Role + Name are much rarer than those of Name + Role. This could be due to shorter NPs preceding longer NPs in English (e.g., salt and pepper, wash and brush-up), or it could be because there is something special about proper names. In our first attempts to establish some basic facts, we asked whether the noncanonical order has any consequences for the production of complex reference objects, for instance, by amplifying the difference already seen for Name + Role compared to Name + Name. Both methodologies were applied to these questions by Morrow, Sanford, and Emmott (2004). Part of the interest in the problem came from an ongoing attempt to see how deviations from canonical formats might be used as a stylistic device in creative writing and literature, and the first task was to establish whether deviations from form have any influence on processing at all.

Materials like those described for problem 2 above (7a, b) were used, except that the first sentences contrasted Name + Role with Role + Name, as in (9a) and (9b); slashes indicate region boundaries, and the numbers indicate regions to the left of the boundaries:

(9) a. *Mary and the landlord 1/painted the room2/.*
     b. *The landlord and Mary 1/painted the room2/.*

Analysis of first-pass times in the first region showed a reliable difference between the two orderings, with Name + Role resulting in shorter times (at 628 ms) than the noncanonical Role + Name ordering (at 690 ms). This suggests that noncanonical ordering information is detected on very early reading. There were no effects on region 2. Also, there were no total time differences in region 1, this being explained by longer second-pass reading times in the Name + Role case than in the Role + Name. We are unsure of the explanation for this, but it may be the case that the processing difficulty for Name + Role obtained in problem 2 is offset in the present study by the longer first-pass time on Role + Name. There were no differences in the difficulty of processing singular and plural pronouns under the two orders.

The presence of an effect of noncanonical ordering provides grounds for the possibility of that ordering being used to cue special effects, for instance, somehow emphasizing the role-described character. However, a continuation task showed no such effect. Instead, there was an overwhelming tendency to refer to the named character in both cases, and there were no differences between the order in terms of the proportions of plural or singular pronouns, or repeat name or repeat role-descriptions produced. As it stands, there is no evidence that the noncanonical order is used to direct attention to different things in terms of discourse focus.

With problem 3, eyetracking reveals some subtle effects that would not be uncovered in overall reading times, and continuations cast doubt on a potential impact of noncanonical ordering on discourse focus, although this requires more investigation.

9.7 CONCLUSIONS

In this paper, we have shown how a number of research questions in plural reference can be addressed using eye-movement recording and continuation-production measures. We have seen how both on-line and off-line experimental techniques can be informative about the representations and processes that are involved.

The continuation method is a production-based measure, which is informative about the nature of the interpretations and inferences that are made after comprehending an initial fragment. As we have seen in the discussion above, this technique is particularly well suited to questions about whether or not some individual or group of individuals is in discourse focus, and it can also be used to probe other aspects of interpretation, for example, the thematic role that has been assigned to a particular noun phrase. It may reveal relatively small differences in preferences, which may be too weak to be revealed by eyetracking measures.

Unlike continuation production, eyetracking during reading does not provide direct evidence about interpretations. Instead, indirect evidence about discourse focus, for example, is available through indications of processing difficulty in the eye-movement record. The obvious advantage of eyetracking is that it allows us to determine which information is available at which time. Moreover, because of the various first- and second-pass eye-movement measures, as well as the ability to divide stimulus sentences into analysis regions, it is possible to detect subtle effects that in the present work were not revealed in less sensitive on-line techniques such as self-paced reading.

In our discussion we have seen several examples of experimental investigations where a full picture of plural reference processes could only be obtained by combining the data from the on-line and off-line experiments. For example, in problem 2 (mixed-description types within groups), we investigated whether referring to two individuals with different description types (e.g., *Mary and the landlord*) as opposed to two named individuals (e.g., *Mary and John*) decreased the usual tendency to form a plural reference object in a conjoined noun phrase. The continuation data did show that the mixed-description types slightly increased the accessibility of the named character. However, the eye-movement data suggested that a plural reference object was nevertheless formed for both description types and that an increased processing load was found in the mixed-description type.

To conclude, continuation is informative about interpretation and role assignment, and may show small trends that are not picked up in eyetracking. Eyetracking may show on-line processing effects that are subtle and do not influence interpretation. In general, we found the techniques to produce converging evidence for the strongest effects.

9.8 ACKNOWLEDGMENT

This research was supported by ESRC Grant R000223497 and AHRB Grant B/IA/AN8799/APN13740.

References

Albrecht, J., & Clifton, C. (1998). Accessing singular antecedents in conjoined phrases. *Memory and Cognition, 26,* 599–610.

Carreiras, M. (1997). Plural pronouns and the representation of their antecedents. *European Journal of Cognitive Psychology, 9*(1), 53–87.

Clifton, C., & Ferreira, F. (1987). Discourse structure and anaphora: Some experimental results. In M. Coltheart (Ed.), *Attention and performance* 10, (pp. 635–654). London: Erlbaum.

Eschenbach, C. C., Habel, C., Herweg., M., & Rehkamper, K. (1989). Remarks on plural anaphora. *Proceedings of 4th conference of European chapter of the association for computational linguistics,* University of Manchester, Manchester, UK, pp. 161–167.

Gordon, P. C., Camblin, C., & Swaab, T. Y. (this volume): *Referential Processing: evidence from eyetracking and ERPs.*

Gordon, P. C., & Hendrick, R. (1998). The representation and processing of coreference in discourse. *Cognitive Science, 22,* 389–424.

Gordon, P. C., Hendrick, R., Ledoux, K., & Yang, C. L. (1999). Processing of reference and the structure of language: An analysis of complex noun phrases. *Language and Cognitive Processes, 14*(4), 353–379.

Grosz, B. J., Joshi, A. K., & Weinstein, S. (1995). Centering: A framework for modelling the local coherence of discourse. *Computational Linguistics, 21,* 203–226.

Huitema, J. S. (1989). *Pronouns and the representation of discourse.* Unpublished master's thesis, University of Massachusetts, Amherst.

Kaup, B., Kelter, S., & Habel, C. (2002). Representing referents of plural expressions and resolving plural anaphors. *Language and Cognitive Processes, 17*(4), 405–450.

Koh, S., & Clifton, C. A. (2002). Resolution of the antecedent of a plural pronoun: Ontological categories and predicate symmetry. *Journal of Memory and Language, 46,* 830–844.

Morrow, L. I., Sanford, A. J., & Emmott, C. (2003). *Canonical ordering and plural reference.* Manuscript in preparation.

Moxey, L. M., Sanford, A. J., Sturt, P., & Morrow, L. I. (2004). Constraints on the formation of plural reference objects: The influence of role, conjunction, and type of description.

Manuscript submitted for publication.

Sanford, A. J., & Garrod, S. C. (1981). *Understanding written language: Explorations of comprehension beyond the sentence.* Chichester, UK: Wiley.

Sanford, A. J., & Garrod, S. C. (1998). The role of scenario mapping in text comprehension. *Discourse processes, 26,* 159–190.

Sanford, A. J., & Lockhart, F. (1990). Description types and method of conjoining as factors influencing plural anaphora: A continuation study of focus. *Journal of Semantics, 7,* 365–378.

Sanford, A., Moar, K., & Garrod, S. C. (1988). Proper names as controllers of discourse focus. *Language and Speech, 31,* 43–56.

Sanford, A. J., & Moxey, L. M. (1995). Notes on plural reference and the scenario-mapping principle in comprehension. In C. Habel & G. Rickheit (Eds.), *Focus and cohesion in discourse.* Berlin: Walter de Gruyter.

Chapter 10
Constituent Order Priming from Reading to Listening: A Visual-World Study

CHRISTOPH SCHEEPERS AND MATTHEW W.
CROCKER

10.1 INTRODUCTION

Studies of sentence generation have repeatedly shown a tendency for language producers to maintain aspects of syntactic structure over consecutive trials, if possible. When participants are restricted in their choice of possible syntactic alternatives in one trial (the *prime*) and are then confronted with a wider range of possible syntactic alternatives in the following trial (the *target*), there is an above-chance likelihood that they will reproduce the structure they have generated in the prime trial, despite the fact that they are free to produce an alternative structure in the target trial (e.g., Bock, 1986; Bock & Loebell, 1990; Pickering & Branigan, 1998; Corley & Scheepers, 2002; among many others). This phenomenon, which is commonly being referred to as *syntactic priming*, has been taken to reflect a mechanism whereby syntactic representations generated in the prime trial retain some residual activation over time which facilitates their reactivation in the following target trial.

The assumption of a similar short-term adaptation mechanism in comprehension is not only plausible (just like production, sentence comprehension requires the activation of syntactic representations, as highlighted in many chapters of this volume), but also widely agreed upon by psycholinguists (at least implicitly, as evidenced, for example, by comments on comprehension studies that do *not* control for syntactic priming). The comprehension of a given sentence structure in one trial may facilitate the comprehension of the same structure in a subsequent trial and, more specifically, syntactic ambiguity resolution within a given sentence may be influenced by the way in which the same (or a similar) ambiguity was disambiguated in the previously encountered sentence. Thus, the way in which sentences are being parsed might be preserved over consecutive trials, which is why it is common practice to have syntactically unrelated "fillers" between the trials of interest when the experimental focus is on general syntactic ambiguity resolution strategies in comprehension.

However, despite a growing body of evidence for syntactic priming in production, experimental findings supporting a similar mechanism in comprehension are still rather sparse and, where available, not very conclusive. They either allow for alternative explanations (lexical or metrical parallelism rather than structural parallelism) or they fail to demonstrate reliable priming effects altogether, partly because of rather crude stimulus presentation techniques (e.g., Frazier, Taft, Roeper, & Ehrlich, 1984; Branigan, 1995; Weskott, 2002). In these studies, structural priming has mostly been measured (more or less successfully) in terms of faster reading times for targets that match the structure of the preceding primes compared to targets that do not match the structure of the primes.

The present study aims at investigating the issue of syntactic priming in comprehension by looking at the resolution of constituent order ambiguity in German. It is a well-established fact that although German allows for variable sequencing of subject and object NPs at the sentence surface, native German speakers reliably prefer a subject-before-object ordering (e.g., Hemforth & Konieczny (Eds.), 2000; see also Fiebach et al., chapter 17, this volume). Furthermore, the German case marking system, which is crucial for designating syntactic function in that language, is partially ambiguous so that, for example, sentence-initial feminine singular NPs like "Die Krankenschwester ... " (The nurse [fem, sing] ...) can be interpreted as either subject (typically the agent) or object (typically the patient). Since the subject-first ordering is generally preferred, this sentence-initial case ambiguity is usually resolved in favor of a nominative (i.e., subject) interpretation of the critical NP (e.g., Hemforth, 1993).

The question we are going to address is whether this preference is subject to priming from a previous trial in which participants have to process either an unambiguous subject-first or object-first sentence. Provided that syntactic priming in comprehension exists, the subject-first preference should be strengthened after having encountered an unambiguous subject-first sentence in the previous trial; conversely, it should be weakened, or even overruled, after having encountered an object-first sentence in the previous trial. (Our experiment will include a baseline condition whereby such modulations of syntactic preference become more explicit). Moreover, we will look at priming effects across different modes of processing. While participants are presented with unambiguous written sentences (for reading) in the prime trials, they will listen to temporarily ambiguous auditory sentences in the target trials. This ensures that potential priming effects must rely upon the preservation of abstract sentence representations rather than low-level perceptual strategies.

In order to measure the critical constituent order preferences in the auditory targets, we will make use of the visual-world eyetracking paradigm (e.g., Cooper, 1974; Tanenhaus, Spivey-Knowlton, Eberhard, & Sedivy, 1995; Altmann & Kamide, 1999; Kamide, Scheepers, & Altmann, 2003; Kamide, Altmann, & Haywood, 2003; Scheepers, Kamide, & Altmann, 2003; see also Boland, chapter 5; Brown-Schmidt et al., chapter 13; and Huettig & Altmann; and Mitchell, chapter 2, this volume). The auditory materials will be concurrently presented with related visual scenes in which an *ambiguous* character (serving both as agent and patient) is pictured together with an unambiguous *agent* character (acting upon the ambiguous character) and an unambiguous *patient* character (being acted upon by the ambiguous character).

(The pictures will actually show two transitive events at the same time.) The case-ambiguous first NP of the auditory sentences will always refer to the ambiguous character.

Previous visual-world research has shown that eye movements around a visual scene are closely time-locked with the related auditory input, and more importantly, that participants are able to *anticipate* forthcoming linguistic reference to objects in the scene. Visual attention is often drawn to critical objects in the scene before these objects are actually mentioned in the auditory input (Altmann & Kamide, 1999; Kamide et al., 2003; Kamide et al., 2003; Scheepers et al., 2003). For example, Kamide et al. (2003) and Scheepers et al. (2003) found that native German partic-ipants rapidly combine unambiguous case-marking information at the first NP (if available) and semantic restrictions provided by the verb in order to predict a second forthcoming NP-argument. In these experiments, participants were presented with visual scenes showing, e.g., a hare, a cabbage, a fox, and a tree (distractor), while at the same time listening to unambiguous subject-first sentences like *Der Hase frisst gleich den Kohl* (The hare [nom] eats shortly the cabbage [acc]) or unambig-uous object-first sentences like *Den Hasen frisst gleich der Fuchs* (The hare [acc] eats shortly the fox [nom]). Note that the critical actions were not displayed in the pictures (unlike in the present study). The main finding was that shortly after the verb was available in the auditory input (and clearly before the second NP was encountered), participants already launched reliably more and longer looks to the appropriate NP2-referents in the picture (i.e., the cabbage in the subject-first condi-tion and the fox in the object-first condition) than to their inappropriate counterparts, suggesting that the most likely forthcoming referent was anticipated on the basis of the linguistic and visual information available. Crucially, in order to be able to display this pattern of anticipatory eye movements, participants must have taken into account which one of the two available argument slots of the verb (subject or object) has already been filled with the first NP and its referent.

Given these findings, we assume that in the present experiment, the interpretation of the ambiguous first-NP referent (as either subject or object) should reveal itself in anticipatory looks to the visually unambiguous characters in the scene. That is, if participants prefer the subject-interpretation of the ambiguous first-NP referent, they should pay more attention to the unambiguous *patient* character (the most likely forthcoming object); however, if they prefer the object-interpretation of the ambig-uous first-NP referent, they should pay more attention to the unambiguous *agent* character (the most likely forthcoming subject). The reasoning behind this assump-tion is that once listeners have committed to a particular role assignment for the ambiguous first-NP referent (which is assumed to proceed very quickly), they should start focusing their attention on a character that is likely to fill the *remaining* argument slot, as was the case in the earlier studies.[1]

A final important point is that all of our auditory target sentences will be disambiguated further downstream, after the case-ambiguous initial NP has been processed. This enables us to investigate potential garden-path effects during listening. Overall, we expect that structures disambiguated towards an object-initial reading will be harder to process than structures disambiguated towards a subject-initial reading (see Hemforth, 1993; Hemforth & Konieczcny [Eds.], 2000), and that this effect should become stronger or weaker, dependent on whether a subject-initial or an object-initial structure has been read in the previous prime trial, respectively. In order to measure garden-path effects during auditory sentence processing, we will look at pupil size changes over time (see details in the following text).

10.2 EXPERIMENT

10.2.1 Method

10.2.1.1 Participants

A total of 48 undergraduates from the Saarland University community were paid for participation. All of them were native German speakers with normal or corrected-to-normal vision. Of these, 33 (69%) had a right-eye dominance as determined via a simple parallax test prior to the experiment.

10.2.1.2 Target Materials

A total of 24 experimental pictures (and another 24 fillers for a different experiment) were created using digital images from commercially available clip art collections. Each visual stimulus showed three human characters: a female character in the center, a male character to the left, and another male character to the right of the central character (cf. Figure 10.1).[2]

The visual scenes always depicted two events at the same time, one in which the female character acted as an agent (e.g., the nurse blow-drying the priest in

(a)

(b)

Figure 10.1. Example picture with (a) left-to-right direction of action and with (b) right-to-left direction of action.

Figure 10.1a and pushing the sportsman in Figure 10.1b) and one in which she acted as a patient (e.g., the nurse being pushed by the sportsman in Figure 10.1a and being blow-dried by the priest in Figure 10.1b). The direction of action was counterbalanced between and within material files, that is, in half of the trials, it was left-to-right (Figure 10.1a), and in the other half of trials it was right-to-left (Figure 10.1b). This was done to ensure that potential viewing preferences for particular characters in the scene (agents vs. patients) were not explainable in terms of a simple left-to-right scanning strategy. Furthermore, the pictures were pretested such that the depicted actions were equally recognizable across conditions.

Each picture was paired with one of two versions of auditory sentences.[3] One version (henceforth the subject–object or SO condition) referred to the event in which the female character acted as the agent (1a,b) and the other version (henceforth the object–subject or OS condition) referred to the event in which the female character acted as the patient (2a,b). Sentences were always consistent with the displayed actions; the (a) and (b) sentence versions apply to the picture versions in Figure 10.1a and 10.1b, respectively.

(1) a. *Die Krankenschwester föhnt offensichtlich den Priester.*
  The nurse [ambig.] *blow-dries apparently the priest* [acc].
 b. *Die Krankenschwester schubst offensichtlich den Sportler.*
  The nurse [ambig.] *pushes apparently the sportsman* [acc].

(2) a. *Die Krankenschwester schubst offensichtlich der Sportler.*
    The nurse [ambig] *pushes apparently the sportsman* [nom].
  b. *Die Krankenschwester föhnt offensichtlich der Priester.*
    The nurse [ambig] *blow-dries apparently the priest* [nom].

The first NP in each sentence always referred to the central (female) character and was therefore ambiguous with respect to case marking (in German, nominative and accusative case feminine NPs are morphologically identical). Thus, locally, this NP could either be interpreted as the subject (typically, the agent) or the object (patient) of the sentence. The earliest point of disambiguation was the (present tense) verb region, which, combined with the visual context, unequivocally indicated the role being played by the central character. The verb was followed by an adverbial and an unambiguously case-marked masculine NP referring to the remaining accusative (patient) or nominative (agent) NP in (1) and (2), respectively.

A cross-splicing procedure ensured that there were no prosodic differences between the SO- and OS-versions of the target sentences up to the onset of the second NP: the final OS-versions were actually generated from the SO-recordings (1) by replacing the original second NPs with the appropriate second NPs from the OS-recordings (2).

10.2.1.3 Priming Materials

The picture–sound target trials were immediately preceded by (lexically and semantically unrelated) prime trials in which participants had to read aloud one of three types of written sentences: SVO primes (P1), OVS primes (P2), or Neutral primes (P3). SVO primes consisted of a masculine singular nominative NP followed by a past tense verb, an adverbial, and a masculine singular accusative NP, resulting in an unambiguous subject–verb–object ordering of constituents. In OVS primes, the assignment of case to the relevant NPs was reversed, which resulted in an unambiguous object–verb–subject order. Neutral primes consisted of intransitive passive constructions, which were considered an unlikely trigger of a particular subject–object sequencing (thus, they provide a baseline with which the effectiveness of SVO/OVS primes can be compared).[4]

(P1) *Der Regisseur lobte insbesondere den Produzenten.*
    The director [nom] *commended in particular the producer* [acc].
(P2) *Den Regisseur lobte insbesondere der Produzent.*
    The director [acc] *commended in particular the producer* [nom].
(P3) *Vor den Wahlen wurde im Fernsehen heftig gestritten.*
    Before the elections there was a lot of debate on TV.

10.2.1.4 Design and Procedure

For each picture version (Figure 10.1a vs. 10.1b), each type of prime (SVO, OVS, Neutral) was paired with each type of sentence condition (SO vs. OS), resulting in a 2 (picture version) × 3 (prime) × 2 (sentence condition) design. Twelve material files were generated such that (a) each of the 24 items appeared exactly once per file, but in different factor-combinations across files and (b) the number of items per factor-combination was balanced within each file. In addition to the prime-target pairs of interest, each material file included 24 visual-world items (pictures combined with auditory sentences) and 12 written sentences (for reading) as fillers. For each of the 12 files, four different quasirandom orders of trials were generated, subject to the constraint that each prime-target sequence was preceded by at least one filler (visual-world or reading trial).

Participants were seated approximately 75 cm from the screen of a 21-in. color monitor that was connected to the participant–PC of an *SMI EyeLink* head-mounted eyetracking system (spatial resolution: < 0.01°, sampling rate: 250 Hz). The participant–PC controlled the presentation of the stimuli and stored the eyetracker output for later analysis. Connected to the sound card of the partici-pant–PC was a Labtec LCS-2414 satellite speaker and subwoofer system for auditory presentation. The stimulus display ran at 120 Hz refresh rate in 1024 × 768 pixel resolution. Viewing was binocular, but only the participant's dominant eye was tracked.

In order to conceal the purpose of the study, the experiment was disguised as the training phase of a picture–sentence recognition test. Participants were told that they would see a random series of trials comprising either written sentences (that they would have to read aloud on encounter) or pictures combined with auditory sentences (to which they would just have to pay attention). They were told that their "task" was to memorize as many of the presented pictures and sentences (written or auditory) as possible; at the close of the experiment, they would be tested on how many of the previously presented stimuli they would recognize from a list containing "old" and "new" stimuli. This testing phase actually never took place (participants were debriefed about the actual purpose of the experiment at the close of each session).

Each trial started with the presentation of a fixation cross in the center of the screen. The participant fixated it so that an automatic drift correction could be performed (the trial would not proceed until the cross was fixated). Then the exper-imenter pressed the space bar of the experimenter-PC keyboard, triggering the presentation of the relevant stimuli. In the case of a reading trial (prime or filler), a written sentence was presented for 5.5 s. The participant read it aloud, and then the next trial was initiated. In the case of a visual-world trial (target or filler), the picture appeared and the corresponding sentence was played 1000 ms after picture onset (the relevant system time stamps were recorded in the tracker output). The participant had to pay attention both to the picture and to the sentence. The sounds typically ended about 2 s before the end of the corresponding picture presentation, which always lasted for 6.5 s before the next trial was initiated.

The eyetracker continuously recorded the temporal onsets and offsets of fixations (as defined in the event-sampling routines of the tracker) together with (a) the corresponding spatial coordinates and (b) the relevant pupil size (video-frame area in pixels).

The experiment started with the camera set-up (which took about 1.5 min) followed by a brief calibration and validation procedure (ca. 30 s) during which the participant had to fixate a crosshair in nine different screen positions. Over the course of the experiment, calibration and validation were repeated once every 20 trials.

10.2.1.5 Data Analysis

The temporal onsets of the words in each target sound file were hand-coded in millisecond resolution using GoldWave. For later analysis, two critical time intervals were chosen, namely NP1 (from sentence onset until the onset of the verb) and V–ADV (from the onset of the verb until the onset of the determiner of NP2, comprising the verb and the adverbial). The average durations were 1105 ms and 1289 ms for NP1 and V–ADV, respectively. Due to cross-splicing (as explained earlier), OS-disambiguated target sentences were identical with their SO-disambiguated counterparts until the onset of the second NP.

The eyetracking data were processed as follows. The temporal onsets and offsets of the fixations within a trial were recalculated relative to the corresponding picture onset by subtracting the picture onset from the relevant fixation onsets and offsets. Extremely short fixations (less than 80 ms between onset and offset, accounting for ca. 2.3% of all fixations) were pooled with the immediately preceding or following fixation if that fixation lay within a Euclidean distance of 12 pixels (ca. 0.5°); otherwise they were eliminated. The time for a blink was added to the immediately preceding fixation. Finally, the spatial coordinates of the fixations were mapped onto the objects in the picture by means of color-coded bitmap templates (1024 × 768 pixels). The data were further processed such that all consecutive fixations on an object before the eyes moved to another object were accumulated into one *gaze*. Besides gaze duration (which will be a primary measure in our analyses), a mean pupil size per gaze was calculated (the *weighted average* of the log-transformed[5] pupil size scores of the constituent fixations; longer fixations contributed proportionally more to the mean pupil size per gaze than shorter ones). Furthermore, a mean X/Y-coordinate per gaze was calculated (the *weighted average* of the X/Y-coordinates of the constituent fixations; again, longer fixations contributed more to the mean X/Y-coordinate per gaze than shorter ones). The mean X/Y-coordinate per gaze will be used as an auxiliary measure for analyzing pupil size (see details in the following text).

In a first set of analyses (focusing on gaze duration), we were interested in the effects of *prime type* (SVO, OVS, Neutral) and *target disambiguation* (SO vs. OS) on looks to the male patient (the priest in Figure 10.1a and the sportsman in Figure 10.1b) and looks to the male agent (the sportsman in Figure 10.1a and the priest in Figure 10.1b) in each of the critical sentence regions (NP1 and V–ADV). As already discussed in the introduction, the rationale behind this was that longer looks to the male patient would indicate a preference for the ambiguous first-NP referent (the female character) to be interpreted as the subject/agent of the target sentence (anticipation of an upcoming object/patient), whereas longer looks to the male agent would suggest that the ambiguous first-NP referent is interpreted as the object/patient of the target sentence (anticipation of an upcoming subject/agent). More specifically, our analyses considered mean gaze durations per target object (a) for gazes launched within NP1 and (b) for gazes launched within V–ADV. In case a picture object was not inspected within a given trial and sentence region, the corresponding gaze duration was scored as missing value; in case a picture object was inspected more than once within a given trial and sentence region, the relevant gazes were treated as separate observations (i.e., the individual gaze durations were averaged). Hence, our measure represents the average uninterrupted viewing time spent on a given picture object in response to the linguistic (and visual) information available in the relevant sentence region.[6] Inferential analyses were based on three-factorial ANOVAs including *prime type* (SVO, OVS, Neutral), *target disambiguation* (SO, OS), and *picture object* (patient, agent) as repeated-measures factors. The data were summarized by participants and items for $F1$- and $F2$-analyses, respectively.

In a second set of analyses, we were interested in *garden-path effects*, specifically, in how difficult the OS-disambiguated versions of the auditory target sentences are in comparison to their SO-disambiguated counterparts, and whether such differences in processing difficulty are modulated by the type of the previously read prime sentence. Obviously, an analysis of looks to different target objects in the scene is not very informative in this respect (it reveals early interpretational preferences rather than processing difficulty associated with the auditory linguistic input). We therefore used the pupil size measure as an indicator of the garden-path effects of interest (cf. Just & Carpenter, 1993; Hoeks & Levelt, 1993; Hyönä & Pollatsek, 2000; Hyönä, Tommola, & Alaja, 1995). Pupil dilation has long been known to correspond with mental processing load (e.g., Beatty, 1982; Kahneman, 1973). An increase in the mental effort associated with a task is typically accompanied by an increase in pupil size. Thus, we expect that sentence conditions which are "hard" to process will be associated with more dilated pupils. Note that changes in pupil size are relatively slow (with a latency of about 200–400 ms), but still fast enough to enable the identification of their triggering events in the sound stream. Further details of the pupil size analysis will be given in the relevant results section in the following text.

10.2.2 Results and Discussion

10.2.2.1 Gaze Durations

The analysis of gazes starting within NP1[7] revealed a reliable *prime type × picture object* interaction in gaze duration ($F1(2, 94) = 3.67$; $p < .03$; $F2(2, 46) = 5.16$; $p < .01$, see Figure 10.2), but no effect of *target disambiguation* ($Fs < 2$). The latter was expected because SO and OS target sentences were identical during this interval. We further resolved the *prime type × picture object* interaction by comparing the gaze duration difference between looks to the male patient and looks to the male agent across prime conditions (Newman-Keuls Tests by participants and items). These tests revealed a reliably stronger patient preference after SVO rather than OVS primes ($p_1 < .01$; $p_2 < .03$), a marginally stronger patient preference after Neutral rather than OVS primes ($p_1 < .03$; $p_2 < .10$), and no reliable effect ($ps > .30$) between SVO and Neutral primes, despite a numerical trend towards a smaller patient preference after Neutral primes (cf. Figure 10.2). Thus, on the assumption that longer gaze durations on the male patient indicate a preference for the ambiguous (female) NP1-referent to be interpreted as a subject/agent, we

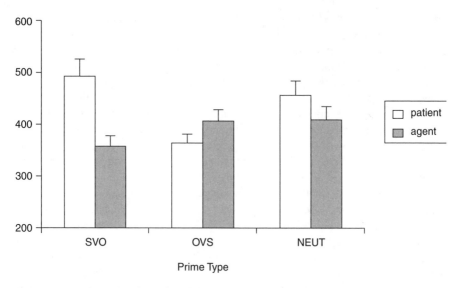

Figure 10.2. Mean durations (in millisecondss, with standard errors) of gazes launched within NP1, by levels of *prime type* (SVO, OVS, Neutral) and *picture object* (male patient, male agent).

conclude that OVS-primes substantially reduced the expectation of a subject-first structure during the NP1 region.

The analysis of gazes launched within V–ADV (these gazes ended about 77 ± 35 ms [95% c.i.] before the onset of the determiner of the case-unambiguous second NP) revealed a significant main effect of *picture object* (longer looks to the male patient rather than agent, $F1(1, 47) = 71.66; p < .001; F2(1, 23) = 70.51; p < .001$, see Figure 10.3). This could reflect a general subject/agent-first preference in interpretation, or alternatively, a visual bias favoring the character that is being faced by the NP1-referent (cf. Scheepers et al., 2003). Note that in all of our target pictures the female character was visually oriented toward the male patient character.

Importantly, there was also a reliable *target disambiguation × picture object* interaction ($F1(1, 47) = 45.37; p < .001; F2(1, 23) = 59.45; p < .001$), due to longer gazes on the male patient in the SO rather than OS target disambiguation condition ($F1(1, 47) = 37.40; p < .001; F2(1, 23) = 51.73; p < .001$) and longer gazes on the male agent in the OS rather than SO condition ($F1(1, 47) = 16.72; p < .001; F2(1, 23) = 18.61; p < .001$), see Figure 10.3. This suggests that verb information, in combination with the visual context, already allows for proper disambiguation of the target structure: participants are obviously able to anticipate the appropriate forthcoming argument (i.e., the object/patient in the SO condition and the subject/agent in the OS condition) before this argument and its case marking are available in the sound stream (cf. Kamide et al., 2003; Scheepers et al., 2003). Effects of prime type were not detected during the V–ADV region ($Fs < 1.5$).

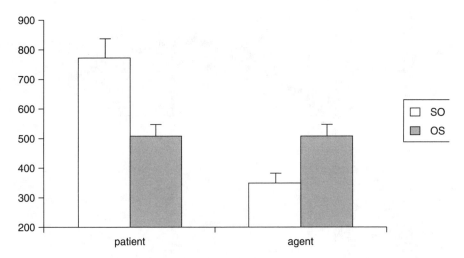

Figure 10.3. Mean durations (in milliseconds, with standard errors) of gazes launched within V–ADV, by levels of *picture object* (male patient, male agent) and *target disambiguation* (SO, OS).

10.2.2.2 Pupil Size

In order to be able to use changes in pupil size as an indicator of on-line processing difficulty, some potential confounds need to be controlled for. As lighting conditions were basically constant across conditions, the most important of these factors was the absolute gaze position of the eye. The eye-monitoring camera was always located at an angle slightly below and further to the outer rim of the dominant eye; hence, the video image of the pupil became systematically smaller as the dominant eye moved further upwards or towards the nose. To account for this, we performed a series of multiple regression analyses (separately for each participant) with mean X and Y gaze position as predictors and mean pupil size per gaze as the criterion, and subtracted the pupil size predicted from the relevant regression equations from the actual pupil size scores. (Recall from the data analysis section that the pupil size measure was already mapped onto a linear scale via log transformation). The calculation of this adjusted pupil size measure not only neutralized any influences of absolute gaze position but also compensated for interindividual differences in pupil size by subtracting the participant-specific intercept.

Figure 10.4a shows a continuous plot of the adjusted pupil size measure over a period of 0–5000 ms after sentence onset (by time steps of 100 ms), separately for SO- and OS-disambiguated target sentences. Figure 10.4b and Figure 10.4c show the difference between the two curves (positive values indicate more dilated pupils in the OS condition) and mark the time steps at which repeated-measures ANOVAs (by participants and items, respectively) revealed a significant (or marginal) main effect of *target disambiguation*. As can be seen, the OS condition was associated with a significant increase in pupil size relative to the SO condition. This can be regarded as the replication of an already well-established garden-path effect for OS-disambiguated structures in German (e.g., Hemforth, 1993;

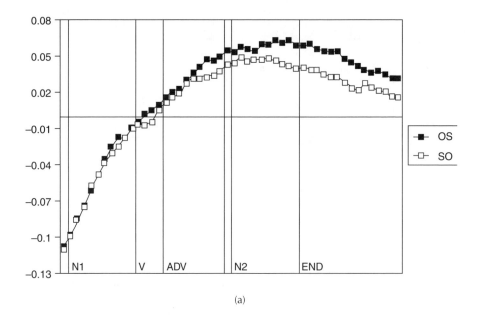

(a)

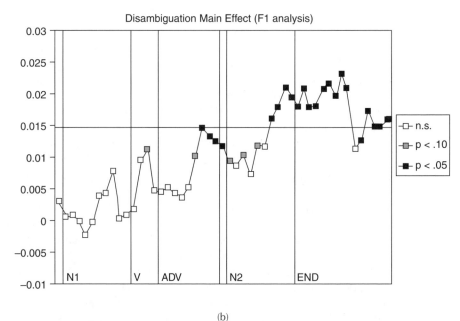

(b)

see also Hemforth & Konieczny [Eds.], 2000). Interestingly, the effect started to emerge even before the second NP became available in the auditory input, namely, towards the end of the adverbial region (approximate word onsets are marked in the plots as well).[8] This suggests that it was triggered, at least during this early time period, by a combination of verb information plus visual context rather than

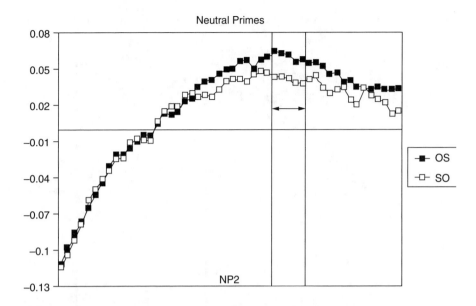

(c)

Figure 10.4. Adjusted pupil size over time (10 Hz resolution), by levels of *target disambiguation* (SO, OS), (a) after SVO primes, (b) after OVS primes, and (c) after Neutral primes

case marking at the second NP (recall that in the given experimental set-up, the verb region already provided all the information necessary to disambiguate the role of the first NP). Also, this seems consistent with the gaze duration findings reported earlier (*target disambiguation × picture object* interaction within the V–ADV region).

Effects of *prime type* on pupil size did not approach significance at any of the considered time steps. However, a suggestion of a priming effect was found within a time period of 700–1200 ms after the onset of the second NP's determiner (i.e. the time period around which pupil dilation reached its overall peak in the OS condition; see Figure 10.5): ANOVAs treating *time step* (five levels, corresponding to the five 100-ms bins of interest) and *target disambiguation* (SO vs. OS) as repeated measures factors revealed a reliable OS garden-path effect after SVO primes ($F1(1, 47) = 5.37$; $p < .03$; $F2(1, 23) = 9.17$; $p < .006$, Figure 10.5a), no effect of *target disambiguation* after OVS primes ($F1 < 1$; $F2 < 2$; Figure 10.5b), and a nearly significant OS garden-path effect after Neutral primes ($F1(1, 47) = 5.36$; $p < .03$; $F2(1, 23) = 4.04$; $p < .06$, Figure 10.5c). Thus, at least within this restricted time period, OVS primes seemed to have reduced the garden-path effect for OS-disambiguated structures relative to the other prime conditions. Effects of *time step* were not reliable within this period ($Fs < 1.5$).

10.3 GENERAL DISCUSSION

The present experiment suggests that language comprehenders make rapid and exhaustive use of various sources of linguistic and nonlinguistic information in order to resolve a temporary constituent-order ambiguity associated with a case-ambiguous

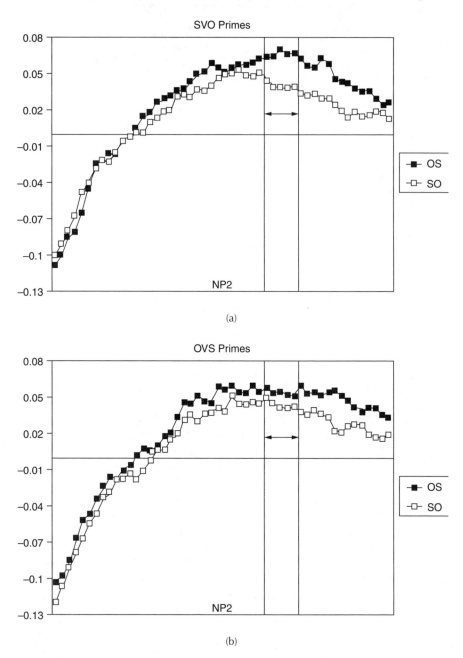

(a)

(b)

NP in sentence-initial position. The gaze-duration findings around the sentence region containing the verb and the adverb (V–ADV), for example, strongly suggest that visual context information (the actually displayed actions) and the verb (referring to one of those actions) enable the prediction of the appropriate forthcoming argument referent, which, in turn, suggests that the role of the case-ambiguous first

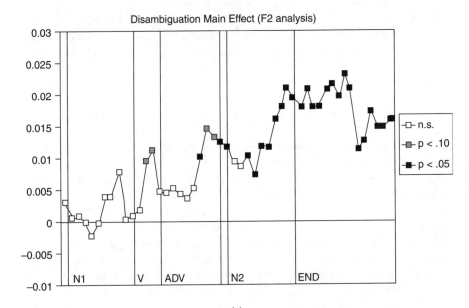

(c)

Figure 10.5. Adjusted pupil size over time (10 Hz resolution): (a) plotted by levels of *target disambiguation* (SO, OS) and (b) and (c) plotted as OS-SO difference scores.

NP (as either subject or object) is likely to have been resolved at this point (crucially, before the case-marked second NP is available; see Knöferle, Crocker, Scheepers, & Pickering, in press, for very similar findings).

Interestingly, the target disambiguation effect showed up not only in gaze durations on the critical unambiguous scene-characters, but also in pupil size changes toward the end of the adverbial region (again, before the case-marked second NP became available). When the verb and the visual context made it clear that the ambiguous first NP must be the object of the sentence (OS-disambiguation), pupils became reliably more dilated than when the verb and the visual context supported the subject-interpretation of the first NP (SO-disambiguation). This is consistent with a garden-path effect for OS-disambiguated structures in German, an already well-documented finding in the literature. The present study is presumably the first to have shown this effect being triggered by visual context and verb information (and, crucially, in the absence of a morphological case marker).

The main findings concern the effect of previous (short-term) linguistic exposure. The present experiment was able to demonstrate that the kind of constituent ordering being processed in a prime trial (where participants had to read unambiguous sentences) reliably affected the constituent ordering preferences in a target trial following immediately (where participants had to listen to temporarily ambiguous sentences). First, gaze durations upon hearing the case-ambiguous first NP in the target trial suggested a substantially reduced tendency to interpret this NP as the subject (or agent) of the sentence after having read an OVS rather than SVO or Neutral prime (as evidenced in reliably shorter gazes on the male patient after OVS primes), suggesting that at least very early interpretational preferences are subject to priming (recall that there were no comparable effects of prime type during the "disambiguating" V–ADV region). Second, changes in pupil dilation revealed that processing difficulty associated with OS-disambiguated target structures tended to be reduced after having read an OVS rather than SVO or Neutral prime (at least within a time frame of about 700–1200 ms after the onset of the case-marked second NP), which, albeit not a very pronounced effect, appears to indicate that garden-path strength can be modulated through prior linguistic exposure (i.e., via some sort of priming mechanism).

A point that is worth further discussion is that relative to the Neutral prime condition, only OVS primes appeared to elicit substantial priming effects. SVO primes, on the other hand, merely induced a numerical but nonsignificant trend in the expected direction (especially in gaze duration around NP1) when compared with Neutral primes. We interpret this as evidence for a general reduction in the magnitude of priming when the prime is consistent with a *preferred* structure. In fact, comparable observations have been made in experiments on priming in production, focusing on rather different syntactic alternations (e.g., Hartsuiker & Westenberg, 2000; Scheepers, 2003). If there was a preference for a given syntactic alternative in the baseline ("Neutral condition"), then the effect associated with preferred structure primes was smaller than the effect associated with non-preferred structure primes. There are at least two plausible reasons for this observation. Either nonpreferred structure primes are more effective because they are more surprising (and thus *salient*) to the language processing system, or they achieve stronger priming effects because they are being processed in a more elaborate fashion (requiring more processing time) than preferred structure primes. At present, it seems too early to decide between these explanatory alternatives. However, we note that priming in comprehension and production may be related at a rather general level.

10.4 CONCLUSION

Of course, a single experiment will hardly be able to give definitive answers to all the questions that we have raised in this paper. For example, are the observed priming effects truly *syntactic* in nature? One potential problem with our present study is that most of the priming sentences employed could have triggered the assumed ordering of syntactic functions (subject-before-object vs. object-before-subject) *as well as* a particular sequencing of thematic roles (agent-before-patient vs. patient-before-agent). Hence, we are currently preparing a follow-up experiment in which functional order priming and thematic order priming will not be confounded in this way (the verbs in the primes will systematically differ in their thematic role assignment properties from the verbs in the targets; cf. Scheepers, Hemforth & Konieczny, 2000, Bornkessel, Schlesewsky, & Friederici, 2003).

Nevertheless, the bottom-line conclusion from the present findings is that on-line sentence comprehension is susceptible to some kind of constituent order priming, either in the form of maintaining syntactic function sequences over consecutive trials or in the form of maintaining thematic role orderings. Hence, the phenomenon of sentence-level priming (i.e., persistence of abstract sentence representations over consecutive trials) does not seem to be confined to language production only.

References

Altmann, G. T. M., & Kamide, Y. (1999). Incremental interpretation at verbs: Restricting the domain of subsequent reference. *Cognition, 73,* 247–264.

Beatty, J. (1982). Task-evoked pupillary responses, processing load, and the structure of processing resources. *Psychological Bulletin, 91,* 276–292.

Bock, J. K. (1986). Syntactic persistence in language production. *Cognitive Psychology, 18,* 355–387.

Bock, J. K., & Loebell, H. (1990). Framing sentences. *Cognition, 35,* 1–39.

Bornkessel, I., Schlesewsky, M., & Friederici, A. D. (2003). Eliciting thematic reanalysis effects: The role of syntax-independent information during parsing. *Language and Cognitive Processes, 18*(3), 269–298.

Branigan, H. P. (1995). *Language processing and the mental representation of syntactic structure.* Unpublished doctoral dissertation, University of Edinburgh, Scotland.

Cooper, R. M. (1974). The control of eye fixation by the meaning of spoken language: A new methodology for the real-time investigation of speech perception, memory, and language processing. *Cognitive Psychology, 6,* 84–107.

Corley, M. M. B., & Scheepers, C. (2002). Syntactic priming in English sentence production: Categorical and latency evidence from an internet-based study. *Psychonomic Bulletin and Review, 9*(1), 126–131.

Frazier, L., Taft, L., Clifton, C., Roeper, T., & Ehrlich, K. (1984). Parallel structure: A source of facilitation in sentence comprehension. *Memory and Cognition, 12,* 421–430.

Hartsuiker, R. J., & Westenberg, C. (2000). Word order priming in written and spoken sentence production. *Cognition, 75,* B27–B39.

Hemforth, B. (1993). *Kognitives Parsing: Repräsentation und Verarbeitung sprachlichen Wissens.* Sankt Augustin, Germany: Infix.

Hemforth, B., & Konieczny, L. (Eds.). (2000). *German Sentence Processing.* Dodrecht, Netherlands: Kluwer.

Hoeks, B., & Levelt, W. J. M. (1993). Pupillary dilation as a measure of attention: A quantitative system analysis. *Behavior Research Methods, Instruments, and Computers, 25,* 16–26.

Hyönä, J., & Pollatsek, A. (2000). Processing of Finnish compound words in reading. In A. Kennedy, R. Radach, D. Heller, & J. Pynte (Eds.), *Reading as a Perceptual Process* (pp. 1–23). Amsterdam: Elsevier.

Hyönä, J., Tommola, J., & Alaja, A. M. (1995). Pupil dilation as a measure of processing load in simultaneous interpretation and other language tasks. *The Quarterly Journal of Experimental Psychology, 48A*(3), 598–612.

Just, M. A., & Carpenter, P. A. (1993). The intensity dimension of thought: Pupillometric indices of sentence processing. *Canadian Journal of Experimental Psychology, 47,* 310–339.

Kahneman, D. (1973). *Attention and effort.* Englewood Cliffs, NJ: Prentice-Hall.

Kamide, Y., Scheepers, C., & Altmann, G. T. M. (2003). Integration of syntactic and semantic information in predictive processing: Cross-linguistic evidence from German and English. *Journal of Psycholinguistic Research, 32*(1), 37–55.

Kamide, Y., Altmann, G. T. M., & Haywood, S. (2003). The time-course of prediction in incremental sentence processing: Evidence from anticipatory eye-movements. *Journal of Memory and Language, 49*, 133–156.

Knöferle, P., Crocker, M. W., Scheepers, C., & Pickering, M. J. (in press). The influence of the immediate visual context on incremental thematic role assignment: evidence from eye-movements in depicted events cognition.

Pickering, M. J., & Branigan, H. P. (1998). The representation of verbs: Evidence from syntactic priming in language production. *Journal of Memory and Language, 39*, 633–651.

Scheepers, C. (2003). Syntactic priming of relative clause attachments: Persistence of structural configuration in sentence production. *Cognition, 89*, 179–205.

Scheepers, C., Hemforth, B., & Konieczny, L. (2000). Linking syntactic functions with thematic roles: Psych-verbs and the resolution of subject–object ambiguity. In B. Hemforth & L. Konieczny (Eds.), *German Sentence Processing* (pp. 95–135). Dodrecht, Netherlands: Kluwer.

Scheepers, C., Kamide, Y., & Altmann, G. T. M. (2003). *The compositional integration of syntactic, semantic, and world knowledge constraints in projecting upcoming arguments in German.* Manuscript submitted for publication.

Tanenhaus, M. K., Spivey-Knowlton, M. J., Eberhard, K. M., & Sedivy, J. C. (1995). Integration of visual and linguistic information in spoken language comprehension. *Science, 268*(5217), 1632–1634.

Weskott, T. (2002, September 19–21). *Information structure and local discourse interpretation: Processing the left periphery of German V2-sentences.* Poster presented at AMLaP 2002, La Laguna, Tenerife, Canary Islands, Spain.

Notes

1. For a more detailed empirical as well as theoretical motivation of the underlying rationale see Knöferle, Crocker, Scheepers, and Pickering (2003) which, in fact, forms the starting point of the present study.

2. We are especially grateful to Pia Knöferle for permission to use her visual-world materials.

3. The recordings were made on MiniDisk (44.1 KHz, mono) in one session by a male native German speaker (CS). They were transferred to a PC via TOSLINK for further editing (see below) and re-mastered into 16-KHz wave files before presentation. The latter had no audible effect on sound quality but saved a considerable amount of disc and memory space.

4. To avoid confusion, we will use the labels SVO, OVS, and Neutral to refer to *prime* conditions, and the labels SO and OS to refer to *target disambiguation* conditions.

5. The log transformation translates proportional pupil size changes into linear ones.

6. Previous findings have shown that this measure corresponds well with gaze frequencies in a visual-world task. The main difference, if any, appeared to be that average gaze durations were more sensitive to linguistic variation and less affected by the visual salience of individual picture objects than gaze frequencies (see Scheepers et al., 2003).

7. On average, these gazes ended about 183 ± 35 ms (95% c.i.) before the onset of the verb. Effects in the relevant gaze durations are therefore unlikely to be affected by disambiguating material becoming available further downstream.

8. To ensure that the early onset of this effect was not an artifact of the rather crude averaging procedure, we carried out an additional analysis focusing only on gazes that ended 1–400 ms before the onset of the NP2-determiner (a subset of the gazes that are responsible for the effect at the end of the adverbial region in Figure 10.4). These gazes revealed mean pupil size scores of 0.029 ±0.007 (*SE*) for the SO condition and 0.049 ±0.006 (*SE*) for the OS condition. The difference was reliable by participants and marginal by items ($t_1(47) = 2.02$; 2-tailed $p < .05$; $t_2(23) = 1.71$; 2-tailed $p < .11$), which confirms a trend towards an OS garden-path effect well before information about the NP2-determiner became available.

Chapter 11
The On-Line Processing of Ambiguous and Unambiguous Words in Context: Evidence from Head-Mounted Eyetracking

FALK HUETTIG AND GERRY T. M. ALTMANN

11.1 BACKGROUND: THE INTERACTION OF LANGUAGE, ATTENTION, AND VISION IN REAL-WORLD BEHAVIOR

A main goal of the study of language processing must be to understand how language processing affects aspects of human behavior. Traditionally, language processing has almost exclusively investigated language in isolation from the environment in which it is usually used. Although one of the defining features of language is that it can be used to refer to objects in their absence, language *is* often used to refer to objects in the immediate environment. From an evolutionary perspective, the sensory environment is likely to have had (and has) an important impact on the evolution of language and, more generally, cognition. Similarly, from a developmental perspective, language acquisition appears to be reliant in large part on a concurrent world with which the infant/child can interact. Notwithstanding this reliance on an external world (and even in its absence language does *refer* to objects and events in that external world), there has been little research that directly explores the interface of language and visual perception and its impact on our interactions with the visual world (but see Henderson & Ferreira, 2003, for reviews of such work).

Many theoretical accounts of language processing have assumed modular semantic or conceptual systems for the representation of knowledge that are theoretically (and possibly physically) distinct from the episodic modality-specific systems that support perception and action. In contrast, recent theories of *embodied* cognition (e.g., Barsalou, 1999; Glenberg, 1997) propose that conceptual representations are grounded in the neural substrate that supports interaction with, and perception of, the external world. Common to all embodied theories of cognition is a rejection of the claim that the human representational system is independent of the biological systems that embody it. This is in contrast with the view that cognition and knowledge can be considered independently of perception and action. Barsalou proposes that the meaning of a word is, in effect, a context-sensitive representation which, when activated, causes the reenactment of previous experiential states. These "simulations" develop through repeated experience of objects, actions, mental states, and so on (see Barsalou, Simmons, Barbey, & Wilson, 2003, for review). The experience may be perceptual or sensory, or motoric, and thus the cognitive representations that ensue are embodied in the neural substrate that supports such experiences. When a word is recognized, the cognitive system activates the simulation of the associated concept, and this may include the reenactment of experiential states that include sensory and motoric components.

Situated accounts of cognition fit well with embodied accounts. Situated cognition refers to theories that propose that the perceptual system "offloads" information by leaving it in the environment (or the "external world") rather than just passively passing information on to the cognitive system for propositional (*amodal*) representations to be created. According to this view, perceptual information in the environment is accessed when needed, with the visual world functioning as a kind of external memory (e.g., O'Regan, 1992). Objects in this situated memory are represented in a spatial data structure which contains "pointers" to the real-world location of the object. Thus, the system need not store internally detailed information about the object, but can instead locate that information, when it has to, by directing attention back to that object in the external world. Note, however, that we assume situated memories to be content-addressable and to contain some information about objects to permit content-addressability, i.e., just enough information to allow the system to acquire the detailed information that was not stored.

In sum, a word's meaning must be represented, according to the embodied cognition approach, across several sensory modalities. In effect, its meaning is composed of different sensory impressions abstracted across multiple experiences of that object in multiple modalities. If one receives a combination of sense impressions with any degree of frequency, simple principles of learning (Hebbian learning, for example) predict that, subsequently, any single member of the combination could trigger the others (see also Calvin & Bickerton, 2000). Embodied and situated theories of cognition propose, therefore, that cognition is perceptually grounded, and that conceptual processing involves perceptual simulation rather than the manipulation of the abstract and arbitrary symbols that are assumed in traditional cognitive science (see Barsalou et al., 2003, for a brief overview of this position).

11.2 THE IMMEDIATE BEHAVIORAL CONSEQUENCES OF THE DISPLAY OF PERCEPTUAL COMPETITORS

If conceptual representations are abstractions across modality-specific experiences, and if language comprehension involves perceptual simulation (the reenactment of embodied experiential states), then variables such as perceptual similarity should affect language-mediated eye movements in our interactions in the visual world. For example, hearing a word such as *cabbage* should give rise to an experiential state that reflects the perception of properties such as roundness and greenness, as well as other properties stemming from a cabbage's typical smell and taste. The reenactment of these experiential states (i.e., the activation of the *perceptual features*) will direct visual attention to objects in the environment which share these same features. (See the following text for an account of the mechanism by which visual attention is directed to these locations.) For the moment, we simply assume that a mechanism *is* in place to direct attention toward a cabbage when the word *cabbage* is heard. The system must presumably match the *simulated properties* against whatever perceptual properties are afforded by the objects in the visual scene, and thus objects that share some (but not necessarily all) of those perceptual properties may attract visual attention more than others that do not share those properties. The experiments that follow explore this prediction. Specifically, we ask whether hearing a word such as *cabbage* causes more eye movements toward objects that share physical shape (roundness) or color than toward objects that do not. Given that the eyes *can* be directed towards cabbages when we hear *cabbage*, we must be matching the perceptual features recovered through hearing *cabbage* against the perceptual features afforded by the objects in the visual environment. What is less clear is whether, when we have identified those objects, we direct our attention on hearing *cabbage* to any of them that, although not cabbages, are nonetheless round or green.

In the studies that follow, participants heard sentences such as *In the beginning, the man watched closely, but then he looked at the snake and realized that it was harmless*. Simultaneously, they viewed a visual scene depicting four objects. The target word, in this example, was *snake*, and the delay between the onset of the sentence (and the concurrent onset of the visual scene) and the onset of this target word, was approximately 5 s. We asked our participants to listen to the sentences carefully. They were told that they could look wherever they want but we asked them not to take their eyes off the screen (i.e., the listeners received no instructions other than to listen to the sentences carefully). We recorded participants' eye movements as they listened to the sentences.

11.2.1 Experiment 1: Visual Form Similarity

In the first study, we created two sets of visual stimuli. The stimuli in one set (the "target" set) consisted of a picture depicting an unambiguous target word (e.g., a snake) and three pictures depicting objects from different semantic/conceptual categories than the target word. These distractor items were chosen so that their names were frequency-matched with the target according to the CELEX (Baayen, Piepenbrock, & van Rijn, 1993) database. The stimuli in the second set (the "visual competitor" set) consisted of the same four pictures in the identical positions except that the target picture (the snake) was replaced with a picture depicting an object with a similar visual form as the target word (e.g., a cable). See Figures 11.1 and 11.2 for examples.

We constructed 21 sentential stimuli in two versions: a neutral context condition and a biasing context condition. For the neutral context condition, the sentence did not provide any contextual bias up until the target word that would favor any of the pictures depicted in the visual scene: *In the beginning, the man watched closely, but then he looked at the snake and realised that it was harmless*. For the biasing context

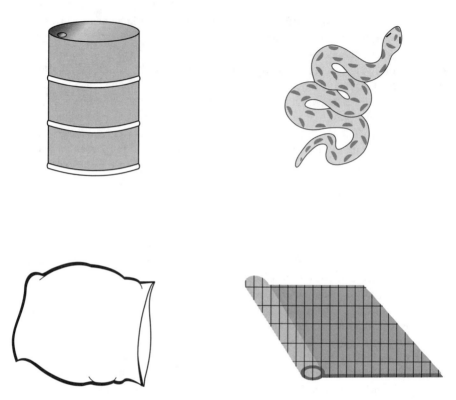

Figure 11.1 An example of a visual stimulus for the target set.

condition, the sentence biased toward the target object (the snake): *In the beginning, the zookeeper worried greatly, but then he looked at the snake and realised that it was harmless*. These sentences were identical to the neutral condition except for a single phrase that biased the upcoming target word (*zookeeper worried greatly*) which replaced the neutral phrase in the neutral condition (*man watched closely*). In the experiment itself, there were three conditions: the neutral sentences with the target stimuli, the biasing sentences with the target stimuli, and the biasing sentences with the visual competitor stimuli. Our rationale for presenting the visual competitor in a biasing context was simply that we wanted to make it relatively unlikely that participants would anticipate, prior to the target word, that the visual competitor would be the object of attention (even though it was not going to be referred to directly). The neutral sentences were included in order to establish a baseline against which the efficacy of the biasing context could be determined; the idea here was that in the neutral context there would be no advantage (in terms of attracting looks) of the target object until the corresponding target word was heard, but in the biasing context (if the attempt to induce a bias were successful), an advantage for the target object should be observed prior to the target word. We return to discussion of these contexts below.

In these first studies we report the percentage of trials in which a saccade was launched towards the target object during the acoustic lifetime of the target word,

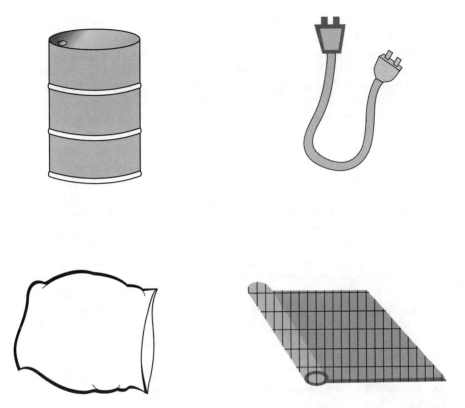

Figure 11.2 An example of a visual stimulus for the corresponding visual competitor set.

and, where appropriate, the percentage of trials on which the different objects were being fixated at the acoustic onset of that word.[1] The latter measure gives an indication of the bias to look toward one object or another before any of the acoustic input pertaining to the target word has been encountered.

In the neutral context condition, there was no significant bias at target word onset to look at the snake any more than at the distractors. During the target word (which averaged 447 ms in duration), participants initiated saccadic eye movements toward the target object (in fact, toward the quadrant within which the target object was depicted) on 45% of trials. Saccades toward the distractors averaged 11% of trials (that is, the three distractors each attracted saccades on 11% of trials). This difference was highly significant in statistical analyses by subjects and by items.[2] In the biasing context condition, there was a significant bias, at target word onset, to fixate *the snake* more than the distractors (target, 39%; distractors, 19%). During the target word, saccades were initiated toward the target object on 32% of trials, and to the distractors on 11% of trials. Again, this difference was highly significant. Although it may seem counter-intuitive that we see *fewer* looks toward the target object when the context biased towards this object, this reflects, simply, the increased likelihood of already fixating *the snake* in the biasing context. The fact that there was a significantly increased bias at target word onset to fixate *the snake* in the biasing context compared to the neutral context (biasing context, 39%; neutral context, 27%) suggests that our contextual manipulation had been successful (although we are less concerned with the magnitude of the bias than with the fact that there is a bias at all). Of critical interest were the data from the visual competitor condition in which *the snake* had been replaced by a cable. At the onset of *snake*, the cable and each of the distractors were being fixated with equal probability. However, postonset, during the lifetime of *snake*, more saccades were initiated toward the cable (35% of trials) than toward any of the distractors (each distractor attracted saccades on 18% of trials). Thus, as *snake* unfolded, participants executed more saccades toward the visual competitor (*the cable*) than to the visually unrelated distractors.

In summary, the patterns of eye movements to the visual competitor closely resembled the eye movements to the target object depicting the target word and did so from the earliest moments in which information from the unfolding target word (*snake*) became available (cf. Dahan & Tanenhaus, 2002; Dahan & Tanenhaus, 2004) although nothing in the linguistic context biased toward the visual competitor. Thus, visual attention during real-time speech processing seems to be directed toward objects in the visual world that match the physical shape of whatever is being referred to by the language. Importantly, the acoustic onset of the target word in these studies occurred on average 5 s after the onset of the visual scene. That is, any eye movements initiated toward *the snake* in response to *snake* most likely were initiated toward that location because participants already knew there was *snake* at that location. Similarly, any eye movements initiated toward the cable in response to *snake* most likely were initiated toward that location *despite* participants knowing that there was a cable at that location.

11.2.2 Experiment 2: Color

Our next study explored whether we could extend this finding to perceptual properties other than shape, such as color. Participants heard sentences such as *The boy turned around carefully, and then he saw the frog and looked happy*, which were designed to be linguistically neutral with respect to any of the visually presented pictures. The concurrent visual stimuli consisted of sets of four line drawings taken from Snodgrass and Vanderwart (1980). In the target condition, the four line drawings included the target object (e.g., a frog) and three distractors that were unrelated conceptually to the target (e.g., a mitten, a pipe, and a suitcase). The target was colored according to its prototypical color (green, in this case), and the distractors were colored in ways that were deemed normal (e.g., a blue mitten, a brown pipe, and a red suitcase). In the color competitor condition, the target object was replaced by a color competitor: for the frog, the color competitor was a lettuce. The procedure in this study was the same as in the previous one. The data were similar: significantly more saccades were initiated during the acoustic lifetime of the target word towards the competitor than towards the other distractors. Thus, in the target condition, the frog engendered saccades on 52% of trials, and each distractor on 12% of trials. In the visual competitor condition, the lettuce engendered saccades on 41% of trials, and the distractors on 26% of trials. There were no advantages of either the target or the competitor prior to the onset of the target word. Thus, participants initiated significantly more saccades during the acoustic lifetime of the target word *frog* toward the picture of the color competitor (*lettuce*) than toward the distractors (*mitten, pipe,* and *suitcase*).

These data, together with those from Experiment 1, demonstrate that language-mediated visual attention is directed immediately toward objects that match on the perceptual properties of form and color. We suggest that information activated during the acoustic lifetime of the target word (including information about visual form and color) causes the activation of stored representations of the visual objects that share such information. Why this engenders immediate looks to those objects will be left until later discussion. First, we consider whether similar effects can occur if the overlap between the target word and the object in the visual field is based not on perceptual properties of real-world objects but on their semantic properties.

11.3 THE IMMEDIATE BEHAVIORAL CONSEQUENCES OF THE DISPLAY OF CONCEPTUAL COMPETITORS

11.3.1 Experiment 3: Conceptual Category

Are the effects we have observed thus far confined to perceptual features or might they generalize to *conceptual* features also. Work by Eiling Yee and Julie Sedivy suggests that it may: they observed increased looks toward a key when the word *lock* was heard (Yee & Sedivy, 2001). In their study, the lock was co-present in the visual scene, and it is possible that looks to the key were initiated once the lock had been attended to. However, like them, we suspect that their finding was the visual equivalent of semantic priming (in this example, mediated by a *functional* relationship between the lock and the key). Our next study was designed to investigate such effects further.

The basic design consisted of three alternative visual scenes each accompanied by the same target sentence: *Eventually, the man agreed hesitantly, but then he looked at the piano and appreciated that it was beautiful.* The target word was *piano*, and the three alternative scenes differed in respect of the objects they portrayed (see Figures 11.3 to 11.5). In each case, the scene was composed of four line drawings. In the first condition, one drawing depicted the referent of the target word (e.g., a piano), and the remaining three drawings were distractors that were unrelated in visual form, prototypical color, or conceptual category. In the second condition, the target from the first condition was replaced by a conceptual competitor (a trumpet), but the three distractors remained the same. The third condition portrayed both the target and the conceptual competitor, as well as two distractors (cf. the Yee and Sedivy study, but see the following text).

The pictures were black and white line drawings from the normed Snodgrass and Vanderwart (1980) set and were matched for picture-naming agreement, familiarity, frequency (of the corresponding name), and other variables. All the pictures for each item were from different conceptual categories. Similarly to Snodgrass and Vanderwart we used the Battig and Montague (1969) category norms as a guide. We used only pictures from the Snodgrass and Vanderwart set that were also

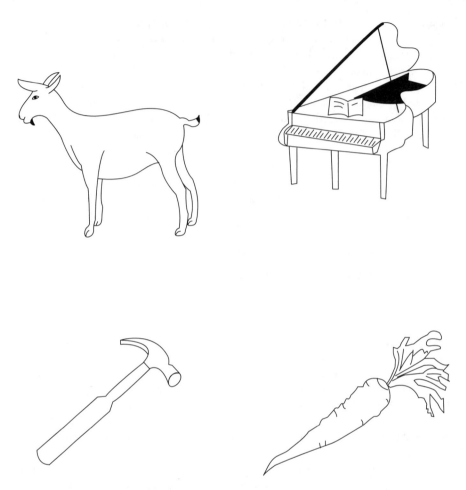

Figure 11.3 An example of a visual stimulus in the first condition (target: *piano* depicted).

members of the Battig and Montague norms. We selected pictures from the following conceptual categories: four-footed animal, furniture, human body part, kitchen utensil, musical instrument, clothing, type of vehicle, part of building, weapon, fruit, carpenter's tool, bird, toy, insect, and vegetable. None of the conceptual competitors were associates of the target words (unlike the lock and key example used by Yee & Sedivy, 2001). We consulted the University of South Florida word association norms (Nelson, McEvoy, & Schreiber, 1998) that typically used hundreds of participants in the collection of the norms for each word. We used a stringent exclusion criterion: if even a single participant produced the competitor after the target, or vice versa, we rejected that item. For example, if only one participant of the several hundreds in that norming study had produced *trumpet* after *piano* or *piano* after *trumpet*, then we would have excluded this item.

We analyzed our data in the same way as in the previous experiments. In the first condition, with just the target (the piano) and three distractors, there were more

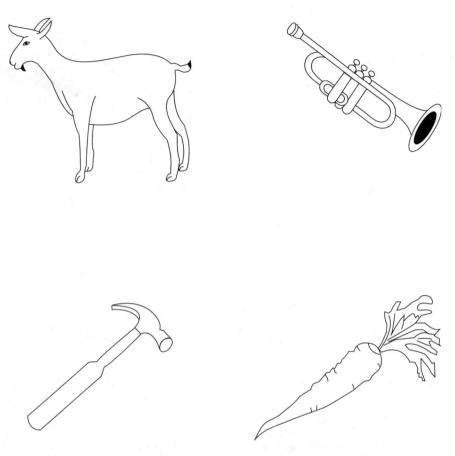

Figure 11.4 The visual stimulus in the second condition (target picture replaced by a picture of the category competitor *trumpet*).

trials with looks initiated toward the piano (39%) than with looks initiated toward the distractors (14% each). In the second condition, which portrayed instead the conceptual competitor (the trumpet), there was a large difference, during the target word, between looks toward the trumpet (36%) and looks to each of the distractors (19%). In both conditions there were no biases by the onset of the target word that favored looks toward any of the drawings (whether target, competitor, or distractor)—all were being fixated at this point with equal probability. Thus, hearing *piano* engenders immediate looks toward the conceptually related trumpet. The data from the third condition were a little more complex because the visual scene portrayed both the target and the competitor and, unsurprisingly, there were more looks towards the target than toward the competitor (41% vs. 17%) but more looks to both of these than to the two distractors (9% each). The likelihood of the distractors being fixated at the onset of the target word was marginally greater than that for the target or conceptual competitor being fixated (27% for the distractors, and 22% for each of the target and conceptual competitor); thus, although it was marginally less likely

Figure 11.5 The visual stimulus in the third condition (target *and* competitor depicted).

at the onset of *piano* that the target and competitor were already being fixated, there were more looks initiated post-onset toward the target and competitor than toward the distractors. The greater advantage of the target relative to the conceptual competitor is accounted for by the fact that the conceptual competitor (*trumpet*) only matched on basic conceptual dimensions, while the target (*piano*) matched on both conceptual and perceptual properties.

Taken together, these data demonstrate that visual attention is directed immediately, as a word unfolds, toward objects that match the target specification of that word on the grounds of conceptual category.[3] The fact that the pictures corresponding to these objects had been on-screen for approximately 5 s suggests that our effects were not due to any confusion regarding the identities of the four portrayed objects. We note in this regard that Dell'Acqua and Grainger (1999) observed unconscious activation of semantic information from picture stimuli after exposures of just 17 ms. Interestingly, visual attention appears to be directed toward conceptually related objects even if they mismatch on other grounds (perceptual shape and color, and conceptual detail). Finally, attention is directed towards such mismatching objects even when an object exists in the visual field which meets the full conceptual and perceptual specifications associated with the critical target word. Before considering the mechanism which causes such effects, we shall turn to one final question that arises following the conceptual competitor data. They concern the locus of the color effect observed earlier.

11.3.2 Experiment 4: Putting Color in Black and White

Why did participants look at the lettuce when they heard *frog*? Is it because they accessed the color information associated with frogs, and their eyes were then attracted to anything that they *saw* was green? Or were their eyes attracted to anything that they *knew* was green? In other words, is the color competitor effect a *semantic* effect, or a *perceptual* one? To explore this, we repeated the logic of the color competitor experiment, but in black and white. Participants were shown a four-picture scene with, for example, a frog, a mitten, a pipe, and a suitcase. We again used line drawings from the Snodgrass and Vanderwart (1980) set. Participants heard either *The boy turned around carefully, and then he saw the frog and looked happy,* or *The boy turned around carefully, and then he saw the spinach and looked happy.* In the first case, the visual scene affords a referent for the target word *frog*, but in the second case, there is no referent for *spinach*, although there is a conceptual color match between spinach and the frog portrayed in the scene. In the *frog* condition, participants initiated a saccadic movement toward the frog, during *frog* on 52% of trials. Each distractor attracted saccades on 12% of trials. In the *spinach* condition, on only 30% of trials did participants look toward the frog during *spinach*. And in this case, the distractors each attracted saccades on 27% of trials. Thus, there was no significant difference between looks to the frog and looks to the distractors in this condition (the numbers add up to more than 100 because there were some trials on which there was more than one fixation within the lifetime of the target word). The difference in looks as a function of the target word (*frog* vs. *spinach*) cannot be explained by any difference in the duration of the two words, as these averaged 480 and 490 ms, respectively.

These data suggest strongly that the color competitor effect is driven by *perceptual*, not *conceptual*, factors (given that prototypical color could be deemed to be a conceptual or semantic feature). In the following section, we offer a tentative explanation of our competitor effects before proceeding to the application of these effects to the study of lexical ambiguity.

11.4 LANGUAGE-MEDIATED EYE MOVEMENTS, "EMBODIED LOCATION," AND COMPETITOR EFFECTS

Why do the eyes move to form, color, or conceptual competitors? And why do they move so quickly? In respect of conceptual competitors, proponents of situated vision would argue, presumably, that the conceptual information that is accessed (or activated) on hearing the target word causes the eyes to move towards the depicted conceptual competitor in order to retrieve the situated memory of what is at that location. In other words, the system has a record that something with particular conceptual features is located at that location, and when the target word is heard, the system needs to retrieve information about that object in order to establish its fit with the target specification as provided by the target word. But if this is the case, what is the *mechanism* by which attention is directed toward that location? The situation in respect of situated vision and the perceptual competitor effects (of form and color) is a little more complex; the word *frog* makes available prototypical color information, and situated memories cause the eyes to move toward something sharing that color in order to recover further details. However, the conceptual competitor effects suggest that enough is known about whatever is in the location to which the eyes will be directed to know that it is of a certain conceptual type (if *piano* causes us to attend to the trumpet, this must be because we know that *piano* refers to a musical instrument, and that a musical instrument is located at the position in the visual field that is in fact occupied by a trumpet). So why, when we hear *frog*, should we move to the lettuce when, evidently, we know that *what we want* is animal-like, and that *what we will get* is vegetable-like?

The answer to these puzzles is to consider how information about location might be encoded within the cognitive system. Within the embodied approach to cognition, the representations of objects in the world are encoded in the same substrate whose activation has supported the experience of those objects (cf. Glenberg, 1997). Presumably, the representation of the *location* of those objects would be encoded in the same substrate whose activation supported the experience of those objects *as mediated by* physical movement with or toward those objects (whether in terms of orientation toward the objects or shifts in visual attention toward those objects). Thus, if one attends to an object, the neural substrate implicated in the corresponding shift in attention towards that object encodes that object's location. The relevance of this embodiment is in terms of what happens when the representation of an object is subsequently reactivated. Activating the representation of an object necessarily activates the embodiment of the experience of that object, and because this experience necessarily includes an attentional component, the embodiment of that attentional component is also activated. We conjecture that reenacting this component will, in the absence of any competing attentional demands, cause the eyes to move automatically toward that object's location. The claim, then, is that the activation of the mental representation of a specific object in the visual scene will automatically cause a shift in attention towards the location at which that object was located (at the time that it was experienced). This in itself does not explain our competitor data. However, little more is required to explain those effects than the same processes implicated in priming. In respect of semantic priming (e.g., McRae & Boisvert, 1998; Moss, Ostrin, Tyler, & Marslen-Wilson, 1995), it is commonly supposed that the activation of a particular semantic feature causes the activation of other concepts that share that feature (where "semantic feature" is shorthand, within the embodied view of cognition, for a particular component of the neural substrate that encodes the relevant abstractions across the multiple experiences that led to the formation of the concept). In respect of our conceptual competitor data, we can suppose that hearing *piano* activates concepts that share experiential features, and in this case, experiential features that correspond to the (emergent) superordinate level category information associated with pianos (i.e., that they are musical instruments). The conceptual representation corresponding to the trumpet shares such information and has associated with it the episodic information corresponding to its experience previously in the visual scene. The ensuing change in activation state of this representation causes the reenactment of the experiential state associated with the trumpet, and hence (according to the previous arguments) the shift in attention toward it.[4]

In respect of the color competitor effects, a similar chain of events is required with one subtle, but as we shall see, perplexing, difference: Hearing *spinach* activates information about the prototypical color of spinach, but it is not information about the prototypical color of the visually presented frog that attracts looks; instead, it is information about the actual colors in the visual scene that attracts looks. In other words, activation does not spread to all things that are prototypically green. If it did, and by extension of the previous arguments, we should have seen looks toward the black and white frog in response to *spinach*. But we did not. Instead, activation of the color information associated with spinach results in orientation towards the location associated with the *perception* of color, rather than the location associated with *conceptual* color. Conceptual, or prototypical, color is a quite different kind of conceptual feature to category membership—a piano is a musical instrument whatever kind of piano it is, but what is its prototypical color? Black? Brown? White? And are apples green or red? And South American tree frogs can be any number of colors, ranging from yellow through red to blue. Further (around the UK) water is rarely *blue*. It is thus unclear what manner of abstraction results from the experience of the different colors of different things (even plants and leaves). Indeed, color appears to be largely context-dependent in a way that category membership is not (which is why, for the majority of their lifetimes, bananas are not yellow, and yet they are still fruit). We suspect that this distinction between category membership and prototypical color is the cause of the behavioral distinction between the corresponding competitor effects.

There is one fact about these data that is particularly noteworthy: Even in the presence of the target object, language-mediated eye movements are directed to objects that share certain characteristics, but not all, with the target specification determined by the unfolding word. That is, the eyes are directed *spuriously* to objects that are not intended by the speaker to attract the hearer's attention. Intriguingly, these spurious shifts in attention occur regardless of conceptual mismatch (as in the visual shape competitor and color competitor studies) or form mismatch (as in the conceptual competitor study). We return to the implications of such spurious eye movements after the next section, in which we use the competitor effects we have identified above (and specifically visual form competitor effects) to study the perceptual and attentional consequences of lexical ambiguity.

11.5 COMPETITOR EFFECTS AND THE ONLINE PROCESSING OF LEXICALLY AMBIGUOUS WORDS

Perceptual and conceptual competitor effects are a useful indication of the functioning of the cognitive processing system. But they can also be used as a tool to explore issues in language processing. The final study we shall describe uses competitor effects to explore issues in the processing of lexical (semantic) ambiguity.

11.5.1 Experiment 5: Semantically Ambiguous Words

The indeterminacy of meaning in our environment is a particularly pervasive problem that faces the cognitive system. The interpretation of a word can vary greatly from context to context, and this is particularly true in the case of homonyms for which the alternative interpretations may be completely unrelated as in *The animal rights activist will locate the animals and then unlock the pen* and *The secretary will write the letter and then put down the pen*. Here, it is simply an accident of the phonology that the two tokens of *pen* can have such differing meanings. Research on lexical ambiguity has centered on the question of how we come to select and integrate into the context the appropriate meaning of an ambiguous word. Duffy, Morris, and Rayner (1988), for example, provided evidence that best supports models in which more than one meaning of an ambiguous word is initially activated, with the degree of activation being influenced by the fit with prior context and by the relative frequencies of the alternative meanings of the ambiguous word. Their data provided evidence against multiple access models that assume that context has no effect on lexical access and evidence against selective access models that assume that sufficiently strong contexts will lead to selective access of only the contextually appropriate meaning. Given the sensitivity of language-mediated eye movements to lexical access (e.g., Allopenna, Magnuson, & Tanenhaus, 1998) and contextual integration (e.g., Kamide, Altmann, & Haywood, 2003), we conducted a series of studies identical in methodology to the competitor studies described above but in which the target words were lexically ambiguous (thus, instead of *spinach*, or *piano*, we used words like *pen* and *diamond*). Specifically, we were interested in the temporal dynamics with which objects in the visual scene that were related to the different meanings of the ambiguous target word would be fixated.

We selected 15 ambiguous words that are highly polarized with respect to the relative frequencies of their alternative meanings. Thus, for the word *pen*, the writing implement meaning is considerably more frequent than the enclosure meaning. We carried out a single word association task to determine the relative frequencies of these meanings. There were three experimental conditions in the first study: a neutral context condition, a biasing context condition, and a visual competitor condition. The neutral context did not bias one meaning or another of the target word: *First, the man got ready quickly, but then he checked the pen and suspected that it was damaged*. The sentences in the biasing and visual competitor conditions were identical but were designed to bias toward one meaning rather than another: *First, the welder locked up carefully, but then he checked the pen and suspected that it was damaged*. The sentences were identical to the neutral condition except for a phrase that biased towards the subordinate meaning of the ambiguous word (*welder locked up carefully*) which replaced the neutral phrase in the neutral condition (*man got ready quickly*). There has been a great deal of controversy about the classification of the strength of linguistic contexts in lexical ambiguity experiments (cf. Tanenhaus & Lucas, 1987). However, there has been little consensus about what constitutes a strong linguistic context. And although we used linguistic contexts that we judged would bias the subordinate meaning of ambiguous words, the evidence for the efficacy of our bias manipulation lies in the empirical data—that is, whether or not the bias increases the likelihood of fixations on the subordinate object (the enclosure) at the onset of the target word *pen* (cf. our use of biasing contexts in the visual competitor study described in the preceding text).

Of primary interest in this study was the presence or absence of visual referents for the alternative meanings of the lexically ambiguous target word and the interaction of eye movements with the sentential context. Each visual stimulus in the neutral and biasing condition portrayed four objects: One corresponded to the dominant meaning of the target word (e.g., a writing pen), one corresponded to the subordinate meaning (e.g., an appropriate enclosure), and two depicted objects from different semantic/conceptual categories. The names of all the objects in the scene were frequency-matched according to the CELEX database. In the visual competitor condition, the object corresponding to the dominant meaning (e.g., *pen*—writing implement) was replaced with a visual competitor of a similar visual form (a needle; see Figure 11.6).

We shall refer to the object corresponding to the dominating meaning as the *dominant object,* and similarly for the subordinate object. The procedure we used

Figure 11.6 An example stimulus of the visual competitor condition (the visual form competitor *needle* is depicted instead of the dominant meaning *pen*—writing implement).

was the same as in the previous experiments. We shall first report the percentage of trials on which each object was already being fixated at the onset of the target word. In the neutral condition, there were no significant differences in fixations to the dominant object, the subordinate object, or the distractor objects (24% on average for each one). Thus, the context was indeed neutral with respect to the likelihood of the dominant or subordinate objects being fixated. In the condition that favored the subordinate meaning, there were no differences in fixation likelihood between the distractors and the dominant object (17% each). However, there was a large increase in the likelihood that the subordinate object was being fixated by target onset (46%). Thus, our biasing contexts, which were designed to bias towards the subordinate meaning of the target word, appear to have been effective.[5] In the visual competitor condition (in which the dominant object was replaced by a visually similar competitor), there was no difference in fixation likelihood at target onset between the visual competitor and the distractors (17% each), but there was again a larger likelihood of fixation on the subordinate object (48%). We turn now to the incidence of saccadic movements during the target word itself (mean duration: 400 ms). In the neutral condition, there were marginally more saccades launched towards the dominant object than toward the subordinate object (26% vs. 17%—statistically significant by subjects but not by items). Both of these attracted more saccades than did the distractors (8% each). In the biasing condition, there were no more saccades launched toward the subordinate object (16%) than towards the dominant object (16%). Again, the distractors attracted fewer saccades (8% each). To the extent that we can interpret the neutral context condition as reflecting the standard dominance effect (with the dominant meaning being more strongly activated than the subordinate meaning), the biasing context suggests that looks toward the dominant object have been suppressed relative to the neutral condition (26% vs. 16%, a statistically significant difference, albeit at $p = .05$ by items). Nonetheless, the dominant object *was* looked at more often than either of the distractors. Of interest, therefore, is what happened in the visual competitor condition where the dominant object was replaced by a visual competitor (in this example, a needle). In the event, there were more looks toward the visual competitor than to either of the distractors (21% vs. 11%—significant by subjects, and approaching significance by items: $p < .1$), with looks to the subordinate object nonsignificantly lower than looks to the visual competitor (17%). The patterns of saccadic eye movements during the target word itself are mirrored more robustly, statistically speaking, in the data on the likelihood of each object being fixated at target word *offset*. In the neutral condition the dominant object was being fixated at this point on 43% of trials, compared to 29% for the subordinate object and 10% for each of the distractors. In the biasing condition, the corresponding figures were 27%, 46%, and 9%, respectively, and in the visual competitor condition, 26%, 50%, and 10%, respectively.

To summarize: We have converging evidence from the patterns of both fixation and saccades that in the neutral context the dominant object attracts more looks than the subordinate, which attracts more looks than the distractors. In the biasing context, the pattern reverses, with more fixations on the subordinate object than on the dominant one. Importantly, this reflects only the fact that there were more fixations to begin with on the subordinate object. In terms of *switched* attention, the dominant and subordinate object attracted equal numbers of saccadic movements, suggesting that the effect of the biasing context is to reduce the otherwise large number of movements toward the dominant object that would occur in the absence of a bias. Of course, one could argue that this pattern of shifting attention is in part an artifact of the fact that both meanings of the target word are represented in the visual scene. Perhaps, in the biasing context, only the subordinate meaning of the ambiguous word would ordinarily be active, but the physical presence in the visual scene of an object corresponding to the dominant meaning causes that meaning to be active also. The visual competitor data address this issue; in this case, there was no dominant object, just a visual competitor. And in that condition, the data patterned almost identically with the case where the dominant meaning *was* represented (the biasing condition). Thus, even in the absence of an object corresponding to the dominant meaning we find strong evidence that conceptual information associated with the dominant meaning, regarding physical form, was accessed during the target word *pen*. Thus, and despite the linguistic and visual context biasing the subordinate meaning, we found compelling evidence of the activation of the dominant meaning of the ambiguous word.

This last finding is open to alternative interpretations. On the one hand, the dominant meaning of *pen* may indeed have been activated in the context that biased the subordinate meaning (as predicted by multiple access models and hybrid models of lexical ambiguity resolution), and this activated representation may then have mediated eye movements toward the object that shared with this representation certain visual form features. On the other hand, the activation of the dominant meaning in the biasing context may have been due in part to the existence in the scene of an object with those form features. This may have activated concepts sharing those features (cf. our earlier account of competitor effects), including the concept associated with the dominant meaning of the ambiguous word (in other words, the activation may have originated through spreading activation from form information portrayed within the visual scene). The current data do not distinguish between these two cases.

Finally, we repeated the biased condition, in which the sentential context originally favored the subordinate meaning of the target word, and in which the visual scene portrayed objects depicting both the dominant and subordinate meanings of *pen*. In the new version of this condition, we modified the sentential contexts to bias the *dominant* meaning. Would we still find increased looks toward both the dominant *and* subordinate objects relative to the distractors? There were indeed significantly more saccades during *pen* to both the dominant and subordinate objects (20% and 14%, respectively) than to the unrelated distractors (7% each). The difference in looks to the dominant and subordinate objects was not statistically reliable.

To summarize: The main finding that goes beyond previous studies using other methodologies is that the presence of a clear and contextually appropriate referent for one meaning of the lexically ambiguous item does not prevent eye movements to a potential referent for the other meaning. This is true irrespective of whether the context biases the subordinate meaning or the dominant meaning. Even more significantly, the presence of such a clear and appropriate referent does not even prevent eye movements to other objects that are *unrelated* conceptually to the alternative meaning (although they must share some features with it; in these cases, it was visual form). These data confirm our previous findings that the activation of meaning has behavioral consequences that go beyond attending only to the intended referent; these consequences include fast eye movements in response to an individual word toward objects that, although related in visual form, color, or conceptual category, are clearly not the intended referent for that word.

11.6 GENERAL DISCUSSION AND CONCLUSION

Our research with regard to lexically ambiguous words provides an important addendum to the literature to date. In some respects, our study with a visual competitor in place of the object corresponding to the dominant meaning of an ambiguous word is simply a visual-world analog of a standard cross-modal priming study. In such a study, the target word would be presented in the auditory modality, and reaction times to a related word presented subsequently in the visual modality would be measured at test. In our studies, we also presented the target word in the auditory modality, although instead of subsequently monitoring reaction times to a related word, we monitored concurrent eye movements to a related object (related through visual form, although we anticipate that we could just as well have used category competitors as in our earlier competitor studies). We observed that the reaction to that object was quantitatively different to the reaction toward unrelated objects. In some respects, therefore, we have simply "ported" one paradigm onto another. And what we have shown is that conceptual representations corresponding to the contextually less preferred meaning are nonetheless activated and nonetheless mediate visual attention about the concurrent visual scene. Importantly, such activation happens even when there is, quite unambiguously, a uniquely identifiable visual referent that corresponds to the intended (contextually biased) meaning.

This last observation is perhaps the most significant. These data, coupled with the competitor effects we described earlier, suggest that even when we know what it is in the concurrent environment that is being referred to, we cannot help but attend to other objects that are related. It is this observation that is in some respects the most challenging. It suggests that, during everyday conversation, there are pressures driving our visual attention spuriously toward objects in the environment that are not the intended ones to which we should be attending. The situation is made all the more dramatic when we consider data by Allopenna and colleagues showing that as a word such as *candy* unfolds, our attention is driven not just towards *candy*, but towards *candles* also (a "cohort competitor" effect; Allopenna et al., 1998). Our data go further in showing that as those mental representations unfold, our attention is driven also to objects that are related in various different ways to the target concept (and we have only just begun to investigate the dimensions of relatedness on which such effects might occur). And when a word has more than one meaning, each of those meanings exerts an influence on where the visual system should attend next, somewhat independently of the context, and certainly independently of whether or not whatever is being attended to matches that meaning on all the relevant dimensions. One challenge that these data present is that there must be some mechanism that prevents the explosion of spurious shifts in attention that would occur if these influences went unchecked during normal conversational dialogue. In the absence of further data, we can only conjecture that such a mechanism must exist. Further research will be required to understand the limits on the effects we have identified here.

Eye movements to perceptual and conceptual competitors are fast, but are they automatic? This largely depends on our definition of automaticity. We do not have anything other than anecdotal reports from the participants themselves that they were unaware of any conscious control over their eye movements. The speed with which these effects manifest themselves (the target words averaged approximately 400 ms in duration) suggests that the eye movements we observed were not under volitional control (at least not in the sense that a conscious decision was made to move the eyes in a particular direction). Furthermore, we also obtained these results when only a small percentage of trials investigated a particular competitor relationship (less than 15%). Nor are our results an artifact of uncontrolled differences between different auditory targets or different visual objects. In one study we observed for the same acoustic target word *lettuce* more looks to a green jacket than toward blue trousers. But we also observed in this study fewer looks to the green jacket after *lemon*. Thus, whether we monitor for the same acoustic target looks toward different objects or, for the same object, looks engendered by different acoustic targets, the pattern is the same.

Traditional methods in experimental psycholinguistics have failed to highlight the behavioral consequences of a conceptual system whose concepts are not indivisible wholes. The major consequence we have highlighted in this chapter is that the conceptual parts that make up the whole can, during spoken word recognition, exert independent influences on how the cognitive system attends to the external world. One of the basic tenets of embodied cognition is that cognition is rooted in the same representational substrate that supports interaction with the external world. A direct consequence of this approach to cognition is that language, as a component part of cognition, must be studied in the context of the interactions it causes between the hearer and the world. One such interaction comprises the manner in which attention is directed, by language, around that world. We believe that, for too long, experimental psycholinguistics has remained modular, encapsulated, and theoretically autonomous with respect to the cognitive processes that serve our interactions with the world around us. Research into the relationship between language and vision attempts to place psycholinguistics at the center of cognition and, conversely, cognition at the center of psycholinguistics.

11.7 AUTHOR/ NOTE ACKNOWLEDGMENTS

Correspondence should be sent to Falk Huettig, Department of Psychology, University of York, York, YO10 5DD, England, UK. Email: F.Huettig@psych.york.ac.uk. FH was supported by a University of York doctoral studentship. The research was also made possible with support from the Medical Research Council (G0000224 awarded to GA). We thank Gareth Gaskell, Graham Hitch, Ken McRae, and Mike

Tanenhaus for constructive discussion of this research, and Chuck Clifton and Manuel Carreiras for their comments on an earlier version of this chapter.

References

Allopenna, P. D., Magnuson, J. S., & Tanenhaus, M. K. (1998). Tracking the time course of spoken word recognition using eye movements: Evidence for continuous mapping models. *Journal of Memory and Language, 38*(4), 419–439.

Altmann, G. T. M., & Kamide, Y. (1999). Incremental interpretation at verbs: Restricting the domain of subsequent reference. *Cognition, 73,* 247–264.

Altmann, G. T. M., & Kamide, Y. (in press). Now you see it, now you don't: mediating the mapping between language and the visual world. In Henderson, J. M., & Ferreira, F. (Eds.). *The interface of language, vision, and action.* New York: Psychology Press.

Baayen, R. H., Piepenbrock, R., & van Rijn, H. (1993). The CELEX lexical database [CD-ROM]. Philadelphia Linguistic Data Consortium, University of Pennsylvania.

Barsalou, L. W. (1999). Perceptual symbol systems. *Behavioral and Brain Sciences, 22,* 577–660.

Barsalou, L. W., Simmons, W. K., Barbey, A. K., & Wilson, C. D. (2003). Grounding conceptual knowledge in modality-specific systems. *Trends in Cognitive Science, 7,* 84–91.

Battig, W. F., & Montague, W. E. (1969). Category norms for verbal items in 56 categories: A replication and extension of the Connecticut category norms. *Journal of Experimental Psychology Monograph, 80.*

Calvin, W., & Bickerton, D. (2000). *Lingua ex machine: Reconciling Darwin and Chomsky with the human brain.* Cambridge, MA: MIT Press.

Cree, G. S., & McRae, K. (2003). Analyzing the factors underlying the structure and computation of the meaning of chipmunk, cherry, chisel, cheese, and cello (and many other such concrete nouns). *Journal of Experimental Psychology: General, 132,* 163–201.

Dahan, D., & Tanehaus, M. (2002). *Activation of conceptual representations during spoken-word recognition.* Poster presented at the 43rd Annual Meeting of the Psychonomics Society, Kansas city.

Dahan, D., & Tanenhaus, M. K. (2004). Continuous mapping from sound to meaning in spoken-language comprehension: Immediate effects of verb-based thematic constraints. *Journal of Experimental Psychology: Learning, Memory & Cognition, 30,* 498–513.

Dell'Aqua, R., & Grainger, J. (1999). Unconscious semantic priming from pictures. *Cognition, 73,* B1–B15.

Duffy, S. A., Morris, R. K., & Rayner, K. (1988). Lexical ambiguity and fixation times in reading. *Journal of Memory and Language, 27,* 429–446.

Glenberg, A. (1997). What memory is for. *Behavioral and Brain Sciences, 20,* 1–55.

Henderson, J. M., & Ferreira, F. (Eds.). (2003). *The interface of language, vision, and action.* New York: Psychology Press.

Kamide, Y., Altmann, G. T. M., & Haywood, S. (2003). The time course of prediction in incremental sentence processing: Evidence from anticipatory eye movements. *Journal of Memory and Language, 49,* 133–156.

Kamide, Y., Scheepers, C., Altmann, G., & Crocker, M. (2002). *Integration of semantic and syntactic information in predictive processing.* Paper presented at the 15th CUNY conference, New York.

McRae, K., & Boisvert, S. (1998). Automatic semantic similarity priming. *Journal of Experimental Psychology: Learning, Memory, and Cognition, 24,* 558–572.

Moss, H. E., Ostrin, R. K., Tyler, L. K., & Marslen-Wilson, W. D. (1995). Accessing different types of lexical semantic information: Evidence from priming. *Journal of Experimental Psychology: Learning, Memory, and Cognition, 21,* 863–883.

Nelson, D. L., McEvoy, C. L., & Schreiber, T. A. (1998). *The University of South Florida word association, rhyme, and word fragment norms.* From http://www.usf.edu/Free-Association/

O'Regan, J. K. (1992). Solving the "real" mysteries of visual perception: the world as an outside memory. *Canadian Journal of Psychology, 46,* 461–488.

Snodgrass, J. G., & Vanderwart, M. (1980). A standardised set of 260 pictures: Norms for name agreement, image agreement, familiarity, and visual complexity. *Journal of Experimental Psychology: Human Learning and Memory, 6,* 174–215.

Tanenhaus, M. K., & Lucas, M. M. (1987). Context effects in lexical processing. *Cognition, 25,* 213–234.

Yee, E., & Sedivy, J. (2001). *Using eye movements to track the spread of semantic activation during spoken word recognition.* Paper presented to the 13th Annual CUNY Sentence Processing Conference, Philadelphia.

Notes

1. However, and in line with other recent work using the visual-world paradigm (see Henderson & Ferreira, 2003, for recent reviews), we, in fact, defined this region as starting 200 ms *after* the onset of the target word and ending 200 ms after its offset. This is to take into account the time it takes to program and initiate a saccadic movement (see Altmann & Kamide, in press, for an empirical investigation into such launch times, and Dahan & Tanenhaus, (2004), for compelling evidence that the 200 ms figure is an accurate estimate).

2. Henceforth, all reported differences in subsequent analyses were significant by both subjects and items unless otherwise described.

3. In collaboration with Ken McRae, we computed the "conceptual distance" between each target and its conceptual competitor (see Cree & McRae, 2003, for a discussion of the relevant semantic feature norms). Of the 30 target-competitor pairs in our study, we could compute such distance scores for 24 of the pairs (that is, existing semantic feature norms existed for both members of the pair). We eliminated a further two pairs whose members were visually very similar. We then correlated the remaining distance scores against the proportion of saccades launched during the target word towards the competitor in the competitor-only condition. The resulting correlation was highly significant ($r = 0.6$), and we are thus confident that our data do, indeed, reflect effects mediated at the level of semantic features.

4. It is the change in activation state that causes the shift in attention, because, although the representation corresponding to the trumpet receives some priming from *piano*, we can suppose that it becomes neither as active as the representation corresponding to whatever is currently being fixated, nor as active as the representation corresponding to *piano*. Thus, we conjecture that it is not *degree* of activation but *change* in activation that drives shifts in attention. However, a full treatment of what drives attention is beyond the remit of this research. Nonetheless, to fully understand how it is that language can mediate visual attention will require an understanding also of attentional control.

5. See also the literature on prediction effects in sentence comprehension (e.g., Altmann & Kamide, 1999; Kamide, Scheepers, Altmann, & Crocker, 2002; McDonald & Shillcock, chapter 5, this volume).

Chapter 12
That Is Not *It* and *It* Is Not *That*: Reference Resolution and Conceptual Composites

SARAH BROWN-SCHMIDT, DONNA K.
BYRON, AND MICHAEL K. TANENHAUS

12.1 INTRODUCTION

This chapter reports work in progress that examines the processing of the personal pronoun *it* and the demonstrative pronoun *that*. The motivation for this work is to understand how addressees combine utterance-based linguistic information and conceptually based properties of potential referents to assign interpretations to anaphoric expressions in spoken-language comprehension. Before turning to the details of our experiment, we briefly review some of the relevant background literature on personal and demonstrative pronouns.

Demonstrative pronouns such as *that* and *these* have received relatively little attention in psycholinguistics and computational linguistics, perhaps because they are less common in text compared to personal pronouns such as *it*. However, recent analyses of conversational speech find that demonstratives occur just as frequently as personal pronouns (Byron & Allen, 1998; Eckert & Strube, 2000). The ubiquity of demonstrative pronouns in conversational speech takes on added importance because most approaches to pronoun resolution assume an initial stage in which the pronoun is linked to a linguistic antecedent. However, demonstrative pronouns often do not have clearly identifiable linguistic antecedents. As a consequence, computational algorithms that work well for assigning interpretations to personal pronouns perform poorly with demonstratives (Byron, 2002).

There is general agreement in the literature that comprehenders tend to assign different interpretations to *it* and *that* though they are not in complete complementary distribution. For example, Schuster (1988) presented participants with different versions of sentences in which only the form of the pronoun was altered. Her participants had different preferred interpretations for *it* and *that*, as illustrated in the discourse in (1) and (2):

(1) *John thought about becoming a street person.*
(2) a. *It would hurt his mother and it would make his father furious.*
     b. *It would hurt his mother and that would make his father furious.*

The use of the personal pronoun *it* in the second conjunct of sentence (2a) maintains the reference established by the first *it* (John's becoming a street person). In contrast, use of the demonstrative pronoun *that* in (2b) changes the interpretation to something like *John's mother being hurt would make his father furious.* In a similar study, Borthen, Fretheim, and Gundel (1997) found the same pattern in both English and Norwegian. This alternation in meaning is typically attributed to the effect of attentional focus: personal pronouns are claimed to prefer referents that are highly salient, whereas demonstrative pronouns prefer less-salient referents.

A similar distinction between *it* and *that* has also been found in several studies of naturally occurring discourse. In a corpus of spoken descriptions of apartment layouts, *it* was used to refer to the room currently being described, which is taken to be the local focus, whereas *that* was used to refer to portions of the apartment outside the current focus of attention (Linde, 1979). Linde found that *it* and *that* were for the most part in complementary distribution. However, a few cases violated this pattern, leading her to conclude that there is some overlap in the conditions for choosing between *that* and *it*. In a set of career counseling interviews, Passonneau isolated two factors that characterize the differences between use of personal and demonstrative pronouns (Passonneau, 1989; 1993). The first is that demonstratives were preferred over personal pronouns when either the pronoun or its antecedent was not the subject of its clause. The second is that when referring to elements described previously by clausal or sentential arguments, the more clause-like the antecedent, the more likely it is to be rementioned with a demonstrative pronoun. Passonneau concluded that each of these conditions indicates that demonstratives are used to refer to entities that are of lower salience than personal pronouns.

Perhaps the most complete proposal for how pronominal forms are related to the cognitive status of the entity being referred to comes from the Givenness Hierarchy proposed by Gundel, Hedberg, and Zacharski (1993) and shown in Table 12.1. A key property of the Givenness Hierarchy is that the cognitive states are organized in a subsumption hierarchy rather than into mutually exclusive categories. Each state entails all lower states. Thus, focused items are also activated, familiar, uniquely identifiable, etc.

The Givenness Hierarchy claims that particular referring expressions conventionally signal specific levels of activation of the referent. Given a referring expression of a specific form to interpret, an addressee utilizes the form as a clue to the likely cognitive status of the referent. According to the Givenness Hierarchy, demon-

Table 12.1. **The Givenness Hierarchy**

Status:	In focus>	Activated>	Familiar>	Uniquely identifiable >	Referential>	Type identifiable
Form:	*It/*	*This/*	*That N/*	*The N*	*This N*	*A N*
	them/	*that*	*This N*		*(indefinite*	
	they				*use)*	

strative pronouns may be used to refer to entities with *activated* status, such as entities that have been evoked into short-term memory by some trigger in either the discourse or the conversational setting. In contrast, unstressed pronouns (personal pronouns) and zero pronouns may only be used to refer to entities with *focused* status. Gundel et al. (1993) define focus as follows: "the entities in focus at a given point in the discourse will be that partially ordered subset of activated entities that are likely to be continued as topics of subsequent utterances" (p. 279), for example, "subjects and direct objects of matrix sentences" (p. 279). The Givenness Hierarchy subsumes the text-based conditions proposed by Passonneau, and in addition it also allows for referents that are activated by virtue of being related to items explicitly mentioned in the discourse or salient in the discourse setting.

Although there is a large psycholinguistics literature on the processing of anaphoric expressions (for review see Garnham, 2001; also see Gordon, Grosz, & Gillom, 1993; van Gompel, Liversedge, & Pearson, chapter 7, this volume), the most detailed proposals for reference resolution have been developed by computational linguists. Although it has long been acknowledged that conceptual constructs should be utilized both in estimating the attentional salience of referents and in determining the acceptability of candidate referents in particular argument positions (Carbonnel & Brown, 1988; Hobbs, 1986; Sidner, 1983), the most effective general purpose algorithms rank the salience of entities using grammatical function to assign salience (Tetreault, 2001). For example, entities referred to by arguments of the main verb are considered to be more salient than other arguments, and items mentioned as simple noun phrases are more salient than referents described by phrase types such as verb phrases and sentential complements. It is important to note that formulations of attentional state based entirely on properties of the discourse are meant to serve as approximations to cognitive status. Thus they do not reflect other factors that might make a particular entity likely to be the topic of upcoming discourse, such as its importance in an ongoing task. However, detailed models of pronoun interpretation that utilize anything other than surface linguistic features are just beginning to be developed (Baldwin, 1997; Eckert & Strube, 2000; Byron & Allen, 1998; Byron, 2002). Moreover, it is unclear whether conceptual factors are used in parallel with linguistic factors or whether reference resolution begins with an initial interrogation of linguistic antecedents and utilizes conceptual factors either to evaluate the relative plausibility of potential referents or when utterance-based procedures do not identify a likely referent.

Demonstratives may prove particularly useful for determining the role of conceptual factors in reference resolution because there is suggestive evidence that demonstratives may be preferred when the entity being referred to is a conceptual composite. Channon (1980) observed that demonstrative pronouns have looser agreement features than personal pronouns. He suggested that speakers may use demonstratives when the antecedent is a composite entity with conflicting or unclear semantic features. In this situation, the speaker may be unable to quickly determine the appropriate agreement features when selecting a pronoun. Thus the more complicated the constituent used to describe the antecedent, the more likely it is to be referred to using *that*, and the less acceptable other pronouns will be.

In summary, personal and demonstrative pronouns have different preferred referents, with the differences related to the activation level of the referent. Although activation can be inferred from utterance-based properties, conceptual factors may also influence the activation of a potential referent. Demonstratives may be a preferred anaphoric form for referring to conceptual composites that do not have clear linguistic antecedents. Taken together, these factors suggest that comparing personal pronouns and demonstratives might provide a promising window into how linguistic and conceptual factors affect reference resolution for different classes of pronouns in spoken-language comprehension.

12.2 OVERVIEW OF THE EXPERIMENT

We examined the eye movements of participants as they followed spoken instructions to manipulate blocks and common objects using the action-based variant of the visual-world paradigm (Tanenhaus, Spivey-Knowlton, Eberhard, & Sedivy, 1995). Critical instructions manipulated the degree to which the potential referents for the pronouns *it* or *that* formed a natural conceptual composite, such as a cup on a saucer. The characteristics of the instructions and objects allowed us to examine the concurrent effects of discourse and pragmatic factors on the on-line interpretation of *it* and *that* in sentence pairs like (6a) and (b):

(6)   a. *Put the cup on the saucer.*
      b. *Now put it off to the side.*

We used an action-based task (Tanenhaus et al., 1995) for three reasons. First, having participants manipulate real objects allowed us to independently vary the linguistic properties of the instruction and the properties of the potential referents. Second, monitoring eye movements provides a moment-by-moment window into reference resolution processes (e.g., Arnold, Eisenband, Brown-Schmidt, & Trueswell, 2000). Third, and perhaps most importantly, the action performed by the participant reveals the interpretation assigned to the anaphor on each particular trial. This allows one to conduct action-contingent analyses (cf. Runner, Sussman, & Tanenhaus, in press) to examine the earliest moments of processing for conditions that result in similar and different interpretations. In contrast, most eye-movement studies investigating reference resolution provide insights into processing difficulty but do not assess what interpretations are assigned. This is potentially problematic when the listener's choice of one of several potential classes of referents for an anaphor differ across trials and the preference for alternative interpretations differs across pronoun forms. These conditions are likely to hold whenever investigators compare ambiguous anaphors that have different distributions of preferred interpretations. Under these circumstances, processing difficulty might provide insight into processes that hold across all interpretations. However, average measures of processing difficulty are just as likely to be misleading because data are being combined across different types of trials. As we will see, action-contingent analyses allow one to distinguish between these alternatives for the pronouns *it* and *that*.

12.3 METHOD

We present eyetracking and behavioral data from 16 participants recruited from the University of Rochester undergraduate community. The experiment lasted approximately 1 hr, and participants were paid for their time. Following eyetracker calibration, participants were seated at a table on which the experimenter placed the experimental stimuli, which included everyday objects and children's blocks. Participants were instructed to follow prerecorded spoken instructions to manipulate the objects. They were told that the task was fairly easy and to simply "do the first thing that comes to mind" when given the instructions. Eye movements were measured using a lightweight, head-mounted ASL Series 5000. Software superimposed fixations on a video-record taken from a 60-Hz camera mounted on the headband. The actions and eye movements of the participants were hand-coded by the experimenters using a digital VCR.

On each trial, participants were presented with a display that consisted of four objects, as illustrated in Figure 12.1. Two classes of objects were used: children's blocks and everyday objects that formed a natural composite, e.g., a cup and saucer.

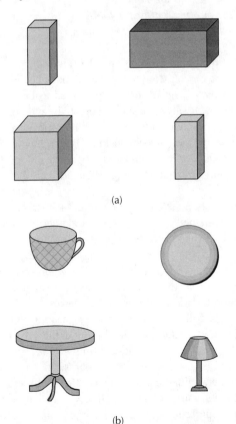

(a)

(b)

Figure 12.1 A 2-D representation of the experimental display, (a) for the blocks and (b) objects conditions.

The children's blocks were six small, brightly colored blocks of different shapes (all cuboids) and colors (yellow, red, purple, blue, orange, green). The everyday objects (see Appendix 1) were slightly larger than the blocks, and more variable in size and shape. The object pairs were items that when placed together would form a coherent whole such as a cup and a saucer, or a toy lamp and a table.

Example sets of instructions from trials using the children's blocks and the objects are presented in examples 7 and 8, respectively.

(7) a. *Put the <u>red block</u> next to the blue block.*
     b. *Now put that on the green block.*
     c. *Put the green block on the yellow block.*
     d. *Now put the blue block on the yellow block.*
        (Scene includes a red, blue, green, and yellow block.)

(8) a. *Put the <u>cup</u> on the saucer.*
     b. *Now put it over by the lamp.*
     c. *Put the table next to the lamp.*
     d. *Now put the cup in front of the table.*
        (Scene includes cup, saucer, table, lamp.)

In both examples, the first sentence (7a and 8a) introduces two discourse entities in the role of theme (the object being moved) and goal (the destination of the moved object). The theme, which is underlined, is predicted to be the most salient entity, henceforth the *focused entity* at the onset of *Now* in 7b and 8b. The second sentence (7b and 8b) contained a pronoun, either *it* or *that*. Eye-movement data were analyzed from the onset of *Now* (in the (b) sentences) and continued until participants completed an action in response to that command. The third and fourth instructions never contained pronouns, and eyetracking data associated with these sentences were not analyzed.

A total of 64 instruction sets, each containing 4 instructions, were used in the study. Of these, 32 contained blocks and 32 contained common objects. Half of these trials contained a pronoun in the second instruction. The stimulus sentences were prerecorded by a female speaker, speaking as naturally as possible, at a fairly quick but intelligible rate. The "natural" stress on *that* was somewhat more pronounced than the stress on *it* (this difference was confirmed by an analysis of word length; *that* was longer than *it* by an average of 88 ms).

We manipulated the following three factors: pronoun type (*it* vs. *that*), object type (everyday objects vs. children's blocks), and the whether the prepositional phrase introducing the goal in the first instruction was *on top of* or *next to*. We will refer to the manipulation of the prepositional phrase as the location manipulation, since the preposition determined the location of the theme with respect to the goal. The object-type manipulation was blocked (first vs. second half of the experiment) and block order was counterbalanced across participants. Pronoun-type and object location factors were both manipulated using a Latin square design. Each participant was presented with a total of 32 target pronoun sentences, 4 in each of the 8 different conditions. The trials using children's blocks were organized into one pseudorandom order. The 6 different colored blocks were randomly assigned to the sentences for two different lists (plus two corresponding reverse-order lists). The trials using everyday objects were organized into a different pseudorandom order and the individual items (such as the trial with the cup, saucer, lamp, and table) rotated through the four conditions, yielding four lists (plus four reverse-order lists).

12.4 RESULTS

Our analyses were guided by five questions: (1) Do *it* and *that* have different preferred interpretations, with *it* more frequently interpreted as the focus than *that*? (2) Does *that* preferentially refer to a mentioned, but not focused, entity, or does it preferentially refer to a conceptual composite? (3) Is there an effect of conceptual coherence on the rate of composite interpretations, with the salience of the composite increasing the degree to which pronouns are interpreted as referring to composites? (4) When *it* and *that* are interpreted as having the same referent (e.g., the theme), does the processing of the pronouns differ? (5) When listeners adopt the preferred interpretation for a particular pronoun, is reference resolution faster when the pronoun refers to the linguistically more salient entity?

Referent choice. We can answer the first three questions by examining the actions performed by the participants. When participants heard instructions such as *Put the cup next to the saucer. Now put it/that ...,* they typically moved either the theme (the cup) or the composite (both the cup and saucer) to the specified location. We will refer to the object they selected as the *referent* of the pronoun. A small number of responses fell into one of three other categories (accounting for 2% of the data): selection of the goal (e.g., the saucer), one of the other two items in the scene (e.g., the lamp or table, in Example 8), or selecting three or more items. Due to the low frequency of occurrence, we will not discuss these trials except to note that the composite, which was not introduced in a linguistic constituent, was preferred to the goal, which did have a linguistically introduced antecedent. This result demonstrates that nonlinguistic referents can be as highly activated as some linguistically introduced antecedents. We return to this point in the discussion.

It and *that* clearly had different preferred referents. Participants tended to interpret *it* as the theme of the preceding utterance (see Figure 12.2a) and *that* as the composite (see Figure 12.2b).

Pragmatic factors clearly guided the interpretation of both *it* and *that*. Placing the theme on top of the goal object increased the number of composite interpretations of both *it* and *that*. This effect was strongest for the conditions with common objects. These observations were confirmed by analyses of variance. Because we observed primarily theme and composite interpretations, we simply analyzed the proportion of theme interpretations as the dependent variable in the following analyses. A lower proportion of theme interpretations thus implies a higher proportion of composite interpretations. An ANOVA including pronoun type (*it/that*), object location (*on top/next to*), and object type (objects/blocks) as factors, and participants as the random variable, was significant for all three main effects, as

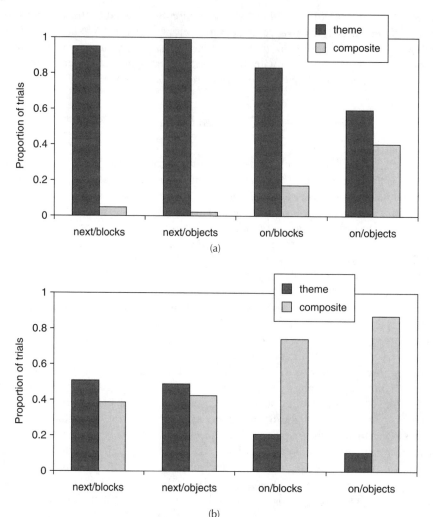

Figure 12.2a–b Interpretations of (a) *it* and (b) *that* by object location (*on top/next to*), and object type (objects/blocks). "Theme" refers to selections of the theme (e.g., the cup) as the referent, and "composite" refers to selections of the composite (e.g., cup and saucer). Bars do not add up to 100% because we do not show other types of referent selections.

well as a significant object type by object location interaction. The remaining three-way and the two-way interactions were not significant (all F's < 1.5). The main effect of the pronoun was due to more theme interpretations for *it* than for *that*, $F(1, 15) = 46.23$, $p < .000$. The main effect of object location was due to more theme interpretations in the *next to* condition compared to the *on top*-of condition, $F(1, 15) = 35.33$, $p < .0001$. The main effect of object type was due to more theme interpretations in the blocks conditions compared to the objects conditions, $F(1, 15) = 6.72$, $p < .05$. The significant object type by object location interaction, $F(1, 15) = 20.54$, $p < .001$, was due to a large preference for the composite interpretation in the *on top*/objects condition, and an approximately equal number of theme and composite interpretations in the blocks condition (but no effect of object type in the *next to* condition).

In summary, the preferred interpretation of *it* was the theme, and the preferred interpretation of *that* was the composite. However, the interpretation of both pronouns was modulated by pragmatic factors that affected how easily the theme and goal could be construed as a composite entity.

Fixations to potential referents. Addressing questions 4 and 5 requires examining the timing with which participants considered potential referents for *it* and for *that*. We first conducted an analysis of eye movements beginning at the onset of *Now* in the phrases containing pronouns [e.g., (7b) and (8b)], and continuing until the participant moved and released an object in response to the command. At the onset of the pronoun, participants were looking approximately equally at the theme and goal objects, with a slight preference for the theme. This preference for the theme increased over the course of the time window we analyzed and was still present at the end of our coding range. About 1200 ms after the onset of *Now*, looks to the destination [e.g., the green block and the lamp in examples (7b) and (8b)] begin to rise. By 2000 ms, participants were equally likely to be looking at the theme and destination.

In order to make sense of the fixation data, we need to consider what patterns of eye movements would be expected if the participants were considering a theme or a composite interpretation. If a participant is considering the theme as the referent, we would expect looks to the theme. However, it is less obvious what the pattern should be when the participant is considering the composite. In this situation, the participants might focus on the goal object, which is at the bottom, or alternate looking between the theme and goal. Thus, while we expect more variability in situations where participants are considering composites compared to when they are considering the theme, we would expect more looks to the goal overall when the participant interprets the pronoun as the composite. Additionally, we can supplement these observations by focusing on the rise in looks to the destination. It is likely that participants would begin looking at the destination location only after deciding which object to move. Thus the timing of looks to the destination should reveal the difficulty in arriving at an interpretation of the pronoun.

We first analyze the proportion of eye movements for the three conditions that we manipulated: type of object, pronoun, and location. Recall, however, that these analyses are confounded by the fact that participants made different numbers of theme and composite choices across conditions. As a partial solution to this problem, we then present action-contingent analyses in which we separately examine trials on which the participants adopted theme and composite interpretations.

Upon the onset of *Now* in critical phrases, fixations were primarily limited to the theme, goal, and destination locations, with few looks to the unrelated object in the scene. In order to simplify our analyses, we present the relative proportion of fixations between these three categories. As an additional simplification, all the figures collapse the data from the two different object types (blocks and objects) together.

Figures 12.3a and 12.3b show the relative proportion of fixations to the theme, goal, and destination for the *next to/it*, and *next to/that* conditions, respectively. As

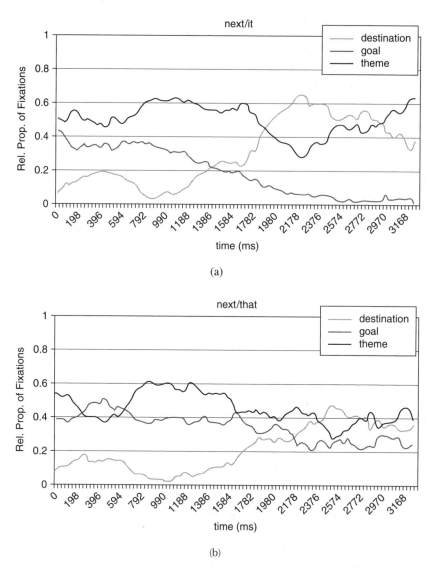

(a)

(b)

with the overall pattern of fixations, initial eye movements were primarily to the theme, followed by a later rise in looks to the destination location. Eye movements associated with the pronoun *that* elicited substantially more looks to the goal object.

In contrast to the *next to/it* condition where looks to the goal fall below 20% at about 1400 ms, in the *next to/that* condition, looks to the goal remained high, reflecting the larger number of composite interpretations in this condition. In the *on top/it* condition, there was an early preference for looks to the theme, followed by a later rise in looks to the destination (see Figure 12.3c). In contrast, fixations associated with the *on top/that* condition showed a completely different pattern (see Figure 12.3d). In the *on top/that* condition, we see an almost equal proportion of

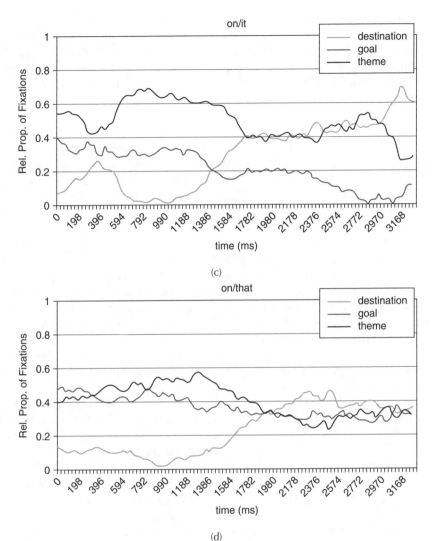

(c)

(d)

Figure 12.3a–d Relative proportion of fixations to theme, goal, and destination for (a) *next to/it*, (b) *next to/that*, (c) *on top/it*, and (d) *on top/that*, for both blocks and objects. 0 ms = onset of *Now*, 316ms and 358ms = average onsets of it and that, respectively.

looks to theme and goal, and sustained looks to the goal which do not drop off as they do in the *it* condition.

We analyzed the eye-movement data in four 400-ms windows, beginning 200 ms after average pronoun onset. Due to differences in the pronoun onset time between *it* and *that* conditions, the windows for the *that* condition begin approximately 40 ms after those for the *it* condition. Our first window began 200 ms following pronoun onset because this is the first place at which we would expect to see fixations driven by the pronoun itself. The first two epochs capture the earliest effects we would expect to see based on participants hearing the pronoun. The onset of the destination location information [e.g., *lamp* in example (8b)] is shortly before the beginning of epoch 3, so we would expect to see destination-related effects primarily in epochs 3 and 4.

Following Arnold et al. (2000), we analyzed the eyetracking data in terms of "theme advantage." We calculated the theme advantage for each segment by taking the total amount of time spent looking at the theme in a given condition and subtracting the total amount of time spent looking at the goal. Fixations to the destination location are analyzed separately (see the following text). For each of the four 400-ms segments, a separate 3-way ANOVA with participants as the random variable was calculated using the pronoun, object type, and object location variables as factors. At the first two epochs, only the pronoun-type effect was significant, with more looks to the theme in the *it* conditions, epoch 1: $F(1, 15) = 5.88$, $p < .05$; epoch 2: $F(1, 15) = 3.36$, $p = .09$. The pronoun-type effect persisted in epoch 3: $F(1, 15) = 19.56$, $p < .001$. In addition, this main effect was qualified by a marginal object-type by pronoun-type interaction, $F(1, 15) = 4.32$, $p = .06$. At Epoch 3, *it* and *that* did not differ in the blocks condition ($p = .58$), but there was a strong theme bias associated with *it* (as compared to *that*) in the objects condition, $F(1, 15) = 15.78$, $p < .01$. One source of this difference may be the increased prominence of the theme for objects compared to blocks. In epoch 4, the same pronoun-type effect continued, $F(1, 15) = 24.70$, $p < .001$. There was also a significant object-type by object-location interaction, $F(1, 15) = 7.52$, $p < .05$. The reason for this interaction was that, in the objects condition, there were significantly more looks to the theme for the *next to* compared to *on top* instructions, $F(1, 15) = 7.25$, $p < .05$. However, in the blocks condition, we did not observe a significant difference between the *next to* and *on top* conditions ($p = .96$).

In summary, these analyses substantiate previous claims that the preferred interpretation of *it* is the theme, as we consistently found more eye movements to the theme for the pronoun *it* as compared to *that*. Additionally, we observed interactions with object location and object type, suggesting that interpretation of both pronouns is affected by pragmatic as well as discourse-based factors.

Looks to the destination. Looks to the destination should reflect the participants' decision to move an object to that location. Thus we would expect the timing of the rise in looks to the destination to provide information about the relative timing of reference resolution across conditions. The onset of the destination phase did not begin until just before the beginning of the time window captured by epoch 3, so we only present analyses for epochs 3 and 4. Looks to the destination in these regions suggest that participants generally arrived at an interpretation of the pronoun earlier in the *it* conditions, as indicated by larger proportion of fixations to the destination. Additionally, this effect was modulated by the pragmatic factors of object kind and location.

At epoch 3, we observed a significant pronoun-type effect, $F(1, 15) = 9.56$, $p < .01$, with more looks to the destination for *it* trials. This main effect was qualified by a significant object-type by pronoun-type interaction, $F(1, 15) = 5.61$, $p < .05$. In the blocks condition, participants looked significantly more to the destination for *it* ($p < .01$). However, we did not see pronoun differences in the objects condition ($p = .54$). At this epoch, we also observed a significant object-type by object-location interaction, $F(1, 15) = 6.55$, $p < .05$, with more looks to the destination for *on top* in the blocks condition ($p < .01$) and no difference between *on top* and *next to* in the objects condition ($p = .6$). Finally, in Epoch 4, we observed a main object-type effect, $F(1, 15) = 10.92$, $p < .01$, with more looks to the destination for the blocks condition, and a main pronoun-type effect, $F(1, 15) = 5.27$, $p < .05$, with more looks to the destination for *it*.

12.5 INTERIM SUMMARY

Taken together, the pattern of looks to potential referents and destinations support two conclusions. First, *it* is interpreted more quickly than *that*. Second, theme interpretations are arrived at more quickly than composite interpretations. This pattern of results is consistent with the hypothesis that participants initially consider the most highly activated linguistic antecedents before considering possible nonlinguistic referents. However, this conclusion should be accepted with caution. First, the low proportion of goal interpretations is inconsistent with the idea that all referents with linguistic antecedents are considered before referents without linguistic antecedents. Second, delayed looks to the destination for *that* may simply reflect the fact that composite interpretations may require participants to look at both the theme and goal in order to carry out the action. This problem is most clearly demonstrated in the *on top/that* condition (see Figure 12.3d) in which participants look back and forth between the theme and goal throughout the time window analyzed.

These differences in the on-line interpretation of *it* and *that* may be characteristic of early processing differences between the pronouns, regardless of their final interpretation. Alternatively, we may observe early distinctions in the eye-movement patterns which reflect the final interpretation. In order to obtain a more accurate picture of how reference resolution proceeds, we conducted action-contingent analysis in which we analyzed eye movements based on the final referent choice.

Action-dependent analyses. In order to understand whether the on-line interpretation of *it* and *that* are qualitatively different, we analyzed the eye-movement data based on referent selection. Due to problems of small sample sizes, we collapsed across the object-type variable and will focus primarily on descriptive analyses. First, we present the data from trials in the *on top/that* condition in which subjects chose the composite (Figure 12.4a) because this condition strongly facilitated composite interpretations. Figure 12.4b presents fixations to trials in the *next to/it* condition in which subjects chose the theme because this is the condition which best supported the preferred interpretation of *it*.

The pattern of fixations in Figure 12.4a shows strong, long-lasting competition between theme and goal, reflecting the fact that the subjects formed composite interpretations on these trials. In contrast, the fixation pattern in Figure 12.4b shows a theme bias from early on in the processing.

Next, consider the processing of *it* in the *on top* condition. Here, participants were equally likely to choose the composite or the theme (Figures 12.5a and 12.5b, respectively). The fixation pattern when subjects chose the theme shows the same pattern as in Figure 12.4b. However, when participants chose the composite

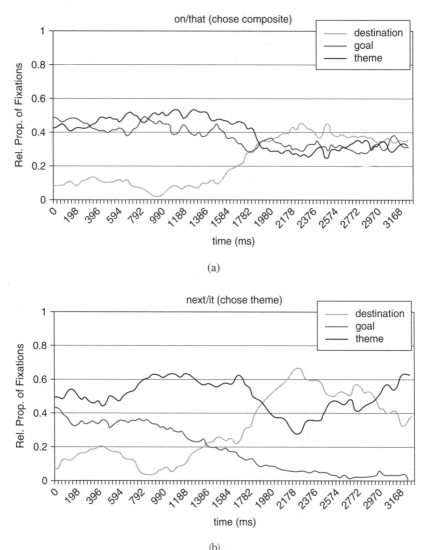

Figure 12.4a–b Relative proportion of fixations to theme, goal, and destination for (a) *on top/that* (chose the composite), and (b) *next to/it* (chose the theme), respectively, for both blocks and objects. 0 ms = onset of *Now*.

interpretation, there was still an initial theme bias, with the composite pattern emerging later. These results suggest that listeners initially considered the theme interpretation for *it* on all trials, and then later rejected the theme interpretation on some proportion of trials when there was also a salient composite referent.

Figures 12.5c and 12.5d show the eye movements associated with the *next to/that* condition on trials where subjects selected the composite or the theme (respectively). When subjects selected the composite (12.5c), we see the standard fixation pattern associated with composites, with looks equally distributed between the theme and

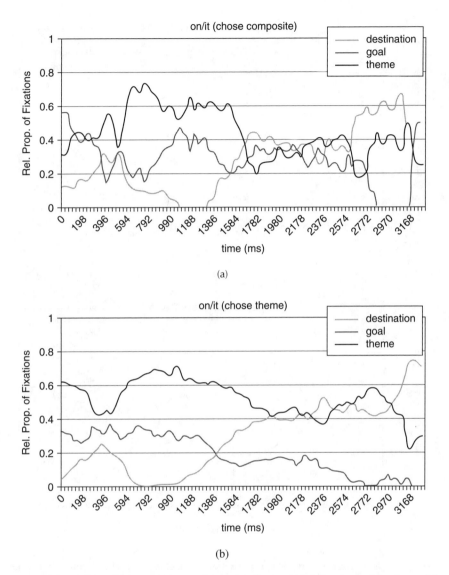

(a)

(b)

the goal. In contrast, when subjects chose the theme (12.5d), we see a substantial theme advantage, comparable to the pattern seen for interpretations of *it* in the *next to* condition (Figure 12.4b).

In both the *next to/that* and *on top/it* conditions, there are two clear patterns of interpretation of the pronoun (as the theme or the composite), which are reflected not only in the behavioral data but also in the early on-line data. When *it* and *that* were assigned theme interpretations, the pattern of early eye movements was very similar, suggesting that similar referents were considered. However, for composite interpretations there was a suggestion of an initial theme bias for *it* but not for *that*.

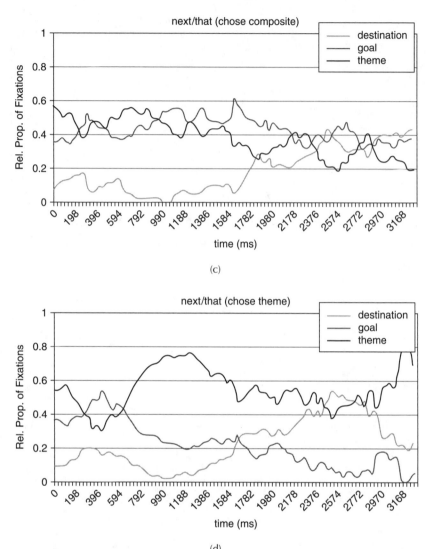

(c)

(d)

Figure 12.5a–d Relative proportion of fixations to theme, goal, and destination for both blocks and objects. Figures 12.5a and 12.5b show the *on top/it* condition where subjects chose the composite and the theme (respectively). Figures 12.5c and 12.5d show the *next to/that* conditions where subjects chose the composite and the theme (respectively). 0 ms = onset of *Now*.

12.6 SUMMARY AND IMPLICATIONS

The interpretation of both demonstrative and personal pronouns was affected by factors such as the type and placement of objects in the scene. Increasing the availability of a conceptual composite in the scene by placing the two most recently mentioned objects on top of one another increased composite interpretations of both pronouns. In addition, using entities which made transparent conceptual groupings (such as a cup and a saucer) increased composite interpretations for both pronouns compared to the conditions with blocks. Contrary to many theories of demonstratives, we rarely observed participants interpreting the demonstrative as the mentioned but nonfocused entity (the goal). Additionally, interpretations of *that* as the theme were frequent in conditions where the pragmatic factors biased this response (e.g., the *next to* condition).

The on-line interpretation of the pronouns showed early and long-lasting differences between the pronoun types. Upon hearing *it*, participants showed early and long-lasting looks to the theme; whereas, upon hearing *that*, participants looked relatively equally to both the theme and goal, reflecting their off-line choices (this difference was also reflected in faster looks to the destination for *it*). We observed the object-type and object-location effects on pronoun interpretation beginning at 800 ms following pronoun onset. The theme bias for *it* was magnified in the objects condition. Additionally, the *next to* condition prompted significantly more looks to the theme for both pronouns, but only when subjects were manipulating objects. The object-type and object-location effects also modulated the rise in looks to the destination.

We also found that the eye-movement patterns were strongly affected by choice of referent. In comparing conditions in which the pronouns were different but participants chose the same referent, we found that the eye movements were similar. In contrast, when participants heard the same pronoun, for instance *that* in the *next to* condition, but chose either the focus or the composite, we found that early differences in eye-movement patterns reflected ultimate referent selection, suggesting that final interpretations of the pronouns are reflected in early processing differences.

These results provide answers to most of the questions that we proposed at the beginning of this chapter. We asked whether *that* has a different interpretation preference than *it*. Our data clearly provide support for previous observations that these pronouns have different interpretation preferences. The most common interpretation of *it* was as the focused entity, while *that* tended to be interpreted as the composite. However, pragmatic factors modulated these interpretation preferences, resulting in frequent interpretations of *it* as the composite, and frequent interpretations of *that* as the theme, depending on the context of the reference. Additionally, the relatively small proportion of goal interpretations suggests that the preferred interpretation of *that* was the conceptual composite, rather than the previously mentioned but not focused entity (the goal). Finally, in cases where *it* and *that* were interpreted as the theme and composite (respectively), we saw a very different eye-movement pattern associated with the two pronouns. When hearing *it*, participants tended to look mostly at the theme, whereas participants hearing *that* tended to look back and forth between the theme and goal.

We also asked whether there are effects of conceptual coherence on the tendency to interpret pronouns as composites. The answer to this question is clearly "yes." There were more composite interpretations for both *it* and *that* when the theme was placed on top of the goal and when the result was more likely to be a coherent composite (e.g., a cup on a saucer). We also examined situations in which *it* is interpreted in the same way as *that* to see whether there was an intrinsic difference in processing difficulty for these pronouns. Our analyses of eye movements in situations where participants interpreted the pronouns in the same way found that the eye-movement patterns were similar, suggesting that the early processing of the pronoun (as evidenced by the eye movements) corresponds to the ultimate interpretation of the pronoun. Finally, we examined whether *it* is processed more easily than *that*. Measurements of the increase in looks to the destination pointed to faster processing times for *it*. However, differences in the eye-movement patterns are strongly affected by the referent that the participant selected, with generally slower responses when selecting the composite. When *it* and *that* were both interpreted as the theme, for example, we observed similar patterns of eye movements, suggesting that in some circumstances the two pronouns may be equally easy to process.

In sum, three major findings emerge from these results. First, *it* and *that* have different preferred interpretations. Second, composite referents are preferred to goal referents for both *it* and *that*. Third, pragmatic factors affect the proportion of composite interpretations for both personal and demonstrative pronouns.

These results have several implications for models of reference resolution. First, the results provide support for earlier hypotheses about the preferred interpretations of *it* and *that*, including claims made by the Givenness Hierarchy. However, contrary to the claims of the Givenness Hierarchy, there was no asymmetry in the ease with which the lower ranking form, *that*, could refer to a more activated referent (the focused entity, the theme) compared to the higher-ranking form *it* referring to a less-activated referent (the composite).

Both demonstrative and personal pronouns were strongly affected by pragmatic–conceptual factors. Moreover, the composite, which did not have a linguistic antecedent, was a more salient referent than the goal, which was introduced linguistically with a noun phrase. This result demonstrates that when identifying the referent of a pronoun, goal-relevant, real-world entities can be as accessible as entities that are introduced linguistically as oblique arguments. Thus the activation of a referent is not primarily a linguistic construct. Moreover, referents with linguistic antecedents are not necessarily easier to refer to than salient entities that are mentioned in the discourse but do not have a linguistic antecedent. This result strongly suggests that reference resolution algorithms cannot relegate conceptual factors to a second stage of processing, as is often assumed by models that adopt text or utterance-based approaches. Models that hope to account for real-time pronoun interpretation will have to incorporate notions of saliency that combine both utterance and conceptual variables.

Finally, there is a methodological take-home message for psycholinguists interested in reference resolution. Real-time processing measures that focus primarily on processing difficulty for anaphors can be misleading when they collapse across conditions that have different preferred referents. Under these conditions, it is important to conduct interpretation-contingent analyses.

12.7 ACKNOWLEDGMENTS

This material is based upon work supported by the National Institutes of Health under award number NIH HD-27206 to M.K. Tanenhaus. We thank Manuel Carreiras and Chuck Clifton for helpful comments that greatly improved the readability of this chapter.

References

Arnold, J. E., Eisenband, J., Brown-Schmidt, S., & Trueswell, J. C. (2000). The rapid use of gender information: Evidence of the time course of pronoun resolution from eyetracking. *Cognition, 76,* B13–B26.

Baldwin, B. (1997). Cogniac: High precision coreference with limited knowlege and linguistic resources. *In Operational Factors in Practical, Robust Anaphora Resolution for Unrestricted Texts (ACL-97* workshop), pp. 38–45, Madrid, Spain.

Borthen, K., Fretheim, T., & Gundel, J. K. (1997). What brings a higher-order entity into focus of attention? Sentential pronouns in English and Norwegian. In R. Mitkov and B. Boguraev (Eds.), *Operational factors in practical, robust anaphora resolution for unrestricted texts* (pp. 88–93). Association for Computational Linguistics, Madrid, Spain.

Byron, D. K. (2002). Resolving pronominal reference to abstract entities. *Proceedings of the 40th Annual Meeting of the Association for Computational Linguistics (ACL~'02),* pp. 80–87, Philadelphia, Pennsylvania.

Byron, D. K., & Allen, J. F. (1998). Resolving demonstrative pronouns in the TRAINS93 corpus. *New Approaches to Discourse Anaphora: Proceedings of the 2nd Colloquium on Discourse Anaphora and Anaphor Resolution (DAARC2),* pp. 68–81, Lancaster, UK.

Carbonell, J. G., & Brown, R. D. (1988). Anaphora resolution: a multi-strategy approach. *Proceedings of the 12th International Conference on Computational Linguistics (COLING~'88),* pp. 96–101, Budapest, Hungary.

Channon, R. (1980). Anaphoric that: A friend in need. In J. Kreiman & A.Ojeda (Eds.), *Papers from the Parasession on Pronouns and Anaphora* (pp. 98–109). Chicago Linguistic Society, Chicago, Illinois.

Eckert, M., & Strube, M. (2000). Dialogue acts, synchronising units, and anaphora resolution. *Journal of Semantics, 17,* 51–89.

Garnham, A. (2001). *Mental models and the interpretation of anaphora.* New York: Psychology Press.

Gordon, P. C., Grosz, B. J., & Gillom, L. A. (1993). Pronouns, names, and the centering of attention in discourse. *Cognitive Science, 17*(3), 311–347.

Gundel, J. K., Hedberg, N., & Zacharski, R. (1993). Cognitive status and the form of referring expressions in discourse. *Language, 69,* 274–307.

Hobbs, J. (1986). Resolving pronoun reference. In *Readings in natural language processing* (pp. 339–352). San Francisco: Morgan Kaufmann.

Linde, C. (1979). Focus of attention and the choice of pronouns in discourse. In T. Givon (Ed.), *Syntax and Semantics 12: Discourse and Syntax.* New York: Academic Press.

Passonneau, R. J. (1989). Getting at discourse referents. *Proceedings of the 27th Annual Meeting of the Association for Computational Linguistics (ACL~'89),* pp. 51–59, Vancouver, Canada.

Passonneau, R. J. (1993). Getting and keeping the center of attention. In M. Bates & R. Weischedel (Eds.), *Challenges in natural language processing* (pp. 179–226). New York: Cambridge University Press.

Runner, J. T., Sussman, R. S., & Tanenhaus, M. K. (2003). Assignment of reference to reflexives and pronouns in picture noun phrases: Evidence from eye movements. *Cognition, 89*(1), B1–B13.

Schuster, E. (1988). *Anaphoric reference to events and actions: Evidence from naturally-occurring data.* (Technical Report MS-CIS-88-13). Philadelphia: University of Pennsylvania, LINC LAB.

Sidner, C. (1983). Focusing in the comprehension of definite anaphora. In M. Brady and R. Berwick (Eds.), *Computational models of discourse* (pp. 363–394), Cambridge, Mass: MIT press.

Tanenhaus, M. K., Spivey-Knowlton, M. J., Eberhard, K. M., & Sedivy, J. C. (1995). Integration of visual and linguistic information in spoken language comprehension. *Science, 268,* 1632–34.

Tetreault, J. R. (2001). A corpus-based evaluation of centering and pronoun resolution. *Computational Linguistics, 27,* 507–520.

12.8 APPENDIX LIST OF OBJECT PAIRS

1. soap   soap dish
2. lamp   table
3. cup   saucer
4. car   road
5. anchor   boat
6. egg   small nest
7. butterfly   flower
8. bird   large nest
9. cheese   cracker
10. dragonfly   lotus plant
11. hamburger   plate
12. candle   candleholder
13. bow   present
14. bee   grapes
15. pot   potholder
16. picture   picture frame

Chapter 13
Sentence Comprehension in a Wider Discourse: Can We Use ERPs To Keep Track of Things?

JOS J. A. VAN BERKUM

13.1 INTRODUCTION

13.1.1 ERPs and Sentence Comprehension

It has been known for a long time that event-related brain potentials (ERPs) can provide valuable information about the nature and time course of sentence comprehension. Brain potential research on sentence comprehension took off in the late 1970s, when Marta Kutas and Steve Hillyard discovered that semantically anomalous words at the end of a sentence, as in *He spread the warm bread with socks,* elicited a conspicuous negative deflection in the ERP at about 400 ms after the offending word (Kutas & Hillyard, 1980). Because this so-called N400 effect was not elicited by a typographic anomaly, as in *He spread the warm bread with BUTTER,* Kutas and Hillyard took the effect to reflect something about the semantic processing of words in relation to the sentence-semantic context. Follow-up experiments soon confirmed this observation. It also became clear that N400 effects reflected graded modulations of an underlying N400 *component,* elicited by every content word, but with its amplitude increasing to the extent that the word was somehow less expected given the sentence-semantic context (see Kutas & Van Petten, 1994, for a review).

The significance of these N400 findings was enhanced by the end of the 80s, when syntactically anomalous or unexpected words were found to elicit a qualitatively very different ERP effect, the so-called P600/SPS effect (Osterhout & Holcomb, 1992; Hagoort, Brown, & Groothusen, 1993). The discovery of these two very different ERP "signatures" raised interesting theoretical questions about the architecture of the sentence comprehension system and the types of representations it computed. However, it also implied that ERPs could be used as a tool to *selectively* keep track of specific aspects of sentence comprehension as a sentence unfolded in real time.

Of course, a process as complex as sentence comprehension was bound to generate more than just two ERP effects. Several other language-relevant ERP phenomena were soon discovered, including another short-lived effect associated with syntactic analysis (the so-called Left-Anterior Negativity or LAN; e.g., Neville, Nicol, Barss, Forster, & Garrett, 1991; Friederici, Hahne, & Mecklinger, 1996), slow ERP shifts associated with verbal working memory (e.g., Kluender & Kutas, 1993; Mueller, King, & Kutas, 1997), and effects that seem to reflect the extent to which the phonology of a word matches some sentence-based expectation (e.g., Connoly & Phillips, 1994; Van den Brink, Brown, & Hagoort, 2001). With this small but growing repertoire of relatively selective ERP effects in hand, EEG researchers have begun to explore the architecture of the sentence comprehension system (see Oster-hout, McLaughlin, Kim, Greenwald, & Inoue, chapter 14, this volume, for review; see also Brown & Hagoort, 2000; Brown, Hagoort, & Kutas, 2000; Friederici, 1998, 2002; Hagoort, Brown, & Osterhout, 1999; Kutas & Federmeier, 2000; Kutas, Federmeier, Coulson, King, & Münte, 2000; Kutas & Schmitt, 2003; Osterhout, McLaughlin, & Bersick, 1997).

In the typical sentential ERP experiment, subjects read or listen to a sequence of totally unrelated sentences, such as *The red-white rocket safely landed on the moon./He spread the warm bread with socks./Max shot at Onno as he jumped over the fence./The broker persuaded to sell the stock was sent to jail./* etc. For many of the issues addressed in this research, this is by all means good enough—after all, people can parse and make sense of a sentence presented in isolation, and there is no *a priori* reason to assume that the basic processes involved here are radically different from those involved in processing sentences in context (but see Clark, 1997, for a different view). On the other hand, of course, this assumption needs to be checked at some point in time. Moreover, if we want to understand how language users integrate their comprehension of an unfolding sentence with their knowledge of the wider discourse, such as a conversation or a piece of written text, we need to go beyond the isolated sentence. The purpose of this chapter is to see whether we can take ERPs up to the level of discourse-dependent comprehension, and what we might gain by doing so.

13.1.2 Taking ERPs Beyond the Single Sentence

Discourse-level comprehension has been studied with a wide range of behavioral measures, including eyetracking, self-paced reading, and concurrent probe response tasks (see Graesser, Millis, & Zwaan, 1997; Kintsch, 1998; and Myers & O'Brien, 1998, for reviews). To date, however, there is very little research in which discourse-level processing has been examined by means of ERPs—or any other neuroimaging measure, for that matter. Of the 130 citations in the Graesser et al. review of discourse comprehension research, for instance, none is to a neuroimaging paper. It is not that Graesser et al. missed an entire body of research. A PsychInfo search on "discourse" ("stories," "text") and "ERP" (or other potentially relevant neuroimaging terms) yields only a handful of studies, most of which appeared after 1997.

One reason why ERP and other neuroimaging researchers may have stayed away from discourse-level comprehension is that working with neuroimaging methods is difficult enough as it is. On the practical side of things, for example, the use of EEG imposes rather severe constraints on one's experiment, one of which is the need to have a much larger number of critical trials per condition (at least ~30–40) than is common in most behavioral designs. With a story in every trial, this can get rather awkward, an issue to which I will return below. However, there is probably more to the story than just practical hurdles. Discourse-level processing is often associated with "everything affecting everything else," a form of intractability that might unfavorably interact with the perceived intractability of ERP waveform interpretation. Also note that compared to, say, parsing, discourse-level comprehension also comes awfully close to the comprehender's "central system," the neurocognition of which was declared to be doomed by Jerry Fodor some 20 years ago in a monograph that was extremely influential amongst psycholinguists (Fodor, 1983).

The few ERP studies that have used discourse-level materials come in several varieties. One of the earliest ERP experiments on the N400 in sentence comprehension (Kutas & Hillyard, 1983) actually used prose passages taken from children's books, and the semantically incongruent words were deliberately made incongruous with respect to the particular sentence in which it occurred as well as with the gist of the entire story. This approach made sense given the research goals at hand, but it also made it impossible to disentangle the respective contribution of the local sentence and the wider discourse. Several other studies have used multisentence text stimuli simply because prose passages happened to provide a natural and convenient way to present large amounts of content and function words (Osterhout, Bersick, & McKinnon, 1997; Brown, Hagoort, & Ter Keurs, 1999).

More relevant here are the handful of ERP studies that were designed to examine comprehension as a function of the wider discourse context. To my knowledge, St. George, Mannes, and Hoffman (1994) were the first to do so, in an elegant ERP experiment. St. George et al. recorded ERPs as subjects were reading passages taken from earlier behavioral research (Bransford & Johnson, 1972; Dooling & Lachman, 1971) designed to make only limited sense when read without their title but perfect sense when the title was given with the passage (e.g., *The procedure for washing clothes*). The words in these passages generated smaller N400s when the title had been given than when the title had not been presented, allowing St. George et al. to infer that the N400 is not only sensitive to local sentence-semantic context, but also to global, discourse-level context.

Several studies have since then supported and extended this N400 claim in a variety of ways (Federmeier & Kutas, 1999a, 1999b; Federmeier, McLennan, De Ochoa, & Kutas, 2002; Van Berkum, Hagoort, & Brown, 1999c; Van Berkum, Zwitserlood, Brown, & Hagoort, 2003b; see also Van Petten, Kutas, Kluender, Mitchiner, & McIsaac, 1991 for indirect evidence). Other recent studies have examined how and when comprehenders establish reference to entities mentioned in the earlier discourse (Van Berkum, Brown, & Hagoort, 1999a; Van Berkum, Brown, Hagoort, & Zwitserlood, 2003a; Streb, Rösler, & Hennighausen, 1999); the extent to which discourse context affects syntactic ambiguity resolution (Van Berkum et al., 1999a, 1999b), and the degree to which comprehenders can use discourse-level information to make inferences (St. George, Mannes, & Hoffman, 1997), or to predict specific upcoming words (Van Berkum, Brown, Hagoort, Zwitserlood, & Kooijman; 2002a; Van Berkum, Kooijman, Brown, Zwitserlood, & Hagoort, 2002b). Finally, in an interesting twist, recent research has examined the

ERP correlates of discourse-level semantic integration by means of stories relayed not in the form of text, but in the form of entirely non-textual cartoons (West & Holcomb, 2002) or videos (Sitnikova, Kuperberg, & Holcomb, 2003).

13.1.3 Goals and Plan of This Paper

The main goal of this paper is to assess whether, in the light of the limited experience gained so far, it makes sense to use ERPs as a tool to track the processes involved in relating a sentence to the wider discourse on-line, as these processes occur. Of course, whether the use of a tool makes sense depends on what people want to do with it. For example, using ERPs to locate a specific discourse-relevant neural generator with 5 mm precision in the brain would not be a good idea. After briefly reviewing the purpose and nature of on-line measurement, I will therefore examine the utility of ERPs for *each of several different types of inferences* one might wish to draw from ERPs, illustrating each with recent discourse-level ERP research. After this relatively detailed analysis, I evaluate the specific pros and cons of using ERPs to track discourse-level comprehension relative to the other measures avaiable in this domain. In a final section, I briefly look at some new EEG-related developments, as well as at what other neuroimaging methods might bring.

13.2 ON-LINE MEASUREMENT—WHAT IS IT AND WHO CARES?

One can learn a great deal about how language comprehension actually works by looking at how the final interpretation changes as a function of the input. For example, a comparison of the ease with which language users arrive at a correct final interpretation of sentences with center-embedded versus right-branching phrase structures tells us that the comprehension process operates in a way that makes the latter easier to process than the former. Unfortunately, such off-line findings have as yet not provided sufficient constraints to pin down the exact nature of the language comprehension process. And, given the complexity of this process, it is unlikely that they ever will. It is generally accepted, therefore, that research on language comprehension also requires so-called on-line measures, which allow the researcher to track the comprehension process *as it unfolds*.

Processes by definition unfold in time but sentential input itself does, too. This confounding can make it hard to see what on-line measurement actually amounts to in the sentence comprehension domain. In the hypothetical example depicted in Figure 13.1, I try to disentangle the two confounding factors. Suppose we are interested in the comprehension processes that deliver a final interpretation for the spoken sentence *SnowWhite kissed a dwarf*. Furthermore, assume for sake of the argument that this sentential input unfolds *instantaneously*, taking 0 ms instead of the usual 1 or 2 s. Keeping the rest of the universe as it is, the sentence comprehension process that takes this "sentence impulse" as its input and delivers an interpretation as its result will, by definition, extend over time. To understand this unfolding comprehension process or "*impulse response*,"[1] it should be examined at various moments in time (Figure 13.1a), particularly if we suspect the process to have a complex internal

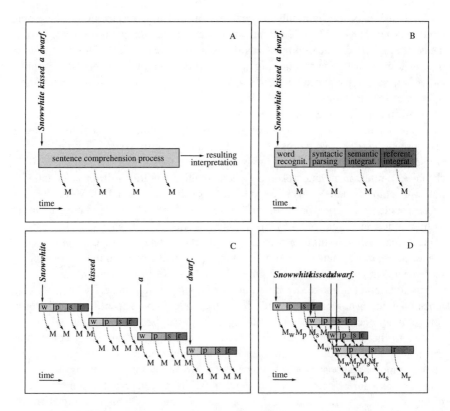

Figure 13.1 On-line measurement in language comprehension. Panel A: Impulse response tracking with instantaneous sentential input and a homogeneous response of the system (M = on-line measurement). Panel B: Impulse response tracking with instantaneous sentential input and an interestingly structured response (hypothetically assumed to consist of word recognition, parsing, semantic integration, and referential integration). Panel C: Incremental impulse response tracking in some ideal world, with word-driven impulse responses that are strictly sequential, nonoverlapping, of the same duration and internal structure, and unambiguously tied to their respective instantaneous word inputs. Panel D: Incremental impulse response tracking in the real world with word-driven impulse responses that are overlapping, of potentially different duration and internal structure, and (for spoken-language input) tied to word input that itself also unfolds and overlaps. Things would become more tractable if the on-line measurements themselves tell us what type of subprocess they are tapping in to (indicated by subscripted Ms).

structure (Figure 13.1b).[2] Note that the assumption of instantaneous sentential input reveals an aspect of on-line measurement that is solely related to *processes* unfolding in time and not to a *sentence* unfolding in time. I refer to this aspect of on-line measurement as *impulse response tracking*.

Of course, we know sentential input is not instantaneous, in that its words come in one after the other for spoken and written sentences alike (ignoring, for the moment, that not every word is fixated in reading, and that more than one word may be processed in a particular fixation; Rayner, 1998). We also know that the sentence comprehension system is highly incremental, in that it processes every in-coming word to at least a considerable extent. Thus, we can remodel the problem of on-line measurement in sentence comprehension as one of *incremental impulse response tracking*, with every word eliciting its own little incremental impulse response, including, say, some word recognition, some parsing, some semantic, and some referential interpretation (Figure 13.1c).

Unfortunately, if the language comprehension system's impulse response to a word takes longer than the unfolding word itself (an empirical issue), the impulse responses to consecutive words of a sentence are going to overlap. To make things worse, the incoming words are usually not driving the system at fixed onset asynchronies, neither in natural reading (where fixation durations differ substantially) nor in listening (where acoustic word durations differ substantially). Moreover, in a spoken sentence, every word itself also unfolds in time, adding deep uncertainty as to how much of the unfolding lexical signal is enough to trigger (specific aspects of) a lexically driven impulse response. In all, measuring on-line in sentence comprehension can be characterized as tracking a sequence of potentially overlapping incremental impulse responses (Figure 13.1d). In plain English: a real mess.[3]

In an attempt to make the situation more tractable, researchers who study sentence comprehension on-line usually focus their attention on specific critical words, for example, one at which some syntactic garden path becomes apparent. However, relative to the situation depicted in Figure 13.1d, things would also become more tractable if the particular on-line measure that is used to track the system's incremental impulse response would tell us whether we are looking at, for instance, some aspect of parsing or some aspect of interpretation, as illustrated schematically by different subscripts in Figure 13.1d. One of the central claims developed in this chapter (see also Osterhout et al., chapter 14, this volume) is that this is precisely what ERPs are good at.

13.3 TYPES OF INFERENCES ONE CAN DRAW FROM ERPS

When comparing ERPs to other neuroimaging methods, the former is often said to have excellent temporal resolution but rather poor spatial resolution. As will be seen below, there is some truth to this. However, the adagium might also incorrectly be taken to suggest that ERPs can *only* be used to make timing inferences. A more careful analysis reveals that ERPs can actually be used to support some very different types of inferences about the language comprehension system—or, for that matter, any other cognitive subsystem (see also Rugg & Coles, 1995). Researchers usually look at the ERP response to some particular manipulation X to draw one or more of the following inferences:

1. *Sensitivity inferences.* Does anything at all happen in response to X, at whatever level of the comprehension system?
2. *Timing inferences.* At what moment in time is the comprehension system sensitive to X, that is, when does it "know" about X?

3. *Identity inferences.* Is whatever happens in the system in response to X, indexed by ERP effect E_X, the same as or qualitatively different from whatever happens in response to Y?

4. *Magnitude inferences.* How exactly does the manipulation X determine the size of the ERP effect E_X?

5. *Neuronal generator inferences.* What specific areas of the brain are involved in the processing of X, that is, where are the neural generators of ERP effect E_X?

To see how ERPs might contribute to the study of discourse-level comprehension, I will illustrate each of these types of inferences with specific ERP experiments on sentence comprehension in discourse. Most examples will be drawn from my own work, conducted in collaboration with Peter Hagoort, Colin Brown and, for the spoken language research, Pienie Zwitserlood. However, other relevant work will be drawn in whenever appropriate. Bear in mind that the purpose of this section is to examine ERPs as a tool and to have a closer look at the methodological issues that come up. For each of the example experiments, therefore, the specific theoretical debate that motivated it will be touched upon only briefly; interested readers are referred to the original literature.

13.3.1 Sensitivity Inferences

By far the simplest thing one can show with ERPs is that the comprehension system is sensitive to some manipulation X. We recently conducted a discourse-level ERP experiment that primarily used ERPs for this purpose (Van Berkum, Brown, et al., 2002a, 2004; Van Berkum, Kooijman, et al., 2002b). The goal of the study was to find out whether people can use their knowledge of the wider discourse to rapidly *predict* specific upcoming words while a sentence is unfolding. For example, do listeners anticipate the word *painting* by the time they have heard the mini-story in (1) up to the indefinite article?

(1)   *The burglar had no trouble whatsoever locating the secret family safe.*
      Of course, it was situated behind a

Note that various phenomena suggest that they might indeed be able to do this. One is that in natural conversation, people can "take over" and finish each other's sentence quite successfully. Another is that when subjects are asked to complete a truncated story like the above in a so-called story completion or *cloze* test, they tend to come up with the same word (in this case, *painting*). Both observations suggest that, in at least some circumstances, people can indeed use their knowledge of the wider discourse to predict specific upcoming words. However, one might object that people may only be able to do this when given ample time, e.g., because the other speaker hesitates, or, in the paper-and-pencil cloze test, because subjects can essentially take all the time they want. The issue is whether people can use their knowledge of the wider discourse *rapidly enough* to predict specific upcoming words "on the fly," as the current sentence is unfolding.

To examine this issue, we created 120 Dutch two-sentence mini-stories like the above example. Each story was relatively predictable in that, in a written cloze pretest, at least 50% of the subjects had used the same noun to complete the story. The predictability of this noun always hinged on the discourse context sentence, as revealed by the fact the same noun was practically never generated if subjects had only seen the incomplete second sentence (*Of course, it was situated behind a* ...).

As in German and French, every Dutch noun has a fixed and essentially arbitrary syntactic *gender* feature, which in indefinite (but not definite) NPs controls an inflectional suffix on the adjective:

> *(2) een groot schilderij*   *a big$_{NEU}$ painting$_{NEU}$*   *neuter gender*   *"zero" suffix*
>   *een grote boekenkast*   *a big$_{COM}$ bookcase$_{COM}$*   *common gender*   *-e suffix*

In the ERP experiment, we used this fact to probe for discourse-based prediction of a noun by *first* continuing the story with an adjective whose inflectional suffix was either congruent or incongruent with the gender of the predictable noun. To make sure we would not be confounding the critical inflection *mismatch* effect with a mere inflection effect (e.g., "e" vs. zero inflection), we counterbalanced the latter across critical condition. Subjects were merely asked to listen to the stories (amid many fillers) as we recorded their EEG. The research logic was simple: If listeners indeed expect a specific noun by the time they have heard the indefinite article, an incongruently gender-inflected adjective should be an unpleasant surprise. The processing consequences of this perturbation might show up as an ERP effect at the adjective.

As can be seen in Figure 13.2, gender-incongruent adjectives indeed elicited a small but reliable ERP effect right at the inflection. Also, the effect disappears when the same critical sentences are heard in isolation, that is, without the discourse context that supports the lexical prediction (see Van Berkum, Brown, Hagoort, Zwitserlood, & Kooijman 2004). Because the ERP effect hinges on the (arbitrary) syntactic gender of an expected but not yet presented noun, it suggests that discourse-level information can indeed lead people to anticipate specific upcoming words "on the fly," as a local sentence unfolds. In addition, the effect suggests that the syntactic gender properties of a strongly anticipated noun can immediately begin to interact with local syntactic constraints (such as the gender inflection of a prenominal adjective).

This effect raises many questions (see Van Berkum et al., 2004 for discussion). For one, why is it so early? Also, is it really a message-level effect rather than some lexical priming effect? And, as it hinges on a syntactic gender agreement violation, why does not the effect look like, say, a P600/SPS effect? We are now pursuing these issues in follow-up research.[4] For current purposes, however, note that the research logic only required *a differential* ERP effect at the adjective, and neither required it to have a specific polarity or identity (P600/SPS, LAN, N400, etc.), nor a particular timing (provided that the features of the ERP effect actually observed are "reasonable"). Because all we needed was evidence for some perturbation of the system at the critical adjective, any other on-line measure might have done the job as well.[5]

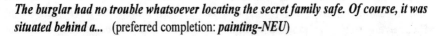

The burglar had no trouble whatsoever locating the secret family safe. Of course, it was situated behind a... (preferred completion: *painting-NEU*)

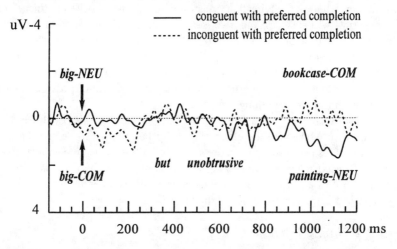

Figure 13.2 ERPs elicited by spoken adjectives whose suffixes are congruent or incongruent with the gender of a predictable noun. Results are shown for a right-temporal site (RT), and for stories with at least 75% cloze probability. Apart from the critical inflection-elicited early positivity, one can also see a discourse-induced N400 effect, elicited if a subsequently presented noun was not the predictable one. Estimated onset of the inflectional suffix is at 0 ms. Negative voltage is up. Data from J. J. A. Van Berkum et al., 2004.

At this point, it is instructive to examine some methodological issues associated with the use of ERPs to assess system sensitivity. First, what if we had not picked up an effect at the critical adjective inflection? As with any other measure, such a null result might indicate that the manipulation did not perturb the comprehension system, either because it *really* did not matter (e.g., people do not predict upcoming nouns), or because it was not strong enough. However, because of several reasons related to the ERP technique and the underlying physiology, there is also a real possibility that the language comprehension system *did* get perturbed by the critical adjective but the ERPs simply did not pick this up. As described in more detail by, for instance, Kutas, Federmeier, and Sereno (1999), the EEG recorded at the scalp reflects tiny changes in postsynaptic potentials that, in order for the associated tiny electrical fields to summate, must occur simultaneously within a very large number of neurons all oriented in the same way. If there are cognitive events—and there might be—for which any of these conditions does not hold, these events will not generate a measurable ERP effect at the scalp.

Furthermore, even cognitive events that do generate a "blip" in the ongoing raw EEG each time they occur may fail to show up in the ERP. The stimulus-tied blips that ERP researchers are after are very small, and therefore usually completely hidden in the much larger fluctuations of the background EEG. They can only be uncovered by computing an ERP, that is, by averaging the raw EEG measured at, say, 50 critical stimulus events assumed to be equivalent in some way (e.g., all are unexpected inflections). Everything that is *not systematically time-locked* to the critical event (e.g., the random background EEG) is going to cancel out in the averaging, whereas the blips that *are* systematically time-locked to the critical event across trials will survive. And here is the catch: If each of our 50 critical trials does indeed generate a blip, but does so at highly variable latencies ("latency jitter") relative to what we take to be the critical event for our EEG segment alignment, the blips are not going to be fully superimposed in the averaging procedure. The consequence is that the resulting ERP effect may be "smeared," possibly even to such an extent that there is nothing left to see.[6]

A final word of caution: Perhaps, in part, because working with EEG is such a bother, those who make the effort can easily be tempted to believe (and suggest) that the EEG is per definition a more sensitive on-line measurement instrument than, say, self-paced reading, eyetracking, or cross-modal probe response time. In fact, and because of all of the reasons listed above, this is an entirely empirical issue, to be assessed anew for every new domain of inquiry.

13.3.2 Timing Inferences

For some issues, it is important to move beyond demonstrating any ERP effect at any (reasonable) time, and to more closely examine *when* the comprehension system is sensitive to some manipulation X. As an example, we recently used ERPs to establish how quickly listeners relate the meaning of incoming words to their knowledge of the wider discourse (Van Berkum et al., 2003b). Following up on a written-language study (Van Berkum et al., 1999c), we presented listeners with the Dutch equivalent of mini-stories such as in (3).

(3)   *As agreed upon, Jane was to wake her sister and her brother at five o'clock in the morning. But the sister had already washed herself, and the brother had even got dressed. Jane told the brother that he was exceptionally* **quick/slow**.

These stories had been designed such that the two alternative critical words (in boldface in the example) were equally coherent with respect to the local sentence context. However, the wider discourse context rendered one of these words semantically incoherent (*slow* in the example), while leaving the other word (*quick*) perfectly acceptable.

When presented in discourse in a spoken-language ERP experiment, discourse-incoherent words elicited a differential ERP effect relative to their discourse-coherent counterparts (Figure 13.3a), which at some electrode sites emerged as early as 150 ms relative to the acoustic onset of the critical word. Also, when the critical sentences were presented in their carrier sentence but without the wider discourse, the differential effect disappeared (Figure 13.3b), showing that it, indeed, hinged on how the critical words related to the discourse. As revealed by a re-analysis of the ERP data for just those stories in which, according to a paper-and-pencil pretest, the *coherent* word had not been expected either (Figure 13.3c), the present discourse-dependent

A: discourse-semantic anomaly effect

----- anomalous in discourse
——— coherent in discourse

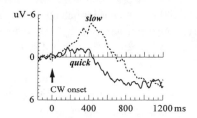

B: control study without the discourse

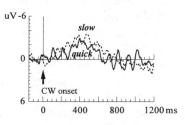

C: effect for low-constraint stories only

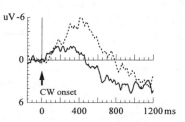

D: effect for sentence-medial words only

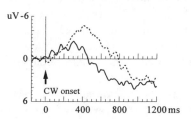

E: effect for long (>550 ms) words only

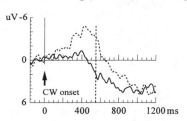

Figure 13.3 Panel A: ERPs to spoken words that were semantically coherent or anomalous with respect to the wider discourse. Panel B: ERPs to the same spoken words, now presented in their local carrier sentence only. Panel C: Discourse-semantic anomaly effect for low-constraint stories in which, next to the anomalous word, the *coherent* word had not been expected either (mean cloze probability of .01, and all below .05). Panel D: Discourse-semantic anomaly effect for sentence- (and clause-) medial words only. Panel E: Discourse-dependent anomaly effect for long words only, with the minimum word duration indicated by a vertical bar. Estimated acoustic onset of the critical words is at 0 ms. Data at Pz, from "When and how do listeners relate a sentence to the wider discourse? Evidence from the N400 effect," by J. J. A. Van Berkum, P. Zwitserlood, C. M. Brown, and P. Hagoort, 2003b, *Cognitive Brain Research, 17,* 701–718.

negativity did *not* depend on the disconfirmation of a strong lexical prediction. Finally, subanalyses revealed that discourse-incoherent words elicited this early ERP effect regardless of whether they were at the end of a main or subordinate clause (not shown) or right in the middle of it (Figure 13.3d).

Note that the ERP data in Figure 13.3 afford two different kinds of inferences about how quickly listeners relate the meaning of incoming words to their knowledge of the wider discourse. One is *how soon in the sentence*, i.e., at which word the effects show up. The fact that a discourse-dependent ERP effect shows up right in the middle of a clause confirms what intuition, earlier written-language ERP work (e.g., St. George et al., 1994; Van Berkum et al., 1999c), and earlier behavioral work (e.g., Marslen-Wilson & Tyler, 1980) already suggested, namely, that the system *incrementally* relates the incoming words to a representation of the wider discourse, as the sentence is unfolding.

In addition, ERPs are particularly good at also simultaneously supporting a second timing inference, which is *how soon after onset of the critical word* the processing consequences of a manipulation show up. The ERP elicited by discourse-incoherent words begins to diverge from that elicited by discourse-coherent words at about 150 ms after acoustic onset of the critical word. The average critical word in our study, however, took about 550 ms to unfold. This suggests that the language comprehension system seems to have detected that a particular word is not going to fit the discourse *long before the offending word itself has been fully heard.*

This is where several cautions should be made. First, remember that ERPs are averages, and not necessarily representative of each of the single-trial blips going into the average. In particular, these little blips need not be completely aligned in time ("latency jitter"). This means that for the result at hand, the early part of the ERP effect might in principle hinge on a few critical words of very short (say, below 150 ms) duration only, in which case our second timing inference would perhaps not be legitimate. To address this issue, we recomputed the ERPs for only those items in which the critical words were of *at least* 550 ms duration. The outcome, displayed in Figure 13.3e, unequivocally confirms that at least some incoming words are really related to the wider discourse well before their offset.

A second caution is related to the possibility that interesting cognitive events may fail to show up in ERPs for reasons discussed before. As noted many times before (e.g., Rugg & Coles, 1995; Kutas et al., 1999), the consequence for timing inferences is that the earliest evidence for a differential effect to manipulation X can in principle only be taken as an *upper-bound* estimate of the time it takes the system to discover about X. For example, we cannot rule out the possibility that the comprehension system already detected a problem with discourse-incoherent words at, say, 100 ms from word onset, and that these earlier processing consequences simply failed to show up in ERPs as they occurred. In such a case, the later effect that we do observe could either be a direct reflection of some later process that *independently* detected the problem or of some downstream process whose operation is changed by the earlier detection.

A final caution relates to the temporal resolution of EEG and its derived measures (e.g., ERPs). EEG is usually advertized as providing continuous measurement with millisecond precision. This is entirely correct, and it is one of the things that give EEG its power as an on-line measure. However, although EEG can be recorded continuously throughout the unfolding sentence, the interpretation of these signals requires them to be anchored to (i.e., averaged relative to) the timing of some predefined critical event. In many ERP studies on sentence comprehension, there is only one such event per critical trial, usually a specific critical word—or morpheme therein—at which something might become apparent to the comprehension system:

a syntactic dead-end, a discourse-semantic anomaly, a lexical prediction shown wrong. Of course, there is the possibility to examine the impulse responses of the system at other words than the critical one, and sometimes this makes sense. In addition, one can examine slow shifts building up in the EEG across the sentence, relative to some critical word therein or the onset of the sentence (e.g., Kutas, 1997; Münte, Schiltz, & Kutas, 1998). But in all but the latter case, the continuous EEG is chopped into discrete segments to study the impulse response of the comprehension system at just one or a few word positions per critical sentence.

Moreover, the extent to which our ERP findings inherit the millisecond precision of EEG depends on how accurately we can define the critical events that elicit the blips going into an ERP average. In most research on sentence comprehension, including the example just discussed, ERPs are computed relative to a word's visual or acoustic onset. With written words flashed on the screen, word onset is not difficult to determine. However, in research with fully connected speech stimuli, there is usually considerable uncertainty as to where a spoken word begins, sometimes up to several tens of milliseconds for a particular word onset. Furthermore, with a spoken word it may take some—and, across items, some variable amount of—time before the truly critical information comes along in the acoustic signal. Researchers can try to locate this critical bit of information in the acoustic signal (e.g., an inflectional suffix) and reaverage relative to this, but if this is not realistic, they will need to accept some additional latency jitter as well as, potentially, some latency bias.[7]

Because coherent ERP effects can be found with spoken language, there is no reason to be overly concerned about the temporal uncertainties introduced by acoustic onset measurement. Also, the problem can sometimes be attenuated by, for example, using the same critical words and the same recordings in two different context conditions. However, it will be clear that the millisecond precision of EEG cannot always be exploited to the maximum.

13.3.3 Identity Inferences

To address the above timing question, all that mattered was the *onset* of the differential ERP effect elicited by words that did not fit the wider discourse, relative to the ERP elicited by fully acceptable words. Nothing in the discussion hinged on the *identity* of the effect, for instance, whether it was an N400 effect, a P600/SPS effect, or something else. However, one of the major strengths of ERPs is that every ERP effect has not only a time course, but also a polarity (Is it a positive or negative deflection?), a morphology (What is the shape of the waveform?), and a scalp distribution (the size of the effect at various recording locations over the scalp). In addition, some ERP effects (e.g., the N400 effect) can be characterized as modulations of some known underlying ERP component.

This rich multidimensional "signature" can provide cues as to the identity of the cognitive event at hand. If the signatures of two observed ERP effects are identical, the most parsimonious inference is that the cognitive processes that gave rise to these two effects are the same. Conversely, if two observed ERP effects have nonidentical signatures, the most parsimonious inference is that the cognitive processes that gave rise to these two effects are different in some way. There is a lot to be said about these two inferences, most of which goes beyond the scope of this chapter (see Rugg & Coles, 1995; Urbach and Kutas, 2002). However, it is important to know that, by and large, the ERP research community interprets nonidentical polarity, morphology, and scalp distribution as reliable cues to the presence of *qualitatively* different cognitive processes (the reason being that if two ERP effects differ in any of these ways, the neural generators that gave rise to them must be at least partially nonoverlapping; Urbach & Kutas, 2002). Furthermore, if two ERP effects are deemed identical in terms of these three features, then (reasonable) differences in their time course or overall magnitude or both are most commonly interpreted as reflecting *quantitative* variations in when and to what extent a single underlying cognitive process is engaged.

The above identity logic can be used to make inferences about the cognitive processes underlying *any* two ERP effects E_X and E_Y observed in response to manipulations X and Y, within or across experiments. However, and quite fortunately, research has revealed that at least some observed ERP effect tokens tend to cluster in *types* such as the N400 effect or the P600/SPS effect, which, in turn, rather reliably map onto interestingly different classes of language comprehension events. Thus, in addition to comparing any two observed ERP effect tokens to each other, we can also compare a single ERP effect token to any of the known effect *types* and draw inferences on the basis of that.

Virtually all of the ERP research on the comprehension of sentences in discourse has posed the identity question in some way. For example, the ERP effect of a discourse-dependent semantic anomaly in Figure 13.3a has been compared to the effect elicited by *sentence*-dependent semantic anomalies, as well as to the effects of discourse-dependent *referential* and *syntactic* problems. I discuss each of these below.

13.3.3.1 Comparing Discourse- and Sentence-Dependent Semantic ERP Effects

One of the reasons for conducting an ERP study with discourse-dependent semantic anomalies was to see whether or not such anomalies would engage the same comprehension subsystem as so-called sentence-dependent semantic anomalies. We know that the latter elicit an N400 effect in ERPs, but would the former also do so? The St. George et al. (1994) research discussed before had already clearly suggested that the N400 is sensitive to global coherence. In our experiments (Van Berkum et al., 2003b) we wanted to have a closer look at this issue in a way that would be more directly comparable to how most of the sentence-semantic N400 research is conducted.

The discourse-dependent ERP effect whose timing we examined in the previous section had all the features of a classic *sentence*-dependent N400 effect (see Kutas & Van Petten, 1994, for review): a monophasic and relatively peaked negative deflection which emerged in the grand average at about 150–200 ms after acoustic word onset, peaked at about 400 ms, lasted for about 800–1000 ms, and reached its maximum over centro-parietal scalp sites. To support the comparison, we obtained a sentential N400 effect in the same lab under similar conditions. Figure 13.4 redisplays the ERP effect of a discourse-dependent semantic anomaly next to the

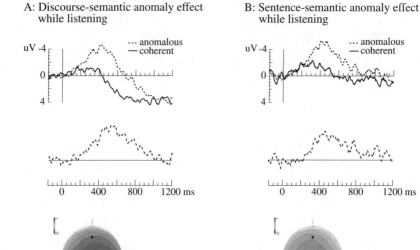

A: Discourse-semantic anomaly effect
while listening

B: Sentence-semantic anomaly effect
while listening

Figure 13.4 Discourse- and sentence-dependent semantic anomaly effects in spoken language comprehension. Top: Grand-average waveforms at Pz for anomalous and coherent words respectively. Middle: Corresponding anomalous–coherent difference waves. Bottom: spline-interpolated scalp distribution of the anomaly effect, based on mean difference-wave amplitude in the 300–500 ms latency range at each of 13 electrodes (6 of which are below the "equator" and therefore not visible; data from "When and how do listeners relate a sentence to the wider discourse? Evidence from the N400 effect," by J. J. A. Van Berkum, P. Zwitserlood, C. M. Brown, and P. Hagoort, 2003b, *Cognitive Brain Research*, 17, 701–718).

N400 effect elicited by sentence-dependent semantic anomalies. As revealed most clearly in the difference waveforms and the associated scalp distributions, the ERP effect of a discourse-dependent semantic anomaly is identical to the classic sentence-dependent N400 effect in polarity, morphology, scalp distribution, and coarse timing. As shown in Figure 13.5, this equivalence was also observed in experiments with *written* language (Van Berkum et al., 1999c).

The equivalence of discourse- and sentence-dependent N400 effects suggests that within the domain of spoken as well as written language processing, the semantic comprehension process indexed by the N400 is *indifferent* to where the semantic constraints originally came from ("local" or "global" context), and simply evaluates the incoming words relative to the widest interpretive domain that is available. We briefly return to this in a later section, but refer to Van Berkum et al. (2003b) for a more detailed discussion.

13.3.3.2 Comparing Discourse-Dependent Semantic, Referential, and Syntactic ERP Effects

Whereas the ERP effect to discourse-dependent semantic problems turned out to be identical to the classic N400 effect observed for sentence-dependent semantic

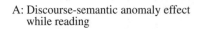

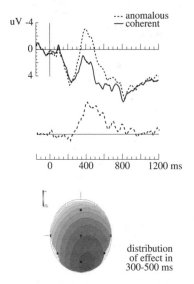
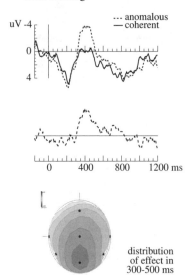

Figure 13.5 Discourse- and sentence-dependent semantic anomaly effects in written language comprehension. (Interpretation as in Figure 13.4; data at Pz, from "Semantic integration in sentences and discourse: Evidence from the N400," by J. J. A. Van Berkum, P. Hagoort, & C. M. Brown, 1999c, *Journal of Cognitive Neuroscience, 11*(6), 657–671).

problems, discourse-dependent *referential* problems elicited a very different ERP effect (Van Berkum, Brown, et al., 1999a; Van Berkum, Zwitserlood, et al., 2003A). The specific problem involved was a referential ambiguity, illustrated in (4), an example translated from Dutch.

(4a) *Just as the elderly hippie had lit up a joint, he got a visit from a friend and a nephew. Even though his friend had had quite a few drinks already, and the nephew had just smoked quite a lot of pot already, they insisted on smoking along. The hippie warned the **friend** that there would be some problems soon.*

(4b) *Just as the elderly hippie had lit up a joint, he got a visit from two friends. Even though one of his friends had had quite a few drinks already, and the other one had just smoked quite a lot of pot already, they insisted on smoking along. The hippie warned the **friend** that there would be some problems soon.*

Whereas in (4a), the critical noun "friend" was referentially unique, *two* equally eligible candidate referents had been supplied by the wider discourse context in (4b). As shown in Figure 13.6a for written-language input (Van Berkum et al., 1999a),

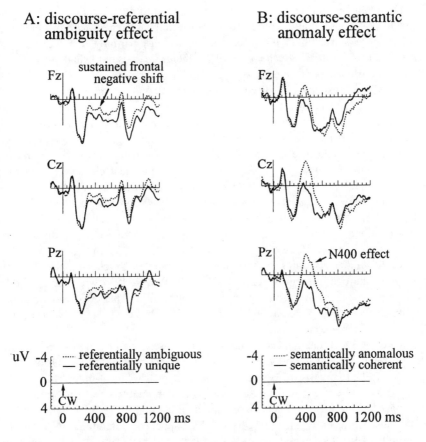

A: discourse-referential
ambiguity effect

B: discourse-semantic
anomaly effect

Figure 13.6 Panel A: ERPs to written words that were referentially unique or ambiguous with respect to the wider discourse. Data from "Early referential context effects in sentence processing. Evidence from Event-Related Brain Potentials," by J. J. A. Van Berkum, C. M. Brown, and P. Hagoort, 1999a, *Journal of Memory and Language*, 41, 147–182. Panel B: ERPs to written words that were semantically coherent or anomalous with respect to the wider discourse. Data from "Semantic integration in sentences and discourse: Evidence from the N400," by J. J. A. Van Berkum, P. Hagoort, and C. M. Brown, 1999c, *Journal of Cognitive Neuroscience, 11*(6), 657–671. Effects are shown for a frontal, central, and parietal midline site.

the processing consequences of such referential ambiguity showed up immediately in ERPs, right at the critical noun.

The early onset of the referentially induced ERP effect reveals that people rapidly discover whether a singular definite NP is referentially ambiguous or not. Moreover, whereas semantically problematic words elicit an N400 effect (redisplayed in Figure 13.6b for the same three midline sites), referentially ambiguous nouns elicited a *qualitatively different* effect: a frontally dominant and sustained negative shift in ERPs, starting at about 300 ms from word onset during reading (Van Berkum et al., 1999a), and about 300–400 ms from acoustic word onset during listening (Van Berkum et al., 2003A). As discussed in more detail elsewhere, this nonidentity suggests that the processing implications associated with difficulties in making sense and establishing reference are at least partially distinct, and that, perhaps not too surprisingly, the N400 effect therefore does not exhaustively reflect *all* aspects of conceptual integration.

In the same experiment, discourse-induced referential ambiguity also had an immediate impact on how the parser analyzed a subsequent local *syntactic* ambiguity. For instance, if *the friend* in *The hippie warned the friend **that** ...* was referentially ambiguous, the parser was more inclined to take the syntactically ambiguous word *that* as the beginning of a referentially restrictive *relative clause* (*... that had had quite a few drinks*) than as the beginning of a complement clause (*... that there would be some problems soon*). This discourse-induced preference for a relative-clause analysis was revealed by the fact that in relative-supporting contexts like (4b), a subsequent critical word that ruled out this analysis by signalling a *complement-clause* continuation (*there* in the example) elicited a P600/SPS effect, indicating that the parser had been led down a garden path by the two-referent discourse context. Conversely, if the discourse context favored a complement-clause analysis at the word *that* (the one-referent context in 4b), a P600/SPS effect was instead elicited by a word that signalled a *relative-clause* continuation. This crossover pattern of P600/SPS results is depicted in Figure 13.7 (see Van Berkum et al., 1999a, for details and two additional conditions).

Words at which the syntactic analysis currently pursued by the parser runs into trouble reliably elicit a P600/SPS effect (see Hagoort et al., 1999; Osterhout & Hagoort, 1999, for a review). Hence, if one predicts—as we did—that certain features of the discourse context will lure the parser into an analysis that runs into a dead end at particular critical words, then one should find P600/SPS effects at those words, and at those words only.[8] This is precisely what happened. Obtaining an *N400* instead of a P600/SPS effect at these critical words would have forced us to revise our interpretation. The *identity* of these ERP effects therefore provides an important constraint on interpretation.

As illustrated by Figure 13.8 for written-language input, the three discourse-dependent ERP effects depicted in Figures 13.5a, 13.6a, and 13.7 were actually obtained in a single ERP experiment (see Van Berkum et al., 1999a, 1999b). ERPs thus allow us to simultaneously yet *selectively* examine how prior discourse modulates the referential, syntactic, and semantic analyses as a local sentence unfolds within the same subjects and the same texts. Given that discourse-level comprehension is bound to involve a complex dynamic interplay of many different processes overlapping with each other as well as with the input (Figure 13.1d), this ability of ERPs to simultaneously yet selectively track at least some of those processes with high temporal precision can be of considerable importance.

Several important cautions remain to be made. If a particular ERP effect observed in some experiment is labeled as, say, a "P145," and there have been no earlier reports using the same label, then the term is probably intended as descriptive of the effect token, meaning no more than a positivity peaking at 145 ms. However, if an observed ERP effect is labeled with the name of a *familiar effect type*, such as an N400 effect, then the researcher usually claims that the observed effect token

A: Complement-clause disambiguation   B: Relative-clause disambiguation

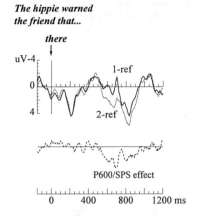
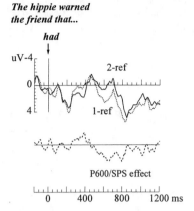

Figure 13.7 Panel A: P600/SPS effect to written complement-clause disambiguation in a two-referent context. Panel B: P600/SPS effect to written relative-clause disambiguation in a one-referent context. Data, at Pz from "Early referential context effects in sentence processing: Evidence from event-related brain potentials," by J. J. A. Van Berkum, C. M. Brown, and P. Hagoort, 1999a, *Journal of Memory and Language, 41,* 147–182.

matches the well-known effect type to a sufficient degree to justify *classifying* the token as an instance of this type. Within a particular domain of inquiry, ERP researchers will often agree on whether the claim is reasonable or not, given the effect type at hand and the variability observed across other accepted instances of the type. However, it is important to realize that the *ERP waveforms themselves do not come with labels*, and that it is the researcher that provides them. Even when backed up by the entire ERP community, the claim that is implicit in such classification may turn out to be wrong, either because the specific effect was misclassified ("It looked exactly like an N400 effect, but it turned out to be a perfect look-alike generated by a completely different process"), or because later research reveals that our partitioning of known effects needs reconsideration.

Related to the latter, note that it is almost never the case that two ERP effect tokens classified as identical *are* in fact completely identical. Many of the differences can be reasonably viewed as "noise" (e.g., residual noise that failed to cancel out in the averaging process), but many others reflect potentially interesting variations that the research community has decided to ignore "for the time being" to keep things tractable.

Finally, clustering ERP effects is more than sorting one's stamp collection on shape and color, for ERP effects that are considered to be equivalent are also considered to reflect the same underlying functional process. Effect classification, hence, always involves a claim about the functional interpretation of the ERP effect (or component) at hand. Those who follow the psycholinguistic ERP literature will have noted that, even for extensively studied phenomena like the N400 and the P600 effect, the exact functional interpretation is still under debate. The fact that one

Just as the elderly hippie had lit up a joint, he got a visit from a friend and a nephew (two friends). Even though his friend (one of his friends) had had quite a few drinks already, and the nephew (the other one) had just smoked quite a lot of pot already, they insisted on smoking along. The hippie warned the **friend** *that* **there** *would be some* **problems/fascists** *soon.*

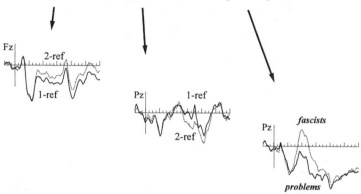

Figure 13.8 From left to right: A sustained frontal negative shift to a discourse-induced referential problem ("friend" is referentially ambiguous in the 2-referent context), a P600/SPS effect to a discourse-induced *syntactic* problem ("there" rules out the provisional relative-clause analysis pursued at "that" in the 2-referent context), and an N400 effect to a discourse-induced *semantic* problem ("fascists" does not fit the wider story context); see text for explanation. The example item is shown here in several variants (1- and 2- referent contexts, coherent/anomalous ending), but any one subject saw only a single variant. Data from "Early referential context effects in sentence processing: Evidence from event-related brain potentials." by J. J. A. Van Berkum, C. M. Brown. & P. Hagoort, 1999a, *Journal of Memory and Language*, 41, 147–182. and from "Semantic integration in sentences and discourse: Evidence from the N400." by J. J. A. Van Berkum, P. Hagoort, & C. M. Brown (1999a). *Journal of Cognitive Neuroscience*, 11(6), 657–671.

cannot as yet *exhaustively* characterize the system that generates, say, the P600 effect, does *not* mean that research cannot exploit the effect at hand to address some psycholinguistically relevant issue (see also note 8). However, our limited understanding of even the "well-known" N400 and P600 effects serves as a reminder that the linking of ERP effects to underlying functional processes is difficult business. In all, the search for meaningful (and manageable) clusters in the set of observable ERP effects is a nontrivial job. The quality of the clusters we have defined at any given point in time will ultimately be judged by whether we make any scientific progress with it or not.

13.3.4 Magnitude Inferences

In none of the examples of ERP research on discourse-level comprehension discussed so far did the *size* of a particular ERP effect matter to the inferences we wanted to draw. So, even if the discourse-dependent N400 effect would have been bigger than the sentence-dependent N400 effect, this would not have prevented us from classifying both as N400 effects, and as such license our inference that both types of anomalies engage the same processing system. However, some inferences do critically depend on the magnitude of an effect. A recent discourse-level ERP study by Federmeier and Kutas (1999a) exemplifies this. Federmeier and Kutas asked subjects to read stories such as the one in (5).

(5) *They wanted to make the hotel look more like a tropical resort.*
     So along the driveway they planted rows of ***palms/pines/tulips***.

   Like the example story, each critical story either ended with a highly expected word (*palms*), a "within-category violation" that belonged to the same semantic category as the expected control word (e.g., *pines*, a tree as well), and a "between-category violation" coming from a different semantic category (e.g., *tulips*). Relative to the expected control word *palms*, both types of anomalous words were semantically incoherent with respect to the wider discourse. And, in line with other work (St. George et al., 1994; Van Berkum et al., 1999c), both elicited a clear discourse-dependent N400 effect. However, the N400 effect elicited within-category violations (e.g., *pines*, a tree as well) turned out to be *smaller* than the N400 effect elicited by semantically incoherent words coming from a different semantic category (e.g., *tulips*). Because in off-line pretests both types of anomalous words had on average been rated as *equally* implausible and unpredictable, Federmeier and Kutas argued that the differential N400 effect could not solely derive from differences in how the words related to the dynamic discourse context, and therefore had to be interpreted as evidence for the context-independent involvement of permanent semantic memory structure. Regardless of whether their interpretation is correct,[9] the work by Federmeier and Kutas illustrates how the magnitude of an ERP effect can support particular inferences about discourse-dependent comprehension.

   Whereas the above inferences require only coarse-grained ordinal differences in the magnitude of an ERP effect, it is sometimes relevant to plot the size of an ERP effect in a more fine-grained manner, as a function of some interval-scale factor (e.g., 10 equidistant increasing levels of cloze probability). Unfortunately, within the domain of discourse-level comprehension, such parametric designs are very difficult to realize. The reason is that to get a relatively noise-free ERP average for conditions $X_1 \ldots X_N$, one needs the raw EEG of a large number of critical trials (say, ~30 at least) *per condition*. Furthermore, if every critical condition needs its own control, the number of required trials doubles. If every trial requires a *piece of discourse*, things really get out of hand. For some issues, the problem can perhaps be attenuated by including multiple critical trials within a single discourse (cf. St. George et al., 1994). In general, however, it will not be easy to use fine-grained parametric factors in a discourse-level ERP experiment.[10]

   Interval-level effect size also matters in another type of ERP design. If the processes that respond to manipulations X and Y are functionally independent, the corresponding ERP effects E_x and E_y should be strictly additive, that is, the effect E_{xy} to a *combined* XY manipulation should equal $E_x + E_y$. Among other things, this additivity logic has been used to study the functional independence of sentence-level semantic and syntactic processing (e.g., Osterhout & Nicol, 1999). Because it often requires a mere 2 x 2 design, it can also be used to study functional independence issues in discourse comprehension. However, as with the classification of ERP effect tokens, there is some uncertainty as to how strict one needs to be in applying the logic to actual ERP datasets (notably, how much divergence from perfect additivity can we do away with as "noise?"). Although this by no means invalidates the approach, it does sometimes make it a little harder to use.

13.3.5 Neuronal Generator Inferences

So far, we have discussed inferences based on the presence, timing, identity, and magnitude of an ERP effect. However, one additional question has been conspicuously absent from the discussion until now: What specific areas of the brain generate a given ERP effect E_x? In order arrive at a complete understanding of language-relevant ERP effects, we need to know what the underlying neural generators are. Unfortunately, it has turned out to be very difficult to determine the neuronal sources of a given scalp-recorded ERP effect from the nature of the effect itself. The reason is that any given ERP effect can be explained by a principally unbounded number of different generator configurations (see Kutas et al., 1999 for a good explanation of this so-called inverse problem; see also Fabiani, Gratton, & Coles, 2000; Urbach & Kutas, 2002). As a consequence, for example, an ERP effect that is largest over Pz need *not* have its generator right below (or even close to) Pz. The N400 effect is a case in point. Within the domain of language comprehension, this effect is usually largest at midline centro-parietal sites (say, close to Pz). Intracranial recordings, however, suggest that the N400 effect is generated by a number of brain areas, bilaterally distributed, and none of which being particularly close to Pz (see Kutas & Federmeier, 2000, and references therein). On their own, therefore, scalp-recorded ERPs do not straightforwardly inform us about which areas of the brain gave rise to them.

One way to use ERPs to make (coarse) spatial inferences without tackling the inverse problem is illustrated a recent discourse-level experiment on *hemispheric processing asymmetries* (Federmeier & Kutas, 1999b). Following up on the ERP study that I used to illustrate magnitude inferences with, Federmeier and Kutas now presented the critical words of stories such as in (5) in either the left or right visual hemifield, causing these words to be initially processed by the right and left hemisphere, respectively. Interestingly, only for words that were initially presented to the *left* hemisphere did within-category violations (*pines*) elicit a smaller N400 effect than between-category violations (*tulips*). For words initially presented to the *right* hemisphere, the N400 effects elicited by within-category violations (*pines*) and between-category violations (*tulips*) were of equal size. Based on these and other aspects of their ERP data, Federmeier and Kutas have proposed that whereas the right hemisphere would engage in discourse-driven plausibility-based integration, the left hemisphere might operate in a more predictive mode of processing, using the ever-changing discourse context as well as the more permanent structure of semantic memory as its source. Whether this specific interpretation is correct remains to be seen (cf. note 9), but these ERP results do suggest an asymmetry in how the two hemispheres contribute to discourse-level comprehension. Note, though, that the critical spatial inference hinges on a differential effect of left/right hemifield presentation, which happened to show up in ERPs but might have shown up in some other measure as well.

13.3.6 What Can We Infer About Discourse-Level Comprehension?

It is beyond the scope of this chapter to discuss the specific theoretical implications of the ERP work on discourse-level comprehension reviewed so far. However, before evaluating the utility of ERPs relative to other available on-line measurement tools, let me just lay out some of the most obvious implications. In a nutshell, the work reviewed suggests that the impact of discourse-level information is immediate, penetrating, proactive and—perhaps, surprisingly, in a chapter like this—maybe not so special. As for the first, the ERP data depicted in Figure 13.8 (as well as all the other discourse-dependent ERP effects observed so far, e.g., St. George et al., 1994) suggest that incremental interpretation holds "all the way up." The words of an unfolding sentence are immediately mapped onto a representation of the wider discourse in terms of their syntactic, their semantic, and their referential implications. Not only does the impact of discourse show up at the very first word where it can be expected in each case, but it also shows up very rapidly, within only a few hundred milliseconds after onset of the word at hand.

Because our P600/SPS data (cf. Figure 13.7) suggest that the analysis of a local syntactic ambiguity is not insensitive to discourse-level referential constraints, the ERP data also suggest that discourse-based comprehension is *penetrating* lower levels of analysis. One may debate about whether the ERP research at hand has tapped the earliest possible stage of parsing or just missed it (see the exchange between Brysbaert & Mitchell, 2000, and Van Berkum, Hagoort, & Brown, 2000 for an example), but the fact remains that discourse extremely rapidly affects the parsing process, being able to affect the provisional resolution of a syntactic ambiguity right at the word at which it emerges and, as discussed in detail elsewhere (Van Berkum et al., 1999b; see also Brown, Van Berkum, & Hagoort, 2000) even before a locally available syntactic gender cue is brought to bear on the analysis. Because the explanation of these findings involves a discourse-based anticipation of plausible syntactic structures, they can also be taken to suggest that discourse-level comprehension is *proactive*. Recent ERP evidence for discourse-based anticipation of specific upcoming words, shown in Figure 13.2, points in the same direction. The ERP effect at hand is relatively fragile and needs to be consolidated in follow-up experiments. However, with the same materials, we have already found that unexpectedly inflected adjectives also slow down the reader in a self-paced reading task (albeit only at a second adjective; see Van Berkum et al., 2002a; 2004). Thus, we have converging evidence from different methods that both listeners and readers can routinely exploit their knowledge of the wider discourse to anticipate upcoming language.

Finally, the equivalence of sentence- and discourse-dependent N400 effects, illustrated in Figures 13.4 and 13.5, can be taken to suggest that, in a sense, discourse-level comprehension *may not be all that special*. The comprehension process indexed by the N400 does not seem to care about whether the semantic constraints come from the first few words of a single unfolding sentence or from some wider discourse. What the data suggest is that it simply evaluates the incoming words relative to the widest interpretive domain available. One way to account for this is to recognize that, although sentence-semantic violations are local or sentence-internal in that it takes a single sentence to elicit them, the unfolding sentence itself draws in a much wider interpretive context, involving knowledge of the world, the language at hand, the present situation, and possibly even the absent speaker (see Van Berkum et al., 2003b , for a discussion in terms of "common ground"; Clark, 1996). If prior discourse simply adds a few more bits of information to this ever-present vast interpretive context, the equivalence of sentence- and discourse-dependent semantic anomaly effects should come as no surprise.

13.4 SO, CAN ERPS BE USED TO STUDY DISCOURSE-LEVEL COMPREHENSION?

One reason why ERP researchers may so far have stayed away from discourse-level comprehension is that working with ERPs is difficult enough as it is. With so many word- and sentence-level issues unresolved, why not get a firm grip on these first before getting into the complexity and potential intractability of discourse-level comprehension? This is a reasonable consideration. However, the work I reviewed shows that ERP research with discourse-level materials is feasible and can lead to systematic, tractable, and interpretable effects which support all of the various types of inferences that ERPs can be used for. Of course, the fact that we can do it does not necessarily mean we should. Working with ERPs is really difficult, and if we can get all the "goodies" with self-paced reading in 6 weeks instead of 6 months, why bother with ERPs? In the end, therefore, the utility of ERPs to track discourse-level comprehension depends on the pros and cons of using this method relative to the other tools available. The purpose of this section is to examine some of these trade-offs.

13.4.1 Advantages

13.4.1.1 Sensitivity Without Artificial Response Task

The language comprehension system did not develop to support timed responses to a concurrent probe word or control the index finger in a self-paced reading task. Of course, artificial response tasks by no means necessarily generate bad data. For example, many of the findings initially obtained with the self-paced reading task turned out to generalize to less artificial reading situations (Mitchell, chapter 2, this volume). However, every artificial response task does carry a risk of bringing artificial response strategies along with it. With ERPs, one can study the processes involved in discourse-level language comprehension by giving subjects just one simple task: read or listen for comprehension. Note that this happens to be what the system is for. This seems like as good a reason as any to consider ERPs as a tool to study discourse-level language comprehension.

As it happens, not everybody agrees that the absence of a secondary task is a virtue. ERP research sometimes faces skepticism because, without having assessed the quality of comprehension (e.g., through comprehension questions), how can we know what the subjects are doing? There may well be situations in which the concern is real. For example, if one's aim is to compute ERPs as a function of whether some difficult sentence was interpreted correctly or not, then this must be independently assessed at every trial. However, the how-do-we-know-what-they-are-doing? concern is often rather overstated. For one, it is not as though *comprehension questions* provide privileged access to what subjects are doing while they work on the input—if so, why need on-line measures to begin with? Also, to the extent that secondary tasks tell us what subjects are doing because *we told them what to do* (a nonnegligible risk, for example, in some types of probe tasks), then what they are doing may not be so interesting.[11]

One advantage of research with discourse-level input is that it is possible to have relatively interesting stimuli (as opposed to, say, a list of unrelated words) that can be used to draw subjects into the natural task of language comprehension. Furthermore, in a well-designed study with non-zero results, the ERP data *themselves* can be used to verify that subjects were drawn into this task to a sufficient degree. An N400 effect elicited by discourse-dependent semantic anomalies, for example, tells us that subjects were interpreting our stories to a sufficient degree to tell an anomalous word from a coherent one. In all, therefore, there is no principal reason why ERP measurements cannot stand on their own.

13.4.1.2 High Temporal Resolution

The ERP research with discourse-dependent semantic anomalies (see Figure 13.3) showed that ERPs are good at supporting two different kinds of inferences about the timing of a discourse-relevant processing event. One is how soon in the sentence, that is, at which word, the effect at hand shows up. In terms of the analysis of on-line measurement supplied in section 2, this type of temporal sensitivity involves establishing *which word-elicited incremental impulse response* turns out to be sensitive to the manipulation at hand. ERPs can do this well, but so can many behavioral measures (see various chapters in this volume for thorough discussion).[12]

However, bearing the caveats made before in mind, ERPs are particularly good at supporting a second type of timing inference, which is how soon after onset of (or some other relevant point within) the critical word the processing consequences of a manipulation show up. In terms of the earlier analysis, this involves establishing *when in the relevant word-elicited impulse response* things begin to happen. ERP effects are immediately linked to differential activity in the associated neuronal generator, with 0 ms delay (see also Osterhout et al., chapter 14, this volume). Hence, if some ERP effect emerges at time t, then we know the manipulation matters to the system at time t. Because behavioral measures tap cognition through its consequences for actual behavior, the timing of a cognitive event must in these measures always be inferred by subtracting some approximate correction factor (e.g., ~ 200 ms estimated saccade programming time). For questions that require precise timing *within* a word's impulse response, therefore, ERPs have a distinct cutting edge over the behavioral alternatives.

13.4.1.3 Selective Tracking and Process Identification

Figure 13.8 reveals what is perhaps the biggest advantage of using ERPs to track discourse-level comprehension as it unfolds: the possibility to *selectively* track specific aspects of the comprehension process. To make the point, consider what would happen if the example item in Figure 13.8 took part in a self-paced reading experiment. If this task is sensitive enough to pick up on referential ambiguity at the noun *friend*, a referentially induced syntactic dead-end at the word *there*, and the semantic problem emerging at *fascists*, we would see three delays in reading time, and that is it. There would be nothing *in the data* telling us that we are looking at three qualitatively different cognitive events. With ERPs, such information comes "for free." Although we do not yet fully understand the nature and the degree of language-specificity of the processes that underlie each of the ERP effects displayed in Figure 13.8, the fact is that within the domain of discourse-dependent language comprehension, ERPs clearly allow one to selectively tap into aspects of the ongoing referential, syntactic, and semantic analyses. If any feature of ERPs is going to help us disentangle and make sense of the many different processes interacting in discourse-level comprehension, it will be this one.

The fact that ERP effects "come in different flavors" also implies that there is information in obtaining *identical* ERP effects. Our finding that sentence- and discourse-dependent anomalies elicit the very same N400 effect (Figures 13.4 and 13.5), for example, clearly suggests that from the perspective of the interpretive process indexed by the N400, there is no functional distinction between a context set up by a single unfolding sentence and one set up by a larger piece of discourse. Also, the equivalent N400 findings with spoken- and written-language input (compare Figures 13.4 and Figure 13.5) suggests that the underlying machinery reflected by this component is basically modality-independent. Now, all this may or may not be considered a big surprise (as it happens, much of this was no surprise to me), but the fact is that the observation of, say, four exactly identical reading time delays would not in itself have licenced these inferences about process equivalence (see Hess, Foss, & Carroll, 1995, for an example of how hard it is to license such inferences by means of response-time methodology).

13.4.1.4 Easy Cross-Modal Investigation

Eyetracking in reading is necessarily limited to the comprehension of written language, and so is self-paced reading. The use of head-mounted eyetracking in a visual-world setting, on the other hand, is limited to the study of spoken-language comprehension. Of all the tools currently used to track sentence comprehension on-line, only ERPs can be used with spoken as well as written language input. In addition, it can be used with sign language, as well as potentially relevant nonlinguistic forms of input (e.g., a cartoon or video sequence; West & Holcomb, 2002; Sitnikova et al., 2003) For issues in which generalizations across modality are important, the possibility to do so within the same measure is highly attractive. Moreover, and returning to the equivalence of discourse-dependent N400 effects across modality exemplified in Figures 13.4 and 13.5, ERPs provide the means to *directly* test to what extent the processes involved in listening and reading are (non-) identical.

Because eye movements generate deflections in the EEG that are much larger than the ERP effects we are looking for, it is important to avoid them while recording EEG. It is for this reason that virtually all ERP research with written sentences uses Serial Visual Presentation (SVP) in which the words of a sentence are consecutively presented in the center of the screen at some fixed rate (e.g., 600 or 250 ms per word). Psycholinguists who examine reading under more natural conditions are often rather skeptical about this way of presenting written language. And, indeed, it does make sense to be concerned about whether SVP might affect the results obtained. As it happens, however, there is now a substantial database of ERP studies that reveal surprisingly comparable findings for fully natural spoken-language input and written-language input presented with SVP (e.g., for discourse-level N400 effects, compare Figures 13.4 and 13.5, derived from Van Berkum, Zwitserlood, et al., 2003b, and Van Berkum, Hagoort, et al., 1999c; see also Federmeier & Kutas, 1999a; Federmeier et al., 2002; for sentence-dependent N400 effects, see, for instance, Hagoort & Brown, 2000a; for P600/SPS effects, see, for instance, Hagoort & Brown, 2000b; Osterhout & Holcomb, 1992, 1993; for memory-related slow ERP shifts, see, for example, Kutas, 1997). Of course, the fact that *some* sentence-level ERP results generalize from SVP to speech input does not guarantee that *every* new result will do the same (prosodic factors being an obvious complication). However, it *does* mean that we can now no longer discard an ERP result simply because it was obtained with SVP.

13.4.2 Drawbacks

13.4.2.1 Many Constraints on Experimental Design

By far the most important drawback of ERPs is that, as with other neuroimaging measures, they severely constrain the shape of an experiment. One such constraint already mentioned before is the need to have a much larger number of critical trials per condition (at least ~30–40) than is common in most behavioral designs. With a single bleep, flash, or word as critical stimulus, this is not too much of a problem. However, with a 25-s mini-story in every trial and, say, 5 s of overhead around each trial, a simple 2 x 2 design is already looking at 60–80 min pure time-on-task, excluding breaks, practice session, and filler trials. This is a severe constraint on the use of ERPs to study discourse-level comprehension.[13] Having subjects come back to the lab several times is one solution, but because of the time lost in applying and removing electrodes (~1–2 hr per session), this is not very practical. It also leaves subjects with plenty of time to think about the experiment and possibly even discuss it with others. The only other way to attenuate the problem is to make the stories as short as possible, or, if possible, to obtain multiple critical measurements in a single story (cf. St. George et al., 1994).

The limited space for filler trials can be a real concern. However, even a complete lack of fillers does not necessarily invalidate one's design (see Van Berkum et al., 2000). Fillers are usually employed to hide critical features of the design and to make sure that unwarranted strategic processing does not pay off. However, both functions can also be implemented in other ways. Also, critical features of the design can often be hidden by having more variation in how particular critical stimulus features are realized (e.g., avoid using the same critical verb in all items) by having intrinsically interesting and maximally variable content, by counteracting the regularities of critical sentences in noncritical sentences elsewhere in the story, and by adding a salient but harmless dummy manipulation (e.g., a semantic anomaly in the tails of some stories) to distract the subject. The joint effectiveness of these measures can be assessed in a well-conducted postsession interview. In addition, one can often quite easily use counterbalancing, as well as many of the measures just mentioned, to make sure that even if critical features *do* get noticed, there would be nothing to be gained by using some unnatural comprehension strategy. So, even though a design without filler trials will make many experimentally trained psycholinguists somewhat uneasy (see Brysbaert & Mitchell, 2000, replied to in Van Berkum et al., 2000), there is no particular reason to stick to a simple "if it ain't at least 50-50, it's no good."

ERPs impose several other constraints that complicate discourse-level research. One is the requirement to sit still during recording. With long trials, the problem can sometimes be attenuated by designating a part of each story as non-critical, and by communicating to the subject this opportunity to relax by means of a visual cue. A more serious consequence of this requirement is that it makes it *very* difficult to have the discourse occur as part of some more realistic setting such as a referential communication task. To me, a huge, and by far the biggest, advantage of eyetracking in so-called visual-world experiments over *all* other on-line measures is that in these experiments linguistic utterances can be made relevant to some larger collaborative project ("Now pick up the queen of spades and put it below the ace ..."). Although the collaborative task may itself be artificial, once it has been accepted as a legitimate task by the subject, it does provide the latter with a strong natural motivation to process language ("language as action," cf. Clark, 1996). It remains to be seen to what extent ERPs can be taken this far beyond the single sentence.

13.4.2.2 No Intuitively Obvious Interpretation

It is sometimes said that relative to behavioral measures, ERPs provide a more direct window onto cognition because ERPs directly tap into the seat of cognition, the brain. In terms of *timing*, and in terms of whether a behavioral response (e.g., a saccade, a button press) mediates between cognition and its measurement, ERPs are indeed much more immediately related to cognitive events than behavioral measures. However, the general claim that brain measures are somehow privileged can also easily be reversed. Cognition evolved for behavior, and, moreover, for adequate and timely behavior. Thus, although the brain did not specifically evolve to tap a space bar in the self-paced reading task, one could argue that *speed and accuracy measures* are in a sense the more privileged windows onto cognition. Note that related to this, speed and accuracy have an intuitively obvious interpretation: If things go slower or result in more errors, the comprehension system is having a harder time. ERPs lack such an intuitively obvious interpretation. Positive ERP deflections do not necessarily mean the system is doing better, and negative deflections do not tell us it is in trouble. Moreover, although accepted by many as a reasonable working assumption, it is not even clear to what extent an increase in the amplitude of some particular ERP component should always be interpreted as evidence that the underlying system "has to work harder." I suspect that this lack of intuitively obvious meaning ("It's just squiggles") is one of the main reasons why ERP research is frequently ignored by other researchers in the field (and why fMRI and PET results are more easily accepted). The upside, of course, is that because ERPs are not unidimensionally tied to more or less trouble, we may also be able to go beyond the associated unidimensionality in our thinking about comprehension (see Mitchell, chapter 2, and Boland, chapter 4, both for a similar point).

13.4.2.3 Slow Research Cycle

A final drawback of ERPs is that it is cumbersome research, taking more time to conduct than the average eyetracking experiment, and much more time than an average self-paced reading experiment. Because an ERP design needs many trials, and hence, in this particular field of application, many carefully handcrafted and pretested discourses, ERP research with discourse-level materials can become a real problem (with sometimes over half a year dedicated to the construction and validation of materials alone!). Apart from the obvious drawbacks for individual researchers, as well as for students looking for a small-scale project, the implication is that it takes a much larger research effort to systematically chart some empirical phenomenon. Hence, even if the community has lots of good ideas to track discourse-level comprehension by means of ERPs, progress will be slow.

As with all other tools available to track discourse-level comprehension as it unfolds, there are some very good reasons to use ERPs, as well as some very good reasons to not exclusively rely on them. Only an adequate understanding of each of the available tools can help the researcher decide which (combination) of them is most appropriate, given the issue at hand.

13.5 WHAT IS ON THE HORIZON?

The field of neuroimaging is changing rapidly. Whereas, up until only a decade or so ago, ERPs were just about "the only neuroimaging game in town" (for a psycholinguist, that is), several new methods have since become available (e.g., MEG, fMRI, and TMS). Other innovations are taking place within the EEG research community itself. To my knowledge, and with the exception of fMRI, most of the new tools have not yet been used to investigate discourse-level comprehension, and I will therefore only briefly comment on their potential. However, I believe it is only a matter of time before measures like MEG and TMS, as well as EEG-based measures that complement the simple computation of ERPs, will begin to enrich our understanding of the architecture and neural substrate of discourse-level comprehension.

13.5.1 EEG

As mentioned before, scalp-recorded ERPs cannot straightforwardly inform us on their own about which areas of the brain give rise to them. However, ERPs are no longer on their own. Our knowledge of the brain is increasing, and so are our capabilities to identify specific areas of the brain that are recruited in, say, a language-comprehension task. With intracranial recordings, for example, progress has been made in locating at least some of the generators of the language-relevant N400 effect. In addition, a sizeable research effort currently focuses on how to use data from other imaging techniques (notably fMRI and MEG) to help identify the neuronal generators of particular EEG phenomena (see also Osterhout et al., chapter 14, this volume; Kutas et al., 1999).

Another interesting development concerns the revival of the so-called background EEG. For quite a long time, researchers only looked at this to examine the energetic state of cognition, i.e., whether somebody was highly attentive, relaxed, drowsy, or asleep. Other than that, it was viewed as noise to be canceled away by averaging. Over the past few years, however, EEG researchers have discovered that EEG oscillations ("brain rhythms") can inform us about much more than the energetic state of an individual (e.g., Pfurtscheller & Lopes da Silva, 1999; Tallon-Baudry & Bertrand, 1999) So far, there have been only a few attempts to examine these oscillatory EEG phenomena during language comprehension (e.g., Bastiaansen, Van Berkum, & Hagoort, 2002a, 2002b; Weiss & Mueller, 2003), and, to my knowledge, none of this work has gone beyond the single sentence. However, this is bound to change in the very near future. EEG oscillations are believed to play an important role in binding various sorts of information distributed across the brain together in a single representation (cf. Tallon-Baudry & Bertrand). They have also been associated with operations involved in episodic memory storage and retrieval (see Bastiaansen & Hagoort, 2003, for a language-oriented review). Both of these associations lead one to expect that oscillatory EEG phenomena will turn out to be relevant to understanding the architecture of discourse-level comprehension.

Recent evidence (Makeig et al., 2002) suggests that at least one very early ERP component might actually be the result of a stimulus-induced short-lived synchronization of the oscillatory EEG, rather than the average reflection of a transient "blip" that has nothing to do with the background EEG. This suggests that, in some cases, there may be a much more intimate relationship between ERPs and EEG background oscillations than traditionally assumed. Because of their shape and time course, language-relevant effects like the N400 and P600/SPS are unlikely to receive a similar reinterpretation. However, the finding does illustrate the importance of exploring ERPs and EEG oscillations in closer relationship.

A final development also concerns the interpretation of ERPs. As discussed before, qualitatively different ERPs are assumed to reflect qualitatively different processes. However, as discussed by Rugg and Coles (1995), it is not always obvious what the latter means in terms of an interesting model of cognition. For example, recent findings (Pulvermüller, 2001) suggest that words whose meaning involves movement of different part of the body (*talking, walking, reaching*) elicit ERPs that differ in scalp distribution in a way that might be associated with different areas of the human motor cortex that control the movements involved. The example should remind us that the brain's electrophysiology also codes *content*, and that, as a result, ERPs cannot always simply be assumed to reflect processes irrespective of the content involved. In other words, we should not expect a simple mapping between the various different ERPs that we see in our data and the various different "boxes" ("modules," "processors") that we define in our information processing models.

13.5.2 Other Imaging Methods

Over the last few years, researchers have begun to use functional magnetic resonance imaging (fMRI) and positron emission tomography (PET) to examine the neural substrates of discourse-level comprehension (e.g., Ferstl & Von Cramon, 2001; Gallagher et al., 2000; Maguire, Frith, & Morris, 1999; Robertson et al., 2000; St. George, Kutas, Martinez, & Sereno, 1999; Tracy et al., 2003; see also Berthoz, Armory, Blair, & Dolan, 2002). It is beyond the scope of this chapter to review the results of this emerging research area (see Gernsbacher & Kashak, 2003, for a brief review). However, both fMRI and PET examine localized changes in neuronal activity in the brain via the associated changes in regional blood flow. Because such hemodynamic changes are intrinsically rather slow (in the order of seconds), the temporal resolution of measures that depend on these changes is intrinsically limited, perhaps not to the order of seconds but at least to the order of several hundreds of milliseconds (with event-related fMRI; Bandettini, Birn, & Donahue, 2000; Buckner & Logan, 2002). It is for this reason that PET and fMRI are usually referred to as having rather poor temporal resolution. To the extent that the configuration of critical neuronal systems engaged by some unfolding discourse varies more rapidly than a scanner can keep track of—an empirical issue—it will not be easy to relate the functional imaging results to the way comprehension unfolds in time.

The ERP data reviewed in this chapter demonstrate that at least some aspects of discourse-level comprehension occur extremely rapidly. To keep track of these with sufficient temporal resolution, methods that more immediately reflect neuronal activity are to be preferred (cf. Osterhout et al., chapter 14, this volume). The latter include not only measures based on EEG (ERPs and event-related oscillatory changes) but also their magnetic counterparts in magneto-encephalography (MEG). The MEG equivalent of an ERP, a so-called event-related magnetic field or ERF, can support similar types of inferences and can, when combined with ERP data, support somewhat more precise inferences about underlying neuronal generators. Another potentially relevant measure is the so-called event-related optical signal, which reflects changes in the optical scattering properties of brain tissue that are concurrent with neuronal activity (EROS) (Gratton & Fabiani, 2001). The EROS technique is still under development, but if the claims for good temporal *and* spatial resolution turn out to be correct, its benefits will be clear.

All the above-mentioned neuroimaging measures share one very important limitation, which is that regardless of all their sophistication, they can only tell us which neuronal events and systems *correlate* with, say, a discourse-dependent comprehension problem. Of course, what we would really like to know is which neuronal events and systems are *responsible for* (i.e., causally involved in) particular aspects of discourse-level comprehension. Until recently, the only way to learn anything about the latter was through lesions caused by, say, a bullet, a cerebral vascular accident, or through the electrical stimulation of pieces of cortex exposed during brain surgery. With the development of transcranial magnetic stimulation or TMS, however, we now have a tool that allows us to noninvasively explore which brain systems are critically involved in some aspect of cognition, as well as when such involvement occurs. TMS can be seen as the inverse of MEG in that rather than picking up the magnetic field caused by neuroelectrical events, external magnetic fields are used to temporarily and harmlessly "mess up" neuronal communication at fairly limited regions of the cortex. Psycholinguists have recently begun working with the technique (e.g., Shapiro, Pascual Leone, Mottaghy, Gangitano, & Caramazza, 2001; Knecht et al., 2002), and TMS is ready to be used to explore the causal structure of discourse-level comprehension.

13.5.3 A Gauntlet Picked Up (Briefly): Why Not Just Do Self-Paced Reading Anyway?

In his thought-provoking contribution to this volume (chapter 2), Don Mitchell observes that many sentence-processing phenomena were first established in the self-paced reading task, subsequently confirmed by eyetracking experiments, and then occasionally corroborated once more in ERP studies. This convergence of findings across on-line measurement tools is reassuring, for each then introduces some unnatural features into the language comprehension situation (button pressing, bite bars, electrode caps, etc.). As Mitchell notes, however, such convergence also does raise the question of why we should spend our valuable resources on complex time-consuming measures such as EEG, MEG, and fMRI, instead of running simple self-paced reading studies all the time. In Mitchell's words, "Why use a 3G video-enabled cell-phone when a Post-It Note will do?"

To me, the most obvious reason is that although several decades of self-paced reading research has uncovered lots of phenomena, it has by no means resolved all the debates that came along with them. Like perhaps all other cognitive systems (cf. Newell, 1973; Anderson, 1978), the language comprehension system is a difficult one to pin down by behavioral data alone. The obvious response to this is to look for additional constraints, by linking domain-specific theories to a theory of generic cognitive system architecture (e.g., Newell, 1990; Rumelhart, McClelland, & the PDP Research Group, 1986), by more careful analyses of what the system is supposed to do (e.g., Marr, 1982; Anderson, 1991; Tooby & Cosmides, 2000), and—most relevant here—by gathering other types of data, such as ERPs and fMRI scans. As for the latter, the growing suspicion that the brain is perhaps not an arbitrarily structured device running algorithms that could not care less about their implementation suggests that neuroimaging data may actually provide some rather useful constraints.[14] This does not mean that we should all run for the scanners. At the same time, however, perhaps we should not all go for self-paced reading either. Post-It Notes have become indispensable, and for good reason. After a while, however, they invariably clutter up one's desk and begin to point in different directions.

13.5.4 The Real Challenges

I hope to have shown that at least one neuroimaging technique, the registration of event-related brain potentials, can help keep track of discourse-level comprehension in a way that justifies the effort. Although it takes some creativity to make it work, ERPs and discourse can be combined in a single feasible experiment to explore the existence, precise timing, identity, degree of involvement, and—to some extent—neural substrate of processes involved in discourse-level comprehension. As illustrated in Figure 13.8, ERPs are particularly good at selectively keeping track of specific aspects of comprehension, doing so with high temporal precision as people read or listen for comprehension. Because discourse-level comprehension is no simple task, being able to tell one process apart from another, to identify which of the many processes one is looking at in a particular study, is no trivial benefit. Of course, as with all other measures, this benefit comes at a cost. It depends on the specific issue at hand whether one outweighs the other or whether some other measure should be used instead.

At least three important challenges are ahead of us. One is to see whether we can *really* take ERPs (and other neuroimaging measures) beyond the sentence. Much of the ERP research that I reviewed was framed in terms of whether discourse modulated some aspect of sentence comprehension (e.g., the parsing of a local syntactic ambiguity). However, discourse is obviously more than a contextual factor affecting sentence comprehension. For many interesting discourse-level phenomena, a minimal one- or two-sentence discourse context will not provide enough leverage, and far richer texts will be required. Moreover, for many really interesting discourse-level phenomena, we will have to move away from "textoids" (Graesser et al., 1997) altogether and enter the true arena of language use (Clark, 1996) where language comprehension is relevant to achieving some private or collective goal. In our lab, we are currently exploring new ways to record EEG in a constrained conversational setting, but it remains to be seen whether we can take ERPs this far.

The second challenge is to keep the importance of on-line measurement in perspective. With comprehension and its input unfolding over time, we need tools to keep track of things as they unfold. However, the availability of such tools should not lure us into pursuing timing questions all the time. Comprehension is about things being understood, and the system that does it is doing more than just meeting deadlines. For this reason, measures that are sensitive to the nature of the representations being constructed or to the identity of the processes involved are indispensable. Some of these measures may be more or less on-line (e.g., ERPs, head-mounted eyetracking in visual-world settings, and concurrent probe tasks), but others may be relatively or even completely off-line (e.g., fMRI, PET, as well as paper-and-pencil cloze tests, plausibility ratings, and comprehension questions). If we do not make good use of such content-sensitive measures, we are never going to understand the nature of comprehension.

The final challenge for us psycholinguists, I believe, is to try to be open-minded about other people's tools to track sentence- and discourse-level comprehension. In my opinion, the field of sentence comprehension research suffers from an unhealthy amount of "dependent variable chauvinism," with occasionally very strong biases towards a single preferred measure (say, eye movements in reading) at the expense of some other measure (say, ERPs). The phenomenon can be seen in polite debates—or, more usually, polite silences—at conferences, in the selective quoting of other people's work, and, more violently, in manuscript and grant proposal reviews. Yes, it is very tempting and very pleasant to believe that one's own method dominates all others, and probably everybody will occasionally fall prey to this, especially if the method involves a lot of hard work that requires justification. However, in view of the rather modest progress we have made with the measures currently at our disposal, there is no reason whatsoever to proclaim any of them as The Measure (or The Invariably Most Cost-Effective Measure; cf. Mitchell, chapter 2, this volume). The problems of discovery that we face are so difficult that it makes sense to welcome *every* feasible and a priori reasonable measure, as long as it provides a new window on the language comprehension system.

13.6 ACKNOWLEDGMENTS

Supported by an NWO Innovation Impulse Vidi grant. I would like to thank Colin Brown and Peter Hagoort for introducing me to the art of sentential ERP research, the research assistants of the Max Planck Institute for Psycholinguistics, the F.C. Donders Centre for Cognitive Neuroimaging, and the University of Amsterdam Psychology Department for helping me out with some very laborious experiments, the AMLaP-2002 organizers for their invitation to give a talk on ERPs and discourse (upon which this chapter is based), and Manuel Carreiras, Chuck Clifton, and Peter Hagoort for comments on an earlier version of this chapter.

References

Anderson, J. R. (1978). Arguments concerning representations for mental imagery. *Psychological Review, 85*(4), 249–277.

Anderson, J. R. (1991). Is human cognition adaptive? *Behavioral and Brain Sciences, 14,* 471–517.

Bandettini, P. A., Birn, R. M., & Donahue, K. M. (2000). Functional fMRI. In J. T. Cacioppo, L. G. Tassinary, & G. G. Berntson (Eds.), *Handbook of psychophysiology* (pp. 978–1014). Cambridge, UK: Cambridge University Press.

Bastiaansen, M. C. M., & Hagoort, P. (2003). Event-induced theta responses as a window on the dynamics of memory./*Cortex,* 39, 967–992.

Bastiaansen, M. C. M., Van Berkum, J. J. A., & Hagoort, P. (2002a). Event-related theta power increases in the human EEG during online sentence processing. *Neuroscience Letters, 323,* 13–16.

Bastiaansen, M. C. M., Van Berkum, J. J. A., & Hagoort, P. (2002b). Syntactic processing modulates the theta rhythm of the human EEG. *NeuroImage, 17,* 1479–1492.

Berthoz, S., Armony, J. L., Blair, R. J. R., & Dolan, R. J. (2002). An fMRI study of intentional and unintentional (embarrassing) violations of social norms. *Brain, 125*(8), 1696–1708.

Bransford, J. D., & Johnson, M. K. (1972). Contextual prerequisites for understanding: Some investigations of comprehension and recall. *Journal of Verbal Learning and Verbal Behavior, 11*(6), 717–726.

Brown, C. M., & Hagoort, P. (2000). On the electrophysiology of language comprehension: Implications for the human language system. In M. W. Crocker, M. Pickering, & C. Clifton, Jr. (Eds.), *Architectures and mechanisms for language processing* (pp. 213–237). Cambridge, UK: Cambridge University Press.

Brown, C. M., Hagoort, P., & Kutas, M. (2000). Postlexical integration processes in language comprehension: Evidence from brain-imaging research. In M. S. Gazzaniga (Ed.), *The new cognitive neurosciences* (pp. 881–895). Cambridge, MA: MIT Press.

Brown, C. M., Hagoort, P., & Ter Keurs, M. (1999). Electrophysiological signatures of visual lexical processing: Open- and closed-class words. *Journal of Cognitive Neuroscience, 11*(3), 261–281.

Brown, C. M., Van Berkum, J. J. A., & Hagoort, P. (2000). Discourse before gender: An event-related brain potential study on the interplay of semantic and syntactic information during spoken language understanding. *Journal of Psycholinguistic Research, 29*(1), 53–68.

Brysbaert, M., & Mitchell, D. C. (2000). The failure to use gender information in parsing: A comment on Van Berkum, Brown, and Hagoort (1999). *Journal of Psycholinguistic Research, 29,* 453–466.

Buckner, R. L., & Logan, J. M. (2001). Functional neuroimaging methods: PET and fMRI. In R. Cabeza & A. Kingstone (Eds.), *Handbook of functional neuroimaging of cognition* (pp. 27–48). Cambridge, MA: MIT Press.

Clark, H. H. (1996). *Using language.* Cambridge, UK: Cambridge University Press.

Clark, H. H. (1997). Dogmas of understanding. *Discourse Processes, 23*(3), 567–598.

Connolly, J. F., & Phillips, N. A. (1994). Event-related potential components reflect phonological and semantic processing of the terminal word of spoken sentences. *Journal of Cognitive Neuroscience, 6,* 256–266.

Dooling, D. J., & Lachman, R. (1971). Effects of comprehension on retention of prose. *Journal of Experimental Psychology, 88*(2), 216–222.

Fabiani, M., Gratton, G., & Coles, M. G. H. (2000). Event-related brain potentials. In J. T. Cacioppo, L. G. Tassinary, & G. G. Berntson (Eds.), *Handbook of psychophysiology* (pp. 53–84). Cambridge, UK: Cambridge University Press.

Federmeier, K. D., & Kutas, M. (1999a). A rose by any other name: Long-term memory structure and sentence processing. *Journal of Memory and Language, 41,* 469–495.

Federmeier, K. D., & Kutas, M. (1999b). Right words and left words: Electrophysiological evidence for hemispheric differences in meaning processing. *Cognitive Brain Research, 8,* 373–392.

Federmeier, K. D., McLennan, D. B., De Ochoa, E., & Kutas, M. K. (2002). The impact of semantic memory organization and sentence context information on spoken language processing by younger and older adults: An ERP study. *Psychophysiology, 39*(2), 133–146.

Ferstl, E. C., & Von Cramon, D. Y. (2001). The role of coherence and cohesion in text comprehension: An event-related fMRI study. *Cognitive Brain Research, 11*(3), 325–340.

Fodor, J. A. (1983). *The modularity of mind.* Cambridge, MA: MIT Press.

Friederici, A. D. (1998). The neurobiology of language comprehension. In A. D. Friederici (Ed.), *Language comprehension: A biological perspective* (pp. 263–301). Berlin: Springer.

Friederici, A. D. (2002). Towards a neural basis of auditory sentence processing. *Trends in Cognitive Sciences, 6*(2), 78–84.

Friederici, A. D., Hahne, A., & Mecklinger, A. (1996). Temporal structure of syntactic parsing: Early and late event-related brain potential effects. *Journal of Experimental Psychology: Learning, Memory, and Cognition, 22*(5), 1219–1248.

Gallagher, H. L., Happé, F., Brunswick, N., Fletcher, P. C., Frith, U., & Frith, C.D. (2000). Reading the mind in cartoons and stories: An fMRI study of 'theory of the mind' in verbal and nonverbal tasks. *Neuropsychologia, 38*(1), 11–21.

Gaskell, M. G., & Marslen-Wilson, W. D. (2001). Lexical ambiguity resolution and spoken word recognition: Bridging the gap. *Journal of Memory and Language, 44,* 325–349.

Gernsbacher, M. A., & Kashak, M. P. (2003). Neuroimaging studies of language production and comprehension. *Annual Review of Psychology, 54,* 91–114.

Graesser, A. C., Millis, K. K., & Zwaan, R. A. (1997). Discourse comprehension. *Annual Review of Psychology, 48,* 163–189.

Gratton, G., & Fabiani, M. (2001). Shedding light on brain function: The event-related optical signal. *Trends in Cognitive Sciences, 5*(8), 357–363.

Hagoort, P., & Brown, C. M. (2000a). ERP effects of listening to speech: Semantic ERP effects. *Neuropsychologia, 38,* 1518–1530.

Hagoort, P., & Brown, C. M. (2000b). ERP effects of listening to speech compared to reading: The P600/SPS to syntactic violations in spoken sentences and rapid serial visual presentation. *Neuropsychologia, 38,* 1531–1549.

Hagoort, P., Brown, C. M., & Groothusen, J. (1993). The syntactic positive shift (SPS) as an ERP measure of syntactic processing. *Language and Cognitive Processes, 8,* 439–483.

Hagoort, P., Brown, C. M., & Osterhout, L. (1999). The neurocognition of syntactic processing. In C. M. Brown & P. Hagoort (Eds.), *The neurocognition of language* (pp. 273–316). Oxford: Oxford University Press.

Hess, D. J., Foss, D. J., & Carroll, P. (1995). Effects of global and local context on lexical processing during language comprehension. *Journal of Experimental Psychology: General, 124*(1), 62–82.

Jongman, A. (1998). Effects of vowel length and syllabic structure on segment duration in Dutch. *Journal of Phonetics, 26,* 207–222.

Kemps, R. J. J. K., Ernestus, M., Schreuder, R., & Baayen, R. H. (2003). *Prosodic cues for morphological complexity*: The case of Dutch plurals. Manuscript submitted for publication.

Kintsch, W. (1998). *Comprehension: A paradigm for cognition.* Cambridge, UK: Cambridge University Press.

Kluender, R., & Kutas, M. (1993). Bridging the gap: Evidence from ERPs on the processing of unbounded dependencies. *Journal of Cognitive Neuroscience, 5*(2), 196–214.

Knecht, S., Floël, A., Draeger, B., Breitenstein, C., Sommer, J., Henningsen, H., Ringelstein, E. B., & Pascual Leone, A. (2002). Degree of language lateralization determines susceptibility to unilateral brain lesions. *Nature Neuroscience, 5*(7), 695–699.

Kutas, M. (1997). Views on how the electrical activity that the brain generates reflects the functions of different language structures. *Psychophysiology, 34,* 383–398.

Kutas, M., & Federmeier, K. D. (1998). Minding the body. *Psychophysiology, 35*(2), 135–150.

Kutas, M., & Federmeier, K. D. (2000). Electrophysiology reveals semantic memory use in language comprehension. Trends in Cognitive Sciences, 12, 463–470.

Kutas, M., Federmeier, K. D., Coulson, S., King, J. W., & Münte, T. F. (2000). Language. In J. T. Cacioppo, L. G. Tassinary, & G. G. Berntson (Eds.), *Handbook of psychophysiology* (pp. 576–601). Cambridge, UK: Cambridge University Press.

Kutas, M., Federmeier, K. D., & Sereno, M. I. (1999). Current approaches to mapping language in electromagnetic space. In C. M. Brown & P. Hagoort (Eds.), *The neurocognition of language* (pp. 359–387). Oxford: Oxford University Press.

Kutas, M., & Hillyard, S. A. (1980). Reading senseless sentences: Brain potentials reflect semantic incongruity. *Science, 207,* 203–205.

Kutas, M., & Hillyard, S. A. (1983). Event-related brain potentials to grammatical errors and semantic anomalies. *Memory and Cognition, 11,* 539–550.

Kutas, M., & Schmitt, B. M. (2003). Language in microvolts. In M. T. Banich & M. Mack. (Eds.), *Mind, brain, and language.* Hillsdale, NJ: Erlbaum.

Kutas, M., & Van Petten, C. K. (1994). Psycholinguistics electrified: Event-related brain potential investigations. In M. A. Gernsbacher (Ed.), *Handbook of psycholinguistics* (pp. 83–143). New York: Academic Press.

Maguire, E. A., Frith, C. D., & Morris, R. G. M. (1999). The functional neuroanatomy of comprehension and memory: The importance of prior knowledge. *Brain, 122*(10), 1839–1850.

Makeig, S., Westerfield, M., Jung, T.-P., Enghoff, S., Townsend, J., Courchesne, E., & Sejnowski, T.J. (2002). Dynamic brain sources of visual evoked responses. *Science, 295,* 690–694.

Marr, D. (1982). *Vision.* Freeman.

Marslen-Wilson, W. D., & Tyler, L. K. (1980). The temporal structure of spoken language understanding. Cognition, 8, 1–71.

Mueller, H. M., King, J. W., & Kutas, M. (1997). Event-related potentials to relative clause processing in spoken sentences. Cognitive Brain Research, 5, 193–203.

Münte, T. F., Schiltz, K., & Kutas, M. (1998). When temporal terms belie conceptual order. *Nature, 395,* 71–74.

Myers, J. L., & O'Brien, E. J. (1998). Accessing the discourse representation during reading. *Discourse Processes, 26,* 131–157.

Neville, H., Nicol, J. L., Barss, A., Forster, K. I., & Garrett, M. F. (1991). Syntactically based sentence processing classes: Evidence from event-related brain potentials. *Journal of Cognitive Neuroscience, 3*(2), 151–165.

Newell, A. (1973). You can't play 20 questions with nature and win. In W. G. Chase (Ed.), *Visual information processing* (pp. 283–308). New York: Academic Press.

Newell, A. (1990). *Unified theories of cognition.* Cambridge, MA: Harvard University Press.

Osterhout, L., Bersick, M., & McKinnon, R. (1997). Brain potentials elicited by words: Word length and frequency predict the latency of an early negativity. *Biological Psychology, 46*(2), 143–168.

Osterhout, L., & Hagoort, P. (1999). A superficial resemblance doesn't necessarily mean you're part of the family: Counterarguments to Coulson, King, and Kutas (1998) in the P600/SPS debate. *Language and Cognitive Processes, 14*(1), 1–14.

Osterhout, L., & Holcomb, P. J. (1992). Event-related brain potentials elicited by syntactic anomaly. *Journal of Memory and Language, 31,* 785–806.

Osterhout, L., & Holcomb, P. J. (1993). Event-related potentials and syntactic anomaly: Evidence of anomaly detection during the perception of continuous speech. *Language and Cognitive Processes, 8*(4), 413–437.

Osterhout, L., & Holcomb, P. J. (1995). Event-related potentials and language comprehension. In M. D. Rugg & M. G. H. Coles (Eds.), *Electrophysiology of mind* (pp. 171–215). Oxford: Oxford University Press.

Osterhout, L., McLaughlin, J., & Bersick, M. (1997). Event-related brain potentials and human language. *Trends in Cognitive Sciences, 1*(6), 203–209.

Osterhout, L., & Mobley, L. A. (1995). Event-related brain potentials elicited by failure to agree. *Journal of Memory and Language, 34,* 739–773.

Osterhout, L., & Nicol, J. (1999). On the distinctiveness, independence, and time course of the brain response to syntactic and semantic anomalies. *Journal of Psycholinguistic Research, 14*(3), 283–317.

Pfurtscheller, G., & Lopes da Silva, F. H. (1999). Event-related EEG/MEG synchronization and desynchronization: basic principles. *Clinical Neurophysiology, 110,* 1842–1857.

Pulvermüller, F. (2001). Brain Reflections of words and their meanings. *Trends in Cognitive Sciences,* 5, 517–524.

Rayner, K. (1998). Eye movements in reading and information processing: 20 years of research. *Psychological Bulletin, 124,* 372–422.

Robertson, D. A., Gernsbacher, M. A., Guidotti, S. J., Robertson, R. R. W., Irwin, W., Mock, B. J., & Campana, M. E. (2000). Functional neuroanatomy of the cognitive process of mapping during discourse comprehension. *Psychological Science, 11*(3), 255–260.

Rugg, M. D., & Coles, M. G. H. (1995). The ERP and cognitive psychology: Conceptual issues. In M. D. Rugg & M. G. H. Coles (Eds.), *Electrophysiology of mind: Event related brain potentials and cognition.* (Vol. 25, pp. 27–39). Oxford: Oxford University Press.

Rumelhart, D. E., McClelland, J. L., & the PDP Research Group. (1986). *Parallel distributed processing.* Cambridge, MA: MIT Press.

Salverda, A. P., Dahan, D., & McQueen, J. M. (2003). The role of prosodic boundaries in the resolution of lexical embedding in speech comprehension, *Cognition,* 90, 51–89.

Shapiro, K. A., Pascual Leone, A., Mottaghy, F. M., Gangitano, M., & Caramazza, A. (2001). Grammatical distinctions in the left frontal cortex. *Journal of Cognitive Neuroscience, 13*(6), 713–720.

Sitnikova, T., Kuperberg, G. & Holcomb, P. J. (2003). Semantic integration in videos of real-world events: An electrophysiological investigation. *Psychophysiology, 40,* 160–164.

St. George, M., Kutas, M., Martinez, A., & Sereno, M. I. (1999). Semantic integration in reading: Engagement of the right hemisphere during discourse processing. *Brain, 122*(7), 1317–1325.

St. George, M., Mannes, S., & Hoffman, J. E. (1994). Global semantic expectancy and language comprehension. *Journal of Cognitive Neuroscience, 6*(1), 70–83.

St. George, M., Mannes, S., & Hoffman, J. E. (1997). Individual differences in inference generation: An ERP analysis. *Journal of Cognitive Neuroscience, 9*(6), 776–787.

Streb, J., Rösler, F., & Hennighausen, E. (1999). Event-related responses to pronoun and proper name anaphors in parallel and nonparallel discourse structures. *Brain and Language, 70*(2), 273–286.

Tallon-Baudry, C., & Bertrand, O. (1999). Oscillatory gamma activity in humans and its role in object representation. *Trends in Cognitive Sciences, 3*(4), 151–162.

Tooby, J., & Cosmides, L. (2000). Toward mapping the evolved functional organization of mind and brain. In M. S. Gazzaniga (Ed.), *The new cognitive neurosciences* (pp. 1167–1177). Cambridge, MA: MIT Press.

Tracy, J., Flanders, A., Madi, S., Natale, P., Delvecchio, N., Pyrros, A., & Laskas, J. (2003). The brain's response to incidental intruded words during focal text processing. *NeuroImage,* 18, 117–126.

Urbach, T. P., & Kutas, M. (2002). The intractability of scaling scalp distributions to infer neuroelectric sources. *Psychophysiology, 39*(6), 791–808.

Van Berkum, J. J. A., Brown, C. M., & Hagoort, P. (1999a). Early referential context effects in sentence processing: Evidence from event-related brain potentials. *Journal of Memory and Language, 41,* 147–182.

Van Berkum, J. J. A., Brown, C. M., & Hagoort, P. (1999b). When does gender constrain parsing? Evidence from ERPs. *Journal of Psycholinguistic Research, 28*(5), 555–571.

Van Berkum, J. J. A., Brown, C. M., Hagoort, P., & Zwitserlood, P. (2003A). Event-related brain potentials reflect discourse-referential ambiguity in spoken-language comprehension. *Psychophysiology, 40,* 235–248.

Van Berkum, J. J. A., Brown, C. M., Hagoort, P., Zwitserlood, P., & Kooijman, V., (2002a). Can people use discourse-level information to predict upcoming words in an unfolding sentence? Evidence from ERPs and self-paced reading. *Proceedings of the 8th International Conference of Cognitive Neuroscience (ICON-8),* Porquerolles, France, September 9-15, p. 105.

Van Berkum, J. J. A., Brown, C. M., Hagoort, P., Zwitserlood, P., & Kooijman, V., (2004). Can people use discourse-level information to predict upcoming words in an unfolding sentence? Evidence from ERPs and self-paced reading. Manuscript submitted for publication.

Van Berkum, J. J. A., Hagoort, P., & Brown, C. M. (1999c). Semantic integration in sentences and discourse: Evidence from the N400. *Journal of Cognitive Neuroscience, 11*(6), 657–671.

Van Berkum, J. J. A., Hagoort, P., & Brown, C. M. (2000). The use of referential context and grammatical gender in parsing: A reply to Brysbaert and Mitchell. *Journal of Psycholinguistic Research, 29*(5), 467–481.

Van Berkum, J. J. A., Kooijman, V., Brown, C. M., Zwitserlood, P., & Hagoort, P. (2002b). Do listeners use discourse-level information to predict upcoming words in an unfolding sentence? An ERP study. *Proceedings of the Cognitive Neuroscience Society 9th annual meeting (CNS-2002),* San Francisco, April 14–16. Supplement to *Journal of Cognitive Neuroscience* (p. 82).

Van Berkum, J. J. A., Zwitserlood, P., Brown, C. M., & Hagoort, P. (2003b). When and how do listeners relate a sentence to the wider discourse? Evidence from the N400 effect. *Cognitive Brain Research,* 17, 701–718.

Van den Brink, D., Brown, C. M., & Hagoort, P. (2001). Electrophysiological evidence for early contextual influences during spoken-word recognition: N200 versus N400 Effects. *Journal of Cognitive Neuroscience, 13*(7), 967–985.

Van Petten, C., Kutas, M., Kluender, R., Mitchiner, M., & Mclsaac (1991). Fractionating the word repetition effect with event-related potentials. *Journal of Cognitive Neuroscience, 3*(2), 131–150.

Weiss, S., & Mueller, H. M. (2003). The contribution of EEG coherence to the investigation of language. *Brain and Language, 85,* 325–343.

West, W. C., & Holcomb, P. J. (2002). Event-related potentials during discourse-level semantic integration of complex pictures. *Cognitive Brain Research, 13*(3), 363–375.

Notes

1. In engineering, the temporally extended response of a system to (something approximating) an infinitely short impulse at its input is termed an *impulse response*, and is considered to be one of the keys to characterizing and analyzing basic system behavior.

2. The hypothetical four-stage compartmentalization of comprehension displayed is chosen to make a methodological point, not to advance a particular model of language processing.

3. In spoken language, sentence-level prosodic cues such as those signaling a pause, a question, or a bit of irony, also drive the system. To the extent that these cues (some of which have a written-language counterpart in punctuation) cannot be tied to specific words, the image of sentence comprehension as a sequence of solely *word-driven* incremental impulse responses is incomplete.

4. Although we know that discourse-dependent ERP effects can have a surprisingly early onset (see the section on timing inferences), the effect displayed in Figure 13.2 begins to emerge somewhere in the first 50 ms from estimated onset of the inflection. We suspect that this rather disconcerting timing may have to do with how we estimated the acoustic onset of the inflection. To determine the latter, we displayed the speech waves of the two alternative adjectives (e.g., *groot* and *grote*) simultaneously on screen, and used this as well as their sound to determine at what point in time the two acoustic signals started to diverge in sound (which, for this example, would be by the end of the "t"). However, this procedure did not take into account such subtle cues as durational changes in the stem vowel (which are known to systematically correlate with the presence of an inflection; e.g., Jongman, 1998), for the simple reason that such cues are very difficult to capture in a practical measurement procedure. Because recent evidence suggests that listeners *can* make use of such early cues to an upcoming inflection in the stem of the word (Salverda, Dahan, & McQueen, 2003; Kemps, Ernestus, Schreuder, & Baayen, 2003; see also Gaskell & Marslen-Wilson, 2001), the estimated inflection onsets that we used for ERP averaging may well have been "too late" to an unknown variable extent (see Van Berkum et al., 2003, for further discussion).

5. In fact, when we presented a subset of the same materials in a noncumulative, moving-window, self-paced reading paradigm (Van Berkum et al., 2002a), readers did *not* slow down at the critical adjective if it had an expectation-incongruent gender inflection. They did slow down several words downstream at a second—and equally incongruently inflected—adjective. Because the latter effect still occurred *before* readers saw the noun, it supports our claim that discourse-level information is routinely used to predict specific upcoming words. At the same time, however, it illustrates that not everything seen in ERPs can also easily be picked up in self-paced reading (cf. Mitchell, chapter 2, this volume).

6. The study just discussed actually provides an interesting illustration of this problem. Because we were looking for an ERP effect tied to adjective *inflections*, the most appropriate ERP analysis was one in which we computed ERPs relative to the acoustic onset of the inflection within the adjective. However, for the same data we also computed ERPs relative to the acoustic onset of the adjective itself. Our adjectives were of variable length, and the critical inflectional suffix was therefore at a variable distance from adjective onset. The ERPs time-locked to adjective onset did reveal some traces of perturbation by incorrectly inflected adjectives. However, consistent with the fact that the (variably later) *inflection* provided the truly critical information, the ERP effect relative to adjective onset was broader, much less articulate, and not statistically significant.

7. The inflection-tied lexical prediction effect discussed in the previous section (Figure 13.2) illustrates the time-locking difficulties posed by spoken-language materials very well, both with respect to latency jitter (see note 6) and with respect to potential bias in one's estimate (see note 4). However, the problem is not specifically tied to ERPs,

and holds for any measure (e.g., eyetracking and probe response times) that must be related to an unfolding acoustic signal.

8. Note that for this logic to work, it is *not* important to know whether the P600 specifically indexes the initial detection of a syntactic problem, its further diagnosis, or subsequent repair. All one needs to assume is that, within the domain of language comprehension, a syntactic dead end reliably elicits a P600 effect (see Van Berkum et al., 2000).

9. To argue that the observed difference in N400 effect size does *not* reflect some aspect of how words like *pines* and *tulips* related to the dynamic discourse context, Kutas and Federmeier need to assume that the equal plausibility and predictability ratings obtained for these words rule out any other N400-relevant difference in how these words relate to the discourse. This is a very strong assumption, which need not be correct. In addition, there seems to be something odd about separating the knowledge encoded in one's representation of a discourse context from the structure of one's semantic memory. The former necessarily always draws upon, and thus incorporates, part of the latter. Moreover, although semantic memory can be said to have a rich *permanent* structure, what is the *relevant* structure may well be *dynamically* co-determined by the discourse context. That is, although a species-based classification will be relevant in many situations, one can easily imagine a context in which *palms* cluster with *tulips* instead of with *pines* (e.g., both *palms* and *tulips* will not be found up high in the mountains).

10. Although the problem is formulated for ERP effect size issues, it also occurs with fine-grained parametric studies of, say, the onset or peak latency of an ERP effect.

11. Because ERPs can be recorded in the presence or absence of an artificial secondary response task, they provide a unique opportunity to study the impact of such tasks. As might be expected, a task in which the subject is asked to evaluate linguistic stimuli on a critical feature (e.g., grammaticality judgments in an experiment looking for P600 effects to grammatical anomalies) can change the outcome of the experiment (see Osterhout & Mobley, 1995, for just such an example). Such task-dependence is not necessarily problematic or uninteresting. However, it does reveal that secondary response tasks can affect the processes involved in a language comprehension experiment (cf. Mitchell, chapter 2, this volume).

12. One might be tempted to argue that the self-paced reading task does not do so well in this respect because the reading time effects in this task frequently show up one or two words downstream from the critical word. However, although this spillover phenomenon is most salient in the self-paced reading task, the downstream displacement of effects is a general problem that affects *all* on-line measures. If the processing consequences to word X_w extend into the temporal domain of subsequent word X_{w+1} or beyond (i.e., the incremental impulse responses overlap), then both the ERP signals timelocked to, and the eye fixation on, the latter word may be contaminated by overlapping effects to the former.

13. In my experience, most subjects do not have a hard time listening to stories over four to five blocks of 15 min each, provided that the stories are sufficiently interesting, and provided that a few other conditions are met. One is that subjects should be given substantial breaks between recording blocks with each break offering some distraction (conversation, coffee, a check of electrode impedances, etc.). Another is to avoid a sleep-inducing environment, such as by *not* dimming the lights to dusk level, by *not* trying to block out all extraneous environmental sounds, and by mixing input modalities (e.g., announcing each visually displayed new discourse by means of a beep). Under these conditions, a 75-min ERP recording session is by no means necessarily

more problematic or arduous than a 15-min self-paced reading experiment (cf. Mitchell, chapter 2, this volume). Related to this, and probably partly due to social-psychological factors, subjects participating in an EEG experiment are very often more committed than their counterparts taking part in a run-of-the-mill 15-min RT task.

14. In discussing the relevance of neuroimaging data to psycholinguistics, Mitchell (chapter 2, this volume) could be taken to suggest that such data provide spatial XYZ-coordinates only and, as such, do not bear on traditional (spatially agnostic) theories of language processing. However, knowing which particular area of the brain is engaged by a particular task or condition (usually more than one) is not merely a matter of spatial localization. We often already know about *other* tasks or conditions that engage the exact same area and about how cognition breaks down if the area at hand is damaged. In addition, we sometimes also know from which other brain systems the area at hand receives input and to what other systems it projects its output. All of this can provide strong additional constraints on traditional theories of language comprehension, even if the latter do not speak about the brain at all.

Chapter 14
Sentences in the Brain: Event-Related Potentials as Real-Time Reflections of Sentence Comprehension and Language Learning

LEE OSTERHOUT, JUDITH MCLAUGHLIN,
ALBERT KIM, RALF GREENWALD, AND
KAYO INOUE

14.1 INTRODUCTION

From the perspective of a person trying to understand a sentence, language is a continuous flow of information distributed over time. Somehow, the listener translates this stream of information into discrete and rapidly sequenced units of sound, meaning, and structure, and does so in real time, that is, nearly instantaneously. The results of these complex analyses are then integrated into a single coherent interpretation, even in the presence of considerable ambiguity.

The challenge facing us is to account for how people accomplish this. Asking the listener or reader for an answer to this question provides little useful information; the relevant processes are not generally available to conscious reflection. We must therefore rely on other methods of investigation. One might surmise that the ideal method would mirror the properties of comprehension itself (Osterhout, McLaughlin, & Bersick, 1997). The ideal method should provide continuous measurement throughout the process of understanding a sentence, have a temporal resolution exceeding that of the relevant processes, and be differentially sensitive to events occurring at different levels of analysis (phonological, syntactic, semantic, etc.). Furthermore, language comprehension is clearly a function of the human brain. Theoretical accounts of some of the most fundamental questions about human language (e.g., the ability of children to acquire language, and the effects of age on language-learning ability) rely explicitly on biological explanations. Compelling tests of these hypotheses necessarily require biological measurement. For these and other reasons, the ideal method should also provide a means for relating the obtained data to brain function.

These properties of the ideal tool amount to a formidable methodological challenge. Unfortunately, few of the available methods have all of these properties, and the absence of even one property can limit significantly the utility of the method. For example, eyetracking provides continuous measurement during comprehension and has been quite useful for modeling certain aspects of reading and spoken language comprehension. However, eye movements respond similarly to events occurring at different levels of linguistic analysis; for example, eye fixations and regressions occur following an anomaly at any linguistic level. Furthermore, eyetracking does not provide any direct information about how language processing is instantiated in the brain. Functional neuroimaging techniques (e.g., PET and fMRI) do provide evidence concerning the relationship between language and brain and have proven helpful in revealing the neurobiology of certain cognitive functions (e.g., visual perception; cf. Tootell, Hadjikhani, Mendola, Marrett, & Dale, 1998). However, nearly all of the currently available imaging methods suffer from a temporal resolution (> 1 s) that is at least an order of magnitude worse than the presumed temporal resolution of the processes of interest (tens and hundreds of milliseconds). The consequences of this and related limitations will be discussed in later sections of this chapter. (Further discussion of the properties of these methods can be found in Mitchell, chapter 2, this volume.)

One method that approximates the ideal method is the recording of event-related brain potentials (ERPs) elicited during language processing (Osterhout et al., 1997). ERPs are scalp-recorded changes in electrical activity that occur in response to a sensory, cognitive, or motor event (Rugg & Coles, 1995; van Berkum, chapter 13, this volume). ERPs are thought to reflect the summed, simultaneously occurring postsynaptic activity within neocortical pyramidal neurons. Topographical features of the ERP are referred to as components and can be described in terms of polarity (positive and negative), amplitude, onset, peak latency, and scalp distribution. ERPs provide a millisecond-by-millisecond record of the brain's electrical activity during the process of interest. ERPs are multidimensional (varying in polarity, latency, source configurations, etc.). Because they are direct reflections of brain activity, ERPs offer the prospect of tying cognitive theories of sentence processing more closely to the underlying neurobiology.

These prospective advantages are insignificant unless ERPs have the necessary sensitivity to the processes of interest. The goal of this chapter is to selectively review evidence (primarily from our laboratory) that ERPs are highly sensitive to the relevant processes, and that this sensitivity can be exploited to illuminate the cognitive and neurobiological underpinnings of sentence comprehension in native speakers and in language learners. In particular, we will demonstrate how the unique properties of ERPs permit novel tests of two fundamental tenets of modern-day psycholinguistics: the belief that syntactic processing always precedes semantic processing, and the belief that success at learning a language in adulthood is limited by an age-related decline in brain plasticity. The ERP evidence we describe here provides novel and perhaps unique perspectives on these widely held assumptions. Ultimately, however, all of the available methods (including ERPs) are imperfect tools. The most compelling conclusions often result from a convergence of evidence coming from very different methods.

14.2 SENTENCE COMPREHENSION IN A NATIVE LANGUAGE

Contemporary linguistic theories posit a number of distinct and largely independent levels of linguistic knowledge (Chomsky, 1986). A standard typology includes the levels of phonology, syntax, and semantics. The task of a linguist is to describe the units at each level and the rules that govern their combination. Psycholinguistic theories need to specify how closely this typology, which is based on linguistic observation and description, describes the cognitive and neurobiological events underlying the comprehension of a sentence. Critically, however, the psycholinguist's task does not end with the description of a simple typology but must extend to an account of how these different sources of knowledge are recruited in the service of comprehending a sentence. This includes, for example, specifying the order in which various sources of information are employed and the interactions (or lack of interactions) between them. The ultimate and most challenging step is to describe how these processes are implemented in the brain.

14.2.1 Syntax and Semantics

Perhaps the most fundamental distinction is the one between sentence structure (syntax) and sentence meaning (semantics). To many linguists, sentences that violate syntactic constraints (such as *The cat will ate the food*) are clearly distinct from sentences that violate semantic constraints (such as *John buttered his bread with socks*). Whether this distinction characterizes accurately the processes underlying sentence comprehension has been a matter of debate. A standard assumption underlying much psycholinguistic work is that a relatively direct mapping exists between the levels of knowledge posited within linguistic theories and the cognitive and neural processes underlying comprehension (Bock & Kroch, 1989; Fodor, 1983; Forster, 1979). Distinct language-specific processes are thought to interpret a sentence at each level of analysis, and distinct representations are thought to result from these computations. However, other theorists, most notably those working in the neural net modeling domain, deny that this mapping exists (Elman, 1990; McClelland, St. John, & Taraban, 1989). Instead, the meaning of the sentence is claimed to be derived directly, without an intervening level of syntactic structure.

This debate is mirrored in the language dysfunction literature. The syndromes known as Broca's and Wernicke's aphasia were initially given motor and sensory interpretations, respectively. This approach gave way to linguistic descriptions in which each disorder was claimed to reflect the loss of a specific type of linguistic information or function (Caramazza & Zurif, 1976). Broca's aphasia was claimed to manifest (in addition to other impairments) an impairment in syntactic function. Wernicke's aphasia was associated with a degradation in the access to lexical semantics. These "linguistic" accounts of aphasia not only accepted the distinction between sentence form and meaning but also localized these aspects of language processing in different parts of the brain. Syntactic processes were claimed to be located in restricted parts of the left inferior frontal lobe, whereas semantic processes were claimed to be located in the posterior portion of the left temporal lobe. However, although this account has been quite influential, a closer inspection of the aphasic syndromes raises questions. The correlations between lesion site and the linguistically described aphasic symptoms turn out to be weak (Caplan, Hildebrandt, & Makris, 1996; Dronkers, 2000), and the aphasic symptoms tend to vary dramatically within a person over time (McNeil & Doyle, 2000). Such considerations have led some researchers to question the accuracy and utility of linguistically based accounts of aphasia (Bates & Dick, 2000; Blumstein & Milberg, 2000; McNeil & Doyle; Milberg & Blumstein, 2000).

14.2.2 Neuroimaging and the Syntax/Semantics Distinction

Neuroimaging methods provide another means for identifying the types of processes used in sentence comprehension and mapping them onto the brain (Fiebach et al., chapter 17, this volume). For example, fMRI allows researchers to measure changes in blood flow (usually by recording changes in the blood oxygenation level dependent [BOLD] response; Jezzard, Matthews, & Smith, 2001) while neurologically intact subjects read or listen to tokens of the language. It is assumed that the BOLD response indirectly reflects neural activity. Although these methods represent major advances for the field of cognitive neuroscience, they are not without complications as tools for studying real-time language comprehension. First, the hemodynamic response to an event is delayed several seconds and evolves over 10 to 15 s. This temporal resolution contrasts starkly with the fact that in normal fluent conversation, speakers produce (on average) three words, four syllables, and 12 phonemes per sec (Levelt, 1999). Furthermore, the processing of a single linguistic unit, for example a word, most likely involves a constellation of processes, each having temporal durations of considerably less than 1 s. In other words, under conditions that approximate normal speaking and reading, it is very difficult to isolate the hemodynamic response to a particular word, much less the (phonological, syntactic, semantic, etc.) processing steps that occur in the processing of that word. In imaging experiments, all of these processes are represented in the time dimension by a single data point. Disentangling them (i.e., associating a specific process with a specific activated area) is not a trivial matter.

Second, because language comprehension is inherently an integrative process, one cannot reasonably assume that successive words and sentences are processed independently. This fact complicates efforts to isolate the response to particular words in a sentence by using event-related fMRI designs (e.g., Burock, Buckner, Woldorff, Rosen, & Dale, 1998). Event-related designs measure the BOLD response to rapidly sequenced individual events and assume that temporally overlapping BOLD responses summate linearly. Although the independence of overlapping hemodynamic functions has been demonstrated for simple visual stimuli (Dale and Buckner, 1997), the same cannot be assumed for words in sentences.

Third, even if the BOLD response to a particular word in a sentence could be isolated successfully, the BOLD response is maximally sensitive to sustained brain events and relatively insensitive to transient events (Savoy et al., 1995). Consequently, sustained brain events will always dominate the BOLD response and potentially obscure the transient language-related events of interest.[1]

These complications notwithstanding, fMRI has been used successfully to elucidate some aspects of word and sentence processing. The most fundamental and consistent finding has been that words and sentences activate the perisylvian areas of the left hemisphere that are classically associated with language dysfunction following brain damage (Bavelier, Corina, Jezzard, Padmanabhan, Clark, Karni, Prinster, Braun, Lalwani, Rauschecker, Turner, & Neville, 1997; Price, 1998). However, it is not unusual for areas in addition to these classical areas to show equally strong activation, and not all of the relevant perisylvian areas are always activated.

The cross-experiment variability in fMRI results increases substantially when specific linguistic processes are examined. For example, studies attempting to localize semantic processing have reported activated areas including most of the left (and sometimes right) temporal lobe and various parts of the frontal lobe (Binder & Price, 2001). Attempts to localize syntactic processes have also varied widely, and have included the left inferior frontal cortex (Broca's area and surrounding cortex) and parietal and temporal regions, sometimes but not always lateralized to the left hemisphere.

Undoubtedly, some of this variation occurs due to differences in stimuli, task, and procedures. It is therefore instructive to examine results obtained in a relatively homogeneous set of studies that employ a common strategy for isolating a particular linguistic process. One seemingly straightforward stimulus manipulation contrasts the BOLD response to anomalies that involve different linguistic levels, for example, syntactic and semantic; the assumption is that the anomaly will engender more processing at the linguistic level of the anomaly, and that this processing will be reflected in a larger BOLD response in the affected areas of the brain. At least six neuroimaging studies employing this strategy have been published recently (Friederici, Ruschemeyer, Hahne, & Fiebach, 2003; Kang, Constable, Gore, & Avrutin, 1999; Kuperberg et al., 2000; Kuperberg, Holcomb, et al., 2003; Newman, Pancheva, Ozawa, Ozawa, Neville, & Ullman, 2001; Ni et al., 2000). Perhaps the most striking aspect of these collective results is the variability in outcome and conclusion (see Kuperberg, Holcomb, et al., for an excellent discussion of this point). For example, Kuperberg et al. (2000) conclude that the left and right temporal lobes are involved in semantic processing but do not identify any areas that are modulated specifically by syntactic anomalies. Ni et al. and Kang et al. conclude that the left inferior frontal lobe is involved in syntactic processing, whereas the posterior temporal lobes are more involved in semantic processing. Newman et al. (2001) conclude that superior frontal regions are involved in syntactic processing and inferior frontal and temporal regions are involved in semantic processing. In the two most recent studies, Kuperberg et al. (2003) conclude that overlapping networks (including inferior frontal and left temporal regions) are modulated in opposite directions by the two types of anomaly, with semantic anomalies evoking a larger BOLD response in this area and syntactic anomalies a weaker response, relative to a nonanomalous sentence condition. Friederici et al. (2003) conclude that syntactic anomalies evoke more activity in inferior frontal and anterior temporal regions in the left hemisphere, whereas semantic anomalies evoke activity bilaterally in the midtemporal regions.

There are a few notable consistencies across these studies. For example, the authors are in agreement (except Kuperberg, Holcomb, et al., 2003) that their syntactic and semantic manipulations identified distinct regions of the brain as being more involved in one level of analysis than the other. However, there is considerable disagreement about which brain regions are involved in syntactic and semantic processing. It is reasonable to speculate that this variance in outcome is due, in part, to the difficulty of isolating specific types of linguistic processes using fMRI when these processes are transient and closely sequenced in time.[2]

14.2.3 ERPs and the Syntax/Semantics Distinction

Unlike fMRI, ERPs have a temporal resolution exceeding that of the processes underlying language comprehension. ERPs are also maximally sensitive to transient events occurring in the brain and much less affected by sustained events. These advantageous properties allow one to hope that ERPs might be more successful at isolating individual processes as they occur in real time during sentence comprehension.

This hope has been fulfilled by two decades of accumulating evidence, much of it investigating the brain responses to syntactic and semantic anomalies. The crucial finding is that syntactic and semantic anomalies elicit qualitatively distinct ERP effects, and that these effects are characterized by distinct and consistent temporal properties. Semantic anomalies (e.g., *The cat will bake the food* ...) elicit a negative wave that peaks at about 400 ms after the anomalous word appears (the *N400 effect*; Figure 14.1A) (Kutas & Hillyard, 1980, 1984; Osterhout & Nicol, 1999). By contrast, syntactic anomalies (e.g., *The cat will eating the food* ...) elicit a large positive wave that onsets at about 500 ms after presentation of the anomalous word and persists for at least half a second (the *P600 effect*; Figure 14.1B) (Hagoort, Brown, & Groothusen, 1993; McKinnon & Osterhout, 1996; Osterhout, 1997; Osterhout & Holcomb, 1992, 1993; Osterhout, Holcomb, & Swinney, 1994; Osterhout & Mobley, 1995; Osterhout, McKinmon, Bersick, & Corey, 1996; Osterhout, McLaughlin, Allen, & Inoue, 2002; Osterhout & Nicol, 1999). In some studies, syntactic anomalies have also elicited a negativity over anterior regions of the scalp, with onsets ranging from 100 to 300 ms (Friederici, 1995; Neville, Nicol, Barss, Forster, & Garret, 1991; Osterhout & Holcomb, 1992; Osterhout & Mobley, 1995). These results are highly reproducible[3] and generalize well across types of anomaly (with anomalies involving phrase structure, agreement, verb subcategorization, and constituent-movement all eliciting P600-like effects), types of languages (including word-order languages such as English, Dutch, and French, and case-marked languages such as Italian and Japanese; Angrilli et al., 2002; Hagoort et al., 1993; Inoue & Osterhout, in preparation; Nakagome et al., 2001), and various methodological factors (including modality of the input, rate of word presentation, and presenting isolated sentences and natural prose; Allen, Badecker, & Osterhout, 2003; McKinnon & Osterhout, 1996; Osterhout & Holcomb, 1993; Osterhout et al., 2002). These robust effects seem to indicate that the brain does in fact honor the distinction between the form and the meaning of a sentence.

Furthermore, the available evidence suggests that the N400, but not the P600, is sensitive to a wide range of word properties, including word frequency, morphological

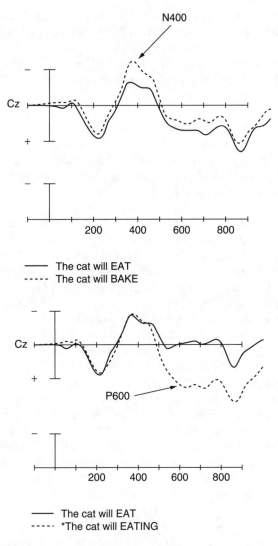

Figure 14.1. (A) ERPs (recorded over the vertex) elicited by semantically anomalous words (dashed line) and nonanomalous control words (solid line) in sentences such as *The cat will eat/bake the food*. (B) ERPs elicited by syntactically anomalous (dashed line) and nonanomalous control words (solid line) in sentences such as *The cat will eat/eating the food*. Onset of the critical word is indicated by the vertical bar. Each hashmark represents 100 ms The vertical calibration bar represents 5 μV. Adapted from "On the distinctiveness, independence, and time course of the brain responses to syntactic and semantic anomalies," by L. Osterhout and J. Nicol, 1999, *Language and Cognitive Process, 14,* 283–317.

content, and semantic relatedness. Conversely, the P600, but not the N400, is sensitive to the syntactic well-formedness of the sentence. A recent study by Allen et al. (2003) nicely illustrates this point. Allen et al. independently manipulated the normative frequency and syntactic well-formedness of verbs in sentences. These factors had independent effects: Word frequency affected N400 amplitude but not P600 amplitude, and syntactic well-formedness affected P600 amplitude but not N400 amplitude (Figure 14.2).

All of this ERP evidence converges on the conclusion that separable lexico-semantic and syntactic processes exist, and that manifestations of this distinction can be observed in scalp-recorded electrical brain activity. Furthermore, the ERP evidence shows quite clearly that the syntactic and semantic (or relevant correlated) processes are temporally distinct and transient events—and that ERPs, unlike fMRI, are capable of temporally isolating these (or correlated) processes as they occur in real time. That is, at a predictable moment in time during comprehension, the ERP waveform is sensitive specifically to lexico-semantic manipulations, whereas at another moment in time the waveform is sensitive specifically to syntactic manipulations.

Ideally, one would like to discern the neural sources of these language-sensitive ERP effects. By doing so, one might be able to isolate the processes of interest in both time and space. Unfortunately, the source of a given ERP effect (known as the "inverse solution") cannot be known with certainty. This follows from the fact that a large number of source configurations could produce an identical pattern of activity across the scalp (Nunez, 1995). Nonetheless, source estimates are possible, given certain limiting assumptions. The traditional approach to source localization has been to search for point dipole sources (Hämäläinen & Sarvas, 1989; Henderson, Butler, & Glass, 1975; Kavanaugh, Darcey, Lehmann, & Fender, 1978). In general, this entails assuming a small number of dipole sources and iterating through all possible combinations of dipole location, orientation, and strength, looking for the best match between the source model and the observed scalp distribution. This method brings with it numerous limitations and caveats (Halgren et al., 2002).

More recently developed alternative methods provide a true tomographic analysis analogous to that provided by neuroimaging methods. For example, Low Resolution Electromagnetic Tomography (LORETA; Pascual-Marqui, Michel, & Lehmann, 1994) estimates the current distribution throughout the entire three-dimensional brain. The primary assumption of this approach is that dramatic changes in current do not occur across contiguous areas of cortex (i.e., in adjacent voxels). The primary limitation is that the maximum spatial resolution is perhaps as low as 1 cm^3, significantly worse than fMRI or PET. The primary advantage, a crucial one, is that LORETA can provide an estimate of current distribution for each sample of brain activity (i.e., one estimate every few ms). Although LORETA should be viewed as a model or estimate rather than as an observation of current distribution, its reliability and validity have been established in some nonlinguistic domains (Anderer, Pascual-Marqui, Smlitsch, & Saletu, 1998; Pascual-Marqui, 1999; Pascual-Marqui, Esslen, Kochi, & Lehmann, 2002).

In our lab, we have been using LORETA to provide estimates of current distribution for the peaks of the N400 and P600 effects. In one study, we recorded ERPs from 20 native English speakers while they read sentences that were well-formed and coherent, or contained a syntactic or semantic anomaly. As expected, the syntactic and semantic anomalies elicited P600 and N400 effects, respectively. We then performed the LORETA analysis on the N400 peak (in both the semantically

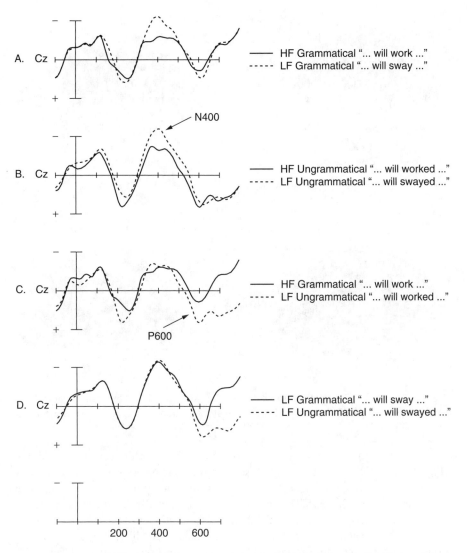

Figure 14.2. (A) ERPs (recorded over the vertex) to high-frequency (solid line) and low-frequency (dashed line) verbs in grammatical sentences such as *The man will work/sway on the platform.* (B) ERPs to high-frequency (solid line) and low-frequency (dashed line) verbs in ungrammatical sentences such as *The man will worked/swayed on the platform.* (C) ERPs to grammatical (solid line) and ungrammatical (dashed line) high-frequency verbs. (D) ERPs to grammatical (solid line) and ungrammatical (dashed line) low-frequency verbs. Note that the factors of word frequency and grammaticality have independent effects on the ERP. Adapted from "Morphological analysis during sentence processing," by M. D. Allen, W. Badecker, and L. Osterhout, 2003, *Language and Cognitive Process,* 18, 405–430.

well-formed and semantically anomalous conditions) and on the P600 midpoint in the syntactically anomalous condition, and on the corresponding sample in the syntactically well-formed condition.[4]

Semantically Well-formed

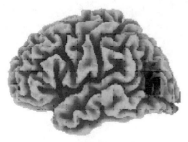 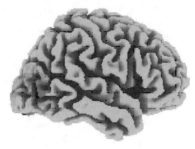

Semantically Ill-formed

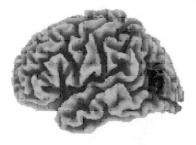 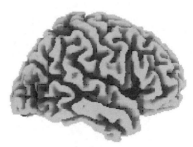

Figure 14.3. LORETA solutions for N400 peak (at 410 ms) elicited by critical words in the well-formed (top panel) and semantically anomalous (bottom panel) condition. See text for more detail.

The results of the LORETA analysis were striking. In the semantic condition (Figure 14.3), the estimated current distribution for the N400 peak (at 410 ms) was largest in the posterior middle temporal lobe and angular gyrus of the left hemisphere [Brodmann's area (BA) 39]. This was true for both the well-formed and semantically anomalous conditions, although the current distribution in this area had greater intensity in the anomalous condition. In the syntactic condition (Figure 14.4), the primary source of current for the P600 midpoint (at 603 ms) was in the left inferior frontal cortex (BA 44, 45, and 47). When the stimulus was syntactically anomalous, the current spread throughout the left prefrontal cortex and into the left anterior temporal lobe.

Our LORETA results are striking because they are highly consistent with the classic lesion-based model of language and brain. The putative source of the N400 component, which is sensitive to properties of words and to meaning relations between words, is located in the part of the brain that, when damaged, produces the most problems with words and meaning (e.g., Dronkers, 2000). The putative source of the P600 effect (and the same time point in the syntactically well-formed condition) is localized to the left inferior frontal cortex, which is classically associated with agrammatism, and to the left anterior temporal cortex, which is the area most

Syntactically Well-formed

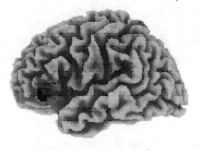 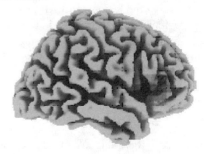

Syntactically Ill-formed

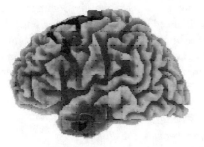 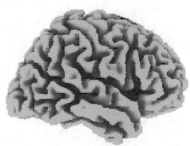

Figure 14.4. LORETA solutions for the P600 midpoint (at 603 ms) elicited by critical words in the well-formed (top panel) and syntactically anomalous (bottom panel) conditions.

commonly damaged in cases of agrammatism (Dronkers). These results are also consistent to a degree with fMRI results. The posterior temporal lobe/angular gyrus region of the left hemisphere (and in particular BA 39) is one of the few regions that is almost always activated in studies attempting to isolate semantic processing (Price, 1998). The inferior frontal lobe of the left hemisphere is frequently activated in studies attempting to isolate syntactic processing (Caplan et al., 1996).[5]

One important caveat is that although the stimulus manipulations affecting the N400 and P600 are well understood, the specific cognitive processes underlying them are not. These effects might be direct manifestations of the syntactic and semantic processes or they might be manifestations of processes that are correlated with, but indeterminately removed from, the linguistic process themselves. Deciding which of these possibilities is correct might turn out to be an intractable problem, as impossible as altering the temporal properties of the brain's hemodynamic response or discovering perfect correlations between a lesion site and deficit patterns. However, what seems to be intractable might become less so given data from other methods of investigation. For example, given both the LORETA estimates of the current distribution for the N400 and P600 effects *and* the lesion data, one could rationally argue that these effects do in fact index specifically semantic and syntactic processing. Similarly, given both the highly variable semantic-processing fMRI results *and* the lesion and ERP results, compelling claims can be made concerning the regions in the brain most implicated in semantic processing. Although an appreciation for the value of converging evidence is an old and perhaps out-of-fashion virtue, its value has only increased with the advent of these new, but imperfect, investigative methods.

14.2.4 Coordination Between Syntax and Semantics in Sentence Processing

Because of their unique constellation of properties, ERPs can also be used to address longstanding issues concerning the coordination of syntactic and semantic processing. Theory regarding this issue has been deeply influenced by a family of syntax-first models of linguistic structure (Chomsky, 1981) and language processing (Ferreira & Clifton, 1986; Fodor & Ferreira, 1998). The psycholinguistic models posit that language comprehension is controlled by an initial stage of purely syntactic processing. As words arrive in the linguistic input, they are rapidly organized into a structural analysis by a process that is not influenced by detailed lexical or semantic knowledge. The output of this syntactic process then guides semantic interpretation. Syntax-first processing has been implicated in accounts of garden-path phenomena, in which readers and listeners initially misanalyze sentences containing temporary syntactic ambiguities. Consider, for example, sentences (1a) and (1b):

(1)   a. *The doctor believed the patient was lying.*
      b. *The doctor believed the patient after hearing the story.*

Readers of sentences like (1a) often initially interpret the second noun phrase (*the patient*) as the direct object of the first verb (*believed*), when it is actually the subject of an embedded clause (*the patient was lying*). Misanalysis is detected in the form of processing difficulty when readers encounter *was*, which is only consistent with the correct analysis. This processing difficulty is manifested in eye-fixation times, regressive eye movements, and P600 effects in the ERP (Ferreira & Clifton, 1986; Osterhout & Holcomb, 1992). Syntax-first models have claimed that, due to the control of initial interpretative commitments by exclusively syntactic mechanisms, garden-path errors occur even in the presence of potentially disambiguating semantic information (e.g., Ferreira & Clifton). In situations of temporary syntactic ambiguity such as (1a, b), processing is controlled by a bias to choose the simplest grammatically licensed structural analysis [in (1a, b), the direct object analysis]. Whenever the simplest structural analysis is not the correct analysis, garden-path effects are predicted.

While garden-path effects have been widely observed, other studies have shown that they can be mitigated or eliminated by some types of nonsyntactic information. For instance, Garnsey, Pearlmutter, Myers, & Lotocky, (1997) found that semantic plausibility affected the likelihood of garden-path effects. Sentences in which the direct-object interpretation is implausible (e.g., *The doctor believed the medication would work*) result in small or nonexistent garden-path effects. Other studies have shown effects of a wide range of constraints, including detailed lexico-syntactic knowledge, semantics, and discourse knowledge (cf. MacDonald, Pearlmutter, & Seidenberg, 1994; Trueswell & Tanenhaus, 1994). The influence of such factors on ambiguity resolution seems inconsistent with the syntax-first prediction that initial processing commitments are not influenced by nonsyntactic knowledge.

To account for these interacting influences of syntactic and nonsyntactic information on sentence processing, theorists have developed a diverse family of constraint-based models. These models posit a probabilistic constraint-satisfaction process in which syntactic knowledge is only one of a number of constraints on interpretation. Syntax-first models have not, however, been completely invalidated by demonstrations of rapid interactivity. The most recent proposals continue to posit an initial stage of purely syntactic processing, albeit one with a short duration (Frazier & Clifton, 1996). According to these proposals, a rapid influence of non-syntactic knowledge on sentence parsing can be explained in terms of re-analysis. For example, if processing difficulty at *was* in (1a) is eased by semantic knowledge, this might mean that a direct-object analysis was initially pursued but rapidly revised using information about plausibility.

Thus, a consensus has emerged concerning the rapid nature of interaction between syntactic and semantic knowledge, without resolving fundamental disagreements about the degree to which syntactic processing controls other aspects of language processing. These theoretical developments have brought the field against some limitations of the standard garden-path paradigm. Garden-path experiments examine the impact of nonsyntactic information exclusively in situations where syntactic cues are indeterminate. The question is usually whether or not syntactic processing is influenced by some nonsyntactic form of knowledge (or whether it is independent).

However, the implicit assumption in all of this work (regardless of theoretical bias) is that unless syntactic cues are indeterminate, syntax always controls the direction of processing. We describe here a recent study in our laboratory (Kim & Osterhout submitted) that examined semantic influences on sentence comprehension in syntactically *unambiguous* situations. The goal of the study was to test the widespread assumption that, in the absence of syntactic uncertainty, syntactic information is "in charge" of sentence processing or, more specifically, that semantic processing is always fundamentally dependent on the output of the syntactic processing system. Kim et al. recorded ERPs while participants read strings containing linguistic violations, as in (2a), and well-formed controls like (2b) and (2c):

(2) a. *The mysterious crime had been <u>solving</u> the detective. (verb violation)*
    b. *The mysterious crime had been <u>solved</u> by the detective. (passive control)*
    c. *The brilliant detective had been <u>solving</u> mysterious crimes for decades.*
      (active control)

In (2a), the first noun phrase *mysterious crime* is highly plausible as the logical object (theme) of the verb *solve* but anomalous as the logical subject (agent). The syntactic cues in the sentence conflict directly with these semantic properties. The *-ing* inflection of the verb is consistent with the anomalous agent interpretation but not the theme interpretation [as opposed to -*ed* as in (2b)]. Sentence (2a) provides a special situation—contrasted with the well-formed (2b) and (2c)—in which syntactic and semantic constraints point toward directly opposed functional outcomes. The interaction of syntactic and semantic processing in such situations can be studied with ERPs. If syntactic processing controls semantic processing, then an agent interpretation of the first noun phrase should be pursued. The implausibility of this interpretation should elicit an enhanced N400 component for violation verbs (2a) relative to control verbs (2b) and (2c). By contrast, semantic processing may operate with some independence from syntactic control such that the plausible theme interpretation of the noun phrase is pursued, even though it directly conflicts with syntactic cues in the string. Because this interpretation is in direct conflict with the syntactic cues in the string, it is possible that readers will encounter *syntactic* processing difficulty at the verb. That is, powerful semantic cues may cause a well-formed string to appear ill-formed. Such a perceived syntactic incongruity might elicit a P600 effect. Note that the two different functional outcomes mentioned above cannot be distinguished by reading time or eyetracking measures, which conflate syntactic and semantic processing difficulty at the anomalous verb.

ERPs to the verbs in each sentence type are shown in Figure 14.5. Violation verbs elicited a robust P600 effect compared to the control conditions, but no increase in N400 amplitude. These results seem to indicate that syntactic processing difficulty occurred at the verb when its inflection conflicted with available semantic cues. At the same time, there is no indication that semantic processing is guided by syntactic cues into the difficult logical-subject interpretation.[6,7]

The idea that syntactic processing precedes and drives semantic interpretation is pervasive in psycholinguistics. Our results clearly do not fit well with that idea. Instead, it appears that at least under some circumstances, semantic processing exhibits a degree of independence from syntactic control and in fact seems to operate in advance of, and drive, syntactic processing. An important theoretical issue raised by this and related work (see Kolk, Chwilla, van Herten, & Oor, 2003; Kuperberg, Sitnikova, Caplan, & Holcomb, 2003) is the notion of processing independence. With respect to the claims of syntax-first models, the Kim and Osterhout results indicate that the independence of semantic processing is greater than predicted and that the independence of syntactic processing is less than predicted.

We suggest that syntactic and semantic processing are indeed separated by a form of independence, but a weak form. The independence of these processes enables them to pursue an internally attractive analysis *even when it is inconsistent with the output of other processes.* Furthermore, rather than operating in a serial fashion (as proposed by the two-stage garden-path theory), syntactic and semantic processing operate in parallel. Finally, it seems likely that these processes undergo a near-constant interaction. Thus, syntactic processing might guide semantic processing in *John was disliked by Mary*, where syntactic information points to the proper thematic role assignments (i.e., the passive morphology indicates that *John* is the theme and not the agent of *dislike*). Semantic processing might guide syntactic processing in *We gave <u>John</u> the money*, where semantic knowledge supports the proper syntactic analysis (indirect vs. direct object) of *John* (i.e., *John* would make an excellent recipient and an unlikely theme for the verb *give*).

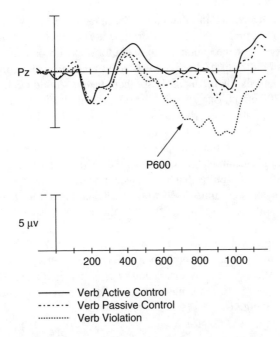

Figure 14.5. ERPs (recorded over the posterior site PZ) elicited by critical words in the two nonanomalous control conditions and in the anomalous verb violation condition (small dashes).

These considerations suggest a potentially rich area of investigation concerning the nature of syntactic and semantic processing. We know that in *The mysterious crime had been solving*, the verb *solving* elicits a P600 effect and not an N400 effect. Presumably, this happens because the syntactic analyzer tries to find an analysis consistent with a "Predicate = *solve*, Theme = *crime*" interpretation. But we also know that in *The cats will bake the food*, the verb *bake* elicits an N400 effect and not a P600 effect (Osterhout & Nicol, 1999, and discussed in the "Syntax and Semantics" section, this chapter). It appears that the implausibility of cats acting as agents in this scenario does not cause the syntactic analyzer to flail away trying to come up with an alternative structure; instead, an implausible but syntactically supported interpretation is pursued, with difficulty.

The above observations raise a compelling paradox. *The crime had been solving* and *The cats will bake* are quite similar; in each scenario, the subject is an implausible Agent for the verb. Why, then, do the verbs in these two sentences elicit such different brain responses? Two hypotheses come to mind. Perhaps the critical factor is that a strong "semantic attraction" exists between the verb *solve* and the theme *crime*, whereas no such attraction exists between the verb *bake* and *cat*. Alternatively, the critical factor might be that the syntax of *The mysterious crime had been solving* can be easily "fixed" to support a semantically plausible interpretation (simply changing the verb's inflection from *-ing* to *-ed*), whereas no such easy fix is available in the sentence *The cats will bake the food*. These two hypotheses can be contrasted by examining sentences containing a strong semantic attraction, one that is inconsistent with the syntax and that cannot be made to fit the syntax with an easy syntactic fix. For example, the sentence fragment *The meal began to devour* does not allow an easy fix of the syntax to conform to a "theme = *meal*" interpretation, but the system might try to find one anyway due to the semantic attraction between the verb *devour* and the theme *meal*. If so, then *devour* should elicit a P600 effect, rather than an N400 effect. Exactly this type of result has been reported in two recent studies (Kolk et al., 2003; Kuperberg, Sitnikova, et al., 2003). Kuperberg, Sitnikova, et al. report that the verb *eat* in the sentence *For breakfast, the eggs began to eat* elicits a P600 effect, rather than an N400 effect. Apparently, strong semantic attractions between predicates and arguments induce the syntactic analyzer to work over-time, searching for a structure that is consistent with the attraction. To phrase it differently: The system commits itself to the semantic attraction (hence the lack of an N400 effect) and insists on trying to "fix" the syntax (hence the presence of a P600 effect).

Obviously, more work is needed to test the plausibility of this model and to more completely understand how and when syntactic and semantic processing influence each other. What is already clear, however, is that ERPs are useful tools for investigating complex issues in sentence comprehension that have been difficult to study using other methods.

14.3 WORD AND SENTENCE PROCESSING IN SECOND-LANGUAGE LEARNERS

One of the standard tenets of modern-day psycholinguistics is that the ability to learn a new language degrades with age. Age-related decreases in language-learning ability have been reported for most aspects of language (including phonemes, words, and grammar), and adults are often claimed to achieve lower levels of second-language proficiency than children. Although the causes of these age effects on proficiency are controversial, two frequently cited theoretical explanations stand out. One explanation involves the putative existence of a critical period for second-language learning. According to this explanation, language learning is constrained by maturational factors (specifically, brain maturation) that circumscribe a critical period (which, according to most accounts, ends around puberty) for native-like attainment. Behavioral studies appear to confirm this notion by showing that the proficiency scores of L2 learners on a variety of language tasks decline with the age of initial exposure to the second language (Johnson, 1992; Johnson & Newport, 1989).

Another explanation attributes the age-related declines in L2 learning to the effects of increasing experience with a first language. Neural network simulations provide a convenient framework for understanding effects of L1 learning on L2 learning. In these simulations, early learning results in the entrenchment of optimal network patterns, after which new learning requires considerable training. Consistent with this view, it has been demonstrated that early experience with phonemes (Kuhl, 2000) and words (Ellis & Lambon Ralph, 2000) seems to degrade the ability to learn new phonemes and words later in life.

Although on the surface these two explanations appear to be quite distinct, they both implicate the same underlying cause for the age-of-acquisition effects on L2 learning, namely, a reduction in neural plasticity that degrades the ability to learn new linguistic information. However, despite a considerable consensus about the accuracy of this claim, there is little direct evidence to support it. The ideal method for investigating the plasticity hypothesis would provide direct measurements of brain responses to L2 words and sentences. This would permit researchers to evaluate changes in brain activity that occur over time as a person attempts to acquire a new language.

Recently, several studies using neuroimaging methods (i.e., PET, MRI) have investigated the "reduction in plasticity" hypothesis by contrasting groups of L2 speakers who acquired the L2 at different ages. A result indicating that, for example, prepubescent learners represent their L1 and L2 similarly, whereas postpubescent learners do not, would be consistent with the critical-period hypothesis. Exactly that type of evidence was reported in one recent study (Kim et al., 1997). Early L2 learners showed highly similar patterns of activation for their L1 and L2, whereas late learners showed differences, most notably in Broca's area (for other studies showing L1/L2 differences see Dehaene et al., 1997; Halsband, Krause, Sipila, Teras, & Laihinen, 2002; Perani et al., 1996; Waterburger et al., 2003). However, other studies have reported no significant effects of age of acquisition (Chee, Caplon et al., 1999a; Chee, Tan et al., 1999b; Hasegawa, Capenter, & Just, 2002; Hernandez, Martinez, & Kohnert, 2000; Illes et al., 1999; Klein, Milner, Zatorre, Zhao, & Nikelski, 1999).

One partial explanation for the inconsistent results implicates the almost universal use of cross-sectional, between-subject designs in prior fMRI (and ERP) work on L2 learning. This design makes it very difficult to properly control numerous subject variables (e.g., L2 fluency and the quantity and quality of L2 experience) that could easily confound the age effects (Chee et al., 2001; Perani et al., 1998). The best way of avoiding such pitfalls is to longitudinally study a group of novice learners as they become increasingly proficient in the L2. A longitudinal design allows one to examine changes in brain activity and behavior relative to responses observed during an initial state of near-total incompetence in the L2 within the same group of learners. By including a group of subjects with native proficiency, one can compare intermediate states of language competence to both the beginning (no competence) and end (native competence) states of language learning. And by confining the study to learners who have had qualitatively and quantitatively similar exposure to the language, one avoids the problems of interpretation introduced by variable linguistic experiences across subject groups. However, even under ideal circumstances, uncertainties often exist (for reasons discussed above) concerning the relationship between the BOLD signal and the transient events underlying language comprehension.

In principle, ERPs provide the temporal resolution and sensitivity needed to reveal how (and potentially where) the L2 is processed, how similar this processing is to L1 processing, and how L2 processing changes as a function of increasing L2 experience. In a series of ERP experiments, we have tracked changes in brain activity that are correlated with increasing exposure to the L2 in adult L2 learners. We describe here two experiments, one involving L2 word learning (McLaughlin, Oster-hout, & Kim, in press), and a second involving sentences (Osterhout et al., in preparation). In both studies, English-speaking novice French learners were studied longitudinally as they progressed through their first year of classroom French instruction. Learners were tested three times: near the beginning, in the middle, and near the end of the instructional period. This design allowed us to track changes in brain activity within a single group of language learners, and ensured that the learners were relatively homogeneous in their initial lack of L2 proficiency and in their subsequent L2 experience.

McLaughlin et al. examined word learning by measuring learning-related changes in N400 amplitude, which is sensitive to both lexical status (i.e., whether or not a letter string is a word) and word meaning (Bentin, 1987; Kutas & Hillyard, 1980). For native speakers, N400 amplitude is largest for pronounceable, orthograph-ically legal nonwords (pseudowords, e.g., *flirth*), intermediate for words preceded by a semantically unrelated context, and smallest for words preceded by a seman-tically related context. Our goal was to determine how much L2 exposure is needed before the language-learners' brain activity elicited by L2 words and word-like stimuli resembles that of a native speaker.

McLaughlin et al. asked adult French learners to make word/nonword judgments to a sequence of French words and pronounceable nonwords. They found that after only 14 hr (roughly two weeks) of L2 instruction, the nonwords elicited a robustly larger-amplitude N400 than did words (Figure 14.6). This was true even though learners showed random behavior (d-prime = 0) when making explicit word/nonword judgments about these stimuli. Furthermore, the correlation between hours of instruc-tion and the word/nonword N400 difference was very robust ($r = .72$), suggesting that the N400 difference was approximately a linear function of the amount of L2 exposure. Effects of word meaning, manifested as smaller-amplitude N400s to words preceded by related than by unrelated words, were observed after approximately 62 hr of instruction. By the end of the instructional period (after approximately 138 hr), the amplitude of the word/nonword differences approximated that typically observed in native speakers, even though learners' conscious lexicality judgments remained very poor (d-prime < 1). Importantly, no N400 differences were observed for a group of subjects who had received no French instruction.

Thus, even for adult learners, the brain response to L2 words and word-like nonwords changes dramatically with very little L2 exposure. Furthermore, these changes are not random, but instead, almost immediately begin to approximate the responses seen in native speakers to analogous stimuli, and occur even while the learner behaves randomly when making conscious lexicality judgments to these stimuli. These results seem to indicate that the brain response to words and word-like strings in the L2 changes dramatically with remarkably little L2 exposure.

A second experiment was motivated by the observation, discussed above, that syntactic and semantic anomalies embedded within sentences elicit distinct ERP effects (the P600 and N400 effects, respectively). With respect to adult L2 learning, several questions immediately come to mind: How much experience with a language is needed for the learner's brain to distinguish between well-formed and ill-formed sentences? How much experience is needed for the learner's brain to distinguish

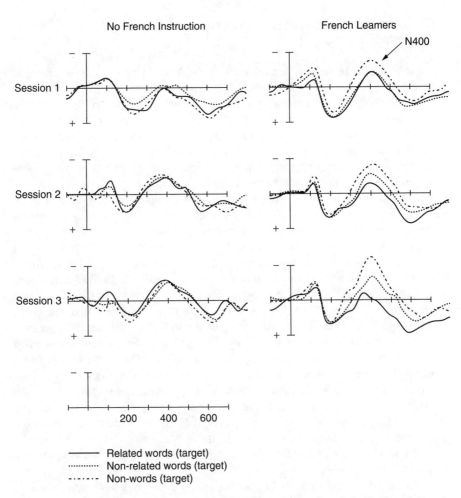

No French Instruction

French Learners

N400

Session 1

Session 2

Session 3

200   400   600

———— Related words (target)
·········· Non-related words (target)
------ Non-words (target)

Figure 14.6. ERPs (recorded over the vertex) for No Instruction (left panel) and French Instruction (right panel) subjects, recorded at the three successive testing sessions. ERPs are plotted for three types of target strings: target words that were semantically related to the prime word (solid line), target words that were not semantically related to the prime word (small dashes), and target nonwords (large dashes). Adapted from "Neural correlates of second-language word learning: Minimal instruction produces rapid change," by J. McLaughlin, L. Osterhout, and A.Kim, in press. *Nature Neuroscience.*

between different types of linguistic anomalies (e.g., syntactic and semantic)? And how much experience is needed for the learner's brain to respond to these anomalies like the brain of a native speaker of the L2? To answer these questions, we presented well-formed French sentences and French sentences containing either a semantic or a syntactic anomaly, as in the below examples:

(3)   *Sept plus cinq*livre font douze.* (semantic condition)
(4)   *Tu adores*adorez le francais.* (verb conjunction condition)

(5) *Tu manges des hamburgers*hamburger pour diner.* (article–noun agreement condition)

In (3), the noun *livre* is semantically anomalous. In (4), the verb *adorez* is conjugated incorrectly, given the preceding sentence fragment. In (5), the noun *hamburger* disagrees with the syntactic number of the plural article. Thus, the anomalous version of (3) is semantically anomalous, whereas the anomalous versions of (4) and (5) are syntactically anomalous. Importantly, the two syntactic rules differ in terms of their relative prevalence in the L1 and L2. Verb conjugation in French is quite similar to that in English; however, article–noun agreement is exceedingly common in French but is much less so in English.

Subjects were native French speakers and a group of novice, adult French learners. Learners were tested after approximately 1 month, 4 months, and 8 months of French instruction. As expected, native French speakers showed an N400 effect to the semantically anomalous words, and very large P600 effects to the two types of syntactic anomalies. The French learners, as is often the case, showed striking individual differences, both in a behavioral "sentence acceptability judgment" task and in the pattern of ERPs elicited by the anomalous stimuli. We then segregated the learners into upper ("fast learners") and lower ("slow learners") halves, based on their performance on the sentence-acceptability judgment task, and averaged the ERPs separately for each group. Results for the "fast learner" group will be discussed here. At each testing session, including the initial session that occurred after just 1 month of instruction, semantically anomalous words elicited a robust N400 effect, and this effect changed minimally with increasing instruction (Figure 14.7). The finding of real interest pertained to the two syntactic conditions. We will describe the verb conjugation condition first (Figure 14.8). After just 1 month of instruction, the learners' brains discriminated between the syntactically well-formed and ill-formed sentences. However, rather than eliciting the P600 effect (as we saw in native French speakers), the syntactically anomalous words elicited an N400-like effect. By 4 months, the N400 effect had largely disappeared and was replaced by a P600-like positivity. By 8 months, this P600 effect increased in amplitude and the N400 effect was entirely absent.

One interpretation of these results is that the learners initially learned about words but not rules. That is, after one month of French instruction they recognized, for example, that the word *adorez* does not fit well in the context "Tu … " but had yet to grammaticalize this knowledge (and hence elicited an N400 effect). With a bit more exposure, this knowledge became codified as a syntactic rule (and hence elicited a P600 effect). Regardless of the validity of this speculation, this experiment, much like the McLaughlin et al. experiment, demonstrates the dramatic changes in the brain responses to tokens of the L2 that occur with very little L2 exposure. As in the McLaughlin et al. study, less than a year of L2 exposure was sufficient to produce brain responses that were qualitatively similar to native-speaker brain responses.[8]

These findings seem to argue in favor of a great deal of brain plasticity, even with minimal adult L2 instruction. However, the results in the article–noun agreement condition clearly demonstrated limits to this plasticity: Learners' judgments concerning the grammaticality of these sentences were uniformly poor (even after

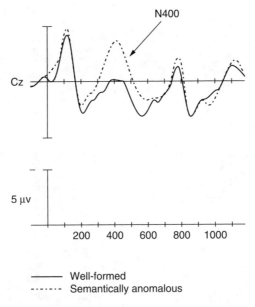

Figure 14.7. ERPs (recorded over the vertex) to critical words in the well-formed (solid line) and semantically anomalous (dashed line) conditions, collapsed over the three testing sessions.

a year of L2 instruction), and no reliable differences were observed in the ERPs to critical words in the grammatical and ungrammatical sentences (Figure 14.9). This was true even though article–noun number agreement is seemingly a simple rule, and even though both rules were encountered at roughly the same (early) point in the instructional period. Informal discussions with the French instructors indicated that learners often have more trouble learning the agreement rule than the conjugation rule. Although the proper interpretation of this set of results is uncertain at the moment, one possibility is that the rate of L2 learning is determined in part by L1–L2 similarity. Those aspects of the L2 that are highly similar to the L1 will be learned very rapidly; those aspects that are sufficiently dissimilar will be learned very slowly. Dissimilarities might include the presence of a rule in one language and its absence in the other language, differences in how the rule is expressed across languages, or differences in the prevalence or salience of that rule across languages. This proposal is not new, as influences of L1–L2 similarity on L2 learning have been documented for many years (Gass & Selinker, 1992; Odlin, 1989, Ringbom, 1987).

In summary, these findings seem to demonstrate that dramatic changes in brain activity occur during the earliest stages of adult L2 learning. Furthermore, these changes are sometimes, but not always, accompanied by increasing accuracy in related behavioral judgments. Finally, the qualitative nature of these changes might reveal important details of what has been learned. Importantly, however, mere exposure to the L2 is not enough to guarantee increasing sensitivity to every aspect of

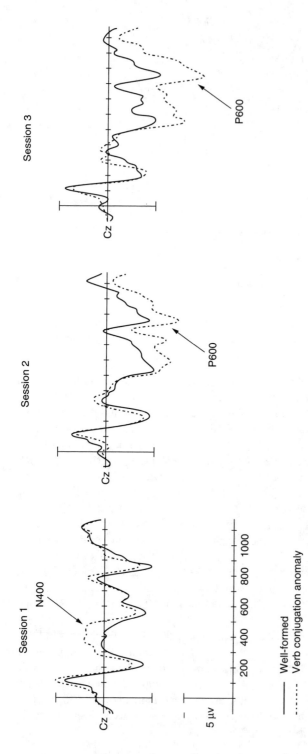

Figure 14.8. ERPs (recorded over the vertex) to critical words in the well-formed (solid line) and verb conjugation anomaly (dashed line) conditions, plotted separately for each of the three testing sessions.

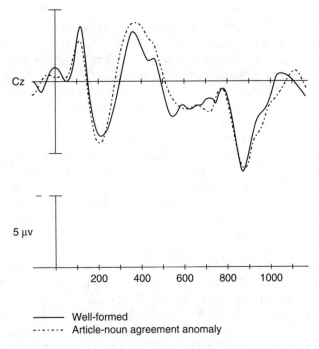

Figure 14.9. ERPs (recorded over the vertex) to critical words in the well-formed (solid line) and article–noun agreement anomaly (dashed lines) conditions, collapsing over the three testing sessions.

the language; these rapid changes in brain activity might depend on similarities across the learner's L1 and L2.

14.4 CAVEATS AND CAUTIONS

As is the case with any method, ERPs have their limitations. The most fundamental limitation is one we noted earlier in this chapter: It is relatively easy to identify the stimulus manipulations (that is, the antecedent conditions) that produce or modulate some ERP effect, but it is often very difficult to identify the precise cognitive events underlying the effect.[9] Misattributing a particular function to a particular ERP effect can have serious consequences, particularly with respect to developing and testing theories of language processing. To illustrate this point, we will discuss two example cases in which particular ERP effects have been tied to specific cognitive processes. In both examples, we present evidence that at the very least raises some questions about the general veracity of these claims. The goal of this exercise is to demonstrate the difficulty of ascertaining with any confidence the precise process made manifest by some ERP effect. We are not claiming that these claims are universally wrong, nor are we disparaging the science that motivates them.

The first example concerns the distinction between content (or "open-class") and function (or "closed-class") words (see Hoen and Dominey, chapter 16, this volume). Content words (nouns, verbs, adjectives, etc.) play a largely referential role in language, whereas function words (articles, prepositions, auxiliary verbs, etc.) play a primarily syntactic role. Neville and colleagues (e.g., Neville, Mills, & Lawson, 1992) have argued that content words elicit a negative-going wave that peaks at about 400 ms (N400), whereas function words elicit a negativity that peaks at about 280 ms (N280). The N400 component is largest over the posterior parts of the scalp, whereas the N280 is largest over anterior portions of the left hemisphere. These areas of maximum amplitude are interesting because they correspond to the lesion sites that putatively produce problems in processing the meaning and form of sentences, respectively. Such evidence has led Neville and colleagues to conclude that the N400 and N280 reflect specifically the semantic and syntactic functions of these two word classes, respectively.

The problem with this claim is that many variables are confounded with the content/function distinction. Most notable in this regard is the confounding between word class, on the one hand, and word length and normative word frequency, on the other. Function words tend to be shorter and more frequent than content words. It could be, then, that the ERP differences between content and function words are due mostly to the physical properties of length and frequency than to their abstract linguistic functions. To investigate this possibility, we asked subjects to read a short essay for comprehension (Osterhout, Allen, & McLaughlin, 2002). We then averaged ERPs in two ways: as a function of word class (content and function) and as a function of word length. When we averaged the ERPs as a function of word class, we replicated the result reported by Neville and colleagues. Function words elicited a negative component at about 300 ms that was largest over anterior portions of the left hemisphere, whereas content words elicited a posterior-maximal N400 component (Figure 14.10A). However, when we averaged the ERPs as a function of word length, we found that the variation in amplitude and latency could be accounted for almost entirely by the single variable of word length (Figure 14.10B). This robust near-linear function is much more consistent with a "word-length" model than a "word-class" model; the word-length model predicts a continuous distribution, whereas the word-class model predicts a bimodal one.

Our second example concerns the observation, noted above, that certain types of syntactic (but not semantic or pragmatic) anomalies elicit a left anterior negativity (LAN) in addition to eliciting a P600 effect. Friederici and colleagues (Hahne & Friederici, 1999; Friederci, 1995, 2002) have proposed a two-stage functional model for these ERP effects. They claim that the LAN effect reflects a fast, automatic syntactic analyzer, and that the P600 effect reflects attempts at syntactic reanalysis.[10] Underlying these claims are three more basic claims: first, that the LAN effect is reliably elicited by violations of syntactic rules; second, that the LAN effect can be associated with a neural source in or near Broca's area (Friederici, Hahne, & von Cramon, 1998; Friederici, von Cramon, & Kotz, 1999; Friederici, Wang, Herrmann, Maess, & Oertel, 2000); and, third, that (on a single trial and within a single subject) the ERP response to syntactic rule violations is biphasic, involving an initial detection of the error (reflected in the LAN) and then an attempt to fix it (reflected in the P600).

Each of these claims is open to debate. First, a critical step in identifying the cognitive processes made manifest by some ERP effect is to identify the antecedent

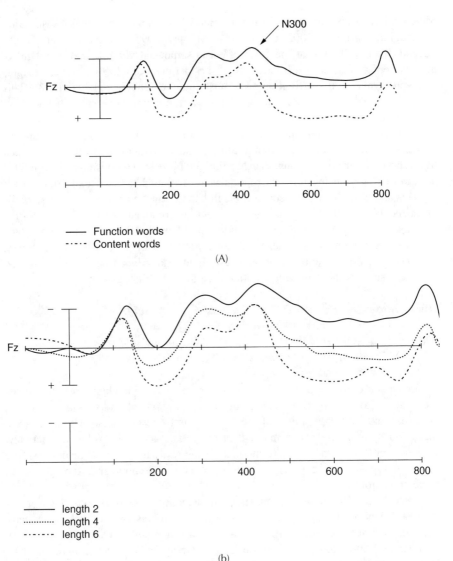

Figure 14.10. (A) ERPs (recorded over anterior midline site Fz) averaged as a function of word class. Adapted from "Words in the brain: Lexical determinants of word-induced brain activity," by L. Osterhout, M. Allen, and J. McLaughlin, 2002, *Journal of Neurolinguistics, 15,* 171–187. (B) ERPs averaged as a function of word length. Adapted from "Words in the brain: Lexical determinants of word-induced brain activity," by L. Osterhout, M. Allen, and J. McLaughlin, 2002, *Journal of Neurolinguistics, 15,* 171–187.

conditions that elicit or modulate it. However, the antecedent conditions that elicit the LAN effect are not clear. Although LAN effects are often reported in the response to a syntactic anomaly, there are a significant number of reports in which they are not reported (e.g., Ainsworth- Darnell, Shulman, & Boland,1998; Allen et al., in press; Hagoort, Brown, & Groothusen, 1993; Kuperberg, Holcomb, et al., 2003;

McKinnon & Osterhout, 1996; Osterhout, Bersick, & McLaughlin, 1997; Osterhout, McLaughlin, & Inoue, 2002; Osterhout & Mobley, 1995; Takazawa et al., 2002). Second, the distribution of the LAN effect is somewhat variable and is not infrequently reported to have a bilateral (e.g., Friederici et al., 1999) or even a right-hemisphere-maximal distribution (e.g., Osterhout & Nicol, 1999, Exp. 2). This variability raises questions about the claim that the neural generators of the effect lie in or near Broca's area.

Third, even given the apparent existence of a LAN effect in the brain response to syntactic rule violations, it is not certain that individual subjects in individual trials show a biphasic response (LAN followed by P600) to these anomalies. This is because ERPs in the relevant reports were averaged (as is usually done) over subjects and trials. Thus, it is conceivable that the syntactic anomalies in Friederici's experiments elicited a negative-going effect in some subjects and a P600-like response in others. Such a finding would be problematic for Friederici's multistage model. A result much like this has been reported in one recent study (Inoue & Osterhout, in preparation). Inoue and Osterhout asked Japanese speakers to read sentences such as the following (written here in an English gloss):

(6a)   *Taro*-NOM *Hanako*-DAT *textbook*-ACC *to-buy said.*
        "Taro told Hanako to buy a textbook."
(6b)   **Taro*-NOM *Hanako*-ACC *textbook*-ACC *to-buy said.*
        "Taro told ??? to buy a textbook/Hanako."

In Japanese, the verb typically appears at the end of the clause, and the nouns are attached to case markers specifying their grammatical and thematic roles. In both (6a) and (6b), the subject of the sentence is followed by two nouns. In (6a), these nouns are appropriately marked for dative and accusative roles, respectively. However, in (6b), both nouns are marked for the accusative role. If readers assume that both nouns are attached to the main verb, the second noun should be perceived to be anomalous.[11]

Therefore, ERPs to the second noun in sentences like (6a) and (6b) were of interest. When we averaged ERPs over all subjects, the response to the syntactically anomalous words seemed to be biphasic, involving both an anterior negativity between 300 and 500 ms, and then a large posterior P600 effect (Figure 14.11A). However, when subjects were divided into two groups based on the magnitude of the anterior negativity effect, ERPs averaged separately for these two groups revealed compelling individual differences: Those subjects who responded with a large negativity to the violations tended to show a very small P600 effect, whereas those that responded with a large P600 effect showed no evidence of a negativity (Figures 14.11B and 14.11C). Furthermore, the "anterior" distribution of the negativity largely disappeared when averages were formed over the two groups; in fact, the timing and distribution of the negativity elicited by these case anomalies were similar in this group of subjects to the timing and distribution of N400 elicited by semantic anomalies. Apparently, the anterior distribution was (at least to a degree) an artifact caused by component overlap (i.e., the posteriorly distributed P600 effect reduced the size of the negativity over posterior sites, but not over anterior sites).

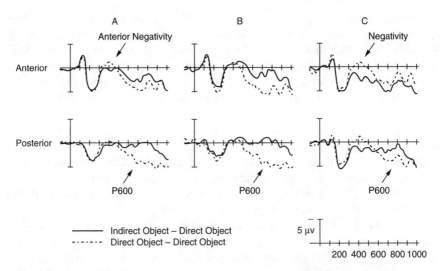

Figure 14.11. (A) ERPs averaged over 20 subjects (recorded over an anterior and a posterior site) elicited by Japanese sentences of the form "Noun-Nominative Noun-Dative Noun-Accusative" (solid line) and "Noun-Nominative Noun-Accusative Noun-Accusative" (dashed line). Readers are predicted to encounter processing problems at the second of two consecutive nouns marked for accusative case. ERPs shown are those elicited to the second post-subject noun (Noun-Accusative) in each sentence type. (B) ERPs averaged over 10 subjects who showed the smallest-magnitude Anterior Negativity. (C) ERPs averaged over 10 subjects who showed the largest-magnitude Anterior Negativity.

Obviously, it is far from clear how this finding relates to prior reports of a "LAN followed by P600" response to different types of syntactic anomalies in English and German. The relevant point, however, is that sometimes the grand average does not accurately reflect what occurs on a single trial or within a single subject. Unfortunately, if the sample is comprised of two or more populations, each of which responds differently to some event, this fact can be obscured by averaging over everyone.[12] This, in turn, can lead to erroneous conclusions about the distribution of an effect across the scalp, the ordering of events during a particular process, and the precise cognitive processes underlying some effect.

Perhaps it will turn out that the LAN effect is reliably elicited by syntactic anomalies, that it has a consistent scalp distribution, and that it is not an artifact of averaging over subjects. Is such evidence sufficient to justify the conclusion that the LAN effect directly manifests a fast, automatic syntactic analyzer? Unfortunately, no. This is because (as we noted above) the processes underlying the LAN effect (or the P600) might be correlated with, but indeterminately removed from, the syntactic processes themselves. One is still limited in the types of inferences that are licensed by the evidence; for example, by localizing the source or the LAN effect or the P600, one has not definitively isolated the source of syntactic processing. In all likelihood, definitive conclusions concerning the cognitive processes underlying these ERP effects will require converging evidence from other methods of investigation.

Friederici and colleagues provide another type of evidence that the LAN effect reflects the detection of a syntactic anomaly, whereas the P600 reflects syntactic reanalysis. They have shown that although the P600 is sensitive to stimulus manipulations (e.g., manipulating the proportion of anomalies within a list) and task manipulations (e.g., monitoring for a syntactic vs. a semantic problem), the LAN effect is not (Hahne & Friederici, 1999, 2002). Such a result is expected if the LAN reflects the actions of a fast, automatic syntactic analyzer, whereas the P600 does not. However, these demonstrations suffer from a potentially serious materials flaw. In both of their experiments, Hahne and Friederici presented their sentences as continuous natural speech. In such a paradigm, ERPs to several successive words will commingle. If these words are different across conditions, confounds are likely. In the Hahne and Friederici experiments, sentences in the control and syntactically anomalous conditions were comprised of sequences such as (1) *Das Brot wurde gegessen* (*The bread was eaten*) and (2) *Das Brot wurde im gegessen* (*The bread was in-the eaten*), respectively. The critical word was the verb *gegessen*. This comparison is problematic. For example, *wurde* and *im* might be different in phonological length and/or normative frequency, and thereby produce differences in ERPs that extend into the critical word epoch. Furthermore, it is likely that ERPs to *Brot* and *wurde* overlapped with the ERPs to *gegessen* in (1), while ERPs to *wurde* and *im* overlapped with the response to *gegessen* in (2). Nouns like *Brot* and high-frequency function words like *wurde* and *im* elicit quite different ERPs (e.g., Neville et al., 1992; Osterhout et al., 2002). Hence, one cannot assume that the reported differences in the ERPs to *gegessen* are due to the ungrammaticality of (2). Importantly, stimulus confounds of this sort would not be influenced by task and stimulus manipulations. This potential problem is not ameliorated by the use of a poststimulus baseline to equate the well-formed and ill-formed conditions (as was done by Hahne and Friederici); whatever preexisting differences are present continue to resolve themselves and continue to contaminate ERPs to the critical words, regardless of the choice in baseline. Although the existence or nonexistence of these confounds could probably be ascertained by examining the prestimulus portion of the epoch elicited by the critical word, Hahne and Friederici go counter to convention and do not plot this portion of the waveform.

It is undeniably true that the more we know about the cognitive events underlying some language-sensitive ERP effect, the more useful that ERP effect becomes. It is also true that erroneous hypotheses of this sort can have serious and unfortunate consequences, especially with respect to theory-building. We would like to be clear about what we are claiming: The hypotheses discussed in this section are useful. Even so, it is important to maintain a cautious and realistic attitude concerning the difficulties in attempting to validate such hypotheses.

Fortunately, these realities do not limit in any profound way the utility of ERPs for studying sentence processing. All that is needed to make progress is the discovery of ERP effects that co-vary systematically with principled stimulus manipulations (cf. Osterhout & Holcomb, 1995). With that in hand, one can use the ERP data to contrast functional claims about sentence processing even if one cannot make clear functional claims about the ERP effects themselves. The preceding two decades of work has provided convincing evidence of such effects and of their utility as tools for studying real-time sentence comprehension (see also chapter 13 by van Berkum, chapter 15 by Barber et al., and chapter 16 by Hoen and Dominey in this volume).

14.5 CONCLUSIONS

In our review, we have attempted to illustrate the advantages of ERPs for studying real-time language comprehension, both in native speakers and in adult language learners. We recognize, of course, that ERPs (like all methods of investigation) imperfectly reflect the cognitive and neural processes underlying human language. Because of this, it is wise to consider possible sources of converging evidence whenever possible.

Nonetheless, sentence comprehension (like all aspects of language comprehension) involves complex events that occur with great speed. A satisfying theory of sentence comprehension will explain how these events occur over time, in real time, as a person is trying to understand a sentence. The same is true for language learning, although in that case the theory must track changes that occur over two vastly different time scales: the time it takes a person to understand a word or sentence and the time it takes a person to learn the facts of the foreign language. A truly compelling theory will link these events to the brain, relying on direct measurement of brain activity. The primary (and perhaps unique) advantage of ERPs is that they provide us with a means for observing reasonably direct manifestations of some of the transient brain events that make up the core of language processing. ERPs also allow us to determine the "response selectivities" of these brain events through careful manipulation of linguistic stimuli. Given recent methodological advances, it appears that we might now be able to more compellingly relate these brain events to their underlying neural sources.

A cynically minded reader might argue that some of the novel insights described above are a bit too novel to be entirely believable. Surely we know that syntax is always first, that critical periods for language learning exist, and that fMRI is better suited than ERPs for localizing neural activity in the brain. We do not mean to espouse dangerously or ludicrously radical ideas. We do mean to suggest, however, that a particular method should be evaluated on the basis of its a priori suitability, its sensitivity to the phenomena of interest, and its ability to generate reproducible and theoretically interesting results. ERPs get high marks along all of these dimensions. ERPs (or any other method) should not be devalued or viewed skeptically simply because the data generated by the method seemingly contradict conventional beliefs. On the contrary, such methods should be valued more highly, as they provide the primary means for advancing our theoretical understanding.

References

Ainsworth-Darnell, K., Shulman, R., & Boland, J. (1998). Dissociating brain responses to syntactic and semantic anomalies: Evidence from event-related brain potentials. *Journal of Memory and Language, 38,* 112–130.

Allen, M. D., Badecker, W., & Osterhout, L. (in press). Morphological analysis during sentence processing. *Language and Cognitive Processes, 18*, 405–430.

Anderer, P., Pascual-Marqui, R. D., Smlitsch, H. V., & Saletu, B. Differential effects of normal aging on sources of standard N1, target N1, and target P300 auditory event-related brain potentials revealed by low resolution electromagnetic tomography (LORETA). *Electroencephalography and Clinical Neurophysiology, 108*, 160–174.

Angrilli, A., Penolazzi, B., Vespignani, F., De Vincenzi, M., Job, R., Ciccarelli, L., Palomba, D., & Stegagno, L. (2002). Cortical brain responses to semantic incongruity and syntactic violation in Italian language: An event-related potential study. *Neuroscience Letters, 322*, 5–8.

Bates, E., & Dick, F. (2000). Beyond phrenology: Brain and language in the next millennium. *Brain and Language, 71*, 18–21.

Bavelier, D., Corina, D., Jezzard, P., Padmanabhan, S., Clark, V., Karni, A., Prinster, A., Braun, A., Lalwan, A., Rauschecker, J., Turner, R., & Neville, H., (1997). Sentence reading: A functional MRI study at 4 tesla. *Journal of Cognitive Neuroscience, 9*, 664–686.

Bentin, S. (1987). Event-related potentials, semantic processes, and expectancy factors in word recognition. *Brain and Language, 31*, 308–327

Bever, T. G., & Townsend, D. J. (2001). Some sentences on our consciousness of sentences. In E. Dupoux (Ed.), *Language, brain, and cognitive development: Essays in honor of Jacques Mehler*. Cambridge, MA: MIT Press.

Binder, J., & Price, C. J. (2001). Functional neuroimaging of language. In R. Cabeza & A. Kingstone (Ed.), *Handbook of functional neuroimaging of cognition*. Cambridge, MA: MIT Press.

Blumstein, S., & Milberg, W. (2000). Language deficit in Broca's and Wernicke's aphasia: A singular impairment. In Y. Grodzinsky, L. Shapro, & D. Swinney (Eds.), *Language and the brain: Representation and processing*. San Diego, CA: Academic Press.

Bock, J. K., & Kroch, A. S. (1989). The isolability of syntactic processing, In G. N. Carlson & M. K. Tanenhaus (Eds.), *Linguistic structure in language processing*. Boston: Kluwer Academic.

Burock, M. A., Buckner, R. L., Woldorff, M. G., Rosen, B. R., & Dale, A. M. (1998). Randomized event-related experimental designs allow for extremely rapid presentation rates using functional MRI. *NeuroReport, 9*, 3735–3739.

Caplan, D., Hildebrandt, N., & Makris, N. (1996). Location of lesions in stroke patients with deficits in syntactic processing in sentence comprehension. *Brain, 119*, 933–949.

Caramazza, A., & Zurif, E. B. (1976). Dissociation of algorithmic and heuristic processes in language comprehension: Evidence from aphasia. *Brain and Language, 3*, 572–582.

Chee, M. W., Caplan, D., Soon, C. S., Sriram, N., Tan, E. W., Thiel, T., et al. (1999a). Processing of visually presented sentences in Mandarin and English studied with fMRI. *Neuron, 23*, 127–137.

Chee, M. W., Hon, N., Lee, H. L., & Soon, C. S. (2001). Relative language proficiency modulates BOLD signal change when bilinguals perform semantic judgments. *Neuroimage, 13*, 1155–1163.

Chee, M. W., Tan, E. W., & Thiel, T. (1999b). Mandarin and English single word processing studied with functional magnetic resonance imaging. *The Journal of Neuroscience, 19*, 3050–3056.

Chomsky, N. (1986). *Knowledge of language*. New York: Praeger.

Dale A. M, Bunker R. L. (1997). Selective averaging of individual trials using fMRI. *Human Brain Mapping, 5*, 329–340.

Dale, A. M., Liu, A. K., Fischl, B. R., Buckner, R. L., Belliveau, J. W., Lewine, J. D., et al. (2002). Dynamic statistical parameteric mapping: Combining fMRI and MEG for high-resolution imaging of cortical activity. *Neuron, 26,* 55–67.

Dehaene, S., Dupoux, E., Mehler, J., Cohen, L., Paulesu, E., Perani, D., et al. (1997). Anatomical variability in the cortical representation of first and second language. *Neuroreport, 8,* 3809–3815.

Donchin, E., & Coles, M. G. H. (1988). Is the P300 component a manifestation of context updating? *Behavioral and Brain Sciences, 11,* 343–427.

Dronkers, N. F. (2000). The pursuit of brain-language relationships. *Brain and Language, 71,* 59–61.

Ellis, A. W., & Lambon Ralph, M. A. (2000). Age of acquisition effects in adult lexical processing reflect loss of plasticity in maturing systems: Insights from connectionist networks. *Journal of Experimental Psychology: Learning, Memory, Cognition, 26,* 1103–1123

Elman, J. L. (1990). Representation and structure in connectionist models. In G. T. M. Altmann (Ed.), *Cognitive models of speech processing.* Cambridge, MA: MIT Press.

Ferreira, F., & Clifton, C. (1986). The independence of syntactic processing. *Journal of Memory and Language, 25,* 348–368.

Fodor, J. A. (1983). *Modularity of mind.* Cambridge, MA: MIT Press.

Fodor, J. D., & Ferreira, F. (1998). *Reanalysis in sentence processing.* Boston: Kluwer Academic.

Forster, K. (1979). Levels of processing and the structure of the language processor. In W. Cooper & E. C. T. Walker (Eds.), *Sentence processing.* Hillsdale, NJ: Erlbaum.

Frazier, L., & Clifton, C., Jr. (1996). *Construal.* Cambridge, MA: MIT Press.

Friederici, A. D. (1995). The time course of syntactic activation during language processing: A model based on neuropsychological and neurophysiological data. *Brain and Language, 50,* 259–284.

Friederici, A. D. (2002). Towards a neural basis of auditory sentence processing. *Trends in Cognitive Sciences, 6,* 78–84.

Friederici, A. D., Hahne, A., & von Cramon, D. Y. (1998). First-pass versus second-pass parsing processes in a Wernicke's and a Broca's aphasic: Electro-physiological evidence for a double dissociation. *Brain and Language, 62,* 311–341.

Friederici, A. D., Ruschemeyer, S., Hahne, A., & Fiebach, C. J. (2003). The role of left inferior frontal and superior temporal cortex in sentence comprehension: Localizing syntactic and semantic processes. *Cerebral Cortex, 13,* 170–177.

Friederici, A. D., von Cramon, D. Y., & Kotz, S. A. (1999). Language related brain potentials in patients with cortical and subcortical left hemisphere lesions. *Brain, 122,* 1033–1047.

Friederici, A. D., Wang, Y., Herrmann, C. S., Maess, B., & Oertel, U. (2000). Localization of early syntactic processes in frontal and temporal cortical areas: A magnetoencephalographic study. *Human Brain Mapping, 11,* 1–11.

Garnsey, S. M., Pearlmutter, N. J., Myers, E., & Lotocky, M. A. (1997). The contributions of verb bias and plausibility to the comprehension of temporarily ambiguous sentences. *Journal of Memory and Language, 37,* 58–93.

Gass, S., & Selinker, L. (1992). *Language Transfer in Language Learning.* Amsterdam: John Benjamins.

Haan, H., Streb, J., Bien, S., & Roesler, F. (2000). Individual cortical current density reconstructions of the semantic N400 effect: Using a generalized minimum norm model with different constraints (L1 and L2 norm). *Human Brain Mapping, 11,* 178–192.

Hagoort, P., Brown, C., & Groothusen, J. (1993). The syntactic positive shift (SPS) as an ERP measure of syntactic processing. *Language and Cognitive Processes, 8,* 439–483.

Hahne, A., & Fiederici., A. D. (1999). Electrophysiological evidence for two steps in syntactic analysis: Early automatic and late controlled processes. *Journal of Cognitive Neuroscience, 11,* 193–204.

Hahne, A., & Friederici., A. D. (2001). Processing a second language: Late learners' comprehension mechanisms as revealed by event-related brain potentials. *Bilingualism: Language and Cognition, 4,* 123–141.

Hahne, A., & Friederici, A. D. (2002). Differential task effects on semantic and syntactic processes as revealed by ERPs. *Cognitive Brain Research, 13,* 339–356.

Halgren, E., Dhond, R. P., Christensen, N., van Petten, C., Marinkovic, K., Lewine, J., & Dale, A. M. (2002). N400-like magnetoencephalography responses modulated by semantic context, word frequency, and lexical class in sentences. *NeuroImage, 17,* 1101–1116.

Halsband, U., Krause, B. J., Sipila, H., Teras, M., & Laihinen, A. (2002). PET studies on the memory processing of word pairs in bilingual Finnish-English subjects. *Behavioral Brain Research, 132,* 47–57.

Hämäläinen, M. S., & Sarvas, J. (1989). Realistic conductivity geometry model of the human head for interpretation of neuromagnetic data. *IEEE Transactions on Biomedical Engineering, 36,* 165–171.

Hasegawa, M., Carpenter, P. A., & Just, M. A. (2002). An fMRI study of bilingual sentence comprehension and workload. *NeuroImage, 15,* 647–660.

Henderson, C. J., Butler, S. R., & Glass, A. (1975). The localization of equivalent dipoles of EEG sources by the application of electrical field theory. *Electroencephalography and Clinical Neurophysiology, 39,* 117–130.

Hernandez, A. E., Martinez, A., & Kohnert, K. (2000). In search of the language switch: An fMRI study of picture naming in Spanish-English bilinguals. *Brain and Language, 73,* 421–431.

Illes, J., Francis, W. S., Desmond, J. E., Gabrieli, J. D., Glover, G. H., Poldrack, R., Lee, C. J., & Wagner, A. D. (1999). Convergent cortical representation of semantic processing in bilinguals. *Brain and Language, 70,* 347–363.

Inoue, K., & Osterhout, L. (in preparation). Brain potentials elicted by case anomalies in Japanese sentences.

Jackendoff, R. (2000). Fodorian and representational modularity. In Y. Grodzinsky, L. Shapiro, & D. Swinney (Eds.), *Language and the brain: Representation and processing.* San Diego, CA: Academic Press.

Jezzard, P., Matthews, P. M., & Smith, S. (2001). *Functional magnetic resonance imaging: Methods for Neuroscience.* Oxford: Oxford University Press.

Johnson, J. S. (1992). Critical period effects in second language acquisition: The effect of written versus auditory materials on the assessment of grammatical competence. *Language Learning, 42,* 217–248.

Johnson, J. S., & Newport, E. L. (1989). Critical period effects in second language learning: The influence of maturational state on the acquisition of English as a second language. *Cognitive Psychology, 21,* 60–99.

Kang, A. M., Constable, R. T., Gore, J. C., & Avrutin, S. (1999). An event-related fMRI study of implicit phrase-level syntactic and semantic processing. *Neuroimage, 10,* 555–561.

Kavanaugh, R. N., Darcey, T. M., Lehmann, D., & Fender, D. H. (1978). Evaluation of methods for three dimensional localization of electrical sources in the human brain. *IEEE Transactions in Biomedical Engineering, 25,* 421–429.

Kim, A., & Osterhout, L. (submitted). The independence of combinatory semantic processing: Evidence from event relates potentials.

Kim, K. H. S., Relkin, N. R., Lee, K-M., & Hirsch, J. (1997). Distinct cortical areas associated with native and second languages. *Nature, 388,* 171–174.

Klein, D., Milner, B., Zatorre, R. J., Zhao, V., & Nikelski, J. (1999). Cerebral organization in bilinguals: A PET study of Chinese-English verb generation. *NeuroReport, 10,* 2841–2846.

Kolk, H. H. J., Chwilla, D. J., van Herten, M., & Oor, P. J. W. (2003). Structure and limited capacity in verbal working memory: A study with event-related potentials. *Brain and Language, 85,* 1–36.

Kounios, J., Smith, R. W., Yang, W., Bachman, P., & D'Esposito, M. (2001). Cognitive association formation in human memory revealed by spatiotemporal brain imaging. *Neuron, 29,* 297–306.

Kuhl, K. P. (2000). Language, mind, brain: Experience alters perception. In S. M. Gazzaniga & E. Bizzi (Eds.), *The new cognitive neurosciences.* Cambridge, MA: MIT Press.

Kuperberg, G. R., Holcomb, P. J., Sitnikva, T., Greve, D., Dale, A. M., & Caplan, D. (2003). Distinct patterns of neural modulation during the processing of conceptual and syntactic anomalies. *Journal of Cognitive Neuroscience, 15,* 272–293.

Kuperberg, G. R., McGuire, P. K., Bullmore, E. T., Brammer, M. J., Rabe-Hesketh, S., Wright, I. C., et al. (2000). Common and distinct neural substrates of pragmatic, semantic, and syntactic processing of spoken sentences. *Journal of Cognitive Neuroscience, 12,* 321–341.

Kuperberg, G. R., Sitnikova, T., Caplan, D., & Holcomb, P. J. (2003). Electrophysiological distinctions in processing conceptual relationships within simple sentences. *Cognitive Brain Research, 17,* 117–129.

Kutas, M., & Hillyard, S. A. (1980). Reading senseless sentences: Brain potentials reflect semantic incongruity. *Science, 207,* 203–205.

Kutas, M., & Hillyard, S. A. (1984). Brain potentials during reading reflect word expectancy and semantic association. *Nature, 307,* 161–163.

Levelt, W. J. M. (1999). *Producing spoken language: a blueprint of the speaker.* Oxford: Oxford University Press.

MacDonald, M. C., Pearlmutter, N. J., & Seidenberg, M. S. (1994). The lexical nature of syntactic ambiguity resolution. *Psychological Review, 101,* 676–703.

McClelland, J., St. John, M., & Taraban, R. (1989). Sentence comprehension: A parallel distributed processing approach. *Language and Cognitive Processes, 4,* 287–336.

McKinnon, R., & Osterhout, L. (1996). Constraints on movement phenomena in sentence processing: Evidence from event-related brain potentials. *Language and Cognitive Processes, 11,* 495–523.

McLaughlin, J., Osterhout, L., & Kim, A. (in press). Neural correlates of second-language word learning: Minimal instruction produces rapid change. *Nature Neuroscience.*

McNeil, M., & Doyle, P. J. (2000). Reconsidering the hegemony of linguistic explanations in aphasia: The challenge for the beginning of the millennium. *Brain and Language, 71,* 154–156.

Menon, R. S., & Goodyear, B. G. (2001). Spatial and temporal resolution of fMRI. In P. Jezzard, P. Matthews, & S. Smith (Eds.), *Functional MRI: An Introduction to Methods.* Oxford: Oxford University Press.

Milberg, W., & Blumstein, S. (2000). Back to the future: Reclaiming aphasia from cognitive neurolinguistics. *Brain and Language, 71,* 160–163.

Mulert, C., Gallinat, J., Pascual-Marqui, R., Dorn, H., Frick, K., Schlattmann, P., et al. (2001). Reduced event-related current density in the anterior cingulated cortex in schizophrenia. *NeuroImage, 13,* 589–600.

Neville, H., Mills, D., & Lawson, D. (1992). Fractionating language: Difference neural subsystems with different sensitive periods. *Cerebral Cortex, 2,* 244–258.

Neville, H. J., Nicol, J. L., Barss, A., Forster, K. I., & Garret, M.(1991). Syntactically based sentence processing classes: Evidence from event-related brain potentials. *Journal of Cognitive Neuroscience, 3,* 151–165.

Newman, A. J., Pancheva, R., Ozawa, K., Neville, H. J., & Ullman, M. T. (2001). An event-related fMRI study of syntactic and semantic violations. *Journal of Psycholinguistic Research, 30,* 339–364.

Ni, W., Constable, R. T., Mencl, W. E., Pugh, K. R., Fullbright, R. K., Schaywitz, B. A., & Gore, J. (2000). An event-related neuroimaging study distinguishing form and content in sentence processing. *Journal of Cognitive Neuroscience, 12,* 120–133.

Nunez, P. L. (1995). *Neocortical dynamics and human EEG rhythms.* Oxford: Oxford University Press.

Odlin, T. (1989). *Language Transfer.* Cambridge, UK: Cambridge University Press.

Osterhout, L. (1997). On the brain response to syntactic anomalies: Manipulations of word position and word class reveal individual differences. *Brain and Language, 59,* 494–522.

Osterhout, L. (2000). On space, time, and language: For the next century, timing is (almost) everything. *Brain and Language, 71, 175–177.*

Osterhout, L., Allen, M., & McLaughlin, J. (2002). Words in the brain: Lexical determinants of word-induced brain activity. *Journal of Neurolinguistics, 15,* 171–187.

Osterhout, L., Bersick, M., & McKinnon, R. (1997). Brain potentials elicited by words: Word length and frequency predict the latency of an early negativity. *Biological Psychology, 46,* 143–168.

Osterhout, L., Bersick, M., & McLaughlin, J. (1997). Brain potentials reflect violations of gender stereotypes. *Memory and Cognition, 25,* 273–285.

Osterhout, L., & Holcomb, P. J. (1992). Event-related brain potentials elicited by syntactic anomaly. *Journal of Memory and Language, 31,* 785–806.

Osterhout, L., & Holcomb, P. J. (1993). Event-related potentials and syntactic anomaly: Evidence of anomaly detection during the perception of continuous speech. *Language and Cognitive Processes, 8,* 413–438.

Osterhout, L., & Holcomb, P. J. (1995). Event-related brain potentials and language comprehension. In M. D. Rugg & M. G. H. Coles (Eds.), *Electrophysiology of mind: Event-related brain potentials and cognition.* Oxford: Oxford University Press.

Osterhout, L., Holcomb, P. J., & Swinney, D. A. (1994). Brain potentials elicited by garden-path sentences: Evidence of the application of verb information during parsing. *Journal of Experiment Psychology: Learning, Memory, and Cognition, 20,* 786-803.

Osterhout, L., McKinnon, R., Bersick, M., & Corey, V. (1996). On the language-specificity of the brain response to syntactic anomalies: Is the syntactic positive shift a member of the P300 family? *Journal of Cognitive Neuroscience, 8,* 507–526.

Osterhout, L., McLaughlin, J., Allen, M., & Inoue, K. (2002). Brain potentials elicited by prose-embedded linguistic anomalies. *Memory and Cognition, 30,* 1304–1312.

Osterhout, L., McLaughlin, J., & Bersick, M. (1997). Event-related brain potentials and human language. *Trends in Cognitive Sciences, 1,* 203–209.

Osterhout, L., & Mobley, L. A. (1995). Event-related brain potentials elicited by failure to agree. *Journal of Memory and Language, 34,* 739–773.

Osterhout, L., & Nicol, J. (1999). On the distinctiveness, independence, and time course of the brain responses to syntactic and semantic anomalies. *Language and Cognitive Processes, 14,* 283–317.

Osterhout, L., McLaughlin, J., & Inoue, K. (in preparation). Acquiring knowledge about syntax and semantics during second-language learning: a longitudal ERP study.

Pascual-Marqui, R. D. (1999). Review of methods for solving the EEG inverse problem. *International Journal of Bioelectromagnetism, 1,* 75–86.

Pascual-Marqui, R. D., Esslen, M., Kochi, K., & Lehmann, D. (2002). Functional imaging with low resolution brain electromagnetic tomography (LORETA); review, new comparisons, and new validation. *Japanese Journal of Clinical Neurophysiology, 30,* 81–94.

Pascual-Marqui, R. D., Michel, C. M., & Lehmann, D. (1994). Low resolution electromagnetic tomography: A new method for localizing electrical activity in the brain. *International Journal of Psychophysiology, 18,* 49–65.

Perani, D., Dehaene, S., Grassi, F., Cohen, L., Cappa, S. F., Dupoux, E., et al. (1996). Brain processing of native and foreign languages. *Neuroreport, 7,* 2439–2444.

Perani, D., Paulesu, E., Galles, N. S., Dupoux, E., Dehaene, S., Bettinardi, V., et al. (1998). The bilingual brain. Proficiency and age of acquisition of the second language. *Brain, 121,* 1841–1852.

Price, C. (1998). The functional anatomy of word comprehension and production. *Trends in Cognitive Sciences, 2,* 281–288.

Ringbom, H. (1987). The role of the first language in foreign language learning. Clevedon, Somerset, UK: Multilingual Matters.

Rugg, M. D., & Coles, M. G. H. (1995). *Electrophysiology of mind—Event-related brain potentials and Cognition.* Oxford: Oxford University Press.

Savoy, R. L., Bandettini, P. A., O'Craven, K. M., Kwong, K. K., Davis, T. L., Baker, J. R., et al. (1995). Pushing the temporal resolution of fMRI: Studies of very brief visual stimuli, onset variability, and asynchrony, and stimulus-correlated changes in noise. *Proceedings of the Society of Magnetic Resonance, 2,* 450.

Takazawa, S., Takahashi, N., Nakagome, K., Kanno, O., Hagiwara, H., Nakajima, H., et al. (2002). Early components of event-related potentials related to semantic and syntactic processes in the Japanese language. *Brain Topography, 14,* 169–177.

Tootell, R. B. H., Hadjikhani, N. K., Mendola, J. D., Marret, S., & Dale, A. (1998). From retinotopy to recognition: fMRI in human visual cortex. *Trends in Cognitive Sciences, 2,* 174–183 .

Trueswell, J. C., & Tanenhaus, M. K. (1994). Toward a lexicalist framework of constraint-based syntactic ambiguity resolution. In. C. Clifton, L. Franzier, & K. Rayner (Eds.), *Perspectives on Sentence Processing.* Hillsdale, NJ: Erlbaum.

Wartenburger, I., Heekeren, H. R., Abutalebi, J., Cappa, S. F., Villringer, A., & Perani, D. (2003). Early setting of grammatical processing in the bilingual brain. *Neuron, 37,* 159–170.

Weber-Fox, C. M., & Neville, H. J. (1996). Maturational constraints on functional specializations for language processing: ERP and behavioral evidence in bilingual speakers. *Journal of Cognitive Neuroscience, 8,* 231–256.

Notes

1. Some event-related designs are probably better than others if the goal is to isolate the BOLD response to a specific word within a sentence. For example, a design in which sentences are identical across conditions except for a single critical word, and in which the hemodynamic response to critical words in successive sentences are

sufficiently separated in time, might be one effective means for isolating word-specific BOLD responses. Also, recent efforts have been made to reduce the effective temporal resolution (or "localization") of fMRI signals (Menon & Goodyear, 2001). However, whether these methods can be successfully applied to psycholinguistic research remains to be seen.

2. These studies did differ in how the fMRI data were treated statistically, which by itself could result in different conclusions across studies, even given similar BOLD signals.

3. Although the N400 and P600 effects to semantic and syntactic processing, respectively, are in fact highly reproduceable, and the antecedent conditions that elicit them are fairly well understood, this is perhaps less so for the LAN and other anterior negativities elicited by syntactic anomalies. These anterior negativities are often not observed under conditions when they should be, according to some theories (e.g., Friederici, 2002). We comment further on this issue in the "Caveats and Cautions" section.

4. We computed the LORETA solutions using a grand-average waveform comprised of approximately 600 trials per condition (20 subjects times 30 trials per condition). The waveform was projected onto the Montreal Neurological Institute averaged brain. LORETA solutions were obtained for a single sample point representing the approximate peak of each ERP effect of interest.

5. Despite these interesting consistencies, the LORETA solutions should be viewed as preliminary until they are replicated. To the best of our knowledge, only two published studies have attempted to localize the N400 component (or the magnetic equivalent) using similar procedures (and none has attempted to localize the P600 effect). These studies produced results that differ from each other and from our results. Haan, Streb, Bien, and Roesler (2000) asked subjects to read pairs of words, some of which were semantically related, and estimated the current distribution for the N400 on an individual-subject basis. They found no consistent pattern across subjects. Dale et al. (2002) asked subjects to read sentences with a sentence-final word that was either fully acceptable or pragmatically implausible given the context. Source modeling placed N400m (the magnetic equivalent) onset (at ~250 ms) in the left posterior temporal lobe, and N400m peak (at 370 ms) in the left anterior orbital and frontopolar cortices. There are numerous procedural differences across studies that could account for these differences in outcome. Most fundamentally, both Haan et al. and Halgren et al. computed solutions on difference waves (in which the responses to the fully acceptable words were subtracted from the responses to the pragmatically anomalous words). However, the difference waveform is a mathematical fiction that might not preserve the underlying source information. Furthermore, Haan et al. presented word pairs rather than sentences, and Halgren et al. presented the critical words at the ends of sentences. It is not clear that these conditions will generalize to the conditions we used, in which the critical words were embedded in sentences. For example, by placing the critical words in sentence-final position, one potentially confounds the response to the anomaly with sentence wrap-up effects (cf. Osterhout, 1997, for more on this important point). Finally, Haan et al. and Halgren et al. both computed LORETA solutions on individual subject data, whereas we chose to compute them using grand-average data. Single-subject solutions probably preserve more precise spatial information; however, they also contain fewer trials and therefore more noise. LORETA cannot discriminate between signal and noise and models both; therefore, the validity of the procedure depends on reducing the noise as much as possible. This is most effectively done by using grand averages over subjects as the basis of the LORETA

procedure. Evaluations of LORETA's reliability must take such methodological variation into account.

6. A reviewer suggested that the garden-path model could also account for these results. Perhaps the N400 effect is elicited only when the final/eventual analysis is implausible. It is conceivable that the implausible interpretation of (2a) is initiated, but rapidly detected as implausible. This could trigger rejection of the initial semantic interpretation before it is integrated along with an attempt to syntactically re-analyze the sentence. The syntactic re-analysis may be manifested in the P600 effect at the verb and the failure to integrate the initial interpretation may explain the absence of an N400 effect. The difficulty with this explanation is that a vast literature shows that N400 amplitude is exquisitely sensitive to pragmatic implausibility, and in fact is roughly linearly related to gradations of plausibility. Furthermore, the N400 effect typically onsets within ~250 ms after presentation of the anomalous word (which leaves little time for additional processing to occur). Therefore, it seems highly unlikely that implausibility would fail to be manifested in the N400 to the verb in sentences like (2a) if the verb was perceived to be pragmatically implausible.

7. It is worth mentioning that the temporal ordering of the N400 and P600 is seemingly inconsistent with the general assumption that syntactic processing precedes semantic processing. Caution is needed in using the temporal qualities of these and other ERP effects to make inferences about the timing of linguistic processes, due to the fact that the specific cognitive events underlying these all ERP-sensitive effects are not known. Nonetheless, it is interesting to note that linguistic (Jackendoff, 2000) and psycholinguistic (Bever & Townsend, 2001) theories have disputed the syntactocentric and syntax-first assumptions so prevalent in the field.

8. Several recent studies have examined ERP responses to linguistic anomalies presented in an L2 (e.g., Hahne & Friederici, 2001; Weber-Fox & Neville, 1996). These studies have in some cases produced results that are seemingly inconsistent with those reported here. For example, Weber-Fox and Neville examined the ERP response to linguistic anomalies in adult Chinese-English bilinguals who had been exposed to English at various ages, ranging from 1 to 16 years. All subjects had lived in the U.S. for a minimum of 5 years. ERPs were obtained in response to English pragmatic anomalies and several types of syntactic anomalies, including phrase structure anomalies. All groups displayed an N400 effect to pragmatic anomalies. However, the phrase structure anomalies elicited a P600-like effect only in bilinguals who were exposed to English before the age of 16; for those subjects who were first exposed to English after the age of 16, the phrase structure anomalies elicited an N400-like response. However, there are many differences between the Weber-Fox and Neville study and the study reported here, including language similarity (English-French vs. Chinese-English), study design (longitudinal vs. cross-sectional), quality and quantity of linguistic experience, the complexity of the stimuli, etc. We take our results as indicating that it is possible to see the rapid development of native-like brain responses to both pragmatic and syntactic anomalies given sufficient similarity between the L1–L2, and especially L1–L2 similarity in the syntactic rules being tested.

9. We want to stress the distinction between claiming that some ERP effect correlates highly with some stimulus manipulation and claiming that some ERP effect manifests some particular process. For example, we have claimed and continue to believe that the P600 effect is highly correlated with syntactic processing difficulty. We do not think that there is good evidence that the P600 effect reflects specifically structural reanalysis, as some have proposed.

10. In its most recent incarnations, Friederici's theory is actually a three-stage theory: the first stage is indexed by an "ELAN" effect between 100 and 300 ms, the second stage by the LAN effect, and the third stage by the P600 effect. These effects are claimed to reflect detection of a word category anomaly, detection of a morphosyntactic anomaly, and syntactic reanalysis, respectively. We have reduced the stages to two for ease of exposition; our reasoning applies equally well to a two- or three-stage model.

11. Predictions about what type of brain response should be elicited by this anomaly depend largely on one's theory of Japanese grammar. Having two nouns assigned the same case (that is, the same thematic role) might be viewed as a syntactic problem or a thematic–semantic problem. The uncertainty about how a Japanese speaker would respond to these anomalies was one of the primary motivations for the experiment.

12. A simple statistical test exists for determining whether a biphasic LAN-P600 response seen in a grand average waveform is biphasic or monophasic for individuals. If subjects show either the LAN or the P600 (but not both) in response to a syntactic anomaly, then the effect sizes (i.e., the amplitude difference between the well-formed and ill-formed conditions) will be negatively correlated (indicating that as one effect gets larger, the other gets smaller). In the Inoue and Osterhout study, the correlation between the LAN and P600 effect sizes was robustly negative. This test can be applied to any relevant data set.

Chapter 15
Gender or Genders Agreement?

HORACIO BARBER, ELENA SALILLAS, AND
MANUEL CARREIRAS

15.1 INTRODUCTION

Gender is an important feature that plays a crucial role in agreement. In Spanish, as in other Romance languages, there are three types of gender, that is, semantic, grammatical, and morphological. Semantic gender refers to the biological sex, masculine or feminine, of the word referent in the real world. Thus, only animate nouns with animate referents (especially with human referents) usually have semantic gender. Grammatical gender is a formal characteristic of many words. Because this is an arbitrary characteristic without any conceptual relationship, different words with closely related referents can have different gender forms (e.g., two synonyms can display different grammatical gender), and the same concept across different languages can be represented through masculine or feminine words.

Words of the same grammatical gender tend to share specific phonological properties. Morphological gender refers to the orthographic and phonological representation of grammatical gender. In Spanish, morphological gender can be marked with several suffixes. The "-a" suffix is mostly associated with feminine gender and the "-o" suffix mainly with masculine gender. There are, however, exceptions to this rule, with some feminine gender words ending in "-o" and some masculine gender words ending in "-a", and there are other less frequent suffixes such as "-dad" for feminine, and even some neutral suffixes such as "-e" that apply to both masculine and feminine gender. Finally, many words can change their suffixes under phonological rules or do not display any suffixes at all (opaque gender).

Consider the following Spanish words:

(1) *Abuelo* (grandfather)
(2) *Faro* (lighthouse_masc_)
(3) *Reloj* (clock_masc_)
(4) *Rey* (king)

According to grammatical gender, the four words are masculine, but from a conceptual point of view, only (1) and (4) have semantic gender because only these gender forms refer to the sex of the referent in opposition to "grandmother" and "queen," respectively. Furthermore, only (1) and (2) have morphological gender because only these words display at the end of the word the suffix "–o," the canonical suffix for the masculine-singular form in Spanish, while (3) and (4) do not show any gender marking. It is worth noting that the gender value at any one of these levels is not a reliable indicator of its value at another level.

Gender features play an important role in determining agreement between words in noun phrases or in the selection of pronominal forms. Gender is marked in nouns, adjectives, articles and pronouns. Establishing agreement relationships between words is a relevant aspect of sentence comprehension and production, especially in Romance languages, which have an overt agreement system among the different elements in sentences. Thus, Spanish relies very heavily on agreement, in contrast to other languages such as English, for which word order is more important than agreement as a grammatical constraint. For instance, in Spanish, all the words in a noun phrase (NP)—determiners, adjectives, and nouns—must agree in number and gender. This way, in the NP *El faro alto* (*The*$_{masc}$ *high*$_{masc}$ *lighthouse*$_{masc}$) the three words are masculine and singular. Similarly, a postverbal adjective has to agree in gender and number with the NP (e.g., *El faro alto es luminoso*; *The*$_{masc}$ *high*$_{masc}$ *lighthouse*$_{masc}$ *is bright*$_{masc}$). The agreement relationships are asymmetrical because adjectives agree with nouns, not vice versa. Consequently, the adjective differs from the noun in that it lacks gender semantic characteristics; in fact, adjectives inherit semantic features from the noun they agree with.

The two different kinds of information carried by the two types of gender (semantic vs. grammatical) can be used to investigate grammatical as opposed to semantic aspects of language processing. Some previous behavioral studies have addressed the use of semantic and grammatical gender information in the interpretation of pronouns in Spanish (Carreiras, Garnham, & Oakhill, 1993; Garnham, Oakhill, Erhlich, & Carreiras, 1995). Sentences were presented containing two antecedents followed by a pronoun referring to one of these. The two antecedents could be of the same gender (e.g., both feminine), thus no gender cue was available, or of two different genders (one masculine and the other feminine), so a gender cue was available for pronoun interpretation. The authors also manipulated whether the two antecedents were of semantic gender or of arbitrary gender. By using a moving-window methodology they found that the sentences containing the pronoun were read faster when the two antecedents were of different gender (gender cue) as compared to when they were of the same gender (no gender cue). This gender cue advantage was similar when the two antecedents were of semantic gender or of grammatical gender. However, questions asked immediately after each sentence only showed a gender cue advantage for semantic gender which led the authors to conclude that semantic gender effects last longer that grammatical gender effects, although the two genders had similar early effects. Nonetheless, another study carried out by Deutsch, Bentin, and Katz (1999) in Hebrew using gender agreement relations between other different constituents has shown that the semantic information carried by semantic gender influenced the agreement processes differently from grammatical gender.

Therefore, comparison between the response to grammatical and semantic gender disagreement using fine-grained methodologies such as ERPs is desirable since it can help to determine the influence of semantic information (semantic gender information) on grammatical agreement processes (see Osterhout et al., chapter 14, this volume, and van Berkum, chapter 13, this volume, for the advantages of ERPs to capture the time course of cognitive processes). This way, the study of the gender agreement process can shed some light on the more general debate regarding how and when semantics and syntax interact during language comprehension. Therefore, let us summarize what has been found in gender agreement using ERPs.

15.1.1 Event-Related Potentials and Gender Agreement

Using the ERP technique, Osterhout and Mobley (1995) compared gender agreement violations between a reflexive pronoun and its antecedent, and between a personal pronoun and its antecedent in English. The effects of gender violations were not different from the effects of number agreement violations but were different from semantic violations. Semantic violations[1] usually produce a significant enhancement of the N400 component, a negative waveform associated with integration processes (Kutas & Hillyard, 1980; Kutas & Federmeier, 2000). The words that violated agreement rules produced an increase of the P600. The P600, also labeled Syntactic Positive Shift (SPS), is a large positive wave with an onset at about 500 ms and a duration of several hundred milliseconds, which has been reported in response to different kinds of syntactic anomalies (Hagoort, Brown, & Osterhout, 1999). The results of Osterhout and Mobley (1995) point to the syntactic nature of gender agreement more as part of the form than the meaning of language, which is note-worthy, since in English gender is semantically based and usually is not marked through overt morphological indicators. Following government and binding theory, the authors propose that gender features, even when semantically based, might become in a sense independent of the lexical item in order to percolate up to the noun phrase node from the nouns within the sentence.

In a later study, Osterhout, Bersick, and McLaughlin (1997) analyzed the effect of social gender stereotypes in English. Gender agreement violations of reflexive pronouns showed effects on the P600 even when the gender of the subject was not explicit but was inferred from the stereotype (e.g., *The doctor prepared herself...*). This supports the idea that even stereotypical gender could be coded in the representation of some words as an autonomous feature involved in grammatical agreement rules.

In contrast to English, languages such as Dutch, German, Spanish, and Hebrew distinguish between semantic and grammatical gender. Some recent investigations have taken advantage of this to investigate whether the same processing mechanisms underlie agreement for both types of gender. Schmitt, Lamers, and Münte (2002) assessed gender agreement during personal pronoun processing in German. They reported N400 and P600 effects in response to the agreement violation between a pronoun and its animate antecedent (semantic gender). In addition, they used dimin-utive nouns as antecedents to try to separate semantic from syntactic aspects in agreement processing. In German, diminutive nouns have neuter gender and agree with neuter pronouns but have masculine/feminine determiners, thus, a mismatch of genders is produced in syntactically well-formed sentences. The authors consider this mismatch a semantic violation in opposition to the purely syntactic agreement violation. They found a P600 effect in response to agreement violations between a gender-marked pronoun and a diminutive neuter noun, indicating that similar syntactic reanalysis processes are engaged during the comprehension of these sentences and the sentences with nondiminutive antecedents. Double violations (a feminine pronoun that disagreed with a diminutive neuter noun with male referent) produced greater amplitudes than single violations (a masculine pronoun that disagreed with a diminutive neuter noun with male referent), pointing to the additive effects triggered by semantic and syntactic factors.

It is noteworthy that the previously described ERP effects were found with violations of semantic gender agreement in pronouns. Hagoort and Brown (1999) manipulated in Dutch the agreement between an article and a noun-within-NP in order to ascertain whether grammatical gender agreement was a semantic or a syntactically based process. Results showed a P600 component effect when violation occurred in the middle of the sentence and an N400–P600 complex at the end of the sentence. Hagoort and Brown concluded that information of grammatical gender agreement processing is not a content-driven process but a syntactic-form-driven process. The N400 effect recorded at the end of the sentence would reflect global sentence integration factors.

In order to study the possible interactions between syntactic and semantic information during agreement processes in German, Gunter, Friederici, and Schriefers (2000) manipulated the cloze probability of a target word and its grammatical gender agreement in the same experimental design. Gender disagreement produced the P600 effect preceded by a left anterior negativity (LAN) effect, while semantic manipulation (cloze probability) produced the classic N400 effect. The LAN effect has been also found with a disparate set of syntactic violations and generally linked to early aspects of syntactic analysis (Friederici, 1995). LAN and N400 share their polarity and sometimes their latency but, while the N400 shows a centro-parietal distribution, the LAN effect is localized in anterior zones and usually lateralized to the left side. In Gunter et als.' (2000) experiment, the N400 effect was not influenced by the syntactic manipulation, and the LAN effect was not influenced by the semantic manipulation. However, there was an interaction between both manipulations in the P600 due to the increase of amplitude of this component for words only with a high cloze probability that violated gender agreement. The authors conclude that syntactic and semantic information are processed autonomously in a first stage, but both types of information interact in a second stage. Moreover, the presence of the LAN effect in this study is interesting as this effect was not present in the gender violations of the experiments described below. A study in Spanish (Demestre, Meltzer, García-Albea, & Vigil, 1999) reported results that could fit in with the LAN-P600 pattern in response to semantic gender agreement violations, although differences in the design (i.e., auditory presentation) and data analysis make comparison with the German study far from straightforward.

Wicha, Moreno, and Kutas (2003) also studied the influence of semantic expectations in grammatical gender agreement in Spanish. They presented a picture in the middle of a sentence, substituting for a word that was semantically predictable or not by the context. They reported a negativity between 500 and 700 ms in response to the nonagreement of the gender associated with the picture and the gender of the preceding article, and this effect was independent from that of semantic expectations. The authors considered this effect to be the result of gender disagreement, although with characteristics different from that of classical syntactic components as the picture was a stimulus of a different nature. The lack of the classical syntactic components has been found also when gender disagreement is produced in Spanish noun–adjective word pairs presented without a sentence context. In this case, only the N400 effect was reported (Barber & Carreiras, 2003).

Finally, in a study closer to the present experiment, Deutsch and Bentin (2001) analyzed the role of semantic and syntactic information during agreement processing by comparing grammatical and semantic gender processing in Hebrew. Participants read sentences in which the sentential subject was an animate or an inanimate noun, and this noun could be morphologically overtly marked or unmarked. In these sentences, the subject–predicate gender agreement was manipulated (e.g., *the woman saw that the boy/diamond*$_{masc}$ *had fallen*$_{masc/fem}$ *into the pond*). An N400 effect was found after gender agreement violation only for the animate condition (semantic gender) and this effect did not interact with markedness. The N400 effect in the animate condition could show the mismatch of the conceptual information carried by semantic gender. In addition, the violation of either semantic or grammatical gender agreement resulted in a P600 effect, but this effect interacted with the markedness as it was only significant for masculine-plural-marked predicates, that is, only marked forms elicited the P600 effect. In contrast with the Gunter et al. (2000) study, the authors claim that the lack of interaction of the P600 with animacy indicates that the process reflected by this component is not sensitive to semantic information. They relate this component to initial on-line syntactic processing and therefore consider that it is not exclusively associated with the reanalysis processes. In addition, a very early negative effect was reported in response to all the disagreement conditions, but this effect did not fit either in latency or in distribution with the LAN effect previously linked with agreement violations.

In summary (see Table 15.1), all the ERP studies showed a P600 effect in response to gender agreement violations with both types of gender (Osterhout & Mobley, 1995; Osterhout et al., 1997; Schmitt et al., 2002; Hagoort & Brown, 1999; Gunter et al., 2000; Demestre et al., 1999; Deutsch & Bentin, 2001). As an exception, the P600 effect was not found with morphologically unmarked words in Hebrew (Deutsch & Bentin 2001). In a Spanish (Demestre et al. 1999) and a German (Gunter et al., 2000) experiment, the P600 effect was preceded by a LAN effect. In addition to these syntactic related indexes, an N400 effect as response to semantic gender violation was reported in a German study (Schmitt et al., 2002) and in the Hebrew study (Deutsch & Bentin, 2001). On the other hand, the N400 effect was not found in other studies that analyzed the semantic gender violation in English (Osterhout & Mobley, 1995; Osterhout et al., 1997) and in Spanish (Demestre et al., 1999).

15.1.2 The Present Experiment

The goal of the present study was to further investigate the agreement processes in Spanish involving grammatical and semantic gender. Previous studies in several

Table 15.1. **ERP Effects Obtained in Gender Agreement Violations**

	Target Word	Language	Gender	P600	N400	LAN
Gunter et al., 2000	noun	German	grammatical	*	—	*
Hagoort & Brown, 1999	noun	Dutch	grammatical	*	—	—
Deutch & Bentin, 2001	adjective	Hebrew	grammatical	*	—	—
			semantic	*	*	—
Smicht et al., 2002	personal pronoun	German	semantic	*	*	—
Osterhout & Mobley, 1995	personal pronoun	English	semantic	*	—	—
Osterhout et al., 1997	reflexive pronoun	English	semantic	*	—	—
Demestre et al., 1999	adjective	Spanish	semantic	*	—	*

languages have shown a mixed picture of semantic and grammatical gender agreement effects (see Table 15.1). Thus, in the present experiment, both types of gender were examined under the same circumstances, with transparent gender, in a very simple agreement relationship in Spanish, a language in which agreement processes are crucial for syntactic analysis. The effects of semantic or grammatical gender agreement were studied in sentences in which agreement rules between the NP and a post-verbal adjective were violated. We used animate nouns in the semantic gender condition[2] while all the nouns were unanimate in the grammatical gender condition. We studied the ERPs associated with agreement in the context of reading sentences presented word by word. According to previous results (Demestre et al., 1999; Gunter et al., 2000), LAN and P600 effects were expected in response to agreement violations with both types of gender. However, possible differences in the N400 component in response to semantic gender disagreement or modulations of the syntactic ERP effects by the type of gender could also be predicted (see Deutsch & Bentin, 2001; Schmitt et al., 2002), which would indicate the influence of semantic information in the agreement processes.

15.1.3 Method

15.1.3.1 Participants

A total of 24 undergraduate students, 14 females and 10 males, participated in the experiment in exchange for course credit. All of them were native Spanish speakers with no history of neurological or psychiatric impairment and with normal or corrected-to-normal vision. Ages ranged from 19 to 26 years (mean = 20.8 years). All participants were right-handed as assessed with an abridged Spanish version of the Edinburgh Handedness Inventory (Oldfield, 1971): LQ > + 50. Five of the participants had left-handed relatives. Data of six additional participants were rejected before the analysis because of too many artifacts in the EEG record.

15.1.3.2 Stimuli

For the study, 160 experimental sentences and 160 filler sentences were generated. Experimental sentences were formed with a noun phrase that had to agree in gender with a predicate adjective (agreement in gender between nouns and adjectives is mandatory in Spanish). This adjective was taken as the target word and its gender was manipulated to produce agreement or disagreement with the noun phrase. Between two and four filler words were included after the adjective in order to avoid wrap-up effects on the target word. The noun phrase in half of the experimental sentences was formed by an inanimate noun with only grammatical gender, so in this case gender was always a strictly morphosyntactic feature without semantic significance. The other half of the experimental sentences was formed with an animate noun with grammatical and semantic gender indicating the biological sex of the referent. Half of these two lists of sentences (with grammatical or semantic gender) included an agreement violation in the adjective gender, and the other half consisted of well-formed sentences. In short, the adjectives were manipulated to create four different conditions:

a) Agreement with grammatical gender.
   El faro es luminoso *y alto.*
   The_{masc} $lighthouse_{masc}$ *is* $bright_{masc}$ *and high.*
b) Disagreement with grammatical gender.
   El faro es luminosa *y alto.*
   The_{masc} $lighthouse_{masc}$ *is* $bright_{fem}$ *and high.*
c) Agreement with semantic gender.
   El abuelo estaba delgado *y débil.*
   The_{masc} *grandfather was* $slim_{masc}$ *and weak.*
d) Disagreement with semantic gender.
   El abuelo estaba delgada *y débil.*
   The_{masc} *grandfather was* $slim_{fem}$ *and weak.*

Nouns and adjectives in all experimental sentences marked the morphological gender with the canonical suffixes, "-a" for feminine and "-o" for masculine. Half the nouns were feminine and half were masculine. Assignment of sentences to conditions in each list was counterbalanced across participants. Thus, each sentence occurred twice across subjects, once in each agreement or disagreement condition so that each subject only saw one form of each sentence during the experiment.

In addition, a list of 160 filler trials was introduced. Some fillers included nouns and adjectives with opaque gender (e.g., the word *reloj* [clock] lacks any explicit morphological mark) or irregular words (e.g., *mano* [hand] ends with the letter "-o" but is feminine). This type of filler was included to prevent participants from using a superficial strategy for solving the task, such as attending just to the suffixes. Half of these filler sentences had a gender agreement violation at the beginning of the sentence, between the determiner and the noun, and half had no gender agreement violation. This way, participants could not focus attention only on the position of the target adjective. In total, each subject received 320 sentences, half of which agreed and the other half disagreed.

15.1.4 Procedure

Participants were seated comfortably in a darkened sound-attenuated chamber. All stimuli were presented on a high-resolution computer that was positioned at eye level 80–90 cm in front of the participant. The words were displayed in black lowercase letters against a gray background.

Participants performed a syntactic judgment task, that is, they said whether the sentence was well-formed or not. A response button was positioned beneath each thumb. For half of the participants the right button was used to signal the "yes" response, and the left button was assigned the "no" response. For the remaining subjects the order was reversed. Thus, the assignment of buttons to hands was counterbalanced across participants.

The sequence of events in each trial is described as follows: First, a fixation point ("+") appeared in the center of the screen and remained there for 300 ms. This fixation point was followed by a blank screen interval of 300 ms, then the sentence was displayed word by word. Each word appeared for 300 ms and was followed by a 300-ms blank interval (SOA = 600 ms). Participants were instructed to respond after the last word of the sentence. At that moment, a question mark was presented and remained there up to a maximum of 2000 ms or until the participant's response. The intertrial interval varied randomly between 2000 and 2500 ms. All sentences were presented in a different pseudorandom order for each participant in two different blocks with a break of 10 min between blocks in which the subject could rest and the impedances were checked.

A total of 10 warm-up sentences were provided at the beginning of the session and were repeated if necessary. Participants were also asked to avoid eye-movements and blinks during the interval when the fixation asterisk was not present, and they were directed to favor accuracy over speed in their responses. Each session lasted approximately 1∫ hr.

15.1.5 EEG Recording

Scalp voltages were collected from Ag/AgCl electrodes using a 128-channel Geodesic Sensor Net. Figure 15.1 shows the schematic distribution of the recording sites. The vertex electrode was used as reference, and the recording was re-referred off-line to linked mastoids. Eye movements and blinks were monitored with supra- and infra-orbital electrodes and with electrodes in the external canthi. Interelectrode impedances were kept below 30 KΩ (amplifiers input impedance >200 MΩ). EEG was filtered with an analogue bandpass filter of 0.01–100 Hz (50 Hz notch filter) and a digital 35 Hz low-pass filter was applied before analysis. The signals were sampled continuously throughout the experiment with a sampling rate of 250 Hz.

15.1.6 Analysis

Epochs of the EEG corresponding to 1200 ms after word onset presentation were averaged and analyzed. Baseline correction was performed using the average EEG activity in the 100 ms preceding the onset of the target word as a reference signal value. Following baseline correction, epochs with simultaneous artifacts in at least

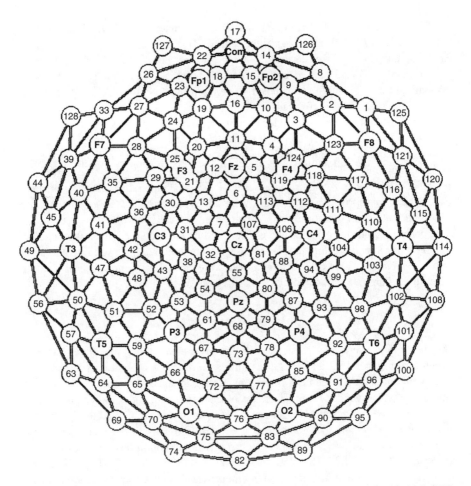

Figure 15.1. Schematic flat representation of the 129 electrode positions from which EEG activity was recorded (front of head is at top). Channel nomenclature is by number. Approximate international 10–20 system localizations are marked.

10 channels were rejected. This operation resulted in the exclusion of approximately 15% of the trials, which was evenly distributed among the different experimental conditions. Furthermore, electrodes with a high level of rejected trials (>10%) were substituted by the average value of the group of nearest electrodes.

Averaging was conducted off-line using only samples recorded in trials in which correct responses had been made in a grammatical judgment task. Separate ERPs were formed for each of the experimental conditions, each of the subjects, and each of the electrode sites.

Nine regions of interest were computed out of the 129 electrodes, each containing the mean of a group of electrodes. The regions were (see electrode numbers in Figure 15.1): midline-anterior (5, 6, 11, and 12), midline-central (7, 55, 107, and 129), midline-posterior (62, 68, and 73), left-anterior (13, 20, 21, 25, 28, 29, 30, 34, 35, 36, and 40), left-central (31, 32, 37, 38, 41, 42, 43, 46, 47, 48, and 50), left-posterior

(51, 52, 53, 54, 58, 59, 60, 61, 66, 67, and 72), right-anterior (4, 111, 112, 113, 116, 117, 118, 119, 122, 123, and 124), right-central (81, 88, 94, 99, 102, 103, 104, 105, 106, 109, and 110), right-posterior (77, 78, 79, 80, 85, 86, 87, 92, 93, 97, and 98).

The analyses were carried out in different temporal windows on the basis of calculations of mean amplitude values. Different repeated measures ANOVAs for each type of measures were performed, including the agreement relation (agreement or disagreement) and the type of gender (grammatical or semantic) as within factors. In addition, electrode regions (anterior, central, and posterior) were entered as another within-subject factor. Separate analyses were carried out for the midline regions and the lateral regions. Analysis of the lateral regions included the hemisphere factor with two levels (left/right). A significance level of .05 was adopted for all the statistical tests. Where appropriate, critical values were adjusted using the Geisser–Greenhouse (1959) correction for violation of the assumption of sphericity. Effects related to the electrode regions factor or hemisphere factor will be only reported when they interact with the experimental manipulations. In cases of interaction of any experimental factor with the *electrode region* or *hemisphere*, data were normalized following the vectorial scaled procedure recommended by McCarthy and Wood (1985).

15.2 RESULTS

The ERP grand averages, time-locked to the onset of the target adjectives, are represented in Figures 15.2 and 15.3 over nine recording sites. Figure 15.2 shows the agreement and the disagreement conditions in the sentences with a noun phrase with only grammatical gender. Grand averages of the agreement and disagreement conditions of sentences with semantic gender in the noun phrase are plotted in Figure 15.3. Visual inspection of both figures reveals clear differences in the responses to the disagreement conditions with respect to the agreement conditions, these differences are observed within the 350 to 450 ms window and in the 500 to 700 ms window as well. Between 350 and 450 ms, disagreement waves showed more negative values than those in the agreement condition. These effects are present at anterior electrodes and especially on the left side of the scalp, fitting with the previously described LAN effect. In both figures, the negative effect is followed by a typical P600 effect, showing larger amplitudes for the disagreement conditions than for the agreement ones. These positive differences have a posterior distribution over the midline, slightly lateralized to the right side at the end of the temporal window.

Statistical analysis supported these observations. The ANOVA with the average values of the 350–450 ms time epoch, including the factor *gender agreement* (agreement and disagreement), the factor *type of gender* (semantic and grammatical), and the factor *electrode regions* (anterior, central, and posterior), indicated a *gender agreement* and *electrode regions* interaction in the midline analysis ($F_{2,22}$ = 3.85; $p < .05$; $\varepsilon = .78$), effect that was maintained after the data normalization ($F_{2,22} = 3.97$; $p < .05$). The lateral regions analysis failed to show any significant effect. Even though the interaction of gender agreement with the factor *electrode* in the lateral analysis was not significant, additional ANOVAs for each electrode area were conducted separately. A *gender agreement* effect was found only in the

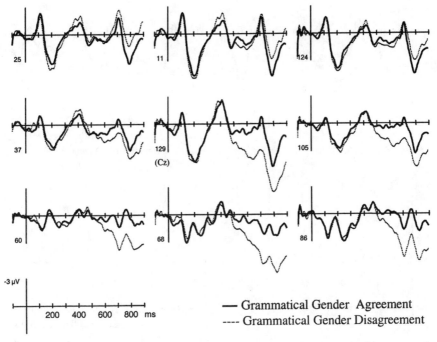

-3 μV

200 400 600 800 ms

—— Grammatical Gender Agreement
---- Grammatical Gender Disagreement

Figure 15.2. Sentences with only grammatical gender in the agreement condition versus the disagreement condition. In this and the following figures, ERPs to the target words (i.e., adjectives) are shown in the three midline, three left, and three right hemisphere electrodes. Onset presentation is at 0 ms and negative amplitude is plotted upward.

anterior area of the midline ($F_{1,23}$ = 4.64; p < .05), in the left anterior area ($F_{1,23}$ = 9.73; p < .01), and the left central ($F_{1,23}$ = 4.36; p < .05) area. No effects of *type of gender* or interactions with this factor were found in any of these analyses.

The ANOVAs for the time epoch from 500 to 700 ms with the same factors as the previous window, *gender agreement, type of gender,* and *electrode regions,* revealed a significant main effect of *gender agreement* in the midline analysis ($F_{1,23}$ = 10.13; p < .01), as well as an interaction between the *gender agreement* and the *electrode regions* factors in the lateral regions analysis ($F_{2,22}$ = 16.30; p < .001), interaction that was maintained after data normalization ($F_{2,22}$ = 18.59; p < .001). Likewise, there was an interaction between the *type of gender* and the *electrode regions* factors both in the midline analysis ($F_{2,22}$ = 7.22; p < .01; ε = .61) and the lateral regions analysis ($F_{2,22}$ = 4.01; p < .05), and this effect was maintained after data normalization in the midline ($F_{2,22}$ = 6.53; p < .05) and was marginally significant in the lateral sites ($F_{2,22}$ = 2.8; p = .09). However, there was no interaction between the factors *gender agreement* and *type of gender*. The different distribution of the two effects was manifested in the ANOVAs realized for each area separately (p < .05); the *gender agreement* effect was present in central and posterior areas both in the midline and the lateral sites, while the *type of gender* effect was present in anterior and central areas of the midline sites as well as in the anterior and central sites of the left side. The type of gender effect will be described in more detail below.

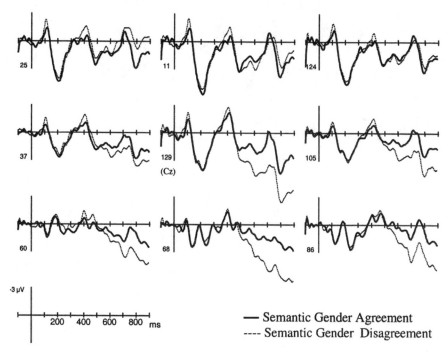

Figure 15.3. Sentences with semantic gender in the agreement condition versus the disagreement condition.

The 700–900 window analysis showed an interaction between the factor *gender agreement* and the *electrode regions* in the midline analysis ($F_{2,22} = 36.76$; $p < .001$; $\varepsilon = .71$; with normalized data, $F_{2,22} = 21$; $p < .001$), as well as a three-way interaction between the factors *gender agreement, electrode regions,* and *hemisphere* in the lateral regions analysis ($F_{2,22} = 5.5$; $p < .01$; $\varepsilon = .77$), and the two-way interaction between *gender agreement and electrode regions* after the data normalization ($F_{2,22} = 4.38$ $p < .001$). This three-way interaction reflects the right-posterior distribution of the effect in this window. The factor *type of gender* did not show any reliable effects in this window.

15.2.1 Type of Gender Effect

The previous analyses have shown differences between sentences with grammatical gender and sentences with semantic gender only in the 500–700 window but this effect did not interact with the agreement violations. Figure 15.4 compares the waves of the two agreement conditions. These differ from each other in the 500–700 temporal window with the semantic condition amplitudes more positive than those of the grammatical condition. Comparison of the two disagreement condition waves can be found in Figure 15.5, showing a similar effect. Importantly, the *type of gender* effects present a different spatial distribution from the violation effects; they are bigger in the central and anterior electrodes. In addition, visual inspection of these figures suggests, in contrast with the *gender agreement* effect, that the onset of the

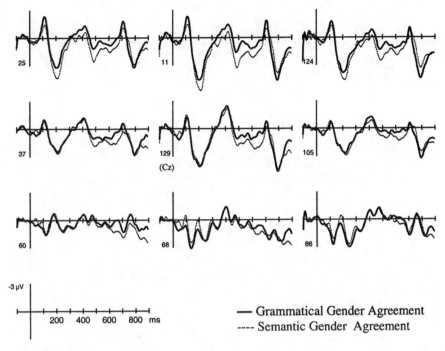

Figure 15.4. Well-formed sentences with only grammatical gender versus well-formed sentences with semantic gender.

type of gender effect could be slightly earlier, around 450 ms. In order to study this possible difference, additional analyses were performed using a short time window from 450 to 500 ms. Analysis in this window again indicated an interaction between the *type of gender* and the *electrode regions* factors both in the midline analysis ($F_{2,22} = 10.89$; $p < .001$; $\varepsilon = .65$) and in the lateral regions analysis ($F_{2,22} = 8.97$; $p < .01$; $\varepsilon = .61$), (normalized data, $F_{2,22} = 22$; $p < .01$ and $F_{2,22} = 3.68$; $p < .01$, respectively). However, in these latencies, there were no effects related with gender *agreement*.

15.3 DISCUSSION

The goal of this experiment was to investigate the role of semantic and morphosyntactic information associated with gender agreement processes. This was done by comparing sentences in which the gender of the noun was only a morphosyntactic characteristic with others in which the gender of the noun also implied conceptual information under two different conditions: well-formed sentences and sentences that violated gender agreement between the noun and the adjective. ERP comparisons showed two main results.

First, violations of both types of gender agreement produced two effects that have been typically associated with syntactic processes: a negativity around 400 ms with a left-anterior distribution that fits with the so-called LAN, and an inverse

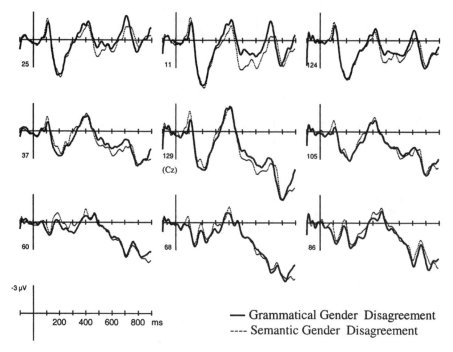

— Grammatical Gender Disagreement
---- Semantic Gender Disagreement

Figure 15.5. Ungrammatical sentences with only grammatical gender versus ungrammatical sentences with semantic gender.

polarity effect that begins around 500 ms and stays for more than 400 ms, which corresponds with the P600. The distribution of the P600 effect until 700 ms is symmetrical in the central and posterior areas, and from that point on it is slightly lateralized towards the right side in the posterior areas. The magnitude of these effects was equivalent for the violations of both kinds of genders.

Second, there were differences between the waves of morphosyntactic gender and semantic gender conditions, both when there was a violation of agreement and when the sentence was well-formed. These differences were reliable between 450 ms and 700 ms and more prominent in the anterior areas. The effect of gender-type and the first phase of P600, although simultaneous in time, presented different distributions across electrodes and were additive in the central areas. The fact that these effects were independent suggests that they may reflect the operation of different processes, which allows us to consider them separately.

15.3.1 Agreement Violations Effects

According to previous interpretations, the LAN effect could be reflecting the detection of a mismatch between the features of the target word (the adjective) and those of the preceding NP (Münte, Matzke, & Johannes, 1997), the difficulty of integrating these characteristics in a syntactic structure (Gunter et al., 2000), or an increase of memory demand implied in these processes (Coulson, King, & Kutas, 1998). In a similar way, the P600 could also reflect the impossibility of a later processing of syntactical integration (Osterhout & Mobley, 1995), the reanalysis and repair processes (Gunter et al. 2000), or a more general activation process associated to anomaly detection (Coulson et al. 1998). In any case, it seems that there is considerable evidence that these two effects are sensitive to manipulations of sentence syntax.

Some behavioral data point to the implication of semantic information in agreement processes (e.g., Deutsch et al., 1999), and some approaches propose continuous interaction between gender and semantic information during language comprehension (Bates, Devescovi, Hernandez, & Pizzamiglio, 1996). The N400 effect has been associated with difficulties in integrating lexical-semantic information, appearing in response to the disruption of conceptual coherence or of the expectations generated during language comprehension (Kutas & Federmeier, 2000). It could be thought that semantic gender information is involved in meaning integration processes during the agreement process, and so semantic gender mismatch could result in an increase in the amplitude of the N400. In fact, this result was reported by Deutsch and Bentin (2001). In an experiment in Hebrew, they presented sentences similar to those of the present study in which agreement between NP and predicate was or was not violated at the same time as subject animacy was manipulated. They found effects on the N400 only when semantic gender agreement was violated. Our data show differences around 400 ms but with a left-anterior distribution, whereas an overlapping between the agreement condition waves and those of disagreement was found in the areas where the N400 component is usually obtained, which suggests that there does not seem to be any modulation of this component. Although Spanish and Hebrew are languages with a richly inflected morphology in which agreement plays a relevant role in building the syntactic structure, there are important differences between the gender systems of both languages that could be producing this discrepancy in the results. In a similar way, Schmitt et al. (2002) reported an N400 effect when semantic gender agreement was violated, but in this work they manipulated anaphoric coreferences that involved long-distance relationships and discourse integration processes, so it is difficult to establish an adequate comparison with our design. In any case, our results fit better with other studies that did not find the N400 effect in gender agreement violations when these implied semantic gender (e.g., Osterhout & Mobley, 1995; Osterhout et al., 1997; Demestre et al., 1999). In this sense, the work of Osterhout et al. that has previously been mentioned is important, in that the nonagreement with the stereotypical gender of the subject produced an effect on the P600 but no effect on the N400. A semantic effect could also be expected because the stereotype associated with the subject of the sentences generated a pragmatic expectation about the gender of the reflexive pronoun that was afterwards violated. Therefore, these results also suggest that semantic information of gender does not seem to be implicated in the agreement process.

Even if semantic gender agreement does not trigger semantic integration processes, another possibility is that it affects syntactic agreement processes at later times. In the case of the P600, Gunter et al. (2000) points out that late syntactic integration processes can be modulated by the previous semantic processes. Nonetheless, the present results do not sustain that semantic gender information is involved in syntactic agreement processes because there was no influence of the semantic characteristics of gender on processes related to syntactic integration, reanalysis, or detection of the nonagreement. The magnitude of the LAN and P600 effects was the same when agreement was violated with an animate subject with semantic gender or with a nonanimate subject with grammatical-only gender. Therefore, our data do not indicate any implication of semantic information in the detection and reanalysis processes of agreement violations, supporting previous claims that gender agreement is exclusively a syntactically driven process (Osterhout & Mobley, 1995; Hagoort & Brown, 1999).

In order to explain the exclusively syntactic nature of agreement processes, we should consider that agreement is based on the matching of gender features of the same nature between two words. In Spanish, as in other languages, determiners, adjectives and pronouns by themselves lack gender semantic characteristics, assuming the gender form of the noun they agree with.[3] In other words, only nouns actually have independent semantic gender characteristics. The integration of semantic gender characteristics is impossible when only one of the parts has these characteristics. Consequently, even in languages in which grammatical gender is almost nonexistent, as in English, the words with semantic gender (even stereotypically) need to have associated autonomous features of grammatical gender that could agree with other words such as pronouns that by themselves lack specific semantic referents.

15.3.2 Type of gender effect

The other intriguing effect is the type of gender. Our data have shown differences in the voltages associated with the adjective when the NP was animate as compared to when it was inanimate, independently of whether there was a grammatical violation of agreement. These differences were found between the 450 and 700 ms with an anterior distribution.

The fact that semantic gender information is not playing a differential role in the agreement process does not mean that such information could not be recovered or activated at the same time as syntactic agreement occurs. Independently of syntactic structure construction, this information is valuable for the creation of a representation of the message because the completion of the meaning of the adjective requires consideration of the information from the noun. Activation of the semantic gender information would not necessarily imply the triggering of agreement in a strict sense (see preceding text), because the adjective would passively assume the semantic gender characteristics of the NP. The effects obtained could reflect the demands of activating the gender information of the noun or of creating a new representation. This representation would have to consider the attributes of semantic gender but not necessarily those of the grammatical gender. For example, if we imagine *a thin grandfather*, the mental representation we would generate will include the attributes of the adjective *thin* applied to a concrete subject (i. e., elderly person) with specific male sex characteristics. On the contrary, the mental representation in the case of an inanimate object, for example, the case of *the high lighthouse,* does not need to incorporate any gender attribute apart from that necessary for establishing agreement. Thus, the present type of gender effect could be related with the differential activation of the information per se, or with the creation of a semantic representation rather than with a matching or agreement syntactic process.

On the other hand, taking into account that the presence of semantic gender is correlated with the animacy of the subject in our sentences, it could be argued that the effect was a more general process of animacy in sentence processing. Some previous studies show that animacy is a characteristic of nouns that is processed very early. ERP changes around 250 ms after the onset between animate and inanimate nouns have been previously observed (Weckerly & Kutas, 1999). Therefore, the differences described in the adjective could have begun much earlier in the sentence, even from the reading of the noun. For this reason, additional analyses were performed using long segments that included all the words from the beginning of the sentence to the word after the adjective, but these analyses failed to find any difference in the words previous to the adjective. Therefore, in our data, the gender effect is associated with processes that occur not earlier than after reading the adjective, and thus, it seems that they refer to activation of semantic gender information—for example, animacy as one of the features associated with semantic gender—rather than different demands in the maintenance of that information.

To sum up, the two main findings reported in the present paper are: (a) both semantic and morphosyntactic gender agreement processes produced LAN and P600 effects, showing that agreement is mainly a syntactic process; (b) differences in the time window from 450 to 700 ms with an anterior distribution were found between semantic and morphosyntactic gender, but they did not affect the agreement processes. Although we cannot be precise about the functional origin of the differences produced by gender type, we propose that they are related to differential gender information activation processes but independent of grammatical agreement processes, or, at least, of those processes involved in the detection and repair of violations which appear to be of a purely syntactic nature and are not affected by semantic gender information.

Further research is needed to investigate whether differences between semantic and morphosyntactic gender representation-activation still occur independently of animacy, what the nature of such differences is, and whether semantic gender influences the agreement process differently in other, more complex structures.

15.4 ACKNOWLEDGMENTS

Preparation of this chapter was supported by grant BSO2000-0862 (Spanish Ministry of Science and Technology). We would like to thank Chuck Clifton for comments on an earlier draft of this chapter.

References

Barber, H., & Carreiras, M. (2003). Integrating gender and number Information in Spanish word pairs: An ERP study. *Cortex, 39.*

Bates, E., Devescovi, A., Hernandez, A., & Pizzamiglio, L. (1996). Gender priming in Italian. *Perception and Psychophysics, 58,* 922–1004.

Carreiras, M., Garnham, A., & Oakhill, J. (1993). The use of superficial and meaning-based representations in interpreting pronouns: Evidence from Spanish. *European Journal of Cognitive Psychology, 5,* 93–116.

Coulson, S., King, J., & Kutas, M. (1998). Expect the unexpect: Event-related brain response to morphosyntactic violations. *Language and Cognitive Processes, 13,* 21–58.

Demestre, J., Meltzer, S., García-Albea, J. E., & Vigil, A. (1999). Identifying the null subject: Evidence from event-related brain potentials. *Journal of Psycholinguistic Research, 28*(3), 293–312.

Deutsch, A., & Bentin, S. (2001). Syntactic and semantic factors in processing gender agreement in Hebrew: Evidence from ERPs and eyes movements. *Journal of Memory and Language, 45,* 200–224.

Deutsch, A., Bentin, S., & Katz, L. (1999). Semantic influence on processing syntactic rules of agreement: Evidence from Hebrew. *Journal of Psycholinguistic Research, 28,* 515–535.

Friederici, A. D. (1995). The time course of syntactic activation during language processing: a model based on neuropsychological and neurophysiological data. *Brain and Language, 50,* 259–281.

Garnham, A., Oakhill, J., Erhlich, M. F., & Carreiras, M. (1995). Representations and processes in the interpretation of pronouns: New evidence from Spanish and French. *Journal of Memory and Language, 34,* 41–62.

Geisser, S., & Greenhouse, S. (1959). On methods in the analysis of profile data. *Psychometrika, 24,* 95–112.

Gunter, T. C., Friederici, A. D., & Schriefers, H. (2000). Syntactic gender and semantic expectancy: ERPs reveal early autonomy and late interaction. *Journal of Cognitive Neuroscience, 12*(4), 556–568.

Hagoort, P., & Brown, C. (1999). Gender electrified: ERP evidence on the syntactic nature of gender processing. *Journal of Psycholinguistic Research, 28,* 6, 715–728.

Hagoort, P., Brown, C., & Osterhout, L. (1999). The neurocognition of syntactic processing. In C. Brown & P. Hagoort (Eds.), *Neurocognition of Language.* Oxford: Oxford University Press.

Kutas, M., & Federmeier, K. D. (2000). Electrophysiology reveals semantic memory use in language comprehension. *Trends in Cognitive Sciences, 4*(12), 463–470.

Kutas, M., & Hillyard, S. (1980). Reading senseless sentences: Brain potentials reflect semantic incongruity. *Science, 207,* 203–205.

McCarthy, G., & Wood, C. (1985). Scalp distributions of event-related potentials: an ambiguity associated with analysis of variance models. *Electroencephalography and Clinical Neurophysiology, 62,* 203–208.

Münte, T. F., Matzke, M., & Johannes, S. (1997) Brain activity associated with syntactic incongruencies in words and pseudo-words. *Journal of Cognitive Neuroscience, 9,* 318–329.

Oldfield, R. C. (1971). The assessment and analysis of handedness: The Edinburgh Inventory. *Neuropsychologia, 9,* 97–113.

Osterhout, L., Bersick, M., & McLaughlin, J. (1997). Brain potentials reflect violations of gender stereotypes. *Memory and Cognition, 25*(3), 273–285.

Osterhout, L., & Mobley, L. A. (1995). Event-related potentials elicited by failure to agree. *Journal of Memory and Language, 34,* 739–773.

Schmitt, B. M., Lamers, M., & Münte, T. (2002). Electrophysiological estimates of biological and syntactic gender violation during pronoun processing. *Cognitive Brain Research, 14,* 333–346.

Weckerly, J., & Kutas, M. (1999). An electrophysiological analysis of animacy effects in the processing of object relative sentences, *Psychophysiology, 36,* 559–570.

Wicha, N. Y., Moreno, E., & Kutas, M. (2003). Expecting gender: An event related brain potential study on the role of grammatical gender in comprehending a line drawing within a written sentence in Spanish. *Cortex, 39.*

Notes

1. It is important to distinguish semantic violations from violation of semantic gender. In this second case we are referring to a gender violation which involves semantic gender in contrast to grammatical gender.
2. Under some circumstances it is possible to dissociate animacy and semantic gender such as in the case of some animals (e.g., *perdiz* [partridge]). However, these variables cannot be dissociated when referring to human beings.
3. Although in our stimuli this circumstance does not happen, there are some adjectives that are statistically or stereotypically associated with referents of one particular sex (for instance: the adjective "bearded" is closely associated with men). In this case, the integration of the adjective with an animate noun may imply the integration of the features associated with the semantic gender of the noun and the semantic characteristics associated to the adjective, and therefore a mismatch between these could produce effects on the N400 (i. e., "the girl is bearded"). However, it should be noted that this effect would be a purely semantic one without any need for grammatical gender violation.

Chapter 16
Evidence for a Shared Mechanism in Linguistic and Nonlinguistic Sequence Processing? ERP Recordings of On-Line Function- and Content-Information Integration

MICHEL HOEN AND PETER F. DOMINEY

16.1 INTRODUCTION

16.1.1 Function Versus Content Processing in Natural Language Comprehension

The comprehension of language in humans allows the individual to perform the on-line mapping from sentences onto a mental representation of their meaning, based on the application of specific structural and generative rules that correspond to the grammar of a particular language. Determining the relevant characteristics of the linguistic input that allow the successful realization of this mapping constitutes a main open question in cognitive neuroscience.

One essential characteristic of human languages that allows the construction of correct associations between sentences and meaning is the existence, within the linguistic input, of two different but complementary levels of information: function information and content information (see also Osterhout et al., chapter 14, this volume, for a discussion of a related issue). Function information is present at different stages of the linguistic stimulus, namely in (a) word categories, (b) morphosyntactic marking, (c) word-order regularities, and (d) prosody (Bates & MacWhinney, 1989). In this chapter, we will particularly concentrate on the three first sources of function information, as prosodic information is absent in the visual modality.

Words can classically be separated in two different categories: function words (or closed-class words) and content words (or open-class words). On the one hand, function words (determiners, prepositions, conjunctions, and auxiliary verbs) principally contain syntactic information reflecting the underlying structure of the sentence. On the other hand, content words (nouns, verbs, adverbs, and adjectives) contain principally semantic information, but the global meaning of content arguments is sentence-specific and context-dependent. Therefore, the particular association between content elements and their meaning in a particular sentence can only be determined after combining function/structural and content information in order to retrieve the thematic roles (agent, object, recipient) of the different arguments. Function items in the form of morphosyntactic markers constitute another instance of this type of structural cues, which can replace the function-word category in certain languages. Likewise, sequential order regularities can be found in numerous human languages in which a preferred word-order exists.

Human languages combine these different sources of function information in varying proportions (Bates & MacWhinney, 1989). In English, for example, word order is predominant with morphosyntactic marking being rather rare, whereas in German, both word order and rich case-marking exist and contribute to the extraction of syntactic structures (See Fiebach et al., chapter 17, this volume). In these languages, as in French, canonical sentence constructions are based on a preferred word order (SVO in these examples), which corresponds to a canonical mapping of thematic roles (agent, object, in this particular sequential order). Syntactically complex sentences, also referred to as noncanonical sentences, rely on a nonpreferred word order (e.g., OVS in passive sentences), which corresponds to a transformation of serial order in the thematic structure (e.g., object, agent). In such sentence types, the reliance on function information is particularly relevant for the retrieval of thematic roles.

Classical psychoclinical research has provided extensive evidence for the relevance of the function versus content distinction in language production and comprehension. Agrammatic aphasic patients typically show specific impairments in the production of function words and function markers and in the processing of function information in sentence comprehension, correlated with great difficulties in assigning thematic roles in sentences with noncanonical (e.g., transformed) thematic structure (Caramazza & Zurif, 1976; Caplan, Baker, & Dehaut, 1985; Bates, Wulfeck, & MacWhinney, 1991). This pattern is in contrast to specific impairments with particular categories of content words that can be observed in anomic patients (see Miceli, Silveri, Villa, & Caramazza, 1984; Damasio & Tranel, 1993; Hillis & Caramazza, 1995, for specific impairments on nouns, or McCarthy & Warrington, 1985; Caramazza & Hillis, 1991, and Hillis & Caramazza 1991a, 1991b, for specific impairments on verbs). These data argue in favor of the existence of distinct neural networks for function- and content-information processing, but only with a technique allowing the direct on-line recording of brain activity during language comprehension could these observations be validated and dynamically characterized in normal readers.

16.1.2 ERP Correlates of Content Versus Function
Processing in Natural Language Comprehension

One of the best ways to explore brain activity reflecting the dissociation between on-line function- and content- information processing during sentence comprehension is by analyzing event-related scalp potentials from subjects involved in a sentence comprehension task. Numerous ERP studies of language have been conducted within the context of the Function–Syntax versus Content–Semantic dissociation (see Osterhout et al., chapter 14, this volume, for another review), and have isolated, in the visual reading modality, essentially three distinct components: the N400, related to semantic integration; the LAN; and the P600 or SPS, both related to various stages of syntactic structure building and complex syntactic structure processing.

The N400 (see Kutas & Federmeier, 2000, for a review), is a centro-parietal negative wave peaking around 400 ms after word onset. It was first related to semantic anomaly detection, as for the word *city* in the sentence *He shaved off his moustache and city* (Kutas & Hillyard, 1980). Further inquiries revealed that it was a reflection of semantic integration, sensitive to a word's cloze probability both in short- (sentence comprehension) (Kutas & Hillyard, 1984) and long-distance (text comprehension) contexts (van Berkum, Hagoort, & Brown, 1999). The N400 component can thus be considered as an ERP marker for content information processing.

When directly addressing the issue of word category, ERP studies have demonstrated the ability to separate content words and function words by two topographically distinguishable negative waves, the above-mentioned N400 and a left-anterior negativity (LAN) respectively, the latter appearing in the same time window as the N400 (Brown, Hagoort, & ter Keurs, 1999). The LAN was reported for phrase structure and specificity constraint violations (Neville, Nicol, Barss, Forster, & Garrett, 1991; see also Barber, Salillas, & Carreiras, chapter 15, this volume), as well as for the processing of syntactically complex sentences (Kluender & Kutas, 1993). When analyzing the effect of word frequency on the category distinction, the LAN was observed only for high-frequency function words (Münte et al., 2001). In fact, previous studies had already shown that the LAN was present only for the processing of function markers or function words indicating a transformation in the thematic structure of sentences (e.g., noncanonical or scrambled thematic structures, Rösler, Pechmann, Streb, Röder, & Hennighausen, 1998; see also Fiebach et al., chapter 17, this volume). This observation suggests the existence of particular parsing mechanisms for sentences with noncanonical thematic structures compared to sentences with canonical thematic structures, though the exact nature of this processing mechanism remains undetermined. In this perspective, the LAN could be considered as a marker for thematic role assignment or morphosyntactic information processing (Friederici, 2002), in the context of processing noncanonical sentences or transformed thematic structures.

Another marker that has been associated with function-information processing is the P600 or SPS for Syntactic Positive Shift (see Stemmer & Whitaker, 1998, for a review; but see also Osterhout et al., chapter 14, this volume). The P600 is a centro-parietal positive component peaking around 600 ms after word onset. Analogous to the N400 effect, it was first associated with the detection of syntactic ambiguities, as for the verb *answer*, following the intransitive verb *to persuade* in the sentence *The woman persuaded to answer the door* (Osterhout & Holcomb, 1992). Again, further inquiries revealed that the P600 was also present when subjects read normal sentences with complex or unusual syntactic structures (Hagoort, Brown, & Groothusen, 1993). Other authors thus argued that it reflected syntactic repair or second-pass syntactic processing (Friederici, Hahne, & Mecklinger, 1996), sensitive to the complexity of the syntactic structure of a sentence (Münte, Szentkuti, Wieringa, Matzke, & Johannes, 1997; Friederici, Steinhauer, Mecklinger, & Meyer, 1998). The P600 can thus be considered as an ERP signature of complex structure processing, repair, and reprocessing.

16.1.3 Transformation Processing Indicated by Function Information: The Case of French Passivization

Compared to other languages, French appears to be a rather simple language with a preferred SVO word-order, two genders (feminine and masculine), and relatively rare case-marking. But, of course, examples of noncanonical syntactic structures implying word-order transformations and morphosyntactic marking do exist. An interesting example, amongst others, is the formation of passive voice sentences, implying, as in English, a movement of the object of the main verb toward a position preceding the verb phrase.

(1) *Le président **a** annoncé un projet (Active–Canonical)*
       S   V   O
       (The president announced a project)
(2) *Un projet a **été** annoncé par le président (Passive–Transformed)*
       O   V   S
       (A project was announced by the president)
(3) *Des élections ont **été** annoncées par le président. (Passive–Transformed and marking)*
       O   V   S
       (Elections were announced by the president)

In French, passivization is accompanied by the appearance of new function words at the surface level, as in (2) or (3), and the auxiliary verb *a* present alone in the active sentence is modified to form an auxiliary group *a été*. The second auxiliary *été* is then the first available cue indicating that the sentence is actually in the passive voice, whereas the first auxiliary *a* present in both sentence types does not unambiguously specify the underlying syntactic structure.

French passivization also triggers an agreement between the verb and the object of the sentence, only for verbs requiring the auxiliary *avoir* (to have). This agreement is realized in the written modality, with regular verbs in French (1st group), by adding an *e* for an agreement in gender with feminine objects and an *s* for an agreement in number with plural objects to the *default* ending *é* that is nonmarked in French. Hence the spelling *annoncées* when the preceding object is [feminine, plural] *élections* (elections), and the spelling *annoncé* when the preceding object is [masculine, singular] *projet* (project).

To summarize, due to these two modifications accompanying passivization in French, it appears that comparing French passive and active sentences can be a used as a good example to study the effects of both function words (auxiliaries) and function marks in canonical versus noncanonical sentences.

16.1.4 Using the Function Information Versus Content Information Distinction to Model Syntactic Comprehension

We have attempted to specify the possible computational mechanisms that allow the processing of noncanonical or transformed sentences by developing a neural-network model of syntactic comprehension, primarily based on a dual-route processing of function versus content information (Dominey, 1997; Dominey, Lelekov, Ventre-Dominey, & Jeannerod, 1998; Dominey, Hoen, Blanc, & Lelekov-Boissard, 2003). The goal in this approach was to design an artificial system that would be able to learn the mapping between sentences with different syntactic structures of increasing complexity (canonical or noncanonical) and their meaning, expressed as the correct assignment of thematic roles to arguments involved in an ongoing action. What these modeling studies suggested is that two minimal properties were required for this artificial system to be successful in the comprehension of English or French sentences: (1) the ability to separate function from content information and (2) the systematic use of serial-order transformations in sequential structures, based on function cues, to retrieve the canonically ordered thematic roles from arguments in noncanonical sentences. In this model, the word-by-word sentence input is directed into two parallel-processing streams based on their lexical category. In the open-class stream, content words are stored in their sequential order of appearance in this particular sentence. In the closed-class stream, function words are integrated to generate a Transformation Index. During training, the model associates this transformation index with the correct transformation of sequential order to be applied to content elements in order to retrieve their thematic roles in the order (1) Agent, (2) Object, (3) Recipient. The model processes syntactically complex sentences by learning to associate the integrated pattern of function words, encoded in the Transformation Index, with the correct sequential-order transformation to be applied to content arguments in order to retrieve the canonical thematic order (see Dominey et al., 2003).

16.1.5 The Equivalence Hypothesis

These observations led us to propose the hypothesis that nonlinguistic sequences constructed using specific transformation rules that are determined by a special class of "function" symbols would to a certain extent be functionally equivalent to language and would therefore be processed, at least partially, by the neurophysiological system underlying this aspect of language processing. Behavioral support for this hypothesis was obtained in the observation that agrammatic aphasic patients were impaired in a highly correlated manner for (a) syntactic comprehension and (b) this type of nonlinguistic sequence processing (Dominey et al., 2003). Following this hypothesis, in the current study we developed a sequencing task that could mimic the two properties mentioned above: (a) existence of distinct function versus content information and (b) systematic use of serial-order transformations in sequential structures, based on function cues.

16.1.6 Transformation Processing Guided by Function Information in Sequences of Abstract Symbols: The Cognitive Sequencing Task

A sequence of abstract symbols like ABCABC (1) can be both described at a serial-structure level and at an abstract-structure level. The serial structure of a sequence concerns the nature and the position of each element in a given sequence, here the letters ABCABC, in this particular order. The abstract structure of a sequence describes the internal relationships existing between the elements it is composed of (Dominey et al., 1998). In our example, sequence (1) can be described as corresponding to the abstract structure 123123, the sequence being composed of one repeated triplet of symbols. This abstract structure can then be arbitrarily associated with the presence of a special "function" symbol (e.g., the letter Y), appearing at the serial level and leading to sequences such as (2): ABCYABC, corresponding to the abstract structure 123Y123 (Hoen & Dominey, 2000). This type of abstract structures is "generative" in the sense that once the abstract structure is known, one can create an open set of sequences corresponding to the same abstract structure, such as FRTYFRT or NGDYNGD. Sequences such as (2) reproduce the first property identified above, that is, the distinction between two classes of information: function (the symbol Y indicating the abstract structure) and content (the different letters or other symbols that can be mapped onto this abstract structure to create new sequences). The second property, systematic use of serial-order transformations triggered by function markers, can be reproduced by introducing a second abstract structure as 123X312, where this time the function symbol X is associated with an abstract structure that requires a transformation in the serial order of elements from the first triplet, leading to sequences such as (3): ABCXCAB or GPMXMGP.

This material was thus used to develop a cognitive sequencing task. In this task, sequences are composed of a series of eight letters presented one at a time. The fourth letter is a "function symbol" that triggers the application of a structural rule that determines the subsequent sequence structure as described above. Function symbols are either Y or X and correspond to two types of structural rules leading to Repetition or Transformation sequences, respectively. In repetition sequences, the function symbol Y indicates that the three subsequent elements are a repetition of the three first letters, as in (2). In this condition, there is no transformation of the serial structure of the second triplet with respect to the first. In transformation sequences, the function symbol X indicates that the three subsequent elements are to be derived from a specific transformation in the serial order of the first three, as in (3). Letter 8 was always a repetition of the function element, either Y or X, indicating the end of a sequence.

Using variants of this task, we have conducted initial experiments that demonstrated P600-like (Lelekov, Dominey, & Garcia-Larrea, 2000; Lelekov-Boissard & Dominey, 2002) and LAN-like (Hoen & Dominey, 2000) effects, but we did not directly compare these responses to those observed for language processing.

16.2 THE PRESENT STUDY

Observations from our modeling studies suggested that nonlinguistic stimuli with the two basic properties such as (1) a distinction between content and function information and (2) the systematic use of serial-order transformations in sequential structure based on function cues would share certain structural characteristics with language and thus would be processed at least in part by language-related cerebral networks. The experiment presented here was thus designed, first, to establish reliable results on transformation processing guided by function information in normal French sentence comprehension and in abstract sequences reproducing the two above-mentioned properties.

Second, this experiment allows us to perform, in the same subjects, a direct comparison between content versus structural processing in French sentences and in nonlinguistic sequences. The equivalence hypothesis predicts that under appropriate conditions, the LAN, P600, and N400 can be generated both by the processing of sentences and nonlinguistic sequences.

16.2.1 Correct Function-Information Processing in Sentences and Abstract Sequences

With respect to the LAN effect, our study was first aimed at characterizing this effect in the context of correct sentence comprehension. The hypothesis was that the LAN effect is not specific for function-word processing alone but for the integration of function information, indicating a transformed thematic structure which would confirm the observation of Rösler et al. (1998). The LAN effect was therefore studied in the context of processing correct sentences only, using correct target words and involving two main factors: their lexical category (open vs. close) and the type of syntactic structure they indicated (canonical agent–object–recipient vs. transformed). Then, in an abstract sequencing task, we hypothesized that the processing of function symbols that would trigger a serial-order transformation in a sequence of letters would be associated to an LAN effect, in contrast to a function symbol that only triggers the recall of three letters, without any supplementary serial-order manipulation.

16.2.2 Violation Detection

The second goal of this experiment was to perform, in the same subjects, a direct comparison of structural versus content violation detection both in a classical sentence-comprehension task and in an abstract sequencing task, attempting to establish whether the N400 and P600 responses classically observed in language studies could be obtained for analogous violations in a nonlinguistic task.

16.3 EXPERIMENT—METHOD

16.3.1 Subjects

A total of 16 subjects (8 male, 8 female), aged 22–30 years, all right-handed and free of neurological impairment or language deficit, with normal or corrected-to-normal vision, entered the study. After being advised of the physical details of the stimulation and recording techniques employed, subjects gave their informed consent.

16.3.2 Stimuli

Linguistic Stimuli—French Sentences (see Table 16.1 for examples)

For the experiment, 160 French sentences were constructed. The different sentences were either 8 words long (active sentences) or 10 words long (passive sentences). They were presented word by word at a central fixation point, words being written in lower case, except the first letter of the first word in a new sentence, which was printed in upper case.

16.3.3 Types

A total of 80 Correct Sentences were constructed, separated into two types:

Table 16.1. **Examples of the Different Stimuli Used in the Correctness Judgment Task**

TYPE	COMPLEXITY	CONDITIONS		
		Correct	**Semantic/Content Violation**	**Structural/Rule Violation**
Sentences	**Active**	Le pianiste a donné un concert au parc (The pianist gave a concert at the park)	Le pianiste a donné un concert au banc (The pianist gave a concert at the bench)	Le pianiste a donné un au concert parc (The pianist gave a at the concert park)
	Passive	Un concert a été donné au parc par le pianiste (A concert was given at the park by the pianist)	Un concert a été donné au banc par le pianiste (A concert was given at the bench by the pianist)	Un concert a été donné parc au par le pianiste (A concert was given park at the by the pianist)
Sequences	**Repetition**	N O P Y N O P Y	N O P Y N O A Y	N O P Y P N O Y
	Transformation	N O P X P N O X	N O P X P N A X	N O P X N O P X

1. Type 1 or Active. Sentences were three argument active sentences.
2. Type 2 or Passive. The same sentences were presented in the passive voice, forming normal French dative-passive sentences. Amongst the passive sentences, half (20) contained a [masculine, singular] object, and hence an unmarked verb, and half (20) a [feminine, plural] object, and hence the morphosyntactic marking -*es* on the main verb, resulting from the agreement in gender and number with the object.

16.3.4 Violations

For the experiment, 80 Violation sentences were constructed, 40 for each type, divided into two conditions:

1. Semantic Violation: The third content argument in the sentence was always replaced by a semantically anomalous content-word in position 8 in active sentences and in position 7 in passive sentences.
2. Structural Violation: The preposition preceding the third content argument was moved to an anomalous position.

Nonlinguistic Stimuli—Letter Sequences (see Table 16.1 for examples)
For the experiment, 160 sequences were constructed, composed of 8 letters, an initial triplet of letters, a function symbol X/Y as the fourth element, a second triplet, and finally a repetition of the function element to indicate the end of the sequence. Sequences were presented letter by letter at a central fixation point, letters being written in upper case.

16.3.5 Types

A total of 80 Correct Sequences were constructed, separated into two types:

1. Type 1 or Repetition. Sequences following the abstract structure 123Y123Y.
2. Type 2 or Transformation. Sequences following the abstract structure 123X312X.

16.3.6 Violations

A total of 80 Violation sequences were constructed, 40 for each type, divided into two conditions:

1. Content Violation: A new, unexpected letter appeared at position 7, violating the former context of the sequence established in the first triplet.
2. Structural Violation: The function symbol/abstract structure correspondence was violated such that a Repetition appeared after the function symbol X or a transformation after the function symbol Y, leading to a structural rule violation, first detectable on letter 5.

16.3.7 Sequence Learning

Before the beginning of the recording phase, subjects were explicitly taught the two sequence structures (123 Y 123 and 123X312) and were trained to manipulate them by studying lists of sequences clearly presenting the correct and the two violated versions of the different sequences for about 10 min. This learning was then assessed and reinforced during a second training period of 10 min, where subjects had to read and judge 20 example sequences in the EEG experimental context.

16.3.8 Stimulus Presentation

Subjects were seated 50 cm in front of a 14-in. video monitor, where stimuli (words or letters) were presented separately for 400 ms, followed by a 400-ms blank-screen pause, yielding an 800-ms stimulus onset asynchrony (SOA). The task consisted in judging if sequences or sentences were well formed or not. At the end of each string, and after a delay of 2 s, a response screen appeared for 2 s, during which participants were asked to give their answer by pressing the correct or incorrect button on a response pad (balanced right–left or left–right for two subject groups).

16.3.9 Trial Blocking and Randomization

For the experiment, 320 trials were presented in 4 different blocks separated by a 5-min break, leading a total recording duration of approximately 90 min. The blocks were composed of a balanced mixing of all conditions and types for either sentences (2 blocks) or sequences (2 blocks).

16.3.10 EEG Recording

Scalp voltages were recorded with a 65-channel Geodesic Sensor Net referenced to Cz and amplified with an AC-coupled, 65-channel, high input impedance amplifier (200 M, Net Amps, Electrical Geodesics Inc., Eugene, OR). Amplified analogue voltages (0.1–200 Hz bandpass) were sampled at 500 Hz. Individual electrodes were adjusted at an impedance of less than 50 kΩ (Tucker, 1993). Trials were automatically rejected from analysis if they contained eye movements, as monitored by two EOG electrodes. The different topographies of the evoked markers were visually represented using the 3-D topographic mapping tool from the BESA 2000 software (MEGIS Software GmbH, Munich).

16.3.11 EEG Preprocessing

EEG recordings were segmented from 100 ms before to 900 ms after the onset of the item of interest in the sequence/sentence. Segments were then filtered by a low-pass filter of 30 Hz, rereferenced to an average reference of the 65 channels, and a normalization was applied, taking the 100 ms preceding the stimulus onset as a voltage baseline.

16.3.12 Statistical Analysis

For the comparison between LAN and N400 effects for function- versus content-information processing during correct active and passive sentence comprehension, we were interested in separating these effects according to their topographic distribution. We therefore extracted 20 electrodes corresponding to two spatial domains, each one consisting of 10 electrodes. The first domain was composed of electrodes typically sensitive to LAN effects and was situated inside a triangle defined by the corresponding 10–20 electrode locations: Nasion, FC1, and F9. The second domain corresponded to electrodes typically sensitive to N400 effects and contained the group of centro-parietal electrodes, behind and around Cz.

For the violation detection part, in order to facilitate statistical analysis, we extracted 20 electrodes, this time homogeneously distributed on the surface of the scalp, corresponding to the 10–20 coordinates : F3, F7, F8, F4, Fz, FCz, C1, C3, C4, C2, Cp1, Cp2, T8, T7, P7, P3, P4, P8, Pz, and POz. To study the N400 effect, mean scalp voltages were obtained in a time window from 250 to 450 ms. The P600 effect was studied in a time window from 450 to 900 ms and the LAN effect was analyzed in a time window from 350 to 550 ms. These data were then analyzed in repeated-measure ANOVAs, taking mean voltage amplitude, expressed in microvolts, as the dependent variable.

16.4 RESULTS

16.4.1 The LAN Effect: Comparing Function Words Indicating or not Indicating a Noncanonical Thematic Structure

In this analysis, we compared the average evoked responses obtained for the processing of the auxiliary *a* in active sentences and the auxiliary *été* in passive sentences. Due to the high regularity of the sentence structures used as stimuli in the experiment, the word *a* in active sentences and the word *été* in passive sentences could only be interpreted as function words, namely auxiliary verbs. While these two words have different length, the comparison of their event-related responses remains valid as no major effect of word length has been reported concerning the LAN effect or other lexical-category-relevant ERP markers (see e.g., Brown et al., 1999). The first auxiliary *a* in active sentences does not predict any transformation in the thematic structure, whereas the second auxiliary *été*, in passive sentences, is the first cue indicating a transformed or noncanonical thematic structure (Figure 16.1)

An initial 2-WayANOVA, discarding topographic information and performed with factors Structure (2:Transformation/No Transformation) $\times$ Electrodes (20), revealed a main effect for Structure [$F(1, 15) = 5, 30; p < .05$] and for Electrodes [$F(19, 285) = 21, 18; p < .05$] as well as a significant interaction [$F(19, 285) = 3, 88; p < .05$], suggesting that the reading of function words was associated with differential-evoked responses in this time window, with different topographic distributions. We thus conducted a second 2-Way ANOVA, restricting the spatial region

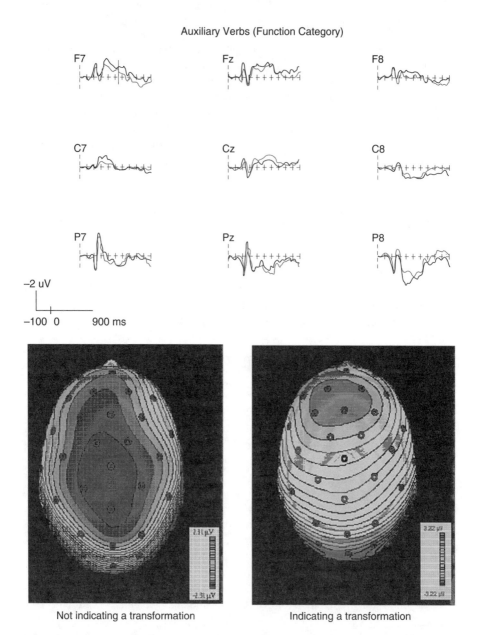

Auxiliary Verbs (Function Category)

Not indicating a transformation   Indicating a transformation

Figure 16.1. **Top:** Grand Average ERPs over 9 left-midline and right sites to the function word *été*, indicating a Transformed thematic structure (dark line), and to the function word *a*, not predicting a transformation (gray line).

Bottom: 2-D pictures of the 3-D interpolations over 65 electrodes, at 450 ms. Right: for the function word *été* indicating a transformed thematic structure (LAN). Left: for the function word *a*, not predicting a function word (N400).

of interest to the LAN domain. This topographic analysis revealed a main effect for Structure [$F(1, 15) = 7, 36; p < .05$], as the scalp voltage for the reading of function words, indicating that a transformed thematic structure was significantly more negative. No main effect for the factor Electrodes was observed [$F(9, 135) = 0, 51; p = .86$] suggesting that this negativity is homogeneously distributed over all the 10 electrodes in the left-anterior region. This was confirmed by the nonsignificant Structure X Electrodes interaction [$F(9, 135) = 0, 94; p = .49$]. Thus, in sentences, the reading of a function word indicating a transformation in the thematic structure, as the auxiliary *été* in French passive sentences, produces a significant LAN effect. In contrast, the reading of a function word not providing any relevant information about the transformation of the thematic structure, as the function word *a* in active sentences, is associated with an N400 component.

16.4.2 The LAN Effect: Comparing Content Words With or Without a Morphosyntactic Mark Confirming a Noncanonical Thematic Structure

The verb *annoncées* in (3) shows a morphosyntactic marking (*-es*) resulting from its agreement in gender and number with the preceding object [feminine, plural]. We compared ERPs obtained for the marked verb to ERPs obtained for verbs agreeing with objects [masculine, singular] showing no additional function marker and ending with (*-é*).

An ANOVA on the factors Function marker (present and absent), Spatial domain (LAN and N400) and Electrodes (20), revealed no main effects either for the F unction marker [$F(1, 15) = 0.19, p > .05$] or for the Spatial domain [$F(1, 15) = 1.27, p > .05$] or Electrodes [$F(6, 90) = 1.07, p > .05$], showing that the reading of the main verb in passive sentences is globally associated with a widely distributed negative wave present in both the LAN and N400 spatial domains (Figure 16.2)

The only significant effect obtained for the Function-mark * Spatial domain interaction is [$F(1, 15) = 8.33, p < .05$], revealing an effect of the presence of a function mark, highly dependent on the spatial location considered. A planned comparison analysis reveals that the Function-mark effect is only significant in the LAN Spatial domain, ($p < .05$) but not in the N400 Spatial domain ($p > .05$). We can interpret these results such that the agreement on the main verb is characterized by the appearance of a LAN component only when it is made overt by morphosyntactic marking.

16.4.3 Processing Abstract Function Elements Implying Serial-Order Transformations and the LAN Effect

Here we contrasted the average evoked response in the cognitive sequencing task for the reading of the function element Y, not triggering any serial-order transformation, with the response obtained for the reading of the function element X, associated with a serial order transformation in the second triplet of the sequence.

As revealed in Figure 16.3, the reading of function elements requiring the processing of a serial-order transformation in sequences (X) is associated with the appearance of a frontal left negativity, in the time window 350 to 550 ms. A 2-Way

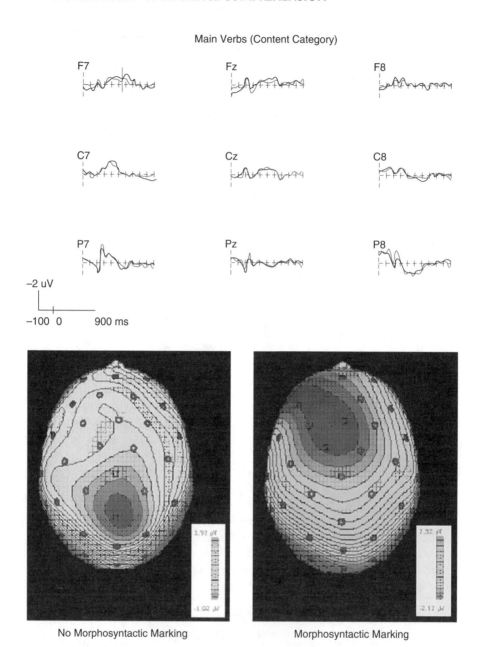

Figure 16.2. **Top:** Grand Average ERPs over 9 left-midline and right sites to the main verb (Content Word), with a morphosyntactic marked ending *-es* (dark line) or without (gray line). **Bottom:** 2-D pictures of the 3-D interpolations over 65 electrodes at 420 ms. Right: for the marked verb (LAN) and Left: for the unmarked verb (N400).

Function Symbols in abstract sequences

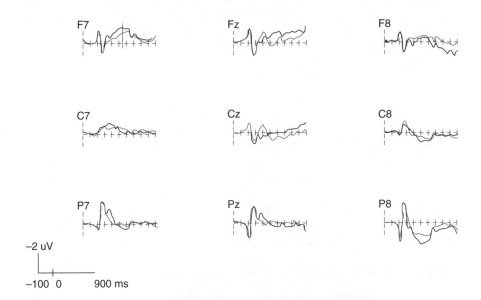

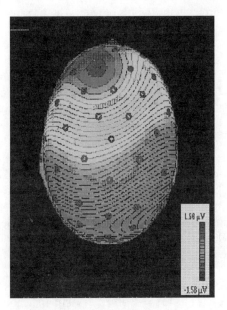

Figure 16.3. **Left:** Grand Average ERPs over 9 left-midline and right sites to the function element X, predicting a Transformation (dark line), and to the function element Y, predicting a Repetition (gray line).
Right: 2-D picture of the 3-D interpolation over 65 electrodes, showing the left-anterior topography of the negative wave at 450 ms for the processing of the function symbol X.

ANOVA with the factors Structure (2:Transformation/No Transformation) ∞ Electrodes (20) revealed a main effect for Structure [$F(1, 15) = 4, 59; p < .05$], reflecting a global enhanced negativity for the reading of the function symbol X that predicted a transformation and a main effect for Electrodes ($F(19, 285) = 10, 24; p < .05$). The significant interaction [$F(19, 285) = 4, 25; p < .05$] suggests that the negativity is not homogeneously distributed amongst the 20 electrodes of interest. We thus conducted a second 2-Way ANOVA, restricting the spatial region of interest to the one previously mentioned, 10 electrodes in the left-anterior region of the scalp. This second ANOVA reveals a main effect for transformation [$F(1, 15) = 19, 35; p < .05$], as the waveform for the reading of the transformation-predicting function symbol was significantly more negative in this scalp region. The absence of a significant main effect for the factor Electrode [$F(9, 135) = 1, 92; p = .06$] and the absence of significant interaction between the two factors [$F(9, 135) = 1, 35; p = .22$] indicate that this negativity is globally present over all electrodes in this region. Thus, the reading of a function symbol that triggers the processing of a transformation in the serial order of items in an abstract sequence is associated with a left-anterior negative wave in the time window 350–550 ms.

16.4.4 Semantic/Content Violation and the N400 Effect

We then contrasted items (words or letters) constituting a content violation with the corresponding correct items (words or letters) at the same place in correct sentences or correct sequences.

As seen in Figure 16.4A and Figure 16.4B, Content/Semantic violations in sequences and sentences led to a centro-parietal negative component in the time range 250 to 450 ms. The spatial distribution of the negativity obtained for Content violations in sequences is strikingly comparable to the one obtained for semantic violations in sentences, suggesting the involvement of a common neural mechanism.

The 3-Way ANOVAs performed with factors Complexity (2:Repetition–Active/Transformation–Passive) × Condition (2:Correct/Violation) × Electrodes (20) for responses in the 250–400 ms range revealed a main effect for Condition, both for Sequences [$F(1, 15) = 8, 44; p < .05$] and Sentences [$F(1, 15) = 27, 9; p < .05$], with waveforms for violating items (letters/words) systematically more negative in this time window. We also observed a main effect for Electrodes both for Sequences [$F(19, 285) = 3, 5; p < .05$] and Sentences [$F(19, 285) = 5, 42; p < .05$], reflecting the spatially selective distribution of voltages over the scalp.

We observed no main effect for Complexity, either for Sequences [$F(1, 15) = 1.97; p = .18$] or for Sentences [$F(1, 15) = 2.57; p = .13$]. There was no interaction between Complexity and Condition, either for Sequences [$F(1, 15) = 3.39; p > .05$] or for Sentences [$F(1, 15) = 3.79; p > .05$], indicating that complexity of the sequence/sentence structure does not significantly modulate this effect in our experiment. Statistical analysis also revealed a significant interaction between Condition and Electrodes, both for Sequences [$F(19, 285) = 10, 9; p < .05$] and Sentences [$F(19, 285) = 4,9; p < .05$], reflecting the specific centro-parietal distribution of the negativity associated with content/semantic violation processing in sequences and sentences.

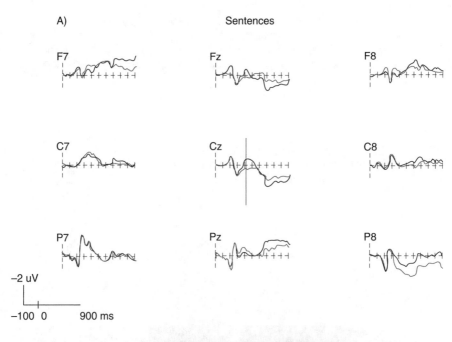

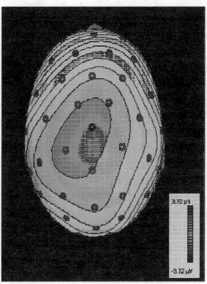

Figure 16.4. **(A) Left:** Grand Average ERPs over 9 left-midline and right sites to semantically anomalous word in sentences (dark line) and to the semantically correct control word (gray line). **Right:** 2-D picture of the 3-D interpolation over 65 electrodes, showing the centro-parietal topography of the N400 component at 300 ms.

In order to directly compare ERP profiles in the sentence and sequence task types, we conducted a 4-Way ANOVA with the same factors as above, adding the

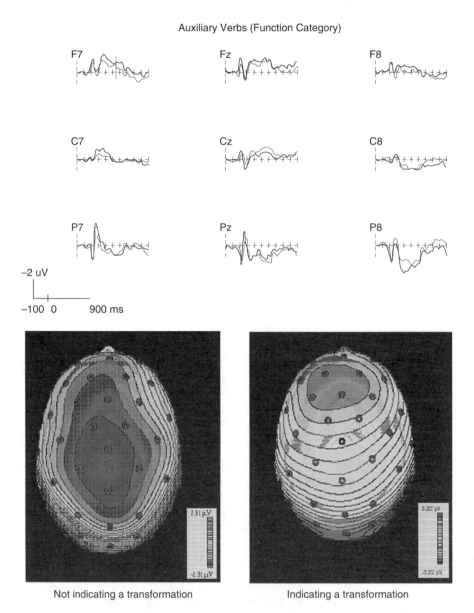

Figure 16.4 (**B**) **Left**: Grand Average ERPs over 9 left-midline and right sites to content violation in sequences (dark line) and to the correct control symbol (gray line). **Right:** 2-D picture of the 3-D interpolation over 65 electrodes, showing the centro-parietal topography of the N400 component at 300 ms.

factor Type (2:Sentence/Sequence). The significant main effect for Type $[F(1, 15)$ $= 12, 7; p < .05]$ demonstrates that letters in sequences, and words in sentences, are globally recognized as different and processed in a distinct manner. Main effects were also observed for Condition $[F(1, 15) = 22, 1; p < .05)]$ confirming the significant effect associated with the detection of the content violation, and for Electrodes $(F(19, 285) = 4, 77; p < .05)$, reflecting the selective spatial distribution of voltage at the surface of the scalp. The Complexity factor showed no main effect $[F(1, 15) = 4, 23; p > .05]$, confirming the observation from the 3-Way ANOVAs. Most interestingly, Type and Condition do not interact significantly $[F(1, 15) = 1, 37; p > .05]$, suggesting that the N400 effect associated with the detection of the content violation is independent of the type of stimuli considered (sentence or sequence). Content violations in sentences as well as in abstract sequences are characterized by the induction of an N400 component.

16.4.5 Structural Violations and the P600 Effect

Finally, we contrasted items constituting a structural or rule violation with their corresponding controls. In sentences, in order to minimize lexical-category effects, we compared the function word appearing at illegal sentence positions with the same function word appearing at its correct place in a correct sentence. In sequences, we compared ERPs obtained for the violating letter to those obtained for the correct letter at the same position in the correct sequences.

As seen in Figures 16.5A and 16.5B, both Rule violations in sequences and Structural violations in sentences led to a late positivity in the 400–900 ms time range. Again, both components have very similar spatial distribution, as both are widely distributed strong positive waves with centro-parietal maxima. The 3-Way ANOVAs performed with factors Complexity (2:Repetition–Active/Transformation–Passive) $\times$ Condition (2:Correct/Violation) x Electrodes (20) revealed a main effect for Condition, both for Sequences $[F(1, 15) = 7, 99; p < .05]$ and Sentences $[F(1, 15) = 30, 55; p < .05]$, with the waveforms for violating items (letters/words) systematically more positive in this late time window. A main effect for the factor Electrodes was observed, both for Sequences $[F(19, 285) = 6, 08; p < .05]$ and sentences $[F(19, 285) = 3, 44; p < .05]$, reflecting the selective local differences in the spatial distribution of scalp voltages. The interactions between Condition and Electrodes for Sequences $[F(19, 285) = 6, 22; p < .05]$ and for Sentences $[F(19, 285) = 8, 96; p < .05]$ reflect the specific centro-parietal distribution of the late positivity associated with structure violation detection in sequences and sentences. We observed no main effect for Complexity either for Sequences $[F(1, 15) = 0, 55; p = .46]$ or for Sentences $[F(1, 15) = 3, 72; p > .05]$. Likewise, there was no interaction between Complexity and Condition, either for Sequences $[F(1, 15) = 0, 001; p = .98]$, or for Sentences $[F(1, 15) = 0.43; p = .52]$, showing that the complexity of the sequence/sentence structure does not modulate significantly this late positivity.

To allow direct comparison of sequence versus sentence processing, we performed a 4-Way ANOVA including the additional Type factor (2:Sentences vs. Sequences). The significant main effect for Type $[F(1, 15) = 44, 86; p < .05]$ indicates that words in sentences and letters in sequences are globally processed in a

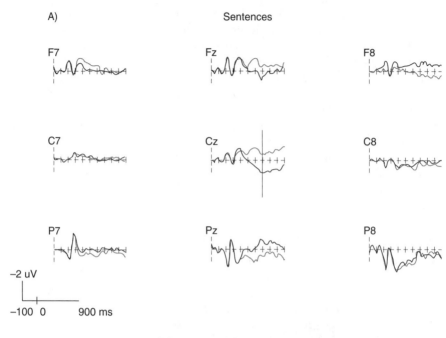

A)   Sentences

F7   Fz   F8

C7   Cz   C8

P7   Pz   P8

−2 uV

−100 0   900 ms

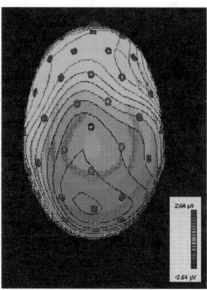

2.64 μV

-2.64 μV

Figure 16.5. (A) **Left:** Grand Average ERPs over 9 left-midline and right sites to syntactically anomalous words in sentences (dark line) and to the syntactically correct control word (gray line). **Right:** 2-D picture of the 3-D interpolation over 65 electrodes, showing the centro-parietal topography of the P600 component at 600 ms for the violating word.

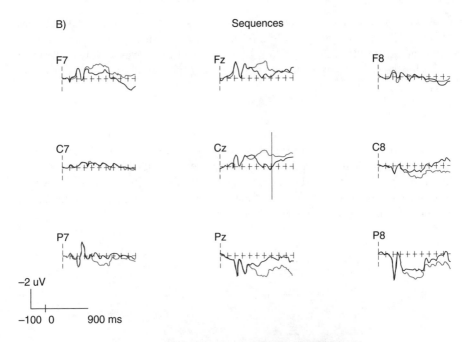

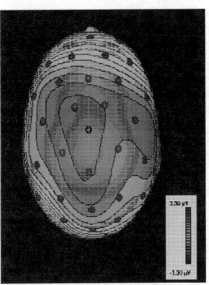

Figure 16.5 **(B) Left:** Grand Average ERPs over 9 left-midline and right sites to rule violation in sequences (dark line) and to the correct control symbol (gray line). **Right:** 2-D picture of the 3-D interpolation over 65 electrodes, showing the centro-parietal topography of the P600 component at 600 ms for the reading of the violating word.

significantly different manner in this time window. The significant Condition effect [$F(1, 15) = 26, 41; p < .05$] reveals the strong effect associated with the detection of the syntactic/structure violations in both cases, and the significant Electrodes effect [$F(19, 285) = 4, 53; p < .05$] reflects the selective spatial location of voltages at the surface of the scalp. Confirming the results of the 3-Way ANOVA, the main effect for the Complexity factor did not reach statistical significance [$F(1, 15) = 0, 55; p = .46$].

The interaction between Type and Condition was significant [$F(1, 15 = 15, 01 ; p < .05$], suggesting the existence of differences between the effects observed for the detection of structural violations in sentences versus sequences. Closer inspection of this interaction (see Figure 16.6) indicates that while a positivity is present both for incorrect sentence and sequence processing, the amplitude of the effect obtained for sentences is significantly greater than the amplitude of any other effects observed in this time window, thus yielding the interaction. Structure violations in sentences as well as in abstract sequences are characterized by the appearance of a late positive component, a classical P600 effect. The effect observed for sentences appears significantly greater in amplitude than that observed for sequences, an observation that will be discussed below.

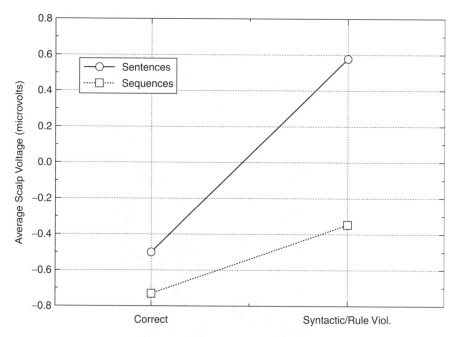

Figure 16.6. Graphic presentation of the interaction Type × Condition considered over all the 20 electrodes of interest and showing the difference in magnitude of the effect. The effect of the violation is significant in both cases, in sentences (LSD test $p < 0.05$) and sequences (LSD test $p < 0.05$). However, the amplitude of the P600 effect observed for syntactic violations in language is significantly higher than the one observed for rule violation for sequences, post-hoc LSD test $p < 0.05$, thus yielding the Type × Condition interaction.

16.5 DISCUSSION

The goal of this experiment was to test the hypothesis that sequential stimuli constructed based on the two basic properties—(a) the presence of a distinction between two types of content and function categories and (b) the systematic use of serial-order transformations in sequential structure based on function cues—would share certain structural characteristics with language and thus would demonstrate at least partially comparable processing dynamics as revealed by the recording of ERPs.

In particular, a specific subclass of elements should indicate the appropriate transformational structure for a given sequence. We thus developed and tested subjects in a new cognitive sequencing paradigm to reproduce language-relevant ERP markers. Using this type of material, three main language-relevant ERP signatures, the N400, the P600, and the LAN, could be reproduced in the context of a single, well-defined cognitive sequencing paradigm.

This is of particular interest because up to now the use of linguistic material or other "cognitively rich" material such as music or arithmetic was essentially the only way to obtain and to study these effects (Patel, Gibson, Ratner, Besson, & Holcomb, 1998; Niedeggen, Rösler & Jost, 1999). Because language is highly structured and complex, it was difficult to isolate the specific processing functions associated with these effects. Here we used a significantly reduced protocol and obtained quite similar results. The advantage of cognitive sequences is that one can precisely manipulate sequence parameters to selectively study the nonlinguistic modulation of language-relevant ERPs. One interest of this approach is that it provides the ability to precisely determine the non-language-specific characteristics of such ERP effects in order to better control language experiments and thus determine what features are specific to language processing.

16.5.1 The LAN Effect

A LAN effect was obtained in the time range 350–550 ms that differentiated function words indicating a transformed (noncanonical) thematic structure from function words that did not predict such a transformed structure in French sentences, reproducing the result obtained by Rösler et al. (1998) in German. In parallel, we replicated our previous observation (Hoen & Dominey, 2000), demonstrating that a LAN effect was induced for the processing of serial-order transformations in a triplet of letters, triggered by the function symbol X in Transformation sequences. This LAN effect is not present when subjects had only to recall three letters with no serial-order transformation, in response to the function symbol Y in Repetition sequences. Importantly, we observed that this LAN effect was similar for both sequences and sentences as revealed by the nonsignificant interaction between functional category and stimulus type. This result demonstrates that working-memory load alone is not sufficient to trigger a LAN, but that manipulation of the working-memory content, specifically that involved in transformation processing, is also required. The question of the specificity of transformational processes and the nature of the transformations leading to the LAN effect are open questions that will lead to further inquiries.

16.5.2 The N400 Effect

In the case of the N400 effect, it has sometimes been argued that this marker is specific for the contextual integration of meaningful stimuli (Kutas and Federmeier, 2000). What abstract sequences show us is that meaning might well be a part of an N400 effect, but meaning is not necessary to obtain an N400 effect. Our results suggest that a reasonably consistent part of the N400 effect might be due to a detection procedure involving the match or mismatch between an expected item and the actual event that occurs within a structured, and thus predictable, sequence of items, independently of the presence or not of semantic meaning associated with this particular item.

16.5.3 The P600 Effect

The question of the nature of the P600 effect is still debated. Is the P600 an isolated effect, specifically due to language processing, or is this late positivity a member of the P3 components, analogous to the P3b effect seen in classical odd-ball tasks (Osterhout, McKinnon, Bersick, & Corey, 1996; Friederici et al., 1996; Münte et al., 1998)? Using sequences of letters, our current protocol could have been considered a typical "oddball" task. What we show, however, is that when the regularity of the baseline stimulus is more complex than simply a homogenous string of identical elements (e.g., sequences of letters that are constructed according to precise rules) and when the oddball constitutes a rule violation rather than a classical "perceptual" oddball, then the positivity appears in a later time window, with onset latency, peak latency, and a spatial topography remarkably homologous to those observed for structural violations in sentences, that is, the P600. The main difference we observed was quantitative rather than qualitative, the voltage amplitude observed for the language-related P600 being significantly greater than that observed for the P600 in sequences.

Several explanations could account for this difference. For example, syntactic violation detection and repair involve, in language, the use of a large set of grammatical rules, whereas our cognitive sequences were built on only two different and very simple rules. Alternatively, the fact that language is a faculty that is highly overtrained in humans, whereas our subjects learned the two rules to judge sequences only 20 min before recording, might well be another explanation of this observation. Our results show that rule violation detection in abstract sequences and sentences involves a comparable dynamic mechanism reflected in a late positivity. Clearly, however, language remains a much more complex system, involving numerous mechanisms other than those isolated by cognitive sequences.

16.5.4 A Cognitive Sequencing Approach to the Function of Language

Our cognitive sequencing approach began with simulation of the cortico-striatal system in sensorimotor sequence learning (Dominey, Arbib, & Joseph, 1995) and the extension of this model to accommodate abstract transformational structure (Dominey, 1997; Dominey et al., 1998). We subsequently demonstrated that the resulting model could simulate infant sensitivity to language-related serial, temporal, and abstract structure (Dominey & Ramus, 2000) and could learn to perform adult syntactic comprehension (Dominey et al., 2003), thus leading us to predict certain commonalties in the neurophysiology of language and sequential cognition.

In the current study, processing involved during the cognitive sequencing paradigm gives rise to electrophysiological responses observed at the scalp level that are very similar to those observed for analogous processing in language comprehension. This suggests that the language system is accessible to nonlinguistic tasks. There are now numerous observations in different scientific areas convergent with this observation and laying the foundations for a new way to approach the neurophysiology of language processing.

Several ERP experiments have demonstrated that markers related to language processing could be observed in nonlinguistic sequences. The P600 effect was observed for structural violations in musical phrases (Patel et al., 1998) and in sequences of geometrical shapes and letters (Lelekov et al., 2000; Lelekov-Boissard & Dominey, 2002). The P600 effect could also be reproduced for the detection of grammatical violations occurring in an artificial language that retained many characteristics of human natural language (Friederici, Steinhauer, & Pfeifer, 2002). The LAN effect could be reproduced for the processing of serial-order transformations in sequences of words that kept a clear semantic content (Rolke, Heil, Hennighausen, Haussler, & Rösler, 2000) as well as in abstract sequences of letters (Hoen & Dominey, 2000). In the domain of neuroimagery, Broca's area has been shown to be involved in processing syntactic relations in music (Maess, Koelsch, Gunter, & Friederici, 2001 using MEG). This area also participates in other nonlinguistic tasks as motor sequencing (Rizzolatti & Arbib, 1998; Jackendoff, 1999), or set-shifting tasks (Konishi et al., 1998).

If language shares some neurophysiological characteristics with other sequencing systems, then one could imagine that an improvement due to training in one modality should transfer to the other one, for example, that cognitive sequencing could improve syntactic processing in aphasic patients. We have recently tested this hypothesis, demonstrating that training with nonlinguistic sequences improves thematic role assignment in a group of agrammatic aphasic patients (Hoen et al., 2003). Further inquiries will be dedicated to the study of the language system and the neurophysiology of the neural networks that may be shared between language and other sequential cognitive processes.

16.6 CONCLUSION

Three main language-relevant ERP signatures, the N400, the P600, and the LAN, were reproduced using a single "cognitive sequencing" paradigm. Cognitive sequences do not constitute an artificial language but they mimic two basic properties of natural language—(a) items appear in temporal sequences that require knowledge of construction rules implying systematic transformation processing, and (b) both the structure and the transformations required to process these sequences are indicated in the stimulus itself by the existence of a specific "function" category of items. We thus observed that the processing of transformations and the detection of different types of violation, respectively, trigger ERP components—the LAN, the N400, and the P600—that are comparable in sentences and abstract sequences. This suggests that the neurophysiological substrate implicated in language comprehension can also be activated by nonlinguistic stimuli, opening a wide range of theoretical, experimental, and practical applications.

16.7 ACKNOWLEDGMENTS

The first author was supported by a doctoral fellowship from the Minister of Research and Technology (Paris). The project was supported in part by the ACI Cognitique (Paris) and the Human Frontier Science Program. We would like to thank Viviane Deprez, Douglas Saddy, and Peter Hagoort for their helpful suggestions at the outset of the project.

References

Bates, E., & MacWhinney, B. (1989). (Eds.) *The cross-linguistic study of sentence processing.* New York: Cambridge University Press.

Bates, E., Wulfeck, B., & MacWhinney, B. (1991). Cross-linguistic research in aphasia: An overview. *Brain and Language, 41*(2), 123–148.

Brown, C. M., Hagoort, P., & ter Keurs, M. (1999). Electrophysiological signatures of visual lexical processing: Open- and closed-class words. *Journal of Cognitive Neuroscience, 11*(3), 261–81.

Caplan, D., Baker, C., & Dehaut, F. (1985). Syntactic determinants of sentence comprehension in aphasia. *Cognition, 21*(2), 117–75.

Caramazza, A., & Hillis, A. E. (1991). Lexical organization of nouns and verbs in the brain. *Nature, 349*(6312), 788–790.

Caramazza, A., & Zurif, E. B. (1976). Dissociation of algorithmic and heuristic processes in language comprehension: Evidence from aphasia. *Brain and Language, 3*(4), 572–582.

Damasio, A. R., & Tranel, D. (1993, June 1). Nouns and verbs are retrieved with differently distributed neural systems. *Proceedings of the National Academy. of Science, USA, 90*(11), 4957–4960.

Dominey, P. F. (1997). An anatomically structured sensory-motor sequence learning system displays some general linguistic capacities. *Brain and Language, 59,* 50–75.

Dominey, P. F., Arbib, M. A., & Joseph, J. P. (1995). A model of cortico-striatal plasticity for learning oculomotor associations and sequences. *Journal of Cognitive Neuroscience, 7*(3), 311–336.

Dominey, P. F., Hoen, M., Blanc, J. M., & Lelekov-Boissard, T. (2003). Neurological basis of language and sequential cognition: Evidence from simulation, aphasia, and ERP studies. *Brain and Language, 86*(2), 207–225.

Dominey, P. F., Lelekov, T., Ventre-Dominey, J., & Jeannerod, M. (1998). Dissociable processes for learning the surface and abstract structure sensorimotor sequences. *Journal of Cognitive Neuroscience, 10*(6), 734–751.

Dominey, P. F., & Ramus, F. (2000). Neural network processing of natural lanuage: I. Sensitivity to serial, temporal and abstract structure of language in the infant. *Language and Cognitive Processes, 15*(1), 87–127.

Friederici, A. D. (2002). Towards a neural basis of auditory sentence processing. *Trends in Cognitive Sciences, 6*(2), 78–84.

Friederici, A. D., Hahne, A., & Mecklinger, A. (1996).Temporal structure of syntactic parsing: Early and late event-related brain potential effects. *Journal of Experimental Psychology: Learning, Memory, and Cognition, 22*(5), 1219–1248.

Friederici, A. D., Steinhauer, K., Mecklinger, A., & Meyer, M. (1998). Working memory constraints on syntactic ambiguity as revealed by electrical brain responses. *Biological Psychology, 47,* 193–221.

Friederici, A. D., Steinhauer, K., & Pfeifer, E. (2002, January 8). Brain signatures of artificial language processing: Evidence challenging the critical period hypothesis. *Proceedings. of the National. Academy. of Sciences, USA, 99*(1), 529–534.

Hagoort, P., Brown, C. M., & Groothusen, J. (1993). The Syntactic Positive Shift (SPS) as an ERP measure of syntactic processing. *Language and Cognitive Processes, 8,* 439–483.

Hillis, A. E., & Caramazza, A. (1991a). Mechanisms for accessing lexical representations for output: Evidence from a category-specific semantic deficit. *Brain and Language, 40*(1), 106–144.

Hillis, A. E., & Caramazza, A. (1991b, October). Category-specific naming and comprehension impairment: A double dissociation. *Brain, 114*(5), 2081–2094.

Hillis, A. E., & Caramazza, A. (1995). The compositionality of lexical semantic representations: Clues from semantic errors in object naming. *Memory, 3*(3, 4), 333–358.

Hoen, M., & Dominey, P. F. (2000). ERP analysis of cognitive sequencing: A left anterior negativity related to structural transformation processing. *Neuroreport, 11*(14), 3187–3191.

Hoen, M., Golembiowski, M., Guyot, E., Deprez, V., Caplan, D., & Dominey, P. F. (2003). Non-linguistic cognitive sequence training improves syntactic comprehension in agrammatic aphasics. *Neuroreport., 14*(3), 495–499.

Jackendoff, R. (1999). Possible stages in the evolution of the language capacity. *Trends in Cognitive Sciences, 3*(7), 272–279.

Kluender, R., & Kutas, M. (1993). Bridging the gap: Evidence from ERPs on the processing of unbounded dependencies. *Journal Of Cognitive Neuroscience, 5,* 196–214.

Konishi, S., Nakajima, K., Uchida, I., Kameyama, M., Nakahara, K., Sekihara, K., & Miyashita, Y. (1998). Transient activation of inferior prefrontal cortex during cognitive set shifting. *Nature Neuroscience, 1*(1), 80–84.

Kutas, M., & Federmeier, K. D. (2000). Electrophysiology reveals semantic memory use in language comprehension. *Trends in Cognitive Sciences, 4*(12), 463–470.

Kutas, M., & Hillyard, S. A. (1980). Reading senseless sentences: Brain potentials reflect semantic incongruity. *Science, 207*(4427), 203–205.

Kutas, M., & Hillyard, S. A. (1984). Brain potentials during reading reflect word expectancy and semantic association. *Nature, 307*(5947), 161–163.

Lelekov, T., Dominey, P. F., & Garcia-Larrea, L. (2000). Dissociable ERP profiles for processing rules vs. instances in a cognitive sequencing task. *Neuroreport, 11*(5), 1129–1132.

Lelekov-Boissard, T., & Dominey, P. F. (2002). Human brain potentials reveal similar processing of non-linguistic abstract structure and linguistic syntactic structure. *Clinical Neurophysiology, 32*(1), 72–84.

Maess, B., Koelsch, S., Gunter, T. C., & Friederici, A. D. (2001). Musical syntax is processed in Broca's area: An MEG study. *Nature Neuroscience, 4*(5), 540–545.

McCarthy, R., & Warrington, E. K. (1985). Category specificity in an agrammatic patient: The relative impairment of verb retrieval and comprehension. *Neuropsychologia, 23*(6), 709–727.

Miceli, G., Silveri, M. C., Villa, G., & Caramazza, A. (1984). On the basis for the agrammatic's difficulty in producing main verbs. *Cortex, 20*(2), 207–220.

Münte, T. F., Heinze, H. J., Matzke, M., Wieringa, B. M., & Johannes, S. (1998). Brain potentials and syntactic violations revisited: No evidence for specificity of the syntactic positive shift. *Neuropsychologia, 36*(3), 217–226.

Münte, T. F., Szentkuti, A., Wieringa, B. M., Matzke, M., & Johannes, S. (1997). Human brain potentials to reading syntactic errors in sentences of different complexity. *Neuroscience Letters, 235*(3), 105–108.

Münte, T. F., Wieringa, B. M., Weyerts, H., Szentkuti, A., Matzke, M., & Johannes, S. (2001). Differences in brain potentials to open and closed class words: Class and frequency effects. *Neuropsychologia, 39,* 91–102.

Neville, H., Nicol, J., Barss, A., Forster, K., & Garrett, M. (1991). Syntactically based sentence processing classes: Evidence from event-related brain potentials. *Journal of Cognitive Neuroscience, 3,* 152–165.

Niedeggen, M., Rösler, F., & Jost, K. (1999). Processing of incongruous mental calculation problems: Evidence for an arithmetic N400 effect. *Psychophysiology, 36*(3), 307–324.

Osterhout, L., & Holcomb, P. J. (1992). Event-related brain potentials elicited by syntactic anomaly. *Journal of Memory and Language, 31,* 785–806.

Osterhout, L., McKinnon, R., Bersick, M., & Corey, V. (1996). On the language-specificity of the brain response to syntactic anomalies: Is the syntactic positive shift a member of the P300 family? *Journal of Cognitive Neuroscience, 8,* 507–526.

Patel, A. D., Gibson, E., Ratner, J., Besson, M., & Holcomb, P. J. (1998). Processing syntactic relations in language and music: an event-related potential study. *Journal of Cognitive Neuroscience, 10*(6), 717–733.

Rizzolatti, G., & Arbib, M. A. (1998). Language within our grasp. *Trends in Neurosciences, 21*(5), 188–194.

Rolke, B., Heil, M., Hennighausen, E., Haussler, C., & Rösler, F. (2000). Topography of brain electrical activity dissociates the sequential order transformation of verbal versus spatial information in humans. *Neuroscience Letters, 282*(1, 2), 81–84.

Rösler, F., Pechmann, T., Streb, J., Röder, B., & Hennighausen, E., (1998). Parsing of sentences in a language with varying word order: Word-by-word variations of processing demands are revealed by event-related brain potentials. *Journal of Memory and Language, 38,* 150–176.

Stemmer, B., & Whitaker, H. A. (1998). *Handbook of neurolinguistics.* San Diego, CA: Academic Press.

Tucker, D. M. (1993). Spatial sampling of head electrical fields: The geodesic sensor net. *Electroencephalography and Clinical Neurophysiology, 87,* 154–163.

van Berkum, J. J., Hagoort, P., & Brown, C. M. (1999). Semantic integration in sentences and discourse: Evidence from the N400. *Journal of Cognitive Neuroscience 11*(6), 657–671.

Chapter 17
Distinct Neural Correlates of Legal and Illegal Word-Order Variations in German: How Can fMRI Inform Cognitive Models of Sentence Processing?

CHRISTIAN J. FIEBACH, MATTHIAS
SCHLESEWSKY, INA D. BORNKESSEL, AND
ANGELA D. FRIEDERICI

Viele mögliche Wortabfolgen erlaubt dem Sprecher die deutsche Sprache. (*Many possible word orders* [direct object] *allows to the speaker* [indirect object] *the German language* [subject].)

Unlike English, which imposes very strict constraints on word order, German—like several other languages such as Russian, Japanese, or Turkish—is characterized by a relatively free ordering of constituents. Thus, a declarative sentence (like the above example in which the objects are encountered before the subject) is grammatical and, importantly, not even uncommon. From the perspective of language comprehension, the interest in examining languages with word-order freedom lies in determining which linguistic properties are drawn upon in the process of establishing syntactic structure (i.e., the required precursor to semantic interpretation).

A case in point that has been investigated repeatedly is *scrambling* in German [i.e., an argument order variation illustrated in example (1)]. In scrambled sentences, objects precede the subject within the clause-medial region that follows the finite verb in second position or the complementizer "dass" (that), the so-called middle-field. This operation renders sentences more complex, but not ungrammatical (e.g., Haider, 2000).

(1) a. *Dann hat der Junge dem Vater den Hammer geholt.* (S-IO-DO-V)
         then has the boy(nom) *the father*(dat) *the hammer*(acc) *fetched*

Then *the boy fetched the hammer for the father.*
b. *Dann hat dem Vater der Junge den Hammer geholt.* (IO-S-DO-V)
   then has the father(dat) *the boy*(nom) *the hammer*(acc) *fetched*

It has been established theoretically (e.g., Lenerz, 1977; Uszkoreit, 1986) and empirically (e.g., Pechmann, Uszkoreit, Engelkamp, & Zerbst, 1994, 1996; Rösler, Pechmann, Streb, Röder, & Henninghausen, 1998; Röder, Schicke, Stock, Heberer, & Rösler, 2000; Schlesewsky, Bornkessel, & Frisch, 2003) that, in unmarked declarative sentences with nonpronominal arguments such as (1), (a) the subject of a sentence precedes the object(s) (see also Bader & Meng, 1999), and (b) the indirect object precedes the direct object. These observations can be formally described in terms of linear precedence rules, for example (Uszkoreit, 1986), but also by considering the number of filler-gap relations involved in such structures (De Vicenzi, 1991; Gibson, 1998). Sentences deviating from the unmarked S-IO-DO word order are less acceptable and more difficult to process. This has been demonstrated using acceptability ratings (Pechmann et al., 1994, 1996; Röder et al., 2000; Meng & Bader, 2000), as well as other behavioral techniques such as delayed articulation, sentence generation (Pechmann et al.), or rapid serial visual presentation followed by sentence comprehension judgments (Pechmann et al.; Röder et al.). In particular, these studies showed a clear correlation between the degree of deviance from the canonical S-IO-DO word order (in terms of the number of scrambled object noun phrases [NPs]) and the unacceptability and processing difficulty induced by these sentences.

Interestingly, complex scrambled sentences (i.e., sentences involving multiple scrambling operations) were shown to exhibit very similar behavior to ungrammatical sentences. For example, two studies (Pechmann et al., 1994; Röder et al., 1996) contrasted scrambled sentences with ill-formed sentences like (2) in which the participle is positioned *clause medially* rather than *clause finally*.

(2) **Dann wird den Hammer holen dem Vater der Junge.* (*DO-V-IO-S)
    then will the hammer(acc) *fetch the father*(dat) *the boy*(nom)

Sentences such as (2) were judged to be slightly less acceptable than the most complex of the grammatical sentence conditions. However, the decrease in acceptability from the grammatical to the ungrammatical conditions was not, as one might expect, significantly greater than the differences among the grammatical conditions that varied in complexity. In the study reported by Pechmann et al., for example, the acceptability of *DO-V-IO-S differed from that of IO-DO-S-V, the most complex grammatical condition, by 0.15 (non sig.) on a 5-point scale, as compared to the significant pairwise differences of 1.07, 0.79, 0.59, or 0.45 among the acceptability ratings for the five grammatical conditions (Pechmann et al., 1996; Table 17.1, p. 267).

The off-line results outlined above therefore suggest that there is a continuum from well-formed to ill-formed sentences, within which possible qualitative differences between "grammatical" and "ungrammatical" structures cannot be unequivocally determined. However, these methods reflect a global integration of numerous parsing operations taking place in the order of a few hundred milliseconds at different positions in the sentences. It is therefore conceivable that processing differences not captured by these global measures will emerge when methods are used that are more informative with regard to the underlying mechanisms giving rise to the surface behavior. This can be achieved, for example, by modern neurocognitive methods such as event-related brain potentials (ERPs) and hemodynamic measures like positron emission tomography (PET) or functional magnetic resonance imaging (fMRI).

While ERPs provide insights into the temporal dynamics of event-related neuronal activity in the order of milliseconds, functional neuroimaging techniques can identify the brain areas involved in cognitive processes. Thus, these methods provide new sources of data that can be used to constrain cognitive models of language processing. With respect to fMRI, the method used in the present study, this means that the neural networks that were activated during the process of interest (i.e., sentence comprehension) can be identified. Thus, although the temporal resolution of fMRI is not as good as that of ERPs, this method yields a more complex picture of the mechanisms underlying overt behavior than off-line behavioral measures. For example, differences in the brain activation patterns elicited during the comprehension of varying sentence types can provide evidence for qualitative distinctions between the processes involved in each case.

Here, we utilize fMRI to determine the brain regions involved in the processing of grammatically correct but complex (scrambled) sentences, as well as ungrammatical sentences similar to those shown in (2). In this way, we will determine whether the processing of complex grammatical sentences and ungrammatical structures—which are indistinguishable on the basis of their surface behavior—will induce a continuous modulation of activity within particular brain regions or, alternatively, give rise to distinct activation patterns. While the former would support the idea of a grammaticality–ungrammaticality continuum, the latter would be indicative of an underlying, qualitative distinction between the processing of the two sentence types.

17.1 AN FMRI-STUDY OF SCRAMBLING IN GERMAN

In the study to be presented here, we investigated the neuroanatomical correlates of the processing of sentences that are syntactically complex and of sentences that are ungrammatical. We included three levels of complexity, namely a canonical word order (S-IO-DO-V), a sentence condition with one scrambled indirect object (IO-S-DO-V), and a condition with two scrambled objects (IO-DO-S-V). Syntactic violations were generated by positioning the participle in the middlefield. An example item set is shown in (3):

(3) a. *Gestern hat der Vater dem Sohn den Schnuller gegeben.* (S-IO-DO-V)
   b. *Gestern hat dem Sohn der Vater den Schnuller gegeben.* (IO-S-DO-V)
   c. *Gestern hat dem Sohn den Schnuller der Vater gegeben.* (IO-DO-S-V)
   d. **Gestern hat der Vater gegeben dem Sohn den Schnuller.* (*S-V-IO-DO)

A behavioral study conducted prior to the fMRI experiment supported the notion that scrambled sentences are less acceptable than canonical sentences and are more difficult to process. Here, participants were presented with 15 sentences per condition using a phrase-by-phrase mode of rapid serial visual presentation (500 ms plus 100 ms intertrial interval). Participants performed a speeded acceptability rating on a six-point scale ranging from "perfectly acceptable" to "totally unacceptable." As Figure 17.1 shows, acceptability decreased and decision times increased with the number of scrambled NPs. In the ungrammatical condition, acceptability decreased only marginally as compared to the most complex correct condition, a result that replicates the findings by Pechmann and collaborators (1994, 1996). The ratings for ungrammatical sentences, however, were given significantly faster than for the most complex correct condition.

In the fMRI study, we measured 20 horizontal slices covering the whole brain while 13 participants read the sentences, which were presented in the same way as in the behavioral experiment. For each condition, 48 sentences were presented. Participants performed a sentence comprehension task on eight of these items. This task procedure was chosen for two reasons. First, it is important to ensure that the effects of interest—that is, the activation differences induced by different sentence types—are not contaminated by hemodynamic responses related to the actual performance of the comprehension task. This danger exists due to a delay of 4 to 6 s between the critical event and the peak of the hemodynamic response. In an earlier study (Fiebach, Schlesewsky, Lohmann, von Cramon, & Friederici, submitted), it was observed that complexity-related activation differences induced by different sentence types were observable on the positive slope (but not at the maximum) of a late peak in the haemodynamic response that was associated with the behavioral task (see also Fiebach, 2001). As this confounding activation from the actual task performance might make it more difficult to detect subtle activation differences between the critical conditions, the present study employed a procedure that allows one to perform the analysis of the fMRI data for nontask items only. Second, the occurrence of trials with behavioral task was not predictable in order to assure that participants remained attentive throughout the experiment. (Note, however, that one cannot exclude the fact that a sentence comprehension judgment might have to be made after reading the sentences could have influenced how participants processed the sentences.) The participants' performance on the 20% task trials was sufficiently good so that no participants had to be excluded from the data analysis.

The four sentence conditions described above [cf. (3)] were presented in a pseudorandom order, thereby allowing for an event-related single trial design analogous to behavioral and ERP studies. In comparison to blocked designs frequently employed in functional neuroimaging, event-related designs allow one to investigate stimulus-evoked brain activation independent of block-wise response strategies.

The neuroanatomical correlates of the complexity manipulation for grammatical sentences were determined by using the acceptability ratings displayed in Figure 17.1 as a predictor variable in a regression analysis (known as *parametric design* in the functional imaging literature; e.g., Friston, 1997). This analysis indicated that the inferior tip of the pars opercularis of the left inferior frontal gyrus correlated best with the empirically determined acceptability of the sentences [Figure 17.2(A)].

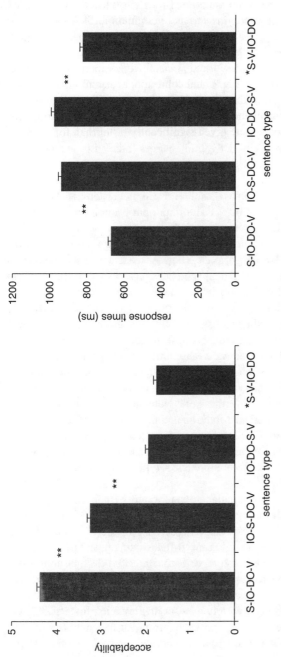

Figure 17.1 Results from the behavioral experiment (n = 24). The left panel displays mean acceptability ratings ranging from 6 (perfectly acceptable) to 1 (totally unacceptable). There was a significant effect of sentence type [$F(2, 46) = 56.4$; $p < .0001$] with all pairwise comparisons among the three grammatical conditions significant (all $F > 30$). Acceptability ratings for ungrammatical sentences (*S-V-IO-DO) did not differ reliably from those for complex correct sentences (IO-DO-S-V; $F < 1$). Decision times displayed in the right panel also showed a main effect of sentence type for grammatical sentences [$F(2, 46) = 19.3$; $p < .0001$]. Responses to ungrammatical sentences, however, were faster than those to complex grammatical sentences [$F(1, 23) = 15.9$; $p < .001$]. **, $p < .001$.

Greater activation was elicited for sentences judged less acceptable. This region of the brain is the inferior portion of the posterior third of the inferior frontal gyrus and is a central part of Broca's area. The same result (i.e., Broca's area activity for complex sentences) was also obtained when adopting the more common analysis strategy of directly contrasting the most complex with the least complex sentence condition. Converging evidence for this complexity effect stems from a recent study in which auditorily presented normal and pseudoword sentences were investigated (Röder, Stock, Neville, Bien, & Rösler, 2002). In this study, the authors also observed greater activation in Broca's area for more complex sentences involving scrambling.

The specific contribution of the present study, which goes beyond previous neuroimaging studies of syntax and Broca's area, is that it allows for a direct comparison of complexity effects with activation changes induced by ungrammaticality. (Note that the results of previous activation studies using syntactic violations are very heterogeneous and that only two out of six studies known to the authors report violation-specific activation in Broca's area [i.e., Embick, Marantz, Miyashita, O'Neil, & Sakai, 2000; Moro et al., 2001].) The important finding that we wish to stress here is that, in comparison to sentences with a canonical word order [S-IO-DO-V], ungrammatical sentences did not induce activation changes in the area which exhibited a complexity effect [see Figure 17.2(B)]. Instead, a specific activation increase for the processing of ungrammatical sentences was observed in a different region of the inferior frontal lobe of the left hemisphere. As the comparison of Figures 17.2(A) and 17.2(B) indicates, the ungrammaticality effect is slightly posterior to the activation observed for the processing of complex grammatical sentences (i.e., deeply in the posterior fronto-opercular region). In addition, increased activity with a more distributed activation in the right than in the left hemisphere was found in the parietal lobe for grammatical versus ungrammatical sentences. As the present report focuses on the left frontal dissociation between complexity and ungrammaticality, this effect will not be discussed further here. Note that, in a direct comparison between the most complex grammatical condition and the ungrammatical condition, the described activations in Broca's area for complex sentences and in posterior opercular (and parietal) regions for ungrammatical sentences are still observable, thereby suggesting that these activations are indeed specifically related to complexity and ungrammaticality, respectively.

Although the posterior fronto-opercular area reported here is not commonly associated with syntactic violations, we believe that the present result is not an accidental one as we observed violation-specific activity in the identical area, as well, for word-category violations in a recent fMRI study on auditory sentence processing (Friederici, Rüschemeyer, Hahne, & Fiebach, 2003). In addition, visual inspection of recent findings by Kuperberg and collaborators (2003) suggests that morphosyntactically anomalous sentences yielded increased activity in a very similar region (see their Figure 6, middle row, left panel). However, as this effect is not discussed in the study by Kuperberg et al., it probably failed to reach a significant cluster size. Thus, to conclude, we observed a dissociation between two left inferior frontal areas modulated by syntactic wellformedness (posterior fronto-opercular cortex) and by syntactic complexity (inferior portion of Broca's area), respectively. These results will be discussed in the following pages with respect to their

A) parametric complexity effect (IO-DO-S > IO-S-DO > S-IO-DO)

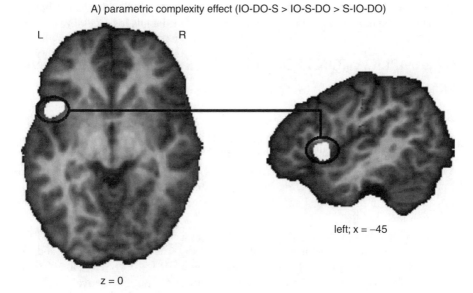

left; x = −45

z = 0

B) ungrammaticality effect (*IO-V-S-DO > S-IO-DO)

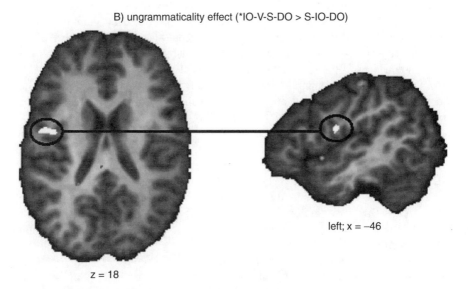

left; x = −46

z = 18

Figure 17.2 Brain activation results for the complexity effect and the ungrammaticality effect in the left inferior frontal cortex. The peak activations for the parametric syntactic complexity effect (A) and for ungrammatical as compared to simple correct sentences (B) are represented in white on a template brain. These activation clusters represent those areas in the brain that showed statistically significant activation differences when applying a statistical threshold of $Z > 2.81$, corresponding to $p < .0025$. Both activations shown are significant when correcting for multiple statistical comparisons at the cluster level using a corrected threshold of $p < .05$. (Note that parietal activity for ungrammatical sentences is not displayed in the figure.)

implications for cognitive models of parsing, as well as in regard to their contribution to an understanding of the neuroanatomical bases of the language processing system.

17.2 IMPLICATIONS FOR COGNITIVE MODELS OF PARSING

Using functional imaging, we have shown that ungrammatical sentences (with an illegal positioning of the verb) and grammatically complex, scrambled sentences are associated with distinct patterns of brain activations. These findings stand in contrast to previous behavioral studies (Pechmann et al., 1994, 1996; Röder et al., 2000) that did not provide evidence for a clear qualitative distinction between the two sentence types in question but rather suggested that both form part of a continuum between "perfect grammaticality" and "outright ungrammaticality." Indeed, a similar pattern was obtained in the speeded acceptability judgment study conducted as part of the research reported here.

The fMRI data indicate that distinct brain regions of the left inferior frontal lobe show increased activation for word-order complexity (inferior Broca's area) and for ungrammaticality (posterior fronto-opercular region). It has to be concluded from these results that although overt acceptability ratings are not qualitatively different between complex and ungrammatical sentences, distinguishable cognitive processes supported by distinct brain systems are recruited to deal with syntactic complexity and ungrammaticality in these sentences. It follows from this conclusion that there should also be differences in the cognitive processes evoked by grammatical and ungrammatical word-order variations, a fact that could not be foreseen on the basis of the behavioral responses to these structures. In the following pages, we will discuss the consequences of these results for cognitive sentence-processing architectures.

The observation of a parametric increase of Broca's area activity that is related to the number of scrambled arguments is in line with a number of models of parsing (e.g., Yngve, 1960; Uszkoreit, 1986; De Vincenzi, 1991; Kemtes & Kemper, 1997). For example, when assuming that syntactic transformation operations underlie the phenomenon of scrambling, it would be plausible to conclude that reconstructing the underlying sentence structure from the perceived surface structure, as it is assumed in classical models of language processing such as the derivational theory of complexity (Miller & Chomsky, 1963; cf. also Fodor, Bever, & Garrett, 1974), is a function of Broca's area. The more syntactic transformations that are required to reconstruct the underlying structure, the greater the activation in this region.

Similarly, the processing cost of parsing scrambled sentences might be related to the increased number of relations between the scrambled noun phrases and the positions in which they were generated. As was proposed in the context of the Minimal Chain Principle (MCP) (De Vincenzi, 1991, 1996), the parser strives to minimize syntactic chains. In the sentences used here, the more chains are constructed the more noun phrases were dislocated. The need to handle more chains than necessary in a canonical sentence structure might also be the cause of the activation increase in Broca's area observed here.

Alternatively, one might argue that the parser generates hypotheses about the to-be-perceived input, as was suggested for example in the context of the syntactic prediction locality theory (Gibson, 1998). According to this approach, the parser makes the minimal prediction of a subject and a verb in order to form a grammatical sentence. This prediction is violated by each scrambled object NP. The creation of new structural positions in the phrase structure representation, due to the violation of syntactic predictions, might therefore be considered as a function of Broca's area.

This type of account would suggest a close link between the activation observed for scrambled sentences in the present experiment and previous ERP studies in which scrambling was shown to induce a fronto-central negativity at the position of the moved object (Rösler et al., 1998; Bornkessel, Schlesewsky, & Friederici, 2002; Schlesewsky et al., 2003). This "scrambling negativity" has been interpreted as a transient mismatch between a syntactic prediction of the parser and the actually perceived input (Friederici, Schlesewsky, & Fiebach, 2003; Schlesewsky et al., 2003). As each scrambled NP elicits a negativity of that sort, one might assume that these negative ERP components sum to the activation difference observed in the present study. More generally, it was suggested that sentential constituents, which index the necessity of transformational processes, elicit negative ERP responses over the left frontal scalp (see Hoen and Dominey, chapter 16, this volume). Thus, as each scrambled NP indicates the need to apply transformational operations in the reconstruction of the underlying structure, these might sum to the parametric complexity effect observed in the present study. This suggestion, however, is difficult to evaluate because of the relatively low temporal resolution of fMRI, which precludes associations between the global activation effects with temporally circumscribed processing regions within a sentence. Although it is possible to detect activation changes in the brain induced by perceptual or cognitive events of only a few milliseconds in length using event-related fMRI (e.g., Dehaene et al., 2001), it is currently not possible to dissociate brief successive events that follow each other rapidly. The parametric activation effect in the left inferior frontal lobe may just as well reflect a global processing effect that does not have to stem from the scrambled constituents themselves.

Thus, with respect to the processing of clause-medial word-order variations, the present fMRI data support previous conclusions drawn from behavioral psycholinguistic studies by showing that subject-first structures are preferred, whereas the processing of sentences with scrambled object arguments induces processing difficulty and increases activation in Broca's area above the level seen for sentences with a canonical word order. Analogous to the behavioral data, the fMRI activation differences are dependent upon the number of object NPs that were scrambled. We therefore suggest that the activation differences observed in Broca's area are associated with the increased number of reconstructions that are required in the process of interpreting a scrambled sentence.

For the purposes of the present discussion, we would like to stress in particular that the inferior frontal mechanisms involved in the processing of complex scrambled sentences are not recruited for the processing of ungrammatical sentences. Although the ungrammatical sentences investigated here are understandable, the reconstruction operations that are necessary for the correct interpretation of scrambled sentences are not initiated for the ungrammatical sentences since no reconstruction is required in these cases. Note, however, that this conclusion should not be taken to specify the temporal dynamics of these cognitive processes and brain regions, as the present fMRI data do not allow us to determine the temporal sequence in which the two inferior frontal areas were activated. Thus, the violation-specific activation observed in the posterior frontal operculum may reflect either (a) the processing failure in cases when reconstruction processes cannot be drawn upon to derive an interpretable input, or (b) an earlier abortion of syntactic processing that blocks the application of syntactic reconstruction processes. Taken together, processing models of sentence comprehension should account for the fact that distinct underlying mechanisms are involved in the processing of sentences with legal, as compared to illegal, syntactic transformations.

17.3 IMPLICATIONS FOR THE FUNCTIONAL NEUROANATOMY OF LANGUAGE PROCESSING

In addition to the implications for parsing models discussed above, the results of the present study also have important implications for the understanding of the neuroanatomical bases of language. Broca's area has been associated with a central representation of syntax involved in both production and perception for some time (e.g., Zurif, Caramazza, & Myerson, 1972; Caramazza & Zurif, 1976; Berndt & Caramazza, 1980). This association was established on the basis of aphasiologic studies and is supported by more recent functional neuroimaging studies. The exact nature of the syntactic processes supported by Broca's area, however, is not yet fully understood. Several neuroimaging studies demonstrated activation differences in this region between sentences of high and low complexity. However, not all complexity variations modulate Broca's area (cf. Cooke et al., 2002; Fiebach, Schlesewsky, & Friederici, 2001; Caplan et al., 2002). Also, the greatest portion of studies of syntactic anomalies did not report activation differences in Broca's area (see also the more detailed discussion by Osterhout and colleagues in chapter 14, this volume).

The present results support the view that Broca's area (i.e., the inferior portion of Brodmann's area 44) is indeed involved in syntactic processing during sentence comprehension. They demonstrate that activation in Broca's area increases when the parser is confronted with sentences with a complex phrase structure. In the present case, this means that new structural positions have to be created in order to correctly interpret the scrambled sentences. This conclusion is in line with the results reported by Röder et al. (2002) for auditory sentence comprehension. Word-order variations as such, however, do not necessarily induce activation increases in Broca's area. In an earlier study (Fiebach et al., 2001), we showed that object- and subject-initial *wh*-questions do not differ in their amount of brain activation. This was most likely due to the fact that in both sentence types, a noun phrase was displaced to the same sentence-initial position. Thus, in sentences that do not differ in terms of the number and type of phrasal nodes, Broca's area is not differentially engaged (see also Cooke et al., 2001, for converging evidence). Broca's area, however, seems to be involved in the processing of *wh*-movement as such (Ben-Shachar, Hendler, Kahn, Ben-Beshat, & Grodzinsky, 2003) and is influenced by the distance over which *wh*-movement took place (Fiebach et al.; Cooke et al.). The latter two studies concluded that Broca's area mediates syntactic working-memory costs induced by syntactic movement operations. In addition, the present study demonstrates that activation in Broca's area is also dependent upon the number of movement operations that underlie a sentence and that, consequently, have to be dealt with when comprehending a complex sentence. We conclude, therefore, that Broca's area (at least the inferior portion of Brodmann's area 44, which is located in the pars opercularis of the left inferior frontal gyrus) is particularly recruited for dealing with phrasal structures that deviate in their complexity from the canonical, underlying structure. Broca's area, under the most general perspective, is thus critical for the hierarchical structuring of the different sentence constituents.

Interestingly, the present results suggest that the detection of a syntactic anomaly is a function of a closely located but distinct left inferior frontal region, located more posteriorly in the deep fronto-opercular region. Assuming a neuroanatomical dissociation between areas involved in detecting ungrammaticalities and areas involved in the transformational processing of complex phrase structures might provide an explanation for the fact that most previous studies did not observe Broca's area activity for syntactic violations. Although the posterior frontal operculum has not as yet received much attention in the context of syntactic processing, the present data and other recent studies (Friederici et al., 2003; Kuperberg et al., 2003; see the preceding text) indicate that it might play a critical role in the detection of syntactic anomalies. Given the fact that lesions resulting in Broca's aphasia are often very extended (Mohr et al., 1978), the two brain regions implicated here for distinct aspects of syntactic processing are very likely to be affected jointly in Broca's aphasia.

17.4 CONCLUSION

To conclude, functional neuroimaging provides a new source of information that can reflect the neural of bases of subcomponents of cognitive processes which are indistinguishable in behavioral data. Here we make use of scrambling in German nonpronominal declarative sentences to demonstrate how fMRI can help to solve open questions regarding cognitive models of sentence processing. We focused on the question of whether or not sentences with grammatically illegal transformations are processed in the same way as grammatically legal but complex sentences, a conclusion that is suggested by off-line behavioral data. The results of the present study indicate that neural activity in two distinct left inferior frontal brain regions is affected by the complexity induced by a word-order variation in the German middlefield and ungrammaticality, respectively. We suggest that these results complement previous behavioral and electrophysiological data.

Despite the apparent continuity in the acceptability of complex and ungrammatical sentences, and despite the fact that scrambled object NPs elicit an ERP response which is quite similar to that seen for syntactic anomalies, complex versus ill-formed constituent permutations activate distinct brain areas in the frontal portion of the left perisylvian language region. The importance of this observation for cognitive models of sentence processing lies primarily in demonstrating that there is no grammaticality–ungrammaticality continuum. This underlying distinction stands in contrast to the surface behavior (acceptability properties) of complex versus ungrammatical structures.

The present data demonstrate how language comprehension models can benefit from considering functional neuroanatomical constraints provided by cognitive neuroimaging. These additional sources of evidence lead to models that specify cognitive processes along several dimensions, including the temporal dynamics of information flow as well as several neuroanatomical stages of information processing (see, for example, the neurocognitive model of sentence processing described by Friederici, 2002), the integration among which is critical for understanding cognitive processes as a function of the workings of the human brain.

17.5 ACKNOWLEDGMENTS

The research reported here was performed as part of research project FI848/1 awarded to CJF and ADF by the German Research Foundation (DFG).

References

Bader, M., & Meng, M. (1999). Subject-object ambiguities in German embedded clauses: An across-the-board comparison. *Journal of Psycholinguistic Research, 28,* 121–143.

Ben-Schachar, M., Hendler, T., Kahn, I., Ben-Beshat, D., & Grodzinsky, Y. (2003). The neural reality of syntactic transformations: Evidence from fMRI. *Psychological Science, 14,* 433–440.

Berndt, R. S., & Caramazza, A. (1980). A redefinition of the syndrome of Broca's aphasia: Implications for a neuropsychological model of language. *Applied Psycholinguistics, 1,* 225–278.

Bornkessel, I. D., Schlesewsky, M., & Friederici, A. D. (2002). Grammar overrides frequency. Evidence from the online processing of flexible word order. *Cognition, 85,* B21-B30.

Caplan, D., Vijayan, S., et al. (2002). Vascular responses to syntactic processing: Event-related fMRI study of relative clauses. *Human Brain Mapping, 15,* 26–38.

Caramazza, A., & Zurif, E. B. (1976). Dissociation of algorithmic and heuristic processes in language comprehension. *Brain and Language, 3,* 572–582.

Cooke, A., Zurif, E. B., Devita, C., Alsop, D., Koenig, P., Detre, J., Gee, J., Piñango, M., Balogh, J., Grossman, M. (2002). Neural basis for sentence comprehension: Grammatical and short-term memory components. *Human Brain Mapping, 15,* 80–94.

Dehaene, S., Naccache, L., Cohen, L., Bihan, D. L., Mangin, J. F., Poline, J. B., Riviere, D. (2001). Cerebral mechanisms of word masking and unconscious repetition priming. *Nature Neuroscience, 4,* 752–758.

De Vincenzi, M. (1991). *Syntactic parsing strategies in Italian.* Dordrecht, Netherlands: Kluwer.

De Vincenzi, M. (1996). Syntactic analysis in sentence comprehension: Effects of dependency type and grammatical constraints. *Journal of Psycholinguistic Research, 25,* 117–133.

Embick, D., Marantz, A., Miyashita, Y., O'Neil, W., & Sakai, K. L. (2000). A syntactic specialization for Broca's area. *Proceedings of the National Academy of Sciences, USA, 97,* 6150–6154.

Fiebach, C. J. (2001). *Working memory and syntax during sentence processing. A neurocognitive investigation with event-related brain potentials and functional magnetic resonance imaging.* Ph.D. Thesis, University of Leipzig, Max Planck Institute of Cognitive Neuroscience: MPI Series in Cognitive Neuroscience.

Fiebach, C. J., Schlesewsky, M., & Friederici, A. D. (2001). Syntactic working memory and the establishment of filler-gap dependencies: Insights from ERPs and fMRI. *Journal of Psycholinguistic Research, 30,* 321–338.

Fiebach, C. J., Schlesewsky, M., Lohmann, G., von Cramon, D. Y., & Friederici, A. D. (2004). Revisiting the role of Broca's area in sentence processing: Syntactic integration vs. syntactic working memory.

Fodor, J., Bever, T., & Garrett, M. (1974). *The psychology of language.* New York: McGraw-Hill.

Friederici, A. D. (2002). Towards a neural basis of auditory sentence processing. *Trends in Cognitive Science, 6,* 78–84.

Friederici, A. D., Rüschemeyer, S.-A., Hahne, A., & Fiebach, C.J. (2003). Localization of syntactic and semantic processing networks: An event-related fMRI study. *Cerebral Cortex, 13,* 170–177.

Friederici, A. D., Schlesewsky, M., & Fiebach, C.J. (2003). Wh-movement vs. scrambling: The brain makes a difference. It did appear. In S. Karimi (Ed.), *Word order and scrambling* (pp. 325–344). Oxford: Blackwell.

Friston, K. (1997). Imaging cognitive anatomy. *Trends in Cognitive Sciences, 1,* 21–27.

Gibson, E. (1998). Linguistic complexity: Locality of syntactic dependencies. *Cognition, 68,* 1–76.

Haider, H. (2000). Scrambling—What's the state of the art? In S.M. Powers & C. Harman (Eds.), *The acquisition of scrambling and cliticization* (pp. 19–40). Dordrecht, Netherlands: Kluwer.

Kemtes, K. A., & Kemper, S. (1997). Younger and older adults' on-line processing of syntactically ambiguous sentences. *Psychology and Aging, 12,* 362–371.

Kuperberg, G. R., Holcomb, P. J., Sitnikova, T., Greve, D., Dale, A. M., & Caplan, D. (2003). Distinct patterns of neural modulation during the processing of conceptual and syntactic anomalies. *Journal of Cognitive Neuroscience, 15,* 272–293.

Lenerz, J. (1977). *Zur Abfolge nominaler Satzglieder im Deutschen.* Tübingen, Germany: Narr.

Meng, M., & Bader, M. (2000). Mode of disambiguation and garden-path strength: An investigation of subject-object ambiguities in German. *Language and Speech, 43,* 43–74.

Miller, G. A., & Chomsky, N. (1963). Finitary models of language users. In R. D. Luce, R. R. Bush, & E. Galanter (Eds.), *Handbook of mathematical psychology* (Vol. 2, pp. 419–491). New York: Wiley.

Mohr, J., Pessin, M., Finkelstein, S., Funkenstein, H., Duncan, G., & Davis, K. (1978). Broca aphasis: Pathological and clinical. *Neurology, 28,* 311–324.

Moro, A., Tettamanti, M., Perani, D., Donati, C., Cappa, S. F., & Fazio, F. (2001). Syntax and the brain: Disentangling grammar by selective anomalies. *NeuroImage, 13,* 110–118.

Pechmann, T., Uszkoreit, H., Engelkamp, J., & Zerbst, D. (1994). *Word order in the German middle field (Report 43).* Computational Linguistics at the University of the Saarland.

Pechmann, T., Uszkoreit, H., Engelkamp, J., & Zerbst, D. (1996). *Wortstellung im deutschen Mittelfeld. Linguistische Theorie und psycholinguistische Evidenz.* In C. Habel, S. Kanngießer, & G. Rickheit (Eds.), *Perspektiven der Kognitiven Linguistik: Modelle und Methoden* (pp. 257–299). Opladen, Germany: Westdeutscher Verlag.

Röder, B., Schicke, T., Stock, O., Heberer, G., & Rösler, F. (2000). Word order effects in German sentences and German pseudo-word sentences. *Zeitschrift für Sprache und Kognition, 19,* 31–37.

Röder, B., Stock, O., Neville, H., Bien, S., & Rösler, F. (2002). Brain activation modulated by the comprehension of normal and pseudo-word sentences of different procesing demands: A functional magnetic resonance imaging study. *NeuroImage, 15,* 1003–1014.

Rösler, F., Pechmann, T., Streb, J., Röder, B., & Henninghausen, E. (1998). Parsing of sentences in a language with varying word order: Word-by-word variations of process-ing demands are revealed by event-related brain potentials. *Journal of Memory and Language, 38,* 150–176.

Schlesewsky, M., Bornkessel, I., & Frisch, S. (2003). The neurophysiological basis of word order variations in German. *Brain and Language, 86,* 116–128.

Uszkoreit, H. (1986). Constraints on order. *Linguistics, 24,* 883–906.

Yngve, V. (1960). A model and a hypothesis for language structure. *Proceedings of the American Philosophical Society, 104,* 444–466.

Zurif, E. B., Caramazza, A., & Myerson, R. (1972). Grammatical judgments of agrammatic aphasics. *Neuropsychologia, 10,* 405–417.

Chapter 18
On-Line Sentence Processing: Past, Present, and Future

MICHAEL K. TANENHAUS

18.1 INTRODUCTION

You know the kind of nightmare that's so realistic that when you wake up the next morning you're not sure whether it was a dream or not? The events in the dream get incorporated into your daily consciousness, so when you meet someone who was in the dream, you are not quite sure whether the conversation in the dream was real or not.

I had a nightmare like that recently. Manolo and Chuck asked me to write a chapter called "On-Line Sentence Processing: Past, Present, and Future," and I agreed. What could be more nightmarish than to publicly misinterpret the past, misunderstand the present, and be hilariously wrong about the future, while exposing my biases, petty grudges, intellectual narrowness, and annoying propensity for didactic pontification? But, after all, it was just a dream. Then the copyright form from Psychology Press showed up in my mailbox.

What follows are some personal thoughts about on-line methodologies in sentence processing: past, present, and future, stimulated by the collection of talks and posters at the special emphasis session, *On-Line Measures for Theoretical Advance: Eye Movements, ERPs, and Beyond,* and the discussion fueled by Don Mitchell's provocative commentary.[1] I will selectively review a bit of the past, comment on the present, and venture some speculations about the future. These observations, comments, and speculations will often be linked by a common theme that can be broadly summarized as follows. Though we have made considerable progress in understanding language processing since we began using on-line measures, and the use of these measures has contributed enormously to that success, progress has often been hampered by the absence of clear linking assumptions. In the next section, I spell out what I mean by linking assumptions. Sections 18.3, 18.4, and 18.5 address the past, present, and future in historical order.

18.2 LINKING HYPOTHESES

The interpretation of any behavioral measure depends upon a theory, or linking hypothesis, that maps the response measure onto the theoretical constructs of interest. Linking hypotheses are a necessary part of the inference chain that links theory to data. Put differently, though we often wish it would be otherwise, there are no "signature" data patterns that provide a direct window into underlying cognitive processes. For example, using cross-modal semantic priming to infer that a noun phrase has been coindexed to an empty category (e.g., Nicol & Swinney, 1989), depends on the following chain of inference. Encountering an anaphor triggers a memory search that identifies the antecedent. The antecedent is then "reactivated." Activation spreads to related or associated lexical concepts, facilitating their recognition and resulting in speeded recognition times compared to unprimed words. The extent to which patterns of priming to words related to antecedents of empty categories can be interpreted as evidence about coindexing in processing depends upon the correctness of these assumptions. Likewise, competing hypotheses about what the N400 component of the ERPs measures are alternative theories about the link between a cognitive process and the brain states that result in the N400.

Linking hypotheses are often stated informally or are left implicit when they seem obvious or intuitive. The magnitude of priming is assumed to index the amount of activation in memory. When the duration and pattern of fixations are used to study sentence processing in reading, the linking hypothesis between fixation duration and underlying processes is that reading times increase when processing becomes more difficult. Nonetheless, our theories of sentence processing will eventually have to combine explicit models of the underlying processes with explicit models of how these processes affect fixations. This will become clear when we consider the link between models of complexity and response measures such as fixation duration and self-paced reading. In fact, I will argue that these complexity measures may introduce a nonlinearity that can actually mask some increases in complexity, raising the possibility that some of these phenomena may be best understood by using off-line measures.

A more general danger is that, in the absence of clear linking hypotheses, we confuse our dependent measure with the (hypothesized) cognitive processes we believe we are measuring. For example, in empty- category experiments, a priming effect does not provide direct evidence that (a) the entity it is associated with has been interpreted as the referent of an anaphor; (b) its antecedent has been reactivated; or (c) that the antecedent has been coindexed with the anaphor. Of course, one can use a priming effect as part of an inference chain to argue that coindexing (a theoretical notion) has taken place. However, this inference chain must include the linking hypothesis. Likewise, one cannot interpret increases in reading times as direct evidence of increased processing complexity, access of multiple linguistic forms, or syntactic misanalysis. Further, evidence that a particular cortical area is more active for two carefully matched classes of sentences that differ only in syntactic complexity (according to some metric) is not direct evidence that that area is involved in syntactic processing.

As researchers continue to use on-line measures to address increasingly fine-grained questions about cognitive microstructure, explicit and quantitative linking hypotheses will become increasingly important. The absence of an explicit linking hypothesis can mean that the logic of superficially clear predictions is actually problematic because the linking hypothesis is fuzzy, undetermined, circular, or simply incorrect. In contrast, the presence of an explicit linking hypothesis can help clarify one's thinking, often making it possible to tease apart subtle differences among competing models. Moreover, making linking hypotheses more explicit can play a central role in helping us understand the nature of our methods.[2]

Let me illustrate why we need to pay more attention to linking hypotheses by addressing and discussing the dangers of two approaches that attempt to finesse the problem. The first assumes that there is a linear relationship between the response measure and the underlying processes. The second approach relies on signature data patterns.

18.2.1 Assuming a Linear Relationship

Why not simply assume that there is a linear relationship between an underlying process and our response measures? Let me illustrate the potential dangers by focusing on a particular issue: the relationship between processing complexity and parsing models. In recent years, there has been considerable interest in developing models that make explicit predictions about processing complexity (e.g., Gibson, 1998). Perhaps the most widely used measure for investigating these effects is self-paced reading, which is generally regarded as a low-tech version of monitoring eye movements—eyetracking on the cheap, as it were. In fact, one can make a strong case that self-paced reading is a better measure of local processing complexity because in unrestricted reading, fixation time is distributed among fixations that come from initial fixations, followed by re-fixations after regressive eye movements. However, both self-paced reading and fixation times are not likely to have a linear relationship to complexity. Readers have a strong tendency to move along at a relatively constant rate, keeping button presses and fixation duration within a restricted range. Thus, both measures will saturate, flattening out the effects of high complexity.

For example, one of the classic observations in sentence processing is that there appears to be a dramatic increase in complexity for center-embedded sentences with two embeddings compared to one embedding, as illustrated in the following examples:

(1) a. *The dog yelped.*
     b. *The dog the cat scratched yelped.*
     c. *The dog the cat the mouse bit scratched yelped.*

In fact, most people will judge (1a) and (1b) to be grammatical and (1c) to be ungrammatical. Moreover, in a magnitude estimation study, people will judge (1b) to be about twice as difficult as (1a), whereas (1c) is judged to be 10 times as difficult as (1a). However, processing time measures will likely restrict the range, attenuating these differences. Without taking this into account, one can draw the wrong conclusions about the underlying process, incorrectly judging some classes of models to be better than others on the basis of goodness of fit to the data when the measure itself has a complex nonlinear relationship to the underlying process. Moreover, a consideration of the linking hypothesis suggests that on-line processing measures may not be appropriate or must be combined with off-line measures when the on-line measure is likely to saturate. Ironically, then, we have a case where we may need to use off-line data to better understand our on-line measure.

18.2.2 Signature Data Patterns

In the absence of explicit linking hypotheses, researchers using on-line measures often resort to using certain data patterns as evidence for an underlying cognitive event. One clear example involves measures of processing time. For example, an increase in the duration of a fixation to the word where a syntactic ambiguity is resolved is taken as evidence for a garden path. If the effect occurs during an initial fixation or during the "first pass" through a region of text, it reflects initial processing; if it occurs after a regression or in a later region, it is an effect of reanalysis. These data patterns are usually established in experiments using materials for which there are pre-theoretical expectations (e.g., *The horse raced past the barn fell* creates a garden path) and then used to resolve theoretical disputes among competing models. These signature effects are taken as evidence that a paradigm is sensitive to a particular level of linguistic processing. They often become stand-ins for the underlying processing; for example, a P600 is a syntactic effect, an N400 is a semantic effect, and so forth. Other examples include referring to an increase in processing as a garden-path effect, a second-pass effect as a reanalysis effect, and priming as evidence for anaphora resolution or lack thereof. On first consideration, this appears fairly innocuous. After all, are we not simply beginning with some clear cases and then building on them? I have three concerns. The first is circularity. The evidence used to diagnose a signature pattern typically comes from pre-theoretical assumptions about the materials. This would be a good first step if the next step were a serious program of research to evaluate this interpretation of the effect. However, what typically happens is that the circle is completed: the effect is used as litmus test for the process that was originally used to define the effect. We then end up chasing our tails because there are multiple interpretations of the linguistic process that motivated the interpretation in the first place. Note, for example, that most disagreements within competing linguistic frameworks are boundary disputes, that is, disputes about how to characterize certain data, and not disputes about the facts. I suspect that this is one reason why attempts to use psycholinguistic data to adjudicate among competing grammatical frameworks are rarely, if ever, successful.

The second problem is that, to my knowledge, there are no clear examples of signature data patterns, at least in the domain of processing load or priming measures. Rather, the interpretation of an effect depends upon the details of linking hypotheses. For example, increases in reading times, or lack thereof, can result from multiple underlying events at multiple levels of representation. For example, in a system in which multiple constraints contribute to ambiguity resolution, the immediate use of a constraint may result in either immediate or delayed effects of that constraint, depending upon the strength and reliability of that constraint and the algorithm that links constraint integration to fixation time. Likewise, a weak constraint may take longer to affect processing, not because its use is delayed, but because its effects are only seen when other constraints come into play. This phenomenon is frequently observed in perceptual domains where we know that multiple cues are at play, for example, motion and depth perception. Tanenhaus, Spivey-Knowlton, and Hanna (2000) develop this argument in detail, focusing on context effects on reading times for locally ambiguous sentences. With an explicit linking hypothesis it becomes clear that data patterns that are traditionally interpreted as support for different classes of models can all arise from the same model simply because the constraints differ in strength. Thus, we argued that in the absence of defining an algorithm that maps processing onto reading times, we become like Thomas Hardy's "purblind doomsters" who determine fate by dicing time (Tanenhaus et al., 2000).

Some may object on the grounds that abandoning signature data patterns makes our theories more difficult to test and more difficult to falsify. However, I think the opposite is likely to be the case. As we develop linking hypotheses, we can often evaluate alternative models using goodness-of-fit metrics. This in turn will let us focus on how much variance we are accounting for, not simply on whether or not a predicted effect reaches significance. This is beginning to happen for models of eye-movement control during reading though these models have yet to be extended beyond low-level and lexical variables (e.g., Reichle, Rayner, & Pollatsek in press). Finally, when we take linking hypotheses seriously, we are more likely to avoid becoming infatuated with a response measure because we think about a particular process. This way, we also avoid being disillusioned when that turns out not to be the case.

18.3 LINKING ASSUMPTIONS: SOME LESSONS FROM THE PAST

The arguments in section 18.2 all had to do with linking hypotheses that relate a dependent measure in a task to an underlying process. As the title of the special session made explicit, on-line measures are useful only insofar as they contribute to advancing theory. Here I would add the caution that both the assumptions that link particular models to particular data patterns and the assumptions that motivate some of the phenomena we take as axiomatic are sometimes more the result of historical associations than of well-articulated arguments. I will try to develop this point by focusing on two such examples: The first is the link between working memory constraints and on-line processing, and the second is the relationship between processing modularity, linguistic representation, and the time course of processing. To foreshadow the argument, we can be suspicious that underspecified linking assumptions are at play when (a) the same first principles are used to motivate different theoretical approaches across different eras, and (b) we cannot point to a clear scientific reason why.

Let us begin with a brief consideration of why on-line measures have become so central to research in sentence processing, focusing on sentence comprehension. To a first approximation, the input for linguistic processing arrives sequentially. This is necessarily true for spoken language, which unfolds over time. For example, the bilabial stop [b] that begins the word *beaker* must *necessarily* be articulated before the velar stop [k], which means that the listeners will encounter its acoustic correlates earlier. This temporal unfolding creates potential ambiguity. The initial phonetic sequence in *beaker* will be consistent with a set of potential lexical candidates, including beaker, beetle, beak, and so forth.

The fact that information unfolds over time also means that information relevant to higher-level language processes may sometimes precede information that disambiguates a lower-level process. For example, pitch accent on a vowel in an anaphoric noun phrase can provide information indicating that the referent is likely to be a given, but not focused, entity, before the noun in that phrase is disambiguated from other potential lexical candidates (Dahan, Tanenhaus, & Chambers, 2002). Ambiguity, of course, holds across multiple levels of representation, including lexical ambiguity, constituent attachment ambiguity, scope ambiguity, and ambiguity of reference, to name a few. The input itself does not unfold over time in reading. However, to a first approximation we know that visual attention is successively directed to the text in word-level units (for a review, see Rayner, 1998).

The fact that the input arrives over time means that response measures that are not time-locked to the input may fail to reveal input-driven processes that are shortlived. This danger was highlighted by two classic studies published by Marslen-Wilson in the early 1970s. The first showed that lexical, syntactic, and contextual information all determine the likelihood that close shadowers (people who can repeat back a message at a lag of about one syllable) will fluently restore a distorted word in running speech (Marslen-Wilson, 1973). The second showed that listeners could monitor a sentence for a target word, a word that rhymed with the target word, or a word that was a member of the semantic category of a target word at an extremely short lag (Marslen-Wilson, 1975a). Response times were faster to words occurring late in a sentence compared to a word occurring early in a sentence. Moreover, there were no differences in response times in rhyme and category monitoring despite the fact that rhyme monitoring would seem to tap phonological processing that would seem to be logically prior to the semantic analysis required for rhyme monitoring (Marslen-Wilson, 1975b).

In retrospect, these results do not seem all that surprising. Why then did they have such enormous impact at the time? One reason was that it was not obvious that language processing would be *that* closely time-locked to the input. In fact, early models of sentence processing assumed that language comprehension was a form of "sophisticated catch-up game."[3] The idea was eminently reasonable. Delaying commitments too long would overload limited-capacity resources, whereas making commitments prematurely would require memory-intensive revisions. In this spirit, early models of "sentence perception" focused on determining which processing units (e.g., phrases or clauses) might best balance these competing constraints. Here is how the problem looked from the perspective of a naïve, second-year graduate student:

Briefly consider the task which the listener faces during speech perception. Armed with an extremely limited short-term memory span, he must convert a (essentially) continuous stream of acoustic input into something meaningful. In order to accomplish this, the listener must periodically process segments of speech and recode them into a form which can be integrated easily with previous and subsequent input and which releases short-term memory for further processing. Thus the first goal for a theory of speech perception is the specification of the perceptual units of speech (Tanenhaus & Carroll, 1975, p. 500).

The catch-up game view was largely abandoned only when studies using time-locked response measures showed that people process language continuously without delaying provisional commitments.

Since then our knowledge of real-time language processing has greatly expanded. Theoretical ideas about language processing that seemed plausible in the 1960s and the 1970s can now be discarded based on a solid body of experimental results. We know that listeners rapidly access and use linguistic knowledge, making provisional commitments at multiple levels of linguistic representation. Access to the semantic representations of spoken words begins as soon as phonetic input is encountered. For example, by the middle of the first vowel in *student*, potential lexical candidates such as student, stool, and stoop become active in memory, along with their associated syntactic and semantic representations. In the absence of strongly constraining context, convergence on the most likely lexical candidate occurs shortly after enough phonetic input is received to distinguish the input from other likely alternatives—often well before the word ends. Constraints based on prior syntactic, semantic, and discourse constraints further increase the speed with which a word is identified, suggesting that semantic integration takes place in parallel with lexical access. Syntactic processing occurs equally quickly. When a sentence becomes syntactically anomalous, processing effects are observed immediately after the word where the anomaly occurs. Moreover, when a sentence that is briefly ambiguous between two or more syntactic alternatives is disambiguated in favor of its less preferred alternative, processing consequences are observed as soon as the disambiguating information is encountered (Frazier & Rayner, 1982; Rayner, Carlson, & Frazier, 1983). Similar effects are observed for semantic and pragmatic information.

18.3.1 Working Memory and Incremental Processing

While most work on sentence processing now takes as axiomatic the observation that language processing is continuous, we have not come all that far in developing plausible theories for why processing is so relentlessly continuous. The relationship between working memory and language processing, which continues to motivate much theorizing, illustrates some of the limits of our current theories. My own informal polling of psycholinguists has not resulted in particularly satisfactory answers. If any explanation for why processing is incremental is offered, it is that continuous processing and provisional commitments are necessitated by the demands of limited working memory.[4] However, as we have just seen, working-memory constraints could, and were, just as plausibly used to argue for delaying syntactic and semantic commitments. To relate this to the linking assumption theme, the link between working memory and real-time language processing continues to be underspecified. While working-memory limitations are often appealed to, the nature of working memory itself is rarely studied. Granted, there is a large literature on how individual differences in working memory affect various aspects of language processing. There is also a vigorous debate about whether language processing draws on a single limited resource pool or a set of specialized resource pools (Just & Carpenter, 1992; Waters & Caplan, 1996; MacDonald & Christensen, 2002). However, there is a dearth of work that seeks to manipulate variables that affect working memory *per se*. It is telling that we do not have an active literature that attempts to measure memory processes during sentence processing to evaluate claims about processing load. Instead, we have a literature that invokes memory load as an explanation for the differences that we observe. I understand that most of us are interested in language processing, and not working memory. Nonetheless, appeals to working-memory constraints will have little explanatory force until the link between working memory and sentence processing is made more explicit.[5] More generally, appeals to working-memory explanations for phenomena in language processing are often no more sophisticated today than they were in the 1960s.

18.3.2 Modularity, Falsifiability, and Linguistic Representation

A second reason for the impact of Marslen-Wilson's results was that he explicitly called into question the mapping between transformational grammar and models of language processing. In the early days of the Derivational Theory of Complexity (DTC), transformational grammar was viewed as the computational engine that drove language processing, providing an explicit theory of both processing and memory for sentences. By the late 1960s, that link was to become increasingly tenuous (for a review, see Tanenhaus & Trueswell, 1995).

Marslen-Wilson directly challenged the incorporation assumption, arguing that the linguistic representations incorporated into the transformational grammars of the time were poorly suited for use in on-line comprehension (cf. Marslen-Wilson, 1975b; see also Bresnan, 1978). The problem was that much of syntactic knowledge was incorporated into ordered rules in a derivation. Moreover, the rules were defined over clause-length sequences. The only natural way to incorporate a transformational grammar into a processing model, then, was to posit that processing was delayed until the end of linguistic units like clauses, which was incompatible with on-line comprehension, or to assume that grammatical relationships are recovered using procedures that do not make direct use of grammatical knowledge (e.g., Bever, 1970; Fodor, Bever, & Garrett, 1974).

Marslen-Wilson argued that linguistic knowledge must be accessible via lexical representations, which could create parallelism at multiple levels of representation. Thus, distributed parallel models were opposed to models that directly relied on the linguistic representations. Of course, Marslen-Wilson's arguments were not accepted without a challenge. In a brilliantly argued paper, Forster (1979) proposed a model of sentence comprehension in which processing was accomplished by a sequence of autonomous subsystems. The crux of Forster's empirical argument was that the types of measures that Marslen-Wilson used might not directly reflect the output of the linguistic subsystems that were responsible for the underlying computations. With a different linking hypothesis, data like Marslen-Wilson's, which seemed to demand parallel access, computation, and unrestricted information flow, could be made compatible with serial models.

Marslen-Wilson's notions are, of course, highly compatible with current linguistic theories, which have increasingly relied on rich lexical representations since Chomsky (1970) reversed course and argued for putting more linguistic knowledge into the lexicon (MacDonald, Pearlmutter, & Seidenberg, 1994). Further, some grammatical frameworks completely eschew transformations. Nonetheless, the association remains. Parallel-distributed interactive models are widely viewed as incompatible with linguistically motivated representations, whereas autonomous serial stage models are seen as more compatible.

Serial models are also often viewed as more constrained and more falsifiable than interactive models. This is a somewhat curious association given that Forster's arguments depended crucially upon making the link between data and theory more obscure, that is, using linking hypotheses that introduced more degrees of freedom. In fact, proponents of parallel constraint-based models throughout the years have typically invoked simple linking hypotheses between theory and data, whereas proponents of serial autonomous models often appealed to more complex linking hypotheses (cf. Norris, McQueen, & Cutler, 2000). However, the association becomes more understandable when we take into account the seminal work by Sternberg (1969) that largely resurrected reaction time as a dependent measure. Sternberg outlined an additive factors methodology in which interactions, or lack thereof, could be used to diagnose stages in information processing. Given a specific set of assumptions, signature data patterns could be used to identify stages and to determine which variables affect those stages, in much the same way as speed–accuracy trade-off functions are now used to identify the time course of memory retrieval—again given certain assumptions.[6] However, proponents of serial models rarely adopt Sternberg's assumptions. Moreover, a complex underspecified linking hypothesis wreaks havoc with the falsifiability of autonomous stage models. Note that I am *not* claiming that parallel interactive models are, in principle, simpler to, or to be preferred to, autonomous serial models. However, the claim that interactive constraint-based models are less easily falsified than autonomous serial models reflects a historical association rather than an actual link between data and theory.

The 1980s saw a methodological synergy emerge between on-line measures and a reenergized link between linguistics and language processing. The notion of modularity played a key role in these developments in psycholinguistics, creating a set of associations that continue to influence our theorizing and use of on-line measures. We can illustrate these associations by considering some well-known studies of lexical ambiguity resolution that used variations of cross-modal lexical priming (e.g., Conrad, 1974; Swinney, 1979; Tanenhaus, Leiman, & Seidenberg, 1979).

Early studies investigating ambiguity focused on the question of whether or not ambiguity complicates processing. Using globally ambiguous sentences, psycholinguists asked whether the presence of lexical and structural ambiguity increased processing difficulty. Many of these studies used the *phoneme monitoring task* introduced by Foss (1969). Phoneme monitoring is a *divided processing load task*.

The participant is instructed to understand the speech while at the same time monitoring for a phoneme. Detection time for a phoneme is assumed to increase as a function of the amount of attention that the listener is required to devote to understanding the sentence. Thus phoneme monitoring times can be used to track processing load at particular points in a sentence. The results for lexical ambiguity were mixed. Some studies suggested that ambiguity complicated processing; other studies suggested that it did not. Interpretation was further complicated by studies that showed that phoneme monitoring was affected by a variety of variables that had not been well controlled in early studies (e.g., Newman & Dell, 1978).

The cross-modal studies took another tack. Building upon classic studies by Meyer and Schvanaveldt (1971) and Warren (1972), associative priming was used to infer which senses of an ambiguous word were activated at a particular point in time. When visual targets were presented at the offset of an ambiguous word, targets related to both contextually appropriate and inappropriate senses were primed. When the target was presented a few syllables later (Swinney, 1979) or after a 200-ms delay (Tanenhaus et al., 1979), only targets related to contextually appropriate senses were primed. These were indeed pretty results. But why did they cause such a stir?

First, they fit neatly within the Posner and Snyder (1975) view of information processing as involving two distinct systems. One system reflected rapid, unconscious, hard-wired, automatic processes. The other system reflected slower, conscious, strategic processes. Associative priming at short time lags was assumed to reflect automatic processing. Expectancy-based priming, which included effects driven by context, was assumed to reflect strategic processes. In the context of this two-stage view, Forster's arguments took on added force. Measures like those used by Marslen-Wilson reflected strategic processes. Response measures that reflected automatic processes could reveal the workings of the language processing system, which was assumed to be automatic. Time course was key to getting at the rapid automatic stuff. Look early enough and you might see the core linguistic stuff. Look too late and you see only the results of strategic processes. The lexical ambiguity results seemed to provide clear evidence for this.

The importance of time course was given a further boost when Fodor (1983) made modularity the centerpiece of a theory of mind. Fodor argued that progress in cognitive science was, and would be, largely restricted to the study of encapsulated input systems. Language was a natural candidate for such an input system and, within the language system, it was possible to envision encapsulated subsystems such as processing modules. This idea resonated with Chomsky's proposal that linguistic knowledge can be understood as arising from the interaction of principles from a small set of separate modules (Chomsky, 1980). Combine Forster's architecture with a modular linguistic theory and the stage was set for a modular theory of language processing that could be tested by using time-course measures to get at the outputs of the modules. Perhaps the most influential example of such an approach is presented in Frazier (1987). Here the elegant theoretical integration of Kimball's ideas by Frazier and Fodor (1977) was combined with studies of eyetracking during reading (e.g., Frazier & Rayner, 1982) and a form of the modularity hypothesis.

Essentially, we have a synthesis of on-line measures, processing modularity, and linguistically motivated processing theories, with striking evidence for distinct modules, a lexical module, and a parsing module, each of which follow different principles. Further, we have a moral: We would never have seen that the system was this structured and this modular if we did not have response measures that distinguished between early and late measures.

Again, however, historical association is at play. As Fodor takes pains to acknowledge, his notion of processing modularity is distinctly different from Chomsky's notion of modularity. Moreover, the issue of information flow in language processing is completely orthogonal to the role of linguistic representation in language processing. More strikingly, Fodor's articulation of the modularity hypothesis (e.g., Fodor, 1983) does not place stringent limitations on the kinds of information available to the "front end" of a modular processing system or the interactions among subsystems that are part of a module. A modular system could in fact involve the simultaneous use of various information sources functioning in either a bottom-up or top-down manner as long as constraints come from representations that are computed at some level of representation within the language module (see, e.g., Fodor, pp. 76–77).

Processing modularity does not entail that lexical access or syntactic parsing will be independent from linguistic context, let alone that linguistic modules will function as processing modules. Moreover, none of the proposed modules in modular theories of language processing have natural linguistic correlates (but see Frazier, 1990, for an outline of what such a model might look like). Most strikingly, however, earlier work on the "psychological reality" of grammar, (e.g., Fodor et al., 1974) was firmly rooted in the "new look in perception" tradition that was challenged by Fodor (1983). Work in the new-look tradition often sought to establish the psychological importance of knowledge representations by showing that they affected low-level perceptual processes (see, for example, the preface to Fodor et al.). In the 1960s and the 1970s, showing interactive effects was taken as evidence for the psychological reality of linguistic representations. In contrast, throughout the 1980s and early 1990s the absence of interaction has been taken as support for models that had strong ties to linguistic theory.

I believe that a serious analysis of linking assumptions results in a somewhat different perspective on alternative theoretical frameworks than the view that arises from historical association. Working memory limits can, and have been, used to support radically different classes of models. Serial autonomous models may or may not be intrinsically more compatible with linguistically motivated representations than parallel constraint-based models, and it is not clear *a priori* which is more easily falsified. Further, modularity, or more accurately, whether or not higher-level representations affect lower-level processes, can be taken as evidence for or against linguistically motivated representations. Of course, one might argue that the shifts that have occurred over the years reflect our deepening understanding of language processing and information processing. This might be the case, but I have yet to see the arguments.

What about the link between early and late measures, automatic and strategic processes, and early and late aspects of linguistic processing, which has fueled much research using on-line measures? I am on more shaky ground here because it is harder for me to be objective given much of my current work. We certainly know that using response measures that are not closely time-locked to the input can result in missing short-lived input-driven processes. The literature provides dozens of plausible examples. However, it is not obvious to me that we have many clear examples where our on-line measures have successfully separated early and late components of processing that are triggered by the same input.

Likewise, it is not clear to me that we have strong evidence for cases in which a more sensitive measure, for example, eyetracking in reading, reveals early short-lived effects that are missed by a less sensitive measure, such as self-paced reading. There are many reasons why it is often preferable to monitor eye movements during reading than to measure button-press times in a self-paced reading task. However, I have yet to see a clear example of a case that has stood the test of time, in which eye movements reveal early processes that self-paced reading misses. Part of the reason is that the interpretation of an effect as "early" or "late" depends upon linking hypotheses. A second reason is research in the 1990s has taught us that when psycholinguists ask the question "What do we use and when do we use it?" the answer more often than not is, "*It's the stimulus.*"

Consider the ambiguity that arises in sentences containing *that*-complements, such as *Bill believed the argument was problematic*. The N(oun) P(hrase), *the argument*, is temporarily ambiguous between the object of the verb, *believe*, and the subject of a complement clause. The verb, *was*, in the complement, disambiguates the NP as the subject of the complement. The ambiguity arises because (a) the verb *believed* can occur with either an NP complement or a S(entence) complement, and (b) the complementizer, *that*, which provides strong probabilistic evidence in favor of an S-complement, is optional.

The experimental literature in the 1980s clearly established that, in the absence of a complementizer, reading times increase at the embedded verb, suggesting that readers were initially biased to assume that *the argument* was an NP complement. However, the literature was less clear on whether that same pattern of results occurred when the main verb typically occurred with an S-complement, as is the case for many "propositional" verbs, such as "say," and verbs of "belief," such as "assumed." Ferreira and Henderson (1990) suggested an elegant solution. They noted that most studies reporting clear effects of verb bias used self-paced reading methods. When Ferreira and Henderson used the same materials with self-paced reading and eye-tracking, they found increased difficulty at the embedded verb using first-fixations and first-pass eye movements, regardless of verb bias, but suggestions of verb-bias effects using later measures. Self-paced reading showed stronger and earlier effects of verb bias. Thus the literature could be unified by assuming that eyetracking measures were sensitive to early processes—in this case, an initial stage of parsing that used only category information—that self-paced reading often failed to detect.

This generalization has fallen by the wayside as psycholinguists have begun to use better-controlled materials. Clear verb effects emerged, regardless of response measure, in studies using norms and statistics from corpora to objectively quantify the frequency with which different verbs occur with different complements as well as the thematic fit between the noun phrase and its potential roles (e.g., Garnsey, Pearlmutter, Meyers, & Lotocky, 1997). The most recent work shows that verb biases are best predicted by frequencies that are tied to verb senses (Hare, McRae, & Elman, in press). Moreover, whether or not a speaker uses a *that* in uttering a sentence with an S-complement (Ferreira & Dell, 2000), and whether or not a writer uses a *that*, is not arbitrary (Roland, Elman, & Ferreira, 2003). Finally, simple constraint-integration models are able to simulate the differences among studies by taking into account the specific properties of the materials used in the studies. Further, learning-based models trained on input from corpora predict the pattern of results in the literature.

When I read the literature on the subject–object ambiguity in sentence complement constructions, I am impressed with the progress we have made. Each article subsumes the results of the preceding article and adds something new. However, the progress is not due to advances in the precision of our on-line methods. Rather, it has been driven by a better understanding of our experimental materials and more explicit models of how processing might map onto response times.

My own view is that a similar story can be told for all of the classic attachment ambiguities that provided the empirical test bed for models of ambiguity resolution through the 1980s and 1990s.

18.4 THE PRESENT

For most of the last two decades, on-line research in sentence processing has been (productively) focused on accounting for a somewhat limited set of phenomena, most of which involved temporarily ambiguous sentences, with English as the primary target language and reading as the preferred modality. Important work on these topics continues. However, the field is rapidly expanding to include a wider range of phenomena, many fueled by developments in our on-line measures and related tools, including theoretical developments in linguistics.

For example, the availability of reliable light-weight head-mounted eyetrackers has made it possible to study real-time spoken language comprehension in natural tasks because eye movements to task-relevant objects are closely time-locked to the unfolding language (Tanenhaus, Spivey-Knowlton, Eberhard, & Sedivy, 1995).[7] Thus we can study language processing in behavioral tasks in which the participant is interacting with the world and participating in an interactive conversation, thus inviting studies of referential issues that lie at the intersection of semantics, pragmatics, and reference. Free-viewing eyetracking has also made it easier to study sentence processing in children (Trueswell, Sekerina, Logrip, & Hill, 1999). For a recent overview see Henderson and Ferreira (in press) and Tanenhaus and Trueswell (in press).

The visual-world paradigm brings with it a new set of concerns about linking hypotheses. For example, how do we interpret eye movements when they are influenced by interactions among language, the visual environment, and the task? One approach is to eliminate the task by using passive listening and then apportion the eye movements into those that are likely to be controlled by properties of the scene and properties of the language. However, I am skeptical. Such a "render-unto-Caesar-what-is-Caesar's" approach to understanding eye movements in visual-world tasks is likely to run into the same problems that plagued the scan-path analyses of scenes (see Vivianni, 1990) after the initial excitement created by the seminal work of Yarbus (1967). Instead, I expect that we will need to use task-based models to understand fixations in much the same way as we need task-based models to understand how eye movements function in scene perception (e.g., Ballard, Hayhoe, Pook, & Rao, 1998; Henderson & Ferreira, in press). This is why I prefer to use task-based variants of the visual-world paradigm.

Having expressed these concerns, I acknowledge that despite my initial skepticism about examining eye movements in passive listening, the line of research initiated by Altmann & Kamide (1999) has proved remarkably successful (see Huettig & Altmann, chapter 11, this volume).

Research using ERPs is becoming increasingly more sophisticated as a stable body of results has emerged and as newer brain imaging techniques have begun to address one of the principle limitations of ERPs—the difficulty of relating the potential measured on the scalp to the region of the cortex where the potential was generated. Increasingly, this reflects a trend to combine different measures, either by using multiple tasks with the same stimuli or by using multiple measures within the same task.

The growing body of work in language production, including paradigms for studying real-time language production, has widened the range of theoretical issues in the field. This includes making comprehension researchers aware of the theoretical implications of two truisms: (a) production creates the input that readers and listeners process (MacDonald, 1999); and (b) interactive conversation requires participants to be both speakers and addressees. A natural outgrowth of these developments has been an increased interest in how naturally occurring features of spontaneously generated utterances, such as disfluency, are used in on-line processing.

Finally, an increased interest in learning has been fueled by numerous developments. These include a growing appreciation of the power of statistical processes in human and machine learning, the lasting impact of network-based learning models, and empirical results demonstrating the plasticity of production and comprehension processes.

The contributions in this volume reflect many of these trends, including those from the invited speakers in the special emphasis session at the Eighth AMLaP Conference held in Adeje, Tenerife, Canary Islands (Pickering, Boland, Osterhout, and van Berkum). The chapter by Martin Pickering (chapter 3) uses processing time measures, both eyetracking and self-paced reading, to explore ideas about interpretation that are drawn from recent work in lexical semantics. The work by Pickering and colleagues suggests that interpretations of nouns are easier to construct when the interpretation uses a stored semantic types interpretation than when it involves shifting semantic types, for example, construing an entity as an event. Type-shifting requires inferences to coerce an interpretation, which increases processing difficulty. The mapping of linguistic input onto event representations is emerging as a central issue within work in sentence processing. Attempts to incorporate pragmatic notions such as coercion and accommodation into real-time sentence processing have been addressed primarily in the context of resolving attachment ambiguity (e.g., Frazier & Clifton, 1996). They emerge as central issues in their own right in the work of Pickering and his colleagues. I anticipate that they will play a major role in research that examines language processing in goal-based tasks, especially those that involve interactive conversation.

The shift away from ambiguity resolution is also reflected in Julie Boland's contribution, which focuses on unambiguous sentences. Boland argues that whereas syntactic selection (i.e., ambiguity resolution) is a constraint-based process, syntactic generation makes use of argument structures stored with lexical representations. She also provides striking evidence for the clear distinction between adjuncts and arguments that is central to her theoretical perspective. If Boland is right, conclusions from work that uses ambiguity resolution as the primary test-bed for developing and testing theories of syntactic processing may miss some important generalizations. Boland also tackles the linking hypothesis between fixations and underlying comprehension processes for both reading and spoken language. She offers some strong hypotheses about the time course with which different processes affect fixations in reading, based on a synthesis of the literature, and provides a road map for how we might understand what aspects of sentence processing drive rapid fixations to objects in scenes.

Lee Osterhout's contribution (chapter 14) summarizes some of the reasons why ERPs are becoming so widely used in the language processing world. His contribution also illustrates the emergence of learning as an important topic in processing. Osterhout exploits ERPs to show powerful effects of learning after brief exposures to a foreign language. What is particularly surprising about the effects is that they are not reflected in concomitant behavioral tasks. The apparent dissociation between what the brain "knows" and what the behavior reflects presents an important theoretical challenge. As Osterhout and his colleagues (and others) take up that challenge, we are likely to learn more about both ERPs and our behavioral measures.

Finally, Jos van Berkum (chapter 13) offers a thoughtful and remarkably balanced evaluation of the strengths and weaknesses of various on-line measures with a focus on measures that reflect brain activity. He also reviews a body of research that illustrates ERPs can be used to examine how lexical, syntactic, and discourse constraints are integrated in real-time comprehension. As an aside, Jos occasionally reminds me that I once expressed some doubts to him about whether ERPs had lived up to their promise by providing us with novel insights into how language is processed. Never before have I so thoroughly enjoyed being wrong.

18.5 THE FUTURE

What will sentence processing look like a decade from now, what role will our current on-line measures play, and what new measures will we be using? The answer to these questions, of course, is that nobody knows. But here are a few of my best guesses.

18.5.1 The Neural Basis of Language

The rest of the current decade and most of the next decade will increasingly be devoted to understanding the neural basis of language, a trend that is clearly reflected in many of the chapters in this volume. I expect that ERPs will continue to be used in these efforts because they have exquisite temporal resolution, and because other brain-imaging techniques will increasingly shed light on what brain regions are responsible for generating the potentials we are measuring. This will partially overcome one of the current shortcomings of ERPs, namely their tenuous link to specific brain mechanisms. As we learn more about the neural basis of ERPs, we may also be able to take more advantage of the fact that ERPs are a multidimensional measure.

I also expect that our understanding of ERPs as an on-line measure will be enhanced as researchers begin to augment research using natural-language stimuli with research that uses artificial languages and nonlinguistic stimuli that incorporate key features of natural language. The use of nonlinguistic analogues will help break the explanatory circle I alluded to earlier. The use of artificial languages will also provide precise control over stimulus properties. Equally important, it will enable us to simultaneously investigate both processing and learning (Hoen & Dominey, chapter 16, this volume).

Other brain-imaging techniques will play an increasingly central role in our understanding of language processing. Clearly PET, fMRI, and event-related fMRI are just the tip of the iceberg. We can expect that the temporal resolution of measures of the hemodynamic response will become better as other techniques such as optical imaging come on-line and as we learn to measure more rapid cellular processes. However, unlike many, I am not particularly troubled by the relatively slow temporal resolution of fMRI. Here is why. Let us assume that different brain-systems are recruited for different aspects of language processing. If this is the case, we can examine how information from one domain that affects processing in one linguistic subsystem affects processing in another subsystem without worrying too much about time course. For example, imagine that interpreting a sentence with a motion verb (e.g., *John kicked the ball*) activates the parts of the cortex that process motion (e.g., MT and MTS, as well as relevant regions of secondary motor cortex). We might then ask whether those areas would also be weakly activated when the verb was a cohort competitor. If so, we might then ask whether this activation still occurred when the syntactic context was inconsistent with a verb. Put more generally, many issues about the interaction of subsystems that are treated as temporal questions in current research in sentence processing might just as easily be construed as spatial questions during the next decade.

As our experimental designs and brain-imaging measures become more sophisticated, we will clearly learn more about what the brain is doing as we learn, produce, and comprehend language. However, I am not optimistic that we will make much progress by simply manipulating the linguistic properties of our stimuli to identify which piece of cortex is most involved in, say, processing more complex sentences compared to less complex sentences, or plausible compared to implausible sentences. I expect that the currently popular coarse-grained "big-picture" models of how the brain processes language, in which different linguistic processes (e.g., first-stage parsing), thematic role assignment, and so forth, are assigned to different pieces of cortex, represent a first, crude step in understanding the neural basis of language. Once we have evidence that a piece of cortex is involved in some aspect of linguistic processing, we have not solved the problem. Rather, we need to understand the computations that engage that system. Studies that use nonlinguistic stimuli are likely to play a major role in these efforts. The move towards including nonlinguistic analogues of linguistic processes might also allow us to address some basic questions using research with animal models. Here is a potential example. Current models of eye-movement control in reading assume that linguistic processing controls the timing of saccade initiation. Models differ primarily in whether they assume serial or parallel processing of the to-be-fixated word and the word in the near periphery. However, a case can be made that cognitive factors primarily affect the no-go system by canceling the next saccade (Yang & McConkie, 2001). Now, neuroscientists examining the eye-movement control system are making considerable progress using saccade, antisaccade, and other tasks to tease apart the neural systems underlying eye-movement control in cognitive tasks (e.g., Schall & Thompson, 1999). It is becoming increasingly clear that there are separate "go" and "no-go" systems. However, we do not know much about how these systems are involved in reading. One could imagine teaching a monkey a reading-like task in which the goal is to visit spatial locations sequentially, picking up information along the way. The complexity and importance of that information and its contingencies would vary. One could then see how the go and no-go systems were coordinated to perform such a task. In particular, such a model might shed light on when cognitive factors mediate saccade initiation (the go system) versus saccade cancellation (the no-go system).

18.5.2 Multiple Measures

Increasingly, psycholinguists will rely upon multiple response measures, compensating for the weaknesses of some measures with complimentary measures. Striking evidence for why it is necessary to combine processing load measures with measures that provide more direct evidence about interpretation is reviewed in Ferreira, Ferraro, and Bailey (2002).

Two of the chapters in this volume illustrate how the multiple-measures approach can shed light on the interpretation of anaphoric expression. Gordon and colleagues use ERPs and eyetracking with the same materials, pairing a processing load measure with a measure that provides additional insight into the type of cognitive processing that might underlie that processing difficulty. Brown-Schmidt and colleagues use the action performed by participants to conduct interpretation-contingent eye-movement analyses to avoid collapsing across trials in which participants assign different interpretations to an anaphor. Other natural pairings of measures include ERPs and fMRI, and monitoring eye movements in spoken language and in reading. However, these represent just the tip of the iceberg.

18.5.3 Integrating Production and Comprehension

Although interactive conversation or dialogue is the most basic form of language use (Clark, 1992, 1996), it has received relatively little attention in the real-time language-processing literature. I expect that will change because we know we have the technology to study real-time processing in interactive conversation. Psycholinguists are currently making forays into dialogue, primarily by examining language processing in participants who are interacting with a confederate who is following a script. Although this class of studies has contributed, and will continue to contribute, important insights, use of confederates eliminates one of the crucial ingredients of spontaneous interactive conversation: interlocutors cooperating to create a relevant discourse, in a task with joint goals. I anticipate that these paradigms will be extended to truly interactive (unscripted) conversation with more complex goal structures as well as to face-to-face interactive conversation. As real-time work on interactive conversation develops, I also anticipate that psycholinguistic work will complement, and be complementary to, work on intelligent communicative systems that make use of spoken language (Allen et al., 2001).

Dialogue systems are beginning to tackle the problem of incremental or continuous generation and understanding in domains that involve interactive conversation with a human user. Because these systems must integrate knowledge of a domain with language processing, they offer the potential for providing a theoretical test bed for explicit computational models of dialogue. Such models will be necessary if psycholinguistic research on dialogue is to seriously address interactive conversation within an explicit theoretical framework. At the same time, our experimental paradigms can provide evaluation tools for practical systems, creating a feedback loop between system development, evaluation, and theory-driven experimental and computational explorations.

Eye movements can play an important methodological role in this research. However, other methods will likely emerge that will help us understand the dynamics of comprehension and production in conversation. For instance, other body movements pertaining to gestures and actions are likely to be highly informative when connected to the timing of speech and eye gaze. As we begin to connect language and action in rich goal-directed tasks, it is likely to influence theoretical developments in natural language processing just as it has begun to enrich theories of perception and cognition. Consider, for example, the question of why we understand incrementally. One possibility is that participants in an interactive dialogue simultaneously play the roles of speaker and addressee. A speaker in an interactive conversation often needs to plan and modify utterances in midstream in response to input from an interlocutor. This type of give-and-take requires incremental comprehension.

18.5.4 The Laboratory of the Future

For the foreseeable future, we will still be monitoring eye movements during reading and imaging the brain by measuring ERPs and blood flow. I also expect that we will be examining spoken language with contingent display changes and using virtual reality to create environments that participants can interact with and that experimenters can control. I also expect that we will be monitoring body movements, both postural and gestural, through various types of sensors, some attached to the body and some not. We will measure comprehension in interaction with other people, with dialogue systems and with avatars. Much of this research will require sophisticated labs and interdisciplinary teams of scientists. However, we will still be collecting response times to press buttons and asking participants to make simple judgments because there are times when those measures may shed more light on a problem than our more expensive, high-technology measures.

18.6 ACKNOWLEDGMENTS

The writing of this chapter was supported by NIH HD-27206 and NIH NIDCD DC005071. Manolo Carreiras and Chuck Clifton provided helpful comments that improved the style and content of this chapter. I would like to thank the members of my lab, past and present, for listening to my rants and for helping me learn most of what (I think) I know about language processing.

References

Allen, J. F., Byron, D. K., Dzikovska, M., Ferguson, G., Galescu, L., & Stent, A. (2001). Towards conversational human-computer interaction. *AI Magazine, 22,* 27–35.

Allopenna, P. D., Magnuson, J. S., & Tanenhaus, M. K. (1998). Tracking the time course of spoken word recognition: Evidence for continuous mapping models. *Journal of Memory and Language, 38,* 419–439.

Altmann, G. T. M., & Kamide, Y. (1999). Incremental interpretation at verbs: Restricting the domain of subsequent reference. *Cognition, 73,* 247–264.

Ballard, D. H., Hayhoe, M. M., Pook, P. K., & Rao, R. P. N. (1997). Deictic codes for the embodiment of cognition. *Behavioral and Brain Sciences, 20*(4), 723–767.

Barsalou, L. W. (1999). Perceptual symbol systems. *Behavioral and Brain Sciences, 22*(4), 577–660.

Bever, T. G. (1970). The cognitive basis for linguistic structures. In J. R. Hayes (Ed.), *Cognition and the development of language.* New York: Wiley.

Bresnan, J. W. (1978). A realistic transformational grammar. In M.Halle, J. W. Bresnan, & G. A. Miller (Eds.), *Linguistic theory and psychological reality.* Cambridge, MA: MIT Press

Chater, N., Crocker, M. J., & Pickering, M. J. (1998). The rational analysis of inquiry: The case of parsing. In M. Oaksford & N. Chater (Eds.), *Rational models of cognition.* Oxford: Oxford University Press.

Chomsky, N. (1970). Remarks on nominalization. In R. Jacobs & P. Rosenbaum (Eds.), *Reading in English transformational grammar.* Waltham, MA: Ginn.

Chomsky, N. (1980). Rules and representations. *Behavioral and Brain Sciences, 3,* 1–15.

Clark, H. H. (1992). *Arenas of language use.* Chicago, IL: University of Chicago.

Clark, H. H. (1996). *Using language.* Cambridge, UK: Cambridge University Press.

Conrad, C. (1974). Context effects in sentence comprehension: A study of the subjective lexicon. *Memory and Cognition, 2,* 130–138.

Cooper, R. M. (1974). The control of eye fixation by the meaning of spoken language. A new methodology for the real-time investigation of speech perception, memory, and language processing. *Cognitive Psychology, 6,* 84–107.

Dahan, D., Magnuson, J. S., & Tanenhaus, M. K. (2001). Time course of frequency effects in spoken word recognition: Evidence from eye movements. *Cognitive Psychology, 42,* 317–367.

Dahan, D., Magnuson, J. S., Tanenhaus, M. K., & Hogan, E. (2001). Subcategorical mismatches and the time course of lexical access: Evidence for lexical competition. *Language and Cognitive Processes, 16,* 507–534.

Dahan, D., & Tanenhaus, M. K. (2004). Continuous mapping from sound to meaning in spoken-language comprehension: Evidence from immediate effects of verb-based constraints. *Journal of Experimental Psychology: Learning, Memory, and Cognition, 30*, 498–513.

Dahan, D., Tanenhaus, M. K., & Chambers, C. G. (2002). Accent and reference resolution in spoken language comprehension. *Journal of Memory and Language, 47*, 292–314.

Ferreira, V., & Dell, G. (2000). Effects of ambiguity and lexical availability on syntactic and lexical production. *Cognitive Psychology, 40*, 296–340.

Ferreira, F., Ferraro, V., & Bailey, K. G. D. (2002). Good-enough representations in language comprehension. *Current Directions in Psychological Science, 11*, 11–15.

Ferreira, F., & Henderson, J. (1990). The use of verb information in syntactic parsing: A comparison of evidence from eye movements and segment-by-segment self-paced reading. *Journal of Experimental Psychology: Learning, Memory, and Cognition, 16*, 555–568.

Fodor, J. A. (1983). *Modularity of mind*. Cambridge, MA MIT Press.

Fodor, J. A., Bever, T. G., & Garrett, M. F. (1974). *The psychology of language*. New York: McGraw Hill.

Forster, K. (1979). Levels of processing and the structure of the language processor. In W. E. Cooper & E. C. T. Walker (Eds.), *Sentence processing*. Hillsdale, NJ: Erlbaum.

Foss, D. J. (1969). Decision processes during comprehension: Effects of lexical item difficulty and position upon decision times comprehension. *Journal of Verbal Learning and Verbal Behavior, 8*, 457–462.

Frazier, L. (1987). Sentence processing: A tutorial review. In M. Coltheart (Ed.), *Attention and performance XII*. Hillsdale, NJ: Erlbaum.

Frazier, L. (1990). Exploring the architecture of the language system. In G. Altmann (Ed.), *Cognitive models of speech processing: Psycholinguistic and computational perspectives*. Cambridge, MA: MIT Press.

Frazier, L., & Clifton, C. (1996). *Construal*. Cambridge, MA:.MIT Press.

Frazier, L., & Fodor, J. D. (1978). The sausage machine: A new two-stage parsing model. *Cognition, 6*, 291–325.

Frazier, L., & Rayner, K. (1982). Making and correcting errors during sentence comprehension: Eye movements in the analysis of structurally ambiguous sentences. *Cognitive Psychology, 14*, 178–210.

Garnsey, S. M., Pearlmutter, N. J., Meyers, E., & Lotocky M. A. (1997). The contributions of verb bias and plausibility to the comprehesnion of temporarily ambiguous sentences. *Journal of Memory and Language, 37*, 58–93.

Gibson, E. (1998). Linguistic complexity: Locality of syntactic dependence. *Cognition, 68*, 1–76.

Hare, M., McRae, K., & Elman, J. L. (in press). Sense and structure: Meaning as a determinant of verb subcategorization preferences. *Journal of Memory and Language*.

Henderson, J. M., & Ferreira, F. (in press). Scene perception for psycholinguists. In Henderson, J. M. & Ferreira, F. (Eds.), *The interface of language, vision, and action: Eye movements and the visual world*. New York: Psychology Press.

Henderson, J. M., & Ferreira, F., (Eds.). (in press). The interface of language, vision, and action: Eye movements and the visual world. New York: Psychology Press.

Jurafsky, D. (1996). A probabilistic model of lexical and syntactic access and disambiguation. *Cognitive Science, 20*, 137–194.

Just, M. A., & Carpenter, P. A. (1992). A capacity theory of comprehension: Individual differences in working memory. *Psychological Review, 99*, 122–149.

Kimball, J. (1973). Seven principles of surface structure parsing in natural language. *Cognition, 2*, 15–47.

Lewis, R. L. (2000). Specifying complete architectures for language processing: Process, control, and memory in parsing and interpretation. In M. W. Crocker, M. Pickering, & C. Clifton (Eds.), *Architectures and mechanisms for language processing*. Cambridge, UK: Cambridge University Press.

MacDonald, M. C. (1999). Distributional information in language comprehension, production, and acquisition: Three puzzles and a moral. In B. McWhinney (Ed.), *The emergence of language*. Hillsdale, NJ: Erlbaum.

MacDonald, M. C., & Christensen, M. (2002). Reassessing working memory: A commentary on Just and Carpenter (1992) and Caplan and Waters (1996). *Psychological Review, 109*, 35–54.

MacDonald, M. C., Pearlmutter, N. J., & Seidenberg, M. S. (1994). The lexical nature of syntactic ambiguity resolution. *Psychological Review, 101*, 676–703.

McClelland, J. L., & Elman, J. L. (1986). Interactive processes in speech perception: The TRACE Model. In D.E. Rumelhart & J. L. McClelland (Eds.), *Parallel distributed processing* (Vol. II.). Cambridge, MA: MIT Press.

McElree, B. (1993). The locus of lexical preference effects in sentence comprehension: A time-course analysis. *Journal of Memory and Language, 32*, 536–571.

Marslen-Wilson, W. (1973). Linguistic structure and speech shadowing at very short latencies. *Nature, 244*, 522–523.

Marslen-Wilson, W. (1975a). Sentence perception as an interactive parallel process. *Science, 189*, 226–228.

Marslen-Wilson, W. (1975b). The limited compatibility of linguistic and perceptual explanations. In R. Grossman, J. San, & T. Vance (Eds.), *Papers from the Parasession on Functionalism* (pp. 499–511). Chicago: Chicago Linguistic Society.

Meyer, D., & Schvanaveldt, R. (1971). Facilitation in recognizing pairs of words: Evidence of a dependence between retrieval operations. *Journal of Experimental Psychology, 90*, 227–234.

Newman, J. E., & Dell, G. S. (1978). The phonological nature of phoneme monitoring: A critique of some ambiguity studies. *Journal of Verbal Learning and Verbal Behavior, 17*, 359–374.

Nicol, J., & Swinney, D. A. (1989). The role of structure in coreference assignment during sentence comprehension. *Journal of Psycholinguistic Research, 18*, 5–19.

Norris, D., McQueen, J. M., & Cutler, A. (2000). Merging information in speech recognition: Feedback is never necessary. *Behavioral and Brain Sciences, 23*, 229–370.

Posner and Snyder (1975). Attention and cognitive control. In R. L. Solso (Ed.), *Inforation processing and cognition: The Loyola symposium* (pp. 55-85). Hillsdale, NJ: Erlbaum.

Rayner, K. (1998). Eye movement in reading and information processing: 20 years of research. *Psychological Bulletin, 124*(3), 372–422.

Rayner, K., Carlson, M., & Frazier, L. (1983). The interaction of syntax and semantics during sentence processing. *Journal of Verbal Learning and Verbal Behavior, 22*, 58–74.

Reichle, E. D., Rayner, K., & Pollatsek, A. (in press). The E-Z Reader model of eye movement control in reading: Comparisons to other models. *Behavioral and Brain Sciences*.

Roland, D. W., Elman, J. L., & Ferreira, V. S. (2003). *Why* that? Poster presented at the 9th Annual Conference on Architectures and Mechanisms for Language Processing, Glasgow, Scotland.

Schall, J. D., & Thomspon, K. G. (1999). Neural selection and control of visually guided eye movements. *Annual Review of Neuroscience, 48*, 269–297.

Sternberg, S. (1969). The discovery of processing stages: Extensions of Dondor's method. In I. W. G. Koster (Ed.), Attention and performance II. *Acta Psychologia, 30*, 276–315.

Swinney, D. A. (1979). Lexical access during sentence comprehension: (Re)consideration of context effects. *Journal of Verbal Learning and Verbal Behavior, 18,* 645–660.

Tanenhaus, M. K., & Carroll, J. M. (1975). The clausal processing hierarchy ... and nouniness. In R. Grossman, J. San, & T. Vance (Eds.), *Papers from the Parasession on Functionalism* (pp. 499–511). Chicago: Chicago Linguistic Society.

Tanenhaus, M. K., Leiman, J. M., & Seidenberg, M. S. (1979). Evidence for multiple stages in the processing of ambiguous words in syntactic contexts. *Journal of Verbal Learning and Verbal Behavior, 18,* 645–659.

Tanenhaus, M. K., Spivey-Knowlton, M. J., Eberhard, K. M., & Sedivy, J. E. (1995). Integration of visual and linguistic information in spoken language comprehension. *Science, 268,* 632–634.

Tanenhaus, M. K., Spivey-Knowlton, M. J., & Hanna, J. E. (2000). Modeling thematic and discourse context effects on syntactic ambiguity resolution within a multiple constraints framework: Implications for the architecture of the language processing system. In M. Pickering, C. Clifton, & M. Crocker (Eds.), *Architecture and mechanisms of the language processing system.* Cambridge, UK: Cambridge University Press.

Tanenhaus, M. K., & Trueswell, J. C. (1995). Sentence comprehension. In J. L. Miller & P. D. Eimas (Eds.), *Handbook of perception and cognition: Vol. 11. Speech, language, and communication* (pp. 217–262). San Diego, CA: Academic Press.

Tanenhaus, M. K., & Trueswell, J. C. (in press). Using eye movements to bridge the language as action and language as product traditions. In J. C. Trueswell & M. K. Tanenhaus (Eds.), *Processing world-situated language: Bridging the language-as-action and language-as-product traditions.* Cambridge, MA: MIT Press.

Trueswell, J. C., Sekerina, I., Hill, N., & Logrip, M. (1999). The kindergarten-path effect: Studying on-line sentence processing in young children. *Cognition, 73,* 89–134.

Vivianni, P. (1990). Eye movements in visual search: Cognitive, perceptual, and motor control aspects. In E. Kowler (Ed.), *Eye movements and their role in vision and cognitive processes.* Amsterdam: Elsevier.

Warren, R. E. (1972). Stimulus encoding and memory. *Journal of Experimental Psychology, 94,* 90–100.

Waters, G. S., & Caplan, D. (1996). A capacity theory of working memory: A critique of Just and Carpenter (1992). *Psychological Review, 103,* 671–772.

Yang, S. -N., & McConkie, G. W. (2001). Eye movements during reading: A theory of saccade initiation times. *Vision Research, 41,* 3567–3585.

Yarbus, A. L. (1967). *Eye movements and vision.* New York: Plenum.

Notes

1. Note the emphasis on personal. This is especially important when I characterize the past. To anticipate a certain type of criticism, let me state for the record that I know historians—in fact one of my brothers, David Tanenhaus, is a historian—and, as he would be happy to confirm, this Tanenhaus is no historian

2. For example, some of my recent work uses eye movements and spoken language in a circumscribed visual context to examine lexical access in spoken-word recognition. A serious concern about this paradigm is that the closed set introduced by the visual world might seriously limit the extent to which the results will generalize to less constrained situations. The use of a linking hypothesis relating lexical activation in TRACE (McClelland & Elman, 1986) to proportion of fixations over time (Allopenna, Magnuson, & Tanenhaus, 1998; Dahan, Magnuson, & Tanenhaus, 2001; Dahan, Magnuson, Tanenhaus, & Hogan, 2001) makes it possible to systematically evaluate

closed set effects, thus helping us better understand both the potential promise and limitations of the paradigm (Dahan & Tanenhaus, 2004; Tanenhaus & Trueswell, in press).

3. I am sure this phrase was used by George Miller, but I have been unable to locate the source (see note 1).

4. Another viable alternative to a working-memory explanation is that continuous integration of constraints, say using a form of Bayesian integration, results in maximally efficient use of information. Surprisingly, the equivalents of ideal observer analyses in vision have not been applied to language processing (but cf. Jurafsky, 1996). Also see, Chater, Crocker, & Pickering (1998) for an application of rational analysis to parsing.

5. Several notable exceptions include work by McElree and colleagues that relate aspects of sentence processing to memory retrieval dynamics, and theoretical work by Lewis which draws on explicit assumptions about memory activation within the ACT-R framework.

6. Note Swinney's (1979) use of the term *exhaustive access*—Sternberg's term for a non-self-terminating serial search.

7. Cooper (1974) first documented the close link between language, spoken language comprehension, and fixations to pictures in an important article that Tanenhaus et al. (1995) were unaware of at the time (see note 1).

Subject Index